Constitutional Law in Hong Kong

Constitutional Law in Hong Kong

Fourth Edition

Anton Cooray

This book was originally published as a monograph in the International Encyclopaedia of Laws/Constitutional Law.

Founding Editor: Roger Blanpain
General Editor: Frank Hendrickx
Volume Editors: André Alen & David Haljan

Wolters Kluwer

Published by:
Kluwer Law International B.V.
PO Box 316
2400 AH Alphen aan den Rijn
The Netherlands
E-mail: international-sales@wolterskluwer.com
Website: lrus.wolterskluwer.com

Sold and distributed by:
Wolters Kluwer Legal & Regulatory U.S.
7201 McKinney Circle
Frederick, MD 21704
United States of America
E-mail: customer.service@wolterskluwer.com

ISBN 978-94-035-3432-9

e-Book: ISBN 978-94-035-3433-6
web-PDF: ISBN 978-94-035-3434-3

The Author

Professor Anton Cooray, Professor of Law at City, University of London, is a Senior Research Associate Fellow at the Institute of Advanced Legal Studies, University of London. He was previously Professor and Associate Dean of Law, City University of Hong Kong. After graduating in law, he obtained his PhD in Law from University of London in 1979. He was awarded a second PhD by the University of Colombo in 1989 for his work on the Sri Lankan Constitution. He has been a Commonwealth Scholar (1975–1979); a Commonwealth Academic Fellow (1986–1987); a British Council Academic Visitor (1992) in the United Kingdom; and a Visiting Professor at University of Aix Marseille and University of Hawaii. He has published extensively especially in constitutional law, comparative law and planning law. His publications include the titles *Town Planning Law* (latest edition 2018), *The Environment* (latest edition 2020), and 'Constitutional Law and Human Rights' (2019) in the series *Halsbury's Laws of Hong Kong* and *Environmental Law in Hong Kong* (2nd edn, Kluwer: 2018). He edits the *Journal of International and Comparative Law* (Sweet and Maxwell).

Part V 'Special Problems', Chapter 2 'The Taxing and Spending Powers' of this work was authored by Professor Michael Littlewood of the Faculty of Law at the University of Auckland. He is a New Zealander but has spent many years in Hong Kong. He has degrees in law and politics from the University of Auckland and a doctorate in tax from the University of Hong Kong. He is admitted as a barrister and solicitor in New Zealand, as a solicitor in England and Wales and as a solicitor in Hong Kong.

The Author

Table of Contents

Table of Contents

Table of Contents

List of Abbreviations

AC	Appeal Cases
ACJ	Acting Chief Justice
ALJR	Australian Law Journal Reports
All ER	All England Law Reports
ALR	Australian Law Reports
BDTC	British Dependent Territories Citizen
BNO	British National (Overseas)
CA	Court of Appeal
CE	Chief Executive of Hong Kong
CFA	Court of Final Appeal
CFI	Court of First Instance
ChD	Chancery Division
CJ	Chief Justice
CJHC	Chief Judge of the High Court
CLR	Commonwealth Law Reports
Crim LR	Criminal Law Review
CUKC	Citizens of the United Kingdom and Colonies
DC	District Court (Hong Kong)/ Divisional Court (England)
HC	High Court
HKC	Hong Kong Cases
HKCFAR	Hong Kong Court of Final Appeal Reports
HKCLR	Hong Kong Criminal Law Reports
HKEC	Hong Kong Electronic Cases
HKLJ	Hong Kong Law Journal
HKLR	Hong Kong Law Reports
HKLRD	Hong Kong Law Reports and Digest
HKPLR	Hong Kong Public Law Reports
HKSAR	Hong Kong Special Administrative Region
HL	House of Lords (UK)

List of Abbreviations

HLC	Clark's House of Lords Cases (UK)
ICCPR	International Covenant on Civil and Political Rights
ICESCR	International Covenant on Economic, Social and Cultural Rights
ICR	Industrial Cases Reports (UK)
ILO	International Labour Organization
Imm AR	Immigration Appeal Reports (UK)
J	Justice
JA	Justice of Appeal
JC&CL	Journal of Chinese and Comparative Law
JICL	Journal of International and Comparative Law
JORC	Judicial Officers Recommendation Commission (Hong Kong since 1997)
JSC	Judicial Service Commission (Hong Kong before 1997)
KB	King's Bench (UK)
LQR	Law Quarterly Review
LegCo	Legislative Council of Hong Kong
LRC	Law Reports of the Commonwealth (UK)
MC	Magistrates Court
NPC	National People's Congress of the People's Republic of China
NPCSC	Standing Committee of the National People's Congress of the People's Republic of China
NPJ	Non-permanent Judge of the Court of Final Appeal of Hong Kong
PC	Privy Council (UK)
PJ	Permanent Judge of the Court of Final Appeal of Hong Kong
PLA	People's Liberation Army of the People's Republic of China
PRC	People's Republic of China
QB	Queen's Bench (UK)
QC	Queen's Counsel (in Hong Kong, before 1997)
SAR	Special Administrative Region
SC	Senior Counsel (in Hong Kong, after 1997)
SC	Supreme Court (UK)
UK	United Kingdom
US	United States
VP	Vice President of the Court of Appeal
WLR	Weekly Law Reports (UK)

General Introduction

Chapter 1. An Outline of Hong Kong's Constitutional History

1. Before the arrival of the British in the 1840s, Hong Kong was part of China and was occupied by a few thousand inhabitants who were governed by Chinese customary laws.[1] By the end of the sixteenth century, the British had established trade links with China, but they had to operate within what they considered to be a stringent and unreasonable Chinese regulatory regime. In the course of the Opium War, British traders had the opportunity of gaining a firm foothold in Chinese territory with the surrender of Hong Kong Island in perpetuity to the British. Formal British occupation of Hong Kong Island took place in January 1841, under the Convention of Chuenpi, a convention which was never ratified. A new treaty, known as the Treaty of Nanking, which was signed in 1842 and ratified in 1843, reaffirmed the British claim to Hong Kong. Through these agreements, Britain laid claim to the Hong Kong Island in perpetuity.

2. The British administration soon felt the need to expand the territorial limits of thriving Hong Kong and was able to obtain additional land in the Kowloon Peninsula in 1860, when it succeeded in forcing the Chinese regional authorities to sign the Treaty of Tientsin. By that treaty, the British secured a perpetual lease of Kowloon and Stonecutters Island. When that treaty was ratified in October 1860, with the signing of the Convention of Peking, the perpetual lease was changed into a more favourable cession in perpetuity.

3. As Hong Kong developed rapidly, the British administration needed more land for expansion. An opportunity for expansion came towards the end of the nineteenth century, when in 1898 the British administration was able to secure a ninety-nine-year lease of a large track of land known as the New Territories under the Second Convention of Peking. It is when the ninety-nine-year lease of the New Territories expired in 1997 that the British administration of Hong Kong had to come

1. For the historical background and relevant constitutional documents, *see* P. Wesley-Smith, *Constitutional and Administrative Law in Hong Kong*, vol. I (Hong Kong: China and Hong Kong Studies, 1987), Ch. 4. For a more detailed account, *see* J.W. Norton-Kyshe, *The History of the Laws and Courts of Hong Kong from the Earliest Period to 1898* (in two volumes) (Hong Kong: Vetch and Lee Ltd, 1971).

to an end. As we shall see, the Chinese Government insisted that Hong Kong be returned to China on 30 June 1997, necessitating the Sino-British negotiations for the purpose of handover.

4. The first two years of British occupation of Hong Kong from 1841 to 1843 was a transitionary period. Soon after occupying Hong Kong Captain Elliot, the Chief Superintendent of Trade, issued two proclamations declaring how Hong Kong was to be governed 'pending Her Majesty's further pleasure'. A Chief Magistrate was appointed, and land sales began. However, as described in paragraph 1, the Convention of Chuenpi secured by Captain Elliot was never ratified, and moreover he was replaced by Sir Henry Pottinger. It was Pottinger who led the military operations in China resulting in the Treaty of Nanking of 1842. On 26 June 1843 when the Treaty of Nanking was ratified, the British Imperial Government proclaimed a Royal Charter dated 5 April 1843, replacing the transitional arrangements that had been in operation.

5. The Royal Charter of 1843 declared Hong Kong to be a Crown Colony and provided for a constitutional framework revolving around a Governor who was assisted by a Legislative Council and an Executive Council, all to be appointed by the Crown. That constitutional arrangement operates, in its essentials, in Hong Kong even today. Hong Kong's constitutional system, just as that of other British colonies, conferred extensive powers to the Governor, who acted as the personal representative of the British Crown. The Governor had the power to make laws for peace, order, and good government with the advice and consent of the Legislative Council. Any legislation so enacted by the Governor could be disallowed by the Crown. Moreover, the Royal Charter reiterated the Imperial Government's power to make laws for Hong Kong by way of Acts of Parliament or Orders in Council. An Executive Council was set up to advise and assist the Governor in the administration of Hong Kong.

6. The Royal Charter gave the Governor the power to make judicial appointments, but it did not set out the judicial system, a matter to be dealt with by local legislation. The Supreme Court Ordinance No. 15 of 1843 established the Supreme Court. Several other ordinances were passed in the early years of Hong Kong providing for the administration of justice. Throughout the British administration, while the powers and functions of the legislative and executive branches of the government were spelled out in the Constitution, the powers and functions of the judiciary were left to be determined by local legislation. Likewise, the Basic Law makes provision for the independence of the judiciary and leaves the task of establishing courts to ordinary legislation.

7. Under the British administration, the principal constitutional document was the Letters Patent, which was supplemented by Royal Instructions.[2] Hong Kong's first Letters Patent was the Royal Charter of 1843, supplemented by the first Royal

2. In *Attorney General v David Chiu* [1992] 2 HKLR 84, (CA), 95, the Court of Appeal described them to be 'effectively our constitution'.

Instructions accompanying it. The updated Letters Patent and Royal Instructions were first published in 1917 and further amended from time to time.[3] In the following paragraphs, we will examine the evolution of Hong Kong's Legislative Council before we proceed to examine the constitutional system in operation at the time of the transfer of sovereignty in 1997.

8. Hong Kong's first Legislative Council consisted of four official members, namely the Governor, the Major General, the Government Legal Adviser and the Chief Magistrate. In June 1844, the Chief Justice took the place of the Chief Magistrate. Until 1850, the Legislative Council consisted only of official members, when two unofficial justices of the peace were appointed. Over the years, the Legislative Council's membership expanded gradually, and for the first time in 1896, unofficial members outnumbered official members by eight to six. The number of unofficial members was gradually increased until 1995 when all sixty members were unofficial members.

9. An elective element was introduced in 1985. Of the fifty-six members of the Council, twenty-four were elected through indirect elections. Twelve of them were returned from functional constituencies, and the remaining twelve from an electoral college consisting of members of the Urban Council (one), the Regional Council (one) and the District Boards (ten). The remaining thirty-two members were the three principal officials, seven official members and twenty-two unofficial members appointed by the Governor. Direct elections were introduced in 1991 when eighteen out of fifty-seven unofficial members were returned from geographical constituencies.

10. All sixty members of the last Legislative Council under the British administration were elected at the Legislative Council elections held in September 1995. Twenty were directly elected from geographical constituencies, thirty from functional constituencies and ten from an Election Committee consisting of all members of the District Boards. Of the thirty functional constituencies, nine were newly created where virtually all eligible voters could participate.

11. The Governor was the President of the Legislative Council until 1993, when the Letters Patent were amended to provide for the election of a President from among members of the Legislative Council. The Chief Justice, who was appointed ex officio from 1844, ceased to occupy a seat in the Legislative Council in 1889. This process of keeping the executive and judicial officers out of the Legislative Council reached its apex in 1995 when no provision was made for any official members to be appointed to the Legislative Council.

12. The Charter of 1843 provided for the appointment by the British Imperial Government of an Executive Council to advise and assist the Governor. The size of the Executive Council was kept small. The first Executive Council which began

3. For Hong Kong's Letters Patent and Royal Instructions as at 1997, *see* the companion volume of constitutional documents for Hong Kong.

operating in 1844 had three official members, in addition to the Governor. In 1872, the number was increased to five, with three ex officio members and two officials. In 1896, the monopoly of the official members ended with the addition of two unofficial members. In 1926, there were six official and three unofficial members, marking the entry of the first Chinese member of the Council. In 1946, there were seven official and four unofficial members. In 1948, there were six official and six unofficial members. The number of unofficial members rose from six in 1948 to eight in 1966. There were ten unofficial members in 1983. In 1989, the number of members was reduced to five official members and nine unofficial members. The number of official members was reduced to four in 1990 and to three in 1995, while retaining the number of unofficial members at nine. The Executive Council today has thirty-two members made up of sixteen official members and sixteen non-official members, in addition to the Chief Executive.[4]

13. Under the British rule, the constitutional system of Hong Kong did not undergo any drastic changes, except possibly for two developments. The first development was the enactment of the Bill of Rights Ordinance in 1991 to incorporate the International Covenant on Civil and Political Rights (ICCPR) into the law of Hong Kong. The amendment of the Letters Patent of that year introduced a new paragraph into Article VII, which dealt with the Governor's power to make laws with the advice and consent of the Legislative Council. The new paragraph, paragraph (5), stated as follows:

> The provisions of the International Covenant on Civil and Political Rights, adopted by the General Assembly of the United Nations on 16 December 1966, as applied to Hong Kong, shall be implemented through the laws of Hong Kong. No law of Hong Kong shall be made after coming into operation of the Hong Kong Letters Patent 1991 (No. 2) that restricts the rights and freedoms enjoyed in Hong Kong in a manner which is inconsistent with the Covenant as applied to Hong Kong.[5]

---

4. Information gathered from G.B. Endacott, *A History of Hong Kong* (2nd edn, Hong Kong; Oxford University Press, 1964), Hong Kong Yearbooks; https://www.yearbook.gov.hk/2019/en/index.html and Webpage of Hong Kong Executive Council, https://www.ceo.gov.hk/exco/eng/index.htm.
5. In *Lau Wong Fat v Attorney General* [1997] HKLRD 533, (CA), Godfrey JA observed that any Ordinance inconsistent with the Hong Kong Bill of Rights would be unconstitutional to the extent of such inconsistency since 'the court would be entitled to declare [such] Ordinance to be of no effect; for the making of the Ordinance would have involved a contravention of art VII(5) of the Letters Patent'. It has been argued that the entrenchment of the Covenant in the Letters Patent was a 'constitutional revolution', in that the courts of Hong Kong were for the first time provided with a set of specific criteria to test constitutionality of legislation. *See* Albert Chen, 'The Interpretation of the Basic Law: Common Law and Mainland Perspectives' (2000) 30 *Hong Kong Law Journal* 380, at 417–418. The Letters Patent came to be inoperative in 1997, when China resumed sovereignty over Hong Kong and brought into force Hong Kong's new constitution, the Basic Law. Section 1(1) of the Hong Kong Act 1985, enacted by the UK Parliament provided that 'As from 1st July 1997, Her Majesty shall no longer have sovereignty or jurisdiction over any part of Hong Kong.'

14. The increasingly representative nature of the Legislative Council resulted in a corresponding increase in the importance of the legislature. As is true of all former British colonies, Hong Kong experienced constitutional changes not only as regards the powers and functions of the Executive Council and the Legislative Council, but also their composition moving towards a stronger popular basis for the formation of the Legislative Council. The speed and enthusiasm with which these changes were brought about varied from colony to colony, principally dependent on the way political developments taking place there and the readiness of the British Government to 'liberate' it. Because of the special circumstances in Hong Kong, especially that Hong Kong was going to be returned to China, constitutional changes could not be directed towards the ultimate aim of self-government. The imminent return of Hong Kong to China prompted rather radical changes in the composition of the Legislative Council steered under the charismatic leadership of Chris Patten, the last British Governor of Hong Kong.[6]

15. The Letters Patent and the Royal Instructions were changed or modified from time to time to reflect any constitutional developments that took place, such as in the composition of the Executive Council and the Legislative Council. Instead of providing a chronological account of the constitutional developments, what is most useful in the space available is to outline the constitutional system that was in operation at the time of the transfer of sovereignty in 1997.

6. For an excellent account of the rise of the Hong Kong legislature under the British rule, *see* Kathleen Cheek-Milby, *A Legislature Comes of Age: Hong Kong's Search for Influence and Identity* (Hong Kong: Oxford University Press, 1995).

Chapter 2. Form of Colonial Government at the Time of the Handover of Hong Kong in 1997

16. Of the two constitutional instruments of the Colony of Hong Kong, the Letters Patent established the office of Governor (Article I), a Legislative Council (Article VI) and an Executive Council (Article V). It set out the Governor's powers including the power to make laws with the advice and consent of the Legislative Council (Article VII), to dispose lands (Article XIII), to grant pardon, remission of fines, etc. (Article XV) and to appoint judges and other public officers (Article XIV).

17. The Legislative Council would debate and pass legislative measures (Bills) which were submitted to the Governor for his approval and assent. A Bill so assented to and proclaimed by the Governor came to be known as 'Ordinances' as in all British colonies. The enacting words of an Ordinance were 'enacted by the Governor of Hong Kong, with the advice and consent of the Legislative Council' (*see* Article XXV(1) of the Hong Kong Royal Instructions). The Governor had discretionary power whether or not to consent to a Bill passed by the Legislative Council, but his discretion had to be subject to any Royal Instructions (Article X of the Letters Patent). The Governor could assent or refuse to assent to a Bill or reserve it for consideration by the Queen (Article X of the Letters Patent). Any Bill that had been assented to by the Governor could be disallowed by the Queen (Article VII of the Letters Patent), signifying the ultimate power over legislation that the British Government retained over Hong Kong.

18. In the exercise of their powers, the Governor and the Legislative Council were required to follow Royal Instructions (Article XII of the Letters Patent). The Royal Instructions provided, among others, for the legislative procedure in the Legislative Council, the right of the Governor to attend sessions of the Legislative Council, the right of a member of the Legislative Council to introduce a private member's bill in addition to Bills introduced by the government and more importantly provided for: (1) the rules and regulations under which Ordinances were to be enacted (Article XXV); and (2) certain classes of Bills not to be assented to by the Governor (Article XXVI).

19. The Governor had the power to appoint judges and other public officers, which he could delegate to any person except for the appointment of judges of the Supreme Court, judges of the District Court, the Chief Secretary, the Attorney General and the Financial Secretary (Article XIV of Letters Patent). He also had the power to dismiss or suspend a judicial officer or a public officer, or exercise disciplinary control over them (except in the case of judges of the Supreme Court and the District Court) (*see* Articles XVI and XVIA). All civil and military officers (but not judicial officers) were required to be obedient to the Governor and to aid and assist the Governor (Article XVIII).

20. The Royal Instructions supplemented the provisions in the Letters Patent. They provided for the formation of the Executive Council consisting of the Chief

Secretary, the Attorney General and the Financial Secretary who were ex officio members and such other persons as the Governor might appoint to be members from among officers of the Crown (official members) or from outside (appointed members) of the Council. The Governor was the President of the Executive Council and could convene meetings of the Council (Articles VII and VIII of the Royal Instructions), and he alone could submit questions for their advice or decision (Article XI of the Royal Instructions). The Governor was required to consult the Executive Council in the execution of his powers and authorities except in cases relating to the appointment, dismissal and disciplinary control of public officers (Article X of the Royal Instructions). He was, however, not bound by their advice or decision, but if he disagreed with the Executive Council, he had to record grounds and reasons for such disagreement (Article XII of the Royal Instructions).

21. Apart from the Letters Patent and Royal Instructions which were especially made for Hong Kong, the Colonial Regulations were also relevant to Hong Kong. The Colonial Regulations contained more detailed provisions regarding the administration of British Colonies which automatically extended to Hong Kong.[7]

§1. The Governor

22. Article I of the Letters Patent established the office of Governor and Commander-in-Chief of Hong Kong, to be appointed by the Queen. Although such a Royal appointment would be at pleasure, the Colonial Regulations provided that as a rule a Governor was to be appointed for a term of five years. The twenty-eighth and last Governor of Hong Kong, Mr Chris Patten, was appointed in July 1992 and held office until the handover on 30 June 1997. Article XVIII made it abundantly clear that the Governor was at the apex of Hong Kong's administration:

> And We do hereby require and command all Our officers and ministers, civil and military, and all other inhabitants of the Colony, to be obedient, aiding and assisting unto the Governor and to any person for the time being administering the Government of the Colony.

7. Colonial regulations are 'directions to Governors for general guidance given by the Crown through the Secretary of State for the Colonies' (Colonial Regulations). The general view that colonial regulations were merely directory (*see* Sir Kenneth Roberts-Wray, *Commonwealth and Colonial Law* (London: Stevens, 1966)) was rejected by the Court of Appeal in *Lam Yuk-ming v Attorney General*, [1980] HKLR 815, (CA). The Court of Appeal held that Colonial Regulations were Royal instructions. The Hong Kong Government had considered Colonial Regulations to be binding on it and changed legislation to be in line with colonial Regulations. For instance, the Pensions Ordinance (Cap. 89) was amended in 1978 in order to reflect a relevant change in 1977 of the Colonial Regulations. *See* Norman Miners, *The Government and Politics of Hong Kong*, (updated 4th edn, Hong Kong: Oxford University Press, 1989), 64. *See* generally P. Wesley-Smith, *Constitutional and Administrative Law in Hong Kong*, (2nd edn, Hong Kong: Longman, 1994), 37–38.

23. The Governor had the power to make 'laws for the peace, order, and good government of the Colony'. He was required to perform this legislative function 'by and with the advice and consent of the Legislative Council'.[8] While the power to debate and pass legislation was vested in the Legislative Council, any legislative measures with financial implications had to be sponsored by the Government.[9] Any Bill passed by the Legislative Council became law when the Governor assented to it. The Governor's power to assent or refuse to assent to a Bill was subject to two limitations. First, the Governor was required to reserve ten classes of legislation for Royal assent. The Governor could assent to any Bill belonging to those classes if: (a) he had previously obtained Royal Instructions; or (b) the Bill contained a clause suspending the operation of the Bill until signification of Royal pleasure; or (c) the Governor was satisfied that 'an urgent necessity exists requiring that such Bill be brought into effect immediately' provided that such Bill was not repugnant to any United Kingdom (UK) legislation or treaty obligation, and the Bill so assented to was sent to the Queen with reason for assenting thereto.[10] A Bill assented to by the Governor contrary to Clause XXVI of the Royal Instructions would have nevertheless been effective as an ordinance.[11] Second, the Crown retained the power to disallow any ordinance that the Governor had assented to. In the first year of the

---

8. Hong Kong Letters Patent 1917–1994, Art. VII(1).
9. *See* Hong Kong Royal Instructions, Cl. XXIV(2) which provided as follows: 'Every Ordinance, vote, resolution or question, the object of which may be to dispose of or charge any part of Our revenue arising within the Colony, shall be proposed only by (a) the Governor, (b) a public officer whom the Governor has designated to make such proposal under Clause XXIB, paragraph (2) or (c) a member of the Legislative Council expressly authorised or permitted by the Governor to make such a proposal.' *See also* the discussion on the Legislative Council below.
10. Clause XXVI of the Royal Instructions sets out ten classes of bills (such as a bill affecting the currency of the colony or relating to the issue of bank notes). In every instance where the Governor assented to a Bill relating to a reserved matter, Royal approval was obtained in advance. *See* N. Miners, *The Government and Politics of Hong Kong*, (updated 4th edn, Hong Kong: Oxford University Press, 1989), 130–131.
11. *See Pong Wai Ting v Attorney General* (1925) 20 HKLR 22, (SC), 27, it was contended that the two ordinances in question, dealing with a reserved matter, were invalid because they did not contain a clause suspending the operation of the two ordinances until the Royal approval had been obtained. It was held that the failure to comply with Royal Instructions did not invalidate the ordinances, and assuming that the ordinances would have been invalid for the lack of compliance with Royal Instructions, they were validated when an express announcement was made of non-disallowance by the Crown. Henry Gollan CJ said: 'If the Governor does not follow instructions, … then he may have to answer to the Sovereign for his neglect; but [section 4 of the Colonial Laws Validity Act, 1865] appears to me specifically to provide that failure on the part of the Governor is not to affect the validity of any law otherwise properly passed by the Legislative Council and assented to by the Governor.' Section 4 of the Colonial Laws Validity Act, 1865, provided as follows: '4. *Colonial laws not void for inconsistency with instructions to Governors*: No colonial law passed with the occurrence of or assented to by the governor of any colony, or to be hereafter so passed or assented to, shall be or be deemed to have been void or inoperative by reason only of any instructions with reference to such law or the subject thereof which may have been given to such governor by or on behalf of Her Majesty, by any instrument other than the letters patent or instrument authorizing such governor to concur in passing or to assent to laws for the peace, order, and good government of such colony, even though such instructions may be referred to in such letters patent or last-mentioned instrument.'

Legislative Council's existence, 1844, four Ordinances were disallowed, including Hong Kong's very first ordinance. Thereafter very few ordinances were disallowed, the last occasion being 1913.[12]

24. Until 1993, the Governor was a member of the Legislative Council and its President. In view of the fact that the Governor was no longer a member of the Legislative Council, an amendment of the Royal Instructions in 1993 permitted him to attend any meeting of the Legislative Council or any of its committees or subcommittees for any of the following purposes:

(1) addressing the Council at any time including during a special sitting;
(2) enabling members of the Council to put questions to him on any public matter for which the Government is responsible and receive answers thereto; and
(3) proposing any policy, measure, bill, vote, resolution, motion or question for debate in the Council or a committee or subcommittee thereof.[13]

25. The Governor could at any time dissolve the Legislative Council,[14] a power that was never exercised.

26. The Governor had the power to suspend any member of the Executive Council and, with Royal approval, revoke the appointment of such member.[15] The Governor was empowered to make provisional appointments to the Executive Council in case of a vacancy in its membership caused by death, resignation, absence from Hong Kong, or suspension from office.[16] The Governor had the power to grant a pardon or remission of sentence.[17]

27. The Governor was given the power to appoint judges and other public officers.[18] He was also given the power to 'dismiss or suspend from the exercise of his office any person holding any public office', or 'take such other disciplinary action as may seem to him desirable'.[19]

---

12. *See* Norman Miners, *The Government and Politics of Hong Kong* (updated 4th edn, Hong Kong: Oxford University Press, 1989), 131.
13. Hong Kong Royal Instructions 1917–1994, Cl. XXIB (1).
14. Hong Kong Royal Instructions 1917–1994, Cl. XXVIIIA.
15. Hong Kong Letters Patent 1917–1994, Art. VI.
16. Hong Kong Royal Instructions, Cl. III.
17. Hong Kong Letters Patent 1917–1994, Art. XV. *See* Cl. XXXIV of the Royal Instructions relating to the Governor's power of pardon in capital cases. *See* Norman Miners, 'The Governor, the Secretary of State and the Prerogative of Mercy' (1987) 17 *Hong Kong Law Journal* 77.
18. Hong Kong Letters Patent 1917–1994, Art. XIV. *See* the discussion below on the judiciary for special provisions relating to the removal or suspension of judges.
19. *Ibid.*, Art. XVI.

28. The Governor was given the power to grant or dispose of land, on behalf of the Queen.[20] This was a very important power in view of the fact that virtually all land in Hong Kong is government owned and disposed of only by way of long-term or short-term leases.[21]

§2. The Executive Council

29. The Executive Council, which was intended to be a consultative body, consisted of three ex officio members and such other number of members appointed by the Queen, as official or unofficial members; the three ex officio members being the Chief Secretary, the Financial Secretary and the Attorney General.[22] The last Executive Council of Hong Kong had ten other members, including one official member.[23] The Governor was required to consult the Executive Council in the execution of his powers, except in trivial matters, or urgent matters, or in cases relating to appointment, dismissal, removal, or disciplinary control of public officers where he considered consultation with the Executive Council to be undesirable.[24] Only the Governor could summon the Executive Council[25] and submit any questions to the Executive Council for their advice or decision.[26] The Governor could act in opposition to the advice given to him by the Executive Council, subject to the condition that he would report such disagreement to the Queen.[27] In addition to considering policy matters, the Executive Council had, in practice, an important part to play in the legislative process. All legislative measures proposed by the government were submitted to the Executive Council for approval. And the Executive Council had a part to play whenever an ordinance provided for any decision or measure to be taken by the Governor in Council, such as entertaining petitions or appeals.

§3. The Legislative Council

30. The last Legislative Council of Hong Kong under the British rule, which was elected in 1995, had sixty members. For the first time in its history, the Hong Kong Legislative Council was fully elected, with no appointed members and no ex officio members. By way of contrast, in the Legislative Council elected in 1991, there were four ex officio members (including the Governor who chose not to attend Legislative Council meetings), eighteen appointed members and thirty-nine elected members. In 1991, the Governor appointed a Deputy President of the Legislative Council

20. Hong Kong Letters Patent 1917–1994, Art. XIII.
21. *See* Anton Cooray, 'Town Planning' in *Halsbury's Laws of Hong Kong*, (2nd edn, 2018), [385.068].
22. Hong Kong Royal Instructions 1917–1994, Cl. II. In practice, the Governor would nominate members, other than the three ex officio members, for the approval of the Secretary of State given on behalf of the Queen.
23. *See Hong Kong 1996* (published by the Hong Kong Government), 7.
24. Hong Kong Royal Instructions 1917–1994, Cl. X.
25. *Ibid.*, Cl. VII.
26. *Ibid.*, Cl. XI.
27. *Ibid.*, Cl. XII.

from among its members to preside at its meetings, as the Governor had decided not to act as its President. In 1993, the Letters Patent were amended to bring to an end the right of the Governor to be a member and President of the Legislative Council. The 1993 amendment provided for a president to be elected by members of the Legislative Council from among its members. Out of the sixty members of the Legislative Council elected in 1995, twenty were elected from single member geographical constituencies, thirty from functional constituencies and ten from an election committee. Of the thirty functional constituency members, nine were elected from functional constituencies made up of all eligible voters in full employment in the relevant profession or industry. The voter base of the other twenty-one functional constituency seats was largely extended. The newly introduced Election Committee consisting of all elected District Board members returned ten Legislative Council Members.[28]

31. The term of a Legislative Council was four years, unless sooner dissolved.[29] However, the Legislative Council elected in 1995 stood dissolved on 1 July 1997, when the Chinese authorities refused to recognize it as the first Legislative Council of Hong Kong under the Basic Law. A Provisional Legislative Council was set up in 1996 to provide for a smooth transition to the new constitutional arrangement under the Basic Law from 1 July 1997, and the first Legislative Council of the Hong Kong Special Administrative Region was formed in 1998.[30]

32. The most important function of the Legislative Council was to debate and pass legislation. A legislative measure, known as a Bill, passed by the Legislative Council became law when it received Royal assent, virtually in all cases given by the Governor on behalf of the Queen. Any bill for the raising or expenditure of public revenue could only be introduced in the Legislative Council by the Governor (who had the right to attend Legislative Council meetings),[31] or by a government official designated by the Governor for that purpose,[32] or by a member of the Legislative Council expressly authorized or permitted by the Governor to introduce such Bill. Any Legislative Council member could introduce a Private Bill, also known as a private member's bill, meaning a bill 'not being a Government measure', subject to certain procedural requirements in case such bill was intended to affect or benefit a particular person, association, or corporate body.[33]

33. The Governor, with the advice and consent of the Legislative Council, could make laws for 'the peace, order, and good government'[34] and those words are said to connote authority 'as plenary and as ample as the Imperial Parliament in the

28. *See*, for a clear account of these constitutional changes, *Hong Kong 1996* (published by the Hong Kong Government).
29. Hong Kong Royal Instructions 1917–1994, Cl. XXVIIIA.
30. *See* further Part II, Ch. 3 'The Legislature'.
31. Hong Kong Royal Instructions 1917–1994, Cl. XXIB (1).
32. *Ibid.*, Cl. XXIB (2).
33. *Ibid.*, Cl. XXVII.
34. Hong Kong Letters Patent 1917–1994, Art. VII (1).

plenitude of its power can bestow'.[35] The legislative power of the Hong Kong Government was only subject to limitations 'imposed on it by the constitutional instruments of the territory itself or by imperial enactments or Orders in Council which are applicable to the territory'.[36] Thus, any legislation passed by the Hong Kong legislature would be invalid to the extent of any inconsistency with imperial legislation which had been extended to Hong Kong,[37] or an Order of Her Majesty in Council.[38]

34. Hong Kong courts have not subscribed to the view that the Legislative Council could not legislate contrary to fundamental principles of justice[39] or treaty obligations.[40] The enactment of the Hong Kong Bill of Rights Ordinance in 1991 and the subsequent amendment of the Hong Kong Letters Patent, which incorporated the ICCPR into Hong Kong's domestic law, introduced limitations on Hong Kong's legislative competence for the purpose of protecting fundamental rights. As will be seen later, the Bill of Rights has no special constitutional status under the Basic Law, although courts continue to regard it as an important source of law for demarcating the scope of fundamental human rights in Hong Kong.

35. Another important function of the Legislative Council was to debate government policies and scrutinize administration.[41] The following description of the role of the unofficial members of the Legislative Council that the Chief Secretary offered in 1975 is apt to describe the perceived role of the Legislative Council itself. 'The task of the unofficial members is not to oppose, but to participate in the formulation of government policy, to improve proposals presented to them, and to monitor their effective implementation. They ensure that the government does not

---

35. *Hodge v R* (1883) 9 AC 117. In *Winfat Enterprises (HK) Co Ltd v Attorney General* [1983] HKLR 211, (HC), Kempster J said: 'The formula "for the peace, order, and good government" of a Colony is, in theory at least, subject to the examination of the court which may hold an ordinance to be beyond the powers so entrusted to the subordinate legislature and void but "such a power has been held to authorize the utmost discretion of enactment for the attainment of the objects pointed to" and a court will not inquire whether any particular enactment of this character does in fact promote the peace, order or good government of the Colony' (quoting from *Chenard & Co v Arissol* [1949] AC 127, (PC), 132).
36. *Winfat Enterprises (HK) Co Ltd v Attorney General* [1984] HKLR 32, (CA), 48.
37. *See Kong Chi-ien (HK) Ltd v Attorney General* (1919) 14 HKLR 48, (HC), 51–52; *Rediffusion (HK) Ltd v Attorney General* [1970] AC 1136, (PC), 1161; [1970] HKLR 231, (PC), 244; and *In Re an Application by the Attorney General* [1985] HKLR 381, (HC), 386.
38. *See TO Wong & Co. Ltd v Leung Pui* [1957] HKLR 417 (FC).
39. *See Li Hong Mi v Attorney General* (1918) 13 HKLR 6, (FC), 22, where Sir William Rees-Davies CJ said: 'The local legislature … has in express and unequivocal terms given to the Governor in Council powers that override the generally accepted principles of the common law of England affecting the liberty of the subject; and in clear language it has provided that these powers cannot be challenged, assuming that the arbitrary procedure laid down by the Ordinance is complied with. This court therefore has no power to override its actions.'
40. *See Winfat Enterprises (HK) Co Ltd v Attorney General* [1983] HKLR 211, (HC), 225, affirmed [1984] HKLR 32, (CA).
41. *See* Norman Miners, *The Government and Politics of Hong Kong* (5th edn, Hong Kong: Oxford University Press, 1995), Ch. 10 'The Legislative Council: Controlling the Administration'.

become divorced from reality or more influenced by the enchantment of its own programmes than by the needs of our citizens.'[42]

36. It was an established constitutional principle in Hong Kong, as it is today, that no measures affecting public revenue could be adopted without Legislative Council approval. Finance control by the Legislative Council through the debate of the annual budget and more particularly by its Finance Committee throughout the year provided an important check on the government.[43]

37. The Legislative Council also played an important part by providing a grievance procedure. Members of the Legislative Council took turns meeting persons aggrieved by government policies, decisions, or procedures.[44] Members also played an important part in the Commissioner for Administrative Complaints scheme by forwarding complaints to be handled by the Commissioner. The scheme was introduced by the Commissioner for Administrative Complaints Ordinance of 1988. Since 1996, it was retitled the Ombudsman Ordinance, and as a result of an amendment in 1994, there is no longer any need to channel complaints to the Ombudsman through a member of the Legislative Council.[45]

§4. The Judiciary

38. The judiciary, the third branch of the state, is significantly separate from the other two branches of the state, the legislature and the executive. The doctrine of separation of powers which is ingrained in the common law system does not envisage the fitting of the three branches of government into watertight compartments. It is true that in modern democracies, legislative and executive functions are to a significant extent vested separately in the legislative and executive branches, but as regards the composition and exercise of each other's functions, the idea of separation of powers can be said to pale into insignificance. In British Colonies, and no less in Hong Kong, the constitutional developments took place from a position where the real power of the government was concentrated in the hands of the Governor, with only a nominal importance given to the legislature. Undoubtedly, the centre of power moved over the course of time towards the legislature, but there continued an inevitable interaction and mutual influence between the executive and legislative branches. While these changes were taking place, the judiciary continued to assert its independence from the other two branches of government.

42. Hong Kong Hansard, 1975–1976, 231.

43. *See* Norman Miners, *The Government and Politics of Hong Kong* (5th edn, Hong Kong: Oxford University Press, 1995), Ch. 9 'Legislative Council: Financial Control'.

44. *See* Legislative Council's Annual Report 1994–1995, Ch. 4 'Redress System'.

45. *See* Anton Cooray, 'Hong Kong's Ombudsman: The First Decade', (1999) 3 *The International Ombudsman Yearbook* 71–88; and 'Some Reflections on the Legislative Context of the Hong Kong Ombudsman', (2009) 17:1 *Asia Pacific Law Review* 53–72. *See also* Johannes Chan, 'Hong Kong's Administrative Complaints System' (1996) 26 *Hong Kong Law Journal* 339–368. For Ombudsman, *see* http://ombudsman.hk.

39. Neither the Governor nor the Legislative Council had any real control over the judiciary, which had its own hierarchical structure, with the Privy Council at its apex, in the sense that there was a final appeal to the Privy Council (which was not part of the domestic courts system of Hong Kong) from Hong Kong judicial decisions. The domestic courts structure consisted of two tiers: (1) superior courts (namely, the Court of Appeal and the High Court) together constituting the Supreme Court; and (2) inferior courts (namely, the District Court, Magistrates Courts) and tribunals such as the Small Claims Tribunal. Judicial officers were appointed by the Governor (magistrates by the Chief Justice in the exercise of power delegated to him),[46] on the advice of a Judicial Service Commission (JSC).[47] Hong Kong Letters Patent fixed the age of retirement for judges of the Supreme Court and the District Court at 65 years, and provided that such a judge could be removed by the Governor only if the Judicial Committee of the Privy Council found that he ought to be removed from office for inability to discharge duties of his office or for misbehaviour, after receiving the report of a judicial tribunal.[48]

46. *See Attorney General v David Chiu Tat-Cheung* [1992] 2 HKLR 84, (CA) where it was held that the Governor could delegate the power of appointment to the Chief Justice, allowing the appeal against the High Court decision in *In Re Tat-Cheong, David v Chiu Te-Ken, Deacon* [1992] 2 HKLR 57, (HC).

47. *See* Judicial Service Commission Ordinance of 1976, (Cap. 92). *See* 'The Process of Appointment of Judges in Hong Kong since 1976', a paper dated 10 April 2001 prepared by Cheung Wai-Lam for the Research and Library Services Division of the Legislative Council Secretariat. http://www.legco.govhk/yr00-01/english/library/0001rp_7.pdf. The title of this Ordinance was changed in 1995 to 'Judicial Officers Recommendation Commission Ordinance' which will be examined when dealing with the judiciary under the Basic Law after 1997.

48. *See* generally P. Wesley-Smith, *Constitutional and Administrative Law in Hong Kong*, (2nd edn, Hong Kong: Longman, 1984), 138–147.

Chapter 3. Form of Government under the Basic Law

§1. Hong Kong in China: 'One Country, Two Systems'

40. When in 1997 the British administration of Hong Kong drew to a close, Hong Kong came to be governed according to the Basic Law, Hong Kong's new constitution.[49] As explained in Chapter 2 of Part I, the Basic Law is founded on the concept of 'One Country, Two Systems', guaranteeing that the Chinese socialist system and policies would not be applied in Hong Kong.[50] The system of government that the Basic Law has introduced is a continuation of the previous system of government, but subject to a number of technical and substantive modifications.[51] Hong Kong's government has been described as an Executive-led system of government, where the Executive initiates financial and other public policies for debate and approval by the Legislative Council and implements them. The executive branch of the government consists of the Chief Executive, as its Head, the Executive Council, appointed by the Chief Executive to advise him, and the public service, consisting of and headed by principal officials who are political appointees since 2002 as distinguished from neutral career civil servants until then. In this set up, the Legislative Council is in many ways subordinate to the executive.

41. The Basic Law draws a clear distinction between government bills, namely bills introduced by the government, and private member's bills, namely bills introduced by members of the Legislative Council. It is only the government that can introduce any bill that relates to 'public expenditure or political structure or the operation of the government'. This is an absolute limitation on private members' competence to introduce legislative measures. A bill relating to government policies may be introduced by a member of the Legislative Council provided that the written consent of the Chief Executive is obtained.[52] This is a qualified limitation on

49. Hong Kong judges especially in the Court of Final Appeal, more particularly Justice Bokhary, have repeatedly referred to the Basic Law as 'our constitution'. *See*, for instance, *Ho Man Kong v Superintendent of Lai Chi Kok Reception Centre*, (2014) 17 HKCFAR 179, (CFA), [27], *Ghulam Rbani v Secretary for Justice* (2014) 17 HKCFAR 138, (CFA) [111], *Kong Yunming v Director of Social Welfare* (2013) 16 HKCFAR 950, (CFA) [155], *W v Registrar of Marriages* (2013) 16 HKCFAR 112, (CFA), [209], [216], [224], [225], (all by Justice Bokhary); *A v Commissioner of Independent Commission Against Corruption* (2012) 15 HKCFAR 362, (CFA), [13] Bokhary and Chan PJJ; *Fok Chun Wa v Hospital Authority* [2008] HKEC 2161, (CFI), [59], Jeremy Poon J. In *Chan Pui Sze v Wang Jue* [2019] HKEC 3355, (CFI), [119], the judge referred to a related bankruptcy proceeding in the USA where the US judge referred to the Basic Law as Hong Kong's constitution.

50. One of the General Principles of the Basic Law is that 'the socialist system and policies shall not be practised in the Hong Kong Special Administrative Region and the previous capitalist system and way of life shall remain unchanged for 50 years': Article 5 of the Basic Law, in Ch. I 'General Principles'.

51. *See* generally Yash Ghai, *Hong Kong's New Constitutional Order: The Resumption of Chinese Sovereignty and the Basic Law*, (2nd edn, Hong Kong: Hong Kong University Press, 1999).

52. Article 74 provides as follows: 'Members of the Legislative Council of the Hong Kong Special Administrative Region may introduce bills in accordance with the provisions of [the Basic Law] and legal procedures. Bills which do not relate to public expenditure or political structure or the operation of the government may be introduced individually or jointly by members of the Council. The written consent of the Chief Executive shall be required before bills relating to government policies

private member's bills.[53] Of course, no bill passed by the Legislative Council becomes law unless it receives the assent of the Chief Executive and is brought into effect by the Chief Executive.

42. The Legislative Council cannot remove the Chief Executive, although there are circumstances where a serious disagreement between the Chief Executive and the Legislative Council might lead to the resignation of the Chief Executive.[54] For its successful operation, Hong Kong's constitutional system relies on close cooperation between the legislative and executive branches. The judicial branch, on the

---

are introduced.' This provision came up for close scrutiny in *Leung Kwok Hung v President of Legislative Council* [2007] 1 HKLRD 387, (CFI), where the question was whether a member of the Legislative Council could introduce an amendment to a bill having an effect on public revenue. In delivering the judgment of the Court of First Instance, Justice Hartmann observed that the stage of introducing a bill in the Legislative Council was a 'preliminary and discrete process' that precedes the law enacting process in the Legislative Council. Article 74 relates to that preliminary stage and not to the legislative procedure on processing a bill in the Council. Thus, while Art. 74 prohibits the introduction of a Private Member's bill of the kind prescribed there, that Article does not apply to a situation where a member proposes an amendment to a bill that has been presented to the Legislative Council having the effect of transgressing the limits of Art. 74. This however did not mean that the Legislative Council could not adopt a rule which prohibits the introduction of an amendment to a bill having the effect for of being contrary to Art. 74. Rule 57(6) of the Rules of Procedure of the Legislative Council provides as follows: 'An amendment, the object or effect of which may, in the opinion of the President or Chairman, be to dispose of or charge any part of the revenue or other public moneys of Hong Kong shall be proposed only by (a) the Chief Executive; or (b) a designated public officer; or (c) a Member, if the Chief Executive consents in writing to the proposal.' In upholding the constitutionality of that rule, which transposes Art. 74 into the bill amendment stage, Justice Hartmann said at [87]: 'In summary, in so far as r. 57(6) diminishes the ability of Hong Kong's legislators, it is a diminishment of long-standing, one inherited by our colonial legislature from Parliament and one, in some like manner, imposed upon legislators in other common law and civil law jurisdictions. It is, I am satisfied, a diminishment founded on the separation of powers, the particular constitutional principle being that no charge on public funds can be incurred except on the initiative of the executive and the administration. It is for those two organs of state to create and propose policies related to the collection and disbursement of public funds; it is for the Legislature to examine and, if thought fit, to approve such proposals.'

53. For a useful discussion on several aspects of the limited competence of private members to initiate legislation, *see* 'A Companion to the history, rules and practices of the Legislative Council of the Hong Kong Special Administrative Region', https://www.legco.govhk/yr13-14/english/counmtg/papers/cm0618as-143-e.pdf. A private member's bill must not be confused with the British idea of a 'private bill' as distinguished from a 'public bill'. A useful statutory definition of a private bill may be found in the Private Bills Ordinance (Cap. 69), which describes a private bill as a bill which 'provides primarily for the particular interest or benefit of any individual, association or body corporate rather than the interest or benefit of the public; and (b) is not a Government measure'. The Private Bills Ordinance (Cap. 69) was enacted to provide for payment of fees by promoters of a private bill. *See also* 'Legislative Procedure on Member's Bills' at http://legco.govhk/general/english/bills/mem-bill.pdf which sets out the procedure for introducing a private bill as well as a public bill. For the British parliamentary practice on private bills, *see* A.W. Bradley & K. Ewing, *Constitutional and Administrative Law*, (12th edn, Harlow, England: Longman, 1997), 210–12.
54. Article 52(2) and (3) envisage two situations where the Chief Executive *must* resign: (a) when after the Legislative Council is dissolved because he or she twice refuses to sign a bill passed by it, the new Legislative Council again passes it by a two-thirds majority of all the Legislative Council members, but he or she still refuses to sign it; and (b) when after the Legislative Council is dissolved because it refuses to pass a budget or any other important bill, the new Legislative Council still refuses to pass the original bill in dispute.

other hand, exists and operates independently of the other two branches of government. The rest of this chapter outlines the relationship between the Chinese Central Authorities and the Hong Kong Government, followed by an outline of Hong Kong's internal constitutional arrangements.

§2. The Relationship Between the Chinese Central Authorities and Hong Kong

43. The Preamble to the Basic Law provides as follows: 'Hong Kong has been part of the territory of China since ancient times; it was occupied by Britain after the Opium War in 1840. On 19 December 1984, the Chinese and British Governments signed the Joint Declaration on the Question of Hong Kong, affirming that the Government of the People's Republic of China will resume the exercise of sovereignty over Hong Kong with effect from 1 July 1997, thus fulfilling the long-cherished common aspiration of the Chinese people for the recovery of Hong Kong. Upholding national unity and territorial integrity, maintaining the prosperity and stability of Hong Kong, and taking account of its history and realities, the People's Republic of China has decided that upon China's resumption of the exercise of sovereignty over Hong Kong, a Hong Kong Special Administrative Region will be established in accordance with the provisions of Article 31 of the Constitution of the People's Republic of China, and that under the principle of "one country, two systems", the socialist system and policies will not be practised in Hong Kong.[55] The basic policies of the People's Republic of China regarding Hong Kong have been elaborated by the Chinese Government in the Sino-British Joint Declaration. In accordance with the Constitution of the People's Republic of China, the National People's Congress hereby enacts the Basic Law of the Hong Kong Special Administrative Region of the People's Republic of China, prescribing the systems to be practised in the Hong Kong Special Administrative Region, in order to ensure the implementation of the basic policies of the People's Republic of China regarding Hong Kong.'

44. Article 1 of the Basic Law states that 'the Hong Kong Special Administrative Region is an inalienable part of the People's Republic of China'. Article 2 provides that 'the National People's Congress of China authorizes the Hong Kong Special Administrative Region to exercise a high degree of autonomy and enjoy executive, legislative and independent judicial power, including that of final adjudication, in accordance with the provisions of [the Basic Law]'. Thus, Hong Kong is not an independent state or a territory, but an integral part of China.[56] If not for the enactment of the Basic Law itself, a national law enacted by People's Republic

55. The Sino-British Joint Declaration clearly set out the position of the People's Republic of China in relation to the 'One Country, Two Systems' policy: desire for national reunification and territorial integrity is an important theme underlying China's recovery of Hong Kong. Hong Kong courts have recognised the importance of Hong Kong an inalienable part of China, but with a unique regional status.

56. The Court of Final Appeal has recognised the importance of Hong Kong being an integral part of China. For instance, in the *Flag Desecration* case, recognising that the place that Hong occupies in

of China, Hong Kong will not have a separate constitutional governmental structure and virtual freedom from China. Just as Macau, the other Special Administrative Region of the People's Republic of China, the Hong Kong Special Administrative Region was created by the Chinese Government under a specific provision of the Chinese Constitution, Article 31, which provides as follows: 'The state may establish special administrative regions when necessary. The systems to be instituted in special administrative regions shall be prescribed by law enacted by the National People's Congress in the light of specific conditions.'

45. The Basic Law is unique among national laws of China, for the reason that the enactment of the Basic Law and its content was agreed between the British Colonial Government and the Chinese Government through the Sino-British Joint Declaration, or 'the Joint Declaration of the Government of the United Kingdom of Great Britain and Northern Ireland and the Government of the People's Republic of China on the question of Hong Kong'. It has therefore been argued that the People's Republic of China has a special international obligation to honour the proper implementation of the Basic Law.[57] While the Basic Law is primarily concerned with Hong Kong's local administrative system, it is also concerned with the constitutional relationship between Hong Kong and Chinese Central Government. The Basic Law maintains a delicate balance between the competence of the Hong Kong Government and the overarching authority of the Chinese Government. For instance, while the appointment of Hong Kong's Chief Executive is a power vested in the Chinese Central Government, the constitutional arrangement is that Hong Kong selects or elects a candidate as the Chief Executive and such person is appointed by the Chinese Government.[58] The use of mandatory words 'shall be selected … and appointed by' in Article 45 suggests that it is mandatory for the Chinese Government to appoint the locally elected person. Even if that obligation is not mandatory, it is inconceivable that the Chinese Government would ignore the selection or election process and refuse to endorse the result. Another important aspect of the fine balance of power between Hong Kong and Chinese Central Authorities relates to the amendment of the Basic Law. As the Basic Law is a national law of China passed by the National People's Congress, the amendment of the Basic Law lies within the sole competence of the National People's Congress. However, Article 159 of the Basic Law lays down the procedure for amending the Basic Law which the National People's Congress of the People's Republic of China (NPC) has to follow.

---

the People's Republic of China, Li CJ said: 'the national flag is the unique symbol of the one country, the People's Republic of China, and the regional flag is the unique symbol of the Hong Kong Special Administrative Region as an inalienable part of the People's Republic of China under the principle of "One country, two systems". These legitimate interests form part of the general welfare and the interests of the collectivity as a whole.' *HKSAR v Ng Kung Siu* (1999) 2 HKCFAR 442, (CFA), 460.

57. *See*, for instance, Roda Mushkat, *One Country, Two International Personalities: The Case of Hong Kong* (Hong Kong: Hong Kong University Press 1997).

58. The Chief Executive of the Hong Kong Special Administrative Region shall be selected by election or through consultations held locally and appointed by the Central People's Government': Basic Law, Art. 45.

46. In relation to the effect of the Basic Law on the central-local relationship, the Court of Final Appeal has boldly asserted the supremacy of the Basic Law: 'What has been controversial is the jurisdiction of the courts of the Region to examine whether any legislative acts of the National People's Congress or its Standing Committee are consistent with the Basic Law and to declare them to be invalid if found to be inconsistent. In our view, the courts of the Region do have this jurisdiction and indeed the duty to declare invalidity if inconsistency is found. It is right that we should take this opportunity of stating it unequivocally.'[59]

47. The Central Government has the authority to pass or extend a national law having effect in Hong Kong. However, the power of the Central Government is restricted by Article 18 which provides as follows: 'National laws shall not be applied in the Hong Kong Special Administrative Region, except for those listed in Annex III of [the Basic] Law.' Laws listed in Annex III do not apply in Hong Kong *ex proprio vigore:* Such laws will have to be applied locally by way of promulgation or legislation 'by the Region' (Article 18, paragraph 2). Apart from this procedural limitation, there is also a substantive limitation: 'Laws listed in Annex III to [the Basic Law] shall be confined to those relating to defence and foreign affairs as well as other matters outside the limits of the autonomy of the Region as specified by [the Basic Law]' (Article 18, paragraph 3). However, in emergency situations, such as war or turmoil in Hong Kong, where the Hong Kong Special Administrative Region is unable to contain threats to national unity or security, the Central Government has the power to extend the application of 'relevant national laws' to the Region (Article 18, paragraph 4).

48. The relationship between the Central Government in China and the regional government in Hong Kong is unique: It is much more sophisticated than the relationship between the Central Government and the local government authorities in a unitary state; but it is not equivalent to the relationships that typically exist between the central (federal) government and the state governments under a federal system of government, such as in India or the United States (US). The Basic Law demarcates the jurisdiction between the Chinese Central Government and Hong Kong's regional Government. Some enumerated powers are primarily within the purview of the Central Government, for instance 'foreign affairs relating to the Hong Kong Special Administrative Region' (Article 13, paragraph 1). However, paragraph 3 of Article 13 goes on to say that 'the Central People's Government authorizes the Hong Kong Special Administrative Region to conduct relevant external affairs on its own in accordance with [the Basic Law]'. Similarly, paragraph 1 of Article 14 provides that 'the Central People's Government shall be responsible for the defence of the Hong Kong Special Administrative Region' while paragraph 2 of that Article goes on to state that 'the Government of the Hong Kong Special Administrative Region shall be responsible for the maintenance of public order in the Region'. Moreover, as stipulated in paragraph 3 of the same Article, 'military forces stationed by the Central People's Government in the Hong Kong special Administrative Region for defence shall not interfere in the local affairs of the Region'. It is

59. *Ng Ka Ling v Director of Immigration* (1999) 2 HKCFAR 4, (CFA), [25]–[26].

only at the request of the Region's Government that the military forces stationed in Hong Kong will become active in Hong Kong for 'the maintenance of public order and in disaster relief' (Article 14, paragraph 3). Paragraph 4 of Article 14 highlights the importance of Chinese national laws and Hong Kong regional laws: 'In addition to abiding by national laws, members of the garrison shall also abide by the laws of the Hong Kong Special Administrative Region.'

49. The Hong Kong Special Administrative Region enjoys legislative, executive and judicial power other than those specifically reserved for the Central Government. Hong Kong's legislative and the executive authorities cannot exercise powers in relation to defence and foreign affairs, except to the extent that the Basic Law provides for, as seen above. Similarly, the judiciary cannot exercise any power that is within the exclusive domain of the Central Chinese Government. For instance, Article 19, paragraph 3 provides as follows: 'The courts of the Hong Kong Special Administrative Region shall have no jurisdiction over acts of state such as defence and foreign affairs. The courts of the region shall obtain a certificate from the Chief Executive on questions of fact concerning acts of state such as defence and foreign affairs whenever such questions arise in the adjudication of cases. This certificate shall be binding on courts. Before issuing such a certificate, the Chief Executive shall obtain a certifying document from the Central People's Government.' In the case of *Democratic Republic of the Congo v FG Hemisphere Associates LLC (No 1)*, the Court of Final Appeal requested the Standing Committee of the National People's Congress of the People's Republic of China (NPCSC) to interpret the relevant Articles of the Basic Law and advise whether the courts of Hong Kong were free to continue to apply the pre-1997 common law practice relating to sovereign immunity. The Standing Committee determined that questions of sovereign immunity fell within the scope of 'foreign affairs' in Article 13 and the meaning of 'acts of state' in Article 22, and therefore it was not a matter which was within the competence of the courts of Hong Kong. The Standing Committee decided that the Hong Kong courts would be bound by an executive certificate issued under Article 19.[60]

50. Where the Hong Kong Special Administrative Region has lawful authority to act, it may exercise such authority without any interference from any department

60. *Democratic Republic of the Congo v FG Hemisphere Associates LLC (No 1)* (2011) 14 HKCFAR 95. The second paragraph of Art. 19 provides as follows: 'The courts of the Hong Kong Special Administrative Region shall have no jurisdiction over acts of state such as defence and foreign affairs. The courts of the Region shall obtain a certificate from the Chief Executive on questions of fact concerning acts of state such as defence and foreign affairs whenever such questions arise in the adjudication of cases. This certificate shall be binding on the courts. Before issuing such a certificate, the Chief Executive shall obtain a certifying document from the Central People's Government.' *See*, for the interpretation issued by the Standing Committee which appears as Instrument 24 appended to the Basic Law, 'Interpretation of Paragraph 1, Article 13 and Article 19 of the Basic Law of the Hong Kong Special Administrative Region of the People's Republic of China by the Standing Committee of the National People's Congress' (adopted by the Standing Committee of the Eleventh National People's Congress at its 22nd Session on 26 August 2011).

of the Central People's Government, any province, autonomous region, or municipality under the Central Government department.[61]

51. The interpretation and amendment of the Basic Law provides a classic example of power distribution and power sharing: Article 158 recognizes that, as under the Chinese Constitution, the power of interpreting the Basic Law is vested in the Standing Committee of the National People's Congress. However, this power of interpretation has been delegated to the Hong Kong Special Administrative Region in relation to the provisions of the Basic Law 'which are within the limits of the autonomy of the Region'. Hong Kong courts may also interpret and apply provisions other than those relating to the matters within the jurisdiction of the Hong Kong Special Administrative Region so long as there is no question about the meaning of such a provision. However, if such an interpretation will affect the determination of a case, the court must seek, through the Court of Final Appeal, a binding interpretation for the resolution of the question of interpretation.[62]

§3. Hong Kong's System of Government: The Executive Branch

52. Within the high degree of autonomy that the Hong Kong Special Administrative Region enjoys, executive power is of prime importance, because what Hong Kong has is an 'Executive-led Government'. The head of the executive is the Chief Executive of Hong Kong who is accountable to both to the Central People's Government and the Hong Kong Special Administrative Region, in accordance with the provisions of the Basic Law.[63] As provided by Article 62 of the Basic Law, the Government of the Hong Kong Special Administrative Region exercises the following powers and functions:

(1) to formulate and implement policies;
(2) to conduct administrative affairs;
(3) to conduct external affairs as authorized by the Central People's Government under the Basic Law;
(4) to draw up and introduce budgets and final accounts;
(5) to draft and introduce bills, motions and subordinate legislations;
(6) to designate officials to sit in on the meetings of the Legislative Council and to speak on behalf of the Government.

61. Article 22 of the Basic Law. Article 22 goes on to provide that if there is a need for any central government department, province, autonomous region or municipality to set up offices in Hong Kong, they must obtain the consent of the Hong Kong Government to do so. Any such office and its personnel must abide by the laws of the Region.
62. *See* below Ch. 2 Interpretation of the Basic Law.
63. Basic Law, Art. 43.

53. The Chief Executive, the head of the executive branch of the Government, is appointed for a term of five years by the Chinese Central Government, after having been selected or elected through consultations held in Hong Kong.[64] As set out in Article 48 of the Basic Law, the Chief Executive of the Hong Kong Special Administrative Region exercises the following powers and functions:

(1) to lead the government of the Region;
(2) to be responsible for the implementation of this Law and other laws which, in accordance with this Law, apply in the Hong Kong Special Administrative Region;
(3) to sign bills passed by the Legislative Council and to promulgate laws; to sign budgets passed by the Legislative Council and report the budgets and final accounts to the Central People's Government for the record;
(4) to decide on government policies and to issue executive orders;
(5) to nominate and to report to the Central People's Government for appointment the following principal officials: Secretaries and Deputy Secretaries of Departments, Directors of Bureaux, Commissioner Against Corruption, Director of Audit, Commissioner of Police, Director of Immigration and Commissioner of Customs and Excise; and to recommend to the Central People's Government the removal of the above-mentioned officials;
(6) to appoint or remove judges of the courts at all levels in accordance with legal procedures;
(7) to appoint or remove holders of public office in accordance with legal procedures;
(8) to implement the directives issued by the Central People's Government in respect of the relevant matters provided for in this Law;
(9) to conduct, on behalf of the Government of the Hong Kong Special Administrative Region, external affairs and other affairs as authorized by the Central Authorities;
(10) to approve the introduction of motions regarding revenues or expenditure to the Legislative Council;
(11) to decide, in the light of security and vital public interests, whether government officials or other personnel in charge of government affairs should testify or give evidence before the Legislative Council or its committees;
(12) to pardon persons convicted of criminal offences or commute their penalties; and
(13) to handle petitions and complaints.[65]

54. As before 1997, the Chief Executive is assisted by the Executive Council in policy making. Article 156 clearly sets out the circumstances in which the Chief Executive is bound to seek the advice of the Executive council: 'Except for the appointment, removal and disciplining of officials and the adoption of measures in

---

64. *Ibid.*, Arts 43, 45 and 59.
65. For an illustration of the procedure for making a petition to the Chief Executive, *see* instructions to a person whose torture claim has been refused: https://www.sb.govhk/eng/special/pdfs/notice_of_petition.pdf.

emergencies, the Chief Executive shall consult the Executive Council before making important policy decisions, introducing bills to the Legislative Council, making subordinate legislation, or dissolving the Legislative Council.' As the Governor was required to do before 1997, the Chief Executive must put down specific reasons if he does not accept a majority opinion of the Executive Council.[66] Many statutes provide for certain powers to be exercised by the Chief Executive in Council.[67]

55. Article 61 of the Basic Law provides that the Government of Hong Kong shall be organized into three departments (Administration, Finance and Justice), and various bureaux, divisions and commissions.[68] Thus, the Basic Law continues to recognize the previous system of organizing the administration under three secretaries (today known as Secretaries of Department): The Secretary for Justice, the Financial Secretary and the Chief Secretary. (1) The Secretary for Justice has only one department under his control, the Department of Justice. (2) The Financial Secretary has four secretaries under him: Secretary for Commerce and Economic Development; Secretary for Development; Secretary for Financial Services and the Treasury; and Secretary for Innovation and Technology. There are three agencies which come directly under the Secretary for Finance, without being under any bureau: Hong Kong Monetary Authority; Office of the Government Economist; and Policy Innovation and Coordination Office. (3) The Chief Secretary directly oversees the operation of the Human Resources Planning and Poverty Co-ordination Office, Administration Wing and Legal Aid Department. The Chief Secretary has under him nine secretaries, such as Secretary for the Civil Service and Secretary for Security, who are each responsible for a bureau and the departments and agencies which belong to the bureau. Article 61 is not prescriptive but facilitates the adoption of an administrative system suitable for the needs of Hong Kong, operating

66. *Ibid.*, Art. 56. *See*, for the working of the Executive Council, www.ceo.govhk/exco/eng/. The Interpretation and General Clauses Ordinance (Cap. 1) states that Chief Executive in Council means the Chief Executive acting after consultation with the Executive Council.
67. For instance, the Chief Executive in Council has the power to make regulations under many Ordinances, such as the Town Planning Ordinance (Cap. 131), s. 14(1), Public Health and Municipal Services Ordinance (Cap. 139), s. 11 and Crimes Ordinance (Cap. 200), s. 23. Examples of other powers are approving land-use plans made by the Town Planning Board (Town Planning Ordinance, s. 9) and appointing authorities for the purpose of certain statutes (designated authorities under Public Health and Municipal Services Ordinance (Cap. 132), s. 3).
68. Basic Law, Art. 60. There are currently 13 policy bureaux, such as Civil Service Bureau; Constitutional and Mainland Affairs Bureau; Security Bureau; Financial and Treasury Bureau; and Innovation and Technology Bureau. Departments and other agencies are grouped within each bureau. For instance, coming under the Food and Health Bureau are: Agriculture Fisheries and Conservation Department; Department of Health, Food and Environment; Hygiene Department; and Government Laboratory. Grouped under the various bureaus, there are thirty-one government departments and a number of agencies, such as the Treasury, Tourism Commission, Registration and Electoral Office, Companies Registry, the Post Office, Hong Kong Property Agency, Official Receiver's Office, Radio Television Hong Kong and Government Flying Service. Certain agencies are directly under one of the three Secretaries, such as the Department of Justice under the Secretary for Justice; Legal Aid Department under the Chief Secretary for Administration; and Hong Kong Monetary Authority under the Financial Secretary. For the Organisation of the HKSAR Government, *see* https://www.govhk/en/about/govdirectory/govchart/index.htm.

under the direction and control of the three secretaries. For instance, in the Development Bureax, the Secretary for Development has under him an Under Secretary for Development and two Permanent Secretaries. Below them are six Deputy Secretaries.[69]

56. The principal officials of the Hong Kong Special Administrative Region must be Chinese citizens who are permanent residents of Hong Kong with no right of abode in any foreign country and have ordinarily resided in Hong Kong for a continuous period of not less than fifteen years.[70]

§4. Hong Kong's System of Government: The Legislative Branch

57. The Legislative Council is the legislature of the Hong Kong Special Administrative Region.[71] At least 80% of the members of the Legislative Council must be Chinese citizens who are permanent residents of Hong Kong with no right of abode in any foreign country.[72] The term of office of the Legislative Council is four years.[73] The Legislative Council has the power:

(1) to enact, amend or repeal legislation;
(2) to examine and approve budgets introduced by the government;
(3) to examine and approve taxation and public expenditure;
(4) to receive and debate the policy address of the Chief Executive (which may be likened to the Queen's speech in the UK);
(5) to raise questions on the work of the government;
(6) to debate any issues concerning public interest;
(7) to endorse the appointment and removal of the judges of the Court of Final Appeal and the Chief Judge of the High Court; (8) to receive and handle complaints from Hong Kong residents;

---

69. https://www.devb.gov.hk/en/about_us/organisation_/index.html.
70. *Ibid.*, Art. 61. The principal officials are the following: the three Secretaries of Departments, Deputy Secretaries of Departments, Directors of Bureaux (known as secretaries) and the following five officials: the Commissioner of Police, Commissioner of the Independent Commission Against Corruption, Director of Audit, Commissioner of Customs and Excise and Director of Immigration Department. *See* Art. 48(5) of the Basic Law and https://www.govhk/en/about/govdirectory/po/index.htm.
71. Basic Law, Art. 66.
72. Basic Law, Art. 67.
73. Basic Law, Arts 66 and 68. The first Legislative Council of the Legislative Council had a two-year term, as provided by Art. 69 of the Basic Law, from 1998 to 2000. The Legislative Council which was elected in 1995 under the British rule was intended by the British and Chinese Governments to have safe passage into the post-1997 era as the first Legislative Council of Hong Kong Special Administrative Region. However, China abandoned this 'through-train' idea when in 1994, Governor Patten introduced a radical direct election element into the Legislative Council, which was incompatible with the composition of the first post-1997 Legislative Council as set out in the Basic Law. The Chinese Government refused to accept the legality of the 1995 Legislative Council and appointed a Provisional Legislative Council before the end of the British rule. The Provisional Legislative Council met in China, and on 1 July 1997 replaced the 1995 Legislative Council and functioned until the first post-1997 Legislative Council was elected in 1998. *See* below paras 254-255.

(9) if a motion initiated jointly by one-fourth of all the members of the Legislative Council charges the Chief Executive with serious breach of law or dereliction of duty and if he or she refuses to resign, the Council may, after passing a motion for investigation, give a mandate to the Chief Justice of the Court of Final Appeal to form and chair an independent investigation committee. The committee shall be responsible for carrying out the investigation and reporting its findings to the Council. If the committee considers the evidence sufficient to substantiate such charges, the Council may pass a motion of impeachment by a two-thirds majority of all its members and report it to the Central People's Government for decision; and

(10) to summon, as required when exercising the above-mentioned powers and functions, persons concerned to testify or give evidence.[74]

58. Any member of the Legislative Council may introduce a bill so long as it does not relate to public expenditure or political structure or the operation of the government. No bill relating to government policies may be introduced in the Legislative Council without the written consent of the Chief Executive.[75] The primacy of the Legislative Council in its relationship with the government is clearly set out in Article 64 of the Basic Law, which provides as follows:

> The Government of the Hong Kong Special Administrative Region must abide by the law and be accountable to the Legislative Council of the Region: it shall implement laws passed by the Council and already in force; it shall present regular policy addresses to the Council; it shall answer questions raised by members of the Council; and it shall obtain approval from the Council for taxation and public expenditure.

§5. HONG KONG'S SYSTEM OF GOVERNMENT: THE JUDICIAL BRANCH

59. If the relationship between the executive and legislative branches of the Hong Kong Government can be described as an 'Executive-led' system, the relationship between the legislative and executive branches on the one hand and the judiciary on the other can be described as one based on a separation of powers, guaranteeing the independence of the judiciary. In fact, the Basic Law is very clear on the independence of the judiciary: 'The courts of the Hong Kong Special Administrative Region shall exercise judicial power independently, free from any interference. Members of the judiciary shall be immune from legal action in the performance of their judicial functions.'[76] Judges are appointed, on the basis of judicial and professional qualifications, by the Chief Executive on the recommendation of an independent commission,[77] namely the Judicial Officers Recommendation

74. *Ibid.*, Art. 73.
75. *Ibid.*, Art. 74.
76. Basic Law, Art. 85.
77. *Ibid.*, Arts 88 and 92.

Commission.[78] A judge may be removed only on the grounds of misbehaviour or inability to discharge his duties. Such removal will be by the Chief Executive on the recommendation of a judicial tribunal, consisting of no less than three local judges, appointed by the Chief Justice of the Court of Final Appeal.[79]

60. The courts of the Hong Kong Special Administrative Region at all levels are the judiciary of the Region exercising the judicial power of the Region.[80] Article 81 provides as follows: 'The Court of Final Appeal, the High Court, district courts, magistrates' courts and other special courts shall be established in the Hong Kong Special Administrative Region. The High Court shall comprise the Court of Appeal and the Court of First Instance.' Article 83 provides that the structure, powers and functions of the courts of the Hong Kong Special Administrative Region at all levels shall be prescribed by law. Just as the Basic Law has guaranteed the continuation of the legal system in operation under the British rule, it also provides for the continuation of the system of courts in existence at the time of the handover, subject to three notable changes: (1) The Privy Council is no longer the highest court of law for Hong Kong, whose place is now taken by the Court of Final Appeal. (2) What was previously known as the Supreme Court of Hong Kong is now known as the High Court and what was known as the High Court is now known as the Court of First Instance. Prior to 1997, the Supreme Court consisted of the High Court and the Court of Appeal. Today the High Court consists of the Court of First Instance and the Court of Appeal. (3) As regards finality of judgments, the Basic Law provides that the power of final adjudication is vested in the Court of Final Appeal, subject to the qualification that the NPCSC retains the ultimate power of constitutional interpretation. Guaranteeing the continuation of the previous judicial practice, Article 84 provides that the courts of the Hong Kong Special Administrative Region shall adjudicate cases in accordance with the laws applicable in the Region as prescribed in Article 8 of the Basic Law [namely, the Basic Law, the laws previously in force in Hong Kong and the laws enacted by the legislature of the Region] and may refer to precedents of other common law jurisdictions.

78. Established in 1995 by the Judicial Officers Recommendation Commission Ordinance (Cap. 92), which amended and replaced the Judicial Service Commission Ordinance, which in 1975 had set up the Judicial Service Commission.

79. Basic Law, Art. 89.

80. *Ibid.*, Art. 80.

Chapter 4. Hong Kong: Territory (Geographic Data)

61. Hong Kong is located to the southeast of the mainland of China, adjoining the Province of Guangdong. Hong Kong covers Hong Kong Island, Lantau Island, the Kowloon Peninsula and the New Territories, including 262 outlying islands. Hong Kong has a land area of 1,104 square kilometres. Less than 25% of the landmass has been developed, and about 40% of the area has been designated as country parks and nature reserves.[81]

62. A striking feature of Hong Kong's landholding system is that the Government is the sole ground landlord. During the British rule, all land in Hong Kong belonged to the Crown, and the Hong Kong Government had authority to lease land on short or long leases or a licence. The Basic Law continues this system. Section 2 of Chapter V 'Economy' of the Basic Law deals with land leases and makes provision for land leases granted during British rule to be honoured and continued after 1 July 1997. The Basic Law provides that all leases of land granted, decided upon, or renewed before the establishment of the Hong Kong Special Administrative Region which extend beyond 30 June 1997, and all rights in relation to such leases, shall continue to be recognized and protected under the law of the Region.[82] It also makes arrangements for the renewal of pre-existing leases.[83] Article 123 of the Basic Law reiterates paragraph 2 of Annex III, 'Land Leases', of the Joint Declaration, which stated that all leases of land granted by the British Hong Kong Government not containing a right of renewal that expire before 30 June 1997, except short-term tenancies and leases for special purposes, may be extended if the lessee so wishes for a period expiring no later than 30 June 2047 without payment of an additional premium. The New Territories Leases (Extension) Ordinance was enacted in 1988 to give effect to this provision.[84]

63. The Basic Law stipulates that the land and land resources within the Hong Kong Special Administrative Region are Chinese State property. The Government of the Hong Kong Special Administrative Region is responsible for their management, use and development and for their lease or grant to individuals, legal persons or organizations for use or development. The revenue derived from any such land grants is exclusively at the disposal of the Hong Kong Government.[85]

---

81. *See* https://www.govhk/en/about/abouthk/facts.htm.
82. Basic Law, Art. 120.
83. *Ibid.*, Arts 121–123.
84. Cap. 150. *See* further Anton Cooray, 'Government as Ground Landlord and Land Use Regulator: The Hong Kong Experience', in T. Kotaka & D.L. Callies (eds), *Taking Land: Compulsory Purchase and Regulation in Asian-Pacific Countries* (Honolulu: University of Hawaii Press, 2002), 96–142.
85. Basic Law, Art. 7.

Chapter 5. Population (Demographic Data)

64. Hong Kong's population, of which about 92% are ethnic Chinese, was approximately 7.49 million in mid-2018.[86] Hong Kong is one of the most densely populated countries in the world and has 6,550 persons per square kilometre. Of the population, 50% live in owner-occupied properties and 32.5% live in public rental housing. Education is a high policy priority of the Hong Kong Government: 18.5% of the government expenditure, equivalent to 3.3% of the gross domestic product (GDP), is spent on education. A total of 22.2% of such expenditure is on primary education, 34.7% on secondary education and 27.4% on post-secondary education. As of May 2016, Hong Kong had a very low unemployment rate of around 3.4%.

65. Census and Statistics Ordinance (Cap. 316) makes provision for the taking of a census of population and the collection, compilation and publication of statistical information concerning Hong Kong. Generally, a population census is taken every ten years and a bi-census taken half way in between. The bi-census of 2016 began on 30 June 2016.[87]

86. The following information was taken from https://www.censtatd.govhk/home/ and https://www.censtatd.govhk/hkstat/sub/so20.jsp.
87. https://www.bycensus2016.govhk/en/index.html.

Part I. Sources of Constitutional Law

Chapter 1. Treaties

66. Today, much more than ever, international treaties are an important source of law. International, regional, multilateral and bilateral treaties play an indispensable part in the global trade, and in cultural and social interdependence. It is widely assumed, but not without reservation, that the present constitutional system of Hong Kong owes its existence to a bilateral treaty: the Sino-British Joint Declaration on the Question of Hong Kong between the Government of the United Kingdom and the Government of the People's Republic of China relating to the Status of Hong Kong after its Reversion to China in 1997. The Chinese Government stipulated in the Joint Declaration its basic policies regarding Hong Kong and set up a Basic Law Drafting Committee to draft Hong Kong's Basic Law founded on those basic policies.

67. Chapter VII of the Basic Law 'External Affairs' recognizes and provides for Hong Kong's participation in international organizations and international agreements either on its own or at the intervention of the People's Republic of China. Article 153 of the Basic Law provides for the application of international treaties that have been concluded either by the British Government or the Chinese Government as follows: 'The application to the Hong Kong Special Administrative Region of international agreements to which the People's Republic of China is or becomes a party shall be decided by the Central People's Government, in accordance with the circumstances and needs of the Region, and after seeking the views of the government of the Region.' It goes on to say that 'International agreements to which the People's Republic of China is not a party but which are implemented in Hong Kong may continue to be implemented in the Hong Kong Special Administrative Region. The Central People's Government shall, as necessary, authorize or assist the government of the Region to make appropriate arrangements for the application to the Region of other relevant international agreements.'[88]

68. Article 150 provides that representatives of the Hong Kong Special Administrative Region may, as part of the Chinese delegation, participate in negotiations at the diplomatic level directly affecting the Region conducted by the National People's Congress. Article 151 provides that the Hong Kong Special Administrative

88. For a complete list of treaties and international agreements that are applicable to Hong Kong, *see* https://www.doj.govhk/eng/laws/treaties.html.

Region may, on its own, using the name 'Hong Kong, China' maintain and develop relations and conclude and implement agreements with foreign States and regions and relevant international organizations in the appropriate fields including the economic, trade, financial and monetary, shipping, communications, tourism, cultural and sports fields. The words 'appropriate fields' suggest that the subject matter of treaties falling within Article 151 must relate to matters within the autonomy of the Region and not within the exclusive competence of the People's Republic of China.[89]

69. Article 152 provides as follows: 'Representatives of the Government of the Hong Kong Special Administrative Region may, as members of delegations of the People's Republic of China, participate in international organizations or conferences in appropriate fields limited to states and affecting the Region, or may attend in such other capacity as may be permitted by the Central People's Government and the international organization or conference concerned, and may express their views, using the name "Hong Kong, China".'[90]

70. Hong Kong subscribes to the dualist system which maintains that an international treaty has legal effect only if it is incorporated into Hong Kong law by legislation.[91] Hong Kong Bill of Rights, which was enacted to incorporate the ICCPR into the law of Hong Kong, is a good example of the application of the dualist system. There are other statutes which give effect to international treaties, such as the Dumping at Sea Ordinance (Cap. 466) which gives effect to the London Convention on the Prevention of Marine Pollution by the Dumping of Wastes at Sea and Recognition of Trusts Ordinance (Cap. 76) which gives effect to the Hague Convention on the Law Applicable to Trusts and on their Recognition.

71. Unlike the International Convention on Civil and Political Rights (ICCPR) which has been incorporated in Hong Kong through the Hong Kong Bill of Rights, no dedicated legislation has been made to incorporate the International Covenant on Economic, Social and Cultural Rights (ICESCR) into the law of Hong Kong, but being a state party to it, Hong Kong is expected to honour the commitments it has

89. Yash Ghai wrote that 'this capacity grows out of the exigencies of the exercise of Hong Kong's autonomy or express delegation and is principally concerned with the maintenance of Hong Kong's economic and cultural systems … .' *See* Yash Ghai, *Hong Kong's New Constitutional Order* (2nd edn, HKUP, 1999) 464.

90. *See* HKSAR External Affairs: 'International intergovernmental organisations limited to states'. https://www.cmab.gov.hk/en/issues/external1.htm.

91. *See* below Part I, Ch. 3, §3 Other Legislative Norms, paras 111-112. While recognizing that international treaties do not have force of law in Hong Kong in the absence of implementing legislation, the Court of Final Appeal in *G A v Director of Immigration* (2014) 17 HKCFAR 60, (CFA), [58], observed citing *Ubamaka v Secretary for Security* (2012) 15 HKCFAR 743, (CFA), [43]: 'It is a principle of construction that where a domestic statute is ambiguous and is capable of bearing different meanings, which may in turn conform or conflict with the treaty, the court will presume that the legislature intended to legislate in accordance with applicable international treaty obligations. But where the statute is clear, the court's duty is to give effect to it whether or not that would involve breach of a treaty obligation.' *See also Comilang Milagros Tescon v Director of Immigration* [2018] HKEC 753, (CA), [103].

undertaken.[92] Two illustrative provisions of the Convention may be reproduced: 'Each State Party to the present Covenant undertakes to take steps, individually and through international assistance and co-operation, especially economic and technical, to the maximum of its available resources, with a view to achieving progressively the full realization of the rights recognized in the present Covenant by all appropriate means, including particularly the adoption of legislative measures' (Article 2 of the Convention); and 'The States Parties to the present Covenant recognize the right of everyone to social security, including social insurance' (Article 9 of the Convention). Some of the provisions of the Convention have found expression through the Basic Law and legislation. The Basic Law provisions are: Article 25 (equal rights of men and women), Article 36 (the right to social welfare), Article 37 (freedom of marriage), Article 137 (freedom of educational institutions), Article 144 (rights of non-governmental organizations) and Article 147 (duty to formulate laws and policies relating to labour). Some of the relevant legislative measures are: Employment Ordinance (Cap. 57), Employment of Children Regulations (Cap. 57B), Labour Tribunals Ordinance (Cap. 25), Labour Relations Ordinance (Cap. 55), Mandatory Provident Fund Scheme Ordinance (Cap. 485), Family Status Discrimination Ordinance (Cap. 527), Marriage Reform Ordinance (Cap. 181), Protection of Children and Juveniles Ordinance (Cap. 243), Education Ordinance (Cap. 279).[93]

72. International treaties which have been incorporated into the law of Hong Kong take effect not as international conventions but as part of Hong Kong law. However, where an ordinance expressly sates that the substantive provisions of an international treaty have force in Hong Kong, then the courts must treat such treaty provisions as forming part of Hong Kong law. *See*, for instance, section 2(1) of the Recognition of Trusts Ordinance (Cap. 76) which states as follows: 'The provisions of the Convention set out in the Schedule shall have the force of law in Hong Kong.' It is of course open to the Hong Kong legislature to modify any such treaty provision in its application to Hong Kong. A good historical illustration which also has constitutional importance is the judicial interpretation of the Convention of Peking,

---

92. *See* for instance, in *Pagtama Victorina Alegre v Director of Immigration* [2016] HKEC 85, (CFI), where the court referred to the practice of the Government to give careful consideration to the ICESCR where appropriate. There is a useful comparative discussion of inspirational value of the Covenant in a paper published by the Research and Library Services Division of the Legislative Council Secretariat, dated April 1995, titled 'The Implementation of the International Covenant on Economic, Social and Cultural Rights in Overseas Jurisdictions and Hong Kong', https://www.legco.govhk/yr97-98/english/sec/library/9495rp02e.pdf.

    In *Ho Choi Wan v Hong Kong Housing Authority* (2005) 8 HKCFAR 628, (CFA), [65]–[67], Bokhary PJ, the only judge to refer to ICESCR, expressed the view that the ICESCR might provide strong support for construing the Housing Ordinance (Cap. 283) as imposing a duty on the Hong Kong Government to provide affordable housing. Dissenting from the majority opinion, Bokhary PJ held that the Housing Ordinance imposes such a duty. *See also* similar observations by Bokhary NPJ (again the only judge to deal with ICESCR) in *Kong Yunming v Director of Social Welfare* (2013) 16 HKCFAR 950, (CFA), [173]–[180].

93. *See* the Fourth Report of the People's Republic of China under the ICESCR, Part Two: Hong Kong Special Administrative Region (February 2020). https://www.cmab.govhk/en/issues/prc_10.htm.

which granted a ninety-nine-year lease of the New Territories to the British Government. One of the treaty provisions declared as follows: 'It is at the same time agreed that within the [Walled City] of Kowloon, the Chinese officials now stationed there shall continue to exercise jurisdiction except so far as they may be inconsistent with the military requirements for the defence of Hong Kong. Within the remainder of the newly-leased territory Great Britain shall have sole jurisdiction.'

73. In *Re Wong Hon*,[94] the question was whether Wong Hon, not being a British subject but a Chinese national and thus an alien, was under the criminal jurisdiction of the colonial government in respect of an offence committed within the Walled City of Kowloon. The argument advanced in support of the application was that the Convention between Great Britain and China dated 9 June 1898, which leased the New Territories to the British Crown for a period of ninety-nine years, excepted therefrom the Walled City of Kowloon or reserved jurisdiction within that area to officials of China and that since Wong Hon was an alien (i.e., not a British subject), the British Courts in Hong Kong could not exercise jurisdiction over him in respect of an offence committed within the area of the Walled City. The court rejected that argument in view of the fact that the British Government had, by an Order in Council made in 1899, clearly manifested its intention to exercise prerogative power in respect of the Walled City. That Order in Council clearly stated that: 'whereas, the exercise of jurisdiction by the Chinese officials in the [Walled] City of Kowloon having been found to be inconsistent with the military requirements for the defence of Hong Kong, it is expedient that … the Chinese officials within the City of Kowloon should cease to exercise jurisdiction therein, and that the said City of Kowloon should become part and parcel of Her Majesty's Colony of Hong Kong for all purposes during the continuance of the term of the lease in the said Convention mentioned.'[95] The Attorney General argued that, whatever might have been the effect of the Convention, the Order in Council was a clear manifestation of the intention to exercise prerogative power, and represented good law. He also argued that Orders in Council made by virtue of royal prerogative were acts of state and were non-justiciable in a court of law. Among the several authorities cited by the court in support of its decision was the judgment of Atkin LJ in *The Fagernes*,[96] where it was said that 'what is the territory of the Crown is a matter of which the Court takes judicial notice. … Any definite statement from the proper representative of the Crown as to the territory of the Crown must be treated as conclusive.' The court in *Re Wong Hon*[97] concluded that: 'on the constitutional aspects of the case the authorities are, in our view, conclusive that in the sphere of municipal law it is not possible to establish, in the face of unqualified assertion of jurisdiction by the Crown, that such jurisdiction does not exist *or that it is subject to some limitation arising from the mode of acquisition of the territory in question'*.[98]

94. *Re Wong Hon* [1959] HKLR 601, (Full Court).
95. *See ibid.*
96. *The Fagernes* [1927] P 311, (CA), 324.
97. *Re Wong Hon* [1959] HKLR 601, (Full Court) at 613.
98. Emphasis added.

74. The legal effect of the Peking Convention was considered in *Winfat Enterprise (HK) Ltd v Attorney General.*[99] The relevant provision of the Convention stated that the land of the inhabitants of the New Territories could be expropriated only for an official purpose and on the payment of a fair price. The applicant, having failed to obtain compensation representing the development value of his land under the Crown Lands Resumption Ordinance,[100] sought to rely on the above provision in the Convention. While conceding that the Convention was not applicable in Hong Kong *ex proprio vigore,* he argued that the Convention had been incorporated into Hong Kong law, particularly through two proclamations made by the Governor in 1899 declaring that property rights of the inhabitants of the New Territories would be respected. Alternatively, he argued that the power of the Hong Kong legislature to make laws 'for peace, order, and good government'[101] did not include the power to pass laws in breach of its treaty obligations. Both of these arguments were rejected:

(1) Regarding the legal effect of the two proclamations, the Court held that they did not have the force of law, because the Governor had not delegated power to legislate of his own motion. The court held that the issuing of the two proclamations was not an exercise of the Royal prerogative power to deny itself the right to enforce the Crown Lands Resumption Ordinance.
(2) Regarding the second argument, Kempster J said:

> In my opinion [the words 'for the peace, order, and good government'], hallowed as they are by long and widespread usage, are clear and unambiguous and must be given effect whether or not they carry out treaty obligations. It has never been held, though it has been suggested, that the laws of a Colonial legislature in breach of international law are void.[102]

75. We may now examine the importance of the Sino-British Joint Declaration in the interpretation of the Basic Law. It has been held that the Joint Declaration does not by itself create any rights in Hong Kong, because it has not been incorporated into the law of Hong Kong.[103] However, Hong Kong courts are justified in referring to the Joint Declaration in interpreting the Basic Law because the Joint

99. *Winfat Enterprise (HK) Ltd v Attorney General* [1983] HKLR 211, (HC).
100. Now Lands Resumption Ordinance (Cap. 124).
101. 'The Governor, by and with the advice and consent of the Legislative Council, may make laws for the peace, order, and good government of the Colony.' Letters Patent 1917–1994, Art. VII (1).
102. *Winfat Enterprise (HK) Ltd v Attorney General* [1983] HKLR 211, (HC), at 225.
103. *See The Home Restaurant Ltd v Attorney General* [1987] HKLR 237, (HC), and *Tang Ping-hoi v Attorney General* [1987] HKLR 324, (HC). In the *Tang Ping-hoi* case at 328 Nazareth J reiterated the well-established rule that courts will not enforce obligations and rights under international treaties, unless they are embodied in the domestic law.

Declaration is part of the history leading to the enactment of the Basic Law.[104] Chief Justice Li said in *Ng Ka Ling v Director of Immigration* that the purpose of the Basic Law is to give Hong Kong a high degree of autonomy in accordance with China's basic policies as set out and elaborated in the Joint Declaration, and that the Joint Declaration was a relevant extrinsic aid in interpreting the Basic Law.[105]

76. There, the Court of Appeal was dealing with the question of right of abode in Hong Kong and did not find the Joint Declaration useful in ascertaining the meaning of Articles 24 and 22(4) of the Basic Law, which relate to the right of abode of persons of Chinese nationality born outside Hong Kong.[106] Professor Yash Ghai points out that according to Chinese practice the Joint Declaration should be applicable in China and that the Basic Law might have to yield to it in case of any inconsistency.[107]

77. The Basic Law specifically refers to the applicability of certain treaties in Hong Kong. Article 39 provides that: 'the provisions of the International Covenant on Civil and Political Rights, the International Covenant on Economic, Social and Cultural Rights and the international labour conventions as applied to Hong Kong shall remain in force and shall be implemented through the laws of the Hong Kong Special Administrative Region'. The second paragraph of that Article states that 'the rights and freedoms enjoyed by Hong Kong residents shall not be restricted unless as prescribed by law. Such restrictions shall not contravene the provisions of the preceding paragraph of this Article.'

78. The relevance of the international conventions referred to in the Basic Law, particularly the ICCPR, has been discussed in several cases. In *HKSAR v Pun Ganga Chandra*,[108] it was unsuccessfully argued that the common law requirement

---

104. It has been said that the Joint Declaration and the Basic Law carry the overwhelming theme of a seamless transition: *HKSAR v Ma Wai Kwan, David* [1997] HKLRD 761, (CA), at 790, per Nazareth VP.
105. *Ng Ka Ling v Director of Immigration* (1999) 2 HKCFAR 4, (CFA), 340. *See also Director of Immigration v Chong Fung Yuen* (2001) 4 HKCFAR 211, (CFA), 225, where Li CJ said: 'External aids are external materials which throw light on the context or purpose of the Basic Law or its particular provisions. Such external materials, generally speaking, include the Joint Declaration, the Explanations on the Basic Law (draft) given at the National People's Congress on 28 March 1990 shortly before its adoption on 4 April 1990, the state of domestic legislation at that time and the time of the Joint Declaration, materials brought into existence prior to or contemporaneous with the enactment of the Basic Law, although it only came into effect on 1 July 1997. (The list of external materials is of course not exhaustive.).'
106. *Ng Ka Ling v Director of Immigration* (1999) 2 HKCFAR 4, (CFA), 347.
107. Yash Ghai, *Hong Kong's New Constitutional Order: The Resumption of Chinese Sovereignty and the Basic Law* (Hong Kong: Hong Kong University Press, 1997), at 70–71. The author says at page 71 that 'the Joint Declaration is effective in Chinese laws, and probably also that it is superior to the Basic law when their provisions conflict'. *See also* Anton Cooray, 'Hong Kong in China: the Promise of "One Country, Two Systems"', (1997) 2 *McGill Law Journal* 42, 751–760 and Roda Mushkat, *One Country, Two International Personalities: The Case of Hong Kong* (Hong Kong: Hong Kong University Press, 1997).
108. *HKSAR v Pun Ganga Chandra* [2001] 2 HKLRD 151, (CA).

as to intention for the offence of murder[109] was arbitrary and unreasonable, and therefore was inconsistent with Article 5 of the Bill of Rights Ordinance (which reproduces Articles 9 of the ICCPR) and 28 of the Basic Law.[110] In *HKSAR v Coady*,[111] it was held that the grievous bodily harm rule[112] did not offend Article 5(1) of the Bill of Rights Ordinance, as reflected in Article 28 of the Basic Law. The Court held that the Common Law requirement was not inconsistent with the relevant provision in the ICCPR. In *HKSAR v Ng Kung Siu and Another*, the Court of Final Appeal upheld the validity of legislation which criminalized desecration of the national flag, as a reasonable restriction of the freedom of expression. The legislation was held to be human rights compliant.[113]

79. The relevance and applicability of international treaties in Hong Kong was explained by Cheung J in *Mok Chi Hung v Director of Immigration.*[114] Cheung stated the following propositions:

(1) An international covenant or treaty, unless it is incorporated into domestic legislation, is not part of the domestic law.[115] The Convention on the Rights of the Child, which the applicant relied upon in the instant case, for instance, was not incorporated into Hong Kong law.
(2) Rectification of an international covenant gives rise to a legitimate expectation, absence statutory or executive indications to the contrary, that administrative decision-makers will act in conformity with the international covenants.[116]
(3) The ICCPR is applicable in Hong Kong through incorporation in the Hong Kong Bill of Rights Ordinance and entrenchment under Article 39 of the Basic Law.[117]

---

109. The *mens rea* of murder is that at the time he killed the deceased, the defendant intended either to kill the deceased or to cause him at least really serious bodily injury.
110. This view was confirmed by the Court of Final Appeal in *Lau Cheong v HKSAR* (2002) 5 HKCFAR 415, (CFA).
111. *HKSAR v Coady* [2000] HKLRD 195, (CA).
112. Namely that a person may be found guilty of murder if his intention was to cause serious bodily injury to the deceased, even though he did not intend to kill the deceased.
113. *HKSAR v Ng Kung Siu and Another* (1999) 2 HKCFAR 442, (CFA). The Court of Final Appeal has in *HKSAR v Koo Sze Yiu*, (2014) 17 HKCFAR 811, (CFA), reaffirmed the correctness of the ruling in *Ng Kung Siu* case. Chief Justice Ma observed in *Koo Sze Yiu* case that 'Article 16 of the Hong Kong Bill of Rights … brings into domestic legislation the provisions of Art. 19 of the International Covenant on Civil and Political Rights.' Cases where reference is made to the effect of ICCPR in Hong Kong are: *Hong Kong Television Network Ltd v Chief Executive in Council* [2016] HKEC 785, (CA); *MS v Director of Social Welfare* [2016] HKEC 344, (CFI); *Television Broadcasts Ltd v Communications Authority* [2016] HKEC 238, (CFI); *Pagtama Victorina Alegre v Director of Immigration* [2016] HKEC 85, (CFI); and *Leung Lai Kwok Yvonne v Chief Secretary for Administration* [2015] HKEC 1034, (CFI).
114. *Mok Chi Hung v Director of Immigration* [2000] 2 HKLRD 514, (CFI).
115. *R v Secretary of State for the Home Department, ex p Brind* [1991] 1 AC 696, (HL).
116. Following two Australian cases, namely: *Minister of State for Immigration and Multicultural Affairs v Teoh* (1994–1995) 183 CLR 273, (HC), and *Tien v Minister for Immigration and Multicultural Affairs* (1998) 159 ALR 405, (Federal Court).
117. The application of the Covenant on Civil and Political Rights through the Basic Law and the Bill of Rights will be further elaborated on later, when dealing with human rights.

(4) The ICESCR, which is referred to in Article 39 of the Basic Law but not incorporated by local legislation, is promotional in nature. It can be used as guidance when the Hong Kong Government considers measures which are within the scope of the ICESCR. Article 39 expressly prohibits any restriction of rights and freedoms in Hong Kong, if any such restriction contravenes the duty of the Hong Kong Government to implement the conventions referred to in that Article.

80. Several international treaties and conventions have been implemented in Hong Kong, in areas not directly relevant to Constitutional Law. For instance, the Whaling Industry (Regulation) Ordinance (Cap. 496) was enacted to give effect to the International Convention for the Regulation of Whaling of 1946. Sometimes an ordinance may provide for the implementation of international conventions through subsidiary legislation. For instance, the Merchant Shipping (Prevention and Control of Pollution) Ordinance (Cap. 413) empowers the Secretary for Economic Services to make regulations for giving effect to the International Convention for the Prevention of Pollution from Ships and other relevant international agreements.

Chapter 2. Constitution (Classification, Nature and Main Features of the Basic Law)

§1. The Relationship Between the Chinese Constitution and Hong Kong's Basic Law

81. The Constitutional relationship between Hong Kong and the People's Republic of China is unique. In the Chinese constitutional framework, Hong Kong is one of the two Special Administrative Regions of China, the other being Macau, which Portugal handed back to China. In order to provide a constitutional and legal framework closely following Hong Kong's previous system of government and law, the Chinese Government enacted the Basic Law of the Hong Kong Special Administrative Region. The Basic Law was promulgated by the NPC on 4 April 1990, founded on the principle of 'One Country, Two Systems'. Although the Basic Law is a national law of the People's Republic of China, it serves as Hong Kong's Constitution. It not only binds the Hong Kong Government and Hong Kong people; it also binds the Chinese Government in that the jurisdiction of the Chinese Government has to be exercised so as not to infringe the provisions of the Basic Law. As Chief Justice Li said in *Ng Ka Ling v Director of Immigration*,[118] Hong Kong courts have the power to examine whether any legislative acts of the NPC or its Standing Committee are consistent with the Basic Law and to declare them to be invalid if found to be inconsistent. 'In our view, the courts of the Region do have this jurisdiction and indeed the duty to declare invalidity, if inconsistency is found. It is right that we should take this opportunity of stating so unequivocally.'[119]

82. Although the Basic Law is a national law of the People's Republic of China, it has a special status because it was drafted and adopted pursuant to an international agreement between the UK and the People's Republic of China. That agreement, the Sino-British Joint Declaration of 1984, set out the basic policies of the Chinese Government regarding Hong Kong. The Basic Law was then enacted in order to implement the basic policies of the People's Republic of China regarding Hong Kong. It has been argued that the Chinese commitment to the proper implementation of the Basic Law is guaranteed by the Chinese commitment under international law to observe its treaty obligations.[120]

83. The constitutional importance of the Basic Law is clearly set out in Article 11 of the Basic Law, the last article in Chapter 1 'General Principles':

> In accordance with Article 31 of the Constitution of the People's Republic of China, the systems and policies practised in the Hong Kong Special Administrative Region including the social and economic systems, the system for

118. *Ng Ka Ling v Director of Immigration* (1999) HKCFAR 4, (CFA).
119. *Ibid.*, at 337.
120. *See* generally Roda Mushkat, *One Country, Two Transnational Personalities: The Case of Hong Kong* (Hong Kong: Oxford University Press, 1997), Ch. 5.

safeguarding the fundamental rights and freedoms of its residents, the executive, legislative and judicial systems, and the relevant policies, shall be based on the provisions of [the Basic Law]. No law enacted by the legislature of the Hong Kong Special Administrative Region shall contravene [the Basic Law].

84. The legislative, executive and judicial branches of the Hong Kong Government are bound by the Basic Law and Hong Kong does not have the power to amend the Basic Law. The power to amend the Basic Law resides with the NPC. What Hong Kong can do is to propose an amendment for consideration by the National People's Congress. Such a proposal has to be submitted by the delegation of the Region to the National People's Congress. The proposal must be supported by two-thirds of the deputies of the Region to the National People's Congress, two-thirds of the members of the Legislative Council, and the Chief Executive.[121]

§2. The Main Features of the Basic Law

85. The Basic Law provides for the establishment of the three principal branches of the Hong Kong Government and their interrelationships. It also sets out the relationship between the Chinese Central Government and the Hong Kong Special Administrative Region. As will be more fully described elsewhere, the Basic Law demarcates matters that are within the autonomy of Hong Kong and matters that are within the province of the Central Authorities. The Basic Law regulates the manner in which Chinese national laws might become applicable in Hong Kong and provides for intervention in Hong Kong affairs by the Central Authorities in certain specified circumstances. Although this outline of the Basic Law has some flavour of a federal constitution, the relationship between the Chinese Central Government and the Hong Kong Special Administrative Region cannot fit into the typical classification of a federal constitution. The Basic Law creates a unique constitutional arrangement that guarantees the continuation of Hong Kong's system of government and way of life, while at the same time Hong Kong remains an integral part of China.[122]

86. Chapter I of the Basic Law, entitled 'General Principles', sets out the basic policies of the Chinese Government regarding Hong Kong. These principles are:

(1) Hong Kong is an inalienable part of China;
(2) the Chinese Central Government authorizes Hong Kong to exercise a high degree of autonomy;
(3) Hong Kong's executive authorities and the legislature must consist of permanent residents of Hong Kong, thereby ensuring that Hong Kong is governed by Hong Kong people;

121. For further details, *see* Part III, Ch. 2, §3 Restrictions upon interpretation and amendment of the Basic Law.
122. For the relationship between the central and regional authorities, *see* Part III, Ch. 1.

(4) the rights and freedoms of people in Hong Kong, including right of private property, will be protected;
(5) the socialist policies will not be practised in Hong Kong and Hong Kong's capitalist system and way of life will remain unchanged for fifty years from 1997;
(6) while land in Hong Kong is State property, their management will be exclusively by the Hong Kong Government;
(7) laws of Hong Kong as previously in force will continue to be maintained, subject to being consistent with the Basic Law;
(8) English and Chinese will be the official languages;
(9) Hong Kong may have a regional flag in addition to the use of the national flag and the national anthem of China.

87. Chapter II of the Basic Law deals with the relationship between the Central Authorities and Hong Kong. Two substantive powers, namely foreign affairs and defence, have been left in the hands of the Central Authorities. However, Hong Kong is authorized to conduct relevant external affairs on its own according to the Basic Law.[123] Similarly, although the Central Government is responsible for the defence of Hong Kong, it is the Hong Kong Government that is responsible for the maintenance of public order in Hong Kong. And although military forces of the Central Government are stationed in Hong Kong, they may 'assist in the maintenance of public order and in disaster relief' at the request of the Hong Kong Government. The members of the garrison have to abide by Hong Kong laws.[124] Hong Kong has legislative power, subject to the limitation that the Chinese Central Government may invalidate any Hong Kong law on the ground that it is not in conformity with provisions of the Basic Law relating to matters not within Hong Kong's jurisdiction or with those provisions relating to the relationship between Hong Kong and the Central Authorities.[125] The only national laws that apply in Hong Kong are those listed in Annex III of the Basic Law. The list may be amended by the Central Government in accordance with the provisions of the Basic Law.[126] Article 22 of the Basic Law has been enacted to ensure that no department of the Central Government and no regional authority in China may interfere with the affairs of Hong Kong.

---

123. Basic Law, Art. 13.
124. *Ibid.*, Art. 14.
125. *Ibid.*, Art. 17. This procedure comes into operation when a law is reported to the Standing Committee (all laws passed by the Hong Kong Special Administrative Region must be reported to the Standing Committee). Where the Standing Committee decides that any law that has been so submitted infringes Art. 17, it may return it to the Hong Kong Special Administrative Region. It has no power to amend the law to make it Basic Law compliant. If the law is returned to Hong Kong Special Administrative Region, it 'shall immediately be invalidated'. The invalidation does not have retrospective effect, unless otherwise provided for in the laws of Hong Kong. The use of the wording suggests that the Standing Committee has discretion in deciding whether a law which is deemed to contravene the Basic Law should or should not be returned to Hong Kong for it to be invalidated.
126. *Ibid.*, Art. 18.

88. Chapter III of the Basic Law deals with Fundamental Rights and Duties of the residents. It protects not only civil and political rights but also cultural and social rights. Article 39 provides a very useful safeguard:

> The provisions of the ICCPR, the International Covenant on Economic, Social and Cultural Rights, and international labour conventions as applied to Hong Kong shall remain in force and shall be implemented through laws of the Hong Kong Special Administrative Region. The rights and freedoms enjoyed by Hong Kong residents shall not be restricted unless as prescribed by law. Such restrictions shall not contravene the provisions of the preceding paragraph of this Article.

89. Chapter IV deals with the political structure. Section 1 deals with the Chief Executive, and section 2 deals with the Executive Authorities. Section 3 is entitled 'The Legislature' and section 4 'The Judiciary'. Section 5 deals with district organizations, and section 6 deals with public servants. These provisions are discussed in appropriate places in this monograph.

90. Chapter V deals with the economy under four sections: Section 1 'Public Finance, Monetary Affairs, Trade, Industry and Commerce', section 2 'Land Leases', section 3 'Shipping', and section 4 'Civil Aviation'. Chapter VI deals with education, science, culture, sports, religion, labour and social services. Chapter VII deals with external affairs. The purpose of these chapters is to enumerate various powers that are within the autonomy of Hong Kong and to highlight how these autonomous rights will have to be accommodated within the equally important principle that China exercises sovereign rights over Hong Kong.

91. Chapter VIII, which deals with the interpretation and amendment of the Basic Law, is the most controversial of the provisions relating to the relationship between central and regional authorities. Articles 158 and 159, which make up this chapter, will be fully discussed later in this monograph.

92. The provisions of the Basic Law are supplemented by three annexes and a number of decisions. The three annexes deal with the procedures for setting up the Legislative Council, the selection of the Chief Executive and the application of national laws in Hong Kong. The Instruments appended to the Basic Law deal with matters preparatory to the establishment of the Basic Law, amendments to the three annexes, explanations of various decisions taken in relation to Hong Kong and constitutional interpretations rendered by the Standing Committee.

Chapter 3. Legislation and Other Equivalent Legal Norms

93. The most important written source of Hong Kong's constitutional law is the Basic Law. Being the constitution of Hong Kong, Basic Law prevails over any Ordinance, subsidiary legislation and unwritten law. There are other statutes that supplement the Basic Law, such as the Hong Kong Bill of Rights (Cap. 383) and the Legislative Council Ordinance (Cap. 542) and thereby constitute sources of constitutional law. Before 1 July 1997, Imperial legislation constituted an important source of Hong Kong's constitutional law, because the Imperial Government had the overriding power to legislate for Hong Kong. In contrast, today Chinese national legislation applies in Hong Kong only as provided by the Basic Law itself. Within those constraints, Chinese national law may provide some assistance in understanding the working of Hong Kong's constitutional system. For instance, the Legislation Law of China may be relevant in understanding the scope of an interpretation given by the Standing Committee of the National People's Congress.[127] Certain provisions of the Chinese Constitution too are relevant to a proper understanding of the operation of the Basic Law.

§1. Chinese National Laws

94. National laws of China apply throughout the territory of Mainland China, other than in the two Special Administrative Regions, Hong Kong and Macau. The application of Chinese national laws in Hong Kong is regulated by the Basic Law. Article 18 of the Basic Law provides two different avenues for them to be extended to Hong Kong. First, China may extend a national law to Hong Kong by including it in Annex III of the Basic Law. Second, China may extend any national law to Hong Kong in an emergency.

95. As regards the first method of extending Chinese national laws to Hong Kong, Article 18 of the Basic Law provides as follows: 'National laws shall not be applied in the Hong Kong Special Administrative Region except for those listed in Annex III to this Law. The laws listed therein shall be applied locally by way of promulgation or legislation by the Region.' Annex III in its original form listed the following national laws:

(1) Resolution on the Capital, Calendar, National Anthem and National Flag of the People's Republic of China.
(2) Resolution on the National Day of the People's Republic of China.
(3) Order on the National Emblem of the People's Republic of China proclaimed by the Central People's Government.
(4) Declaration of the Government of the People's Republic of China on the Territorial Sea.
(5) Nationality Law of the People's Republic of China.

127. *See*, Lin Feng, 'The Duty of Hong Kong Courts to Follow the NPCSC's Interpretation of the Basic Law: Are There Any Limits?' (2018) 48 *Hong Kong Law Journal* 167.

(6) Regulations of the People's Republic of China concerning diplomatic privileges and immunities.

96. Article 18 of the Basic Law further provides that the NPCSC may add to or delete from the list of laws in Annex III after consulting its Committee for the Basic Law of the Hong Kong Special Administrative Region and the government of the Region. Laws listed in Annex III to [the Basic Law] shall be confined to those relating to defence and foreign affairs as well as other matters outside the limits of the autonomy of the Region as specified by [the Basic Law]. The NPCSC has amended the list of national laws in Annex III (by adding to or deleting from the list) on five occasions, and they are found in the decisions which appear as Instrument 5 (dated 1 July 1997), Instrument 6 (dated 4 November 1998), Instrument 7 (dated 27 October 2005), Instrument 8 (4 November 2017) and Instrument 9 (30 June 2020).

97. On 1 July 1997, Instrument 5 added the following national laws to Annex III:

(a) Law of the People's Republic of China on the National Flag;
(b) Regulations of the People's Republic of China concerning consular privileges and immunities;
(c) Law of the People's Republic of China on the National Emblem;
(d) Law of the People's Republic of China on the Territorial Sea and the Contiguous zone; and
(e) Law of the People's Republic of China on the garrisoning of the Hong Kong Special Administrative Region.

Instrument 5 deleted the Order on the National Emblem of the People's Republic of China proclaimed by the Central People's Government from the list and replaced that with the national law on the Design of the national emblem, notes of explanation and instructions for use.

98. On 4 November 1998, Instrument 6 added another national law to the list, the Law of the People's Republic of China on the Exclusive Economic Zone and the Continental Shelf.

99. On 27 October 2005, Instrument 7 added the Law of the People's Republic of China on Judicial Immunity from Compulsory Measures Concerning the Property of Foreign Central Banks.

100. On 4 November 2017, Instrument 8 added the Law of the People's Republic of China on the National Anthem.

101. On 30 June 2020, Instrument 9 added the Law of the People's Republic of China on Safeguarding National Security in the Hong Kong Special Administrative Region.

102. National laws that are listed in Annex III do not apply automatically in Hong Kong. They have to be brought into effect by the Hong Kong Government by way of proclamation or legislation. The national laws originally listed in Annex III, together with some national laws added in 1997, were brought into effect in Hong Kong by way of Proclamations published in 1997.[128] The national laws that were added subsequently were also similarly brought into effect by way of Proclamation.[129] Promulgation simply requires the Hong Kong Government to state that the promulgated national law will apply in Hong Kong, in the form in which it was enacted in China.

103. A national law has to be made applicable in Hong Kong by way of passing an ordinance, if it is necessary to adapt the national law to Hong Kong's peculiar circumstances. An instance where local legislation is appropriate to give effect to a national law of China is provided by the enactment of the National Flag and National Emblem Ordinance.[130] When, on 1 July 1997, the Chinese authorities added the People's Republic of China Law on the National Flag to Annex III, the local legislature passed the National Flag and National Emblem Ordinance because there was a need to adapt the national law for application in Hong Kong. For instance, the Ordinance deals with the power of the Chief Executive to stipulate the organizations that must display or use the national flag and the other places at which, the occasions on which, the manner in which, and the conditions under which, the national flag must be displayed or used.[131]

104. Even where a national law of China has been brought into effect through a Proclamation, there may be a need to pass supplementary legislation in Hong Kong. A good illustration is provided by the Chinese Nationality (Miscellaneous Provisions) Ordinance (Cap. 540), which was passed in 1997 to provide for matters relating to the operation in Hong Kong of the Nationality Law of the People's Republic of China. It deals with the manner in which applications for Chinese nationality should be made and dealt with. The promulgation of the National Security Law of 2020 provides another example. At the same time as promulgating the National Security Law on 30 June 2020, Hong Kong Government passed a set of administrative regulations and Implementation Rules for Article 43 of the National Security Law (relating to measures that the law enforcement authorities, especially the

128. *See* Legal Notices 379 and 386 of 1997.

129. *See*, for instance, Legal Notice of 1998. For promulgation of the Law of the People's Republic of China on Safeguarding National Security in the Hong Kong Special Administrative Region by Gazette on 30 June 2020, *see* https://www.news.gov.hk/eng/2020/07/20200706/20200706_204612_065.html.

130. Ordinance No 116 of 1997. This Ordinance has not been given a chapter number and appears on Hong Kong e-Legislation as Instrument A401. For a discussion of this Ordinance, *see HKSAR v Ng Kung Siu and Another* (1999) 2 HKCFAR 442, (CFA), and *Hong Kong Special Administrative Region v Koo Sze Yiu* (2017) HKCFAR 811, (CFA) (reaffirming *Ng Kung Siu* decision).

131. National Flag and National Emblem Ordinance (Instrument A401), s. 3(2). Article 7 of the Law of the People's Republic of China on Safeguarding National Security in the Hong Kong Special Administrative Region, added to Annex III of the Basic Law on 30 June 2020 states that Hong Kong shall complete, as early as possible, legislation for safeguarding national security as stipulated in the Basic Law and 'shall refine relevant laws'.

police, have to take, such as search and interception of communications under the National Security Law), to take effect on 7 July 2020.[132]

105. The national laws listed in Annex III include laws relating to the capital, the calendar, the national anthem, the national emblem and the national flag of the People's Republic of China,[133] and laws relating to the territorial sea, the contiguous zone, the exclusive economic zone and the continental shelf of China. Regulations of the People's Republic of China concerning consular privileges and immunities are an important entry in Annex III. The Law of the People's Republic of China on the Garrisoning of the Hong Kong Special Administrative Region and, most importantly, the 2020 Law on Safeguarding National Security in Hong Kong are national laws that were made especially for Hong Kong, which will be discussed elsewhere in this work.[134]

106. As regards the second method of extending Chinese national laws to Hong Kong, Article 18 provides as follows: 'In the event that the Standing Committee of the National People's Congress decides to declare a state of war or, by reason of turmoil within the Hong Kong Special Administrative Region which endangers national unity or security and is beyond the control of the government of the Region, decides that the Region is in a state of emergency, the Central People's Government may issue an order applying the relevant national laws in the Region.'[135] The Chinese Government has not so far extended any Chinese laws to Hong Kong under this provision.

§2. Hong Kong Legislation

107. Article 23 of the Basic Law requires the Hong Kong Government to enact laws for the following purposes:

(1) to prohibit any act of treason, secession, sedition, subversion against the Chinese Central Government or theft of state secrets;

132. *See* the press release of the Hong Kong Government on 6 July 2020. https://www.info.gov.hk/gia/general/202007/06/P2020070600784.htm?fontSize=1. National Security Law is dealt with in some details under 'Security Legislation'.

133. In *HKSAR v Ng Kung Siu* (1999) HKCFAR 442, (CFA), the Court of Final Appeal dealt with an offence under the National Flag and National Emblem Ordinance No 116 of 1997 (Instrument A401), which was enacted to give effect to the People's Republic of China Law on the National Flag.

134. For Garrison Law, *see* 477-478, below. For National Security Law, *see* §2, I. The National Security Law, paras 869-892.

135. As regards the rest of China, Art. 67(21) of the Chinese Constitution authorizes the Standing Committee of the National People's Congress to decide on entering a state of emergency nationwide or in particular provinces, autonomous regions or cities directly under the Central Government jurisdiction. Article 89(16) authorizes the State Council to decide, in accordance with the provisions of law, on entering a state of emergency in parts of provinces, autonomous regions and cities directly under the Central Government jurisdiction.

(2) to prohibit foreign political organizations or bodies from conducting political activities in Hong Kong; and
(3) to prohibit political organizations or bodies of Hong Kong from establishing ties with foreign political organizations or bodies.

108. In September 2002, the Security Bureau of the Hong Kong Government published a consultation paper on the proposed legislation to implement Article 23. This led to widespread public concern and attracted much international attention. The consultation was followed by the publication of a legislative measure on 14 February 2003, namely the National Security (Legislative Provisions) Bill. There was widespread opposition to the Bill which was reflected in the Legislative Council debates and which led to the resignation of the Secretary for Security in July 2003. The government was compelled to withdraw the Bill from the Legislative Council. So far there has been no serious attempt to introduce legislation to comply with Article 23.[136]

109. The Hong Kong Bill of Rights Ordinance continues to be an important constitutional document. When passed in 1991, the Bill of Rights Ordinance enjoyed a quasi-constitutional status for two reasons: First, any legislation in existence at the time that the Bill of Rights Ordinance came into effect, namely 8 June 1991, stood repealed to the extent that such legislation did not admit a construction consistent with the Ordinance.[137] Second, the courts were required to interpret any legislation passed subsequent to the enactment of the Bill of Rights Ordinance to be consistent with the ICCPR as applied to Hong Kong.[138] The Hong Kong Bill of Rights contained in Part II of the Hong Kong Bill of Rights Ordinance substantially reproduces the ICCPR as applied to Hong Kong. It must be noted, however, that the NPCSC deleted sections 2(3), 3 and 4 of the Bill of Rights. The intention of that amendment was to remove the effectiveness of the Bill of Rights Ordinance as an aid to interpretation of legislation. However, it has been argued that the Bill of Rights would still have the effects originally intended regardless of the 1997 amendments.[139] Courts do in fact continue to make reference to the Bill of Rights Ordinance in determining cases dealing with human rights.[140]

136. *See* for the enactment and extension to Hong Kong of the National Security Law by the National People's Congress in 2020, to fill this gap, paras 870-873 below.
137. Bill of Rights Ordinance (Cap. 383), s. 3(2). The following are examples of cases where the Bill of Rights Ordinance was invoked successfully to question the validity of pre-existing legislation: *R v Sin Yau-ming* [1992] 1 HKCLR 127, (CA) (presumptions contained in the Dangerous Drugs Ordinance (Cap. 134)); *R v Chong Ah-choi* [1994] 2 HKCLR 263, (CA) (s. 17 of the Summary Offences Ordinance (Cap. 228), which created the offence of possession of an offensive weapon without a satisfactory explanation); *R v Man Wai-keung (No 2)* [1992] 2 HKCLR 207, (CA), (s. 83XX(3)(a) of the Criminal Procedure Ordinance (Cap. 221), which stated that a defendant who on appeal succeeded in obtaining a retrial was not entitled to costs).
138. *Ibid.*, s. 4.
139. *See,* e.g., P. Wesley-Smith, 'Maintenance of the Bill of Rights' (1997) 27 *Hong Kong Law Journal* 15 and Johannes Chan, 'The Status of the Bill of Rights in the Hong Kong Special Administrative Region' (1998) 28 *Hong Kong Law Journal* 152.
140. *See,* e.g., *Tse Kwan Sang v Pat Heung Rural Committee* [1999] 3 HKRLRD 267, (CFI), where Chueng J said at 274: 'The ICCPR is implemented by the Hong Kong Bill of Rights Ordinance.'

110. Legislation is an important supplementary source in areas such as powers and privileges of the Legislative Council, election of the Chief Executive and Legislative Council elections, and the powers and functions of courts of law. A particularly important legislative measure is the Emergency Regulations Ordinance (Cap. 241). That Ordinance empowers the Chief Executive to make any regulations whatsoever that he may consider desirable in the public interest, whenever the Chief Executive in Council considers that there is an occasion of emergency or public danger. The ambit of regulations that he may make is plenary, as appears from the list of purposes in section 2(2): (a) censorship and the control and suppression of publications, writings, maps, plans, photographs, communications and means of communication; (b) arrest, detention, exclusion and deportation; (c) control of the harbours, ports and waters of Hong Kong, and the movements of vessels; (d) transportation by land, air or water, and the control of the transport of persons and things; (e) trading, exportation, importation, production and manufacture; (f) appropriation, control, forfeiture and disposition of property, and of the use thereof; (g) amending any enactment, suspending the operation of any enactment and applying any enactment with or without modification; (h) authorizing the entry and search of premises; (i) empowering such authorities or persons as may be specified in the regulations to make orders and rules and to make or issue notices, licences, permits, certificates or other documents for the purposes of the regulations; (j) charging, in respect of the grant or issue of any licence, permit, certificate or other document for the purposes of the regulations, such fees as may be prescribed by the regulations; (k) the taking of possession or control on behalf of the Chief Executive of any property or undertaking; (l) requiring persons to do work or render services; (m) payment of compensation and remuneration to persons affected by the regulations and the determination of such compensation; and (n) the apprehension trial and punishment of persons offending against the regulations or against any law in force in Hong Kong.[141] An emergency regulation or any order or rule made in pursuance of such a regulation has effect notwithstanding anything inconsistent therewith contained in any enactment. Any provision of an enactment that may be inconsistent with such regulation, order or rule has no effect to the extent of such inconsistency, as long as such regulation, order or rule is in operation.[142] It must be noted that currently there are no regulations made under the Ordinance in force. All the existing regulations made by the Governor were repealed in 1995.

§3. Other Legislative Norms

111. Before 1997, the Queen had the prerogative power to pass legislation for Hong Kong. Under the Basic Law the Central Chinese Government or, by way of

Chief Justice Ma observed in *Leung Fuk Wah Oil v Secretary for Justice* [2015] HKEC 1752, (CFA), footnote 7, that 'Article 39 states that the provisions of the International Covenant on Civil and Political Rights remain in force in Hong Kong. The relevant provision is Article 14.1 of the ICCPR, implemented into Hong Kong's laws as Article 10 of the Bill of Rights by the Hong Kong Bill of Rights Ordinance (Cap 383).'

141. Emergency Regulations Ordinance (Cap. 241), s. 2(2)(g).

142. *Ibid.*, s. 2(4).

delegation, the Chief Executive of Hong Kong has any prerogative power to make law. Therefore, the only primary legislation in Hong Kong consists of ordinances passed by the Hong Kong legislature and Chinese laws that are made applicable in Hong Kong. Article 39 of the Basic Law refers to certain international treaties as providing standards for legislation in Hong Kong. These treaties are the ICCPR, the ICESCR and international labour conventions as applied to Hong Kong. Hong Kong is obliged to implement them through its laws. More importantly, rights and freedoms of Hong Kong residents cannot be restricted in contravention of such obligation.[143]

112. Hong Kong follows the dualist approach, and as in the UK no international treaties take effect in Hong Kong until they are incorporated into the domestic law. Initially the English courts adopted a strict view of the need for incorporation. For instance, in *R v Chief Immigration Officer, Heathrow Airport and Another, Ex parte Salamat Bibi*,[144] the Court of Appeal held that the immigration officers performed their functions under the Act in accordance with the rules made by the Secretary of State and were not under any further duty to apply the principles laid down in the European Convention on Human Rights, for even if it were practicable for them to do so the Convention had not yet been made law by Parliament and was therefore not part of the law of the UK, though, as the UK was a party to the Convention, Parliament when enacting a statute or a Minister when making rules would be presumed to have had regard to its provisions. Lord Denning said:

> The position as I understand it is that if there is any ambiguity in our statutes, or uncertainty in our law, then these courts can look to the Convention as an aid to clear up the ambiguity and uncertainty, seeking always to bring them into harmony with it. Furthermore, when Parliament is enacting a statute, or the Secretary of State is framing rules, the courts will assume that they had regard to the provisions of the Convention and intended to make the enactment accord with the Convention: and will interpret them accordingly. But treaties and declarations do not become part of our law until they are made law by Parliament. I desire, however, to amend one of the statements I made in *R v Secretary of State for Home Affairs, ex p Bhajan Singh* [1976] Q.B. 198, 207. I said then that the immigration officers ought to bear in mind the principles stated in the Convention. I think that would be asking too much of the immigration officers. They cannot be expected to know or to apply the Convention. They must go simply by the immigration rules laid down by the Secretary of State, and not by the Convention.[145]

143. For instance, in *Gurung Kesh Bahadur v Director of Immigration* [2001] 3 HKLRD 32, (CA), the court held that the provisions of the Immigration Ordinance (Cap. 115), s. 11(10) were unlawful in so far as they contravened the right of freedom to travel contained in the Basic Law, Art. 31. This was affirmed by the Court of Final Appeal (2002) 5 HKCFAR 480, (CFA). *See also Official Receiver v Zhi Charles* (2015) 18 HKCFAR 467, (CFA). *See* further Part IV, Ch. 2 'Fundamental Rights and Liberties'.

144. *R v Chief Immigration Officer, Heathrow Airport and Another, Ex p Salamat Bibi* [1976] 1 WLR 979, (CA).

145. *Ibid.*, 984.

113. The Australian and New Zealand courts pioneered a liberal view of international conventions as creating not substantive rights but procedural rights, which has been approved in both the UK and Hong Kong. In *Minister of State for Immigration and Ethnic Affairs v Rah Hin Teoh*, it was held that, while courts would be greatly reluctant to allow backdoor entry to international conventions which have not been incorporated into the domestic law, ratification of a convention is a positive statement by the executive government that it will act in accordance with the Convention. That positive statement is an adequate foundation for a legitimate expectation that administrative decision-makers will act in conformity with the Convention, absent statutory or executive indications to the contrary.[146]

114. The Court of First Instance preferred the Australian and New Zealand approach in *Chan Mei Yee v Director of Immigration* where Cheung J said:

> In my view, the approach of the High Court of Australia and Court of Appeal in New Zealand should be adopted. This approach clearly recognised that the international covenants and conventions are not part of the domestic law. However, a husband and a child who are Hong Kong permanent residents clearly have the legitimate expectation that when the Government is to remove their wife or mother, it should take into account the international covenants on the importance of family and welfare of the children. … Where legitimate expectation is invoked by reference to the international covenants, the court is, of course, dealing this concept in the context of procedural propriety and not as a matter of substance.[147]

115. Under the Basic Law, there is no provision for the Chief Executive to make laws independent of the Legislative Council, although emergency regulations made by him under the Emergency Regulations Ordinance may override any Hong Kong legislation.[148] An area where the Chief Executive may exercise a power that is legislative in nature is when he issues 'executive orders' as provided by Article 48 of the Basic Law. The Chief Executive has made several instruments in the exercise of that power.

116. In *Association of Expatriate Civil Servants of Hong Kong v Chief Executive of the Hong Kong Special Administrative Region*,[149] the Court of First Instance

146. *Minister of State for Immigration and Ethnic Affairs v Teoh* [1994–1995] 183 CLR 273, (HC).
147. *Chan Mei Yee v Director of Immigration* [2000] HKEC 788, (CFI). In *Mok Chi Hung v Director of Immigration* [2001]2 HKLRD 125, (CFI), the Court of First Instance affirmed the principle that ratification of an international covenant gave rise to a legitimate expectation, in the absence of statutory or executive indications to the contrary, that administrative decision-makers would act in conformity with the international covenants. In *R v Secretary of State for the Home Department ex p Mohammed Hussain Ahmed* [1999] Imm AR 22, (CA), Lord Woolf MR happily adopted the *Teoh principle*.
148. *See* below, Part V, Ch. 3. Emergency Laws.
149. *Association of Expatriate Civil Servants of Hong Kong v Chief Executive of the Hong Kong Special Administrative Region* [1998] 1 HKLRD 615, (CFI).

considered the legality of the Public Service Administration Order 1997 (which deals with the Chief Executive's powers in relation to the appointment, dismissal, interdiction and retirement of public servants in the public interest) and the Public Service (disciplinary) Regulation (which was made under the Public Service Administration Order to deal with disciplinary procedures). These two instruments had been made to replace the Colonial Regulations, which were the Crown's Instructions to the Governor, and the Civil Service Regulations, which the Governor had made to supplement the provisions of the Colonial Regulations. It was argued that under the system that prevailed in Hong Kong before 1 July 1997, the procedures by which public servants were appointed and dismissed had been established by the legislature or with legislative approval, and that the existing system could not be replaced solely by an executive order. It was also argued that the procedures did not amount to 'legal' procedures of the kind contemplated by Article 48(7) which it was argued required legislative approval. It was contended that the word 'legal' in Article 48(7) meant 'prescribed by law', and that 'prescribed by law' meant prescribed by legislation.

117. The Court of First Instance rejected that line of argument and held that 'legal procedures' for this purpose need not necessarily be made by an ordinance. Noting that, as held by the Court of Appeal in *Lam Yuk-Ming v Attorney General*, during the British colonial period regulatory powers in relation to the civil service were exercised not by way of legislation but by way of Colonial Regulations, which were prerogative legislation, and regulations made by the Governor, which were subsidiary legislation, the Court held that the executive orders provided a lawful way of prescribing the relevant procedures for decision-making.[150] Following the *Lam Yuk-Ming* case, the court held that the hallmark of the previous system was that, where procedures were to be established locally, they were established by the Governor by executive action; and that while there were undoubtedly constitutional differences between Hong Kong's previous system and the current system, the maintenance of the previous system did not require the current system to have legislative approval. The court in *Association of Expatriate Civil Servants of Hong Kong v Chief Executive of the Hong Kong Special Administrative Region* also observed that although there was no clear pattern as to the rationale behind the use of one phrase and not another in the Basic Law, the meaning of which depended very much on its context, it was important to note that the phrase 'prescribed by law' was used in a number of its provisions. Accordingly, when the Basic Law contemplated that a particular course of action had to be prescribed by law, it said so. The fact that Article 48(7) spoke of 'legal' procedures, rather than of procedures 'prescribed by law' was an indication that a meaning other than 'prescribed by law' was intended. The principle that can be gathered from this case is that the order in question in that case was not an exercise of legislative power by the Chief Executive. Thus, the decision in that case is no authority that the Chief Executive may exercise legislative power in the guise of an executive order. In *Rowse v Secretary*

150. *Association of Expatriate Civil Servants of Hong Kong v Chief Executive of the Hong Kong Special Administrative Region* [1998] 1 HKLRD 615, (CFI), citing *Lam Yuk-Ming v Attorney General* [1980] HKLR 815, (CA).

for Civil Service, the Court of First Instance reiterated that the Public Service Administrative Order of 1997 was not legislation.[151]

118. That the Chief Executive cannot exercise legislative power by issuing an executive order is authoritatively laid down in the following litigation on the system of covert surveillance, particularly secret monitoring of private communications, under the Telecommunications Ordinance (Cap. 106). The Court of First Instance in *Leung Kwok Hung v Chief Executive of Hong Kong Special Administrative Region* [2006] HKEC 239, (CFI), affirmed by the Court of Appeal [2006] HKEC 816, (CA), held that an Executive Order issued by the Chief Executive in August 2005, which was intended, 'to set out the legal procedures in accordance with which covert surveillance may be carried out by or on behalf of officers of government departments which undertake law enforcement investigations or operations' could not be regarded as equivalent to 'legal procedures' for the purposes of Article 30 of the Basic Law, which prohibits invasion of freedom and privacy of communication except that relevant authorities may inspect communications in accordance with legal procedures to meet the needs of public security or of investigation into criminal offences (paragraphs 150–151). The court held that the order was no more than 'a set of administrative directions given to employees of the Government by the Head of the Government' (paragraph 141). The Executive Order was not meant to bind Hong Kong residents generally and did not purport to be legislation (paragraph 141). The Court rejected the argument that the Executive Order was passed to seek the legislative vacuum created by the non-implementation of the Interception of Communications Ordinance, which was passed in 1997, and the Executive Order has legislative effect because it was intended to authorize and regulate secret surveillances of all kinds (paragraphs 142-143).[152]

---

151. *Rowse v Secretary for Civil Service* [2008] 5 HKLRD 217, (CFI).

152. *Leung Kwok Hung v Chief Executive of Hong Kong Special Administrative Region* [2006] HKEC 239, (CFI) affirmed by the Court of Appeal [2006] HKEC 816, (CA).

Chapter 4. Jurisprudence

119. Hong Kong's constitutional principles and rules are to be found in the Basic Law and Constitution-related legislation. Judges in the common law tradition perform an important function in the interpretation and application of constitutional norms and rules. Unlike in certain other countries, such as Sri Lanka under its previous Constitution of 1972,[153] there is no special Constitutional Court in Hong Kong. Matters of constitutional interpretation may be raised in any court of law, and the final determination of constitutional issues will rest with Hong Kong's highest court, the Court of Final Appeal. Exceptionally, the NPCSC will have the right to interpret certain types of provisions in the Basic Law. Decisions of Hong Kong courts and interpretations handed down by the Standing Committee will be an important source of Constitutional Law.

120. Before we examine the rules and judicial practices of constitutional interpretation it is useful to briefly examine the main canons of statutory interpretation. The starting point of statutory interpretation is the Interpretation and General Clauses Ordinance (Cap. 1), which is referred to at several places in this work. The wider general context is provided by the common law rules of interpretation that have evolved through judicial interpretation of legislation in England and the rest of the common law world, which are helpfully and authoritatively collected in *Bennion on Statutory Interpretation.*[154] The central provision in the Interpretation and General Clauses Ordinance on statutory interpretation is section 19: 'An Ordinance shall be deemed to be remedial and shall receive such fair, large and liberal construction and interpretation as will best ensure the attainment of the object of the Ordinance according to its true intent, meaning and spirit.' This is reflected in the general judicial practice of giving a generous and purposive and interpretation to legislation, as well as constitutional documents.[155] Ma CJ has explained the well-settled principles of statutory interpretation relevant to giving a contextual and purposive interpretation: '(1) In construing statutory provisions, the court does not merely look at the relevant words. It construes the relevant words having regard to their context and purpose; (2) The context of the relevant statutory provision should be taken in its widest sense and will of course include the other provisions of the statute. It may also be relevant in any given case to look at the history of the relevant provisions; (3) Ascertaining the purpose of the statutory provision is obviously relevant, not only to help provide the relevant context, but to give meaning to the words used. In this latter respect, it is to be observed that often the meaning of words by themselves will not be clear unless regard is paid to context and purpose. Words have to be construed but they must not be construed in a vacuum; (4) In ascertaining the purpose of a statutory provision, the court adopts a flexible and

153. Anton Cooray, 'Three Models of Constitutional Litigation: Lessons from Sri Lanka', (1992) 21 *Anglo-American Law Review* 430–448.

154. *Bennion on Statutory Interpretation* (8th edn, LexisNexis, 2020, retitled as *Bennion, Bailey and Norbury on Statutory Interpretation*).

155. *See*, for instance, Ma CJ in *Yung Chi Keung v Protection of Wages on Insolvency Board* (2016) 19 HKCFAR 469, (CFA), [22]: 'statutory construction requires a purposive approach to be adopted; in other words, the words of a statute must be construed in the light of their purpose'.

open-minded approach. The purpose may be clear from the provision itself or it may be necessary to look at the Explanatory Memorandum to the bill introducing the provision or a ministerial or official statement may be utilised for this purpose.'[156]

121. One common manifestation of this liberal interpretation approach is that the courts construe statutes as conferring on a pubic authority not only the powers expressly stated in the ordinance but also any other powers which are necessary to carry out such powers.[157] Section 40 of the Interpretation and General Clauses Ordinance gives statutory expression to one important aspect of that principle: 'Where any Ordinance confers upon any person power to do or enforce the doing of any act or thing, all such powers shall be deemed to be also conferred as are reasonably necessary to enable the person to do or enforce the doing of the act or thing.'[158]

122. In the interpretation of the Basic Law and Hong Kong's constitutional system, courts adopt the common law approach to interpretation and, as a result, it is legitimate, and indeed essential, to make reference to cases decided by Hong Kong courts before 1997 as well as to judicial decisions from other common law jurisdictions on constitutional issues.[159] Indeed, Article 8 of the Basic Law provides that the laws previously in force in Hong Kong, that is, the common law, rules of equity, ordinances, subordinate legislation and customary law, shall be maintained, except for any that contravene [the Basic Law], and subject to any amendment by the legislature of the Hong Kong Special Administrative Region. Article 84 provides that the courts of the Hong Kong Special Administrative Region may refer to precedents of other common law jurisdictions. It is important to note that in determining human rights cases, courts will not hesitate to refer to decisions and opinions of international tribunals and advisory bodies that dwell on human rights similar to those recognized and enforced in Hong Kong.[160]

While the Basic Law does not confer an exclusive constitutional jurisdiction on any particular court, it is possible for an ordinance that supplements Hong Kong's Constitution to confer a particular jurisdiction on a particular court. For instance,

---

156. *Town Planning Board v Town Planning Appeal Board* (2017) 20 HKCFAR 196, (CFA), [29].
157. In the oft-cited words of Lord Selborne LC in *Attorney-General v Great Eastern Railway Co* (1880) 5 App Cas 473, (HL), 478: 'whatever may fairly be regarded as incidental to, or consequential upon, those things which the Legislature has authorised, ought not (unless expressly prohibited) to be held, by judicial construction, to be *ultra vires*'. For a recent Hong Kong judicial decision which relied on this principle, *see Lui Chi Hang Hendrick v Independent Police Complaints Council (No 2)* [2020] 2 HKLRD 911, (CFI).
158. For an instance where s. 40 was relied on, *see Leung Kwok Hung v Secretary for Justice* [2020] HKEC 533, (CA), [270].
159. *See*, e.g., the decisions of the Court of Final Appeal in *Ng Ka Ling v Director of Immigration* (1999) 2 HKCFAR 4, (CFA), (Basic Law) and *HKSAR v Ng Kung Siu* (1999) 2 HKCFAR 442, (CFA), (human rights). In the recent case of *Tong Ying Kit v HKSAR* [2020] HKEC 2586, (CFI), the Court of First Instance emphasized that in interpreting the National Security Law of 2020 (a Chinese national law especially made for Hong Kong), Hong Kong courts would be guided by common law rules of interpretation as in the interpretation of the Basic Law, itself being a national law of China. This case is discussed in the discussion of the National Security Law in Part V, Ch. 3, §2 Legislation on Security.
160. *See* Anton Cooray, 'Bills of Rights and Constitutional Interpretation', in J. Hatchard & P. Slinn (eds) *Parliamentary Supremacy and Judicial Independence: A Commonwealth Approach* (London

Part 7 of the Legislative Council Ordinance (Cap. 542) confers on the Court of First Instance jurisdiction in respect of election petitions (with a right of appeal directly to the Court of Final Appeal). Section 67(3) of the Legislative Council Ordinance in its original form contained a finality clause.[161] In *Mok Charles v Tam Wai Ho* the Court of Final Appeal held the finality clause to be an unjustified ouster of the right to appeal.[162] Section 67(3) was amended in 2011.[163] It was through an amendment of the Court of Final Appeal Ordinance (Cap. 484) in 2011 that a discretionary right of appeal was provided to the Court of Final Appeal against the determination of the Court of First Instance.[164] The Legal Practitioners Ordinance (Cap. 159) provides another example of a situation where the denial of a further appeal to the Court of Final Appeal was held to be unconstitutional. Section 13(1) of the Legal Practitioners Ordinance (Cap. 159) provided that an appeal shall lie to the Court of Appeal against any order of the Solicitors Disciplinary Tribunal and that 'the decision of the Court of Appeal on any such appeal shall be final'. The Court of Final Appeal held that this limitation on the Court of Final Appeal's final power of adjudication was not a proportionate limitation.[165] Section 13(1) of the Legal Practitioners Ordinance (Cap. 159) was amended in 2005, removing the objectionable words.

123. The interpretation of the Basic Law calls for special skills particularly because the Basic Law is a Chinese national law and has no counterpart in any common law jurisdiction.[166] As seen in Part III, Chapter 2 'Interpretation of the Basic

---

and Sydney: Cavendish Publishing Co, 1999), 59–64 and Anton Cooray, 'International and Domestic Sources of Human Rights in Harmony? The Hong Kong Experience', (1999) 4 *Year Book Law & Legal Practice in East Asia* 71–94. *See Shum Kwok Sher v HKSAR* (2002) 5 HKCFAR 381, (CFA).

161. Section 67(3) of the Ordinance as originally enacted provided as follows: 'At the end of the trial, the Court must certify the determination of the Court in writing. The judge must sign the certificate and ensure that the seal of the Court is applied to the certificate. The determination, as certified, is final as to the matters at issue concerning the election petition.'
162. *Mok Charles v Tam Wai Ho* (2010) 13 HKCFAR 762, (CFA). At [73], Ma CJ said: 'Accordingly, in my judgment, the burden to demonstrate that the restriction in s. 67(3) of the [Legislative Council Ordinance] satisfies the proportionality test, has not been discharged. It therefore follows that s. 67(3) of the [Legislative Council Ordinance] must be declared unconstitutional as being inconsistent with Art. 82 of the Basic Law (insofar as the finality aspect is concerned). It may be that suitable changes can be made to the legislation to ensure that any restrictions or limitations on the right of appeal are indeed no more than necessary, but this is a matter for the Government and the Legislature to consider, taking into account no doubt those provisions in comparable legislation to which reference has been made.'
163. Section 67(3) now reads: 'At the end of the trial of an election petition, the Court must announce its determination by means of a written judgment.' (amended 18 of 2011 s. 9)
164. Section 22(1)(c) of the Court of Final Appeal Ordinance (Cap. 484). *See* 'Election Petition Mechanism under the Legislative Council Ordinance and related issues' LC Paper No CB(2)798/10-11(03), of the Legislative Council Panel on Constitutional Affairs (undated) explaining the proposed legislative changes in response to *Mok Charles v Tam Wai Ho* (2010) 13 HKCFAR 762, (CFA). https://www.legco.govhk/yr10-11/english/panels/ca/papers/ca0117cb2-798-3-e.pdf.
165. *Solicitor and Law Society of Hong Kong v Secretary for Justice* (2003) 6 HKCFAR 570, (CFA).
166. *See* generally Albert H.Y. Chen, 'The Interpretation of the Basic Law – Common Law and Mainland Chinese Perspectives' (2000) 30 *Hong Kong Law Journal* 380–431 and Johannes Chan et al. (eds) *Hong Kong's Constitutional Debate: Conflict over Interpretation* (Hong Kong: Hong Kong University Press, 2000).

Law', the ultimate power of constitutional interpretation vested in the NPCSC adds a complication to the interpretation of the Basic Law.

124. The rules of interpretation appropriate for Hong Kong's constitutional system go to the root of constitutional jurisprudence. We may now outline those rules of interpretation.

125. In line with courts of other common law jurisdictions, Hong Kong courts have adopted a 'generous and purposive approach' to the interpretation of the Basic Law, particularly for the protection of human rights,[167] while strictly construing any restrictions on human rights. In *Ng Ka Ling v Director of Immigration* Chief Justice Li succinctly describes the purposive approach: 'The adoption of a purposive approach is necessary because a constitution states general principles and expresses purposes without condescending to particularity and definition of terms. Gaps and ambiguities are bound to arise and, in resolving them, the courts are bound to give effect to the principles and purposes declared in, and to be ascertained from, the constitution and relevant extrinsic materials. So, in ascertaining the true meaning of the instrument, the courts must consider the purpose of the instrument and its relevant provisions as well as the language of its text in the light of the context, context being of particular importance in the interpretation of a constitutional instrument.'[168]

126. While constitutional provisions which confer rights have to be given a liberal, wide and purposive interpretation, any constitutional provision that appears to place a restriction on such a right must be given a restrictive interpretation. Referring to the right conferred by Article 24(3) and the limitation prescribed in Article 22(4) of the Basic Law,[169] Li CJ explained how purposive interpretation and restrictive interpretation work hand in hand: 'the right to enter or, as defined in the statute,

167. *See Ng Ka Ling v Director of Immigration* (1999) 2 HKCFAR 4, (CFA), reaffirmed by the Court of Final Appeal in *Ubamaka v Secretary for Security* (2012) HKCFAR 743, (CFA), [5]. For the application of the generous and purposive approach to the Letters Patent (*Attorney General v David Chiu Tat-Cheung* [1992] 2 HKLR 84, (CA)) and to the Bill of Rights (*R v Sin Yau-ming* [1992] 1 HKCLR 127, (CA)), which approach courts should adopt today in relation to the Basic Law: *Wong Kei Kwong v Principal Assistant Secretary for Civil Service* [2008] HKEC 261, (CFI), [53]), *Secretary for Justice v Lau Kwok Fai* (2005) 8 HKCFAR 304, (CFA), and *Law Society of Hong Kong v Solicitor* [2004] HKEC 1423, (CA).

168. *Ng Ka Ling v Director of Immigration* (1999) 2 HKCFAR 4, (CFA), 28. In *W v Registrar of Marriages* (2013) 16 HKCFAR 112, (CFA), [115], the Court of Final Appeal referred to the Basic Law and the Hong Kong Bill of Rights as 'living instruments intended to meet changing needs and circumstances' calling for 'a more generous interpretation of a fundamental right'.

169. Article 22(4) requires people from other parts of China to obtain approval of the Mainland Chinese authorities to enter Hong Kong. The question was whether a child born in China, of Chinese nationals who are permanent residents of Hong Kong, needed such approval to enter Hong Kong. Li CJ explained how the right of abode would be eroded if Art. 22(4) was not given a restricted meaning: 'Article 24(3) confers the right of abode in unqualified terms on permanent residents. If the argument that Art. 22(4) qualifies the right of abode in Art. 24(3) is correct, the right of abode of persons who are undoubtedly permanent residents but who are residing on the Mainland is a most precarious one. The Region's Constitution, whilst conferring the constitutional right of abode in the Region on the one hand, would have with the other hand subjected that right to the discretionary

the right to land, is an essential element of the right of abode. We have concluded that having defined the class of permanent residents, a generous approach should be adopted to the interpretation of the constitutional provisions guaranteeing their rights. The right of abode is ... a core right. Indeed, without it and the right to enter which is an essential element, the rights and freedoms guaranteed can hardly be enjoyed, including in particular the right to vote and to stand for election. Applying the generous approach, the Court should, in our view, scrutinise with the greatest care any submission that art 22(4) encroaches on that core right.'[170]

127. Article 24(3) of the Basic Law provides that 'persons of Chinese nationality born outside Hong Kong' of permanent residents of Hong Kong, are entitled to permanent residence in Hong Kong. Article 22(4) of the basic Law provides that, 'For entry into the Hong Kong Special Administrative Region, people from other parts of China must apply for approval.' In reconciling these two provisions of the Basic Law, the Court of Final Appeal held that the limitation prescribed in Article 24(3) does not operate so as to prevent a child who is entitled to claim permanent residence under Article 24(3) from entering Hong Kong. Adopting this restricted meaning of Article 22(4), the Court of Final Appeal declared unconstitutional the relevant provisions of the Immigration Ordinance which gave effect to an unrestricted meaning of Article 22(4).[171] As Chan ACJ observed in *HKSAR v Chow Nok Hang*, any law which purports to restrict a fundamental right must be narrowly interpreted and the restriction must satisfy the test of necessity and proportionality. In construing the relevant statutory provisions which have the effect of restricting such right, the court must have regard to competing public interests, including the maintenance of public order and the rights and freedoms of others. The right balance has to be struck between the preservation of public order and the exercise of the individual's rights and freedoms and between the competing rights and freedoms of individuals or groups of individuals.[172]

---

control of the Mainland authorities, that discretionary control being beyond the authority of the Region.' *Ng Ka Ling v Director of Immigration* (1999) 2 HKCFAR 4, (CFA), 34.

170. *Ng Ka Ling v Director of Immigration* (1999) 2 HKCFAR 4, (CFA), 34. For similar sentiments on the need for a generous interpretation of rights and a restrictive interpretation of limitations imposed on rights, *see also Gurung Kesh Bahadur v Director of Immigration* (2002) 5 HKCFAR 480, (CFA), [24]; *Leung Kwok Hung v Hong Kong Special Administrative Region* [2005] 8 HKCFAR 229, (CFA), [6], where the court observed: 'Needless to say, in a society governed by the rule of law, the courts must be vigilant in the protection of fundamental rights and must rigorously examine any restriction that may be placed on them'; and *HKSAR v Chow Nok Hang* (2013) 16 HKCFAR 837, (CFA), [2].

171. *See* below, Part IV, Ch. 1, §3 Right of Abode.

172. *HKSAR v Chow Nok Hang* (2013) 16 HKCFAR 837, (CFA), [2]. On proportionality, *see HKSAR v Ng Kung Siu* (1999) 2 HKCFAR 442, (CFA), 461. *See also Ming Pao Newspapers Ltd v A-G of Hong Kong* [1996] AC 907, (PC), at 917D-E. In *Leung Kwok Hung v HKSAR* (2005) 8 HKCFAR 229, (CFA), [58], the Court of Final Appeal applied the proportionality test to restrictions on the freedom of assembly as follows: 'The Commissioner has a discretion to restrict the right of peaceful assembly, by objecting to or by imposing conditions on a notified public procession. In deciding whether and if so what restriction to impose in the exercise of his discretion, the Commissioner must consider: (1) whether a potential restriction is rationally connected with one or more of the statutory legitimate purposes; and (2) whether the potential restriction is no more than is necessary to accomplish the legitimate purpose in question.'

128. A canon of statutory interpretation that is of particular relevance to constitutional interpretation is that courts will not rule on a question of constitutional interpretation, unless such a ruling is necessary for the determination of the dispute before the court. This is aptly referred to as the doctrine of ripeness or live controversy.[173] However, just as the US courts, Hong Kong courts have not regarded this as a fixed constitutional requirement, and in appropriate circumstances made declarations of law in the absence of a concrete controversy needing resolution.[174]

129. Where the court finds a statute unconstitutional, it will limit the ruling of unconstitutionality only to the extent justified in the context of the case. It will refuse to make any broader statement of the law.[175] Similarly, where a legislative provision appears to be unconstitutional the court will try to interpret the objectionable legislative provision restrictively so that it does not offend the constitution, unlike when it is given a wider interpretation.[176] The court may sever an offending provision or parts of it in order to make the rest of the legislation is constitutional.[177] This practice of remedial interpretation is widely known in common law jurisdictions.[178]

130. When the court holds that a legislative or administrative measure is unconstitutional, the ruling will have retrospective effect. In other words, the court declares the statute or administrative decision null and void, with the result that anything done in the past under authorization given by such unconstitutional legislative or executive measure would be unlawful. In circumstances whereby the retrospective effect of a judicial decision would result in great hardship and inconvenience, there are certain solutions that the courts may make use of. The first solution is to make a prospective overruling, that is to specify that the declaration of invalidity would apply only with prospective effect. This is a rather extreme measure, which the courts in the UK and Hong Kong have referred to as a possible solution but not in fact invoked so far.[179] Declaration of temporary validity and suspension of the declaration of invalidity are less radical exceptions to the retrospective effect rule.[180]

---

173. For the very American roots of this restrained judicial approach, *see* Gene R. Nichol, 'Ripeness and the Constitution' (1987) 54:1 *The University of Chicago Law Review* 153.
174. *See* below paras 592-595.
175. *See Pang Yiu Hung v Commissioner of Police* [2003] 2 HKLRD 125, CFI, where the court declined to issue a broadly worded declaration of unconstitutionality of legislation.
176. *See* below paras 615-617 where remedial interpretation is discussed in some detail in relation to human rights protection.
177. *Leung Kwok Hung v HKSAR* (2005) 8 HKCFAR 229, (CFA), [82]–[85].
178. *See*, for the theory and practice of remedial interpretation in Canada and South Africa, Robert Leckey, 'Remedial Practice Beyond Constitutional Text' (2016) 64:1 *The American Journal of Comparative Law* 1.
179. *See* below paras 621-622. For the jurisprudential underpinning of this unique US invention and how it would sit in the UK legal landscape, *see* Wolfgang Friedmann, 'Limits of Lawmaking and Prospective Overruling' (1966) 29:6 *Modern Law Review* 593.
180. *See also* below para. 620.

131. A court may declare a legislative or executive measure unconstitutional and of no legal effect but may allow a brief period of time for the legislature or the executive to amend the law or administrative regulation or policy to make it constitution-compliant. This could be achieved by declaring the legislative or administrative measure invalid but grant it temporary validity. Alternatively, the court may suspend the coming into effect of its ruling of unconstitutionality for a short period of time. Both temporary validity and suspension are intended to give the legislature or the executive a reasonable, but short, period of time to amend the legislation or the executive measure, such as subsidiary legislation or an administrative practice set out in regulations or guidance notes.

132. Where the legislative or executive measure in question can be put right by corrective legislation or executive arrangements,[181] the court might suspend the coming into effect of the declaration of invalidity giving the government sufficient time to expeditiously take remedial measures, generally on the lines suggested by the court. A good illustration of suspension in respect of an executive/ administrative arrangement is the recent case of *Leung Chun Kwong v Secretary for Civil Service (No 2).*[182] There the Court of Final Appeal, following its finding in *Leung Chun Kwong v Secretary for Civil Service*[183] that the Civil Service had discriminated against the applicant-civil servant who was in a same-sex marriage by not extending to him tax and health benefits which are available to civil servants who are in a marriage between a man and a woman as recognized by Hong Kong law, declared the remedies that the court would grant. In order to give a reasonable time to the Civil Service to update their guidelines and computer databases, etc., the Court suspended its orders for a period of six months, observing that the grant of this suspension would not affect the applicant and any other similarly situated persons, as the six-month period would expire before the end of the tax year during which the changed rules had to be applied to the relevant civil servants.

133. Temporary validity is slightly different from suspension: The court declares the legislative or executive arrangement unconstitutional but declares that such arrangement will continue to have validity for a limited period of time so that the government could put it right. The difference seems to be that unlike in the case of suspension, when the court makes a temporary validity order, it may be suggesting to the government that it can continue with the unlawful arrangement without any fear of judicial sanction, since the court has positively sanctioned it for a limited period of time.[184]

---

181. In *Koo Sze Yiu v Chief Executive* (2006) 9 HKCFAR 441, (CFA), [18], Bokhary PJ said: 'If temporary validity or suspension is to be justified that will have to be done on considerations so fundamental as to transcend the distinction between legislation and executive action.'
182. (2019) 22 HKCFAR 282, (CFA).
183. (2019) 22 HKCFAR 127, (CFA).
184. In *Koo Sze Yiu v Chief Executive* (2006) 9 HKCFAR 441, (CFA), the Court of Final Appeal ordered suspension in place of temporary validity, which the Court of Appeal had adopted. For the distinction that Bokhary PJ drew between temporary validity and suspension, *see* [32]–[41]. Sir Anthony Mason NPJ did not *see* any significant difference between temporary validity and suspension: [56]–[58].

134. The judiciary, tasked with the interpretation and upholding of the law, considers cases as objectively as possible, without being answerable to the legislature or the executive. This is different from decisions of the legislature that often reflect the majoritarian view. Where an infringement of a minority right is in question, courts do not consider to be relevant the absence of a majoritarian view in favour of remedying such infraction of right.[185] The view that the judiciary is entitled to take its own view uninfluenced by the will of the legislature or the majoritarian view is counterbalanced by deference to the legislative and executive branches of the government that the judiciary pays in appropriate circumstances.[186] Judicial deference is most visible in areas where the legislation is framed to give effect to important public policy objectives. Judges are reluctant to interfere unless such policy constitutes a glaring infringement of fundamental rights.[187] Where the policy intrudes into the area of fundamental rights the court would come to an independent conclusion without undue deference.[188]

135. Judicial deference is also referred to as allowing the legislature or the executive a margin of appreciation, a concept that has evolved in the jurisprudence of the European Union where member states are given some room to deviate from rules that have union-wide application, without infringing them, where local circumstances may justify such deviation. 'On democratic grounds, the judiciary should defer to the opinion of the elected body or person. This standard may be particularly relevant where "the Court recognises that the originator of the impugned measure is better placed to assess the appropriate means to advance the legitimate aim espoused. This has occurred in cases involving implementation of the legislature's or executive's political, social or economic policies but the principle is not

185. 'Reliance on the absence of a majority consensus as a reason for rejecting a minority's claim is inimical in principle to fundamental rights. … . How can resort to the will of the majority dictate the decisions of a court whose role is to interpret universal and indivisible human rights, especially minority rights?' *W v Registrar of Marriages* (2013) 16 HKCFAR 112, (CFA), [116]. This was recently cited with approval by the Court of Final Appeal in *Leung Chun Kwong v Secretary for Civil Service* (2019) 22 HKCFAR 127, (CFA), [55]–[56], where it was held unconstitutional the denial of employment benefits, which are available to persons in a heterosexual marriage, to persons in a same-sex marriage. The majoritarian view which disapproved same-sex marriages was not a relevant consideration in deciding whether there was unjustified discrimination.

186. *See* for the jurisprudential basis of judicial deference, T R S Allan, 'Judicial Deference and Judicial Review: Legal Doctrine and Legal Theory' (2011) LQR 96. *See also* Jeffrey Jowell, 'Judicial Deference: Servility, Civility or Institutional Capacity?' (2003) *Public Law* 592–601.

187. As Nicholls of Birkenhead put it in *Ghaidan v Godin-Mendoza* [2004] 2 AC 557, (HL), [19]: 'Parliament is charged with the primary responsibility for deciding the best way of dealing with social problems. The court's role is one of review. The court will reach a different conclusion from the legislature only when it is apparent that the legislature has attached insufficient importance to a person's Convention rights. The readiness of the court to depart from the view of the legislature depends upon the subject matter of the legislation and of the complaint.' For Hong Kong, *see*, for instance, *Fok Chun Wah v Hospital Authority* (2012) 15 HKCFAR 409, (CFA), [66].

188. As Nicholls of Birkenhead went on to say in *Ghaidan v Godin-Mendoza* [2004] 2 AC 557, (HL), [19]: 'where the alleged violation comprises differential treatment based on grounds such as race or sex or sexual orientation the court will scrutinise with intensity any reasons said to constitute justification. The reasons must be cogent if such differential treatment is to be justified.' For Hong Kong, *see*, for instance, *Fok Chun Wah v Hospital Authority* (2012) 15 HKCFAR 409, (CFA), [71] and [76].

confined to such cases".'[189] In such cases courts allow a broad margin of appreciation, but in areas involving fundamental rights court would allow, if at all, a narrow margin of appreciation.[190]

136. Courts of Hong Kong adopt the common law approach in interpreting the Basic Law. This is in line with two provisions of the Basic Law. Article 8 provides for the continuation of common law in Hong Kong, and Article 18 authorizes courts to refer to precedents from other common law jurisdictions. 'In essence, the Basic Law provides for a separate legal system in the Hong Kong Special Administrative Region based on the common law.'[191]

137. The task of the court is 'to construe the language used in the text of the instrument in order to ascertain *the legislative intent as expressed in the language.* Their task is not to ascertain the intent of the lawmaker on its own. Their duty is to ascertain *what was meant by the language used* and to give effect to *the legislative intent as expressed in the language.* It is the text of the enactment which is the law and it is regarded as important both that the law should be certain and that it should be ascertainable by the citizen. The courts do not look at the language of the article in question in isolation. The language is considered in the light of its context and purpose.'[192] 'The context of a particular provision is to be found in the Basic Law itself as well as relevant extrinsic materials including the Joint Declaration. Assistance can be also gained from any traditions and usages that may have given meaning to the language used.'[193] Relevant extrinsic materials include the Explanations on the Basic Law (draft) given at the National People's Congress on 28 March 1990 shortly before the adoption of the Basic Law on 4 April 1990.

138. Once the courts conclude that the meaning of the text when construed in the light of its context and purpose is clear, they are bound to give effect to the clear meaning of the language. The courts will not on the basis of any extrinsic materials depart from that clear meaning and give the language a meaning which the language cannot bear.[194]

139. An important contribution to Hong Kong's constitutional jurisprudence is made by the Standing Committee of the National People's Congress, which has the power to interpret the Basic Law. This power has been vested in general and unqualified terms in the sense that: (1) the Standing Committee has the power to

---

189. *HKSAR v Yu Lik Wai William* [[2019] 1 HKLRD 1149, (CA), [183], quoting *Hysan Development Co Ltd v Town Planning Board* (2006) 19 HKCFAR 372, (CFA), [139].
190. *Q v Commissioner of Registration* [2019] 1 HKLRD 1244, (CFI), [43]. As Ma CJ observed in *Fok Chun Wa v Hospital Authority* (2012) 15 HKCFAR 409, (CFA), [79]: 'where the subject matter of the challenge has to do with fundamental concepts, in contradistinction to rights associated with purely social and economic policies, the courts will be particularly vigilant to protect the rights associated with such concepts, and consequently much less leeway or margin of appreciation will be accorded to the authority concerned.'
191. *Director of Immigration v Chong Fung Yuen* (2001) 4 HKCFAR 211, (CFA), 222, per Li CJ (CFA).
192. *Ibid.*, 223.
193. *Ng Ka Ling v Director of Immigration* (1999) 2 HKCFAR 4, (CFA), 28, per Li CJ, (CFA).
194. *Director of Immigration v Chong Fung Yuen* (2001) 4 HKCFAR 211, (CFA), 225, per Li CJ.

interpret any provision of the Basic Law and (2) the Standing's Committee's power of interpretation does not have to be exercised in the context of litigation. In other words, its power of interpretation is free-standing.[195] There are two avenues for the Standing Committee to exercise its power of interpretation. First, the courts of Hong Kong have no authority to give a final interpretation of any provisions of the Basic Law concerning affairs that are the responsibility of the Central People's Government or concerning the relationship between the Central Authorities and the Region.[196] If an interpretation of such a provision affects the determination of a case, the courts of the Region must, before the making of a final decision, seek an interpretation of the Basic Law provision in question. Once the Standing Committee gives an interpretation, the courts are bound to follow it.[197] Second, since the power of interpretation of the Basic Law is vested in the Standing Committee, it can render an interpretation of any provision of the Basic Law on its own, without the need for a reference from Hong Kong courts.

140. Mention may be made here of the importance of Decisions, other than interpretations, made by the NPCSC in relation to Hong Kong. We have discussed in appropriate places of this work the Standing Committee's decisions in relation to the implementation of the Basic Law, such as on changes to the method of electing the Chief Executive and the Legislative Council. There are two recent examples of this power of issuing decisions. The first is the Decision of the NPCSC, which is discussed elsewhere in this work in relation to the extension of the term of office of the sixth Legislative Council, which was due to end on 30 September 2020, by not

195. The Standing Committee's power of interpretation is 'plenary in that it covers all the provisions of the Basic Law; this power may be exercised in the absence of litigation'. Yash Ghai, *Hong Kong's New Constitutional Order: The Resumption of Chinese Sovereignty and the Basic Law*, (2nd edn, Hong Kong: Hong Kong University Press, 2000), 198, cited in *Lau Kong Yung v Director of Immigration* (1999) 2 HKCFAR 300, (CFA), 345. Chief Justice Li, at 345, referred to the Standing Committee's power of interpretation as a 'general and free-standing power of interpretation' under Art. 67(4) of the Constitution of the People's Republic of China and Art. 158(1) of the Basic Law.

196. Basic Law, Art. 158(2).

197. *Ibid.*, Art. 158(3). *See Democratic Republic of the Congo v FG Hemisphere Associates LLC (No 2)* (2011) 14 HKCFAR 95, (CFA), where the Court of Final Appeal decided to request the NPCSC to make an interpretation. Where a question of constitutional interpretation is raised by a party, which the court considers might be reasonably arguable but does not think is necessary for the resolution of the dispute before it, the court will not give a ruling on such issue. Nor would it refer it to the NPCSC if the question involves a matter beyond the competence of Hong Kong SAR. *See Commissioner for Registration v Registration of Persons Tribunal* [1999] 3 HKLRD 199, (CFI), where the court found it unnecessary to decide whether the rule in para. 1(4)(b) of Sch. 1 of the Immigration Ordinance (Cap. 115) that a person cannot be said to be settled in Hong Kong unless he was ordinarily resident in Hong Kong for 'a continuous period of seven years … immediately before' his application for permanent residence was inconsistent with Art. 24(4) of the Basic Law. Keith JA said at 212: 'Questions relating to the compatibility of domestic legislation with the Basic Law are questions of great importance in Hong Kong's new constitutional order. Individual cases should not be regarded as an opportunity for the court to decide all the issues which may arise from a particular provision in the Basic Law. Broadly speaking, a court should only decide those issues which have an impact on the case which it is trying.' On appeal, the Court of Appeal decided that there was no inconsistency between para. 1(4)(b) of Sch. 1 of the Immigration Ordinance and Art. 24(4) of the Basic Law. *See Commissioner for Registration v Registration of Persons Tribunal* [2000] 2 HKLRD 523, (CA).

less than one year.[198] The second is the decision of the Standing Committee relating to the operation of the Guangzhou-Shenzhen-Hong Kong Express Rail Link.[199] Mainland of China and Hong Kong had entered into a cooperation arrangement whereby a person embarking on a train journey to China could have customs, visa and quarantine checks carried out in the Hong Kong terminal at West Kowloon Railway Station not only by the Hong Kong authorities but also by the Chinese authorities who would grant entry clearance, which would have normally been carried out at the destination railway station in China. This is known as the 'co-location arrangement'.[200] These checks by the Chinese authorities are carried out in the Mainland Port Area inside the West Kowloon train terminus, which is subject to Chinese law, other than in respect of reserved matters, which are within the jurisdiction of Hong Kong. Rejecting the argument that it would be unconstitutional for the Chinese Government to enforce Chinese laws in Hong Kong, albeit in a specific location and for a specific purpose, the court confirmed that decisions of the NPCSC have legal effect in Hong Kong. The court adopted the following reasons given by a Mainland Chinese legal scholar:

(1) Article 67(1) of the PRC Constitution provides that the NPCSC has the power to supervise the implementation of the Constitution, and such power extends to Article 31 of the PRC Constitution which implements the 'One Country, Two Systems' principle under which the HKSAR was established. Accordingly, under the PRC Constitution, the NPCSC has the power to decide whether a particular matter is compliant with the 'One Country, Two Systems' principle and the Basic Law.
(2) The NPCSC also has the power, under the Basic Law (by virtue of, or having regard to, Articles 2, 17(2) and (3), and 158(1)), to supervise its implementation and decide whether an arrangement is compliant with it.
(3) The NPCSC may exercise such supervisory power by means of issuing 'decisions', and the NPCSC Decision is one such 'decision.'

---

198. *See* para. 267 below.
199. *Leung Chung Hang Sixtus v President of Legislative Council* [2019] 1 HKLRD 292, (CFI). *See* the English translation of the Explanation of the Draft NPCSC Decision given by the Director of Hong Kong and Macao Affairs Office of the State Council at https://www.thb.gov.hk/eng/policy/transport/policy/colocation/EN%20Explanations%20(2%20Jan).pdf.
200. As the Government had explained in a Legislative Council paper cited in the judgment at [7]: 'Co-location arrangement means conducting clearance procedures of two different jurisdictions successively in one place. This contrasts with a traditional separate-location arrangement similar to that adopted for the current Hong Kong-Guangzhou Intercity Through Trains, under which clearance procedures are conducted at the places of departure and arrival in two different jurisdictions respectively. Under a co-location arrangement, passengers can complete clearance procedures of both Hong Kong and the Mainland at the West Kowloon station in one go. Passengers departing from Hong Kong can go to all cities on the national high-speed rail network without having to undergo clearance procedures again on the Mainland. Passengers coming to Hong Kong can board trains at any station of their choice on the national high-speed rail network, and go through Mainland departure clearance and Hong Kong arrival clearance at the WKS. They will not be constrained by whether a particular Mainland city has clearance facilities.'

(4) As such, the NPCSC Decision, which addresses specifically the question of the Cooperation Arrangement's consistency with the Basic Law, has legal effect and is binding on governmental authorities in the Mainland.
(5) The NPCSC Decision is also binding on the HKSAR, including the Hong Kong courts, because:

(i) the NPCSC exercises the will of the State;
(ii) the NPCSC has the power to supervise the implementation of the PRC Constitution; and
(iii) the NPCSC is part of the sovereign body which authorized the establishment of the HKSAR and its governmental authorities.[201]

141. Andrew Chow J did not wish to give a ruling on the exact legal effect of a Decision of the NPCSC in Hong Kong law: 'It would not be appropriate for me, sitting at first instance, to determine questions concerning the status and legal effect of the NPCSC Decision under Hong Kong laws which may have far reaching implications but are not strictly necessary for my decision. In my view, whatever may be said about the precise status and effect of the NPCSC Decision under Hong Kong laws, it must at least rank as "post-enactment materials" which the Court of Final Appeal in [*Director of Immigration v Chong Fung Yuen* (2001) 4 HKCFAR 211] did not exclude as being potentially admissible or relevant for the purpose of construing the Basic Law where its meaning is not free from ambiguity.'[202]

142. The courts of Hong Kong contribute to the development of constitutional jurisprudence through interpretation of the Basic Law as well as the Hong Kong Bill of Rights. In the exercise of its constitutional jurisdiction, courts will have to consider whether an administrative or legislative measure is incompatible with the Basic Law, and thus unconstitutional. Since the Bill of Rights reproduces the provisions of the ICCPR as applied to Hong Kong (Article 39), Hong Kong courts have relied heavily on international jurisprudence on fundamental rights. The Court of Final Appeal has emphasized the importance of its duty to interpret the Basic Law and to uphold the Basic Law as Hong Kong's fundamental law:

> In exercising their judicial power conferred by the Basic Law, the Courts of the Region have a duty to enforce and interpret that law. They undoubtedly have the jurisdiction to examine whether legislation enacted by the legislature of the Region or acts of the executive authorities of the Region are consistent with the Basic Law and, if found to be inconsistent, to hold them to be invalid. The exercise of this jurisdiction is a matter of obligation, not of discretion so that if inconsistency is established, the courts are bound to hold that a law or executive act is invalid at least to the extent of the inconsistency.[203]

201. *Leung Chung Hang Sixtus v President of Legislative Council* [2019] 1 HKLRD 292, (CFI), [53].
202. *Ibid.*, [61].
203. *Ng Ka Ling v Director of Immigration* (1999) 1 HKCFALR 4, (CFA), 25, per Li CJ.

Chapter 5. Customary Law, Unwritten Law and General Principles of Law

§1. Introduction

143. Just as customs are a source of private law, conventions, or unwritten constitutional practices, play an important part in the Westminster system of responsible government. They are of the greatest importance in Britain where there is no written constitution, but they are of notable importance also in countries that have adopted a written constitution based on the English experience, which are said to practise the 'Westminster Model' system. In England, constitutional conventions are unwritten, whereas in countries that have adopted a written constitution based on the English experience, the written constitution may incorporate the main constitutional conventions as express provisions of the constitution. In the 'Westminster Model' of government, constitutional conventions operate mainly to ensure that executive powers of the Head of State are exercised on the advice of the Prime Minister who is accountable to the popularly elected legislature. Hong Kong does not operate a 'Westminster Model' system of government, which is descriptive of the constitutional framework of former British colonies that have been granted self-government. References to 'Westminster Model' in some Hong Kong cases are simply to the application of the separation of powers doctrine. For instance, Hartmann J in *Yau Kwong Man v Secretary for Security* observed as follows: 'It has not been disputed that the Basic Law is founded on what is commonly called the "Westminster Model". As such, the powers of the legislature, the executive and the judiciary are separate. In terms of Art. 80, judicial power is vested in those appointed to hold judicial office. That being so, what the legislature cannot do, consistent with the separation of powers, is to place judicial power in the hands of the executive.'[204] In *Koon Wing Yee v Financial Secretary*, Fok J referred to Hartmann J's observation and said that he did not regard that observation as controversial.[205]

144. In the absence of a constitutional arrangement of executive-legislative relationship of the British or Westminster Model type, such as that the nominal Head of State (Governor-General or the President) acts on the advice of the Prime Minister, Hong Kong does not have such an important place for constitutional conventions. However, a number of constitutional usages and practices can be found in the constitutional history of Hong Kong under the British administration. Since Hong Kong's system of government under the Basic Law is to a large extent a continuation of the previous system of government, it is possible to argue that similar constitutional usages and practices would continue to be observed. The following paragraphs contain an examination of some constitutional conventions before and after 1997.

204. *Yau Kwong Man v Secretary for Security* [2002] HKEC 1142, (CFI), [38].
205. *Koon Wing Yee v Financial Secretary* [2013] 1 HKLRD 76, (CA), [47].

§2. The Operation of Conventions in the Crown Colony of Hong Kong

145. Article II of the Letters Patent provided that the Governor had to exercise his powers in accordance with the Letters Patent and any instructions that might be given to him. However, as time went by, the Imperial Government generally refrained from issuing instructions on Hong Kong's internal affairs. Similarly, while the Imperial Government had the legal authority to legislate for Hong Kong, such power was sparingly exercised. Thus, local affairs were conducted principally on the basis of policies formulated in Hong Kong and legislation passed in Hong Kong. While the Queen had the power to disallow any legislation passed by the Hong Kong Legislative Council and assented to by the Governor, the power of disallowance was never used after 1913.[206]

146. The Queen had the power to appoint members of the Executive Council, but such appointments were generally made on the recommendation of the Governor. While according to Article V of the Letters Patent, all the members of the Executive Council were to hold office during Her Majesty's pleasure, Clause II of the Hong Kong Royal Instructions, provided that an appointed member of the Executive Council (i.e., any member other than an ex officio member) should be appointed for a renewable period of five years or such other shorter period as may be specified in the instrument of appointment. In practice, appointed members were appointed for shorter periods than five years but many of them had their terms renewed. The Executive Council being an advisory body, the Governor was not bound to accept its advice. However, in practice the Governor rarely, if ever, acted against its advice. Between 1920 and 1948, there were apparently only two occasions when the Governor refused to accept the majority view of the Executive Council.[207]

147. The oldest convention in Hong is said to be the practice that unofficial Justices of the Peace were entitled to select one of their number to sit on the Legislative Council. This practice began in 1849 and was followed until 1973, when the Governor decided to put an end to that practice.[208] As by this time all the unofficial members of the Legislative Council were also Justices of the Peace, the convention

206. The contents of this paragraph and the following paragraphs on conventions during the British period draw on Norman Miners, *The Government and Politics of Hong Kong*, (5th edn, Hong Kong: OUP, 1995), particularly 61–63.

207. Norman Miners, *The Government and Politics of Hong Kong*, (5th edn, Hong Kong: Oxford University Press, 1995), 84, n. 14.

208. Norman Miners, *The Government and Politics of Hong Kong* (5th edn, Hong Kong: Oxford University Press, 1995), 62. Certain government officials were made Justices of the Peace by virtue of their office. They were known as Official Justices of the Peace. Unofficial Justices of the Peace refers to those persons who are appointed as Justices of the Peace, but who are not government officials. The Justices of the Peace Ordinance (Cap. 510) of 1997 recognises the two categories. Section 3 provides that the Chief Executive may from time to time appoint: (a) any person holding any office in the public service whom he considers to be fit and proper [who will hold office until he leaves public office: s. 4(1)(b)]; or (b) any other person whom he considers to be fit and proper [who will hold office unless and until his appointment is revoked: s. 4(1)(a)], to be a justice of the peace on such terms and conditions as the Chief Executive may determine.

did not any longer serve a useful purpose. A breach of a long-established convention occurred in 1978, when 118 police officers and a customs officer were summarily dismissed, for corrupt practices, while it had been long been assumed that this power would be used in case of espionage or other acts of disloyalty towards the Crown.[209]

148. Article XVIII of the Letters Patent required all officers and inhabitants of Hong Kong to obey the Governor. There were, however, by convention, certain decisions that the Governor would permit to be taken without interference. First, the Attorney General decided whether or not to institute a prosecution, and the Governor was expected not to give any direction to the Attorney General in that regard.[210] Second, the Public Service Commission advised the Governor regarding appointments to the public service, and it was uncommon for the Governor to disregard such advice.[211]

149. Article XV of the Letters Patent empowered the Governor to grant a pardon to any accomplice in a crime who agreed to give information leading to the conviction of the principal offender, or to any person convicted of an offence a free or conditional pardon. There was no requirement for the Governor to take advice from an appropriate person, except where he was exercising his power of pardon in respect of a person condemned to death. In such a case, he had to seek the advice of the Executive Council, having received a report from the judge who presided at the relevant criminal trial. In 1973 the British Government intervened to grant a reprieve to a person sentenced to death, who had been denied a pardon by the Governor acting on the advice of the Executive Council. Ever since, the Governor had routinely commuted death sentence to life imprisonment,[212] until 1993 when capital punishment was abolished by Crimes (Amendment) (No. 3) Ordinance.

§3. CONVENTIONS UNDER THE BASIC LAW

150. Unlike the Governor, who had to act in accordance with Imperial instructions, the Chief Executive is not required to take instructions from the Chinese Central Authorities. Article 48(8) provides, however, that the Chief Executive must implement directives issued by the Central People's Government 'in respect of the relevant matters provided for in this law'. It is not quite clear what such 'relevant matters' are. Five possible instances would be:

---

209. *Ibid.*
210. *Ibid. See* Norman Miners, 'The Governor, the Secretary of State and the Prerogative of Mercy' (1987) 17 *Hong Kong Law Journal* 77. *See* generally on prosecutorial discretion, Albert Chen, 'Prosecutorial Discretion, Independence and Accountability' (1998) 28 *Hong Kong Law Journal* 406–411. *See Re Lau Hei Wing* [2016] 3 HKLRD 652, (CFI).
211. *Ibid.* Public Service Commission Ordinance (Cap. 93), s. 6 lists the matters regarding which the Public Service Commission advises the Chief Executive.
212. *Ibid.*, 221.

(1) where the Central Government adds a Chinese law to Annex III of the Basic Law, and it becomes the duty of the Hong Kong Government to implement it locally by way of promulgation or legislation;[213]
(2) where the Chinese Central Government returns to Hong Kong any Hong Kong ordinance which in its view is inconsistent with Basic Law provisions relating to powers of Central Authorities such law 'shall immediately be invalidated';[214] it may be that local legislation is required to formally repeal such an invalidated ordinance;
(3) where the Chief Executive has been requested by courts to issue a certificate concerning an act of state, he must obtain a certifying document from the Central Government, which is binding on him;[215]
(4) foreign warships may access the ports of Hong Kong only with special permission of the Central Authorities and the Chief Executive must implement any directives he receives from the Central Authorities in this regard;[216]
(5) Hong Kong has been authorized to maintain its previous system of civil aviation management and keep its own aircraft register in accordance with provisions laid down by the Central Authorities concerning nationality marks and registration marks of aircraft and foreign state aircraft may enter Hong Kong only with the Central Government's permission; the Chief Executive must implement any directives received by him in this regard.[217]

151. Unlike before 1997, when the Executive Council was appointed by the Queen, today the Chief Executive has the power to appoint members of the Executive Council, and the term of office of Council members cannot extend beyond the expiry of the appointing Chief Executive's term of office.[218] Although it is strictly unnecessary for the Chief Executive to consult the Central Government before making appointments to the Executive Council, it is likely that he would so consult. Such a practice is likely, particularly because appointment of certain principal government officers is in the hands of the Central Government, although the appointments are made on the Chief Executive's recommendation.[219]

152. The Basic Law provides that legislative measures relating to government policies, government structure and public revenue must be sponsored by the government. However, since no legislative measures can be passed without the support

---

213. Basic Law, Art. 18. Yash Ghai thinks that if the Hong Kong Legislative Council refuses to enact necessary legislation to implement a national law, the Central Authorities may issue a directive under Art. 48(8). *See* Yash Ghai, *Hong Kong's New Constitutional Order: The Resumption of Chinese Sovereignty and the Basic Law* (Hong Kong: Hong Kong University Press, 1977), 365.
214. Basic Law, Art. 17.
215. *Ibid.*, Art. 19.
216. *Ibid.*, Art. 126. The fourth and fifth instances were suggested to me by Professor Lin Feng of City University of Hong Kong.
217. *Ibid.*, Art. 129.
218. *Ibid.*, Art. 55.
219. *Ibid.*, Art. 48(5).

of the Legislative Council, it is likely that the practice of government officials lobbying Legislative Council members for support will continue. It will also be desirable for the government to take serious note of policy proposals made by Legislative Council members and to reach consensus on policy matters with them. Although the Basic Law provides that the Chief Executive may dismiss a non-compliant Legislative Council, it is unlikely that the Chief Executive will encourage hostility between the legislative and executive branches of the government.[220]

153. During the period of British administration, it was a tradition for the Governor to deliver an annual address to the Legislative Council reviewing the progress in the previous year and setting out the Government's policy plans for the coming year. This practice originated in the British practice of the Queen's speech. There was no specific provision in the Letters Patent or the Royal Instructions relating to the annual policy address. The Chief Executive today follows the Governor's practice of presenting an annual policy speech. Although there is no specific provision for this purpose, the Basic Law contains provisions, which by implication recognize this practice. Article 48(4) states that the Chief Executive must 'decide on government policies'. Article 64 states that the government of Hong Kong must 'present regular policy addresses to the Council'. One of the powers and functions of the Legislative Council set out in Article 73 includes the power to 'receive and debate the policy addresses of the Chief Executive'.[221] Thus today the convention of the Head of State, the Chief Executive, presenting the annual policy address continues to operate, in a context where the constitution impliedly but strongly recognizes the convention.

154. As the Head of the Region, the Chief Executive has the power to give directions to any administrative authority. It is, however, unlikely that he would try to influence the Secretary for Justice's prosecutorial discretion,[222] or that he would act contrary to advice given to him by the Public Service Commission or the Judicial

---

220. *Ibid.*, Art. 50.
221. *Ibid.*, Art. 73(4).
222. *See* generally Albert Chen, 'Prosecutorial Discretion, Independence and Accountability' (1998) 28 *Hong Kong Law Journal* 406–411. Nor will the judiciary interfere with prosecutorial discretion. As Fuad V-P said in the Court of Appeal case of *Keung Siu Wah v A-G* [1990] 2 HKLR 238, (CA), 255: 'In my judgment it is a constitutional imperative that the Courts do not attempt to interfere with the Attorney General's discretion to prosecute, but once the charge or indictment comes before a Court for hearing, it can consider whether the prosecution should be allowed to continue if grounds amounting to an abuse of process are raised.' *See also RV v Director of Immigration* [2008] HKEC 412, (CFI), where Hartmann J rejected the argument that the control of criminal prosecutions by the Secretary for Justice is today a constitutional duty and that the scope of that duty, and the manner in which it may be lawfully exercised, must therefore be subject to the scrutiny of the courts which themselves have a constitutional duty to interpret the provisions of the Basic Law insofar as those provisions concern matters which fall within the autonomy of the Region. Hartmann J said: 'Whatever the developments in the law in other jurisdictions, it seems to me that I remain bound by the judgment of the Court of Appeal in *Keung Siu Wah v A-G* [1990] 2 HKLR 238, (CA), unless it can be shown that, on a true construction, the Basic Law now provides that the power of the Secretary for Justice to control criminal prosecutions is amenable to judicial review.'

Appointments Recommendation Commission in making public or judicial appointments. In 2001, a Legislative Council motion requiring the Chief Executive to disclose confidential minutes of the Honours Committee was rejected. The motion was put forward to find out if and why the Chief Executive had acted on his own, when he conferred an honour on a person not recommended by the Committee. The Chief Secretary for Administration, who chaired the Committee, told the Legislative Council that the system allowed the Head of the State to delete or add to the names recommended by the Committee. He assured that there was no departure from the previous practice.[223]

223. 'Tung survives vote over medal to leftist riot leader', *South China Morning Post*, 1 November 2001.

Chapter 6. Subordinate Rules and Regulations

§1. Introduction

155. 'The delegation of law-making power by Parliament to other persons or bodies is no new practice, although it has greatly increased in frequency and importance in the nineteenth and twentieth centuries and will continue to increase in this century.'[224] This statement made in relation to Britain is no less true of Hong Kong.[225]

156. There are four legitimate reasons for the use of delegated legislation:[226]

(1) *Pressure on parliamentary time*. Much time can be saved if the legislature discusses and approves essential principles of legislation, leaving subordinate matters of detail to be filled in by the executive branch of the government. For instance, the Air Pollution Control Ordinance (Chapter 311) has eighty sections and is supplemented by nineteen sets of subsidiary legislation (one of which has since been repealed).
(2) *Technicality of subject matter*. Technical matters, as distinct from broad policy, are not susceptible to discussion in the legislature. Delegation to the executive enables it to consult experts and interested parties while the delegated legislation is in the draft stage. For instance, the Noise Control Ordinance (Chapter 400) enables the Secretary for the Environment and Food to make regulations for the purpose of specifying emissions standards to be met by motor vehicles.[227]
(3) *Flexibility*. By nature, legislation is difficult to amend, because parliamentary procedure is both cumbersome and time consuming. In large and complex matters it may be appropriate to delay making of detailed provisions until a later time because it is difficult to foresee all the contingencies and local conditions. Delegated legislation will enable detailed rules to be made and amended expeditiously when new situations arise and as circumstances change. For instance, the Water Pollution Control Ordinance, which came into effect in 1981, was intended as an enabling statute which would be brought into effect only with the declaration of water control zones and the enactment

224. O. Hood Phillips & Paul Jackson, *Constitutional and Administrative Law*, (8th edn, London: Sweet & Maxwell, 2001), 665.
225. *See* generally David Clark & Gary McCoy, *Hong Kong Administrative Law*, (2nd edn, Hong Kong: Butterworths, 1993) especially 407–418.
226. *See* O. Hood Phillips & Paul Jackson, *Constitutional and Administrative Law*, (8th edn, London: Sweet & Maxwell, 2001), 668–669.
227. *See* Anton Cooray, 'The Environment' (2020 reissue), in *Halsbury's Laws of Hong Kong*, Ch. 4 'Noise Control', [160.194] 'Introduction' and Anton Cooray, *Environmental Law in Hong Kong* (2nd edn, The Netherlands: Wolters Kluwer, 2018) [540].

of necessary regulations. The first water control zone was brought into effect in 1987 together with the enactment of the Water Pollution Control (General) Regulation in 1987.[228]

(4) *Emergency powers*. In emergencies such as war and economic crisis, there can be no serious objection to conferring on the executive power to make delegated legislation. The Emergency Regulations Ordinance (Chapter 241) confers power on the Chief Executive in Council to make regulations on occasions of emergency or public danger. Any regulation or order or rule so made by the Chief Executive 'shall have effect notwithstanding anything inconsistent therewith contained in any enactment'.[229] The Full Court in *Li Bun v R*,[230] while recognizing the principle that the legislature cannot abdicate its legislative power by setting up a rival legislative body, upheld the validity of the Emergency Regulations Ordinance on the ground that the Governor (today the Chief Executive) would be able to exercise such legislative powers only on occasions of public danger or emergency.

§2. Definitions

157. 'Subsidiary legislation and subordinate legislation mean any proclamation, rule, regulation, order, resolution, notice, rule of court, by-law or other instrument made under or by virtue of any Ordinance and having legislative effect.'[231] This definition makes it clear that, while subsidiary legislation may be made only under authority given by legislation, any instrument made under the authority given by an ordinance is not to be regarded as subsidiary legislation unless it has legislative effect. Thus any power of an administrative, judicial or quasi-judicial nature will not be considered a delegated legislative power. In *Julita F Raza v Chief Executive in Council*,[232] the Court of Appeal held that the approval by the Chief Executive in Council of a labour importation scheme in terms of section 14(3) of the Employees Retraining Ordinance (Cap. 423) was an exercise of administrative function and did not amount to subsidiary legislation. The scheme that the Chief Executive approved was an employment levy on employers of foreign domestic workers. The Court of Appeal held that the Chief Executive merely identified a category of employer to whom the levy would be applied and thereby gave effect to the Ordinance in a particular way. He was not making law but executing it.

158. The Court of Appeal was aware that the line between a legislative act and an administrative action is not easy to demarcate. Citing De Smith, Woolf and Jowell's *Judicial Review of Administration* the court observed as follows:

228. *See* Anton Cooray, 'The Environment' (2020 reissue), in *Halsbury's Laws of Hong Kong*, Ch. 3 'Water Pollution Control', [160.109] 'Legislative Framework' and Anton Cooray, *Environmental Law in Hong Kong* (2nd edn, The Netherlands: Wolters Kluwer, 2018), [264]–[265].

229. The Emergency Regulations Ordinance (Cap. 241), s. 2(4). All the regulations that had been made under this Ordinance were repealed in 1995. No regulations have been made thereafter.

230. *Li Bun v R* [1957] HKLR 89, (Appellate Jurisdiction).

231. Interpretation and General Clauses Ordinance (Cap. 1), s. 3.

232. *Julita F Raza v Chief Executive in Council* [2006] HKEC 1339, (CA).

> The distinction often made between legislative and administrative acts is that between the general and the particular. A legislative act is the creation and promulgation of a general rule of conduct without reference to particular cases; an administrative act cannot be exactly defined, but it includes the adoption of a policy, the making and issue of a specific direction, and the application of a general rule to a particular case in accordance with the requirements of policy of expediency or administrative practice. Legal consequences flow from this distinction. Since the general shades off into the particular, to discriminate between the legislative and the administrative by reference to these criteria may be a peculiarly difficult task, and it is not surprising that the opinions of judges as to be proper characterisation of the statutory function is at variance.[233]

159. Sometimes legislation may expressly provide that certain administrative acts, which resemble delegated legislation, must not be treated as delegated legislation. For instance, the Air Pollution Control Ordinance (Cap. 311) specifically states that technical memoranda made under the Ordinance are not subsidiary legislation, notwithstanding the fact that they must be subjected to Legislative Council control as in the case of subsidiary legislation.[234] Vocational Training Council Ordinance (Cap. 1130) states that rules made by the Vocational Training Council are not to be regarded as subsidiary legislation for the purposes of section 34 of the Interpretation and General Clauses Ordinance (Cap. 1), thereby excluding the need for Legislative Council approval.[235]

160. There are judicial decisions where it was unsuccessfully argued that certain administrative acts were subsidiary legislation. For instance, it has been held that Outline Zoning plans made by the Town Planning Board under the Town Planning Ordinance (Cap. 131) are not subsidiary legislation for two reasons: (1) the Town Planning Ordinance which contains express provisions for the making of regulations does not provide for the making of land-use plans as subsidiary legislation and (2) unlike regulations made under the Ordinance land-use plans are not required to be laid before the Legislative Council for approval.[236]

233. De Smith, Woolf and Jowell's *Judicial Review of Administration* (Sweet & Maxwell, 1995), at page 1006, [A-011]–[A-012]. Latham CJ said in *Commonwealth v Grunseit* (1943) 67 CLR 58, (CA), 82: 'It is not always easy to draw [a distinction between orders, rules etc. of a legislative character and orders, rules etc. which are of an executive character]. The general distinction between legislation and the execution of legislation is that legislation determines the content of a law as a rule of conduct or a declaration as to power, right or duty, whereas executive authority applies the law in particular cases.'

234. *See* Anton Cooray, 'The Environment' (2020 reissue), in *Halsbury's Laws of Hong Kong*, Ch. 2 (Hong Kong LexisNexis), 'Air Pollution Control', [160.042] 'The Effect of a Technical Memorandum' and Anton Cooray, *Environmental Law in Hong Kong*, (2nd edn, The Netherlands: Wolters Kluwer, 2018) [84]–[86].

235. *See* Vocational Training Council Ordinance (Cap. 1130), s. 20(3).

236. *See Kwan Kong Co Ltd v Town Planning Board* [1995] (1995) 5 HKPLR 261 (HC), affirmed by the Court of Appeal [1996] 2 HKLR 363, (CA) and *Wah Yick Enterprises Co. Ltd v Building*

161. Delegated legislation has a long history in England. For instance, in 1531, the Statute of Sewers delegated legislative powers to the Commissioners of Sewers.[237] In Hong Kong, the first set of delegated legislation appears to be Regulations made by the Governor in Council under section 8 of the Suppression of Piracy Ordinance No. 1 of 1868, which authorized the making of regulations to prevent the carrying of arms in fishing vessels. The other regulations made in the early years of Hong Kong include regulations made under the Dangerous Goods Ordinance of 1873 exempting certain substances from the provisions of the Ordinance, Supreme Court Fee Order 3 of 1873, and regulations made under Merchant Shipping Ordinance No. 10 of 1899. The frequency and volume of subsidiary legislation has since then steadily increased over the years.

162. Subsidiary legislation assumes a variety of names. 'Regulations' is the most common title of subsidiary legislation in Hong Kong. Taking legislation in the area of environmental protection, we find that the Chief Executive[238] or the Secretary for the Environment and Food[239] may make regulations. Other common titles are by-laws,[240] orders,[241] rules,[242] statutes,[243] notices,[244] directions,[245] instructions,[246] and decrees.[247] Subsidiary legislation may be made by many other government officers and agencies, such as the Financial Secretary.

163. Generally, an enabling ordinance does not require any particular procedure to be followed in the preparation of subsidiary legislation. Occasionally, an ordinance may require consultation to be carried out before subsidiary legislation is made. For instance, the Air Pollution Control Ordinance, the Noise Control Ordinance and the Environmental Impact Assessment Ordinance require the Secretary for the Environment and Food to consult the Advisory Council on the Environment,

---

Authority [1999] 1 HKLRD 237, (CA) where it was held that therefore rules of statutory interpretation are not relevant to the interpretation of an Outline zoning Plan. This view has been followed in *Hero v The Director of Planning* [2011] HKEC 1305, (CFI), affirmed by the Court of Appeal [2012] HKEC 991, (CA).

237. H.W.R. Wade & C.F. Forsyth, *Administrative Law*, (11th edn, Oxford: Clarendon Press, 2014), 724.

238. Water Pollution Control Ordinance (Cap. 358), s. 46(1) and (2); Waste Disposal Ordinance (Cap. 354), s. 33(1).

239. Noise Control Ordinance (Cap. 400), s. 27; Air Pollution Control Ordinance (Cap. 311), s. 43(1).

240. *See,* e.g., Airport Authority Bylaw made under the Airport Authority Ordinance (Cap. 483).

241. Airport Authority (Map of Airport Area) Order, made under the Airport Authority Ordinance (Cap. 483).

242. Arbitration (Appointment of Arbitrators and Umpires). Rules made under the Arbitration Ordinance (Cap. 341).

243. Statutes of the University of Hong Kong, published as Schedule of University of Hong Kong Ordinance (Cap. 1053).

244. *See* Fisheries Protection (Specification of Apparatus). Notice made under the Fisheries Protection Regulations (Cap. 171 sub leg A).

245. *See* s. 11 of the Public Finance Ordinance (Cap. 2).

246. *Ibid.*

247. The Chinese University of Hong Kong Ordinance (Cap. 1109) provides that the Council and Senate of the University may, subject to the Ordinance and the University's Statutes, make decrees and regulations.

when making regulations.[248] Similarly, the Water Pollution Control Ordinance and the Waste Disposal Ordinance require the Chief Executive to consult the Advisory Council on the Environment when making regulations.[249]

§3. Control of Subordinate Legislation

164. A strict application of the separation of powers doctrine would demand that the law-making power remain exclusively in the domain of the legislative branch of the government. The reality, however, is that the executive and to a lesser extent the judiciary perform legislative functions. The executive and judicial branches of the government directly exercise legislative power when making delegated legislation.[250] Local government bodies vested with law-making authority, which are in one sense local legislatures, also contribute to the immense body of delegated or subordinate legislation.[251]

165. The doctrine of supremacy of Parliament requires the legislature to be the ultimate law-making authority. Therefore, delegated legislation must operate in the context of the primacy of legislation: 'It must readily be appreciated that the complexity of modern life often entails legislative bodies legislating in general terms, leaving the details of legislation to be filled in, as it were, by regulations and other such subsidiary legislation. But the principle must always be maintained that what the delegate does must come within the four corners of the powers vested in him, if it is to have effect as law. Otherwise he is assuming a power to legislate.'[252]

166. To reconcile supremacy of Parliament and the inescapable and ever-increasing need for delegated legislation, constitutional doctrine requires the legislature to have ultimate control over delegated law-making:

(1) The power to make delegated legislation can only be derived from primary legislation and delegated legislation must be consistent with the enabling statute.
(2) Legislature can at any time amend or repeal any delegated legislation, and it is usual to require delegated legislation to receive approval of the legislature.
(3) Legislature can delegate some of its legislative power within specified limits, but cannot abdicate its legislative power altogether.

---

248. Air Pollution Control Ordinance (Cap. 311), s. 43(1); Noise Control Ordinance (Cap. 400), s. 27; Environmental Impact Assessment Ordinance (Cap. 499), s. 32.
249. Water Pollution Control Ordinance (Cap. 358), s. 46(1); Waste Disposal Ordinance (Cap. 354), s. 33.
250. Section 54 of the High Court Ordinance (Cap. 4) authorizes the Rules Committee of the High Court to make rules of court regulating and prescribing the procedure and practice to be followed in the High Court.
251. The Regional Councils and Urban Councils, which were abolished in 1999, had delegated law-making powers. *See*, for instance, *Ng Enterprises Ltd v The Urban Council* [1997] AC 168, (PC). The District Councils, the only form of local authority in Hong Kong, have no delegated law-making powers. *See* Part IV, Ch. 3 District Administration.
252. *The Attorney General v Tsang Kwok-kuen* [1971] HKLR 266, (FC), 278 per Mills-Owens J.

167. Delegated legislation must therefore be subordinate to the legislative power of Parliament (in Hong Kong the Legislative Council). The subordinate lawmaker must act within the power conferred by the parent legislation. It is in this sense that the term 'subordinate legislation' or 'delegated legislation' is to be understood.

168. The general rule that subsidiary legislation plays a subordinate role to the primary legislative function that is performed by legislature gives way to the need for extraordinary measures during time of war or emergency. As in many jurisdictions, special legislation has been enacted in Hong Kong to provide for taking special, and sometimes drastic measures, in times of emergency. The relevant statute, the Emergency Regulations Ordinance (Cap. 241), was enacted as far back as in 1922, during the time of British colonial administration, conferring extensive powers of law-making on the Governor in Council.[253] When the Basic Law came into effect, the Emergency Regulations Ordinance continued to be in force in Hong Kong.[254] The powers conferred on the Governor in Council in 1922 are now vested in the Chef Executive in Council. The powers given to the Chief Executive in Council under this Ordinance are extraordinarily wide. Section 2(1) of the Emergency Regulations Ordinance provides that, 'On any occasion which the Chief Executive in Council may consider to be an occasion of emergency or public danger he may make any regulations whatsoever which he may consider desirable in the public interest.' Section 2(2) goes on to say that 'without prejudice to the generality of the provisions of subsection (1), such regulations may provide for' a list of fourteen matters, including: '(a) censorship, and the control and suppression of publications, writings, maps, plans, photographs, communications and means of communication; (b) arrest, detention, exclusion and deportation; (c) control of the harbours, ports and waters of Hong Kong, and the movements of vessels; (d) … (e) trading, exportation, importation, production and manufacture; and (f) appropriation, control, forfeiture and disposition of property, and of the use thereof'.

169. More significantly section 2(2)(g) provides that regulations may be made 'amending any enactment, suspending the operation of any enactment and applying any enactment with or without modification'. Section 2(4) emphasizes that, 'A regulation or any order or rule made in pursuance of such a regulation shall have effect notwithstanding anything inconsistent therewith contained in any enactment; and any provision of an enactment which may be inconsistent with any regulation or any such order or rule shall, whether that provision shall or shall not have been amended, suspended or modified in its operation under subsection (2), to the extent of such inconsistency have no effect so long as such regulation, order or rule shall remain in force'. Section 2(3) provides that 'any regulations made under the provisions of this section shall continue in force until repealed by order of the Chief

253. Cap *See* Norman Miners, 'The Use and Abuse of Emergency Powers by the Hong Kong Government' (1996) 26 *Hong Kong Law Journal* 47, for the legislative history of the Emergency Regulations Ordinance (Cap. 241) and for occasions when emergency regulations were made.

254. Emergency Regulations Ordinance (Cap. 241) was not one of those Ordinances that the Standing Committee of the National People's Congress identified as ordinances that would not be adopted in the Hong Kong Special Administrative Region. *See* the Decision of the Standing Committee dated 23 February 1997. This appears as Instrument 18 appended to the Basic Law.

Executive in Council'. section 3(1) provides that 'without prejudice to the powers conferred by section 2, regulations made hereunder may provide for the punishment of any offence (whether such offence is a contravention of the regulations or an offence under any law applicable to Hong Kong) with such penalties and sanctions (including a maximum penalty of mandatory life imprisonment but excluding the penalty of death), and may contain such provisions in relation to forfeiture, disposal and retention of any article connected in any way with such offence and as to revocation or cancellation of any licence, permit, pass or authority issued under the regulations or under any other enactment as to the Chief Executive in Council may appear to be necessary or expedient to secure the enforcement of any regulation or law or to be otherwise in the public interest.' Section 3(2) adds that 'any person who contravenes any regulation made under this Ordinance shall, where no other penalty or punishment is provided by such regulations, be liable on summary conviction to a fine of $5,000 and to imprisonment for 2 years'.

170. An important feature of the Emergency Regulations Ordinance is that it does not require the Chief Executive in Council to first make a declaration of emergency before he proceeds to make emergency regulations. Nor is there a requirement that he must inform the Legislative Council that an emergency has been declared and/or regulations have been made. Resultantly the Legislative Council is not even indirectly involved in the emergency regulation-making process. During the time of British colonial rule, a number of emergency regulations had been made that could be brought into effect by the Governor at a time of emergency. All those regulations were, however, repealed in 1995. The first and only occasion in which the Hong Kong Special Administrative Region invoked the Emergency Regulations Ordinance was in 2019, faced with a serious challenge to law and order arising out of the protest movement.[255]

171. The power of the Head of the Government, the Governor before 1997 and the Chief Executive after 1997, to pass emergency regulations were challenged in court during the British period as well as after Hong Kong became a Special Administrative Region of China. Some reference may be made to the following cases decided during the British colonial administration: *R v To Lam Sin* (1952) 36 HKLR 1; and *R v Li Bun* [1957] HKLR 89. Declaring that the delegation of powers was *intra vires* Howe CJ said in *R v To Lam Sin*: 'Wide though the powers may be, the Legislative Council retains a very firm and close control by virtue of Section 14 of the Interpretation Ordinance (Cap. 1). No regulation involving the imposition of the

255. The protests started in June 2019 as a mass movement against the proposed Extradition Bill which would have allowed extradition of suspected criminals to countries with which Hong Kong had not concluded an extradition treaty such as China and Taiwan. In the face of widespread opposition, the Government unwillingly withdrew the Bill. But, by this time the protest movement had taken a much wider significance as a popular call for full democracy for Hong Kong often resulting in violence and destruction of public and private property. In order to be able to identify those causing such serious breaches of the peace, the Chief Executive passed a regulation under the Emergency Regulations Ordinance in October 2019, Prohibition on Face Covering Regulation (Reg K), banning persons participating in any public assembly or procession from fully or partially covering their faces.

death penalty can become of force or effect without the prior approval of the Legislative Council – this is provided specifically by the Emergency Regulations Ordinance as well. All other regulations must be laid on the table at the first meeting of the Legislative Council after their publication in the Gazette and the Council may repeal or amend any of them. There is in addition the overriding power to repeal or amend the Ordinance itself. We *see* nothing there which can be called effacement as we understand it.'[256] In *R v Li Bun* Hogan CJ followed *To Lam Sin*. He agreed with *To Lam Sin* but would not place the same reliance on section 14 of the Interpretation Ordinance, as ensuring the control of the legislature over regulations made under the Emergency Regulations Ordinance since that section itself was liable to be repealed by the Governor in Council under section 2(3) of the Emergency Regulations Ordinance.[257]

172. The question of constitutionality of the Emergency Regulations Ordinance was comprehensively examined by the Court of Final Appeal in 2020, when it examined the validity of the anti-mask regulation, Prohibition on Face Covering Regulation (Reg K), in *Kwok Wing Hang v Chief Executive*.[258] The Court of Final Appeal upheld the legality of Chief Executive's power to make emergency regulations for the reason that Chief Executive's power to make regulations is sufficiently and effectively restricted in the following manner: when section 2 of the Emergency Regulations Ordinance provides that 'on any occasion which the Chief Executive in Council may consider to be an occasion of emergency or public danger he may make any regulations whatsoever which he may consider desirable in the public interest', it must be established, on an objective standard, that there was indeed such an occasion of emergency or public danger and that the making of the regulation was in the public interest; emergency regulations are subsidiary legislation and therefore the Emergency Regulations Ordinance, which empowers the Chief Executive to make emergency regulations, does not infringe the constitutional rule that primary legislation may be made only by the Legislative Council; emergency regulations are subject to the approval of the Legislative Council through the negative vetting procedure;[259] an emergency regulation may be repealed or modified by the Legislative Council; emergency regulations are subject to judicial control on traditional grounds of review such as reasonableness and good faith; any emergency regulation that the Chief Executive makes must not be inconsistent with the Basic Law, especially the provisions relating to fundamental rights read together with the Bill of Rights; particularly, any restriction placed on a constitutionally protected right must be a necessary and justifiable restriction which satisfies the proportionality test, authoritatively set out by the Court of Final Appeal in *Hysan Development Co Ltd v Town Planning Board*.[260]

256. *R v To Lam Sin* (1952) 36 HKLR 1, (SC).
257. *R v Li Bun* [1957] HKLR 89, (Appellate Division) 97.
258. (2020) 23 HKCFAR 518, CFA.
259. On negative vetting procedure, *see* above para. 177, below.
260. (2016) 19 HKCFAR 372, CFA. This is discussed in paras 673, 766 and 778, below.

173. The Court of Final Appeal upheld the validity of the Prohibition on Face Covering Regulation (Cap. 241K) as a proportionate restriction on the freedom of assembly, procession and demonstration (Article 27 of the Basic Law and Article 17 of the Bill of Rights), freedom of speech and expression (Article 27 of the Basic Law and Article 16 of the Bill of Rights), and the right to privacy (Article 14 of the Bill of Rights). There was no appeal against the decision of the Court of Appeal, that section 5 of the Prohibition on Face Covering Regulation, concerning the power of a police officer to require a person using a facial covering in a public place to remove the facial covering, is a disproportionate restriction of the protected rights in question.[261]

174. Reference may be made here to a recent development in the UK permitting the amendment of primary legislation by orders made by Ministers of the Crown. The first instance of such subsidiary legislation occurred in 1994 when the Deregulation and Contracting Act of that year gave Ministers power to amend or repeal any existing Act of Parliament in order to reduce or remove a statutory burden on a trade, business, profession or individual. The Regulatory Reform Act 2000 is of the same type, under which a Minister may amend Parliamentary legislation to impose new burdens or increase existing burdens affecting persons carrying out any activity, provided that the order also has the effect of removing or reducing a burden. The Human Rights Act of 1998 also permits the amendment of Acts of Parliament by Ministerial Order. Where a UK court has declared any provision of legislation to be incompatible with a Convention right under section 4 of the Human Rights Act 1998, a Minister may, if he considers that there are compelling reasons to do so, amend such legislation in order to remove the incompatibility. This amending power may also be exercised where, as a result of a judgment of the European Court of Human Rights, a legislative provision has become incompatible with an obligation of the UK arising from the Convention (*see* section 10 of the Human Rights Act 1998).

I. Legislative Control of Subsidiary Legislation

175. Many Hong Kong Ordinances do not expressly provide that subsidiary legislation made under them must be submitted to the Legislative Council for approval. This omission is supplied by the Interpretation and General Clauses Ordinance (Cap. 1), which provides the framework for legislative control of subsidiary legislation. Section 34(1) requires all subsidiary legislation to be laid on the table of the Legislative Council[262] at the next sitting thereof after the publication in the Gazette of that subsidiary legislation.[263] Where subsidiary legislation has been so laid on the

261. *See Hysan Development Co Ltd v Town Planning Board* (2016) 19 HKCFAR 372, (CFA), [106]. The decision of the Court of Appeal is reported as *Leung Kwok Hung v Secretary of State* [2020] HKEC 533.

262. Presenting a document to the legislature constitutes laying it before the legislature: *R v Immigration Appeal Tribunal ex p Joyles* [1972] 1 WLR 1390, (DC).

263. Interpretation and General Clauses Ordinance (Cap. 1), s. 34(1). Section 28(2) requires all subsidiary legislation to be published in the Gazette.

table, the Legislative Council may amend it. The Legislative Council may exercise such power of amendment by way of resolution passed at a meeting held not later than twenty-eight days after the sitting at which the subsidiary legislation was so laid. Any such resolution must be published in the Gazette no later than fourteen days after the passing thereof, or within such period as the Chief Executive may allow in a particular case.[264] Any amendment of subsidiary legislation by resolution becomes effective as from the date of the publication in the Gazette of such resolution.[265]

176. Where any ordinance provides that subsidiary legislation shall be subject to the approval of the Legislative Council, or contains words to the like effect, then:

(1) the subsidiary legislation must be submitted for the approval of the Legislative Council; and
(2) the Legislative Council may by Resolution amend the whole or any part of such subsidiary legislation.[266]

177. The Legislative Council scrutiny of subsidiary legislation may take the form of positive vetting or negative vetting. Positive vetting refers to situations where subsidiary legislation takes effect only once the Legislative Council has approved it, after scrutiny. Negative vetting refers to the situations where subsidiary legislation continues to be effective from the time of making and would cease to be effective if the Legislative Council decides not to approve it. A designation order under the Country Parks Ordinance to designate a country park is subject to negative vetting.[267] While subsidiary legislation subject to negative vetting may take effect from the date of its date of publication in the Gazette, there is an understanding between the government and the Legislative Council that any subsidiary legislation which is controversial and/or of sufficient importance to merit close scrutiny by Legislative Council should not take effect until after the scrutiny period has expired; and where it is necessary for such subsidiary legislation to take effect immediately or before the expiry of the scrutiny period, the relevant bureau should explain to members the reason for such urgency.[268]

---

264. Interpretation and General Clauses Ordinance (Cap. 1), s. 34(5).
265. *Ibid.*, s. 34(2).
266. *Ibid.*, s. 35. For instance, s. 27(4) of the Noise Control Ordinance (Cap. 400) provides that noise control regulations made by the Secretary for the Environment and Food are subject to approval of the Legislative Council.
267. *See Re Thomas Lai* [2014] HKEC 334, (CFI).
268. Paragraph 1.8 of *the Handbook for the Chairman of Subcommittees on Subsidiary Legislation/ other Instruments of the Legislative Council* http://www.legco.govhk/general/english/procedur/sc_handbook.htm.

178. It is not uncommon for an ordinance to provide that subsidiary legislation prepared under it need not be gazetted or laid before the Legislative Council, particularly if the ordinance relates to a private institution.[269] It was held in *English Schools Foundation and Another v Bird* that section 10(1) of the English Schools Foundation Ordinance (Cap. 1117) unquestionably delegated extensive powers to the Foundation to 'legislate' on all matters pertaining to its functions and operations. The fact that there was an express provision which exempted the regulations from having to be published and subjected to Legislative Council approval as set out in Interpretation and General Clauses Ordinance (Cap. 1) did not affect the nature of that power or the character of the regulations made pursuant to it. The exemption could not, on any rational basis, operate by implication to strip regulations made in exercise of delegated powers of 'legislative effect' if they would otherwise have that attribute. The regulations made by the Foundation were subsidiary legislation and had the binding force of law.[270] The Handbook for the Chairman of Subcommittees on Subsidiary Legislation/other Instruments of the Legislative Council provides as follows: 'Where an ordinance provides that sections 34 and 35 of Cap. 1 do not apply to the subsidiary legislation made under the ordinance, the subsidiary legislation is not required to be tabled in the Legislative Council, and the Legislative Council has no power to repeal or propose any amendment to the subsidiary legislation. Nevertheless, the House Committee may form a subcommittee to examine issues relating to such category of subsidiary legislation.'[271]

179. Control of subsidiary legislation on the floor of the Legislative Council is supplemented by scrutiny in committee. One of the important functions of the House Committee of the Legislative Council is to scrutinize primary and subsidiary legislation. It may appoint subcommittees on subsidiary legislation to study in greater detail some of the subsidiary legislation tabled in the Legislative Council or presented to the Legislative Council for approval.[272] The referral of subsidiary legislation to a committee allows the committee to examine the effect of the proposed legislative measure and propose any amendment for the Legislative Council's consideration.

II. Judicial Control of Subsidiary Legislation

180. In addition to Parliamentary control over delegated legislation, there is another safeguard in the form of judicial control. The courts in their traditional function of interpreting and applying law may refuse to enforce any delegated legislation that is flawed in substance or in respect of procedure. Delegated legislation is

---

269. For instance, regulations made by the Executive Council of the English Schools Foundation need not be published in the Gazette or laid before the Legislative Council: English Schools Foundation Ordinance (Cap. 1117), s. 10(2).
270. *Bird v English Schools Foundation and Another* [1998] HKLRD (Yrbk) 513, (CA).
271. *See* Handbook for chairmen of subcommittees on subsidiary legislation/other instruments, para. 1.16. This is available on the LegCo website: www.legco.gov.hk.
272. For a detailed account of the procedure in scrutinizing subsidiary legislation, *see* the Handbook referred to in the previous footnote.

defective in substance if it is outside the scope given to it by the enabling legislation and in procedure if, for instance, the requirement of public consultation before making the subsidiary legislation has not been observed.

181. In the exercise of its inherent supervisory jurisdiction over administrative authorities, courts may question the validity of subsidiary legislation. As Mills-Owens J once said: 'Has the delegate exceeded the authority [granted by the Legislative Council to make regulations], and thus purported to make a regulation that he was not authorized to make? If so, that regulation is ultra vires and of no legal effect. It is a fundamental distinction between an Ordinance passed by the Legislative Council and subsidiary legislation that the validity of an Ordinance cannot (ordinarily) be challenged in the courts whereas the validity of subsidiary legislation may be challenged.'[273] The Interpretation and General Clauses Ordinance expressly provides that 'no subsidiary legislation shall be inconsistent with the provisions of any Ordinance'.[274]

182. The *vires* or validity of subsidiary legislation may be impugned on the grounds of procedural impropriety. Subsidiary legislation may be declared invalid if it has not been made in due compliance with a mandatory procedural requirement.[275] An area where procedural ultra vires would be relevant is represented by legislation, which requires the delegated lawmaker to have consultations before exercising its legislative powers. Environmental legislation, for example, stipulates that the Secretary for the Environment and Food may make regulations 'after consultation with the Advisory Council on the Environment'.[276] It is a common practice in Hong Kong for the administration to consult relevant consultative authorities as well as parties who are likely to be affected by proposed subsidiary legislation.[277] Where prior consultation is mandatory, subsidiary legislation may be declared invalid if no proper consultation has taken place.[278] Whether consultation

273. *The Attorney General v Tsang Kwok-kuen* [1971] HKLR 266, (FC), 277, 278. Validity of legislation could before 1997, and can today, be questioned on the ground of unconstitutionality.

274. The Interpretation and General Clauses Ordinance (Cap. 1), s. 28(1). Exceptionally, emergency regulations made by the Chief Executive override any inconsistent legislation.

275. The distinction between mandatory and directory procedural requirements was considered in the context of an administrative decision in *Asia Dyeing Co Ltd and Others v The Authority* [1990] 1 HKLR 263, (CA).

276. *See* Air Pollution Control Ordinance (Cap. 311), s. 43(1), Water Pollution Control Ordinance (Cap. 358), s. 46(1), Noise Control Ordinance (Cap. 400), s. 27, Waste Disposal Ordinance (Cap. 354), s. 33, Environmental Impact Assessment Ordinance (Cap. 499), s. 32.

277. For instance, before introducing the Dangerous Drugs Ordinance (Amendment of First Schedule) (No 2) Ord. 2000, the administration consulted the Action Committee Against Narcotics and Pharmacy and Poisons Board. More information is available on the Hong Kong Legislative Council website www.Legco.govhk.

278. *See Agricultural, Horticultural and Forestry Industry Training Board v Aylesbury Mushrooms Ltd* [1972] 1 WLR 190, (QB), where a ministerial order establishing an Agricultural, Horticultural and Forestry Industry Training Board was held not applicable to persons engaged in the growing of mushrooms because the Minister had failed to consult the Mushroom Growers Association, as required by the parent statute. The Minister had consulted the National Farmers Union to which the Mushroom Growers Association belonged. Notwithstanding that, Donaldson J observed, at 196:

is mandatory or directory may also depend on whether the proposed delegated legislation frustrates a legitimate expectation that a certain government policy will remain unchanged.[279]

183. Subsidiary legislation must be made by the authority that has been authorized to do so, and not by any other person or body. In *Attorney General v Chan Foo*,[280] the Court of Appeal held that the imposition of conditions on a licence issued by the Governor had to be by way of regulations made by the Governor. Therefore, the Governor had acted ultra vires when he authorized the Licensing Authority, by regulation, to attach conditions on licences granted by the Governor.

184. The doctrine of substantive ultra vires requires that subsidiary legislation be within the limits set out in the enabling statute:

> Among the grounds upon which subsidiary legislation may be challenged is the ground that it is defective in substance by reason of it being ultra vires – that is to say, outside the scope of the enabling power. ... The principle must always be maintained that what the delegate does must come within the four corners of the powers vested in him, if it is to have effect as law. Otherwise he is assuming a power to legislate. ... It is in the matter of ascertaining or establishing the extent of the delegate's authority that difficulties arise, that is to say in construing the scope or extent of the enabling legislation – the legislation under which the delegate derives his power to make the subsidiary legislation in question.[281]

185. In determining whether a subsidiary law is intra vires the parent statute the court must adopt a benevolent interpretation. The intention of the legislature, as indicated in the enabling statute, is the prime guide to the meaning of the subsidiary

'Prima facie consultation with the parent body undoubtedly constitutes consultation with its constituent parts, but I think that this general rule is subject to an exception where, as here, the Minister has also attempted and intended direct consultation with a branch. The association's complaint has very little merit, because it seems to have been completely blind to all that was going on around it. Nevertheless, it is important that statutory powers which involve taxation shall be strictly construed and, so construed, I consider that the association should have been consulted and was not consulted.' Cf. *R v Secretary of State for Social Services exp Association of Metropolitan Authorities* [1986] 1 WLR 1, (QB), where the validity of the ministerial order was upheld notwithstanding the failure to consult.

279. '[W]hen a public authority has promised to follow a certain procedure, it is in the interest of good administration that it should act fairly and implement its promise, so long as implementation does not interfere with its statutory duty.' *Attorney General of Hong Kong v Ng Yuen Shiu* [1983] 2 AC 629, (PC), 638 per Lord Frazer.
280. *Attorney General v Chan Foo* [1990] 2 HKLR 428, (CA).
281. *The Attorney General v Tsang Kwok-kuen* [1971] HKLR 266, (FC), 278.

legislation. In particular, the court will prefer a construction that results in the subsidiary legislation being lawful and that avoids any conflict between the enabling statute and the subsidiary legislation.[282]

Substantive ultra vires has been invoked in the following circumstances.

186. A subordinate law will be valid only if there is express statutory authority to make it. In *The Attorney General v Tsang Kwok-kuen*,[283] the court held that the Commissioner for Transport did not have the power to make a regulation cancelling the registration of vehicles. Cancellation being in the nature of a penalty, an intention to penalize innocent persons is not to be lightly imputed to the legislature and for subsidiary legislation to so provide requires the most explicit enabling legislation.[284] Subsidiary legislation is invalid if it seeks to enlarge the scope of the enabling statute and thereby attempts to exercise legislative power of the Legislative Council. In *Chau Hon-leung v Kong Kwok-choi and others*,[285] the Full Court found that the Supreme Court Ordinance permitted any person affected by a decision of the Registrar of the Supreme Court to appeal to a judge in chambers, while a rule made by the Supreme Court permitted any person affected by an assessment of damages by the Registrar to appeal to the Full Court. The rule of court was struck down as a usurpation of the primary legislation power vested in the Legislative Council.[286] Similarly, in *Pang Tak Kwai v Commissioner of Correctional Services and the Chief Executive*,[287] a subordinate law was held to be invalid because it provided for the punishment of prison officers for any offence, whereas the enabling legislation envisaged rules for punishment only in respect of disciplinary offences. It must be noted, however, that as long as there is no inconsistency with an ordinance, it is permissible for subsidiary legislation to expand the scope of primary legislation. After all, the purpose of subsidiary legislation is to supplement primary legislation. Subsidiary legislation is invalid if it conflicts with any statutory provision. In *Mohan v McElney*,[288] a rule of the Supreme Court was held to be invalid because it conflicted with the Limitation Ordinance.

---

282. *See Bennion on Statutory Interpretation*, 7th Edition, s. 3.13. *See Export-Import Bank of China v Taifeng Textile Group Co Ltd* [2018] HKEC 2210, (CFI), [84].
283. *The Attorney General v Tsang Kwok-kuen* [1971] HKLR 266, (FC). Regulation 17(D) of the Road Traffic (Registration and Licensing of Vehicles) Regulations was held to be invalid, to the extent that it enabled the Commissioner to cancel registration of a motor vehicle, because the primary legislation did not confer power to make regulations cancelling the registration of vehicles.
284. *Ibid.*, 285.
285. *Chau Hon-leung v Kong Kwok-choi and others* [1975] HKLR 529, (FC).
286. *See also Mohan v McElney* [1983] HKLR 308, (CA). *See also Wong Hoi Tang v Hospital Authority* [2001] HKEC 1468, (CFI). There, s. 19 of the Legal Aid Ordinance (Cap. 91), provided that a costs order may be made against a legally aided person in the same manner as against any other person, while the Order 62 rule 4(1) of the Rules of High Court excluded a legally aided person from having a costs order made against him. This subsidiary legislation was held to be invalid as being incompatible with the primary legislation.
287. *Pang Tak Kwai v Commissioner of Correctional Services and the Chief Executive* [2000] HKEC 1298, (CFI), affirmed by the Court of Appeal [2001] HKEC 1139, (CA).
288. *Mohan v McElney* [1983] HKLR 308, (CA). *See also Registrar of Hong Kong Institute of Certified Public Accountants v Wong Tak Man Stephen* [2016] HKEC 1859, (CA), [5.7].

187. Subsidiary legislation will be invalid if it is inconsistent with legislation. This is especially true of inconsistency between a subsidiary law and the Bill of Rights Ordinance. For instance, a subsidiary legislative provision that fails to comply with the Bill of Right's requirement of an impartial and fair hearing would be invalid.[289] Inconsistency may arise because the subsidiary legislation has the effect of imposing restrictions on a right given by an ordinance. In *Chiu Koon-kwong v R*,[290] the Full Court of the High Court found that while section 2(2) of the Road Traffic Ordinance permitted the use of dual-purpose vehicles (vehicles that may be used to carry goods or to carry passengers) for the carriage of passengers, Regulation 29(2) made under the same Ordinance imposed restrictions on that right. The regulation was held to be ultra vires.[291]

188. However, subsidiary legislation may regulate an activity that is lawful under primary legislation as long as the regulatory provision does not amount to a prohibition of what is lawful under statute. For instance, the Privy Council in *Ng Enterprises v The Urban Council*[292] held that trade licensing requirements contained in a by-law were valid, as they fell short of prohibiting trading activities. Courts give a generous interpretation to subsidiary legislation and save it if it can be interpreted in a way to be consistent with primary legislation.[293] The recent case of *Horsfield Leslie Grant v Chief Executive of HKSAR*[294] concerned the legality of a regulation made by the Chief Executive in Council permitting an authorized person to place a person arriving in Hong Kong under quarantine (Compulsory Quarantine of Persons Arriving at Hong Kong from Foreign Places Regulation (Cap. 599E)). The applicants for judicial review, a family of Hong Kong permanent residents, who returned from a designated country were placed under quarantine during the COVID-19 pandemic. They argued that the Chief Executive did not have the power to make a regulation under the Prevention and Control of Decease Ordinance (Cap. 599) to provide for the making of such quarantine orders. The argument was that the grant of specific power to the Secretary for Food and Health to make regulation for this kind of situation (isolation and quarantine of persons) excluded the power of the Chief Executive to make such a regulation under his general power to 'make regulations for the purposes of preventing, combating or alleviating the effects of the public health emergency and protecting public health'. Rejecting this argument the Court of First Instance held as follows: (1) the scope of the power of the Chief Executive to make regulations is to be determined by construing the parent statute; (2) a purposive and context-based approach must be adopted in construing a statute; (3) adopting such an approach it cannot be concluded that the conferment on the Secretary of power to make regulations on a specific matter

289. *Lam Siu Po v Commissioner of Police* (2009) 12 HKCFAR 237, (CFA).
290. *Chiu Koon-kwong v R* [1969] HKLR 254, (FC).
291. *See also Ng Che-foon and Another v R* [1968] HKLR 439; *Cowie v Attorney General* (1948) 32 HKLR 156, (SC).
292. *Ng Enterprises v The Urban Council* [1997] AC 168, (PC).
293. *R v Li Tat* [1993] 2 HKCLR 203, (CA), provides a good illustration of the application of this principle.
294. [2020] HKEC 971, (CFI).

excludes the general power of the Chief Executive to make a similar regulation;[295] (4) the legislature could not have intended that the general power of the Chief Executive must not cover a subject of the Secretary's competence. As Anderson Chow J said: 'Such quarantine measures are obvious means of prevention and control of spread or transmission of contagious diseases. It is, I consider, unthinkable that they could have passed unnoticed by the legislature.' In *Syed Agha Raza Shah v Director of Health* it was held that placing a person arriving in Hong Kong under quarantine constitutes a restriction on personal liberty but was justified as a proportionate measure taken to protect public health. The Public Health Department was held to have had acted lawfully under the relevant regulation.[296] Subsidiary legislation may be invalid if it provides for the punishment of persons in violation of the rules of natural justice. An intention to penalize innocent persons is not to be lightly imputed to the legislature and for subsidiary legislation to so provide requires the most explicit enabling legislation.[297] Therefore, unless the parent ordinance expressly or by implication authorizes the delegate to act in contravention of rules of natural justice, subsidiary legislation offending the rules of natural justice will be ultra vires.[298] It must be noted that if any subsidiary legislation is inconsistent with any rights guaranteed by the Basic Law, it will be of no avail to say that such subsidiary law is within the powers granted by the enabling ordinance because the courts have the power to declare the enabling statute unconstitutional.[299]

189. Unreasonableness is a ground on which the validity of subsidiary legislation may be challenged. It was at one time thought that unreasonableness is applicable only to by-laws made by elected local government authorities.[300] However, it is now accepted that unreasonableness, as an aspect of ultra vires, would apply to all subsidiary legislation.[301]

---

295. Anderson Chow J said: 'as mentioned in §36 of the Bills Committee Report, "the reason for only empowering the Chief Executive in Council to make a public health emergency regulation on an occasion of public health emergency is because the whole Government will need to be mobilised to combat and control the emergency situation to which the Government will be held wholly accountable". Hence, on an occasion of a public health emergency, it is more appropriate for the necessary public health and safety measures to be provided for by regulations made by the Chief Executive in Council instead of by the Secretary.'

296. *Syed Agha Raza Shah v Director of Health* [2020] HKEC 802, (CFI). The relevant regulation was the Compulsory Quarantine of Persons Arriving at Hong Kong from Foreign Places Regulation (Cap. 599E), made by the Chief Executive in Council, the same regulation the legality of which was upheld in *Horsfield Leslie Grant v Chief Executive of HKSAR* [2020] HKEC 971, (CFI).

297. *Attorney General v Tsang Kwok-kuen* [1971] HKLR 266, (FC), 285, per Mills-Owens J. *See also Lau Ping v R* [1970] HKLR 343 (FC) and *Wong Pun Cheuk v Medical Council of Hong Kong and the Attorney General* [1964] HKLR 47 (HC).

298. Today, any statute that permits infringement of the rules of natural justice is unlikely to be considered constitutional. *See* Part IV, Ch. 2 'Fundamental Rights and Liberties'.

299. *See Lam Siu Po v Commissioner of Police* (2009) 12 HKCFAR 237, (CFA).

300. *Kruse v Johnson* [1898] 2 QB 91, (QB).

301. *See*, e.g., *Commissioner of Customs and Excise v Cure and Duley Ltd* [1962] 1 QB 340, (QB), and *R v Immigration Appeal Tribunal ex p Begum Manshoora* [1986] Imm AR 385, (QB). Rigby CJ in *The Attorney General v Tsang Kwok-kuen* [1971] HKLR 266, (FC), considered unreasonableness to be but an aspect of the doctrine of ultra vires. This reflects what was said by Lord Russell in

190. Subsidiary legislation is invalid if it is vague and ambiguous. In *Agrila Ltd and Others v Commissioner of Rating and Valuation*,[302] the Lands Tribunal observed that Regulation 2 of the Rent Regulation was ambiguous and would lead to absurdity if interpreted literally. However, by interpreting it in its proper context, the Lands Tribunal was able to uphold its validity.

191. Subsidiary legislation is invalid if it is inconsistent with the general law of the land: 'A by-law is not repugnant to the general law merely because it creates a new offence. It is repugnant if it makes unlawful that which the general law says is lawful. Again, a by-law is repugnant if it adds something inconsistent with the provisions of a statute creating the same offence; but if it adds something not inconsistent, that is not sufficient to make the by-law bad as repugnant.'[303]

192. It was held in *Wong Kwong-shing trading as Ka Wah Motors Co. v The Attorney General*[304] that where subsidiary legislation is only partially inconsistent with the parent statute or the general law of the land, the court will as far as possible declare only such inconsistent provisions invalid, upholding the validity of the rest of the subsidiary legislation. Regulation 18B of the Road Traffic (Registration and Licensing of Vehicles) Regulations had provided that '(1) Without prejudice to

---

Kruse v Johnson [1898]2 QB 91, (QB), 100: the unreasonableness must be such that the court might as well say 'Parliament never intended to give authority to make such rules: they are unreasonable and ultra vires.'

302. *Agrila Ltd and Others v Commissioner of Rating and Valuation* [1999] HKEC 1486, (LT), affirmed by the Court of Appeal [1999] HKEC 793, (CA).

303. *Gentel v Rapps* [1902] 1 KB 160, (KBD), 166. *See Powell v May* [1946] 1 KB 330, (KBD), for a classic statement of the relevant principle. *See also Pan World Airways Incorporated Ltd v The Queen* [1959] HKLR 366, (FC). *See also Cowie v Attorney General* (1948) 32 HKLR 156, (FC), where a subsidiary law which infringed the common law right of access to courts. There the Supreme Court held that a by-law is invalid if it enables a government servant to be dismissed on the basis of a decision by a Departmental Board of Inquiry, denying access to courts to question the correctness of the Board's determination. Today even a statutory provision excluding access to courts would have no legal effect, it being contrary to the rights protected by the Basic Law. *See Lee Yee Shing Jacky v Inland Revenue Board of Review* [2012] 2 HKLRD 981, (CA), where it was unsuccessfully argued that s. 69 of the Inland Revenue Ordinance (Cap. 112) was unconstitutional because it permitted an appeal to the Court of First Instance against a decision of the Inland Revenue Board of Review on a ground involving only a question of law. The Court of Appeal held that the absence of a right of appeal at large, which includes appeal against the factual findings of the Review Board, was not a denial of the right of access to courts. Tang VP quoted the following observation of Ribeiro PJA in *Kwong Mile Services Ltd v Commissioner of Inland Revenue* (2004) 7 HKCFAR 275, (CFA), [31]: 'Appeals from the Board of Review to the courts lie only on questions of law. But intervention in an appeal on law only is not confined to instances in which it is apparent on the face of the record that the determination appealed against resulted from a specifically identifiable error of law. Just because there is no appeal on facts, it does not mean that the appellate court is precluded from detecting and correcting errors of law buried beneath conclusions ostensibly of fact. Sometimes, as Lord Radcliffe put it in *Edwards (Inspector of Taxes) v Bairstow* [1956] AC 14 at p. 36, "the true and only reasonable conclusion contradicts" the determination appealed against. If so, the appellate court will assume that the determination resulted from an error of law. And that opens the way for the appellate court to intervene on the ground of an error of law.'

304. *Wong Kwong-shing, trading as Ka Wah Motors Co. v The Attorney General* [1975] HKLR 654, (HC).

any other enactment the Commissioner by notice in the Gazette may limit the number of motor vehicles which may be registered or licensed as (a) public omnibuses; (b) public light buses; (c) taxis; or (d) public cars.' It was held that the provision must be read down as empowering the Commissioner to limit the number of such vehicles, provided that he does not set the limit below the existing number of such class of licensed vehicles. Reading down a by-law to bring it within the limits of statutory authority as a form of severance has been reaffirmed by courts of Hong Kong relying on English judicial decisions.[305]

193. Courts will not strike down subsidiary legislation lightly, because unlike an administrative order or decision, which affects only a limited class of persons, subsidiary legislation affects the whole community. Courts will declare invalid a subsidiary legislation that has come into effect only if there are special circumstances making it desirable to do so.[306] The court will try to give a construction that will save the subsidiary legislation from being invalid,[307] and the court will lean against any construction that would render any subsidiary legislation ultra vires.[308] It was held in *Bertschy v R*[309] that in construing words used in subsidiary legislation, courts must try to give them their natural meaning and not a restricted meaning, unless the legislative context required them to do so. There, a transit passenger at the Hong Kong airport was caught carrying gold bars. When prosecuted, the defendant argued that, as he was taking the gold to his ultimate destination, he could not be said to have imported gold into Hong Kong. Rejecting this argument, the court gave section 2 of the now-defunct Importation and Exportation Ordinance (Cap. 50) its ordinary meaning. That section defined 'import' to mean 'to bring or cause to be brought into the Colony by land, air or water'. The court found that in interpreting the words in section 2 and in subsidiary legislation made under the Ordinance there was no reason for imposing any narrower meaning than was required by these words when used in their natural sense. The court also found that the relevant provision in the

---

305. *See Attorney General v Cheung King-chow* [1990] 1 HKLR 659, (HC), 662G–664G following *Dunkley v Evans* [1981] 3 All ER 285, (QB).

306. *R v Secretary of State for Social Services ex p Association of Metropolitan Authorities* [1986] [1986] 1 WLR 1, (QB), 175. This was a case where the Secretary of State had failed to follow the mandatory requirement of consulting affected local authorities. The court declined to make a declaration that the regulations were ultra vires because there was a public interest in not upsetting regulations unless good reason could be shown for doing so; it would be disruptive and would lead to uncertainty and delay; these were regulations which the respondent was perfectly entitled to make and no useful purpose would be served in quashing them.

307. *See R v Chu Kwok-fai* [1973] HKLR 107, (HC). Pickering J said: 'The real reason for the validity of the regulation lies in the presumption against legislation being intended to provide for what is inconvenient or unreasonable; the intention which appears to be most in accord with convenience, reason, justice and legal principles will, in all cases of doubtful significance, be presumed to be the true one.' *See also Re Tse Cho* [1979] HKLR 339, (HC).

308. *Cheung Kong Holdings Ltd v Chan Wai Yip Albert* [2001] HKEC 307, (CFI). The Court of First Instance held that s. 5 of the Official Languages Ordinance (Cap. 5) which permits the use of either or both of the official languages in any proceedings must be read subject to rule 4(1) of the High Court Civil Procedure (Use of Language) Rules which require pleadings to be filed in only one language.

309. *Bertschy v R* [1967] HKLR 739, (FC). *See also Pan American Airways Inc v R* [1959] HKLR 366, (FC).

Ordinance did not require any mens rea to be established and therefore imposed absolute liability for the offence of bringing any goods without a permit, where required.

194. The validly of a subsidiary legislation must be tested against the enabling statute at the time the subsidiary legislation was passed. Section 36(1) of the Interpretation and General Clauses Ordinance (Cap. 1) states that where any Ordinance repeals in whole or in part any former Ordinance and substitutes other provisions therefor; or repeals in whole or in part any former Ordinance and re-enacts such former Ordinance with or without modification, any subsidiary legislation made under the former Ordinance and in force at the commencement of the repealing Ordinance shall, so far as it is not inconsistent with the repealing Ordinance, continue in force and have the like effect for all purposes as if made under the repealing Ordinance. Subsection (2) adds that where any subsidiary legislation is continued in force by virtue of subsection (1), such subsidiary legislation may be from time to time amended as if it had been made under the repealing Ordinance. While the subsidiary legislation is *intra vires* the original enabling Ordinance, the court may decide that the subsidiary legislation has become impliedly revoked by the subsequent amendment.[310]

195. Subsidiary legislation which is consistent with the parent statute may become ineffective if the parent statute is later declared to be unconstitutional. In *Lam Siu Po v Commissioner of Police*,[311] an absolute bar to legal representation in disciplinary hearings contained in a regulation made in 1977 under the Police Force Ordinance (Cap. 232) was in question. The Court of Final Appeal agreed that at that time such an absolute limitation was regarded as valid, supported by the English Court of Appeal decision in *Fraser v Mudge* [1975] 1 WLR 1132, (CA). However, the enactment of the Bill of Rights in 1991, which the Court of Final Appeal said incorporated the ICCPR,[312] challenged such a view. Legal representation was now a matter of discretion. Justice Bokhary held that the regulations in question had either become impliedly revoked as in *Attorney General v Chan Kei-lung* [1977] HKLR 312, (CA), if not repealed by the Bill of Rights.[313] The more acceptable view

310. *See Attorney General v Chan Mei kei-lung* [1977] HKLR 312, (CA) where the court held that by-laws 5(1) and 56(1) of the Hawker By-laws were not ultra vires the Ordinance. Although they were entirely compatible with s. 83B prior to its amendment in 1973, they were impliedly revoked by the amending Ordinance of 1973 to the extent that they were inconsistent with the new provisions. This view has been affirmed by the Court of Final Appeal in *Lam Siu Po v Commissioner of Police* (2009) 12 HKCFAR 237, (CFA), [25].

311. *Lam Siu Po v Commissioner of Police* (2009) 12 HKCFAR 237, (CFA).

312. Justice Bokhary PJ said at [15]: 'As is well established, the Bill of Rights is the embodiment of the application to Hong Kong of the International Covenant on Civil and Political Rights ("the ICCPR") from which it is taken almost verbatim. Consequently the Bill of Rights is – and has always been – entrenched. Today it is entrenched by Art. 39 of the Basic Law which provides, relevantly to present purposes, that the ICCPR as applied to Hong Kong shall remain in force and that the rights and freedoms thereunder may not be restricted.'

313. Note, however that s. 3(2) of the Bill of Rights Ordinance was not adopted for application in Hong Kong under the Basic Law. That section provided as follows: 'All pre-existing legislation that does not admit of a construction consistent with this Ordinance is to the extent of the inconsistency

was expressed by Justice Ribeiro PJ at paragraph 142: 'In my view, it is appropriate and just that regulations 9(11) and 9(12) be declared unconstitutional and invalid with the result that the tribunal, as master of its own procedure at common law, is able to exercise a discretion unfettered by those regulations to permit legal or other forms of representation where fairness requires this.'

§4. Scope and Effect of Subsidiary Legislation

196. Section 38 of the Interpretation and General Clauses Ordinance provides that where an Ordinance confers power on any person to make any subsidiary legislation and the Ordinance prescribes conditions, subject to the observance, performance, or existence of which such power is to be exercised, such conditions shall be presumed to have been duly fulfilled if the subsidiary legislation states that it has been made in pursuance of powers given by such Ordinance.[314,315]

197. Legislation may specifically enable subsidiary legislation made thereunder to modify, or to grant exemptions from, the provisions of the legislation. Section 28(2)(s) of the Legal Aid Ordinance (Cap. 91) provides that regulations made by the Chief Executive may modify any provision of the Legal Aid Ordinance as long as it appears to be necessary to meet the circumstances where a person seeking or receiving legal aid is, for example, not resident in Hong Kong. The Dangerous Goods Ordinance of 1873 enabled regulations to be made to exempt certain substances from provisions of the Ordinance.

repealed.' Justice Bokhary referred to the case of *R v Man Wai-Keung (No 2)* [1992] 2 HKCLR 207, (CA), in support of his view on repeal by the Bill of Rights. In *Man Wai-keung* case, the Court of Appeal (with Justice Bokhary as one of the judges) relied on s. 3(2) of the Bill of Rights Ordinance to declare that a pre-existing primary legislation which was inconsistent with the Bill of Rights had been repealed. That decision is correct because at that time s. 3(2) was in the statute book. It is a general principle of statutory interpretation that a statute will stand impliedly repealed to the extent that it is incompatible with a subsequent statute.

314. *See R v To Lam Sin* (1952) 36 HKLR 1, (SC), (emergency regulations); *R v Ng Shing-man* [1960] HKDCLR 211, (DC), (dangerous drugs orders), where it was said that the court must assume, at least in the absence of evidence to the contrary, that the conditions imposed by the statute had been complied with.

315. The repealing statute may impliedly revoke subsidiary legislation made under the repealed statute. *Attorney General v Chan Kei-lung* [1977] HKLR 312, (CA).

Chapter 7. Constitutional Structure of Hong Kong: An Overview

§1. Introduction

198. Hong Kong was a Crown Colony from 1843 to 1997. When China resumed sovereignty over Hong Kong in 1997, Britain and China agreed that Hong Kong's new constitutional system would be based on the colonial model. The following paragraphs outline how the essentials of the colonial system of government continue today, with modifications necessitated by the change of sovereignty. Under the colonial form of government, which has been discussed in the introduction to this monograph, legislative, executive and judicial powers were distributed among the Governor, the Executive Council, the Legislative Council and the judiciary. The doctrine of separation of powers was at work in Hong Kong's colonial government, but it did not mean that powers were strictly compartmentalized.[316]

199. Legislative power was to be exercised by the Governor and the Legislative Council. Unlike in a 'Westminster Model' system of government, where assent to legislation by the Head of State is a mere formality, in Hong Kong the Governor was not bound by any convention to assent to bills passed by the Legislative Council. The requirement of the Governor's assent to laws passed by the Legislative Council was intended to be a check on the Legislative Council. The Governor had a substantial role to play in law-making, because no legislative measure affecting public revenue could be introduced in the Legislative Council unless it was sponsored or approved by the Governor. He had no power to assent to certain types of bills, such as a bill dealing with divorce,[317] and he had a discretionary power to reserve any bill for Royal assent.[318] Moreover, the Queen could disallow any law passed in Hong Kong.[319]

200. Under the Basic Law, legislative power is exercised by the Chief Executive (the Governor under British administration) and the Legislative Council. Unless supported by the Chief Executive, no bill relating to public expenditure, political structure, the operation of the government or government policies may be introduced in the Legislative Council. The Chief Executive may refuse his assent to a bill passed by the Legislative Council, and the Basic Law provides how a deadlock between the Chief Executive and the Legislative Council may be resolved.[320] Legislation passed by the Hong Kong legislature need not be approved by the Chinese Central Government. Nor does the Chinese Central Government exercise any general power of veto over Hong Kong legislation. However, where the Hong Kong legislature has overstepped its legislative authority, the Chinese Central Government may take steps to invalidate it. Article 17 of the Basic Law provides that laws

316. *See*, for references to the relevance of separation of powers to Hong Kong, *R v Ng Tung-Fong* [1992] 1 HKCLR 114, (CA); *Rediffusion (Hong Kong) Limited v The Attorney General and Others* [1968] HKLR 277, (HC).
317. Hong Kong Royal Instructions 1917–1994, Cl. XXVI.
318. Hong Kong Letters Patent 1917–1994, Art. X.
319. *Ibid.*, Art. VIII.
320. *See* Arts 49 and 50.

passed by the Hong Kong legislature must be reported to the NPCSC for record, but that the reporting for record does not affect the entry into force of such laws. Article 17 goes on to say: 'If the Standing Committee … considers that any law enacted by the legislature of the Region is not in conformity with the provisions of [the Basic Law] regarding affairs within the responsibility of the Central Authorities or regarding the relationship between the Central Authorities and the Region the Standing Committee may return the law in question but shall not amend it. Any law returned by the Standing Committee of the national People's Congress shall immediately be invalidated. This invalidation shall not have retrospective effect, unless otherwise provided for in the laws of the Region.'

201. Before the handover in 1997, while legislative power in Hong Kong was to be exercised by the Governor and the Legislative Council, executive authorities did indeed exercise delegated legislative powers. It has been pointed out elsewhere that the emergency law-making power of the Governor had the flavour of primary legislation rather than delegated legislation. The legislative power of the Governor and the Legislative Council was not exclusive in the sense that the British Parliament and the Queen retained the power to legislate for Hong Kong. These features of the colonial government are present today, with necessary modifications. However, unlike the British Government previously, the Chinese Government does not have a free hand to legislate for Hong Kong.[321]

As before 1997, today the doctrine of separation of powers is more stringently applied in relation to the Judiciary.[322] The Judiciary is independent of the legislative and executive branches of the government. The Legislature or the Executive is not expected to exercise judicial power. In *Yau Kwong Man v Secretary for Security* it was held that where a young offender guilty of murder has been given an indeterminate term of imprisonment, it would be unconstitutional for the Chief Executive to have the power to prescribe a minimum period of imprisonment that such person should serve, before he could be considered for release.[323] However, it is a common practice for administrative tribunals to perform adjudicatory functions, which have been traditionally within the jurisdiction of ordinary courts of law. The principle of open justice applies to such tribunals. This principle was upheld in *Ng Shek Wai v*

---

321. As has already been explained above, the Chinese Government has no power to extend its laws to Hong Kong, except as provided in Annex III of the Basic Law or in emergency situations, for which *see* Art. 18 of the Basic Law.
322. As was said in *Lau Cheong v Hong Kong Special Administrative Region*, (2002) 5 HKCFAR 415, (CFA). [101]: 'The Basic Law enshrines the principle that there must be a separation of powers as between the executive, the legislature and the judiciary. The legislature is constitutionally entitled to prescribe by legislation what conduct should constitute criminal offences and what punishment those found guilty by the courts should suffer: *Hinds v R* [1977] AC 195, (PC), 225G-226D. But in the exercise of their independent judicial power, the courts have the duty to decide whether legislation enacted is consistent with the Basic Law and the Bill of Rights. If found to be inconsistent, the duty of the courts is to hold that legislation invalid: *Ng Ka Ling v Director of Immigration* (1999) 2 HKCFAR 4, (CFA), 25G-I.'
323. *Yau Kwong Man v Secretary for Security* [2002] HKEC 1142, (CFI). Hartmann J said at [67]: 'I am satisfied that s. 67C, whatever its form, in substance gives to the Chief Executive the power to exercise what is an inherently judicial power.' Section 67C of the Criminal Procedure Ordinance (Cap. 221) was amended in 2004 to confer the power on the judge to determine the minimum period the offender should serve before he may be considered for release.

Medical Council of Hong Kong, where the Medical Council had refused to disclose the names of the members of a disciplinary committee, the counsel for the Council and the medical practitioner against whom the inquiry in question had been conducted.[324] The Court of First Instance held that the Council had failed to take a relevant consideration into account, namely the requirements of open justice, and remitted the matter to the Council. The Court observed that common law regards open justice as a constitutional right. While there is no absolute right to access to information concerning a 'public judicial hearing', it does not lie entirely in the discretion of the tribunal whether or not comply with a request for information. Whether access was warranted in the circumstances of a particular case is ultimately for the court to decide. The Court observed that the failure to disclose information was due to a misinterpretation of the data protection law, and therefore instead of issuing an order of mandamus, it quashed the decision and remitted it to the Council to arrive at a decision in the light of the judgment.[325] This case is also illustrative of judicial deference to administrative tribunals, whenever that is possible.

While executive powers are within the realm of the administration, the courts sometimes do exercise some powers that can be described as administrative powers rather than judicial powers. Judges perform administrative rather than judicial functions when they serve on commissions of inquiries and other advisory bodies. To that extent, the Executive and the Judiciary perform each other's functions. Judges exercise legislative powers when they make delegated legislation. Judges are also said to make law when they interpret the law or when they create new law for instance by developing the common law.

§2. CONSTITUTIONAL AUTHORITY

202. The Basic Law is the constitution of Hong Kong. Subject to the ultimate constitutional authority of the People's Republic of China, Hong Kong exercises a high degree of autonomy and enjoys executive, legislative and judicial power, in accordance with the provisions of the Basic Law.[326] In addition to laying down the essentials of constitutional government, the Basic Law provides for the maintenance of laws previously in force in Hong Kong, namely the common law, rules of equity, ordinances, subordinate legislation and customary law, as long as they are not inconsistent with the Basic Law.[327] Article 160 of the Basic Law provides as follows: 'Upon establishment of the Hong Kong Special Administrative Region, the laws previously in force in Hong Kong shall be adopted as laws of the Region, except for those which the Standing Committee of the National People's Congress declares to be in contravention of [the Basic Law]. If any laws are later discovered to be in contravention of [the Basic Law], they shall be amended or cease to have

324. *Ng Shek Wai v Medical Council of Hong Kong* [2015] 2 HKLRD 121, (CFI). The request for disclosure of information was made by a member of the public.

325. *Ibid.*, [88]–[89].

326. Basic Law, Art. 2.

327. *Ibid.*, Art. 8.

force in accordance with the procedure as prescribed by [the Basic Law].' Thus, all laws in existence in Hong Kong must conform to the Basic Law.

203. Basic Law being the paramount law, no law of Hong Kong may contravene it. The courts have the power to determine the constitutionality of any legislative or administrative action that is in conflict with the Basic Law. The next in the hierarchy of laws would be primary legislation followed by subordinate legislation. Common law and customs are the other important sources of law. It must be noted that international treaties and other international legal principles play an important part in Hong Kong's legal system.[328]

204. Being an integral part of the People's Republic of China, Hong Kong is also subject to the Constitution of China. It must be noted, however, that the Chinese constitutional system operates in Hong Kong subject to the arrangements set out in the Basic Law. Thus, Hong Kong courts have held that they have the power to declare invalid any action taken by the Central Authorities that is inconsistent with the Basic Law.[329] Laws of the People's Republic of China (commonly referred to as 'Chinese national laws') do not apply in Hong Kong unless expressly extended to the Region.

§3. The Courts

205. Under the Basic Law, the Court of Final Appeal is the highest court of law in Hong Kong, which replaced the Privy Council.[330] Next in order is the High Court, consisting of the Court of Appeal and the Court of First Instance.[331] At the next level are the District Courts[332] and Magistrates Courts.[333] There are several other judicial and administrative tribunals, such as the Small Claims Courts[334] and the Labour Tribunals.[335] By local legislation, criminal and civil jurisdiction in an original and appellate capacity is distributed among these courts and tribunals.

206. In terms of constitutional jurisdiction, special mention may be made of the Court of Final Appeal and the Court of First Instance.[336] In adjudicating cases, it is the Court of Final Appeal, as the highest Court of Appeal, that has the power to authoritatively interpret the provisions of the Basic Law relating to matters within Hong Kong's autonomous jurisdiction. However, this jurisdiction is subject to the

328. *See* Part I, Ch. 1 'Treaties'.
329. *See Ng Ka Ling v Director of Immigration* (1999) 2 HKCFAR 4, (CFA), 337.
330. *See* Hong Kong Court of Final Appeal Ordinance (Cap. 484).
331. *See* High Court Ordinance (Cap. 4).
332. *See* District Court Ordinance (Cap. 336).
333. *See* Magistrates Ordinance (Cap. 227).
334. *See* Small Claims Tribunal Ordinance (Cap. 338).
335. *See* Labour Tribunals Ordinance (Cap. 25).
336. The court system and constitutional jurisdiction of courts is dealt with in Ch. 5 'Judiciary' in Part II of this monograph.

free-standing jurisdiction of the Standing Committee of the National People's Congress.[337] The Court of First Instance, being the highest court of original jurisdiction, has an inherent supervisory jurisdiction over inferior courts and administrative authorities. In the exercise of that jurisdiction, the Court of First Instance exercises the power of judicial review over administrative authorities. Judicial review runs to the core of administrative law, which together with constitutional law constitutes public law.[338]

§4. JURISDICTIONAL CONFLICTS

207. Hong Kong does not have a domestic constitutional structure akin to a federal relationship as in Australia or the USA. In that sense, Hong Kong's is a unitary system of government, as far as the internal constitutional arrangements are concerned. There being no more than one system of courts, there is no room for jurisdictional conflicts between domestic courts of Hong Kong, as in Australia. Nor is there a constitutional relationship between China and Hong Kong of a federal nature. However, Hong Kong is an integral part of China, and Hong Kong's Basic Law operates within the wider parameters of the Chinese constitutional system. Legislative, executive and judicial conflicts could therefore arise between the Chinese Central Authorities and the Hong Kong authorities. Two possible jurisdictional conflicts have so far surfaced. The first conflict is the demarcation of jurisdiction between the NPCSC and the Final Court of Appeal of Hong Kong regarding the power of interpreting the Basic Law. The second conflict relates to the power of the Hong Kong courts to question the legality of action taken by the Chinese Government which is inconsistent with the Basic Law.[339]

337. *See* Part III, Ch. 1.
338. *See* Part IV, Ch. 4 'Judicial Control of Administrative Action'.
339. These issues are discussed in Chs 1 and Ch. 2 of Part III.

Part II. Form of Government

Chapter 1. General

§1. Introduction

208. Hong Kong is a Special Administrative Region of the People's Republic of China, and for that reason a study of Hong Kong's constitutional law involves an examination of Chinese constitutional law as it relates to Hong Kong. Hong Kong's internal constitutional arrangements revolve around Hong Kong's constitution, the Basic Law. Since Hong Kong is not an independent State but a region of the People's Republic of China, Chinese constitutional law and practice will be relevant. Particularly where the Chinese authorities have jurisdiction either to legislate for Hong Kong[340] or to take executive[341] or judicial[342] decisions applicable to Hong Kong, it might be necessary to refer to Chinese constitutional law and practices.

209. The form of government that the Basic Law has established is a continuation of the form of government that operated at the time of the handover in 1997, albeit subject to some significant changes. It is by examining the manner in which the doctrine of separation of powers operates in Hong Kong that we can understand the interaction between the three branches of the government.

210. Regarding the exercise of executive powers, the first point to remember is that Hong Kong does not enjoy a system of representative government where a Prime Minister and a Cabinet of Ministers drawn from an elected legislature would be at the apex of the government. Hong Kong's Chief Executive who leads the Hong Kong SAR is appointed by the Chinese Central Authorities, after a selection or election process in Hong Kong. He is assisted by an Executive Council appointed by him, which need not necessarily have any Legislative Council members serving on it. The Executive Council is a consultative body whose advice the Chief Executive generally follows. Government policies are not initiated in the Legislative Council

340. The authority of the Chinese Government to legislate for Hong Kong is limited. *See* Part 1, Ch. 3, §1 'Chinese National Laws'.
341. For instance, where the Chinese Government accedes to a request of the Hong Kong Government to assist in the maintenance of public order and in disaster relief, as provided by Art. 14 of the Basic Law.
342. The right of the Standing Committee of the National People's Congress to interpret the Basic Law is considered a legislative function in China. However, common law would regard it as a judicial function.

but are presented and promoted by the Chief Executive. Many policies, for instance in relation to land-use planning, commerce and telecommunications, are made by various government departments and bureaux, who come under the leadership of the Chief Executive. The principal government officials may be public servants or political appointees. A ministerial system was introduced in 2001, under which some of the principal officials (Secretaries of Departments and Heads of bureaux) could be political appointees selected from the civil service or from outside the civil service.[343] This ministerial accountability system has been refined over time. As of July 2020, there were twenty-one principal officials consisting of three Secretaries of Departments, thirteen Directors of Bureaux and five others including the Commissioner of Police and the Director of Audit. Some of the ministers are career civil servants and some are non-civil servants.

211. Legislative power may be said to be vested in the Legislative Council, in the sense that it has the exclusive power to pass primary legislation. Article 66 of the Basic Law provides that the Legislative Council of the Hong Kong Special Administrative Region shall be the legislature of the Region. Article 73 lists the powers of the Legislative Council including the power to enact, amend or repeal laws. While it is a common occurrence for administrative authorities to make delegated legislation, the exercise of such subordinate law-making power is subject to control by the Legislative Council.[344] The Legislative Council's law-making power is not unrestrained. It is subject to the following limitations:

(1) Legislative measures concerning government policies, or the political structure, or those having public revenue implications, have to be sponsored or supported by the government.
(2) The Chief Executive may refuse to assent to a bill passed by the Legislative Council, in which event it will not become law.
(3) The Legislative Council must act within the limitations imposed on its legislative competence, such as provisions relating to the protection of fundamental human rights.
(4) The NPCSC may invalidate certain types of legislation.

212. Judicial power is vested in the Judiciary. Article 80 of the Basic Law provides that the courts of Hong Kong Special Administrative Region at all levels shall be the judiciary of the Region exercising the judicial power of the Region. The Basic Law guarantees judicial independence, particularly by providing that judges will be appointed on the basis of judicial and professional qualities, that judicial

343. The Chief Executive proposed a quasi-ministerial system in his annual policy address in the Legislative Council on 10 October 2001. *See* 'Erring Officials Must Pay', *South China Morning Post* Editorial, 28 October 2001.

344. For subordinate legislation, *see* above Part I, Ch. 6 'Subordinate Rules and Regulations'.

appointments must be made on the recommendations of an independent commission, and that removal of judges must be for proved misbehaviour or inability to discharge judicial duties. Article 85 of the Basic Law provides that the courts of the Hong Kong Special Administrative Region shall exercise judicial power independently, free from any interference.

§2. Political Parties, Lobbies and Interest Groups

213. The Basic Law makes no specific reference to political parties and their participation in the government. Political parties do not enjoy an important position in Hong Kong as they do in fully democratic societies. However, political parties are increasingly becoming the most important political force in Hong Kong, exercising powers of persuasion or public protest to demand policy changes. Political parties will become a decisive force when the Chief Executive and the Legislative Council become elected through universal franchise.

214. The Chief Executive Election Ordinance (Cap. 569), No. 21 of 2001, clearly spells out that the nomination paper of a candidate must be accompanied by a declaration that he stands for election in an individual capacity.[345] It requires a person declared elected as the Chief Executive to make a public declaration to the effect that he is not a member of a political party and to give a written undertaking that he will not become a member of any political party or do any act that has the effect of subjecting himself to the discipline of any political party.[346] For the purpose of the Ordinance, a political party has been defined as:

(1) a political party or organization (whether operating in Hong Kong or elsewhere) which purports to be a political party; or
(2) a body or organization the principal function or main object of which is to promote or prepare a candidate for election as a member of the Legislative Council or any District Council.[347]

The effect of these statutory provisions is to ensure that the Chief Executive will not belong to or be directly influenced by a political party.

215. In the Legislative Council, there is a limited but increasing role for political parties. Although the Legislative Council Ordinance does not provide specifically for the participation of political parties in the Legislative Council elections, there is active participation of political parties in the elections, especially in the geographical constituencies. When direct election of a limited number of Legislative Council members was introduced in 1991: 'the challenges and impacts it brought had finally made even its conservative opponents admit that consensus politics,

345. Chief Executive Election Ordinance (Cap. 569), s. 16(7)(a)(i).
346. *Ibid.*, s. 31(1).
347. *Ibid.*, s. 31(2).

which had long been practised in the Legislative Council, had come to an end. It had given way to party politics, a new mechanism characterised by conflict and confrontation.'[348]

216. The Executive Council is not an elective body and therefore political parties do not have a direct role in relation to its composition. The members of the Council are appointed by the Chief Executive 'from among the principal officials of the executive authorities, members of the Legislative Council and public figures'.[349] The Basic Law recognizes that the members of the Executive Council are personal appointees of the Chief Executive when it provides that the term of office of members of the Executive Council shall not extend beyond the expiry of the term of office of the Chief Executive who appoints them. The Basic Law does not explicitly prohibit the appointment of members of political parties to the Executive Council. It does not, however, envisage an Executive Council that draws all its members from a single political party or an alliance of political parties. In contrast, in a 'Westminster Model' system the Cabinet of Ministers would be representative of a single political party or an alliance of political parties.

217. There is no constitutional or legislative provision for lobbies or interest groups. However, there is an important part for them to play in Hong Kong:

> The changes in the political environment since the Sino-British negotiations had a double-edged effect on the development of pressure group politics. On the one hand, pressure groups were transformed firstly into political groups and later came to form political parties. On the other hand, grassroots organisations and community-based pressure groups withdrew from electoral politics and looked for new niches for survival. Meanwhile, new pressure groups, like environmental groups and women's groups, emerged to articulate issues that had not been adequately addressed by politicians and political parties in the establishment. It is true to say that the politicisation of the political environment has not facilitated a transformation of pressure groups. Indeed, the boundary between party politics and pressure group politics is now clearly marked. Pressure groups will play a rather limited role in the post-1997 political development in the sense that major political issues like democratisation are firmly in the grasp of political parties. However, in the domains of local interests and broader social causes like gender equality and environmental protection, pressure groups are still actively articulating their demands.[350]

348. I.C. Choy, 'Political Parties and Political Participation in Hong Kong', in Joseph Y.S. Cheng (ed.) *Political Participation in Hong Kong: Theoretical Issues and Historical Legacy* (Hong Kong: City University of Hong Kong Press, 1999) 121–147, at 128. *See also* Richard Cullen, 'Regulating Political Parties in Hong Kong' (February 2005), LC Paper No. CB(2)911/04-05(01), (2006). http://www.legco.govhk/yr04-05/english/panels/ca/papers/ca0226cb2-911-1e.pdf.
349. Basic Law, Art. 55.
350. T. Lui, 'Pressure Group Politics in Hong Kong', in Joseph Y.S. Cheng (ed.) *Political Participation in Hong Kong: Theoretical Issues and Historical Legacy* (Hong Kong: City University of Hong Kong Press, 1999). 149–174, at 169–70.

§3. Miscellaneous (Referendum, Popular Initiative)

218. Hong Kong has not, and never had, any constitutional provisions requiring referenda or other popular initiatives. The absence of constitutional provisions does not, however, rule out the possibility that the government might consider that a particular decision needs to be approved by the people directly at a referendum. What can safely be stated is that, as the Basic Law stands, the referendum is not a recognized means of law-making.

Chapter 2. Head of State

§1. The Organ of State (Designation)

219. The Head of State of the Hong Kong Special Administrative Region is the Chief Executive. He is appointed by the Chinese Central Government and is accountable to it and to Hong Kong, in accordance with the Basic Law.[351] In the absence of an express provision enabling the Chinese Government to remove the Chief Executive from office, such a power may be implied as long as such a removal is not inconsistent with the Basic Law or the Chinese Constitution.[352] Although the powers and functions of the Chief Executive are quite similar to those held by his predecessor, the Governor under the British colonial administration, his constitutional position is rather different. Whereas the Governor was appointed by the Queen as her personal representative in Hong Kong, the Chief Executive is appointed by the Chinese Central Government, not as a local representative of the Chinese President, but as the head of the Hong Kong Special Administrative Region 'who shall represent the Region'.[353]

220. The Chief Executive of Hong Kong is selected or elected by the people of Hong Kong, and not nominated by the Chinese Government: In contrast, the Governors of Hong Kong were chosen by the British Government, meaning that the Queen made the appointment on the advice of the British Prime Minister. The Chief Executive is accountable to Hong Kong, as he is accountable to the Chinese Government.[354] This accountability is meaningful because the Legislative Council may force him to resign from office.[355] The Governor before 1997 was not accountable to Hong Kong in that sense, in the absence of any provision enabling the Legislative Council to dismiss him or force him to resign.

221. In line with the understanding that Hong Kong must be governed by Hong Kong people, the Basic Law requires the Chief Executive of the Hong Kong Special Administrative Region to be a Chinese citizen of not less than 40 years of age, who must be a Hong Kong permanent resident with no right of abode in any foreign country. The Chief Executive must have been ordinarily resident in Hong Kong for a continuous period of not less than twenty years.[356] He must be a person of integrity, dedicated to his duties.[357]

351. Basic Law, Art. 43.
352. Section 4 of the Chief Executive Election Ordinance, No 21 of 2001 (Cap. 569), expressly recognizes the possibility that the Chinese Central Government may remove him.
353. Basic Law, Art. 43.
354. *Ibid.*
355. *See* Part II, Ch. 3, VI 'Terms of Office and Vacancies'.
356. Basic Law, Art. 44.
357. *Ibid.*, Art. 47.

§2. THE SELECTION AND APPOINTMENT OF THE CHIEF EXECUTIVE

222. Article 46 of the Basic Law provides that the Chief Executive is elected for a term of five years and may serve not more than two consecutive terms. The Chief Executive is selected by election or through consultations held locally and appointed by the Central Chinese Government.[358] When assuming office, the Chief Executive must take the oath of allegiance.[359] The method of selecting the Chief Executive must be specified in the light of the actual situation in Hong Kong and in accordance with the principle of gradual and orderly progress. The ultimate aim is the selection of the Chief Executive by universal suffrage upon nomination by a broadly representative nominating committee in accordance with democratic procedures.[360]

223. The method for electing the first Chief Executive in 1997 for a five-year term from 1997 to 2002 was set out in the Decision of the NPC on the method of formation of the first Government and the first Legislative Council of the Hong Kong Special Administrative Region.[361] That decision declared that the NPC should in 1996 establish a Preparatory Committee for the Hong Kong Special Administrative Region, which shall be responsible for preparing the establishment of the Hong Kong Special Administrative Region and shall prescribe the specific method for the formation of the first Government and the first Legislative Council. The Preparatory Committee was to consist of mainland members and of Hong Kong members who shall constitute not less than 50% of its membership. Its chairman and members were to be appointed by the Standing Committee of the National People's Congress.

224. The Preparatory Committee for the Hong Kong Special Administrative Region was to be responsible for preparing the establishment of the Selection Committee for the First Government of the Hong Kong Special Administrative Region (hereinafter: the 'Selection Committee'). The Selection Committee was to be a broadly representative body composed entirely of permanent residents of Hong Kong. It included Hong Kong deputies to the National People's Congress, representatives of Hong Kong members of the National Committee of the Chinese People's Political Consultative Conference, persons with practical experience who had

358. The Chief Executive Election Ordinance (Cap. 569), which provides for the conduct of Chief Executive elections, provides avenues to challenge the elections, just as there are provisions for challenging the election of members of the Legislative Council and District Councils. The election of a Chief Executive may be challenged, as appropriate, by an election petition or a judicial review application. *See Leung Chun Ying v Ho Chun Yan Albert* (2013) 16 HKCFAR 735, (CFA).

359. Basic Law, Art. 104. *See Kwok Cheuk Kin v Leung Chun Ying* [2017] HKEC 926, (CFI), where an unsuccessful attempt was made to question the validity of the oath of allegiance taken by the Chief Executive in 2012, when he inadvertently did not read out one word of the oath. The court also considered that it could not condone the long delay in instituting the judicial review application.

360. Basic Law, Art. 45.

361. 'Decision of the National People's Congress on the Method for the Formation of the First Government and the First Legislative Council of the Hong Kong Special Administrative Region (adopted at the Third Session of the Seventh National People's Congress on 4 April 1990).' This appears as Instrument 14 appended to the Basic Law.

served in Hong Kong's executive, legislative and advisory organs prior to the establishment of the Hong Kong Special Administrative Region, and persons representative of various strata and sectors of society. The decision set out the composition of the Selection Committee as follows: One hundred members each from the following four categories of representatives: (1) industrial, commercial and financial sectors; (2) the professions; (3) labour, grassroots, religious and other sectors; (4) former political figures, Hong Kong deputies to the NPC and representatives of Hong Kong members of the National Committee of the Chinese People's Political Consultative Conference. The selection committee was required to recommend a candidate for the first Chief Executive through local consultations or through nomination and election after consultation and report the recommended candidate to the Chinese Central Government for appointment. Mr Tung Chee Hwa was elected by the Election Committee as the first Chief Executive of Hong Kong (1997–2002).

225. The selection of the second Chief Executive, who assumed office in 2002 for a five-year term was by a selection committee of 800 members, which was established according to Annex 1 of the Basic Law. The four groups of persons from which 200 members each were to be chosen were not dissimilar to the four groups of members of the Selection Committee for the 1997 selection of the Chief Executive: (1) industrial, commercial and financial sectors; (2) the professions; (3) labour, social services, religious and other sectors; (4) members of the Legislative Council, representatives of district-based organizations, Hong Kong deputies to the NPC and representatives of Hong Kong members of the National Committee of the Chinese People's Political Consultative Conference.

226. Hong Kong enacted the Chief Executive Election Ordinance, No. 21 of 2001, to provide for the finer details of the election process.[362] The Ordinance was intended to delimitate the various sectors, the organizations in each sector eligible to return election committee members and the number of such members returned by each of these organizations in accordance with principles of democracy and openness.[363] Candidates for the office of the Chief Executive could be nominated jointly by not less than one-hundred members. The election committee was required to elect a Chief Executive designate from among such candidates by secret ballot on the basis of one-person-one-vote. The specific method of election was left to be prescribed by legislation.[364] Mr Tung Chee Hwa was elected by the Election Committee to serve a second term as Chief Executive of Hong Kong (2002–2007). He resigned from office in 2005 and his successor Mr Donald Tsang (who at that time was the Chief Secretary of Hong Kong Special Administrative Region) held office for the remaining two years of the term of office of the outgoing Chief Executive.

362. Such as the system of voting providing for the conduct of more than one round of voting until one candidate obtains more than half of the total number of valid votes cast. *See* Part V of the Ordinance.
363. Basic Law, Annex I, s. 3.
364. Basic Law, Annex 1, ss 4 and 5.

227. Annex 1 of the Basic Law provides that if there is a need to amend the method for selecting the Chief Executive for the terms subsequent to the year 2007, such amendments must be made with the endorsement of a two-thirds majority of all the members of the Legislative Council and the consent of the Chief Executive. The amendment must be reported to the NPCSC for approval.

228. The NPCSC decided on 26 April 2004 that the election of the Chief Executive for the third term in 2007 would not be by universal suffrage but by an election committee as before.[365] Mr Donald Tsang, who held office as a succeeding Chief Executive from 2005 to 2007, was elected by the Election Committee for a term of five years in 2007.

229. The NPCSC decided on 29 December 2007 that the election of the Chief Executive for the fourth term in the year 2012 shall not be implemented by the method of universal suffrage. The composition of the Election Committee was expanded so as to consist of 1,200 members with 300 members from each of the four sectors, consisting of representatives as in the previous election. Mr Leung Chunying was elected by the Election Committee as the Chief Executive in 2012.

230. The Decision of the NPCSC of 29 December 2007 went on to provide that the election of the Chief Executive in 2017 may be implemented by the method of universal suffrage. It went on to provide that at an appropriate time prior to the selection of the Chief Executive by universal suffrage, the Standing Committee would make a determination after receiving a report from the Chief Executive on the issue of amending the method for selecting the Chief Executive.[366] The Decision also stated that if the Legislative Council failed to pass the necessary legislation by a two-thirds majority to give effect to such determination, the Chief Executive shall continue to be selected in accordance with the procedure used for the preceding term.[367]

231. As envisaged by the Decision of 29 December 2007, the Chief Executive of Hong Kong Special Administrative Region submitted a report to the Standing Committee 15 July 2014 on the question of introducing election of the Chief Executive by universal suffrage in 2017. The NPCSC considered the report and came to a Decision on 31 August 2014.[368] While it reaffirmed its intention to introduce universal suffrage as the means of electing the Chief Executive in 2017, the Standing Committee also emphasized how important it was that the Chief Executive should be someone 'who loves the country and loves Hong Kong'. It went on to say: '[the Chief executive being a person who loves both China and Hong Kong] is a basic requirement of the policy of "one country, two systems". It is determined by the legal status as well as important functions and duties of the Chief Executive and is

365. This decision appears as Instrument 21 appended to the Basic Law.
366. The Chief Executive made a report as required on 15 July 2014, which was considered by the Standing Committee. *See* the next paragraph for the decision of the Standing Committee.
367. This decision appears as Instrument 23 appended to the Basic Law.
368. This decision appears as Instrument 25 appended to the Basic Law.

called for by the actual need to maintain long-term prosperity and stability of Hong Kong and uphold the sovereignty, security and development interests of the country. The method for selecting the Chief Executive by universal suffrage must provide corresponding institutional safeguards for this purpose.' The Standing Committee therefore laid down the ground rules for the election of the Chief Executive in 2017 as follows:

(1) A broadly representative nominating committee shall be formed. The provisions for the number of members, composition and formation method of the nominating committee shall be made in accordance with the number of members, composition and formation method of the Election Committee for the Fourth Chief Executive.
(2) The nominating committee shall nominate two to three candidates for the office of Chief Executive in accordance with democratic procedures. Each candidate must have the endorsement of more than half of all the members of the nominating committee.
(3) All eligible electors of the Hong Kong Special Administrative Region have the right to vote in the election of the Chief Executive and elect one of the candidates for the office of Chief Executive in accordance with law.
(4) The Chief Executive–elect, after being selected through universal suffrage, will have to be appointed by the Central People's Government.

232. The Standing Committee went on to stipulate that the Hong Kong legislature needed to specify the specific method of universal suffrage for selecting the Chief Executive as an amendment to Annex I of the Basic Law, to be approved by not less than a two-thirds of all the members of the Legislative Council and consented to by the Chief Executive. The decision stipulates that if the specific method of universal suffrage for selecting the Chief Executive is not adopted in accordance with legal procedures, the method used for selecting the Chief Executive for the preceding term shall continue to apply.

233. There was considerable agitation in Hong Kong against the limitations that the Standing Committee had imposed on the right of Hong Kong people to directly elect their Chief Executive, especially the continuation of the Election Committee which was required to nominate two or three candidates for the post of Chief Executive. On 18 June 2015, the Legislative Council rejected the government's electoral reform proposal for the 2017 elections by twenty-eight to eight votes.

234. Hong Kong having failed to come up with a proposal for direct election of the Chief Executive in line with the Decision of the Standing Committee, the selecting method of the 2017 Chief Executive remained unchanged: Carrie Lam, the former Chief Secretary for Administration was elected as the Chief Executive, the first woman and the second former Secretary for Administration to become the Chief Executive. She was selected in accordance with the same system that operated in 2012, election by a 1,200-member Election Committee.

235. The term of office of the Chief Executive is five years, and he may not serve more than two consecutive terms.[369] The Chief Executive must resign under any of the following circumstances:

(1) when he loses the ability to discharge his duties as a result of serious illness or other reasons;
(2) when, after the Legislative Council is dissolved because he twice refused to sign a bill passed by it, the new Legislative Council again passes by a two-thirds majority of all the members the original bill in dispute, but he still refuses to sign it; and
(3) when, after the Legislative Council is dissolved because it refuses to pass a budget or any other important bill, the new Legislative Council still refuses to pass the original bill in dispute.[370]

236. The Legislative Council may impeach the Chief Executive. Article 73(9) provides as follows:

> If a motion initiated jointly by one-fourth of all the members of the Legislative Council charges the Chief Executive with serious breach of law or dereliction of duty and if he or she refuses to resign, the Council may, after passing a motion for investigation, give a mandate to the Chief Justice of the Court of Final Appeal to form and chair an independent investigation committee. The Committee shall be responsible for carrying out the investigation and reporting its findings to the Council. If the Committee considers the evidence sufficient to substantiate such charges, the Council may pass a motion of impeachment by a two-thirds majority of its members and report to the Central People's Government for decision.

237. According to this provision, if a motion is signed by one-fourth of all the Legislative Council members, the Chief Executive may decide to resign. If the Chief Executive does not resign, a judicial investigation followed by a two-thirds majority vote in the Legislative Council will be needed to take the matter further. The Legislative Council's censure does not automatically result in the removal of the Chief Executive, though. It can only report its decision to the Central Government, which has the authority to remove the Chief Executive.

238. The office of the Chief Executive will become vacant:

(1) on the expiry of the term of office of the Chief Executive;
(2) if the Chief Executive dies; or
(3) if the Chinese Central Government removes the Chief Executive from office in accordance with the Basic Law.[371]

369. Basic Law, Art. 46.
370. *Ibid.*, Art. 52.
371. Chief Executive Election Ordinance (Cap. 569), s. 4.

239. If the office of the Chief Executive becomes vacant, a new Chief Executive must be selected within six months.[372] When in 2005 Mr Tung Chee Hwa resigned from the office of Chief Executive, there was no clear constitutional provision whether a new Chief Executive should be elected to serve the unexpired term of the outgoing Chief Executive or for a fresh five-year term. The Hong Kong Government took the view that the new Chief Executive would serve only the remaining two years and the NPC endorsed that view.[373] If the Chief Executive is temporarily unable to perform his duties, his duties must be assumed for such temporary period by the Administrative Secretary, the Financial Secretary or the Secretary for Justice in that order of precedence.[374]

§3. Competence

240. The principal powers and functions of the Chief Executive in relation to the Legislative Council are:

(1) He may request the President of the Legislative Council to call an emergency session of the Council.[375]
(2) He makes an annual policy address in the Legislative Council, which the Legislative Council will debate.[376]
(3) He has the power to approve the introduction of motions regarding revenues or expenditures to the Legislative Council[377] and may give written consent to the introduction in the Legislative Council of any bill relating to government policies.[378]
(4) No legislation passed by the Legislative Council will become law until signed by the Chief Executive.[379]
(5) The Chief Executive may refuse to sign a bill passed by the Legislative Council if he considers that such bill is not compatible with the overall interests of Hong Kong. If the Legislative Council passes such returned bill again with a two-thirds majority, the Chief Executive must sign and promulgate the bill.[380]
(6) If the Chief Executive refuses to sign and promulgate a bill passed a second time by the Legislative Council as stipulated in Article 49 or the Legislative

372. Basic Law, Art. 53.
373. *See* the Interpretation of Art. 53(2) of the Basic Law of the Hong Kong Special Administrative Region by the Standing Committee of the National People's Congress, dated 27 April 2005. Consequently, s. 3 of the Chief Executive Election Ordinance (Cap. 569) was amended in that year to provide that a person, who is appointed by the Central People's Government as the Chief Executive to fill the vacancy before the expiry of the term of office of a Chief Executive elected for a full five-year term, shall hold office for the unexpired period of the outgoing Chief Executive.
374. *Ibid.* Art. 53 refers to 'Administrative Secretary' and 'Secretary of Justice'. However, these officers are commonly referred to as 'Chief Secretary for the Administration' and 'Secretary for Justice'.
375. Basic Law, Art. 72(5).
376. *Ibid.*, Art. 73(4). *See* Part 1, Ch. 5 'Customary Law, Unwritten Law, General Principles of Law'.
377. *Ibid.*, Art. 48(10).
378. *Ibid.*, Art. 74.
379. *Ibid.*, Art. 76.
380. *Ibid.*, Art. 49.

Council refuses to pass a budget or any important bill introduced by the Government, he must try to resolve the impasse through negotiation. If no consensus can be reached through consultation, the Chief Executive may dissolve the Legislative Council. Such power of dissolution can be exercised only once in each term of his office.[381]

241. The powers and functions of the Chief Executive in the executive sphere are:

(1) The Chief Executive leads the Government of Hong Kong.[382]
(2) He is responsible for the implementation of law in Hong Kong.[383]
(3) He has the duty of implementing any directives issued by the Chinese Central Government in respect of relevant matters provided for in the Basic Law.[384]
(4) He conducts, on behalf of the Hong Kong Government, external affairs and other affairs as authorized by the Chinese Central Authorities.[385]
(5) He decides on government policies and has the power to issue executive orders.[386]

---

381. *Ibid.*, Art. 50.
382. *Ibid.*, Art. 48(1).
383. *Ibid.*, Art. 48(2). In *Leung Kwok Hung v Chief Executive of Hong Kong Special Administrative Region* [2006] HKEC 239, (CFI), it was held that the Chief Executive had not failed to comply with his duty to implement laws of Hong Kong when for more than eight years he did not bring into force the Interception of Communications Ordinance (Cap. 589), which was passed by the Legislative Council and approved by the Governor on the eve of Hong Kong's handover to China. The Court found that the Chief Executive had not determined that he would never bring the Ordinance into operation but that he was considering the appropriate manner in which the legislation could be implemented, including the possibility of amendments to the Ordinance. This decision of the Court of First Instance was affirmed by the Court of Appeal in *Leung Kwok Hung v Chief Executive of Hong Kong Special Administrative Region* [2006] HKEC 816, (CA). That Ordinance was subsequently enacted as Interception of Communications and Surveillance Ordinance (Cap. 589) and brought into effect on 9 August 2006. In *Chan Noi Heung v The Chief Executive in Council* [2009] HKCU 377; [2009] 3 HKLRD 362, (CA), the Court of Appeal held that the Chief Executive had not failed in his duty to implement laws when he failed to fix minimum wages under the Trade Boards Ordinance (Cap. 63). The Court of Appeal held that the relevant provision empowered the Chief Executive to fix minimum wages, but it did not impose any obligation on him to do so. The Court of Final Appeal refused leave to appeal against that decision. *See Chan Noi Heung v The Chief Executive in Council* [2009] HKEC 459, (CFA).
384. *Ibid.*, Art. 48(8). *See* Part I, Ch. 5 'Customary Law, Unwritten Law andGeneral Principles of Law'.
385. *Ibid.*, Art. 48(9).
386. *Ibid.*, Art. 48(4). *See*, for instance, *Chan Tak Shing v Chief Executive of the Hong Kong Special Administrative Region* [1999] 2 HKLRD 389, (CA), where the Court of Appeal dealt with Executive Order 1 of 1997. Executive Orders are a means by which the Chief Executive may discharge his executive functions. *See*, for instance, the Public Service (administration) Order, which was discussed in *Rowse v Secretary for the Civil Service* [2008] 5 HKLRD 217, (CFI). It has been held that there is nothing in the Basic Law or in the Hong Kong Reunification Ordinance No 110 of 1997 (Hong Kong e-Legislation, Instrument A601), which impliedly prevents the Chief Executive's executive orders taking effect retrospectively (*The Association of Expatriate Civil Servants of Hong Kong v The Chief Executive of Hong Kong Special Administrative Region* [1998] 1 HKLRD 615, (CFI), 623 per Keith J. In *Leung Kwok Hung v Chief Executive of Hong Kong Special Administrative Region* [2006] HKEC 239, (CFI), the Executive Order issued by the Chief Executive in August 2005, which according to its Explanatory Note was intended 'to set out the

(6) He nominates certain principal officials for appointment by the Chinese Central Government and appoints holders of public office.[387]
(7) He has the power to handle petitions and complaints.[388] Some ordinances specifically provide a right of appeal or petition to the Chief Executive.[389]
(8) The Chief Executive may also exercise any other powers given to him by any legislation. For instance, he has the power to appoint members of the Pharmacy and Poisons Board (section 3(2) of Pharmacy and Poisons Ordinance (Cap. 138) and the Air Transport Licensing Authority (Regulation 4(1) of Air Transport (Licensing for Air Services) Regulations (Cap. 448A)), to make a deportation order under the Immigration Ordinance (Cap. 115),[390] to approve a railway scheme (section 11 of the Railways Ordinance (Cap. 519)), to grant a broadcasting licence (section 10 of the Broadcasting Ordinance (Cap. 562)), and to direct the Town Planning Board to make or amend a land-use development plan and to approve it.[391] The Chief Executive may exercise a variety of powers under a particular ordinance. For instance, under the Air Pollution Control Ordinance (Cap. 311) the Chief Executive in Council may declare any part of Hong Kong to be an air control zone for the purposes of the ordinance.[392] He makes appointments to the Appeal Board Panel[393] and has the power to review an Appeal Board decision.[394] The Air Pollution Control Authority must consult the Chief Executive in exercising certain powers such as cancelling or varying a licence.[395]

242. The principal powers and functions of the Chief Executive in relation to the judicial branch of the Government are as follows:

---

legal procedures in accordance with which covert surveillance may be carried out by or on behalf of officers of Government departments which undertake law enforcement investigations or operations' was considered by the Court of First Instance to be no more than 'a set of administrative directions given to employees of the Government by the Head of the Government'.

387. *Ibid.*, Art. 48(5) and (7).
388. *Ibid.*, Art. 48(13).
389. For instance, s. 17 of the Animal and Plants (Protection of Endangered Species) Ordinance (Cap. 187) (repealed) provided that a person aggrieved by a licensing decision made under the Ordinance may appeal to the Chief Executive. Section 33 of the Pension Benefits (Judicial Officers) Ordinance (Cap. 401) enables a person who is aggrieved by a decision made under ss 29 or 31 to petition the Chief Executive against the decision. The Administrative Appeals Board Ordinance of 1994 (Cap. 442) set up an administrative appeal board and several pre-existing ordinances were amended to transfer the appeal jurisdiction of the Chief Executive to the newly set up appeals board. Such amended ordinances include the Chinese Temples Ordinance (Cap. 153), the Miscellaneous Licences Ordinance (Cap. 114), and the Employment Ordinance (Cap. 57). The Town Planning Ordinance (Cap. 131) is an example of an Ordinance that has set up a special tribunal (in this case the Town Planning Appeal Board) to take the place of appeals to the Chief Executive.
390. Section 20. *See Akram v Secretary for Security* [2000] 1 HKLRD 164, (CFI).
391. Town Planning Ordinance (Cap. 131), s. 3. *See also* Anton Cooray, 'Town Planning' (2018 reissue), in *Halsbury's Laws of Hong Kong*, [385.192]–[385.215].
392. Air Pollution Control Ordinance (Cap. 311), s. 6.
393. *Ibid.*, s. 32.
394. *Ibid.*, s. 35.
395. *See* Anton Cooray, *Environmental Law in Hong Kong* (2nd edn, Wolters Kluwer: 2018), [133].

(1) The Chief Executive has the power to appoint and remove judges of courts at all levels in accordance with legal procedures.[396]
(2) He cannot, however, interfere with the judiciary, because Hong Kong courts must exercise their power independently, free from any interference.[397]
(3) He has the power to pardon persons convicted of offences or commute their penalties.[398]

243. The Chief Executive has important legislative powers during a time of emergency. The Emergency Regulations Ordinance (Cap. 241) confers powers on the Chief Executive in Council to make regulations in times of emergency or public danger. The scope of his regulation-making power is virtually unlimited: 'He may make any regulations whatsoever which he may consider desirable in the public interest.'[399] Moreover, in the event of an inconsistency between an Enactment and any emergency regulation (or even an order or rule made under such a regulation), the Enactment must yield,[400] contrary to the general rule that primary legislation prevails over subordinate legislation.[401]

244. The Public Order Ordinance confers important powers on the Chief Executive. For instance, he may prohibit any gatherings for the prevention of serious public disorder, and the failure to comply with such a prohibition is a punishable offence.[402] The Chief Executive may, in the interest of public order, issue a curfew order, violations of which are punishable offences.[403] Although such an order must be published in the Government Gazette as soon as reasonably practicable, there is no requirement that the persons likely to be affected by a curfew was aware of the order.[404] Other powers of the Chief Executive include the power, in the interest of public order, to prohibit the movement of aircraft and vessels,[405] or to declare a place a closed area, where he reasonably believes that it is necessary for the protection of national security or public safety, or the protection of public order or public health.[406]

245. Legislative power that the Chief Executive may exercise by issuing executive orders has given rise to much judicial discussion. As set out in Article 48 of the Basic Law, one of the functions of the Chief Executive is 'to decide on government policies and issue executive orders'. The nature and scope of executive orders came up for discussion in a decisive way in *The Association of Expatriate Civil Servants of Hong Kong v Chief Executive of HKSAR*, in the very first year of the Hong Kong

---

396. *See* Part II, Ch. 5 on the judiciary.
397. Basic Law, Art. 85.
398. *Ibid.*, Art. 48(12).
399. Emergency Regulations Ordinance (Cap. 241), s. 2(1).
400. *Ibid.*, s. 2(4).
401. *See* Part I, Ch. 6 'Subordinate Rules and Regulations'.
402. Public Order Ordinance (Cap. 245), s. 17E.
403. *Ibid.*, s. 31.
404. *Kwan Yiu-wing v R* [1996] HKLR 752, (Appellate Jurisdiction).
405. Public Order Ordinance (Cap. 245), s. 34.
406. *Ibid.*, s. 36.

Special Administrative Region.[407] The making of the executive order was necessitated by the need to replace the several Colonial instruments that regulated the civil service, which lapsed on 30 July 1997, on the eve of the establishment of the Hong Kong SAR. The executive order, Public Service (Administration) Order 1997, came into effect on 9 July 1997 and provided for the appointment, dismissal and disciplinary control of public servants. The executive order was accompanied by the Public Service (Disciplinary) Regulation, made under the Order. Rejecting the argument that the regulation of the public service was done under legislation before 1997, it was held that the previous system was set up by the Crown in the exercise of prerogative powers and by the Governor acting, under the Letters Patent and Colonial Regulations, as the representative of the Crown. The hallmark of the previous system was that, where procedures were to be established locally, they were established by the Governor by executive action. While there were undoubtedly constitutional differences between Hong Kong's previous system and the current system, the maintenance of the previous system did not require the current system to have legislative approval. Therefore, under the Basic Law the linear successor of the governor, the Chief Executive could exercise such power, and this meant that the Chief Executive could make necessary legal procedures in relation to the public service. The argument that the executive order was invalid as it had retrospective effect was too rejected: As the first meeting of the Executive Council after the establishment of the Hong Kong Special Administrative Region was on 8 July 1997, it was entirely rational for the instruments to be expressed to have come into operation on 1 July 1997 to prevent an undesirable lacuna in the management of the public service.

246. The application for judicial review in *The Association of Expatriate Civil Servants of Hong Kong v Chief Executive of HKSAR* succeeded on one ground, that a restriction on a fundamental right protected by the Basic Law or the Bill of Rights (here the right to leave Hong Kong) could only be valid if it is contained in a law passed by the legislature, or in the common law. Although the restriction was part of the previous system of law, such a restriction being in an administrative provision did not pass the new requirement of Hong Kong Special Administrative Region that a restriction on a fundamental rights, assuming it is justifiable, must be expressed in legislation or common law.[408]

407. [1998] 1 HKLRD 615, (CFI).

408. *Ibid.*, 624–626. Section 17 of the Executive Order, which imposed the limitation which conflicted with the Bill of Rights, was declared invalid. Executive orders are further discussed in paras 115-118, 241 and 245 above.

§4. Privileges and Immunities, Inviolability, Personal Power

247. The Basic Law does not grant the Chief Executive any special immunities. There is no provision, for instance, granting him immunity from judicial proceedings for acts done in his official or private capacity while he holds office.[409] A particular legislative enactment may, however, preclude the possibility of judicial review of his action. For instance, section 64(3) of the Interpretation and General Clauses Ordinance (Cap. 1) states that, 'the conferring by any Ordinance of a right of appeal or objection to the Chief Executive in Council shall not prevent any person from applying to the High Court for an order of mandamus, certiorari, prohibition, injunction or any other order, instead of appealing or making an objection to the Chief Executive in Council, where an application for such an order would lie, but no proceedings by way of mandamus, certiorari, prohibition, injunction or other order shall be taken against the Chief Executive in Council in respect of any such appeal or objection to the Chief Executive in Council or any proceedings connected therewith'.[410] There are cases where decisions taken by the Chief Executive in some official capacity have been challenged. Examples of such decisions include a decision to retire a police officer[411] and an order to surrender a fugitive.[412]

---

409. For instance, Art. 35 of the Constitution of Sri Lanka provides as follows: 'While any person holds office as President no proceedings shall be instituted or continued against him in any court or tribunal in respect of anything done or omitted to be done by him either in his official or private capacity.'

410. *See Akram v Secretary for Security* [2000] 1 HKLRD 164, (CFI). The Court of First Instance held in *Gurung Bhakta Bahadur v Director of Immigration and Another* [2001] 3 HKLRD 225, (CFI), that a person aggrieved by an administrative decision, which is subject to an appeal or objection to the Chief Executive, may either make use of the administrative appeal/objection on the merits of the decision or seek judicial review of the impugned decision for procedural defects. However, if aggrieved person appealed to the Chief Executive and is not satisfied with that decision, there is no further review on merit. However an aggrieved person could judicially review the decision of the Chief Executive in Council if it can be shown that the Chief Executive in Council 'has done or failed to do something in the course of the [appeal] inquiry which is of such a nature that its decision is a nullity'. This means that judicial review does not provide an alternative means of reviewing merits of the decision. The Court followed *Anisminic Ltd v Foreign Compensation Commission (No 2)* [1969] 2 AC 147, *O'Reilly v Mackman* [1983] 2 AC 237, (HL). *A-G v Ryan* [1980] AC 718, (PC), *South East Asia Fire Bricks Sdn Bhd v Non-Metallic Mineral Products Manufacturing Employees Union* [1981] AC 363, (PC), and *R v Secretary of State for the Home Department, ex p Fayed* [1998] 1 WLR 763, (CA).

411. *Chan Tak Shing v The Chief Executive* [1999] 2 HKLRD 389, (CA).

412. *Chen Chong Gui v The Chief Executive* [1999] 1 HKLRD 693, (CFI).

Chapter 3. The Legislature

§1. The Organ of State

248. The principal provisions of the Basic Law of the Hong Kong SAR relating to the legislature are found in Chapter IV, section 3: 'The Legislature'. The Legislature of the Hong Kong SAR of the People's Republic of China is known as the Legislative Council (Article 66 of the Basic Law).

I. Role of the Head of State in the Legislative Process

249. Chapter IV of the Basic Law is entitled 'Political Structure' and is divided into six sections: section 1 'The Chief Executive' (Articles 43–58); section 2 'The Executive Authorities' (Articles 59–65); section 3 'The Legislature' (Articles 66–79); section 4 'The Judiciary' (Articles 80–96); section 5 'District Organizations' (Articles 97 and 98); and section 6 'Public Servants' (Articles 99–104). Section 1 contains provisions dealing with the relationship between the Chief Executive and the Legislative Council. The Chief Executive has an important part to play in the legislative process. While any member of the Legislative Council may introduce a legislative measure for consideration by the Legislative Council, he may not introduce any bill that relates to 'public expenditure or political structure or the operation of the government'. The written consent of the Chief Executive is required for introducing any bill relating to government policies.[413] The Chief Executive has the power to approve the introduction of motions regarding revenue or expenditure to the Legislative Council and to sign bills and budgets passed by the Legislative Council.[414] The Basic Law provides for resolution of conflicts that may arise if the Chief Executive refuses to sign a bill passed by the Legislative Council.[415]

II. Hong Kong's Legislative Council: An Introduction

250. Hong Kong's Legislative Council is a unicameral legislature that exercises legislative functions that are within the competence of the Hong Kong Special Administrative Region. The Basic Law provisions relating to the composition, powers and functions of the Legislative Council are found in section 3 'The Legislature' in Chapter IV 'Political Structure'. Annex II of the Basic Law provides the method for the formulation of Hong Kong's Legislative Council and its voting procedures. Annexed to the Basic Law is the Decision of the NPC on the method for the formation of the first government and the first Legislative Council of the Hong Kong Special Administrative Region.[416]

413. Basic Law, Art. 74.
414. *Ibid.*, Art. 48(10) and (3).
415. *See ibid.*, Arts 49–52.
416. *See* Part III of this monograph, 'Composition of the Legislative Council'.

III. Composition of the Legislative Council

251. The Basic Law requires the Legislative Council to be constituted by election. It sets out the manner in which members of the Legislative Council should be selected in its first two terms. It stipulates that the method for forming the Legislative Council in later terms of office should be determined by taking into account the actual situation in Hong Kong and in accordance with the principle of gradual and orderly progress. It states that the ultimate aim is the election of all the members of the Legislative Council by universal suffrage.[417]

252. The Basic Law provides for the continuation of the political system prevailing under the British colonial administration. The original understanding between the British and Chinese governments was that the last Legislative Council elected under the British administration in 1995 would continue till the end of its four-year term, surviving the transfer of sovereignty in 1997. For this to be accomplished, the composition of the Legislative Council to be elected in 1995 had to be the same as that of the first Legislative Council under the Basic Law. Thus reflecting the composition of the last Legislative Council under the British rule, the first Legislative Council under the Basic Law was to be composed of sixty members, with twenty members returned from geographical constituencies, ten members returned by an election committee and thirty members returned by functional constituencies.[418] In 1990, when the Basic Law was promulgated and the decision regarding the composition of the first Legislative Council was taken,[419] Hong Kong had a Legislative Council consisting of eighteen members directly elected from geographical constituencies, twenty-one members elected from functional constituencies, eighteen appointed members and three ex officio members. The electors of the functional constituencies were a very small number.[420]

253. The Chinese Government was prepared to let the last Legislative Council to be elected in 1995 to continue until the expiry of its term of office in 1999. In order to allow a 'through train' the Legislative Council in existence as at 1 July 1997

---

417. Basic Law, Art. 68.
418. *See* the 'Decision of the National People's Congress on the Method for the Formation of the First Government and the First Legislative Council of the Hong Kong Special Administrative Region': Instrument 14 appended to the Basic Law.
419. *See* 'Decision of the National People's Congress on the Method for the Formation of the First Government and the First Legislative Council of the Hong Kong Special Administrative Region': Instrument 14 appended to the Basic Law.
420. At the 1991 Legislative Council elections, the total number of eligible voters in the twenty-one functional constituencies was just over 100,000 or less than 0.2% of the population. Under the Patten Reforms voting in the existing functional constituencies was changed from corporate to personal, and in the newly created nine constituencies (such as agriculture, textile, manufacturing, hotels and catering, transport and communication, financing insurance real estate and business services) all workers belonging to those categories had the right of vote – effectively universal suffrage for the employed of around 2.7 million. Yash Ghai, *Hong Kong's New Constitutional Order: The Resumption of Chinese Sovereignty and the Basic Law*, (2nd edn, Hong Kong: Hong Kong University Press, 1998), at 234.

had to be constituted on the same model as the Basic Law envisaged.[421] To enable this to happen the term of office of the Legislative Council was extended from three years to four years with effect from the Legislative Council election to be held in 1991. The expectation was that the Legislative Council to be formed in 1995 would have the following composition: twenty members directly elected from geographical constituencies, thirty members returned from functional constituencies and ten members elected from newly introduced Election Committee. The general expectation was that functional constituencies would continue to be limited to a small number of eligible electors and the Election committee would be a small body of persons appointed by the government. While the Basic Law did not specify the composition of the Election Committee for the purposes of the 1995 Legislative Council Election, the Chinese position was that the composition of the election committee would be similar to the Election Committee established by Annex I of the Basic Law for the election of the Legislative Council for the second and third terms in 1999 and 2003, which was a broadly representative body of 800 persons. However, the arrival in 1992 of Christopher Patten, the last Governor of Hong Kong, moved the political developments in a new direction. Interpreting the Basic Law as providing for further democratization of Hong Kong, Christopher Patten was minded to democratize Hong Kong's political system 'to the maximum extent within the terms of the Joint Declaration and the Basic Law'.

254. As regards the 1995 Legislative Council Election this resulted in using the functional constituencies and Election Committee arrangement as a means of providing for more direct participation in the election by the people of Hong Kong. While reflecting the 20:10:30 ratio between members elected from geographical constituencies, members returned by the election committee and members elected through functional constituencies, Chris Patten's political reform package opened the way for far greater voter participation than was in the contemplation of the Chinese Government.[422] The Chinese Government considered these reforms to be inconsistent with the phase of democratic reform the Basic Law envisaged and

421. The relevant part of the 'Decision of the National People's Congress on the Method for the Formation of the First Government and the First Legislative Council of the Hong Kong Special Administrative Region': Instrument 14 appended to the Basic Law, provided as follows: 'If the composition of the last Hong Kong Legislative Council before the establishment of the Hong Kong Special Administrative Region is in conformity with the relevant provisions of this Decision and the Basic Law of the Hong Kong Special Administrative Region, those of its members who uphold the Basic Law of the Hong Kong Special Administrative Region of the People's Republic of China and pledge allegiance to the Hong Kong Special Administrative Region of the People's Republic of China, and who meet the requirements set forth in the Basic Law of the Region may, upon confirmation by the Preparatory Committee, become members of the first Legislative Council of the Region.'

422. For instance, the newly created nine functional constituencies threw open voting to over 2.7 million voters who were employed in the relevant functional constituencies; and the Election Committee, instead of being a small nominated body, consisted of all the members of the District Boards, thus providing an indirect form of direct election. *See* generally, on the 1995 election Lo Shiu Hing, 'An Analysis of Sino-British Negotiations Over Hong Kong's Political Reform' (1994) 16:2 *Contemporary Southeast Asia* 178–209.

decided that the Legislative Council elected in 1995 should not survive the handover and took steps to form a Provisional Legislative Council that would take over on 1 July 1997 from the Legislative Council elected in 1995.

255. In March 1996, the Chinese Government decided to establish a Provisional Legislative Council. The task of establishing a provisional legislature was given to the Preparatory Committee, created by the Decision of the NPC of 4 April 1990, for the purpose of preparing for the establishment of the first government and the first Legislative Council.[423] As required by that decision, a preparatory committee was appointed in November 1996 which appointed the Provisional Legislative Council in December 1996. From then until the handover of Hong Kong to China on 1 July 1997, two legislative councils were in operation. While the Legislative Council elected in 1995 operated formally in Hong Kong, the Provisional Legislative Council met in the territory of China to debate and pass legislative measures, which would formally be adopted soon after 1 July 1997. The Provisional Legislative Council formally became Hong Kong's legislature on 1 July 1997 as a stop gap measure and was intended to operate until such time as the establishment of the First Legislative Council of Hong Kong, but in any event only up until and including 30 June 1998. As Chan CJHC observed in *Hong Kong Special Administrative Region v Ma Wai Kwan, David*, which upheld the validity of the Provisional Legislative Council:

> The Provisional Legislative Council is not the first Legislative Council [of Hong Kong Special Administrative Region for the purposes of the Basic Law]. It was only set up to do specific acts. It is also specified that the laws examined and passed by the Provisional Legislative Council before 1 July 1997 will only come into force from the day the Hong Kong Special Administrative Region is established. It will operate until the first Legislative Council of the Hong Kong Special Administrative Region is formed, which may not be later than 30 June 1998. It is clear that the terms of reference of the Provisional Legislative Council set out in the 1996 Decision of the Preparatory Committee are necessary and incidental to the initial operation of the first Government of the Hong Kong Special Administrative Region.[424]

256. The elections for the first Legislative Council of the Hong Kong Special Administrative Region were held on 24 May 1998, to hold office for a term of two years from 1 July 1998.[425] The term of office of the second Legislative Council,

423. 'Decision of the National People's Congress on the Method for the Formation of the First Government and the First Legislative Council of the Hong Kong Special Administrative Region': Instrument 14 appended to the Basic Law.

424. *HKSAR v Ma Wai Kwan, David* [1997] HKLRD 761, (CA), 785. The Court of Final Appeal expressed a similar view in *Ng Ka Ling v Director of Immigration* (1999) 1 HKCFAR 4, (CFA).

425. For an excellent analysis of the 1998 election, *see* Shiu-Hing Lo and Wing-yat Yu, 'Election and Democracy in Hong Kong: The 1998 Legislative Council Election' (1999) 4 *Contemporary Asian Studies* 1–68.

which commenced on 1 October 2000, and the term of office of any subsequent Legislative Council, is four years. This is in keeping with Article 69, which provides that the term of office of the Legislative Council of the Hong Kong Special Administrative Region is four years, except the first term, which is two years.

257. The Legislative Council of the Hong Kong Special Administrative Region must be composed of Chinese citizens who are permanent residents of the Region with no right of abode in any foreign country. Permanent residents of the Region who are not of Chinese nationality or who have the right of abode in foreign countries may also be elected members of the Legislative Council. However, the proportion of such members must not exceed 20% of the total membership of the Council.[426]

258. Until 2012, the Legislative Council of the Hong Kong Special Administrative Region consisted of sixty members. In the first term, the Legislative Council was to be formed in accordance with the 'Decision of the National People's Congress on the Method for the Formation of the First Government and the First Legislative Council of the Hong Kong Special Administrative Region'.[427] Of the sixty members of the First Legislative Council (1 July 1998–30 June 2000), twenty members were returned from geographical constituencies. Thirty members were elected from functional constituencies, with the remaining ten members being returned by an election committee.[428] The composition of the Legislative Council in its second term (from 1 October 2000 to 30 September 2004) was as follows: twenty-four members returned by geographical constituencies, thirty members returned by functional constituencies and six returned by the election committee. The Legislative Council in its third term (from 1 October 2004 to 2008) consisted of thirty members elected from geographical constituencies and thirty members returned by functional constituencies, there being no provision for an election committee.[429] The Legislative Council formed after the elections in 2012 consisted of seventy members, half of it elected directly from geographical constituencies with the other half elected from functional constituencies.[430] This number of members remained unchanged for the 2016 election.

259. Following on from Article 68 of the Basic Law which provides that the method for the forming of the Legislative Council would be specified in the light of

426. Basic Law, Art. 67.
427. *See* Annex II of the Basic Law, 'Method for the Formation of the Legislative Council of the Hong Kong Special Administrative Region and Its Voting Procedures'.
428. *See* the 'Decision of the National People's Congress on the Method for the Formation of the First Government and the First Legislative Council of the Hong Kong Special Administrative Region': Instrument 14 appended to the Basic Law.
429. *See* Annex II of the Basic Law, 'Method for the Formation of the Legislative Council of the Hong Kong Special Administrative Region and Its Voting Procedures'.
430. This change was brought about by an amendment of Annex II of the Basic Law made by the Standing Committee of the National People's Congress on 28 August 2010. *See* Instrument 4 appended to the Basic Law.

the actual situation in the Hong Kong Special Administrative Region and in accordance with the principle of gradual and orderly progress, while the ultimate aim is the election of all the members of the Legislative Council by universal suffrage, Annex II of the Basic Law prescribes the composition of the Legislative Council with some of the members being directly elected from geographical constituencies. As seen above, in the second term (2000–2004) of the Legislative Council twenty-four out of sixty directly elected and in the third term (2004–2008) of the Legislative Council thirty out of sixty directly elected.[431]

260. Gradually increasing the number of directly elected members from twenty in the first term (1998–2000), twenty-four in the second term and to twenty-four in the third term, as set out in Annex II, the next step was how Hong Kong should progress towards a fully directly elected legislature commencing from 2008. The amendment of Annex II in 2010 increased the number of the members of the Legislative Council to seventy with effect from the 2012 elections.[432] Little progress, however, has been made to elect all members of the Legislative Council through universal franchise.

261. The Decision of the NPCSC that the method of forming the Legislative Council would not change (i.e., election of all members through universal franchise will not be introduced) at the 2008 election was given on 26 April 2004.[433] The Decision of the NPCSC that the manner of forming the Legislative Council would not change at the 2012 election was given on 29 December 2007.[434] The Decision of the NPCSC that the manner of forming the Legislative Council would not change at the 2016 election was given on 31 August 2014.[435]

262. We may briefly examine the decision not to introduce a fully directly elected legislature in 2016, and the reasons given for making no change in the current composition of the legislature (thirty-five of seventy members directly elected from geographical constituencies based on universal franchise). Article III of Annex

---

431. Annex II of the Basic Law, 'Method for the Formation of the Legislative Council of the Hong Kong Special Administrative Region and Its Voting Procedures'.
432. This change was brought about by an amendment of Annex II of the Basic Law made by the Standing Committee of the National People's Congress on 28 August 2010. *See* Instrument 4 appended to the Basic Law.
433. *See* the Decision of the Standing Committee of the National People's Congress on Issues Relating to the Methods for Selecting the Chief Executive of the Hong Kong Special Administrative Region in the year 2007 and the Forming of the Legislative Council of the Hong Kong Special Administrative Region in the year 2008 (dated 6 April 2004): Instrument 21 appended to the Basic Law.
434. *See* the Decision of the Standing Committee of the National People's Congress on Issues Relating to the Methods for Selecting the Chief Executive of the Hong Kong Special Administrative Region and the Forming of the Legislative Council of the Hong Kong Special Administrative Region in the year 2012 and on issues Relating to Universal Suffrage (dated 29 December 2007): Instrument 23 appended to the Basic Law.
435. *See* the Decision of the Standing Committee of the National People's Congress on Issues Relating to the Methods relating to the Selection of the Chief Executive of the Hong Kong Special Administrative Region by Universal Suffrage and the Method for Forming of the Legislative Council of the Hong Kong Special Administrative Region in the year 2016 (dated 31 August 2014): Instrument 25 appended to the Basic Law.

II of the Basic Law stipulates that 'with regard to the method for forming the Legislative Council of the Hong Kong Special Administrative Region … if there is a need to amend the provisions of this Annex, such amendments must be made with the endorsement of a two-thirds majority of all the members of the Council and the consent of the chief Executive, and they shall be reported to the Standing committee for the record'.

263. The Standing Committee set out in its Decision of 29 December 2007 the procedure that would have to be followed if a change in the Legislative Council was needed so as for it to become a fully directly elected legislature:

> At an appropriate time prior to the election of all the members of the Legislative Council of the Hong Kong Special Administrative Region by universal suffrage, the Chief Executive shall make a report to the NPCSC as regards the issue of amending the method for forming the Legislative Council and the issue of whether any corresponding amendment should be made to the procedures for voting on bills and motions in the Legislative Council in accordance with the relevant provisions of the Hong Kong Basic Law and 'The Interpretation by the Standing Committee of the National People's Congress of Article 7 of Annex I and Article III of Annex II to the Basic Law of the Hong Kong Special Administrative Region of the People's Republic of China'; a determination thereon shall be made by the Standing Committee of the National People's Congress. The bills on the amendments to the method for forming the Legislative Council and its procedures for voting on bills and motions and the proposed amendments to such bills shall be introduced by the Government of the Hong Kong Special Administrative Region to the Legislative Council; such amendments must be made with the endorsement of a two-thirds majority of all the members of the Legislative Council and the consent of the Chief Executive and they shall be reported to the Standing Committee of the National People's Congress for the record.[436]

264. As regards the procedure to be followed in amending Annex II was explained by the NPCSC in its interpretation of Article III of Annex II, dated 6 April 2004. The prescribed procedure involves the Chief Executive submitting a report to the Standing Committee, the Standing Committee making a determination and the legislature of Hong Kong passing necessary legislation to give effect to the amendments as proposed by the Standing Committee. The relevant extract of the Interpretation is as follows:

436. The Decision of the Standing Committee of the National People's Congress on Issues Relating to the Methods for Selecting the Chief Executive of the Hong Kong Special Administrative Region and the Forming of the Legislative Council of the Hong Kong Special Administrative Region in the year 2012 and on issues Relating to Universal Suffrage (dated 29 December 2007): Instrument 23 appended to the Basic Law.

> The provisions in [Annex I and Annex II] that any amendment must be made with the endorsement of a two-thirds majority of all the members of the Legislative Council and the consent of the Chief Executive and shall be reported to the Standing Committee of the National People's Congress for approval or for the record mean the requisite legislative process through which the method for selecting the Chief Executive and the method for forming the Legislative Council and its procedures for voting on bills and motions are amended. Such an amendment may take effect only if it has gone through the said process, including the approval or recording ultimately given or made by the Standing Committee of the National People's Congress in accordance with law. The Chief Executive of the Hong Kong Special Administrative Region shall make a report to the Standing Committee of the National People's Congress as regards whether there is a need to make an amendment; and the Standing Committee of the National People's Congress shall, in accordance with the provisions of Articles 45 and 68 of the Basic Law of the Hong Kong Special Administrative Region of the People's Republic of China, make a determination in the light of the actual situation in the Hong Kong Special Administrative Region and in accordance with the principle of gradual and orderly progress. The bills on the amendments to the method for selecting the Chief Executive and the method for forming the Legislative Council and its procedures for voting on bills and motions and the proposed amendments to such bills shall be introduced by the Government of the Hong Kong Special Administrative Region into the Legislative Council.[437]

265. Following the procedure set out above, the Chief Executive submitted a report to the Standing Committee on 15 July 2014, regarding whether there was a need to change the method of electing the Chief Executive and the formation of the Legislative Council. As regards the need for changes in the composition of the Legislative Council, the report made the following submission:

> The public generally agrees that since the successful implementation of universal suffrage of the Chief Executive election in 2017 is a pre-condition for the election of all the Members of the LegCo by universal suffrage, efforts should now be focused on the proper handling of universal suffrage for the Chief Executive election. Moreover, as relatively substantial amendments had been made to the method for forming the LegCo in 2012, it is generally agreed that there is no need to amend Annex II to the Basic Law regarding the method for forming the LegCo in 2016.[438]

437. The Interpretation by the Standing Committee of the National People's Congress of Art. 7 of Annex I and Art. III of Annex II to the Basic Law of the Hong Kong Special Administrative Region of the People's Republic of China, (dated 6 April 2004): Instrument 20 appended to the Basic Law.
438. Available at: http://www.2017.govhk/en/report/index.html.

266. Having considered the report submitted by the Chief Executive, the NPCSC decided as follows:

> The existing formation method and voting procedures for the Legislative Council as prescribed in Annex II to the Hong Kong Basic Law will not be amended. The formation method and procedures for voting on bills and motions of the fifth term Legislative Council will continue to apply to the sixth term Legislative Council of the Hong Kong Special Administrative Region in 2016. After the election of the Chief Executive by universal suffrage, the election of all the members of the Legislative Council of the Hong Kong Special Administrative Region may be implemented by the method of universal suffrage. At an appropriate time prior to the election of the Legislative Council by universal suffrage, the Chief Executive elected by universal suffrage shall submit a report to the Standing Committee of the National People's Congress in accordance with the relevant provisions of the Hong Kong Basic Law and the Interpretation by the Standing Committee of the National People's Congress of Article 7 of Annex I and Article III of Annex II to the Basic Law of the Hong Kong Special Administrative Region of the People's Republic of China as regards the issue of amending the method for forming the Legislative Council. A determination thereon shall be made by the Standing Committee of the National People's Congress.[439]

267. The sixth Legislative Council elected in 2016 was due to come to an end on 30 September 2020 and arrangements had been made for the holding of the general election on 6 September 2020 for the formation of the seventh Legislative Council. However, on 28 July 2020, the Chief Executive made a regulation under the Emergency Regulations Ordinance (Cap. 241), which came into effect on 1 August 2020.[440] The Regulation revoked the specification that the Chief Executive had made on 12 June 2020 for the holding of the election on 6 September 2020 and stated that all arrangements that had been made in respect of the election would cease to be of effect. The regulation provided for the postponement of the election by twelve months so that the general election would now take place on 5 September 2021. While the regulation does not specify a reason why the elections are postponed, the official reason for it is the prevalence of the COVID-19 pandemic.[441] The postponement of the election would mean that from 1 October 2020, Hong Kong

439. Paragraph IV of the Decision of the Standing Committee of the National People's Congress on Issues Relating to the Methods relating to the Selection of the Chief Executive of the Hong Kong Special Administrative Region by Universal Suffrage and the Method for Forming of the Legislative Council of the Hong Kong Special Administrative Region in the year 2016 (dated 31 August 2014): Instrument 26 appended to the Basic Law.

440. Emergency (Date of General Election) (Seventh Term of the Legislative Council) Regulation, Legal Notice 152 of 2020. https://www.legco.gov.hk/general/english/intro/2020ln152-e.pdf.

441. *See* the press release issued by the Hong Kong Government on 31 July 2020. https://www.info.gov.hk/gia/general/202007/31/P2020073100898p.htm. The Decision of the NPCSC, which is discussed immediately below states that the reason for postponing the Legislative Council elections was the COVID-19 situation.

would be without a Legislative Council, there being no provision in the Basic Law authorizing the Chief Executive or any other agency of the Hong Kong Government to extend the four-year term of the Legislative Council. The Chief Executive submitted 'an urgent report to the Central People's Government seeking its support and guidance'.[442] The State Council complied with the request and asked the NPCSC for a decision on how to deal with this situation. The NPCSC made a Decision on 11 August 2020 declaring that after 30 September 2020, the Sixth Legislative Council would 'continue to discharge duties for not less than one year' until the seventh term of the Legislative Council begins.[443]

IV. Franchise

268. Provisions regarding Legislative Council elections are to be found in the Electoral Affairs Commission Ordinance (Cap. 541), the Legislative Council Ordinance (Cap. 542) and regulations made thereunder.

269. The relevant regulations made under the Electoral Affairs Commission Ordinance relating to Legislative Council elections are given below preceded by the regulation number: (A) the Electoral Affairs Commission (Registration of Electors) (Legislative Council Geographical Constituencies) (District Council Constituencies) Regulation, (B) the Electoral Affairs Commission (Registration) (Electors for Functional Constituencies) (Voters for Election Committee Subsectors) (members of Election Committee) Regulation, (C) Electoral Affairs Commission (Nominations Advisory Committees) (Legislative Council) Regulation, (D) Electoral Affairs (Electoral Procedure) (Legislative Council) Regulation, (L) Electoral Affairs Commission (Electoral Procedure) (Election Committee) Regulation, (M) Electoral Affairs Commission (Particulars Relating to Candidates on Ballot Papers (Legislative Council and District Councils) Regulation, (N) Electoral Affairs Commission (Financial Assistance for Legislative Council Elections and District Council Elections) (Application and Payment Procedure) Regulation.

270. Regulations made under the Legislative Council Ordinance, preceded by the regulation number, are: (A) Declaration of Constituencies (Legislative Council) Order 1997, (B) Registration of Electors (Appeals) Regulation, (C) Legislative Council (Subscribers and Election Deposit for Nomination) Regulation, (F) Legislative Council (Formation of Election Committee) (Appeals) Regulation, (G) Declaration of Geographical Constituencies (Legislative Council) Order 1999, (I) Declaration of Geographical Constituencies (Legislative Council) Order 2003, (J)

---

442. *See* Government press release of 11 August 2020, 'CE expresses gratitude to NPCSC for sixth-term LegCo to continue to discharge duties'. https://www.info.gov.hk/gia/general/202008/11/P2020081100677.htm?fontSize=1. *See also* 'Chinese Central Government's Statement on Postponement of HKSAR LegCo Election' Xinhua news agency, 1 August 2020. http://en.people.cn/n3/2020/0801/c90000-9717193.html.

443. Decision of the Standing Committee of the National People's Congress on the Continuing Discharge of Duties by the Sixth Term Legislative Council of the Hong Kong Special Administrative Region: Legal Notice 154 of 2020, Instrument A216.

Declaration of Geographical Constituencies (Legislative Council) Order 2007, (K) Declaration of Geographical Constituencies (Legislative Council) Order 2011, and (L) Declaration of Geographical Constituencies (Legislative Council) Order 2015.

271. For the direct election of twenty members of the Legislative Council in its second term, Hong Kong was divided into five multi-member geographical constituencies.[444] For the election of thirty members from functional constituencies, twenty-eight functional constituencies were established, each constituency returning one member, except the labour functional constituency, which was entitled to return three members.[445] For the purpose of returning ten members, an Election Committee consisting of 800 members was established.[446] The 800 members were drawn from four sectors, 200 from each sector. Each sector had a number of sub-sectors, each electing a fixed number of members. For instance, in the first sector each of the sub-sectors such as catering and hotel returned eleven members, while each of the sub-sectors such as insurance and transport returned twelve members. In the 2004 and 2008 elections, the thirty directly elected members continued to be returned from the five multi-member geographical constituencies.

272. As shown above the membership of the Legislative Council has been expanded to seventy members from 2012, half of which are to be elected through direct elections. Since 2004, half the members of the Legislative Council are elected from functional constituencies and the other half from geographical constituencies.

273. To qualify for registration as an elector in a geographical constituency, a person has to be a permanent resident of Hong Kong of at least 18 years of age and ordinarily resident in Hong Kong.[447] A person who is qualified to be registered as an elector in a geographical constituency is entitled to vote in a functional constituency if he is registered for it. For instance, a university lecturer is entitled to vote in a geographical constituency as well as in the education functional constituency. Certain corporate bodies and unincorporated associations are entitled to vote in certain functional constituencies. For instance, the electors for the insurance functional constituency are bodies that are insurers authorized or deemed to be authorized under the Insurance Companies Ordinance (Cap. 41). The electors of the accountancy functional constituency are professional accountants. The electors of the agriculture and fisheries functional constituency include corporate members of certain bodies, such as the Joint Association of Hong Kong Fishermen, and certain named corporate bodies such as the Fishery Development Association (Hong Kong) Ltd and unincorporated associations such as the Aberdeen Fisherman Friendship Association.

---

444. *See* Legislative Council Ordinance, s. 18 and the Declaration of Geographical Constituencies (Legislative Council) Order 1997 (for the 1998 elections) and the Declaration of Geographical Constituencies (Legislative Council) Order 1999 (for the 2000 elections).
445. *See* Legislative Council Ordinance, s. 20 and s. 21.
446. *See ibid.*, s. 22 and Sch. 2.
447. Legislative Council Ordinance (Cap. 542) ss 24, 27, 28, 29, and 30.

V. Legislative Powers Concerning Elections

274. The Basic Law provides only the skeletal provisions relating to the election of members of the Legislative Council. Supplementary provisions had to be made by the legislature to implement the relevant Basic Law provisions. The laws that have been so passed have already been referred to above. The Basic Law has clearly set out the composition of the Legislative Council in its second term (2000–2004) and third term (2004–2008). The question of the composition of the Legislative Council as from 2008 had to be determined by an amendment of Annex II of the Basic Law. Article III of Annex II of the Basic Law 'Method for the Formation of the Legislative Council of the Hong Kong Special Administrative Region and Its Voting Powers' provides that if there is a need to amend the provisions of Annex II with regard to the method for forming the Legislative Council subsequent to the year 2007, such amendment has to be endorsed by not less than two-thirds of all members of the Legislative Council and approved by the Chief Executive. Such amendments must be reported to the NPCSC for the record. As noted above, the NPC decided in 2004, 2007 and 2014 that the Legislative Council would not be fully directly elected from 2008, 2012 and 2016. The only difference that was made by the NPCSC was to increase the number of members from sixty to seventy with effect from 2012, with thirty-five members elected from functional constituencies and thirty-five from geographical constituencies.

VI. Term of Office and Vacancies

275. The term of office of the Legislative Council is four years.[448] The Chief Executive may, however, dissolve the Legislative Council any time before the expiration of the full term of office, in the following situation:

> If the Chief Executive of the Hong Kong Special Administrative Region considers that a bill passed by the Legislative Council is not compatible with the overall interests of the Region, he or she may return it to the Legislative Council within three months for reconsideration. If the Legislative Council passes the original bill again by not less than a two-thirds majority of all the members, the Chief Executive must sign and promulgate it within one month, or act in accordance with the provisions of Article 50 of [the Basic Law].[449]

276. Article 50 provides as follows:

> If the Chief Executive of the Hong Kong Special Administrative Region refuses to sign a bill passed a second time by the Legislative Council, or the

448. Basic Law, Art. 69.
449. *Ibid.*, Art. 49.

Legislative Council refuses to pass a budget or any other important bill introduced by the government, and if consensus still cannot be reached after consultations, the Chief Executive may dissolve the Legislative Council. The Chief Executive must consult the Executive Council before dissolving the Legislative Council. The Chief Executive may dissolve the Legislative Council only once in each term of his or her office.

277. The Chief Executive's power to dissolve the Legislative Council is therefore restricted, unlike under a 'Westminster Model' Constitution where the Head of State has the power to summon, prorogue, or dissolve Parliament at any time, subject of course to relevant constitutional conventions.[450] The Chief Executive's power to dissolve the Legislative Council is counterbalanced by the Legislative Council's power to compel the Chief Executive to resign from office. Article 52 of the Basic Law provides that the Chief Executive must resign, *inter alia*:

(1) when after the Legislative Council is dissolved because he or she twice refuses to sign a bill passed by it, the new Legislative Council again passes it by a two-thirds majority of all the Legislative Council members, but he or she still refuses to sign it; and
(2) when after the Legislative Council is dissolved because it refuses to pass a budget or any other important bill, the new Legislative Council still refuses to pass the original bill in dispute.

278. A person returned as a member of the Legislative Council at a general election or a by-election holds office until the end of the term of the Legislative Council to which he was elected,[451] unless he ceases to be a member as a result of his death, or resignation from office, or ceasing to be qualified any longer for Legislative Council membership.[452] Newly elected Legislative Council Members must take the prescribed oath. Any person who fails to do so forfeits his office.[453] Article 79 of

450. *See* generally S.A. de Smith, 'Westminster's Export Models: The Legal Framework of Responsible Government' (1961) 1 *Journal of Commonwealth Political Studies* 2. Under the British colonial administration, the Governor could at any time dissolve the Legislative Council. *See* Hong Kong Royal Instructions, Cl. XXVIIIA. No Governor of Hong Kong has ever exercised this prerogative power of dissolution.
451. Legislative Council Ordinance (Cap. 542), s. 12.
452. *Ibid.*, s. 15.
453. The Legislative Council oath is as follows: 'I swear that, being a member of the Legislative Council of the Hong Kong Special Administrative Region of the People's Republic of China, I will uphold the Basic Law of the Hong Kong Special Administrative Region of the People's Republic of China, bear allegiance to the Hong Kong Special Administrative Region of the People's Republic of China and serve the Hong Kong Special Administrative Region conscientiously, dutifully, in full accordance with the law, honestly and with integrity': s. 16(d) and Sch. 2 of the Oaths and Declarations Ordinance (Cap. 11). As a constitutional and mandatory requirement, a member-elect of the Legislative Council must properly and validly take the Oath of Allegiance both in form and in substance as required by the law before he could assume office: *Chief Executive of HKSAR v President of Legislative Council* [2017] 4 HKLRD 115, (CFI), affirmed by the Court of Appeal: [2019] HKEC 417, (CA). Once a member is disqualified by his failure to take the oath, there is no possibility of his retaking the oath to validate his appointment: *Chief Executive of HKSAR v President*

the Basic Law states that the President of the Legislative Council must declare that a member of the Legislative Council is no longer qualified for such membership in any of the following circumstances:

(1) when he or she loses the ability to discharge his duties as a result of serious illness or other reasons;
(2) when he or she, with no valid reason, is absent from meetings for three consecutive months without the consent of the President of the Legislative Council;
(3) when he or she loses or renounces his or her status as a permanent resident of Hong Kong Special Administrative Region;
(4) when he or she accepts a government appointment and becomes a public servant;
(5) when he or she is bankrupt or fails to comply with a court order to repay debts;
(6) when he or she is convicted and sentenced to imprisonment for one month or more for a criminal offence committed within or outside the Hong Kong Special Administrative Region and is relieved of his or her duties by a motion passed by two-thirds of the members of the Legislative Council present;[454] and
(7) when he or she is censured for misbehaviour or breach of oath by a vote of two-thirds of the members of the Legislative Council present.

---

of Legislative Council [2016] HKEC 2487, (CFI), affirmed by the Court of Appeal: [2017] 1 HKLRD 460, (CA). It is a necessary condition that a person who wishes to be nominated as a Legislative Council election candidate must take the oath: *Wong Ti Hoi v Au Nok Hin* [2018] 2 HKLRD 789, (CFI). The invalidity of a nomination because of invalid oath of allegiance may be raised, not by way of a judicial review application, but by way of an election petition questioning the validity of his election to the Legislative Council. The applicant sought judicial review challenging the election of a Legislative Council member on the ground that the Returning Officer ought to have rejected the nomination on the ground that he did not seriously intend to be bound by the oath of allegiance. The Court of First Instance observed that to allow a register voter to bring a judicial review application might be to allow him to circumvent the statutory standing requirement for an election petition, namely the need for ten persons together to submit the election petition. In *Chan Ho Tin v Ying Ki Alan* [2018] 2 HKLRD 7, (CFI), a candidate whose nomination form had been rejected on the ground of adequate compliance with the oath of allegiance requirement unsuccessfully challenged that decision in an election petition. It must be noted that on 7 November 2016, while the question of the legality of incomplete or altered oath was being judicially considered, the Standing Committee of the National People's Congress issued an interpretation under Art. 158(1) on the meaning of Art. 104 of the Basic Law which provides that: 'When assuming office, the Chief Executive, principal officials, members of the Executive Council and of the Legislative Council, judges of the courts at all levels and other members of the judiciary in the Hong Kong Special Administrative Region must, in accordance with law, swear to uphold the Basic Law of the Hong Kong Special Administrative Region of the People's Republic of China and swear allegiance to the Hong Kong Special Administrative Region of the People's Republic of China.' *See* Instrument 27 annexed to the Basic Law of Hong Kong. This interpretation was held to be binding on courts of Hong Kong including in *Yau Wai Ching v Chief Executive of HKSAR* (2017) 20 HKCFAR 390, (CFA) and *Secretary for Justice v Leung Kwok Hung* [2019] HKEC 417, (CA), (leave to appeal to the Court of Final Appeal was refused [2019] HKEC 1830).

454. The Legislative Council resorted to this provision in 1998. The affected candidate brought an unsuccessful application for judicial review to halt the process. *See Chim Pui Chung v President of the Legislative Council* [1998] 2 HKLRD 552, (CFI).

279. If on the hearing of an election petition, the court determines that a person who was originally declared to have been elected as a Member of the Legislative Council at an election was not duly elected, that person ceases to be a member, and that person's office as a member becomes vacant.[455]

280. The Clerk to the Legislative Council must, by notice published in the Gazette, declare the existence of a vacancy in the membership of that Council within twenty-one days after becoming aware of such vacancy,[456] and the Electoral Affairs Commission must arrange for a by-election.[457] A by-election to fill a vacancy occurring in the membership of the Legislative Council is not to be held: (a) within four months preceding the end of that Council's current term of office, or (b) if the Chief Executive has published in the Gazette an order dissolving that Council in accordance with the Basic Law.[458]

VII. Qualifications of a Member of the Legislative Council

281. At least 80% of the members of the Legislative Council must be Chinese citizens who are permanent residents of Hong Kong.[459] To achieve this end, section 37(2) of the Legislative Council Ordinance provides that, except in the case of twelve Functional Constituencies named in section 37(3), every candidate at an election must be a Chinese citizen with permanent residence in Hong Kong. A person is eligible to be nominated as a candidate at an election for a geographical constituency or functional constituency, only if the person:

(1) has reached 21 years of age;
(2) is both registered and eligible to be registered as an elector for a geographical constituency;
(3) has ordinarily resided in Hong Kong for the three years immediately preceding the nomination; and
(4) is not disqualified from being an elector under section 39 of the Ordinance or any other law.[460]

455. Legislative Council Ordinance (Cap. 542), s. 72(1). *See*, e.g., *Chiang Lai Wan v Tang Siu Tong* [1998] HKEC 225, (CFI).
456. Legislative Council Ordinance (Cap. 542), s. 35.
457. *Ibid.*, s. 36.
458. *Ibid.*, s. 36(2).
459. Basic Law, Art. 67.
460. *See* Legislative Council Ordinance (Cap. 542), s. 37. The disqualified persons specified in s. 39 include judicial officers and prescribed public officers; a person who is a member of any legislative body outside Hong Kong, other than a member of a People's Congress or people's consultative body of the People's Republic of China; a person sentenced to imprisonment unless he has served his sentence or received a free pardon; a person who on the date of nomination is serving a sentence of imprisonment; and a person who has been sentenced to imprisonment for a term exceeding three months within the preceding five years, and a person who has been convicted of treason. Section 21 of the District Councils Ordinance (Cap. 547) and s. 23 of the Rural Representative

282. A candidate at an election for a functional constituency must additionally prove that either he is eligible to be registered as an elector for the constituency or that he has a substantial connection with the constituency. A guidance note specifies who are eligible to be registered as an elector of each of the functional constituencies.[461]

283. A person may not be nominated as a candidate for a constituency if that person is currently nominated as a candidate for another constituency.[462] Before the election of some members of the Legislative Council through the Election Committee was abolished in 2004, a person could not be nominated as a candidate for election by the Election Committee, if such person was currently nominated as a candidate for a geographical or functional constituency.[463] These provisions ensure that no person is able to secure election to more than one seat in the Legislative Council. The Legislative Council Ordinance also provides that no person may become or continue to be a member of the Hong Kong Legislative Council if he is a member of any national, regional, or municipal legislature, assembly, or council of any place outside Hong Kong. This prohibition does not apply to membership of a people's congress or people's consultative body of the People's Republic of China, whether established at the national or local level.[464] An important disqualification was added in 2012 which prohibits a person who resigns from his office as a member of the Legislative Council from contesting at an election held within six months of such resignation, unless such election is a general election. The intention was to prevent any members of Legislative Council resigning from his seat in order to force a by-election and seek re-election.[465]

284. Election petitions are heard by the Court of First Instance, with an appeal to the Court of Final Appeal. If on an election petition the Court of First Instance

Election Ordinance (Cap. 576) are all in similar terms to s. 39 of the Legislative Council Ordinance (Cap. 542) and set out various categories of persons who are disqualified from being nominated as a candidate at an election and from being elected as a member of a District Council, and a Rural Representative for a Rural Area.. In *Wong Ho Ming v Secretary for Justice* [2020] HKEC 1132, the Court of First Instance recognised the importance and legality of disqualifying certain persons from becoming members of the Legislative Council and District Councils and rural representatives.

461. Legislative Council Ordinance (Cap. 542), s. 37(2)(b). 'Guidance Notes: Application for Registration as an Elector in a Functional Constituency and as a Voter in an Election Committee Subsector'. https://www.reo.gov.hk/pdf/gn/gn-full_e.pdf.
462. Legislative Council Ordinance (Cap. 542), s. 41(1).
463. *Ibid.*, s. 41(2).
464. *Ibid.*, s. 39(1)(h).
465. *Ibid.*, s. 39(2A). This provision was held to be compatible with the right to stand for election guaranteed under Art. 26 of the Basic Law and Art. 21 of the Bill of Rights Ordinance: *Kwok Cheuk Kin v Secretary for Constitutional and Mainland Affairs* [2014] 2 HKLRD 283 (CFI), affirmed by the Court of Appeal [2015] 5 HKLRD 881, (CA), and on further appeal by the Court of Final Appeal (2017) 20 HKCFAR 353, (CFA). The restriction imposed by s. 39 (2A) of the Legislative Council Ordinance was held to be a reasonable one as being proportionate to the mischief it sought to prevent.

(or on appeal the Court of Final Appeal) determines that a Member of the Legislative Council was not duly elected as a Member, the determination does not invalidate acts purporting to have been done by him as a Member before the date on which the written judgment of the court (or the Court of Final Appeal as the case may be) is handed down.[466] An elector or the Secretary for Justice may bring proceedings in the court against any person who is acting or claims to be entitled to act as a Member, on the ground that the person is disqualified from acting as such.[467] If in such a proceeding it is proved that the defendant acted as a Member while disqualified from acting in that office, the court may:

(1) make a declaration to that effect;
(2) grant an injunction restraining the defendant from so doing; and
(3) order the defendant to pay the Government a sum not exceeding HKD 5,000 for each occasion on which the person so acted while disqualified.[468]

VIII. Disputes

285. An election petition may be lodged, in the case of an election for a geographical or functional constituency: (a) by ten or more electors entitled to vote at the election, or (b) by a person claiming to have been a candidate at the election.[469] Prior to the discontinuation of the return of some members of the Legislative Council by the Election Committee in 2004, an election petition could be lodged in the case of an election by the Election Committee: (a) by ten or more members of that Committee, or (b) by a person claiming to have been a candidate in the election.[470] Any person whose election is questioned and the Returning Officer in respect of the election may be made a respondent to the petition.[471] Two or more candidates at an election may be made respondents in the same election petition.[472]

286. An election to return a Member of the Legislative Council may be questioned on any ground specified in section 61 of the Legislative Council Ordinance or any other enactment. The grounds specified in section 61 of the Legislative Council Ordinance are: (a) that the person was ineligible to be, or was disqualified from being, a candidate at the election; or (b) that a corrupt practice was engaged in by or in respect of that person at or in connection with the election; or (c) that corrupt or illegal practices were generally prevalent at or in connection with the election; or (d) that a material irregularity occurred in relation to the election, or to the polling or counting of votes at the election.

466. Legislative Council Ordinance (Cap. 542), s. 71.
467. *Ibid.*, s. 73(1).
468. *Ibid.*, s. 73(3).
469. *Ibid.*, s. 62(1).
470. *Ibid.*, s. 62(2).
471. *Ibid.*, s. 63(1).
472. *Ibid.*, s. 63(2).

287. An election petition is heard by the Court of First Instance in open court[473] and, unless the Chief Justice otherwise directs, before one judge.[474] At the end of the trial, the court must determine whether the person declared elected was or was not duly elected and if not duly elected whether some other person was duly elected instead.[475] The determination must be given in writing.[476] If the court determines that the election of the respondent as a member is invalid, that person's office as a member becomes vacant from the date of the determination.[477] If the court determines that a person was duly elected as a member in place of a person that the court has determined not to have been duly elected, such person becomes a member from the date of the determination.[478] Where the court does not declare any person duly elected as a member in place of the member whose membership was declared invalid, the Electoral Commission must conduct a by-election.[479]

IX. Procedure

288. The Basic Law contains only a few provisions relating to the procedure in the Legislative Council and enables the Legislative Council to make its own rules of procedure.[480] The Legislative Council has the power to enact, amend or repeal laws in accordance with the provisions of the Basic Law and legal procedures. In the exercise of these powers, the Legislative Council is answerable to no one so long as those rules are compatible with the Basic Law.[481] As the Court of Appeal held in *Leung Kwok Hung v President of the Legislative Council (No. 1),* Article 73(1) did not confer on a member of Legislative Council a constitutional right to participate in its legislative process by speaking. The purpose of Article 73 of the Basic Law was to confer certain powers and functions on Legislative Council as a law-making body but not on its individual members. This conclusion was supported by Articles 75 and 72 which respectively indicated that Legislative Council was to have exclusive authority in determining its procedure, and that the President was to exercise his power to 'preside over meetings' under Article 72 so as to ensure the orderly, efficient and fair disposition of Legislative Council's business.[482] In *Leung Kwok case*, it was argued unsuccessfully that the President of the Legislative Council was

473. That is, the Court of First Instance. Legislative Council Ordinance (Cap. 542), s. 3 'Interpretation'.
474. Legislative Council Ordinance, s. 64(2).
475. *Ibid.*, s. 67(1) and (2).
476. *Ibid.*, s. 67(3).
477. *Ibid.*, s. 72(1).
478. *Ibid.*, s. 72(2).
479. *See* paras 280 and 283 above.
480. Basic Law, Art. 75.
481. *Leung Kwok Hung v President of Legislative Council* [2007] 1 HKLRD 387, (CFI), [10], where Hartmann J concluded that so far as jurisdiction is concerned, the courts of the Hong Kong Special Administrative Region do have jurisdiction under the Basic Law to determine, by way of declaratory relief, whether Rules of Procedure enacted by the Legislative Council are consistent with the Basic Law. Yet, it is a jurisdiction which, having regard to the sovereignty of the Legislative Council under the Basic Law, 'should only be exercised in a restrictive manner'.
482. *Leung Kwok Hung v President of the Legislative Council (No 1)* (2014) 17 HKCFAR 689, (CFA), [21]–[25]. The Court of Final Appeal observed that under the doctrine of separation of powers the legislature has the exclusive authority to manage its own internal affairs. The courts would not

wrong to restrict the right of members to speak in the Legislative Council who allegedly dragged on the legislative debate in order to filibuster a bill that was being debated in the Legislative Council. The Court of Final Appeal asserted the well-established common law principle that courts do not interfere with the inner working of the legislature, 'the principle of non-intervention', so long as the legislative proceedings did not contravene the Constitution. The Court observed that although the common law principles have their origin in the power, privileges and characteristics of Parliament, in particular the House of Commons, in the UK, and in the recognition by the courts of the exclusive authority of Parliament to determine its own internal procedures, it is preferable now to regard the relationship between a legislature and the courts as an outcome of the application of the doctrine of the separation of powers.[483]

289. The doctrine of 'non-intervention', that the courts do not inquire into proceedings of the legislature, is not an absolute rule. 'In a jurisdiction like Hong Kong where a written constitution (that is, the Basic Law), rather than the legislature, is supreme, where the rule of law reigns and where the courts are given under the constitution the independent power of adjudication, this principle of non-intervention has its own inherent limit. First and foremost, the supremacy of the Basic Law means that no one – the legislature included – is above the Basic Law. ... In other words, where a constitutional requirement under the Basic Law is in issue, even the legislature cannot act contrary to that requirement under the Basic Law. Secondly, given that the courts are given under the constitution the independent power of adjudication of the Special Administrative Region, the question of whether that constitutional requirement has been complied with or breached is a matter which it is both the power and responsibility of the courts to decide.'[484]

290. The Basic Law provides that the President of the Legislative Council, the equivalent of the Speaker of the British House of Commons, must be elected by and

---

intervene to determine whether there has been any irregularity in the internal processes of the legislature but would leave it to determine exclusively for itself matters of this kind. This principle of 'non-intervention' rested not only on principle and authority but also on public policy. The courts may determine the existence of a power, privilege or immunity of Legislative Council, but would not exercise jurisdiction to determine the occasion or the manner of exercise of any such powers, privileges or immunities. *See* [28]–[29] and [32]–[43].

483. *Leung Kwok Hung v President of the Legislative Council (No 1)* (2014) 17 HKCFAR 689, (CFA), [27].

484. *Chief Executive of HKSAR v President of the Legislative Council* [2017] 1 HKLRD 460, (CA), [23] and [25], Cheung CJHC. It was held that the courts have jurisdiction to inquire into whether a Legislative Council member has taken a valid oath of allegiance under Art. 104 of the Basic Law. *See also Leung Kwok Hung v President of Legislative Council* [2007] 1 HKLRD 387, (CFI) [10], quoted in footnote 482 above. The application of the non-intervention principle in Hong Kong was succinctly explained by Andrew Cheung J in *Cheng Kar Shun v Li Fung Ying* [2011] 2 HKLRD 555, (CFI), [220]; 'the courts of the Hong Kong Special Administrative Region do not, as a rule, interfere with the internal workings of the Legislature. Exceptionally, where questions of whether the Legislative Council, in going about its business, has acted in contravention of the provisions in the Basic Law arise, the courts do have jurisdiction to intervene. But the jurisdiction must be exercised with great restraint, having regard to the different constitutional roles assigned under the Basic Law to different arms of the Government.'

from among the members of the Legislative Council.[485] The President exercises the following powers and functions: (1) to preside over meetings; (2) to decide on the agenda, giving priority to government bills for inclusion in the agenda; (3) to decide on the time of meetings; (4) to call special sessions during the recess; (5) to call emergency sessions, during a time when the Legislative Council stands dissolved,[486] on the request of the Chief Executive; and (6) to exercise other powers and functions as prescribed in the rules of procedure of the Legislative Council.[487]

291. The Chief Executive must convene at least one ordinary session of the Legislative Council in each calendar year.[488] The consideration of any bill or other business of the Legislative Council is not to be affected by the end of a session and may be resumed at any subsequent meeting, but is to lapse at the end of a term of office or on a dissolution of the Legislative Council.[489] The quorum for the meeting of the Legislative Council is not less than one-half of all its members.[490] The passage of bills introduced by the Government requires at least a simple majority vote of the members of the Legislative Council present. The passage of motions, bills and amendments to government bills introduced by individual members of the Legislative Council requires a simple majority vote of each of the two groups of members present: (1) members returned by functional constituencies and (2) members returned by geographical constituencies through direct elections and by the Election Committee.[491]

292. The Legislative Council adopted its Rules of Procedure on 2 July 1998, which has been amended from time to time.[492] There are 103 rules grouped under the following headings: (A) Members and Officers of the Council, (B) Sessions, Meetings and Adjournments of the Council, (C) Arrangement of Business, (D) Petitions and Papers, (E) Questions to the Government, (F) Statements and Personal Explanations, (G) Motions, (H) Rules of Speaking, (I) Rules of Order, (J) Voting, (JA) Procedure for Particular Motions, (JB) Reports of House Committee on Subsidiary Legislation and other Instruments and related Matters, (K) Procedure on Bills, (L) Financial Procedure, (M) Committees, and (N) Miscellaneous Matters. Its Schedule contains the procedure for the election of the President of the Legislative Council. The Rules and Procedure of the Legislative Council are supplemented by the following documents that the Legislative Council has adopted: (1) House Rules, (2) Finance Committee Procedure, (3) Establishment Subcommittee Procedure, (4)

---

485. *Ibid.*, Art. 71. Under the British administration, the Governor was the presiding officer of the Legislative Council until 1993, when the Royal Instructions were amended to provide for the election of a President of the Legislative Council from among its members. *See* Cl. XXI of the Hong Kong Royal Instructions, in *Hong Kong: Text of Constitutional Documents*.
486. *See* Legislative Council Ordinance (Cap. 542), s. 11(1).
487. Basic Law, Art. 72.
488. Legislative Council Ordinance (Cap. 542), s. 9(1).
489. *Ibid.*, s. 9(4).
490. Basic Law, Art. 75.
491. Annex II of the Basic Law 'Method for the Formation of the Legislative Council of the Hong Kong Special Administrative Region and Its Voting Procedures', para. II.
492. The information that follows about the work of the Legislative Council is taken from the website of the Legislative Council: http://www.legco.govhk/general/english/about/index.html.

Public Works Subcommittee Procedure, and (5) Their Procedures and Practices and Related papers. There are several other documents adopted by the Legislative Council in relation to its procedure, such as procedures relating to the nomination of Select Committees.

293. One important aspect of the Legislative Council procedure relates to the power of the President of the Legislative Council or the Chairman of a Committee to rule on matters of procedure. Such rulings are useful precedents on the interpretation of the rules of procedure. The President's rulings in recent years have been very important in relation to the validity of bills or bill amendments proposed by members, in the light of the Basic Law prohibition that members cannot propose legislative measures relating to public expenditure or political structure or the operation of the Government.[493] In *Leung Kwok Hung v President of Legislative Council*, the Court of First Instance rejected a challenge to a ruling by the President of the Legislative Council that certain proposed amendments to the Interception of Communications and Surveillance Bill could not be introduced by a Member of the Legislative Council, because he had not obtained the prior approval of the Chief Executive.[494] The reason for disallowance was rule 57(6) of the Rules of Procedure of the Legislative Council. That rule provides that any committee stage amendment to a bill whose effect is to 'dispose of or charge any part of the revenue or other public moneys of Hong Kong' could only be introduced by: (a) the Chief Executive or (b) a designated public officer or (c) a Member, if the Chief Executive consents in writing to the proposal. It was held that rule 57(6) was not inconsistent with the Basic Law and therefore was valid.

294. An important aspect of the working of the Legislative Council is its committee system.[495] The House Committee, which consists of all the members of the Legislative Council other than the President, coordinates matters relating to the business of Council meetings, scrutinizes bills and subsidiary legislation. It may form a Bills Committee to scrutinize bills or appoint subcommittees to study subsidiary legislation in greater detail. It has set up a number of subcommittees. They include subcommittees on subsidiary legislation, the Parliamentary Liaison Subcommittee and the Subcommittee on proposed senior judicial appointments. There are three Standing Committees, namely, the Finance Committee (which scrutinizes public expenditure proposals), Public Accounts Committee (which considers the reports of the Director of Audit on the accounts) and the Committee on Members' Interests (which deals with declaration of interests by Members of the Legislative Council). The responsibility of the Committee on Rules and Procedure is to review the Rules of Procedure of the Council and the committee system and to propose necessary changes. The House Committee may set up a number of Bills Committees.

---

493. *See* Basic Law, Art. 74.
494. *Leung Kwok Hung v President of Legislative Council* [2007] 1 HKLRD 387, (CFI).
495. The delegation of its work to committees makes the exercise of the legislative power more effective: *Cheng Kar Shun v Hon Li Fung Ying* [2011] 2 HKLRD 555, (CFI).

The responsibility of a Bills Committee is to consider the general merits and principles as well as the detailed provisions of a bill referred to it. The House Committee may also set up committees called Panels (such as the Panel on the Administration of Justice and Legal Services, the Panel on Constitutional Affairs, the Panel on Commerce and Industry, the Panel on Economic Development, the Panel on Education, the Panel on Financial Affairs, the Panel on Environmental Affairs, the Panel on Health Services, the Panel on Housing, the Panel on Transport and the Panel on Welfare Services) to monitor and examine policy matters referred to it by a Panel member or the House Committee. The Council may appoint Select Committees (such as the Select Committee appointed in November 2014 to inquire into the background of and reasons for the delay of the construction of the Hong Kong section of the Guangzhou-Shenzhen-Hong Kong Express Rail Link) to consider in depth matters or bills that the Council may refer to them. Select Committees are a useful means of inquiring into matters of public interest so that preventive or remedial measures may be proposed or taken.

§2. Legal Status (Powers, Privileges and Immunities)

295. The Basic Law provides that members of the Legislative Council are immune from legal action in respect of their statements at meetings of the Council and that members of the Legislative Council should not be subject to arrest when attending or on their way to meetings of the Council.[496] Detailed provisions regarding powers and privileges of the Legislative Council are to be found in the Legislative Council (Powers and Privileges) Ordinance (Cap. 382). That Ordinance aims to 'declare and define powers, privileges and immunities of the Legislative Council and of the members and officers thereof and of the Chief Executive and public officers designated by him in relation to attendance at sittings of the Legislative Council and committees thereof; to secure freedom of speech in the Legislative Council; to make provision for regulating admittance to and conduct within the precincts of the Chamber of the Legislative Council; to provide for the giving of evidence in proceedings before the Legislative Council or committees thereof, and for offences in respect of such proceedings and related matters; and for purposes incidental to or connected therewith'.[497]

296. The Legislative Council (Powers and Privileges) Ordinance guarantees the freedom of speech and debate in the Legislative Council or proceedings before a committee. Such freedom of speech and debate is not liable to be questioned in any court or place outside the Council.[498] No civil or criminal proceedings may be taken against any member for words spoken before, or written in a report to, the Council

496. Basic Law, Arts 77 and 78.
497. Legislative Council (Powers and Privileges) Ordinance (Cap. 382), the Long Title.
498. Legislative Council (Powers and Privileges) Ordinance (Cap. 382), s. 3. For the nature and extent of the freedom of speech and debate, *see* A. Bradley & K. Ewing, *Constitutional and Administrative Law* (13th edn, London and New York: Pearson Education, 2003), 215–220.

or a committee, or by reason of any matter brought by him therein.[499] No member is liable to be arrested for any civil debt while going to, attending, or returning from a sitting of the Council or committee, or for any criminal offence while attending a sitting of the Council or a committee.[500] These powers and privileges conferred on Legislative Council members will be available to: (a) the Chief Executive when present at a sitting of the Council or a committee and (b) any public officer designated by the Chief Executive for the purpose of attending sittings of the Council or any committee, while so designated and attending such sitting.[501] The Ordinance provides that it is an offence to interfere with members and officers of the Legislative Council or witnesses called by the Council, by way of assault obstruction threats etc.[502]

297. Sittings of the Legislative Council are open to the public, subject to the Rules of Procedure or any resolution of the Council limiting or prohibiting the enjoyment of such right. The President of the Legislative Council is authorized to take such measures as are necessary to ensure proper behaviour and decorum of persons within the precincts of the Council[503] and may issue administrative instructions.[504] Any person who enters or attempts to enter the precincts of the Legislative Council in contravention of any Rule of Procedure or any relevant resolution of the Council commits an offence.[505] Similarly, a person who contravenes any administrative instruction issued by the President, or any direction given under it, commits an offence.[506]

298. Article 73(10) of the Basic Law gives the Legislative Council the power to summon persons to testify or give evidence. The Council or a Standing Committee may order any person to attend before it and to give evidence or produce any document.[507] It may take evidence on oath and compel attendance of witnesses.[508] Any person who refuses to attend a meeting or produce a document when required by the Council or a committee to do so commits an offence. Similarly, a person who refuses to be examined by the Council or committee or to answer any lawful and relevant questions put to him by the Council or committee commits an offence.[509] Any person who intentionally gives false answers or produces any false documents

499. Legislative Council (Powers and Privileges) Ordinance (Cap. 382), s. 4.
500. *Ibid.*, s. 5.
501. *Ibid.*
502. *See HKSAR v Leung Hiu Yeung* (2018) 21 HKCFAR 20, (CFA), where the court upheld the conviction for 'obstructing an officer of the Legislative Council in the execution of his duty' of a person who tried to enter the premises of the Legislative Council forcefully. For legality of administrative instructions for regulating admittance to precincts of the Legislative Council and conduct of persons, *see HKSAR v Fong Kwok Shan Christine* (2017) 20 HKCFAR 425, (CFA).
503. Legislative Council (Powers and Privileges) Ordinance (Cap. 382), s. 8.
504. *See* 'Administrative Instructions for Regulating Admittance and Conduct of Persons', subsidiary legislation A made under Legislative Council (Powers and Privileges) Ordinance (Cap. 382).
505. Legislative Council (Powers and Privileges) Ordinance (Cap. 382), s. 20.
506. *Ibid.*
507. Legislative Council (Powers and Privileges) Ordinance (Cap), s. 9(1). Such power may be exercised by any other committee that has been authorized by the Council to exercise such powers.
508. *Ibid.*, ss 11 and 12.
509. *Ibid.*, s. 17.

with intent to deceive the Council or committee commits an offence.[510] It was held in *Cheng Kar Shun v Hon Li Fung Ying*[511] that the provisions in the Legislative Council (Powers and Privileges) Ordinance (Cap. 382), which are summarized in this paragraph, are consistent with Article 73(10) of the Basic Law. These powers may therefore be exercised by a committee of the Legislative Council, as set up under Part III of the Legislative Council (Powers and Privileges) Ordinance (Cap. 382), although Article 73(10) of the Basic Law only refers to Legislative Council and there is no express reference to its committees.

299. The Council, the President or any officer of the Council is not subject to the jurisdiction of any court in respect of the lawful exercise of any power conferred on or vested in the Council, the President or such officer by or under the Legislative Council (Powers and Privileges) Ordinance or the Rules of Procedure.[512]

300. Within the precincts of the Legislative Council, every officer of the Council has, for the purpose of the Legislative Council (Powers and Privileges) Ordinance and the application of the criminal law, all the powers, and every officer has all the privileges of a police officer.[513]

301. The Legislative Council of Hong Kong has no powers to punish any person for a breach of its powers or privileges, unlike in Britain and many Commonwealth jurisdictions.[514] The power of punishment remains with the courts of law. No prosecution for an offence under the Legislative Council (Powers and Privileges) Ordinance may be instituted without the consent of the Secretary for Justice.[515]

§3. Competence

I. Legislative Power

302. The legislative competence of the Legislative Council of the Hong Kong Special Administrative Region is set out in the Basic Law, which intends to confer a 'high degree of autonomy' on Hong Kong.[516] The laws in force in Hong Kong are

510. *Ibid.*, s. 18.
511. *Cheng Kar Shun v Hon Li Fung Ying* [2011] 2 HKLRD 555, (CFI).
512. Legislative Council (Powers and Privileges) Ordinance (Cap. 382), s. 23.
513. *Ibid.*, s. 24. *HKSAR v Wong Yeung Tat* [2015] HKEC 2796, (CFI), concerns a successful criminal charge of unlawful assembly in the precincts of the Legislative Council. There, the security officers of the Legislative Council had asked the protestors to leave, unable to force their eviction. *See also HKSAR v Fong Kwok Shan Christine* (2017) 20 HKCFAR 425, (CFA), and *HKSAR v Cheung Kwai Choi* [2018] HKEC 2910, (CFI), where protesters were found guilty of unlawful assembly in the precincts of the Legislative Council.
514. For the position in Britain, *see* A.W. Bradley & K.D. Ewing, *Constitutional and Administrative Law*, (13th edn, London and New York: Pearson Education, 2003), 221–223.
515. Legislative Council (Powers and Privileges) Ordinance (Cap. 382), s. 26.
516. Basic Law, Art. 2.

the Basic Law, laws previously in force in Hong Kong[517] and laws enacted by the legislature of Hong Kong.[518] Legislation operative in Hong Kong are ordinances passed by the Hong Kong Legislative Council. National laws of the People's Republic of China, except those listed in Annex III of the Basic Law,[519] are not applicable in Hong Kong.[520] The NPCSC may, after consulting its Committee for the Basic Law of the Hong Kong Special Administrative Region, add to or delete from the list of laws in Annex III. Laws listed in Annex III must be confined to those relating to defence and foreign affairs as well as other matters outside the limits of the autonomy of Hong Kong.[521] Where the NPCSC decides that Hong Kong is in a state of emergency, the Central Government may issue an order applying the relevant national laws in Hong Kong.

303. The Legislative Council of Hong Kong has the power to enact, amend or repeal laws in accordance with the provisions of the Basic Law and legal procedures.[522] The Basic Law contains many provisions recognizing Hong Kong's authority to formulate policies and legislate on a variety of subjects. These provisions do recognize a range of rights and privileges of individuals as well as various communities and organizations, and to that extent impose limitations on Hong Kong's legislative and administrative competence. These limitations do not have the effect of transferring any jurisdiction in those subject areas to the Chinese Central Government. What they do is to require the Legislative Council and the government to comply with the guarantees set out in the Basic Law. In the following paragraphs, we examine some Basic Law provisions that are illustrative of the legislative competence of the Legislative Council as well as the possible limitations on the Legislative Council's power in those subject areas. Thereafter, we examine the implications of the fact that Hong Kong's Legislative Council has to operate within an 'Executive-led system of government' where the Legislative Council does not have plenary legislative competence because of certain procedural limitations.[523]

304. The Basic Law demarcates the legislative competence of Hong Kong's Legislative Council by way of expressly enumerating the legislative powers of the Chinese Central Government. Matters that are not expressly reserved to the Central Government are understood to lie within the 'high degree of autonomy' of the Hong

---

517. Meaning the Common Law, rules of equity, ordinances, subordinate legislation and customary law in force in Hong Kong on 1 July 1997.
518. Basic Law, Art. 18.
519. They relate to, e.g., the Capital, National Anthem, National Flag and National Day of the People's Republic of China; territorial sea of People's Republic of China; Nationality Law of the People's Republic of China; and regulations of the People's Republic of China concerning diplomatic privileges and immunities.
520. Basic Law, Art. 18.
521. *Ibid.*
522. *Ibid.*, Art. 73(1).
523. For a thorough and scholarly treatment of these issues, *see* Yash Ghai, *Hong Kong's New Constitutional Order: The Resumption of Chinese Sovereignty and the Basic Law,* (2nd edn, Hong Kong: Hong Kong University Press, 1998).

Kong Special Administrative Region. The only two areas in respect of which the Central Government has retained jurisdiction are defence and foreign affairs.

II. Foreign Affairs and Defence

305. Even in respect of foreign affairs and defence, what one finds is not an exclusive vesting of power in the Central Government, but a delicate balance between Hong Kong's high degree of autonomy and the sovereignty of the People's Republic of China. The Chinese Central Government is responsible for foreign affairs relating to the Hong Kong Special Administrative Region. However, the Central Government authorizes the Hong Kong Special Administrative Region to conduct relevant external affairs on its own in accordance with the Basic Law.[524] Note the difference in terminology: The Central Government is responsible for 'foreign affairs', while the Hong Kong Government is authorized to exercise 'relevant external affairs'. Chapter VII of the Basic Law deals with 'External Affairs' and provides, for instance, that the Hong Kong Government may participate, as members of the Chinese Government's delegation, in negotiations at the diplomatic level directly affecting the Region conducted by the Central Government,[525] that it may participate in conferences not limited to States,[526] that it may establish economic and trade missions in foreign countries,[527] and that it may maintain and develop relations and implement agreements with foreign states and international organizations.[528]

306. The Chinese Central Government is responsible for the defence of Hong Kong, while the Hong Kong Government is responsible for the maintenance of public order in Hong Kong. The military forces stationed by the Central Government in Hong Kong for defence must not interfere in Hong Kong's local affairs, but the Hong Kong Government may ask the Central Government for assistance from the garrison in the maintenance of public order and in disaster relief. Moreover, the members of the garrison must, in addition to abiding by national laws, abide by the laws of Hong Kong.[529]

III. Public Finance

307. It is a basic principle of constitutional law in the Anglo-American tradition that the government may not collect or spend public revenue without the approval of the legislature. The Basic Law recognizes that principle when it enacts that the Government must obtain approval from the Legislative Council for taxation and

524. Basic Law, Art. 13.
525. *Ibid.*, Art. 150.
526. *Ibid.*, Art. 152.
527. *Ibid.*, Art. 156.
528. *Ibid.*, Art. 151.
529. *Ibid.*, Art. 14.

public expenditure,[530] and that the Legislative Council has the power to examine and approve budgets introduced by the government and to approve taxation and public expenditure.[531] The Legislative Council's paramount authority over public finance is also clear from Article 51 of the Basic Law, which provides that if the Legislative Council refuses to pass the budget introduced by the government, the Chief Executive may apply to the Legislative Council for provisional appropriations. The only occasion when the Chief Executive may approve public expenditure without the Legislative Councils approval arises when the Legislative Council has been dissolved. At such a time the Chief Executive may, prior to the election of the new Legislative Council, approve provisional short-term appropriations. There is, however, a limit on such appropriations: They must be according to the level of the previous fiscal year.

308. Hong Kong has its own independent finances and is not required to hand over any of its finances to the Chinese Central Government.[532] The Legislative Council's right to levy taxes is exclusive, the Central Government having no power to levy any tax in Hong Kong.[533] Hong Kong will have its independent taxation system and may enact laws on its own concerning types of taxes, tax rates, tax deductions, allowances and exemptions, and other matters of taxation.[534] These provisions are clearly enabling provisions, strengthening the legislative power of the Hong Kong Legislative Council. The only limitation appears to be the reference in Article 108 that in enacting tax legislation, the Hong Kong Legislative Council must take 'the low tax policy previously pursued in Hong Kong as reference'. It is a moot question whether the Hong Kong Legislative Council will act in contravention of this provision if it were to increase tax out of line with the previous tax regime.

IV. Hong Kong's Financial System

309. Article 110 provides that the monetary and financial system of the Hong Kong Special Administrative Region shall be prescribed by law (law in this context means Hong Kong law). The power given to Hong Kong in this regard is an exclusive one: 'The Government of the Hong Kong Special Administrative Region shall, on its own, formulate monetary and financial policies, safeguard the free operation

530. *Ibid.*, Art. 64. This reflects Annex I 'Elaboration by the Government of the People's Republic of China of the Basic Policies Regarding Hong Kong', s. V 'Finance', of the Sino-British Joint Declaration: 'The systems by which taxation and public expenditure must be approved by the legislature, and by which there is accountability to the legislature for all public expenditure, and the system for auditing public accounts shall be maintained.'
531. *Ibid.*, Art. 73(2) and (3). *See PCCW-HKT Telephone Ltd v The Secretary for Commerce and Economic Development* [2016] HKEC 1089, (CA), where the Court of Appeal upheld the legality of the power of an administrative authority to prescribe fees by way of subsidiary legislation, which are subject to legislative scrutiny. In *Hui Sin Hang v Chief Executive in Council* [2016] HKEC 608, (CFI), it was argued unsuccessfully that the Airport Authority could not impose certain fees, the court holding that there was ample legislative approval for the scheme.
532. *Ibid.*, Art. 106.
533. *Ibid.*, Art. 106.
534. *Ibid.*, Art. 108.

of business and financial markets, and regulate and supervise them in accordance with the law.'[535] Although the primary importance of this provision lies in the guarantee that the Chinese Central Government will not have any legal power to regulate the monetary and financial system of Hong Kong, it is also important as an illustration of the scope of Hong Kong's legislative competence.

310. Article 107 provides that the Hong Kong Special Administrative Region must follow the principle of keeping expenditure within the limits of revenues in drawing up its budget and must strive to achieve fiscal balance, avoid deficits and keep budget commensurate with the growth rate of its GDP. Although not couched in terms of a prohibition, the principles set out in that article must impose some limitation on Hong Kong's legislative competence.[536] Article 111 is more compulsive: 'The Hong Kong dollar, as the legal tender in the Hong Kong Special Administrative Region, shall continue to circulate. The issue of Hong Kong currency must be backed by a 100 per cent reserve fund.' Regarding matters pertaining to the economy, Article 119 seems to impose an obligation on Hong Kong to formulate policies to promote and coordinate the development of various trades paying due regard to the protection of the environment. Article 112 clearly imposes a restriction.

311. No foreign exchange control policies shall be applied in the Hong Kong Special Administrative Region. The Hong Kong dollar shall be freely convertible. Markets for foreign exchange, gold, securities, futures and the like shall continue. The Government of the Hong Kong Special Administrative Region shall safeguard the free flow of capital within, into and out of the Region.

V. Aviation and Shipping

312. Article 128 of the Basic Law states that the Hong Kong Special Administrative Region 'shall provide conditions and take measures for the maintenance of the status of Hong Kong as a centre of international and regional aviation'. If this provision is taken as imposing an obligation on the Hong Kong Government, it will operate as a limitation on Hong Kong's legislature insofar as it cannot legislate inconsistently with such obligation. Article 129 provides that Hong Kong must continue the previous system of civil aviation management in Hong Kong. Hong Kong may keep its own aircraft register in accordance with provisions laid down by the Chinese Central Government concerning nationality marks and registration marks of aircraft. This provision, while enabling Hong Kong to continue its civil aviation management system, requires it to operate within parameters set by the National Government.

535. *Ibid.*, Art. 110.

536. In *Lau Kwok Fai v Secretary for Justice* [2003] HKEC 711, (CFI), [110], Hartmann J said that Art. 107 imposes a 'broad constitutional obligation ... The language used is, of course, ample. It allows for the necessary use of financial discretion. But that said, Art. 107 directs Hong Kong to a particular course. It employs forceful language: The Government shall "strive" to achieve a fiscal balance.'

313. Article 124 of the Basic Law provides that Hong Kong shall maintain Hong Kong's previous systems of shipping management and shipping regulation, including the system for regulating conditions of seamen. Hong Kong may, on its own, define its specific functions and Article 125 provides that the Central Government authorizes Hong Kong to maintain a shipping register and issue related certificates under Hong Kong legislation, using the name 'Hong Kong', China.

VI. Hong Kong's Social, Economic and Political System

314. The Basic Law, being founded on the concept of 'One Country, Two Systems', strives to ensure that the economic, social, and political system of Hong Kong will remain unchanged. Article 5 of the Basic Law sets out the general principle that the Chinese socialist system and policies will not be practised in Hong Kong and that the previous capitalist system and way of life will remain unchanged for fifty years from 1997. Several provisions of the Basic Law are intended to give expression to that policy in respect of particular matters. These provisions, which were intended as a guarantee of Hong Kong's stability, also may be considered as indirect limitations on Hong Kong's competence. Here we examine those provisions.

VII. Education

315. The Basic Law makes provision to ensure that Hong Kong's previous system of education will continue unchanged under Chinese sovereignty. Article 136 provides that on the basis of the previous educational system, the Hong Kong Special Administrative Region's government has the power to formulate educational policies on its own. Articles 136 and 137 go on to provide certain guarantees to educational institutions. For instance, Article 137 provides that 'educational institutions of all kinds may retain their autonomy and enjoy academic freedom' and that 'schools run by religious organizations may continue to provide religious education, including courses on religion'. These guarantees, in turn, would operate as limitations on the legislative competence of the Hong Kong Legislative Council. The Basic Law safeguards the continuation of the 'previous educational system' in the sense that it cannot be completely overhauled. The government, however, has the power and a duty to formulate policies on its own for the 'development and improvement of education'.[537]

316. In *Catholic Diocese of Hong Kong v Secretary for Justice*, the Court of Final Appeal reaffirmed the correctness of the decision of the Court of First Instance. The Court recapitulated the appellant's argument as follows: 'Article

537. *See Catholic Diocese of Hong Kong v Secretary for Justice* [2007] 4 HKLRD 483, (CFI), especially [94]–[96]. There the Court of First Instance had no reservation that the Hong Kong Government had the power to introduce amendments to a pre-1997 legislation resulting in some restrictions on the control that the Catholic Church had exercised on the schools it managed.

136(1) places a constitutional limit on the kinds of educational policy that the government is allowed to formulate. Such policies must rest "on the basis of the previous educational system", meaning the system in place just before 1st July 1997. Since (so the appellant argues) the policy leading to the enactment of the 2004 amendments was "a brand new policy", it was not one "based on the previous educational system". The government therefore acted beyond those constitutional limits in promoting the 2004 amendments so that they must be struck down as unconstitutional.'[538] At paragraph 61, the Court of Final Appeal observed as follows: 'In *Secretary for Justice v Lau Kwok Fai* (2005) 8 HKCFAR 304, this Court had occasion to consider the meaning of Article 103 of the Basic Law which provides for the "previous system of recruitment, employment, assessment, discipline, training and management for the public service" to be maintained. It was held that the Article was designed to preserve the continuity of the system as a whole and not to prevent changes to elements of the system which could be expected to occur under any system governing public service. As Sir Anthony Mason NPJ put it [at para 66], a constitutional provision in such terms would only inhibit a development which was "such a material change that it resulted in the abandonment of the previous system".'

317. The second paragraph of Article 137 seems to impose another limitation, when it provides that 'Students shall enjoy freedom of choice of educational institutions and freedom to pursue their education outside the Hong Kong Administrative Region.'

VIII. Miscellaneous Matters

318. The Basic Law recognizes the legislative competence of the Legislative Council in respect of several other areas of law. Article 138 provides that community organizations and individuals may provide various medical and health services in accordance with the law.[539] Article 143 provides that non-governmental sports organizations may continue to exist and develop in accordance with the law. These provisions, while they have been intended as guarantees to the organizations concerned, are also illustrative of the wide scope of the Legislative Council's legislative competence. Article 145 of the Basic Law provides that on the basis of the previous welfare system, the Government of Hong Kong Special Administrative Region shall, on its own, formulate policies on the development and improvement of this system in the light of economic conditions and social needs.

---

538. *Catholic Diocese of Hong Kong v Secretary for Justice* (2011) 14 HKCFAR 754, (CFA), [45].

539. *See Re Financial Services and Systems Ltd* [2007] HKEC 1230, (CFI), where the Court of First Instance upheld the constitutionality of a regulatory legislation relating to Chinese medical practitioners, where Barnabas Fung J said: 'A rational and fair minded person would recognize a genuine need for allowing only appropriately qualified CMPs to be given the rights and responsibilities to perform the medical functions and issue the medical certificates under the relevant Ordinances. It is within the Government's power under Art. 138 of the Basic Law to formulate policies for the development of Chinese medicine. Hence, the decision of the legislature was reasonable, rational and proportional to attain a legitimate social objective.'

319. In *Kong Yunming v Director of Social Welfare* the Court of First Instance held that the Hong Kong Government was entitled to make payment of social welfare benefits dependent on a seven-year residence requirement, without violating Article 145, Article 25 (equality before the law) or Article 36 (right to social welfare).[540] The Court of Final Appeal, while conceding that the Hong Kong Government was competent to replace the one-year resident requirement that was applicable at the time of the hand over in 1997, was of the opinion that the seven-year period was not a justifiable restriction, and thus a disproportionate, restriction placed on the right to receive welfare benefits. The seven-year rule was, accordingly, held to be invalid.[541] In *Yao Man Fai George v Director of Social Welfare*, the applicant was a 66-year man who had worked continuously in Hong Kong from 1962. In 2006, the employer sent him to China to work there. In 2008, his employment was terminated. He returned to Hong Kong and immediately but unsuccessfully applied for social welfare benefits. The Court of First Instance held that the requirement that a permanent resident of Hong Kong should have been resident in Hong Kong for one year immediately before applying for social security assistance was discriminatory and unconstitutional for two reasons: (1) there was no justification for the different treatment of permanent residents on the basis of residence immediately before making an application, because imposing such a rigid residence requirement was not proportionate to the achieving of the objective of proper management of the social security system, there was no evidence to show that the residence requirement served any other possible legitimate aim, and the relevant guidelines did not permit consideration of personal circumstances of the applicant in determining if he could waive the residence requirement; (2) The continuous residence requirement that an applicant must not have been away for more than fifty-six days in the immediately preceding one year imposed an unreasonable restriction on the right to travel.[542]

IX. Fundamental Rights and Freedoms

320. Perhaps the most significant limitation on the autonomous legislative power of the Hong Kong Legislative Council is the recognition of fundamental rights and freedoms. Chapter I of the Basic Law, which sets out the General Principles, contains the two fundamental provisions: 'The Hong Kong Special Administrative Region shall safeguard the rights and freedoms of the residents of the Hong Kong Special Administrative Region and of other persons in the Region in accordance with law.'[543] 'The Hong Kong Special Administrative Region shall protect

540. *Kong Yunming v Director of Social Welfare* [2009] HKCU 912, (CFI). Appeal was dismissed by the Court of Appeal in [2012] HKEC 229, (CA). Reversed by the Court of Final Appeal in *Kong Yunming v Director of Social Welfare* (2013) 16 HKCFAR 950, (CFA).

541. *Kong Yunming v Director of Social Welfare* (2013) 16 HKCFAR 950, (CFA). *See also MS v Director of Social Welfare* [2016] HKEC 344, (CFI), which following the Court of Final Appeal decision in *Kong Yunming* held that non-residents (in this case) were not entitled to social welfare benefits.

542. *Yao Man Fai George v Director of Social Welfare* [2011] 1 HKLRD A2, (CFI).

543. Basic Law, Art. 4.

the right of private ownership of property in accordance with law.'[544] Article 11 provides the crucial procedural framework for the protection of fundamental rights: 'In accordance with Article 31 of the Constitution of the People's Republic of China, the systems and policies practised in the Hong Kong Special Administrative Region, including the social and economic systems, the system for safeguarding the fundamental rights and freedoms of its residents, the executive, legislative and judicial systems, and the relevant policies, shall be based on the provisions of [the Basic] Law.' Chapter III of the Basic Law is entitled 'Fundamental Rights and Duties of Residents' and sets out not only civil and political rights, but also economic, social, and cultural rights. The protections that Chapter III provide are supplemented by certain other provisions such as Article 141, which provides that the Government of the Hong Kong Special Administrative Region shall not restrict the freedom of religion, interfere in internal affairs of religious organizations or restrict religious activities that do not contravene laws of Hong Kong.

321. Article 39 states that the provisions of the ICCPR, the ICESCR, and international labour conventions as applied to Hong Kong will remain in force and 'shall be implemented through the laws of the Hong Kong Special Administrative Region'. It goes on to say that rights and freedoms enjoyed by Hong Kong residents cannot be restricted unless as prescribed by law. No such restriction may contravene the duty imposed on Hong Kong to implement the international conventions referred to above. Notwithstanding that it is contained in an ordinary statute (the Bill of Rights Ordinance) passed before Hong Kong's handover to China in 1997, the Hong Kong Bill of Rights continues to be referred to in constitutional litigation for the reason that the content of the Bill of Rights is very similar to the ICCPR, which is entrenched by Article 39 of the Basic Law. The scope and impact of fundamental rights protection on legislative competence is further discussed in Part IV, Chapter 2 'Fundamental Rights and Liberties'.

322. Article 41 of the Basic Law provides that the lawful traditional rights and interests of the indigenous inhabitants of the 'New Territories'[545] must be protected by the Hong Kong Special Administrative Region. The question arises whether the indigenous inhabitants' rights must take precedence where their rights are in conflict with Hong Kong's duty to protect and promote fundamental human rights such as equality and the right to participate in elections. Hong Kong courts have leaned in favour of upholding fundamental rights in several cases dealing with the legality of Chinese customary laws that discriminate against women or customary practices that do not allow anyone other than indigenous Chinese people to be elected as village representatives.[546]

544. *Ibid.*, Art. 6.
545. The term 'New Territories' refers to that part of Hong Kong that was leased by the Chinese Government to the British Government for ninety-nine years in 1898.
546. *See* Anton Cooray, 'International and Domestic Sources of Human Rights in Harmony? The Hong Kong Experience', (1999) 4 *Yearbook Law and Legal Practice in East Asia* 71, at 78, n. 24.

X. Constituent Power

323. It is important to bear in mind that the Hong Kong Legislative Council does not have constituent power. The power to amend the Basic Law belongs to the National People's Congress. The following have the power to propose a bill for the amendment of the Basic Law: (1) the Standing Committee of the National People's Congress; (2) the State Council of China; and (3) the Hong Kong Special Administrative Region. An amendment bill from Hong Kong may be submitted to the NPC by the delegation of the Region to the National People's Congress. Such proposed amendment must be supported by two-thirds of the deputies of the Region as well as two-thirds of all members of the Hong Kong Legislative Council.[547] Such proposed amendment will also have to be supported by the Chief Executive. Thus, it is not only that the Hong Kong Legislative Council has no power to amend the Basic Law, but also that it does not have the legal power to initiate an amendment acting on its own: It is the delegation of the Region to the NPC that can submit an amendment Bill, which has to be supported by: (1) a two-thirds majority in the Legislative Council; (2) two-thirds of the deputies of the Region to the National People's Congress; and (3) the Chief Executive.

XI. Procedural Limitations on Legislative Competence

324. We have so far examined what appear to be substantive limitations on Hong Kong's legislative competence. Now we turn to procedural limitations imposed on Hong Kong's Legislative Council. We have already seen that any important legislation has to be introduced by the government and that no bill passed by the Legislative Council will become law unless the Chief Executive approves it. We noted that while legislation introduced by the government may be passed by a simple majority of members of the Legislative Council present and voting, any bill introduced by a member of the Legislative Council will have to be passed in a different way. Such a bill must be passed by a majority of the two groups of members present: (1) functional constituency members and (2) members elected from geographical constituencies. In the Legislative Councils that were elected in 1998 and 2000, there were some members who were returned by an Election Committee. During this period (1998–2004), members who were returned by the Election Committee were grouped with the functional constituency members for the purpose of voting procedure. There are no members elected by an Election Committee in the Legislative Council since 2004. We also saw that the Chief Executive may dissolve the Legislative Council if he is unable to reach consensus with the Legislative Council on

547. Basic Law, Art. 159.

any legislation.[548] Thus, Hong Kong's Legislative Council does not enjoy legislative sovereignty in the sense that the term is understood in the 'Westminster Model' system, where the nominal Head of State has little control over Parliament's legislative powers.

§4. WORKING

325. The position of the Legislative Council in the government structure is different from the position that Parliament occupies in the British system of government. While in Britain the executive branch is responsible and answerable to Parliament through the cabinet of ministers who are members of Parliament, what we have in Hong Kong is a system of 'Executive-led Government'. The principal officers of the government other than some non-civil service Ministers are civil servants and none of them owe their tenure to the Legislative Council. As more fully described in the chapters on the Head of State and the Executive, policy formulation is the responsibility of the government. While policy formulation may be within the remit of the administration, the executive must seek Legislative Council's approval for giving legislative effect to government policies and other initiatives.

326. One of the powers and functions of the Legislative Council listed in Article 73 of the Basic Law is to receive and debate the policy addresses of the Chief Executive. It is possible for the Legislative Council not only to criticize government policies at such debates but also to record its disapproval of any government policy. Because the government would need financial provision and enabling legislation to implement its policies, the Legislative Council is in a position to veto implementation of government policies. As we have seen above: (a) laws may only be passed by the Legislative Council, and the Chief Executive possesses no power to legislate by proclamation or decree as in some other countries; and (b) without the Legislative Council's approval, the executive cannot raise or spend public revenue.

327. One of the important functions of the Legislative Council is to receive and handle complaints from Hong Kong residents.[549] The Legislative Council operates a 'Legislative Council Redress System' to receive and handle complaints from members of the public who are aggrieved by government actions or policies. It also deals with public representations on government policies and legislation as well as

---

548. 'If the Chief Executive of the Hong Kong Special Administrative Region refuses to sign a bill passed the second time by the Legislative Council, or the Legislative Council refuses to pass a budget or any other important bill introduced by the government, and if consensus still cannot be reached after consultations, the Chief Executive may dissolve the Legislative Council. The Chief Executive must consult the Executive Council before dissolving the Legislative Council. The Chief Executive may dissolve the Legislative Council only once in each term of his or her office.' (Art. 50 of the Basic Law)
549. Basic Law, Art. 73(8).

other matters of public concern. The Legislative Council may raise these issues in the council and generally monitor and scrutinize the working of the government.[550]

328. Matters regarding the conduct of business of the Legislative Council are governed by relevant provisions of the Basic Law, particularly Articles 71, 72, 74 and 75, as well as by the Rules of Procedure of the Legislative Council. The Legislative Council made these Rules of Procedure on 2 July 1998 in pursuance of Article 75 of the Basic Law, which states as follows: 'The rules of procedure of the Legislative Council shall be made by the Council on its own, provided that they do not contravene this law.' Part A of the Rules deals with members and officers of the Council and recognizes the right of the Chief Executive to attend the meetings of the Council and also provides for public officers to attend meetings of the Council or its committees. Part B deals with sessions, meetings, and adjournments of the Council. Among the sixteen parts of the Rules are those dealing with rules of speaking (Part H), voting (Part J) procedure on bills (Part K) and committees (Part M). The procedure of the Legislative Council has been discussed in this chapter under §1, IX Procedure.

550. On the redress system, *see* http://www.legco.govhk/general/english/sec/corg_ser/redress.htm.

Chapter 4. The Executive

§1. Introduction

329. The Executive branch of the Hong Kong Government consists of the Chief Executive, who is at the apex of the government structure; the Executive Council, which mainly serves as a consultant and advisor to the Chief Executive; and the civil service that helps formulate and implement government policy and carry out law into effect. Section 2 of Chapter IV of the Basic Law, containing Articles 59–65, is entitled 'The Executive Authorities'. Article 59 states that the Government of Hong Kong shall be the executive authority of the Region. Article 60 states that the Chief Executive is the Head of Hong Kong. Article 61 refers to principal officials of the government. Article 62 sets out the powers of the Hong Kong Government and Article 64 sets out the primacy of the Legislative Council in relation to the government. These provisions, read together with the Basic Law provisions relating to the Chief Executive and the Executive Council, provide the basic structure of the Executive.

§2. The Chief Executive

330. The Chief Executive is the Head of the Hong Kong SAR and represents the Region.[551] He is responsible for the implementation of the Basic Law and the laws that apply in Hong Kong. He decides on government policies and directs legislation to be moved in the Legislative Council for debate and passage. A law passed by the Legislative Council will not become law unless the Chief Executive signifies his assent to it. The Chief Executive must approve the introduction of motions regarding revenue and expenditure to the Legislative Council. He has been given the power to nominate principal government officials for appointment by the Chinese Central Government and he has the power to appoint and remove judges according to law.[552] The Chief Executive provides an important link between the Chinese Central Government and Hong Kong and is accountable to the Central Government and to the Hong Kong Special Administrative Region. The Chief Executive is required to implement any directive issued by the Central Government in respect of matters specified in the Basic Law.[553]

331. Chinese military forces stationed in Hong Kong will intervene in disaster relief and maintenance of public order, only at the request of the Hong Kong Government, a request which is presumably given by the Chief Executive.[554] When it is

551. Basic Law, Art. 43.
552. *Ibid.*, Art. 48. For further discussion of the powers and functions of the Chief Executive, *see* Part II, Ch. 2 'The Head of State'.
553. *Ibid.*, Art. 48.
554. *Ibid.*, Art. 14.

appropriate for the Chief Executive to issue a certificate regarding acts of state at the request of a court of law, he must obtain 'a certifying document', from the Central Government.[555]

§3. The Executive Council

332. The Executive Council is the rough equivalent to the Cabinet of Ministers in a 'Westminster Model' system, but there are significant differences between them. Unlike a Cabinet of Ministers in a 'Westminster Model' system, drawn from and answerable to the Legislature, the members of the Executive Council are all appointees of the Chief Executive. Unlike before 1997, there is no constitutional requirement to appoint official members to the Council.[556] However, the practice has been to appoint the three principal secretaries (administration, finance and justice) and other secretaries to the Executive Council, who are described as Official Members, currently numbering sixteen. Currently, there are sixteen others, who are described as Non-official members, of which six are Legislative Council Members while one other member is a former Legislative Council member.[557] The Basic Law recognizes the possibility of having Legislative Council Members in the Executive Council by permitting the Chief Executive to make appointments to the Executive Council 'from among the principal officials of the executive authorities, members of the Legislative Council, and public figures'.[558]

333. The Executive Council is weaker than a Cabinet of Ministers because the Chief Executive, unlike a Prime Minister, is not bound by advice given by his Executive Council. The Chief Executive is required (except for the appointment, removal and disciplining of officials and the adoption of measures in emergencies),[559] to consult the Executive Council before making important policy decisions, introducing bills to the Legislative Council, making subordinate legislation or dissolving the Legislative Council. He is not bound to accept the majority opinion of the Council,[560] but if he disagrees, he must put down specific reasons on

555. *Ibid.*, Art. 19.

556. *See* Hong Kong Royal Instructions 1917–1994, Cl. II. The ex officio members in the last years of British rule were the Chief Secretary, the Attorney General and the Financial Secretary.

557. *See* http://www.ceo.govhk/exco/eng/membership.html. The bio-data of the members can be accessed through this link.

558. Basic Law, Art. 55.

559. *See The Association of Expatriate Civil Servants of Hong Kong v The Chief Executive of Hong Kong Special Administrative Region* [1998] 1 HKLRD 615, (CFI) where Keith J said: 'The Chief Executive could reasonably regard the establishment of procedures for the appointment and removal of holders of public office as an important policy decision, requiring him to consult the Executive Council' (at p. 623).

560. *See Sung Man Cho v The Superintendent of Prisons* (1931) HKLR 62, at 66 (FC): 'The act of the Governor in Council is the act of the Governor and not the act of the Executive Council. It is he who makes the order, after taking the advice of the Council, but not necessarily in accordance with that advice.' This observation continues to be accurate under the Basic Law too.

record.[561] The established convention during the British period was that the Governor would generally not go against the majority view of the Executive Council, and there is no reason to assume that the Chief Executive would depart from such practice.[562] In any event, since the Chief Executive is free to remove any Council member,[563] it is possible for him to ensure that the Council members do not hold views fundamentally opposed to his.

334. The Cabinet of Ministers in a 'Westminster Model' system is at the apex of the government, and the Prime Minister is only 'the first among equals'. In Hong Kong, the Executive Council does not enjoy such a position of power and influence and is only 'an organ for assisting the Chief Executive in policy-making'.[564] It is the Chief Executive who is the head of the Hong Kong SAR and represents the Region.[565]

335. It has been the practice for the Executive Council to have minimal control over financial matters. Financial decisions are generally within the jurisdiction of the Secretary for Finance, to be taken in consultation with the Chief Executive, subject to the Legislative Council's approval. The annual budget is disclosed to the Executive Council only at a very late stage, although the Executive Council might then propose changes. The Executive Council would assume an important role only in respect of major policy matters with long-term implications.[566] There is no reason to believe that there will be any drastic departure from these practices, which were developed under the British rule.

§4. Executive Authorities

336. Hong Kong's Government shall be Hong Kong's executive authorities.[567] There must be established in the government a department of administration, a department of finance, a department of justice and various bureaux, divisions and commissions.[568] The organizational arrangement of the executive authorities is as follows. There are three secretaries, namely the Chief Secretary for the Administration (who is the head of the civil service), the Financial Secretary and the Secretary for Justice. There are policy bureaux under the Financial Secretary and the Chief

---

561. Basic Law, Art. 56.
562. Yash Ghai says, however, that 'there would be little justification for the convention that the Chief Executive should accept the advice of the [Executive] Council, since unlike the Governor, the Chief Executive is accountable to China and the Legislative Council and may have to negotiate difficult and complex issues with them'. Yash Ghai, *Hong Kong's New Constitutional Order: The Resumption of Chinese Sovereignty and the Basic Law*, (2nd edn, Hong Kong: Hong Kong University Press, 1998), at 242.
563. *Ibid.*, Art. 55.
564. *Ibid.*, Art. 54.
565. *Ibid.*, Arts 43 and 60.
566. *See* Norman Miners, *The Government and Politics of Hong Kong* (updated 4th edn, Hong Kong: OUP, 1989), 84.
567. Basic Law, Art. 59.
568. *Ibid.*, Art. 60.

Secretary. Various government departments are under these two secretaries. The only department under the Secretary for Justice is the Department of Justice.[569]

337. The powers and functions of the Hong Kong Government are:

(1) to formulate and implement policies;
(2) to conduct administrative affairs;
(3) to conduct external affairs as authorized by the Chinese Central Government;
(4) to draw up and introduce budgets and final accounts;
(5) to draft and introduce bills, motions and subordinate legislation; and
(6) to designate officials to sit on the meetings of the Legislative Council and to speak on behalf of the government.[570]

§5. COMPETENCE

338. The executive authorities of Hong Kong wield extensive powers, because Hong Kong's political system is executive-dominated rather than legislative-centred as in a Parliamentary democracy. The executive authorities exercise legislative powers not only in the sense that they may exercise delegated legislative functions (mainly by enacting subsidiary legislation), but also in the sense that they initiate all the important legislative measures to be taken up in the Legislative Council. Although in a technical sense it is the Legislative Council that passes legislation, the Legislative Council cannot pass legislation concerning government policies or those relating to finances or the government structure unless they are government sponsored.

339. The powers of the executive authorities are primarily executive. The executive arm of the government is responsible for implementing laws passed by the Legislative Council. They also perform an important executive function when they propose policies to be adopted by the Chief Executive and the Executive Council. Unlike in a Parliamentary democracy where policies are adopted by the legislature (although policies often initiate in government departments), in Hong Kong policies are formulated by the government and any input that the Legislative Council could make is indirect and by way of persuasion only.

340. Executive authorities are required to act in cooperation with the Legislative Council. This is particularly important because although the executive authorities have the power to propose bills and make subordinate legislation, such legislative measures require Legislative Council approval. Similarly, although financial measures are proposed and drafted by the government, they require Legislative Council approval. Article 64 of the Basic Law therefore provides that the government must implement laws passed by the Legislative Council; that it must

569. For the organizational chart of the Hong Kong Government, *see* https://www.govhk/en/about/govdirectory/govchart/index.htm.
570. Basic Law, Art. 62.

present regular policy addresses to the Council; that it must answer questions raised by Legislative Council members; and that it must obtain approval from the Legislative Council for taxation and public expenditure.

341. The executive authorities also exercise what are called quasi-judicial powers through tribunals and appeal bodies. Tribunals are a characteristic of the modern state and have replaced ordinary courts of law in dispute resolution.[571] Illustrative are Land Tribunals and the Administrative Appeals Board, which will be further discussed elsewhere in this monograph. While the doctrine of separation of powers, which is a basic feature of Hong Kong's constitutional arrangement, dictates that judicial power may be exercised only by judicial officers, tribunals which have in effect replaced ordinary courts as the dispute resolution forum are so well recognized in the common law world, they are well entrenched in Hong Kong. An important check on procedural fairness in such tribunals is guaranteed by appeal to courts of law, statutory review or judicial review as appropriate in the circumstances.

§6. Legislative Control

342. Legislative control of the executive takes place in the following manner. While the executive authorities may formulate policy and draft legislative measures, such measures may pass into law only if they are approved by the Legislative Council. While executive authorities may make subordinate legislation, they are subject to legislative control in two ways. First, subordinate legislative power must be exercised within the confines prescribed in the enabling legislation. Second, all subordinate laws take effect subject to the ultimate power of the Legislative Council to approve, amend or repeal them. Although the executive authorities make policies, they must make regular policy addresses in the Legislative Council, enabling the Council members to debate and question such policies. Members of the Legislative Council can direct questions to the executive authorities, and the questions must be answered by designated officers who attend Legislative Council meetings. It must be noted, however, that the Chief Executive may decide, in the light of security and vital public interests, that a government official or other personnel in charge of government affairs should not testify or give evidence before the Legislative Council or its committees.[572] While the Legislative Council has no power to remove any public officer, it may record its dissatisfaction with any such officer by passing a non-binding motion of no confidence.

§7. Judicial Control

343. Common law vests an inherent supervisory jurisdiction in the highest court of original jurisdiction over inferior judicial bodies as well as administrative bodies.

571. For the role of tribunals and appeal bodies, *see* Part II, Ch. 6 'Independent, Non-political Agencies in the Legislative or Executive Branch'.
572. Basic Law, Art. 48(11).

The Court of First Instance exercises this supervisory jurisdiction by way of judicial review of administrative action. Where the Chief Executive or any executive authority acts inconsistently with a statutory provision or any recognized common law requirement such as the rules of natural justice, courts have the power to intervene and grant an appropriate remedy, including an award of damages. This matter is discussed in detail in the chapter on judicial control of administrative action.

344. The manner in which the Hong Kong Government operates has been thoroughly examined by academics, the leading work being *The Government and Politics of Hong Kong* by Norman Miners.[573] The proceedings of the Executive Council are confidential, and as a result, the contemporary minutes of the Executive Council are not available for examination.[574] The members of the Executive Council are bound by collective responsibility and as a result there are no detailed accounts of what happens in the Executive Council. The procedures for dealing with appeals and petitions to the Chief Executive in Council are, however, well established.

§8. THE ADMINISTRATION AND BUREAUCRACY

345. Currently the civil service has about 180,000. The overall responsibility for the management of the civil service rests on the Civil Service Bureau, one of thirteen policy bureaux under the Government Secretariat. The Civil Service Bureau has overall policy responsibility for the management of the civil service, including such matters as appointments, pay and conditions of service, staff management, manpower planning, training, discipline and use of the official languages in the civil service. Management of the civil service is governed mainly by three instruments:

573. Norman Miners, *The Government and Politics of Hong Kong* (5th edn, Hong Kong: OUP, 1995).

574. They may be made available to courts or the Legislative Council. *See*, for instance, *Hong Kong Television Network Ltd v Chief Executive in Council* [2015] HKEC 646; [2015] 2 HKLRD 1035, (CFI), where the Chief Executive in Council disclosed all the memoranda and minutes of the relevant meetings of its meetings in order for the court to determine whether the decision made by the Chief Executive was in keeping with government policy. Although the Chief Executive in Council did not supply the reasons for his decision in refusing to grant the applicant a domestic free television licence, the Chief Executive in Council supplied the minutes of the Executive Council in the judicial review proceedings showing that how the Chief Executive in Council had come to make such decision. As there was no reason for the court not to accept the minutes as a contemporaneous record containing the reasons underlying the decision, it refused to quash the decision of the Chief Executive in Council on the ground of failure to provide reasons. *See Chang Lan-Sheung v The Attorney General* [1968] HKLR 487, (FC), where the court refused to order disclosure of the minutes of the Executive Council as being contrary to public interest. Huggins J at page 488 observed as follows: 'I have always been of the view that the courts must be jealous to ensure that their duty to give justice to a subject is not made impossible of fulfilment by reason of some wholly unjustified fear of damage to the interests of the state. But one must not be unrealistic and overlook the fact that the power of the courts to do justice is interdependent upon the ability of the Executive to perform its functions efficiently. The efficient carrying out of the executive function requires that a degree of secrecy should sometimes be afforded.'

the Public Service (Administration) Order, the Public Service (Disciplinary) Regulation and the Civil Service Regulations, all made with the authority of the Chief Executive.[575]

346. Public servants in all government departments must be permanent residents of Hong Kong,[576] provided that the government may employ British and other foreign nationals previously serving in the public service in Hong Kong, or those holding permanent identity cards of the region to serve as public servants.[577] However, the following posts can be held only by Chinese citizens, who are permanent residents of Hong Kong and who do not have the right of abode in any foreign country: the Secretaries and Deputy Secretaries of Departments, Directors of Bureaux, Commissioner Against Corruption, Director of Audit, Commissioner of Police, Director of Immigration, and Commissioner of Customs and Excise.[578]

347. The appointment and promotion of public servants must be on the basis of their qualifications, experience and ability. Hong Kong's previous system of recruitment, employment, assessment, discipline, training and management for the public service, including special bodies for their appointment, pay and conditions of service will be maintained, except for any provisions for privileged treatment of foreign nationals.[579] The Public Service Commission, first set up in 1950 under the Public Service Commission Ordinance (Cap. 93), continues to perform an important function in maintaining independence of the public service. It is an independent statutory body that advises the Chief Executive on appointment, promotion and disciplinary control of public servants. In 2007 a new improved pay adjustment mechanism was introduced.[580]

348. Public servants have a right to make representations of a public or private nature to the Chief Executive under the Public Service (Administration) Order, which provides that the Chief Executive may appoint a review board to advise him on any such representations relating to appointment, dismissal and discipline of public servants.[581] In the 1990s, the Government introduced a performance pledge programme, modelled on the UK Citizen's Charter initiative. The aim of this programme is to require government agencies to set performance targets and monitor the extent to which the targets have been met. Each service provider has set up an internal monitoring and grievance procedure. The consumers may, in addition to directing complaints to such unit, address their complaints to the Ombudsman. These initiatives have to a great extent made public services more transparent and accountable to people.[582]

---

575. *See* the website of the Hong Kong Civil Service Bureau: https://www.csb.govhk/eindex.html.
576. Basic Law, Art. 99.
577. *Ibid.*, Art. 101.
578. *Ibid.*
579. *Ibid.*, Art. 103.
580. *See* Civil Service Bureau website: https://www.csb.govhk/english/admin/pay/2209.html.
581. Section 20. This is an Executive Order made by the Chief Executive of Hong Kong.
582. *See* the following writings by Anton Cooray: 'Ombudsman in Asia: A Case-Study of Hong Kong and Sri Lanka' in Roy Gregory & Philip Giddings (eds) *Righting Wrongs: The Ombudsman in Six*

Chapter 5. The Judiciary in Hong Kong

§1. INTRODUCTION

349. Hong Kong, though it is now an integral part of mainland China, continues to be a common law jurisdiction. Indeed, the Basic Law explicitly guarantees the continuation of the existing legal system including the common law.[583] Courts play an important indispensable part in the common law system, by interpreting and applying the law to resolve disputes, and in the process in fact make law. To ensure that judicial decisions are consistent as far as possible with each other courts have developed the doctrine of binding precedent, which provides certainty of law at the same time providing a mechanism to develop the law in response to changing social circumstances. While Hong Kong courts are only bound by previous judicial decisions of Hong Kong courts, the idea of persuasive judicial precedent enables Hong Kong courts to cite and follow judicial decisions from the UK, Australia, USA, Canada and other common law jurisdictions.

350. In the case of *Solicitor (24/07) v Law Society of Hong Kong,*[584] the Court of Final Appeal considered the continuing relevance and authority of judicial decisions of the Privy Council, the highest Court of Appeal for many Commonwealth jurisdictions, and the House of Lords of the UK (whose jurisdiction has, with effect from October 2009, been transferred to the Supreme Court of England and Wales). Chief Justice Li observed that under Article 84 of the Basic Law, the courts may refer to judicial decisions of other common law jurisdictions, as was done before 1997. Because of the Imperial connection between Hong Kong and the UK, until 1997 decisions of the Privy Council on appeal from Hong Kong were binding on Hong Kong courts. Decisions of the Privy Council from jurisdictions other than Hong Kong were of persuasive authority and so were the decisions of the House of Lords. After the handover in 1997, being the highest judicial body, the Court of Final Appeal is not bound by decisions of any court, in Hong Kong or elsewhere. Chief Justice Li emphasized, however, that the Court of Final Appeal will generally follow its own previous decisions and decisions of the Privy Council on appeal from Hong Kong. Decisions of the Court of Final Appeal, but not decisions of the Privy Council, are binding on all Hong Kong courts. Given the similarities between English law and Hong Kong law, the Court of Appeal and lower courts in Hong

---

Continents (Netherlands, IOS, 2000) 75–91 'Toward More Efficient Administration: Citizen's Charter in the United Kingdom and Hong Kong's Performance Pledge Programme', (1993) *Hong Kong Public Administration* 159–176; 'Accountability and Choice: New Directions in the Delivery of Public Services' in J. Lee & A. Cheung (eds) *Public Sector Reform in Hong Kong: Future Directions* (Hong Kong: Chinese University of Hong Kong Press, 1994), 209–230; 'Public Sector Reform in Hong Kong: Some Legal Aspects', (1999) 8 *Public Administration and Policy* 23–36; 'Hong Kong's Ombudsman: The First Decade', (1999) 3 *The International Ombudsman Yearbook* 71–88; and 'Some Reflections on the Legislative Context of the Hong Kong Ombudsman', (2009) 17:1 *Asia Pacific Law Review* 53–72.

583. Basic Law, Art. 8. Also *see* the website of the Efficiency Unit: http://www.eu.govhk/en/our-work/management-consultancy/performance-measurement.html.

584. *Solicitor (24/07) v Law Society of Hong Kong* (2008) 11 HKCFAR 117, (CFA).

Kong should treat decisions of the Privy Council and the Supreme Court of England and Wales (which has replaced the House of Lords) with great respect. They may have persuasive authority depending on all relevant circumstances, including in particular, the nature of the issues in question and the similarity of any relevant statutory or constitutional provisions.

351. The current position in relation to judicial precedents from other common law jurisdictions may be stated as follows:

(1) Decisions of the Privy Council on appeal from Hong Kong have the highest degree of persuasion. The Court of Final Appeal, while it is not bound by its own decisions or decisions of the Privy Council on appeals from Hong Kong, will hesitate to deviate from such decisions, in order not to disturb the settled law.
(2) Decisions of the Privy Council on appeal from Hong Kong are not binding on the Court of Appeal and lower courts of Hong Kong, because the Privy Council is no longer the highest Court of Appeal for Hong Kong. However, such decisions will be treated with respect and will serve as persuasive authority, not automatically, but depending on the circumstances of the case.
(3) Decisions of the Privy Council on appeal from other common law jurisdictions and decisions of the House of Lords and its successor the Supreme Court of England and Wales may exert persuasive authority on all Hong Kong courts depending on the circumstances of the case.[585]
(4) Hong Kong courts may refer to judicial decisions of other common law jurisdictions, such as Australia and New Zealand, and follow them as persuasive authority.
(5) Hong Kong Courts may refer to decisions of supranational judicial tribunals such as the European Court of Human Rights, and arguably even to decisions of non-common law jurisdictions, where such is relevant and appropriate.

352. The highest court in Hong Kong's judicial structure is the Court of Final Appeal,[586] followed by the Court of Appeal, the Court of First Instance,[587] the District Court, and the Magistrate Court. In addition, there are a number of tribunals exercising limited jurisdiction in certain specified matters.

585. Hong Kong judiciary may follow Privy Council decisions from other jurisdictions in preference to Privy Council decisions from Hong Kong. *See HKSAR v Pang Hiu San* (2014) 17 HKCFAR 545, (CFA); *HKSAR v Tse Hin Yeung* [2016] HKEC 1524, (CA).
586. Created by the Hong Kong Court of Final Appeal Ordinance (Cap. 484).
587. The Court of Appeal and the Court of First Instance constitute the High Court, *see* High Court Ordinance (Cap. 4), s. 3(1).

§2. The Court of Final Appeal

I. Constitution

353. The Court of Final Appeal came into operation on 1 July 1997. Until 30 June 1997, the Privy Council sitting in London was the highest judicial tribunal for Hong Kong. The replacement of the Privy Council by a local Court of Final Appeal was a necessary consequence of the change of sovereignty from Britain to China.[588]

354. The judges of the Court of Final Appeal can be divided into two categories, namely permanent judges and non-permanent judges.[589] The Head of the Hong Kong Judiciary[590] is the Chief Justice,[591] who is also the President of the Court of Final Appeal. The judges of the Court of Final Appeal are the Chief Justice and not less than three other permanent judges.[592] The Court may as required invite non-permanent judges from Hong Kong or other common law jurisdictions to sit on the court. Two lists of non-permanent judges are maintained, one list of non-permanent Hong Kong judges and the other of judges from other common law jurisdictions.[593]

II. Jurisdiction of the Court of Final Appeal

355. The Court of Final Appeal is the highest Court of Appeal and exercises unlimited jurisdiction in both civil and criminal matters. It also has power to make rules of court, acting through its Rules Committee.[594] While the power of final adjudication rests with the Court of Final Appeal, where Article 158 comes into play an interpretation given by the NPCSC will be definitive.

---

588. 'Its symbolism as an instrument of British domination was no doubt too potent for the [Privy Council] to survive the change of sovereignty', Peter Wesley-Smith, *Constitutional and Administrative Law* (Longman Asia Ltd 1995) 140. For an excellent account of the Court of Final Appeal, *see* Simon N.M. Young & Yash Ghai, *Hong Kong's Court of Final Appeal: The Development of the Law in China's Hong Kong* (Cambridge University Press, 2014).
589. Hong Kong Court of Final Appeal Ordinance (Cap. 484), s. 5.
590. As such, the Chief Justice is charged with the administration of the judiciary and such other functions as may from time to time be lawfully conferred on him. *See* Hong Kong Court of Final Appeal Ordinance, s. 6(2).
591. The qualifications for a person to be eligible for appointment as Chief Justice are laid down in s. 12(1) of the Hong Kong Court of Final Appeal Ordinance: (i) a permanent judge; (ii) the Chief Judge of the High Court, a Justice of Appeal or a judge of the Court of First Instance; or (iii) a barrister who has practised as a barrister or solicitor in Hong Kong for a period of at least ten years. Section 12(2), which was repealed in 2005, provided that a retired Chief Judge of the High Court, a retired Justice of Appeal or a retired judge of the Court of First Instance may be appointed as the first Chief Justice of the Court of Final Appeal. In the end however, Mr Andrew Li, QC, a practicing barrister, was appointed as the first Chief Justice of the Hong Kong Special Administrative Region.
592. Hong Kong Court of Final Appeal Ordinance, s. 5(1) and s. 5(2).
593. *Ibid.*, s. 8(1) and s. 9(1). Section 10 of the Court of Final Appeal Ordinance provides that the number of non-permanent judges (from Hong Kong and other common law jurisdictions) on the list should not exceed thirty.
594. *Ibid.*, s. 40.

356. In *Solicitor and Law Society of Hong Kong v Secretary for Justice* the Court of Final Appeal held that it would be unconstitutional for the legislature to oust the final adjudicatory power of the Court of Final Appeal, except where such exclusion could be justified.[595] The Court declared invalid section 13(1) of the Legal Practitioners Ordinance (Cap. 159) which provided that a decision of the Court of Appeal on appeal from an order of the Solicitors Disciplinary Tribunal 'shall be final'. The Court of Final Appeal observed that Article 82 of the Basic Law vested the final power of adjudication in the Court of Final Appeal. Any limitation on this power by the Legislature must pursue a legitimate purpose, and there must be reasonable proportionality between the limitation and the purpose sought to be achieved. In ascertaining the purpose of the limitation, matters such as the subject matter of the dispute, whether it concerned fact or law, whether it related to substantive rights and obligations or only procedural matters, what was at stake, the need for speedy resolution and the cost implication of dispute resolution, including any possible appeals, would have to be considered. The legitimacy of any purpose would depend on whether it was consistent with the public interest, which had many facets, including the proper administration of justice. The Court held that the finality provision in the Legal Practitioners Ordinance was unconstitutional although an appeal to the Court through section 22(1)(b) of the Hong Kong Court of Final Appeal Ordinance (Cap. 484) was available. The reason is that such an appeal was available only at the discretion of the Court of Appeal or the Court of Final Appeal 'if, in the opinion of the Court of Appeal or the Court, as the case may be, the question involved in the appeal is one which, by reason of its great general or public importance, or otherwise, ought to be submitted to the Court for decision'.[596] However, there is no immutable right appeal to the Court of Final Appeal. To be valid, 'the limitation imposed must pursue a legitimate purpose and there must be reasonable proportionality between the limitation and the purpose sought to be achieved ... it is the duty of the courts to review any legislation enacted which seeks to impose any limitation on the power of final adjudication vested in the Court by art 82 and to consider whether the limitation satisfies the proportionality test'.[597] The Court of Final Appeal observed that: 'Whether a particular limitation imposed by statute satisfies the proportionality test will depend on an examination of all the circumstances. There may be instances where a statutory limitation providing that a decision of the Court of Appeal or the Court of First Instance on appeal, whether from a statutory tribunal or a lower court, shall be final may be able to satisfy that test.'[598] The occasion arose in *Incorporated Owners of Po Hang Building v Sam Woo Marine Works Ltd* for the Court of Final Appeal to uphold the validity of a

---

595. *Solicitor and Law Society of Hong Kong v Secretary for Justice (*2003) 6 HKCFAR 570, (CFA).
596. *Ibid.*, [30], [31] and [23]. Section 13(1) was later amended deleting the world 'shall be final'. On the meaning of 'public importance', *see Max Share Ltd v Ng Yat Chi* [1997] HKLRD 1255, (CFA). *See also Association of Expatriate Civil Servants of Hong Kong v Secretary for the Civil Service* [1998] 1 HKLRD 701, (CFA). Cf. *Oriental Daily Publishers Ltd v Comr for Television and Entertainment Licensing Authority* [1998] 1 HKLRD 253, (CA).
597. *Solicitor v Law Society of Hong Kong* [2003] 6 HKCFAR 570, (CFA), [31]–[32]. *See also Mok Charles v Tam Wai Ho* (2010) 13 HKCFAR 762, (CFA), discussed in relation to election petitions.
598. *Ibid.*, [34].

restriction on appeal to the court of Final Appeal.[599] There the provision in the District Courts Ordinance which ruled out any appeal to the Court of Final Appeal from a refusal of the Court of Appeal to grant leave to appeal against a decision of the District Court. The Court of Appeal would not grant leave unless there was a reasonable prospect of success or there was some other reason in the interests of justice for hearing the appeal. The Court of Appeal upheld the restriction on appeal to Court of Final Appeal, having satisfied itself that the restriction served legitimate aims and was no more than necessary.[600]

357. There are instances where an appeal lies against the decision of the Court of First Instance directly to the Court of Final Appeal, leapfrogging the Court of Appeal. Section 22(1)(b) of the Court of Final Appeal Ordinance (Cap. 484) provides a direct appeal from Court of First Instance to the Court of Final Appeal 'at the discretion of the Court of Appeal or [the Court of Final Appeal] in any civil cause or matter, ... if in the opinion of the Court of Appeal or [the Court of Final Appeal], ... the question involved in appeal is one which, by reason of its great general or public importance, or otherwise, ought to be submitted to the [Court of Final Appeal] for decision'.[601] Section 22(1)(c) of the Court of Final Appeal Ordinance (Cap. 484) provides that there shall be an appeal from a determination of the Court of First Instance in an election petition under section 37(1) of the Chief Executive Elections Ordinance,[602] and a determination of the Court of First Instance in an election petition under section 67 of the Legislative Council Ordinance.[603]

358. Appeals are to be heard by a five-member bench of the Court of Final Appeal comprising: (a) the Chief Justice or a permanent judge designated to sit in his place who will act as President of the Court; (b) three permanent judges nominated by the Chief Justice; and (c) one non-permanent Hong Kong judge or one judge from another Common Law jurisdiction selected by the Chief Justice and

599. *Incorporated Owners of Po Hang Building v Sam Woo Marine Works Ltd* (2017) 20 HKCFAR 240, (CFA).

600. *Ibid.*, [35]–[54]. *See China International Fund Ltd v Dennis Lau & Ng Chun Man Architects & Engineers (HK) Ltd* [2015] 4 HKLRD 609, (CA), where a restriction on the right to appeal in s. 84(3) of the Arbitration Ordinance (Cap. 609) was upheld as a proportionate limitation. That section provided that the Court of First Instance could, after determining an appeal against an arbitration award, refuse to grant leave to appeal to the Court of Appeal against its decision. In arriving at this decision, the Court of Appeal took into account the nature of the arbitration process, as well as its, though limited, jurisdiction to allow an appeal in its discretion. The Court of Final Appeal refused leave to appeal against the decision of the Court of Appeal: [2015] HKEC 2707, (CFA).

601. This provision was used famously in *Town Planning Board v Society for Protection of the Harbour Ltd* [2003] HKEC 1207, (CFA).

602. *See Re Ho Chun Yan Albert* (2012) 15 HKCFAR 686, (CFA).

603. Section 67(c) of the Legislative Elections Ordinance, as originally enacted, provided that 'the determination of the Court [of First Instance], as certified, is final as to the matters at issue concerning the election petition'. In *Mok Charles v Tam Wai Ho* (2010) 13 HKCFAR 762, (CFA), this finality clause was held to be an unjustifiable ouster of the right to appeal. In response to that decision, the Ordinance was amended in 2011 removing the objectionable words. In the same year, s. 22(c)(iii) was added to the Court of Final Appeal Ordinance against providing for a discretionary appeal from the determination of the Court of First Instance in an election petition.

invited by the Court.[604] On appeal, the Court of Final Appeal may confirm, reverse or vary the decision of the court.[605] The Court may exercise any powers of the court from which the appeal lies, including the power to order a retrial, or may remit the case to that court.[606]

359. Until 2004, an appeal in civil cases[607] was available as a matter of right from any final judgment[608] of the Court of Appeal where the subject matter exceeded a prescribed monetary limit.[609] Where the subject matter of the dispute fell below such monetary limit an appeal could be made subject to the discretion of the court. Section 22(a) which provided for an appeal as of right where a monetary limit was exceeded was repealed by Ordinance No. 20 of 2014. Now, an appeal lies to the Court of Final Appeal 'at the discretion of the Court of Appeal or the Court [of Final Appeal], from any judgment of the Court of Appeal in any civil cause or matter, whether final or interlocutory, if, in the opinion of the Court of Appeal or the Court [of Final Appeal], as the case may be, the question involved in the appeal is one which, by reason of its great general or public importance, or otherwise, ought to be submitted to the Court [of Final Appeal] for decision'.[610] An appeal lies to the Court of Final Appeal at its discretion from a determination of the Court of First Instance in respect of several matters.[611]

360. An appeal in a 'criminal cause or matter' is always at the discretion of the Court of Final Appeal.[612] Such an appeal lies at the instance of any party to the criminal proceedings from: (a) any final decision of the Court of Appeal; and (b) any decision of the Court of First Instance, (not being a verdict or finding of a jury), from which no appeal lies to the Court of Appeal.[613] In criminal cases, no appeal will be admitted unless leave has been granted by the Court of Final Appeal.[614] The Court of Final Appeal will not grant leave unless it is certified by the Court of

---

604. Hong Kong Court of Final Appeal Ordinance, s. 16(1).
605. *Ibid.*, s. 17(1).
606. *Ibid.*, s. 17(2).
607. The civil jurisdiction of the Court of Final Appeal is governed by Part II ss 19–27 of the Hong Kong Court of Final Appeal Ordinance (Cap. 484).
608. According to s. 19 of the Hong Kong Court of Final Appeal Ordinance judgment includes decree, order or decision.
609. Hong Kong Court of Final Appeal Ordinance, s. 22(1)(a). This was repealed by Ordinance No 20 of 2014, s. 8.
610. *Ibid.*, s. 22(1)(b), as amended by Ordinance No 20 of 2014, s. 8. On the meaning of 'public importance', *see Max Share Ltd v Ng Yat Chi* [1997] HKLRD 1255, (CFA). *See also Association of Expatriate Civil Servants of Hong Kong v Secretary for the Civil Service* [1998] 1 HKLRD 701, (CFA). *Cf. Oriental Daily Publishers Ltd v Comr for Television and Entertainment Licensing Authority* [1998] 1 HKLRD 253, (CA). For very rare instance where leave to appeal was granted, *see Commissioner of Inland Revenue v Perfekta Enterprises Ltd* [2018] HKCFAR 36, (CFA).
611. *Ibid.*, s. 22(c). *See also* s. 27B.
612. Hong Kong Court of Final Appeal Ordinance, s. 31.
613. *Ibid.*, s. 31(a) and (b).
614. *Ibid.*, s. 32(1).

Appeal or the Court of First Instance, as the case may be, that a point of law of great and general importance is involved in the decision or it is shown that substantial and grave injustice has been done.[615]

§3. THE HIGH COURT

361. The High Court consists of the Court of Appeal and the Court of First Instance.[616] Subject to the provisions of the High Court Ordinance, the High Court is a court of unlimited civil and criminal jurisdiction.[617]

362. The predecessor of the High Court was the Supreme Court of Hong Kong, which was first created in 1844 by an Ordinance to Establish a Supreme Court of Judicature.[618] This Ordinance was replaced in 1976 by the Supreme Court Ordinance,[619] which provided for the first time separate judges to sit in the High Court and the Court of Appeal.

363. The Court of Appeal consists of the CJHC and such Justices of Appeal as the Chief Executive may appoint.[620] The CJHC is the President of the Court of Appeal.[621] The Chief Judge may appoint one or more of the Justices of Appeal as vice-presidents of the Court of Appeal.[622] A judge of the Court of First Instance may, on the request of the Chief Justice, sit as an additional judge of the Court of Appeal, in which case he has the jurisdiction, powers and privileges of a judge of the Court of Appeal.[623]

364. The Court of First Instance consists of:

615. *Ibid.*, s. 32(2). For a rare instance where leave was granted on the ground of 'substantial or grave injustice', *see HKSAR v Shum Wai Kee* [2018] HKEC 2225, (CFA), a case concerning false declaration to obtain registration as a nurse. Subsequently in the substantive hearing of the appeal the Court of Final Appeal upheld the argument that substantial and grave injustice was caused to the defendant when her evidence was no admitted to show of a common law defence he had: 'In the light of the conclusions that: (i) in answer to the question of law for which leave to appeal was granted, a defendant's state of mind as to the falsity of the declaration was relevant and that the mental element of the offence would not be made out where a defendant held an honest and genuine belief that the declaration was not false and that (ii) substantial and grave injustice was done to the appellant in disbelieving his evidence that he held such an honest and genuine belief, it follows that the appeal must be allowed and his conviction set aside.' *HKSAR v Shum Wai Kee* [2019] HKCFAR 11, (CFA), [33].
616. High Court Ordinance (Cap. 4), s. 3(1).
617. *Ibid.*, s. 3(2).
618. Supreme Court of Judicature, Ordinance No 15 of 1844.
619. Now renamed the High Court Ordinance (Cap. 4).
620. High Court Ordinance, s. 5(1)(a) and (b). Justices of Appeal are appointed by the Chief Executive on the recommendation of the Judicial Officers Recommendation Commission, *see* Basic Law, Art. 88.
621. High Court Ordinance., s. 5(3).
622. *Ibid.*, s. 5(1A).
623. *Ibid.*, s. 5(2).

(1) the Chief Justice of the High Court;
(2) such judges as the Chief Executive may appoint;
(3) such recorders as the Chief Executive may appoint; and
(4) such deputy judges as the Chief Justice may appoint.[624] A Justice of Appeal may sit in the Court of First Instance and act as a judge thereof whenever the business of the Court of First Instance so requires, in which case he will have all the jurisdiction, powers and privileges of such a judge.[625]

I. Civil Jurisdiction of the Court of Appeal

365. The Court of Appeal is a superior court of record.[626] It has unlimited appellate jurisdiction in both civil and criminal cases.

366. The civil jurisdiction of the Court of Appeal consists of: (a) appeals from any judgment or order of the Court of First Instance in any civil cause or matter; (b) appeals from judgments, decisions or orders of the District Court; and (c) any other jurisdiction conferred upon it by law.[627] The Court of Appeal must exercise its jurisdiction in every cause or matter before it so as to secure that, as far as possible, all matters in dispute between the parties are completely and finally determined and all multiplicity of legal proceedings with respect to any of those matters is avoided.[628]

367. It is expressly provided that the Court of Appeal,[629] when exercising jurisdiction in any civil cause or matter, must continue to administer both law and equity on the basis that, whenever there is any conflict or variance between the rules of equity and common law, the rules of equity will prevail.[630]

368. In the exercise of its civil jurisdiction, the Court of Appeal is duly constituted if it consists of an uneven number of Justices of Appeal not less than three.[631] A Bench of two judges may hear and determine certain appeals, which are set out in the next paragraph. Where an even number of Justices of Appeal decide an appeal and the Court is equality divided, the appeal must be reargued before a court consisting of an uneven number of judges not less than three, before any appeal to the Court of Final Appeal may be taken.[632]

369. Two Justices of Appeal sitting in the Court of Appeal have jurisdiction over the following matters:[633]

---

624. *Ibid.*, s. 4(1).
625. *Ibid.*, s. 4(2).
626. *Ibid.*, s. 3(1).
627. *Ibid.*, s. 13(2).
628. *Ibid.*, s. 16(2)(b).
629. The same applies to the Court of First Instance.
630. High Court Ordinance, s. 16(1).
631. *Ibid.*, s. 34B(2).
632. *Ibid.*, s. 34(5).
633. *Ibid.*, s. 34B(4).

(1) hearing and determining any appeal against an interlocutory order or judgment;
(2) hearing and determining any appeal against a decision of a single Justice of Appeal acting within the jurisdiction conferred upon him by the High Court Ordinance;
(3) hearing and determining any appeal where all the parties have before the hearing filed a consent to the appeal being heard and determined by two Justices of Appeal;
(4) hearing the remainder of, and determining, any appeal where part of it has been heard by three or more Justices of Appeal of whom one or more is or are unable to continue and all the parties have consented to the remainder of the appeal being heard, and the appeal being determined, by two remaining Justices of Appeal; and
(5) hearing and determining an appeal of any such description or in any such circumstances not covered under the categories mentioned above as may be prescribed for these purposes by an order made by the Chief Justice.

370. In civil matters, a single judge of the Court of Appeal sitting in court or in chambers may make an order or direction not involving the determination of the appeal.[634] Similarly, a single judge may make any interim order that he may think fit to prevent any prejudice to the claims of any party pending an appeal.[635]

371. As a general rule, an appeal lies as of right to the Court of Appeal from every judgment or order of the Court of First Instance in any civil cause or matter.[636] There are, however a number of statutory restrictions on the right of appeal.[637]

372. In some situations leave to appeal to the Court of Appeal is required;[638] Leave must be sought from the court or tribunal in question or from the Court of Appeal. An application for leave to appeal may be determined by a single judge of the Court of Appeal.[639]

373. The Court of Appeal is empowered to hear appeals from judgments, decisions and orders made by the District Court.[640] If any party to any proceedings in the District Court is dissatisfied with a determination or direction of a judge on a point of law or upon the admission or rejection of any evidence or on any question of fact, the party aggrieved by the judgment, direction, decision or order may, within

634. *Ibid.*, s. 35(1).
635. *Ibid.*, s. 35(1).
636. *Ibid.*, s. 14(3). An appeal also lies as a matter of right from any judgment or order of a judge in chambers to the Court of Appeal (*ibid.*, s. 14(1)) and also from any judgment, order or decision made by a master (*see* RHC Ord 14 rule 6(2), Ord 36 rule 1, Ord 37, Ord 49B, Ord 58 rule 2(a), (b), (c), (d), (e), Ord 84A rule 3).
637. *See* High Court Ordinance, s. 14(3).
638. *Ibid.*, s. 14(3)(e) and 14(3)(f).
639. *Ibid.*, s. 35(1).
640. *Ibid.*, s. 13(2)(b).

twenty-eight days thereafter,[641] apply to a district judge for leave to appeal or, if such judge refuses leave, within a further fourteen days from the date of such refusal[642] to the Court of Appeal.[643]

374. On any appeal from the District Court, the Court of Appeal may draw any inference of fact and may: (a) order a new trial on such terms as it thinks just; or (b) order judgment to be entered for any party; or (c) make a final or other order on such terms as it thinks proper to ensure the determination on the merits of the real question in controversy between the parties.[644]

375. Further, on appeal, the Court of Appeal may reverse or vary, in favour of a party seeking to support the judgment or order of the District Court in whole or in part, any determinations made by the District Court on questions of fact, notwithstanding that the appeal is on a point of law only, or any such determinations on points of law, notwithstanding that the appeal is an appeal on a question of fact only.[645]

376. Appeals to the Court of Appeal from the decisions of tribunals may be made in two ways. First, an appeal lies from the decision of a tribunal to the Court of Appeal if such an appeal is expressly provided by statute.[646] Second, an appeal by way of case stated to the Court of Appeal will lie where legislation so provides.[647]

II. Criminal Jurisdiction of the Court of Appeal

377. The criminal jurisdiction of the Court of Appeal is entirely statutory.[648]

---

641. The time limit may be extended by the district judge, *see* District Court Ordinance (Cap. 336), s. 63(5).
642. The time period can be extended by the Court of Appeal, *ibid.*, s. 63(5).
643. *Ibid.*, s. 63(1).
644. District Court Ordinance (Cap. 336), s. 64(1)(a), (b) and (c).
645. *Ibid.*, s. 64(2).
646. For examples of such appeals, *see* the Lands Tribunal Ordinance (Cap. 17), s. 11(2); the Legal Practitioners Ordinance (Cap. 159), s. 13(1) (appeal from Solicitors Disciplinary Tribunal) and s. 37B (appeal from Barristers Disciplinary Tribunal).
647. *See*, e.g., the Administrative Appeals Board Ordinance (Cap. 442), s. 24(1) (the Board may before an appeal is determined, refer any question of law arising in the appeal to the Court of Appeal for determination by way of case stated); the Inland Revenue Ordinance (Cap. 112), s. 69A (in cases where, by reason of the amount of tax in dispute or of the general or public importance of the matter or its extraordinary difficulty, there is provision for appeal by way of case stated from the Inland Revenue Board of Review to the Court of Appeal with the leave of the Court of Appeal); and the Buildings Ordinance (Cap. 123), s. 53C, which provides that the Building Appeal Tribunal may by way of case stated refer to the Court of Appeal for its decision any question of law relating to an appeal to the Appeal Tribunal.
648. Common law does not recognize an inherent jurisdiction in courts to entertain an appeal, where a right of appeal is not given by statute. In contrast, courts have an inherent supervisory jurisdiction which is exercised by way of judicial review.

The appellate criminal jurisdiction of the Court of Appeal as laid down in statute consists of:

(1) appeals from the Court of First Instance or District Court under certain provisions of the Criminal Procedure Ordinance;[649]
(2) appeals from a judgment or order of the Court of First Instance given or made in the exercise of the powers of mandamus, prohibition or certiorari[650] and relating to a criminal cause or matter;[651]
(3) the consideration of questions of law reserved for the court;[652]
(4) the consideration of applications by the Secretary for Justice for the review of any sentence;[653]
(5) the consideration of references by the Secretary for Justice of questions of law to the court;[654]
(6) appeals by way of case stated from the District Court;[655]
(7) appeals against an order of court that the proceedings should be conducted in a closed court, where it appears to the court that it is necessary to do so in the interests of justice or public order or public security;[656] and
(8) any other jurisdiction conferred on it by any law.[657]

378. In criminal appeals, the Court of Appeal is duly constituted for the purposes of determining any appeal if the court consists of an uneven number of Justices of Appeal being not less than three.[658]

379. The court is duly constituted for the purposes of determining an appeal against sentence only if it consists of two Justices of Appeal.[659]

380. Where an appeal is heard by two judges of the Court of Appeal and the two judges cannot reach agreement, then the judgment or order appealed from will be disturbed only in as far as it may be modified or affected by any order they make as to which the two Justices of appeal do not disagree.[660] If the judgment or order appealed from is not so modified or affected, it will be deemed to be the judgment or order of the Court of Appeal and, if the judgment or order is so modified or affected, it will, as so modified or affected, be deemed to be the judgment or order of the Court of Appeal.[661]

649. Criminal Procedure Ordinance, (Cap. 221), Part IV (ss 80–832).
650. *See* High Court Ordinance, s. 21I(1).
651. High Court Ordinance, s. 13(3)(aa).
652. *Ibid.*, s. 13(3)(b) and Criminal Procedure Ordinance, s. 81(1).
653. *Ibid.*, s. 13(3)(b) and Criminal Procedure Ordinance, s. 81A(1).
654. *Ibid.*, s. 13(3)(c)(1) and Criminal Procedure Ordinance, s. 81.
655. *Ibid.*, s. 13(3)(d) and Criminal Procedure Ordinance, s. 84.
656. Criminal Procedure Ordinance, s. 123(1B)(a).
657. High Court Ordinance, s. 13(3)(e).
658. *Ibid.*, s. 34(2).
659. *Ibid.*, s. 34(2A).
660. *Ibid.*, s. 34(5).
661. *Ibid.*, s. 34(5) *proviso* (a) and (b).

381. Where a Court of Appeal consisting of three or more Justices of Appeal sits, the judgment or order which is that of the majority of the Justices of Appeal sitting is deemed to be the judgment or order of the Court of Appeal, but if there is no judgment or order which is that of a majority of the Justices of Appeal sitting, the judgment or order appealed from will be deemed to be the judgment or order of the Court of Appeal.[662]

382. In the case of an appeal under the provisions of the Criminal Procedure Code,[663] if two Justices of Appeal agree as to the judgment or order to be made, the judgment or order of the trial judge, or where there is no such judgment or order, the judgment or order of the President will be deemed to be the judgment of the Court of Appeal.[664]

383. Some of the other important powers of the Court of Appeal in the exercise of its criminal jurisdiction include:

(1) The power to order a retrial: Where the Court of Appeal allows an appeal against conviction and it appears to the Court of Appeal that the interest of justice so requires, it may order that the appellant be retried.[665]
(2) The application by a Secretary for Justice for a review of sentence: The Secretary for Justice may, with the leave of the Court of Appeal, apply to the Court of Appeal for the review of any sentence, other than a sentence fixed by law, passed by any court on the grounds that the sentence is not authorized by law, is wrong in principle, or is manifestly excessive or manifestly inadequate.[666] The courts are generally reluctant to interfere with a sentence passed by the trial court.[667]
(3) The reservation of a question of law for Court of Appeal: A judge of a trial court may reserve for the consideration of the Court of Appeal any question of

662. *Ibid.*, s. 34(4).
663. That is, Criminal Procedure Ordinance, Part IV.
664. High Court Ordinance, s. 34(6).
665. Criminal Procedure Ordinance, s. 83E(1). For the restrictions imposed by law on retrial, *see ibid.*, s. 83E(2)(a)–(c).
666. *Ibid.*, s. 81A(1).
667. *Re Applications for Review of Sentence* [1972] HKLR 370, (Appellate Jurisdiction), 414. For an instructive statement of the relevant legal principles and practice, *see Secretary for Justice v Wong Chi Fung* (2018) 21 HKCFAR 35, (CFA), where the court held that as the wording of s. 81A of the CPO showed, the Court of Appeal could only interfere with the sentence under review if it thought that the sentence was: (a) not authorized by law; (b) wrong in principle; (c) manifestly excessive; or (d) manifestly inadequate. But the power to review a sentence, particularly to increase it, did not confer on the Secretary for Justice an analogous right to that of a convicted person appealing against sentence. A review of sentence was also procedurally different to an appeal by a convicted person against conviction or sentence. Further, the ambit of the power of review of sentence was subject to the constitutionally protected right against double jeopardy under Art. 11(6) of the Hong Kong Bill of Rights and the Court of Appeal typically applied a discount to an increased sentence. The Court referred to and applied the reasoning in the following cases: *Re Applications for Review of Sentences by Attorney General* [1972] HKLR 370; *Secretary for Justice v Buk Chui Ying* [2008] 5 HKLRD 185, (CA), where a community order for conviction of theft was increased to two years of imprisonment; *HKSAR v Chan Pak Hoe* (2012) HKEC 941, (CFA), where it was held that a

law which may arise or the trial of any indictment.[668] In exercising this power, the judge may act on his own motion or on the application of the Secretary for Justice or the Secretary for Defence.[669]

(4) The reference of a question of law by the Secretary for Justice to the Court of Appeal following acquittal: Where a person tried on indictment has been acquitted, whether in respect of the whole or part of the indictment, the Secretary for Justice may, if he desires the opinion of the Court of Appeal on a question of law which has arisen in the case, refer the question to the Court of Appeal which must consider the point and give its opinion on it.[670] A reference under this provision does not affect the acquittal of any accused person at the trial.[671]

§4. THE COURT OF FIRST INSTANCE

384. The Court of First Instance is a superior court of record.[672] The civil jurisdiction of the Court of First Instance consists of:

(1) original jurisdiction and authority of a like nature and extent as that held and exercised by the Chancery, Family and Queen's Bench Divisions of the High Court of Justice in England; and
(2) any other jurisdiction, whether original or appellate jurisdiction, conferred on it by any law.[673]

I. Original Civil Jurisdiction of the Court of First Instance

385. The Court of First Instance also exercises original jurisdiction in the following matters:

(1) The court exercises exclusive jurisdiction in Admiralty matters.[674]

---

pending appeal against one part of a magistrate's decision does not preclude a review by that magistrate of another part of her or his decision in the same case; *Secretary for Justice v Lo King Fat* [2015] HKEC 2688, (CA), where the terms of imprisonment imposed on defendants for bribery offences were increased with a discount.

668. Criminal Procedure Ordinance, s. 81(2).
669. *Ibid.*, s. 81(2). Upon consideration of the question so reserved the Court of Appeal may affirm or quash the conviction or order a new trial and make such other order as may be necessary to give effect to its decision: s. 81(4).
670. *Ibid.*, s. 81D(1).
671. *Ibid.*, s. 81D(4).
672. High Court Ordinance, s. 12(1).
673. *Ibid.*, s. 12(2).
674. *Ibid.*, s. 12A.

(2) The Court of First Instance exercises a wide jurisdiction in matrimonial matters.[675] The Court also has wardship jurisdiction. No infant may be made a ward of the court except by an order made by the Court of First Instance.[676]
(3) Cases may be transferred from the District Court[677] or a tribunal[678] to the Court of First Instance.

386. As a general rule, every civil trial in the Court of First Instance and all business arising therefrom must be heard and determined by a judge of the Court of First Instance sitting alone.[679] The Chief Justice may direct that any proceeding or class of proceeding in the Court of First Instance be heard and determined by two or more judges of the Court of First Instance.[680]

II. Appellate Civil Jurisdiction of the Court of First Instance

387. An appeal in civil cases will lie to the Court of First Instance in any case where legislation so provides.[681] A number of statutes provide a right of appeal from the decision of an inferior tribunal.[682]

III. Original Criminal Jurisdiction of the Court of First Instance

388. The criminal jurisdiction of the Court of First Instance consists of original jurisdiction of a like nature and extent as that held and exercised in criminal matters by the High Court of Justice and the Crown Court in England respectively and any other original jurisdiction conferred upon it by any law.[683] Jurisdiction in respect of criminal offences is governed by the territorial principle. Thus, as a general rule the

675. In certain circumstances, this jurisdiction must first be exercised by the District Court, which may transfer appropriate cases to the Court of First Instance. (Matrimonial Causes Ordinance (Cap. 179), s. 10A; Matrimonial Proceedings and Property Ordinance (Cap. 192), s. 2A(1)). In addition to these two statutes, other relevant statutes conferring matrimonial jurisdiction include Domestic Violence Ordinance (Cap. 189). Guardianship of Minors Ordinance (Cap. 13); Parent and Child Ordinance (Cap. 429); Separation and Maintenance Ordinance (Cap. 16).
676. High Court Ordinance, s. 26(1).
677. *See* District Court of Ordinance, ss 38 and 39.
678. Lands Tribunal Ordinance (Cap. 17), s. 8A(1); Small Claims Tribunal (Cap. 338), ss 7 and 11; Labour Tribunal Ordinance (Cap. 25), s. 10(2); Inland Revenue Ordinance (Cap. 112), s. 67(3).
679. High Court Ordinance, s. 32(1).
680. *Ibid.*, s. 32(1).
681. *Ibid.*, s. 12(2)(b).
682. *See,* e.g., the Small Claims Tribunal (Cap. 338), s. 28; Labour Tribunal (Cap. 25, s. 32(1); Copyright Tribunal (Cap. 528), s. 176(1); Inland Revenue Ordinance (Cap. 112), s. 69(1); Trade Mark Ordinance (Cap. 43), ss 48 and 50; Buildings Ordinance (Cap. 123), s. 7(4)(a); Arbitration Ordinance (Cap. 341), s. 23.
683. High Court Ordinance, s. 12(3)(a), (b).

Hong Kong courts are entitled to exercise jurisdiction over criminal offences committed within the territorial limits of the Hong Kong Special Administrative Region. However, the courts may be given extra-territorial jurisdiction by statute.[684]

389. The Basic Law provides that the principle of trial by jury previously practised in Hong Kong shall be maintained.[685] Basic Law does not create a new right to a trial by jury but merely guarantees that the pre-existing judicial practice will continue to be maintained. It is well established in Hong Kong that there is no right to a trial by jury.[686] Every person to be tried before the Court of First Instance must be tried on an indictment[687] and usually before a single judge and jury.[688] At common law, the verdict of the jury must be unanimous. However, this requirement has been relaxed and under the Jury Ordinance a majority verdict is binding. Normally a jury consists of seven jurors, but the court may direct that the jury consist of nine members. Where the jury consists of seven jurors the verdict must be supported by at least five of them, and where the jury consists of nine jurors at least seven of them must agree.[689]

IV. Appellate Criminal Jurisdiction of the Court of First Instance

390. The Court of First Instance has such appellate jurisdiction as may be conferred upon it by law.[690] The appellate criminal jurisdiction of the High Court as conferred by statute relate to:

(1) Appeal from a Magistrate by case stated as regards a point of law following trial of summary offence.[691]
(2) Appeal from a Magistrate by the defendant.[692]
(3) An application for review by the Chief Executive following conviction by a Magistrate, which would then be dealt with as if it were an appeal by the defendant.[693]

684. *See,* e.g., Crimes Ordinance (Cap. 200), ss 19–22 23(B)(1); 23(B)(2), 23(B)(4); Dumping at Sea Ordinance (Cap. 466); Criminal Jurisdiction Ordinance (Cap. 461).
685. Basic Law, Art. 86.
686. *Chiang Lily v Secretary for Justice* [2009] HKEC 1562, (CA), referring to *David Lam Shu-Tsang v Attorney General* [1977] HKEC 140, (CA), [5] where Pickering JA reviewed the case law and said: 'The scheme of the [Magistrates Ordinance] was clear beyond a peradventure and it entailed, with equal clarity, the deprivation of the former common law right to trial by jury.'
687. Criminal Procedure Ordinance, s. 41(1).
688. *Ibid.*, s. 41(2).
689. Jury Ordinance (Cap. 3), s. 24(3).
690. High Court Ordinance, s. 12(3)(b).
691. Magistrates Ordinance (Cap. 227), s. 105.
692. *Ibid.*, s. 113.
693. *Ibid.*, s. 113(1)(a).

V. Supervisory Jurisdiction of Court of First Instance

391. As the highest court of original jurisdiction, the Court of First Instance exercises supervisory jurisdiction over inferior courts such as the District Court, Magistrates Courts, coroner's courts and tribunals. In the exercise of its supervisory jurisdiction, the Court of First Instance is empowered to grant relief by way of judicial review. Such relief includes the remedies of *mandamus*, prohibition, *certiorari*[694] and injunction.[695] It may issue a writ of habeas corpus[696] and may grant declaratory relief.[697] In certain cases, the Court is also empowered to grant damages.[698] An application for judicial review cannot be made without the leave of the Court of First Instance first obtained.[699]

§5. The District Court

392. The District Court was first established in 1953 by the District Court Ordinance[700] as a court of record. The Court has such civil and criminal jurisdiction as are conferred upon it by the District Court Ordinance or any other Enactment.[701]

I. Original Civil Jurisdiction of the District Court

393. The District Court has jurisdiction to hear and determine any action founded upon contract, quasi-contract or tort where the amount of the plaintiff's claim does not exceed HKD 3,000,000.[702] The monetary limit of HKD 3,000,000 excludes: (a) any set-off or any debt or demand the defendant claims or may recover from the plaintiff; (b) any compensation, as defined in section 3 of the Employees' Compensation Ordinance (Cap. 282) paid to the plaintiff under that Ordinance; and (c) any contributory negligence.[703] In cases where the amount or value of the matter in dispute does not exceed HKD 3,000,000, the District Court has jurisdiction to hear and determine any proceedings by way of interpleader.[704]

394. The District Court has jurisdiction to have and determine any action for the recovery of land where the annual rent or the rateable value of the land, determined

694. High Court Ordinance, s. 211(1).
695. *Ibid.*, s. 21J(1).
696. *Ibid.*, s. 22A.
697. *Ibid.*, s. 21K(2).
698. *Ibid.*, s. 21K(4).
699. *Ibid.*, s. 21K(3).
700. District Court Ordinance (Cap. 336), s. 3(1). The District Court Ordinance was amended by the District Court Ordinance No 28 of 2000 to significantly enhance the jurisdiction of the District Court in civil matters.
701. *Ibid.*, s. 3(2).
702. *Ibid.*, s. 32(1).
703. *Ibid.*, s. 32(2).
704. *Ibid.*, s. 32(3).

in accordance with the Rating Ordinance (Cap. 116) or the annual value of the land, whichever is the least, does not exceed HKD 3,200,000.[705]

395. The District Court has jurisdiction to hear and determine any action in which the title to an interest in land comes into question.[706] The District Court has the equitable jurisdiction of the Court of First Instance in the following proceedings:[707]

(1) proceedings relating to or for the administration of the estate of a deceased person;
(2) proceedings for the execution of any trust or for a declaration that a trust subsists or proceedings under section 3 of the Variation of Trusts Ordinance (Cap. 253);
(3) proceedings for the foreclosure or redemption of a mortgage or for enforcing a charge or lien;
(4) proceedings for the specific performance, or for the rectification, rescission or delivery up or cancellation of an agreement for the sale, purchase or lease of property;
(5) proceedings for the maintenance or advancement of an infant;
(6) proceedings for the dissolution or winding up of a partnership, whether or not the existence of the partnership is in dispute;
(7) proceedings for relief against fraud or mistake.

396. The above equitable jurisdiction of the District Court is subject to monetary limits.[708]

397. The District Court has jurisdiction and powers of the Court of First Instance conferred by section 6 of the Married Persons Status Ordinance.[709]

398. The District Court Ordinance makes detailed provisions for the transfer of cases from and to the District Court.[710]

399. In the exercise of its jurisdiction, the District Court has the same power as the Court of First Instance in any proceedings before it to grant such relief, redress or remedy or a combination of remedies, either absolute or conditional, and to give effect to every ground of defence or counterclaim, equitable or legal.[711] In the exercise of the above jurisdiction, the Court has to apply both law and equity, and in the event of conflict between the two, the rules of equity will prevail.[712]

705. *Ibid.*, s. 35.
706. *Ibid.*, s. 36(a) and (b).
707. *Ibid.*, s. 37.
708. *Ibid.*, s. 37(2).
709. *Ibid.*, s. 38. Married Persons Status Ordinance (Cap. 182).
710. *See* District Court Ordinance (Cap. 336), ss 41–44.
711. *Ibid.*, s. 48(1)(a) and (b).
712. *Ibid.*, s. 48(2).

400. The District Court has the power to grant and to enforce injunctions of whatsoever nature and as the case may require and to make binding declarations of right, for instance in all matters affecting movable property subject to an upper monetary value of HKD 3 million, with respect to any apprehended distress.[713]

401. The District Court has the jurisdiction to make an order prohibiting a person from leaving Hong Kong to facilitate the enforcement, securing, or pursuance of a judgment against that person.[714]

II. Original Criminal Jurisdiction of the District Court

402. Being principally a court of civil jurisdiction, the District Court enjoys only a limited criminal jurisdiction. It may exercise jurisdiction when the Secretary for Justice refers criminal charges as he may lawfully do according to the provisions of the District Court Ordinance.[715]

403. A charge or complaint may be transferred to the District Court under the Magistrates Ordinance.[716] Under the provisions of the Magistrates Ordinance, whenever any person is accused before a Magistrate of any indictable offence,[717] upon application made by the Secretary for Justice the Magistrate must make an order transferring the charge or complaint to the District Court.[718] Where an indictment has been preferred against a person and before he is arraigned, the Secretary for Justice may apply to the Court of First Instance for an order that the proceedings against the accused person be transferred to the District Court.[719]

404. The sentencing powers of the District Court are limited by law. The maximum period of imprisonment that can be imposed by the District Court is seven years in respect of one offence. Where two or more consecutive terms of imprisonment are imposed by the court the aggregate of the terms of imprisonment must not exceed seven years.[720] Any sentence of imprisonment imposed in default of payment of a fine must not exceed one year.[721]

405. Examples of jurisdiction conferred on the District Court include:

713. *Ibid.*, s. 52(1)(a)(b)(c) and (d).
714. *Ibid.*, s. 52E. For the requirements to be satisfied before such a Prohibition Order can be obtained, *see* District Court Ordinance, ss 52E (2) and (3).
715. District Court Ordinance (Cap. 336), s. 74 which clarifies that the term 'lawfully prefer' refers to the provisions of s. 75 of the District Court Ordinance and offences under s. 41 of the Labour Tribunal Ordinance.
716. That is, Part IV of the Magistrates Ordinance (Cap. 227). *See also* the Magistrates Ordinance, Sch. 2, Part III for the list of offences over which the District Court has no jurisdiction.
717. This excludes offences specified in the Magistrates Ordinance, Sch. 2 Part III.
718. *Ibid.*, s. 88(1)(a).
719. Criminal Procedure Ordinance (Cap. 221), s. 65F(1).
720. District Court Ordinance, s. 82(2)(a).
721. *Ibid.*, s. 82(2)(b).

(1) Jurisdiction to award costs to the prosecutor in criminal cases.[722]
(2) Jurisdiction to award compensation to any aggrieved party (victims of crime). Such an order may be made against the convicted person.[723]
(3) Jurisdiction to order restitution of property in case of conviction.[724]
(4) Jurisdiction to order seizure of property.[725]
(5) Jurisdiction to make a criminal bankruptcy order.[726]

406. The District Court has sufficient powers to punish offenders for contempt of court.[727] On being found guilty of contempt, the offender may be sentenced to a term of imprisonment not exceeding two years or to a fine for every such offence.[728]

407. Under the Labour Tribunal Ordinance if in any proceedings before the Labour Tribunal it appears to the presiding officer that a person has interfered with a witness or committed perjury, the presiding officer may order such person to appear before a judge of the District Court to answer to the charge.[729]

§6. The Magistracies

408. Magistrates Courts were formally recognized for the first time by the Basic Law.[730] Prior to this, there was no statutory reference to Magistrates Courts, although the Governor was empowered to appoint Magistrates to exercise prescribed jurisdiction. The Magistrates Ordinance expressly provides for the constitution of magistrates rather than Magistrates Courts.[731] Magistrates Courts were popularly known as magistracies, a term that continues in currency today. The Long Title of the Magistrates Ordinance states that the objective of the Ordinance is 'to provide for the jurisdiction of magistrates and the procedure and practice before magistrates in relation to offences punishable on summary conviction, the transfer of charges to the District Court and the committal of persons charges with indictable offences and other purposes'. The Hong Kong Reunification Ordinance provided for the continuation in office of magistrates holding office immediately before 1 July 1997 as magistrates of the Hong Kong Special Administrative Region.[732]

722. Costs in Criminal Cases Ordinance (Cap. 492), s. 12.
723. Criminal Procedure Ordinance, s. 73(1). *See also* Theft Ordinance (Cap. 210), s. 30(1)(c).
724. Criminal Procedure Ordinance, s. 84(1).
725. *Ibid.*, s. 103.
726. *Ibid.*, s. 84A(3).
727. District Court Ordinance, s. 20(1)(a) and (b).
728. *Ibid.*, s. 20(i) and (ii).
729. Labour Tribunal Ordinance (Cap. 25), s. 41(2); District Court Ordinance, s. 74.
730. Basic Law, Art. 81.
731. Part I of the Magistrates Ordinance (Cap. 227) is entitled 'Constitution of Magistrates' and provides for the appointment of permanent and special magistrates.
732. Hong Kong Reunification Ordinance, No 110 of 1997 (Cap. A601), s. 9(1) provides as follows: 'The District Court, magistracies and every other court (apart from the Supreme Court), statutory tribunal or statutory board in existence immediately before 1 July 1997 are on that date established

Magistrates are divided into two categories – permanent and special. In the case of special Magistrates, their jurisdiction and powers are limited by the terms of their appointment.[733]

409. The Magistrates Courts are inferior courts of record with exclusive jurisdiction in criminal cases. Magistrates exercise a wide and varied jurisdiction. These include:

(1) Issuing summonses[734] and warrants of arrest.[735]
(2) The conduct of trials of both summary[736] and indictable offences.[737]
(3) Determining applications for extradition.[738]
(4) Execution of judgments.[739]
(5) Power to award compensation[740] and restitution of property in certain cases.[741]
(6) Power to revise their own decisions.[742]

410. A permanent Magistrate is empowered to exercise all the jurisdiction and powers conferred on a Magistrate by any enactment in force in Hong Kong and also such jurisdiction and powers as may from time to time be conferred on a permanent Magistrate.[743]

411. A special Magistrate can, subject to the provisions of his warrant of appointment, exercise all the jurisdiction conferred on a Magistrate by any enactment, but his powers of imposing imprisonment and fine will, in the case of any enactment in force on 20 May 1949, be subject to the limitation as to the maximum term or terms of imprisonment and the maximum fine that such Magistrate might lawfully impose under the Magistrates Ordinance as amended from time to time and, in the case of any enactment coming into force after 20 May 1949, be so subject unless such enactment expressly provides to the contrary.[744]

---

as the District Court, magistracies, courts, statutory tribunals and statutory boards, as the case may be, of the Hong Kong Special Administrative Region.'

733. *See* Magistrates Ordinance, s. 5(1) and (3).
734. *Ibid.*, s. 8.
735. *Ibid.*, s. 9.
736. *Ibid.*, Part II, ss 7–68.
737. *Ibid.*, Part IV, ss 91–94A.
738. Fugitive Offenders Ordinance (Cap. 503), ss 7 and 10(1).
739. Magistrates Ordinance, ss 51, 52, 59 and 60.
740. *Ibid.*, ss 98 and 100(1).
741. Criminal Procedure Ordinance (Cap. 221), ss 84(1) and (2).
742. Magistrates Ordinance, s. 104(9); *Attorney General v Chan Wah-chuen* [1988] 2 HKLR 559, (HC); *HKSAR v Chan Pak Hoe* [2012] HKEC 941, (CFA).
743. *Ibid.*, s. 5(2).
744. Magistrates Ordinance, s. 5(3).

§7. Independence of the Judiciary

412. The rule of law and the separation of powers, which underlie Hong Kong's constitutional system, demand that the judiciary be protected from legislative and executive interference and influence. Judicial independence is vital for the success of Hong Kong's unique constitutional arrangement of 'One Country, Two Systems' and the high degree of autonomy guaranteed to Hong Kong under the Basic Law.

413. The principal function of the judiciary is settlement of disputes. In order to ensure that disputes are settled by a competent and unbiased judiciary, it is important that judges are appointed solely on the basis of their competence and experience and that adequate provision be made to secure their independence. The Basic Law clearly intends to safeguard independence of the judiciary.[745] Article 85 of the Basic Law sets out the importance of the independence of the judiciary in the performance of its duties: 'The courts of the Hong Kong Administrative Region shall exercise judicial power independently, free from any interference. Members of the judiciary shall be immune from legal action in the performance of their judicial functions.' This provision has two limbs: (1) No person or entity shall interfere with the exercise of the judicial power, which is exclusively vested in the judiciary.[746] This is of particular importance in relation to the other two branches of the government, who are in a position to influence judiciary by threats or favours. (2) Judges are immune from legal action in the performance of their judicial functions.

414. The first limb insulates the judiciary from outside influence and interference and for this purpose special provision has been made to ensure impartial decision-making in relation to appointment, transfer and disciplinary control of judges. Other safeguards include prohibiting the unjustified criticism of the judiciary which constitutes contempt of court.[747] 'Contempt can take many different forms. A disruptive outburst in the courtroom itself is one example; a refusal to be sworn or to answer questions is another.[748] Outside the courtroom, contempt may

745. *See* Basic Law, s. 4 'The Judiciary', especially Arts 85, 88, 91 and 92.
746. *See Secretary for Justice v Leung Kwok Hung* [2020] HKEC 1118, (CA), [72] where, while recognising the Legislative Council's exclusive jurisdiction to deal with its internal matters, including penal jurisdiction in respect of contempt of the Legislative Council, the Court of Appeal observed that in relation to certain matters the legislature's exclusive jurisdiction did not affect the judicial power of the courts: 'By virtue of the criminal offences in Part IV, both the Legislative Council and the courts have different, overlapping, jurisdiction over contempt of legislature. Legislative Council can take disciplinary proceedings against the person guilty of such contempt; the courts can try him for the crime. That being the case, careful consideration must be given to see if a prosecution is warranted for a particular case. For example, if the Legislative Council has already commenced disciplinary proceedings against an offending member, careful consideration should be given to as to whether a prosecution is in the public interest. Accordingly, section 26 of the Legislative Council (Powers and Privileges) Ordinance (Cap 382) provides that no prosecution for an offence under the Ordinance shall be instituted except with the consent of the Secretary for Justice. The Secretary must consider if it is in the public interest to bring the prosecution.'
747. *See* Tom Allen, 'Scandalising the Court: The Impact of the Bills of Rights' (2002) 10:1 *Asia Pacific Law Review* 1.
748. Or giving false statements: *Mathnasium Center Licensing LLC v Chang Chi Hung (no 2)* [2019] 4 HKLRD 565, (CFI).

be committed by refusing to obey a court order[749] or by obstructing court process or officers. [It may take] the form of a publication which interferes with the administration of justice. This may also take several forms. Sub judice contempt involves a publication which creates a real or substantial risk of prejudicing the conduct of a fair trial. Scandalising the court applies after the trial is over, where the only risk is to the administration of justice generally. If a publication contains criticism or imputations of wrongdoing that are serious enough to interfere with the administration of justice, a contempt has been committed.'[750]

415. The second limb of Article 85 of the Basic Law provides as follows: 'Members of the judiciary shall be immune from legal action in the performance of their judicial functions.' The principle of judicial immunity, a long established principle of common law, means that when a member of the judiciary of any rank performs his judicial functions, he is protected against liability in a civil action for damages, even where he may be mistaken in fact or in law.[751] The immunity of judges and judicial officers is absolute.[752] The purpose of the principle of judicial immunity is not to protect the personal interests of judges, but to protect the public interest in an independent and impartial justice system. In performing their judicial functions, judges must be able to make decisions without fear. Any errors they make may be corrected on appeal, but they should not have to fear that they may be threatened by dissatisfied litigants with civil actions alleging malice, bias, or excess of jurisdiction.[753] 'Judicial functions are not limited to deciding cases. In view of society's demands and expectations of the judicial system, most of the time, judges and other judicial officers have to conduct hearings on case management and to make decisions on related arrangements, so as to ensure the fair disposal of cases quickly and effectively. The hearings and decisions made on procedural matters by members of

749. *See* for instance, *Kao, Lee and Yip v Donald Koo Hoi Yan* (2009) 12 HKCFAR 830, (CFA) and *BT v CBY* [2020] HKEC 1300, (CA).

750. Tom Allen, 'Scandalising the Court: The Impact of the Bills of Rights' [2002] 10:1 Asia Pacific Law Review 1. For instance, in *Wong Yeung Ng v Secretary for Justice* [1999] HKEC 1330, (CFA), the Court of Final Appeal found the editor of the Oriental Daily News in contempt in respect of a campaign of harassment directed at members of the Obscene Articles Tribunal and the judiciary. At [11] the Court observed as follows: 'The constitutional right of free speech as contained in the Basic Law, adopting the norms set out in the International Covenant on Civil and Political Rights, is not an absolute right. Every civilized community is entitled to protect itself from malicious conduct aimed at undermining the due administration of justice. It is an important aspect of the preservation of the rule of law. Where the contemnor goes way beyond reasoned criticism of the judicial system and acts in bad faith, as the applicant has done in this case, the guarantee of free speech cannot protect him from punishment.'

751. *Ma Kwai Chun v Queeny KY Au-Yeung* [2002] CHKEC 4914, citing *Sirros v Moore* [1975] 1 QB 118, (CA).

752. *Ma Kwai Chun v Leong Siu Chung* [2001–2003] HKCLRT 286, (CA).

753. *Royer v Mignault* (1988) 50 DLR (4th) 345, cited in *Ma Kwai Chun v Queeny KY Au-Yeung* [2002] CHKEC 4914 (CFI). *See also Tam Kei Kam v HSBC International Trustee Ltd* [2014] HKEC 1189, (CA), [5], where the Court of Appeal reiterated the absolute nature of judicial immunity: 'The common law principle of judicial immunity is both ancient and well settled. That a judge is absolutely immune from personal civil liability for any judicial act done in his capacity as a judge, irrespective of whether he acted under gross error or negligence, or was actuated by envy, hatred and malice and all uncharitableness is well recognized by the law.'

the judiciary are actually part of the process of the court in the enforcement of judgments which are inseparable.'[754] An action against an individual judge challenging his decision would be a violation of judicial immunity, and the result would be the same if the action is brought against the judiciary.[755]

I. Appointment and Removal of Judges of the Court of Final Appeal

416. The Head of the Hong Kong Judiciary[756] is the Chief Justice[757] who is also the President of the Court of Final Appeal.[758] The Chief Justice is appointed by the Chief Executive acting on the recommendation of the Judicial Officers Recommendation Commission.[759] It is a mandatory requirement that the Chief Justice be a Chinese citizen with no right of abode in any foreign country. A Justice of Appeal or a judge of the Court of First Instance appointed as Chief Justice must cease to be a Justice of Appeal or a judge of the Court of First Instance.[760] Where the Chief Justice is unable to perform his duties due to illness or is absent for any reason, the Chief Executive must appoint the next most senior permanent judge, who is eligible to be appointed as the Chief Justice, to act as Chief Justice, with all the powers and functions of the Chief Justice.[761]

417. A permanent judge[762] of the Court of Final Appeal is appointed by the Chief Executive acting on the recommendation of the Judicial Officers Recommendation Commission.[763] If the office of any permanent judge becomes vacant by death or otherwise, and the number of permanent judges is reduced to less than three, the Chief Executive, acting in accordance with the recommendation of the Judicial Officers Recommendation Commission, must as soon as reasonably possible after the office becomes vacant appoint a replacement.[764]

---

754. *Ma Kwai Chun v Queeny KY Au-Yeung* [2002] CHKEC 4914, (CFI), [17].
755. *T v The Judiciary* [2018] CHKEC 709, (DC). The above view of judicial immunity was recently endorsed by the Court of Appeal in *Chong Yu On v Kwan SH Susan* [2020] 2 HKLRD 407, (CA).
756. As the head of the Hong Kong judiciary, the Chief Justice is charged with the administration of the judiciary and such other functions as may from time to time be lawfully conferred on him; *see* Hong Kong Court of Final Appeal Ordinance, s. 6(2).
757. The qualifications for a person to be eligible for appointment as Chief Justice are laid down in the Hong Kong Court of Final Appeal Ordinance, s. 12(1): (i) a permanent judge, (ii) the Chief Judge of the High Court, a Justice of Appeal or a judge of the Court of First Instance, or (iii) a barrister who has practised as a barrister or solicitor in Hong Kong for a period of at least ten years.
758. Hong Kong Court of Final Appeal Ordinance, s. 16(2).
759. *Ibid.*, s. 6(1).
760. *Ibid.*, s. 6(3).
761. *Ibid.*, s. 5(6). For determination of seniority, *see* s. 11.
762. The following persons are eligible for appointment as a permanent judge, namely: (a) the Chief Judge of the High Court, a Justice of Appeal, or a judge of the Court of First Instance or (b) a barrister who has practised as a barrister or solicitor in Hong Kong for a period of at least ten years. However, special provisions were made in respect of eligibility for appointment for the first permanent judges prior to the hearing of the first appeal, so that a retired Chief Judge of the High Court, Justice of Appeal or a judge of the Court of First Instance was eligible for appointment.
763. Hong Kong Court of Final Appeal Ordinance, s. 7(1).
764. *Ibid.*, s. 7(2).

418. The non-permanent judges are appointed by the Chief Executive on the recommendation of the Judicial Officers Recommendation Committee.[765]

419. A person who has been appointed as the Chief Justice, a permanent judge or a non-permanent judge are thereafter not entitled to practise as a barrister or solicitor in Hong Kong.[766]

420. The Chief Executive must obtain the endorsement of the Legislative Council in respect of the appointment of all judges of the Court of Final Appeal, and he must also report the appointment to the NPCSC of the People's Republic of China in accordance with the provisions of the Basic Law.[767]

II. Security of Tenure of Judges of the Court of Final Appeal

421. It is a well-established principle in common law jurisdictions that judges, especially those of the superior courts, hold office during good behaviour. The Court of Final Appeal Ordinance gives clear recognition to this principle when it states that a judge may be removed from office only for inability to discharge his duties, whether arising from infirmity of body or mind or from any other cause, or for misbehaviour.[768] The Chief Justice may be removed only by the Chief Executive on the recommendation of a tribunal of judges appointed by the Chief Executive and consisting of not fewer than five members each of whom is either a permanent judge or a non-permanent judge of the Court of Final Appeal.[769] A permanent judge or a non-permanent judge of the Court of Final Appeal may be removed only by the Chief Executive on the recommendation of a tribunal of judges appointed by the Chief Justice and consisting of not fewer than three members each one of whom is either a permanent judge or a non-permanent judge of the Court of Final Appeal.[770] Provision is made to suspend a judge from office pending the investigation by the tribunal.[771] To what extent the tribunal procedure is effective in safeguarding security of tenure and thereby judicial independence remains to be seen.[772]

422. The age of retirement of the Chief Justice and the other permanent judges of the Court of Final Appeal is 65 years. The terms of office of the Chief Justice or a permanent judge may be extended for not more than two periods of three years.[773] There is no retiring age for non-permanent judges, who are appointed for a term of

765. *Ibid.*, s. 8(2) and s. 9(2).
766. *Ibid.*, s. 13.
767. *Ibid.*, s. 7A(1) and Basic Law, Art. 90.
768. *Ibid.*, s. 14(6).
769. *Ibid.*, s. 14(7).
770. *Ibid.*, s. 14(8).
771. *Ibid.*, s. 14(9).
772. The Malaysian experience of 1987 whereby a number of judges of the Supreme Court of Malaysia were removed by the tribunal procedure highlighted the weakness of the system.
773. Hong Kong Court of Final Appeal Ordinance, s. 14(2)(a).

three years, which may be extended for one or more periods of three years.[774] The Chief Executive must obtain the endorsement of the Legislative Council for the removal of any judge of the Court of Final Appeal and must report the removal to the NPC in accordance with the provisions of the Basic Law.[775]

III. Appointment and Removal of Judges of the High Court

423. The office of the CJHC was created for the first time with effect from 1 July 1997. Like the Chief Justice, it is also a requirement that the CJHC must be a Chinese citizen who is a permanent resident of Hong Kong with no right of abode in any foreign country.[776] The Chief Judge is appointed by the Chief Executive on the recommendation of the Judicial Officers Recommendation Committee.[777] His appointment must be endorsed by the Legislative Council and reported to the NPCSC for the record.[778] Similarly, the other judges of the High Court are also appointed by the Chief Executive on the recommendation of the Judicial Officers Recommendation Committee.[779] The Basic Law expressly provides that all judges in Hong Kong must be chosen on the basis of their judicial and professional qualities and may be recruited from other common law jurisdictions.[780] Provision is also made for the appointment of recorders[781] and deputy judges. A person who is eligible to be appointed as a judge of the High Court may be appointed a Recorder of the Court of First Instance by the Chief Executive.[782] A recorder is appointed for a period as specified in the instrument by which the appointment is made. A recorder is entitled to exercise all the powers, privileges, and jurisdiction of a judge of the Court of First Instance.[783] Similarly, a person who is eligible to be appointed as a judge of the High Court may be appointed as a deputy judge of the Court of First Instance by the Chief Justice. Such appointments may be made if the office of any judge of the Court of First Instance becomes vacant for any reason or if the Chief Justice considers that the interests of the administration of justice require that a deputy judge be appointed temporarily.[784] Further, the Chief Justice may appoint a deputy judge for the purpose of a specified case or class of cases only, or for a specified period only.[785] The appointment of a deputy judge may be terminated at any

774. *Ibid.*, s. 14(4).
775. *Ibid.*, s. 7A and Basic Law, Art. 90.
776. Basic Law, Art. 90.
777. Judicial Officers Recommendation Commission Ordinance (Cap. 92), s. 6 and Sch. 1. For qualifications necessary for the appointment of Chief Judge of the High Court and the other judges of the High Court, *see* High Court Ordinance, s. 9.
778. Basic Law, Art. 90.
779. High Court Ordinance, s. 6(1).
780. Basic Law, Art. 92.
781. First introduced in 1994 by the Supreme Court (Amendment) Ordinance 1994 (No 80 of 1994).
782. High Court Ordinance, s. 6(A)(1).
783. *Ibid.*, s. 6(A)(3).
784. *Ibid.*, s. 10(1)(b).
785. *Ibid.*, s. 10(3)(a)(b).

time by the Chief Justice.[786] Justices of Appeal are appointed by the Chief Executive on the recommendation of the Judicial Officers Recommendation Commission.[787]

424. The retirement age of a judge of the High Court is 65 years.[788] However, provision is made for the term of office of a High Court judge to be extended for a specified period or periods not exceeding five years in the aggregate.[789] This extension is made by the Chief Executive acting on the recommendation of the Judicial Officers Recommendation Tribunal.[790] A High Court judge may only be removed for inability to discharge his or her duties or for misbehaviour.[791] Removal is effected by the Chief Executive acting on the recommendation of a tribunal appointed by the Chief Justice of the Court of Final Appeal consisting of not less than three local judges.[792]

IV. Appointment and Removal of Judges of the District Court and Magistrates

425. The District Court consists of two or more district judges appointed by the Chief Executive[793] acting on the recommendation of the Judicial Officers Recommendation Commission.[794] The qualifications necessary for appointment as a District Court judge are prescribed in the Ordinance.[795] Provision is also made for the appointment of a deputy district judge by the Chief Justice if: (a) the office of any district judge becomes vacant for any reason, or (b) the Chief Justice considers that the interests of the administration of justice require that a deputy district judge should be appointed temporarily.[796] The Chief Justice is also given the power to appoint a deputy District Judge for: (a) a specified case or class of cases only or (b) for a specified period only.[797] The Chief Justice may terminate the appointment of a deputy district judge at any time.[798] A deputy district judge is entitled to exercise all the jurisdiction, powers and privileges and perform all the duties of a district judge.[799] A district judge must vacate his office when he reaches the age of retirement.[800] Notwithstanding the fact that a district judge has attained the retiring age,

786. *Ibid.*, s. 10(4).
787. Basic Law, Art. 88.
788. High Court Ordinance, s. 114(1), (5).
789. *Ibid.*, s. 11(A)(3)(b).
790. *Ibid.*
791. Basic Law, Art. 89.
792. *Ibid.*
793. District Court Ordinance (Cap. 336), s. 4(1).
794. Judicial Officers Recommendation Commission Ordinance, s. 6, Sch. 1.
795. District Court Ordinance, s. 5.
796. *Ibid.*, s. 7(1).
797. *Ibid.*, s. 7(3).
798. *Ibid.*, s. 7(4).
799. *Ibid.*, s. 7(2).
800. *Ibid.*, s. 11A(1). The retirement age for judges appointed before 1 January 1987 is 60 years of age and for those appointed after that date is 65 years of age (*ibid.*, s. 11A(3)). The term of office of

he may continue in office for so long after attaining retirement age as may be necessary to enable him to deliver judgment or do any other thing in relation to proceedings that had commenced before he attained that age.[801]

426. Magistrates, both permanent and special, are appointed by the Chief Executive.[802] The removal of a Magistrate from office is governed by the Judicial Officers (Tenure of Office) Ordinance.[803] This Ordinance sets out the procedure for disciplinary control and removal of judges of inferior courts and tribunals.[804] If a Magistrate is to be removed from office, the Chief Justice must notify the Magistrate of the particulars of the charge against him and call for a written explanation.[805] If the Magistrate does not furnish a written explanation or fails to provide a justifiable explanation, the Chief Justice must appoint a tribunal of two High Court judges to investigate the matter.[806] On completion of the investigation, the tribunal must submit a report to the Judicial Officers Recommendation Commission, which, based on the report, can recommend to the Chief Executive that the Magistrate be dismissed.[807]

427. Security of tenure of district judges is guaranteed by the Basic Law. A district judge may be removed only for inability to perform his duties or for misbehaviour.[808] Removal is effected by the Chief Executive acting on the recommendation of a tribunal appointed by the Chief Justice of the Court of Final Appeal.[809]

§8. Constitutional Jurisdiction

428. The Basic Law expressly recognizes the constitutional jurisdiction of Hong Kong courts. Article 11 of the Basic Law provides that no law enacted by the legislature of the Hong Kong Special Administrative Region may contrive the Basic Law. The issue of inconsistency of a law passed by the Legislature Council with the Basic Law therefore can be raised before any court in Hong Kong. In addition, Article 158 expressly states *inter alia*:

those district judges retiring with 60 years may be extended for a specified period or for periods not exceeding five years in the aggregate by the Chief Executive acting on the Recommendation of the Judicial Officers Recommendation Commission (*ibid.*, s. 11(3)).

801. *Ibid.*, s. 11A(2).
802. Magistrates Ordinance (Cap. 227), s. 5.
803. Judicial Officers (Tenure of Office) Ordinance (Cap. 433).
804. *Ibid.*, Long title: 'An Ordinance to provide procedures for discipline of judicial officers of certain courts and tribunals.'
805. *Ibid.*, s. 3.
806. *Ibid.*, s. 3(2).
807. *Ibid.*, s. 8.
808. Basic Law, Art. 89.
809. *Ibid.*

> The Standing Committee of the National People's Congress shall authorize the courts of the Hong Kong Special Administrative Region to interpret on their own, in adjudicating cases, the provisions of this Law which are within the limits of the autonomy of the Region.

429. It is further laid down that the courts of the Hong Kong Special Administrative Region may also interpret other provisions of the Basic Law in adjudicating cases.[810]

The interpretation of the Basic Law is crucial to the survival of the 'One Country, Two Systems' principle that underlies Hong Kong's new status as a Special Administrative Region of China. As Yash Ghai explained:[811]

> The Basic Law is a detailed document, with several (and frequently vaguely worded) normative provisions which limit the competence of the legislature and the executive of the region. Furthermore, the Basic Law establishes the relationship between the Central Authorities of the People's Republic of China and the Hong Kong Special Administrative Region; some of these provisions are obscurely worded, necessitating their elaboration through interpretation. The precise demarcation of powers between the Central Authorities and the Hong Kong Special Administrative Region is uncertain, and yet the operation of many provisions of the Basic Law depends on a clear understanding of the division of powers. A crucial task of interpretation must be to maintain the boundaries between the economic, social and political systems of the Hong Kong Special Administrative Region and the rest of China.

430. The Hong Kong Bill of Rights[812] has de facto constitutional status.[813] While the Hong Kong Bill of Rights Ordinance is an ordinary law of Hong Kong and therefore has no special status in the hierarchy of laws, Hong Kong courts consider that the Bill of Rights is a reflection of the ICCPR which continues to be operative in Hong Kong as provided by the Basic Law. There have been a number of cases where important constitutional questions have come up for judicial resolution finding their way into the Court of Final Appeal.[814]

431. The constitutional jurisdiction of the Court of Final Appeal is subject to the provisions of Article 158 of the Basic Law. According to this article, the power of

---

810. *See ibid.*, Art. 158 for a detailed treatment on issues relating to the interpretation of the Basic Law, *see* Yash Ghai, *Hong Kong's New Constitutional Order* (2nd edn, Hong Kong: University Press, 1999), Ch. 5.
811. Yash Ghai, *Hong Kong's New Constitutional Order* (2nd edn, Hong Kong: Hong Kong University Press, 1999) Ch. 5, 189.
812. Embodied in the Hong Kong Bill of Rights Ordinance (Cap. 383).
813. *See* Part IV, Ch. 2 'Fundamental Rights and Liberties'.
814. *See Ng Ka ling v Director of Immigration* [1999] 1 HKCFAR 4, (CFA); *Chan Kam Nga v Director of Immigration* (1999) 2 HKCFAR 82, (CFA); *Lau Kong Yung & Ors v Director of Immigration* (1999) 2 HKCFAR 300, (CFA).

interpretation of the Basic Law shall be vested in the Standing Committee of the National People's Congress. This is plenary in that it covers all the provisions of the Basic Law and it can be exercised in the absence of litigation.[815] This view was endorsed by the Court of Final Appeal in *Lau Kong Yung and Ors v Director of Immigration*.[816] Commenting on the power of interpretation vested in the Standing Committee of the National People's Congress, Li CJ stated:[817]

> It is clear that the Standing Committee has the power to make the interpretation. This power originates from Article 67(4) of the Chinese Constitution and is contained in Article 158(1) of the Basic Law itself. The power of interpretation of the Basic Law confined by act 158(1) is in general and unqualified terms. That power and its exercise is not restricted or qualified in any way by Article 158(2) and 158(3).

432. Following the decision of the Court of Final Appeal in *Ng Ka Ling v Director of Immigration*,[818] the Hong Kong Government requested a reinterpretation of the relevant provisions of the Basic Law relating to the right of abode in Hong Kong.[819] In *Lau Kong Yung & Ors v Director of Immigration*, the Court of Appeal accepted the power of the NPCSC to interpret any provision of the Basic Law.[820] The cumulative effect of the NPCSC's reinterpretation and its unequivocal acceptance by the Court of Final Appeal in *Lau Kong Yung* is that in constitutional matters, the ultimate and final power of interpretation of the Basic Law is exercised not by Hong Kong courts but by a political body, namely the Standing Committee of the National People's Congress. Sir Anthony Mason NPJ said:[821]

> The Standing Committee's power to interpret laws is necessarily exercised from time to time otherwise than in the adjudication of cases. So the expression in adjudicating cases [in Article 158 of the Basic Law] makes it clear that the power of interpretation enjoyed by the courts of the Region is limited in that way and differs from the general and free-standing power of interpretation enjoyed by the Standing Committee under Article 67(4) of the People's Republic of China Constitution and Article 158(1) of the Basic Law. This conclusion may seem strange to a common lawyer but, in my view, it follows inevitably

815. Yash Ghai, *Hong Kong's New Constitutional Order*, (2nd edn, Hong Kong: Hong Kong University Press, 1999) Ch. 5, 198.
816. *Lau Kong Yung and Ors v Director of Immigration* (1999) 2 HKCFAR 300, (CFA), 332–334.
817. *Ibid.*, 332–334.
818. *Ng Ka Ling v Director of Immigration* (1999) 2 HKCFAR 300, (CFA), 332–334.
819. For the text of the interpretation, *see* www.scmp.com/special/right of www.abode/index.asp. On this point, *see* Mark Elliot & Christopher Forsyth, 'The Rule of Law in Hong Kong: Immigrant Children, the Court of Final Appeal and the Standing Committee of the National People's Congress', (2000) 8:1 *Asia Pacific Law Review* 53, 67–73 and Albert H.Y. Chen, 'The Interpretation of the Basic Law– Common Law and Mainland Chinese Perspectives' (2000) 30 *Hong Kong Law Journal* 380.
820. *Lau Kong Yung & Ors v Director of Immigration* (1999) 2 HKCFAR 300, (CFA), 332–334 per Li CJ 341 per Ching PJ, 344–345 per Sir Anthony Mason NPJ.
821. *Ibid.*, 820–821.

from a consideration of the text and structure of Article 158, viewed in the light of the context of the Basic Law as the constitution for the Hong Kong Special Administrative Region embodied in a national law enacted by the People's Republic of China.

§9. Judicial Review

433. It is ingrained in the common law system that courts have an inherent jurisdiction to review administrative decisions.[822] Common law recognizes that the highest court of original jurisdiction (in the case of Hong Kong, the Court of First Instance) has an inherent supervisory jurisdiction over inferior courts and administrative agencies and this supervisory jurisdiction is exercised mainly through judicial review of administrative action. The jurisdiction of the court is invoked by way of application for judicial review under the Rules of the High Court.

822. *See* Part IV, Ch. 4 'Judicial Control of Administrative Action'.

Chapter 6. Independent, Non-political Agencies in the Legislative or Executive Branch

§1. Statutory and Non-statutory Bodies Related to Government Functions

434. The Basic Law provides for the continuation of the previous system of establishing advisory bodies.[823] Hong Kong has developed a network of statutory and non-statutory advisory bodies, which facilitate consultation and assist the government in carrying out its various duties. Some of these advisory bodies help coordinate work between different government agencies (such as the non-statutory Advisory Committee on Arts Development, coordinating the work of the Home Affairs Bureau and the Leisure and Cultural Services Department), perform an important advisory function (such as the statutory Advisory Council on the Environment), or act as adjudicatory agencies (such as the statutory Town Planning Appeal Board).[824]

435. Currently there are over 470 statutory and non-statutory bodies. Statutory bodies include the Administrative Appeals Board, the Town Planning Board, Consumer Council, Heung Yee Kuk (an advisory board on affairs of rural Chinese), Personal Date (Privacy) Advisory Committee and Solicitors' Disciplinary Tribunal Panel. Permanent non-statutory bodies with official and unofficial members include Advisory Committee on Agriculture and Fisheries, Criminal and Law Enforcement Injuries Compensation Boards, Land and Development Advisory Committee, Research Grants Council, Road Safety Research Committee and Trade and Industry Advisory Board. The permanent non-statutory bodies with official members only include Accommodation Strategy Committee, Police Force Council, Senior Civil Service Council and Tender Boards/Consultants Selection Boards.[825]

436. Norman Miners has categorized these statutory and non-statutory bodies as follows:[826]

(1) Those bodies that have been set up to provide expert advice and guidance to the government. These include statutory bodies such as the Exchange Fund Advisory Committee,[827] the Standing Committee on Legal Education and

823. Basic Law, Art. 65.
824. *See* http://www.hab.govhk/en/policy_responsibilities/District_Community_and_Public_Relations/advisory.htm.
825. As of 30 June 2016, there were some 470 advisory bodies. They are listed in the web link in the previous footnote, with links to their webpages.
826. Norman Miners, *The Government and Politics of Hong Kong* (5th edn, Hong Kong: Oxford University Press, 1995), 106–107.
827. Set up under the Exchange Fund Ordinance (Cap. 66), s. 3(1).

Training,[828] Antiquities Advisory Board,[829] and non-statutory bodies such as the Aviation Advisory Board and Advisory Committee on Agriculture and Fisheries.

(2) Those bodies which stimulate action by businesses and other interests in directions which the government considers desirable. They include the Hong Kong Productivity Council and Hong Kong Trade Development Council.

(3) Those bodies that have been set up to take politically embarrassing decisions for which the government prefers to avoid direct responsibility. A good example is the Standing Commission on Civil Service Salaries and Conditions of Service, established in 1979.

(4) Those bodies that have been set up with a view to improving services provided by various government agencies and authorities. They include the Aviation Advisory Board, the Port Operations Committee and the Transport Advisory Committee.

(5) Those bodies that ensure cooperation of voluntary agencies which provide services on the government's behalf. They include the Social Welfare Advisory Committee and the Education Commission.

(6) The government may appoint a committee to inquire into certain matters and advise the government on appropriate measures to be taken. A recent example is the Commission of Inquiry into Excess Lead Found in Drinking Water with the following terms of reference: (a) to ascertain the causes of excess lead found in drinking water in public rental housing developments; (b) to review and evaluate the adequacy of the present regulatory and monitoring system in respect of drinking water in Hong Kong; and (c) to make recommendations with regard to the safety of drinking water in Hong Kong. The commission submitted its report to the Chief Executive in Council in May 2016. The enabling legislation is the Commissions of Inquiry Ordinance (Cap. 86).

437. There are a number of statutory bodies that perform important public functions. The Town Planning Board, which consists of official and unofficial members appointed by the Chief Executive, makes land-use plans and grants planning permission. While the government formulates land-use planning policies, the Town Planning Board adopts any plans proposed by the Planning Department and conducts public consultation before they are passed on to the Chief Executive for approval. No statutory plans may be introduced without the Board's approval. Similarly, no land-use developments that require planning permission may be undertaken without the Board's approval. The other statutory bodies of this type are the Film Censorship Authority set up under the Film Censorship Ordinance (Cap. 392), Consumer Council set up under the Consumer Council Ordinance (Cap. 216), Country and Marine Parks Board set up under the Country Parks Ordinance (Cap. 208), and Antiquities Advisory Board set up under the Antiquities and Monuments Ordinance (Cap. 53).

---

828. Set up under the Legal Practitioners Ordinance (Cap. 159), s. 74A.
829. Set up under the Antiquities and Monuments Ordinance (Cap. 53), s. 17.

438. The Equal Opportunities Commission, set up by the Sex Discrimination Ordinance (Cap. 480), is an important statutory body in the context of the protection of fundamental rights. The aims of the Commission are to promote equality and work towards elimination of discrimination. The Commission is tasked with the implementation of the Sex Discrimination Ordinance (Cap. 480), the Disability Discrimination Ordinance (Cap. 487), the Family Status Discrimination Ordinance (Cap. 527) and the Race Discrimination Ordinance (Cap. 602). The Commission seeks to achieve these aims through legislative reform, education and research. The Commission receives complaints from aggrieved persons, whom it assists by giving advice or by facilitating conciliation or judicial proceedings. It also coordinates and communicates with government and non-government organizations on issues of equal opportunities. It issues codes of practice and guidelines on elimination of discrimination and promotion of equal opportunities.

439. There are a number of statutory tribunals that assist in the smooth operation of government. They include appeal boards that entertain appeals against decisions taken by statutory bodies. The Town Planning Appeal Board, set up under the Town Planning Ordinance (Cap. 131) is an independent statutory body to which any applicant for planning permission who is aggrieved by a decision of the Town Planning Board may appeal. The Environmental Impact Assessment Appeal Board, set up under the Environmental Impact Assessment Ordinance (Cap. 499), entertains appeals against decisions made under the Ordinance. Appeal Boards have been set up under numerous other ordinances such as the Amusement Game Centres Ordinance (Cap. 435), the Clubs (Safety of Premises) Ordinance (Cap. 376) and the Consumer Goods Safety Ordinance (Cap. 456).

440. The most important of the tribunals is the Administrative Appeals Board, which may entertain appeals against statutory decisions taken under a number of ordinances specified in the Administrative Appeals Board Ordinance (Cap. 442). The Administrative Appeals Board Ordinance was enacted in 1994 in order to provide an independent tribunal that would hear appeals that previously were heard by the Governor in Council. It was intended that by creating the new tribunal, the Governor in Council (now, the Chief Executive in Council) would be relieved of appellate responsibility in respect of statutory decisions of minor importance. Decisions against which an appeal may be made to the Board are set out in the Schedule to the Ordinance and include refusal to issue or renew or revoke a licence under a number of ordinances. The Administrative Appeals Board has no power to award compensation, but it may refer a case back to the authority against whose decision the appeal was made, where it considers that the appellant deserves to be compensated. It may award costs of the appeal. The tribunal's hearings are held in public and its decision is final, subject to judicial review.[830]

830. *See*, for instance, *Li Wai Hung Cesario v Administrative Appeals Board* [2016] HKEC 1325, (CA) and *Cheung Moon Hoi Jeff v Administrative Appeals Board* [2016] HKEC 1241, (CA).

§2. NON-GOVERNMENTAL ORGANIZATIONS

441. Hong Kong has a number of Quangos (quasi-autonomous, non-government organizations), and they perform a particularly important function in the social organization. These, such as the Society for the Prevention of Cruelty to Animals, being private bodies, are not generally subject to public law. Where, however, there is a public interest in granting a public law remedy, they may be subject to judicial review proceedings.

442. The Basic Law contains several provisions that promote civil society. Article 144 provides as follows:

> The Government of the Hong Kong Special Administrative Region shall maintain the policy previously practised in Hong Kong in respect of subventions for non-governmental organizations in fields such as education, medicine and health, culture, art, recreation, sports, social welfare, and social work. Staff members previously serving in subvented organizations in Hong Kong may remain in their employment in accordance with the previous system.

443. Article 146 provides that voluntary organizations providing social services in Hong Kong may, on their own, decide their forms of service. Article 148 provides that the relationship between non-governmental organizations in fields such as education, science, technology, culture, art, sports, the professions, medicine and health, labour, social welfare and social work, as well as religious organizations in Hong Kong, will be based on the principles of non-subordination, non-interference and mutual respect. Such non-governmental organizations may maintain and develop relations with their counterparts in foreign countries and regions and with relevant international organizations.[831]

444. The Basic Law provides that while the government may formulate policies in areas such as education,[832] professional qualifications,[833] sports[834] and social welfare,[835] non-governmental organizations may run educational institutions,[836] non-governmental professional organizations may assess and confer professional qualifications,[837] non-governmental sports organizations may continue to exist and

831. Basic Law, Art. 149. However, the Hong Kong Government is under a duty under Art. 23 of the Basic Law to enact legislation to prohibit foreign political organizations or bodies from conducting political activities in Hong Kong, and to prohibit political organizations or bodies of Hong Kong from establishing ties with foreign political organizations or bodies. No law has so far been made in pursuance of Art. 23.
832. *Ibid.*, Art. 136.
833. *Ibid.*, Art. 142.
834. *Ibid.*, Art. 143.
835. *Ibid.*, Art. 145.
836. *Ibid.*, Art. 136.
837. *Ibid.*, Art. 142.

develop,[838] and voluntary organizations providing social services in Hong Kong may decide on their forms of service.[839] An important provision is Article 141 of the Basic Law, which protects religious freedom. It provides that religious organizations may, according to their previous practice, continue to run seminaries and other schools, hospitals, and welfare institutions and to provide other social services. Such organizations and believers may maintain and develop their relations with religious organizations and believers elsewhere.

445. Clubs are a form of social organization. They cover not only sports or recreational clubs but also include trade unions and professional associations, which are important public movements. While clubs derive their power from a contract between members and are therefore governed by private law, there may be appropriate circumstances when public law remedies may be applicable.[840]

838. *Ibid.*, Art. 143.
839. *Ibid.*, Art. 146.
840. *See Ho Man-fat (No 2) v The Royal Hong Kong Jockey Club* (1976) HKLR 452, (HC), where in a private action the court inquired into whether there had been a breach of rules of natural Justice. In *Divisional Commissioner v The Jockey Club exp. Aga Khan* [1993] 1 WLR 909, (CA), where public law remedies were held to be inapplicable. *See also Hong Kong Rifle Association v Hong Kong Shooting Association (No 2)* [2013] HKEC 980, (CA), where the Court of Appeal held that the refusal by the Hong Kong Shooting Association (HKSA) to renew the rifle association's membership in it was not susceptible to judicial review. The Court of Appeal reasoned that the power to decide whether to admit or reinstate a member was derived from its memorandum and articles of association and was consensual and contractual in nature. It could not be said that in making the decision, the HKSA was exercising a public law function or its decision had public law consequences.

Part III. The State and Its Subdivisions

Chapter 1. The Relationship Between the Chinese Central Authorities and the Hong Kong Special Administrative Region

§1. Introduction

446. 'The Government of the United Kingdom of Great Britain and Northern Ireland and the Government of the People's Republic of China have reviewed with satisfaction the friendly relations existing between the two Governments and peoples in recent years and agreed that a proper negotiated settlement of the question of Hong Kong, which is left over from the past, is conducive to the maintenance of the prosperity and stability of Hong Kong and to the further strengthening and development of the relations between the two countries on a new basis.' So begins the Sino-British Joint Declaration of 1984 which led to the establishment of the Special Administrative Region of Hong Kong as an integral part of China but enjoying a high degree of autonomy. In the Joint Declaration, the transfer of sovereignty was described by the Chinese Government as 'resumption' of Hong Kong fulfilling the common aspiration of the entire Chinese people and as 'restoration of Hong Kong to China' by the UK. With the implementation of this agreement, Hong Kong ceased to be a British colony and began its new chapter as a special administrative region of China.

447. The Preamble to the Basic Law is unequivocal about the sovereignty of the People's Republic of China over Hong Kong: 'Hong Kong has been part of the territory of China since ancient times; [the signing of the Sino-British Joint Declaration fulfils] the long-cherished common aspiration of the Chinese People for the recovery of Hong Kong. ... Upholding the national unity and territorial integrity ... the People's Republic of China has decided that upon China's resumption of the exercise of sovereignty over Hong Kong ... [and] hereby enacts the Basic Law ... to ensure the implementation of the basic policies of the People's Republic of China regarding HK.' The ultimate supremacy of the People's Republic of China over Hong Kong is also explicit in the second of the basic policies of the People's Republic of China regarding HK: 'The HK Special Administrative Region will be directly under the authority of the Central People's Government of the People's Republic of China.' This is, however, balanced by the second part of that basic policy: 'The HK

Special Administrative Region will enjoy a high degree of autonomy, except in foreign and defence affairs which are the responsibilities of the Central People's government.' The basic policies are referred to in the next paragraph.

448. Article 3 of the Joint Declaration sets out the basic policies of the People's Republic of China, which were intended to be enshrined in the Basic Law,[841] and begins by declaring that in creating the Hong Kong Special Administrative Region, the Chinese Government emphasizes the importance of upholding national unity and territorial integrity, while at the same time taking account of the history of Hong Kong and its realities. The 'One Country, Two Systems' policy reflects the need to balance Hong Kong's new status as an integral part of China and its unique historical development. Thus, while it comes directly under the authority of the Central People's Government of the People's Republic of China, the Hong Kong Special Administrative Region enjoys a high degree of autonomy, except in foreign and defence affairs which are the responsibilities of the Central People's Government.

449. The background was thus set for Hong Kong to begin a new lease of life, largely free of Chinese Central control, but as an integral part of China. Hong Kong's unique constitutional status is a result of the Chinese authorization for Hong Kong to exercise a high degree of autonomy unique in Chinese local government structure. The termination of the constitutional status of Hong Kong as a British Crown Colony in 1997 did not usher in an era of self-government as in the rest of the former British colonies – for instance, India or Sri Lanka. What took place in 1997 was a transfer of sovereignty over Hong Kong from the UK to the People's Republic of China. Just as Hong Kong was subject to final authority of the government of the UK in all three respects, legislature, executive and judiciary, Hong Kong continues to be subject to the final authority of the Chinese Government in respect of legislative, executive and judicial powers. In this chapter, what we will see is the ironic continuation of the colonial system, subject to some significant changes which grants Hong Kong a degree of autonomy that Hong Kong did not enjoy under the British colonial rule.

450. Hong Kong was not granted self-government completely free of all external control: But it was given a high degree of autonomy which may be likened to a form of quasi self-governance, with a promise of its continuation at least for fifty years from 1997. The guarantee is not that the Hong Kong's way of life will be guaranteed only for fifty years, but at least for fifty years. If the relationship between China and Hong Kong proceed smoothly, Hong Kong will not only continue to enjoy its way of life beyond fifty years but Hong Kong's governance will further improve through appropriate amendments of the Basic Law.

---

841. 'The above-stated basic policies of the People's Republic of China regarding Hong Kong and the elaboration of them in Annex I to this Joint Declaration will be stipulated, in a Basic Law of the Hong Kong Special Administrative Region of the People's Republic of China, by the National People's Congress of the People's Republic of China, and they will remain unchanged for 50 years': Sino-British Joint Declaration of 1884, Art. 3(12).

451. The creation of the Hong Kong Special Administrative Region was accomplished by the enactment of the Basic Law which is a national law of the People's Republic of China, adopted on 4 April 1990 by the Seventh NPC. The creation of the Hong Kong Special Administrative Region was facilitated by Article 31 of the Constitution of People's Republic of China, which sets out one of the general principles of the constitution:

> Article 31. The State may establish special administrative regions when necessary. The systems to be instituted in special administrative regions shall be prescribed by law enacted by the National People's Congress in the light of specific conditions.

452. This provision was adopted, with the constitutional amendment of 1982, to facilitate the unification of China, by bringing into its fold Hong Kong and Macau, and at a future stage Taiwan. The creation of the special administrative regions of Hong Kong and Macau (a former Portuguese colony) is now complete. In order to understand the status of the Basic Law of Hong Kong, as a national law of the People's Republic of China and the Constitution of Hong Kong, it is useful to briefly set out the constitutional context in which China's supreme legislative body, the NPC, operates.

453. The People's Republic of China is a unitary state, and not a federal state, where Hong Kong would have the status of a Member State, such as Texas or Arkansas in the USA. Article 2 of the Constitution of the People's Republic of China provides that 'All power in the People's Republic of China belongs to the people. The organs through which the people exercise state power are the National People's Congress and the local people's congresses at different levels.' Article 57 of the Constitution of the People's Republic of China provides that 'The National People's Congress of the People's Republic of China is the highest organ of state power. Its permanent body is the Standing Committee of the National People's Congress.' Article 58 provides that the National People's Congress and its Standing Committee exercise the legislative power of the State. Article 59 provides that the National People's Congress is made up of deputies elected from the provinces, autonomous regions, municipalities directly under the Central Government, and special administrative regions, and of deputies elected from the armed forces. It goes on to affirm that all the minority nationalities are entitled to appropriate representation. Articles 60 and 61 provide that the National People's Congress, which is elected for a term of five years, meets in session once a year and is convened by its Standing Committee.

454. As provided in Article 62, its powers include the power: (1) to amend the Constitution; (2) to supervise the enforcement of the Constitution; (3) to enact and amend basic laws governing criminal offences, civil affairs, the State organs and other matters; and (4) to decide on the establishment of special administrative regions and the systems to be instituted there. The NPC also has constitutive power: As provided in Article 64 amendments to the Constitution are to be proposed by the

NPCSC or by more than one-fifth of the deputies to the NPC and adopted by a vote of more than two-thirds of all the deputies to the National People's Congress.

455. The legislative functions in China are exercised by the NPC and its Standing Committee. Article 62(3) of the Chinese Constitution provides that the NPC has the power to enact and amend basic laws concerning criminal offences, civil affairs, the state organs and other matters: Article 67(2) provides that the Standing Committee has the power to enact and amend statutes with the exception of those which should be enacted by the National People's Congress. The Standing Committee also has the power to interpret the Constitution and supervise its enforcement: Article 67(2). It exercises the power of interpreting statutes and performs a legislative gap-filling function: As provided in Article 67, it has the power: (1) to interpret statutes; (2) to enact, when the NPC is not in session, partial supplements and amendments to statutes enacted by the NPC provided that they do not contravene the basic principles of such laws; and (3) to annul those local regulations or decisions of the organs of state power of provinces, autonomous regions and municipalities directly under the Central Government that contravene the Constitution, the statutes or the administrative rules and regulations.[842]

456. While legislative power is vested in the NPC and its Standing Committee, administrative power is vested in the State Council, which operates under the supervision of the National People's Congress. The State Council, that is, the Central People's Government, is the executive body of the highest organ of state power and the highest organ of state administration (Article 85). As stated in Article 89 the State Council has the power to do the following:

(1) to adopt administrative measures, enact administrative rules and regulations and issue decisions and orders in accordance with the Constitution and the statutes;
(2) to submit proposals to the National People's Congress or its Standing Committee;
(3) to lay down the tasks and responsibilities of the ministries and commissions of the State Council, to exercise unified leadership over the work of the ministries and commissions and to direct all other administrative work of a national character that does not fall within the jurisdiction of the ministries and commissions;
(4) to exercise unified leadership over the work of local organs of state administration at different levels throughout the country, and to lay down the detailed division of functions and powers between the Central Government and the organs of state administration of provinces, autonomous regions and municipalities directly under the Central Government;
(5) to draw up and implement the plan for national economic and social development and the state budget;

842. The distribution of legislative power between the National People's Congress and its Standing Committee is further elaborated in Legislation Law of the People's Republic of China of 2000, as amended in 2015.

(6) to direct and administer economic work and urban and rural development;
(7) to direct and administer the work concerning education, science, culture, public health, physical culture and family planning;
(8) to direct and administer the work concerning civil affairs, public security, judicial administration, supervision and other related matters;
(9) to conduct foreign affairs and conclude treaties and agreements with foreign States;
(10) to direct and administer the building of national defence;
(11) to direct and administer affairs concerning the nationalities and to safeguard the equal rights of minority nationalities and the right of autonomy of the national autonomous areas;
(12) to protect the legitimate rights and interests of Chinese nationals residing abroad and protect the lawful rights and interests of returned overseas Chinese and of the family members of Chinese nationals residing abroad;
(13) to alter or annul inappropriate orders, directives and regulations issued by the ministries or commissions;
(14) to alter or annul inappropriate decisions and orders issued by local organs of state administration at different levels;
(15) to approve the geographic division of provinces, autonomous regions and municipalities directly under the Central Government, and to approve the establishment and geographic division of autonomous prefectures, counties, autonomous counties and cities;
(16) in accordance with the provisions of the law, to decide on entering into the state of emergency in parts of provinces, autonomous regions and municipalities directly under the Central Government;
(17) to examine and decide on the size of administrative organs and, in accordance with the law, to appoint, remove and train administrative officers, appraise their work and reward or punish them; and
(18) to exercise such other functions and powers as the National People's Congress or its Standing Committee may assign it.

457. In this scheme of things, the role of the Chinese judiciary is fairly muted. The people's courts of the People's Republic of China are the judicial organs of the State (Article 123). People's courts exercise judicial power, in accordance with the law, independently and are not subject to interference by administrative organs, public organizations or individuals (Article 126). The highest judicial organ is the Supreme People's Court, which supervises people's courts at various local levels and special courts, while people's courts at higher levels supervise people's courts at lower levels (Article 127). The Supreme People's Court is responsible to the NPC and its Standing Committee while local people's courts at various levels are responsible to the organs of state power which created them (Article 128). While administration of justice is in the hands of the judiciary, it has not been given power to interpret the Constitution or to invalidate legislative or administrative actions taken by the NPC or the State Council on account of unconstitutionality.

458. It is important to keep in mind that just as much as Hong Kong would like to emphasize the 'Two Systems' part of the 'One Country, Two Systems' formula,

China emphasizes the primacy of the 'One Country' part. A whitepaper entitled 'The Practice of the 'One Country, Two Systems' Policy in the Hong Kong Special Administrative Region' (issued on 10 June 2014 by the Information Office of the State Council of the PRC) asserted:

> As prescribed in the Constitution of the People's Republic of China and the Basic Law of the Hong Kong Special Administrative Region, the organs of power by which the central leadership directly exercises jurisdiction over the Hong Kong Special Administrative Region are the National People's Congress and its Standing Committee, the President of the state, the Central People's Government and the Central Military Commission. The National People's Congress decided on the establishment of the Hong Kong Special Administrative Region, formulated the Basic Law of the Hong Kong Special Administrative Region to prescribe the system to be instituted in the Hong Kong Special Administrative Region and has retained the power to amend the Basic Law. The National People's Congress Standing Committee has the power of interpretation regarding the Basic Law of the Hong Kong Special Administrative Region, the power of decision on revising the selection methods of the Chief Executive and the Legislative Council of the Hong Kong Special Administrative Region, the power of supervision over the laws formulated by the legislative organs of the Hong Kong Special Administrative Region, the power of decision on the Hong Kong Special Administrative Region entering a state of emergency and the power of making new authorization for the Hong Kong Special Administrative Region. The Hong Kong Special Administrative Region comes directly under the Central People's Government and its Chief Executive is accountable to the Central People's Government. The Central People's Government appoints the Chief Executive and the principal officials, is responsible for foreign affairs relating to the Hong Kong Special Administrative Region in accordance with the law and issues directives to the Chief Executive. The Central Military Commission is the leading body of the Hong Kong garrison, and performs defence and other duties. The Central Authorities perform overall jurisdiction and constitutional duties as prescribed in the Constitution of the People's Republic of China and in the Basic Law of the Hong Kong Special Administrative Region, and exercise effective administration over the Hong Kong Special Administrative Region.

459. The above description of the background to the creation of Hong Kong Special Administrative Region and the constitutional system of the People's Republic of China provides the backdrop against which the relationship between Central Authorities of the People's Republic of China and Hong Kong Special Administrative Region may be properly understood. At the outset, it must be kept in mind that the authority that China has over Hong Kong is significantly less than the authority it has over municipalities and other local authorities elsewhere in Mainland China that operate directly under the overarching central control of the Chinese Government. The Hong Kong Special Administrative Region is different from provinces, municipalities and ethnic autonomous regions of China. It operates under a specially created constitutional arrangement which guarantees that to a significant extent Hong Kong operates on its own in the exercise of its unique high degree of autonomy.

460. Upon resumption of sovereignty over Hong Kong, the Mainland Chinese Government did not fully integrate Hong Kong into the socio-economic-political and legal structure of Mainland China. Hong Kong was given a special status in the Chinese constitutional framework as a Special Administrative Region with a high degree of autonomy. In constitutional terms this means that Hong Kong is governed by the Basic Law of Hong Kong, subject to some specified measures of ultimate control left in the hands of the Chinese Central Authorities. The laws of Hong Kong are those laws that are passed by the local legislature and unwritten common law, conventions, customs and judge-made law. While the NPC has the authority to extend Chinese national laws to Hong Kong, the conditions under which that power may be exercised is clearly spelt out in the Basic Law. Hong Kong exercises a high degree of autonomy not under a constitution that binds China and Hong Kong equally: Hong Kong enjoys such autonomy because the Chinese Government has so willed: 'the National People's Congress authorizes the Hong Kong Special Administrative Region to exercise a high degree of autonomy'.[843] This carefully chosen terminology emphasizes the fact that Hong Kong's 'high degree of autonomy' did not flow from a surrender of some of the powers of the People's Republic of China to Hong Kong, as the UK did when it granted independence to its former colonies. Prima facie, an authorization given by China to Hong Kong is capable of being taken back by China. However, in view of the clearly expressed intention of the Chinese Government that Hong Kong is to enjoy a constitutional and legal system different from the rest of China, buttressed by the promises made in the Sino-British Joint Declaration, it is far from reality that the Chinese authorities would act contrary to the letter and spirit of the Basic Law and indeed the Joint Declaration. The arrangements made in the Basic Law not being intended to be binding on China in perpetuity but for a limited period of at least fifty years,[844] there is little likelihood that China would seek a complete overhaul of Hong Kong's constitutional arrangement. The Chinese and the Hong Kong economic foundations being different, the Chinese policy of 'One country, Two Systems' that underpins the Basic Law guarantees that the Chinese socialist system will not be practised in Hong Kong, which embraces capitalism and a western style democracy.[845]

461. The significance of the 'One Country, Two Systems' formula has been recognized by courts of Hong Kong. Referring to the interrelation between the Hong

843. *Ibid.*, Art. 2 in 'Chapter I: General Principles'.

844. Clause 3(12) of the Sino-British Joint Declaration states: 'The above-stated basic policies of the People's Republic of China regarding Hong Kong and the elaboration of them in Annex I to this Joint Declaration will be stipulated, in a Basic Law of the Hong Kong Special Administrative Region of the People's Republic of China, by the National People's Congress of the People's Republic of China, and they will remain unchanged for 50 years.'

845. For a useful introduction to Chinese constitutional law, *see* Lin Feng, *Constitutional Law in China* (Hong Kong: Sweet & Maxwell Asia, 2000).

Kong Government and Central Chinese Government, Li CJ said in *Lau Kong Yung v Director of Immigration*: '(1) Article 67(4) of the Constitution [of the People's Republic of China] confers on the NPCSC [the power to interpret statutes], including the Basic Law which is a national law. [Article 158(1) of the Basic Law of Hong Kong] also provides that the power to interpret the Basic Law shall be vested in the NPCSC; (2) In interpreting the Basic Law, the NPCSC functions under the Mainland system, which is different from the system in Hong Kong; (3) When the NPCSC makes an interpretation of a provision of the Basic Law, whether under Article 158(1) or 158(3) [of the Basic Law], the courts of Hong Kong are bound to follow it. Thus, the authority of the NPCSC to interpret the Basic Law is fully acknowledged and respected in the Hong Kong. This is to give effect to the Basic Law implementing the "one country, two systems" principle. Both systems being within one country (of which, we emphasise, Hong Kong is an inseparable part), the NPCSC's interpretation made in conformity with Article 158 under the Mainland system is binding in and part of the system in Hong Kong.'[846] In the flag desecration case, *HKSAR v Ng Kung Siu*,[847] Chief Justice Li emphasized that Hong Kong was an inalienable part of the People's Republic of China and that Hong Kong's constitutional arrangement is founded on the unique concept of 'One Country, Two Systems'. Li CJ said: 'As to the time, place and circumstances with which we are concerned, Hong Kong has a new constitutional order. On 1 July 1997, the People's Republic of China resumed the exercise of sovereignty over Hong Kong being an inalienable part of the People's Republic of China and established the Hong Kong Special Administrative Region under the principle of "One country, Two systems". The resumption of the exercise of sovereignty is recited in the Preamble of the Basic Law, as "fulfilling the long-cherished common aspiration of the Chinese people for the recovery of Hong Kong".' Relating that to the importance of respecting the national and regional flags, Li CJ continued to observe as follows: 'In these circumstances, the legitimate societal interests in protecting the national flag and the legitimate community interests in the protection of the regional flag are interests which are within the concept of public order (*ordre public*). … [T]he national flag is the unique symbol of the one country, the People's Republic of China, and the regional flag is the unique symbol of the Hong Kong Special Administrative Region as an inalienable part of the People's Republic of China under the principle of "one country, two systems".'[848]

846. *Lau Kong Yung v Director of Immigration* (1999) 2 HKCFAR 300, (CFA), 322. In *Yau Wai Ching v Chief Executive of HKSAR* [2017] 20 HKCFAR 390, (CFA), the Court of Final Appeal observed, citing *Director of Immigration v Chong Fung Yuen* (2001) 4 HKCFAR 211, (CFA), '6.2 The Effect of Interpretation by the Standing Committee' at 222–223, that any interpretation of the Basic Law of Hong Kong by the National People's Congress may indeed supplement the law of Hong Kong: 'The exercise of interpretation of the Basic Law under PRC law is one conducted under a different system of law to the common law system in force in the Hong Kong Special Administrative Region, and includes legislative interpretation which can clarify or supplement laws. An interpretation of the Basic Law issued by the NPCSC is binding on the courts of the Hong Kong Special Administrative Region. It declares what the law is and has always been since the coming into effect of the Basic Law on 1 July 1997': *Yau Wai Ching v Chief Executive of HKSAR* (2017) 20 HKCFAR 390, (CFA), [35].

847. *HKSAR v Ng Kung Siu and Another* (1999) 2 HKCFAR 442, (CFA).

848. *Ibid.*, 460.

462. In *Leung Kwok Hung v Legislative Council Secretariat*[849] the Court of First Instance upheld the sanctity of the oath of office the Chief Executive, members of the Legislative Council, judges and other senior public officers must swear or affirm when assuming office. In doing so, the Court observed that oath takers are required to swear allegiance to Hong Kong Special Administrative Region which, according to the Basic Law, is an integral part of, and not independent of, the People's Republic of China. The oath taking is mandated by Article 104 of the Basic Law which provides as follows: 'When assuming office, the Chief Executive, principal officials, members of the Executive Council and of the Legislative Council, judges of the courts at all levels and other members of the judiciary in the Hong Kong Special Administrative Region must, in accordance with law, swear to uphold the Basic Law of the Hong Kong Special Administrative Region of the People's Republic of China and swear allegiance to the Hong Kong Special Administrative Region of the People's Republic of China.' The Court of First Instance rejected the argument that an amended version of the oath of allegiance could be used instead of the authorized version, where the amended version was inconsistent with the requirements of Article 104 of the Basic Law.

463. *Chief Executive of HKSAR v President of Legislative Council*[850] came before the Court of First Instance when two members of the newly elected Legislative Council, following the general election in September 2016, took the oath at the first meeting of the Council on 12 October 2016 in such a way that it did not amount to taking the oath as required by Article 104 or in a solemn and sincere manner as required by the Oaths and Declarations Ordinance (Cap. 11).[851] They had either changed the wording of the oath to emphasize that they were advocating self-governance for Hong Kong and thus undermining the supremacy of the People's Republic of China or pronounced in Cantonese the words 'China' and 'People's Republic of China' in a contemptuous way.

464. The Clerk to the Legislative Council refused to accept the validity of the oath, and six days later, the President of the Legislative Council offered them an opportunity to take the oath afresh, if they made a written request, which they did the same day. However, before a new oath taking could be arranged, the Secretary for Justice, representing the Chief Executive, successfully moved the court for a declaration that the oath taken by the two new members at the first sitting of the Council was invalid. The Court of First Instance upheld the judicial review application on 15 November 2016 and declared that the two newly elected members of

---

849. *Leung Kwok Hung v Legislative Council Secretariat* [2004] HKEC 1203, (CFI).

850. *Chief Executive of HKSAR v President of Legislative Council* [2016] HKEC 2487, (CFI), affirmed by the Court of Appeal [2017] 1 HKLRD 460, (CA).

851. Schedule 2 of the Oaths and Declarations Ordinance (Cap. 11) requires newly elected Legislative Council member to swear that he will uphold the Basic Law, bear allegiance to the Hong Kong Special Administrative Region and to the People's Republic of China, 'conscientiously, dutifully, in accordance with the law, honestly and with integrity'. Thomas Au J in *Chief Executive of HKSAR v President of Legislative Council* [2016] HKEC 2487, (CFI), observed that the oath must be taken solemnly and sincerely is an undisputed requirement of the common law.

the Legislative Council were disqualified from holding office as members of the Council and that the office each of them was elected to was vacant.

465. While the case was pending before the Court of First Instance, the Central Chinese Government issued an interpretation of Article 104 of the Basic Law on 7 November 2016, clarifying that: (1) an oath taker must take the oath 'sincerely and solemnly' and must accurately, completely and solemnly read out the oath prescribed by law; (2) an oath taker who intentionally reads out words which do not accord with the wording of an oath prescribed by law, or takes the oath in a manner which is not sincere or not solemn, shall be treated as declining to take the oath; and (3) if the administrator of the oath refuses to accept the oath as having been read out in the prescribed manner, such purported oath is invalid and no arrangements must be made for retaking the oath.

466. Thomas Au J having held that an interpretation issued by the NPCSC is binding on courts of Hong Kong proceeded to determine the case in accordance with the interpretation of Article 104 pronounced by the Standing Committee on 7 November 2016. The judge, however, agreeing with the government's submission, held that his decision would be the same even in the absence of guidance from the interpretation of Article 104. This decision was upheld by the Court of Appeal.[852]

467. The desecration of flag case and the two oath of office cases lend support in two specific contexts to the supremacy of the People's Republic of China and the nature of the degree of autonomy that Hong Kong enjoys, emphasizing the special relationship created by the Basic Law between Chinese Central Authorities and Hong Kong's regional authorities.

468. Being intended to set out the constitutional arrangements for Hong Kong, the Basic Law does not make a strict demarcation of constitutional power between the central and regional authorities, and impliedly leaves room for any powers that are not specifically referred to in the Basic Law to be left in the competence of the People's Republic of China.[853] Not engaging in the ongoing political debate on the competence or propriety of the Central Government in controlling local affairs of Hong Kong, what we propose to do is to examine the provisions of the Basic Law which are aimed at upholding Hong Kong's high degree of autonomy.

469. Two articles of the Basic Law reflect the special position of Hong Kong. Article 2 of the Basic Law provides that 'the National People's Congress authorizes the Hong Kong Special Administrative Region to exercise a high degree of

852. *Chief Executive of the HKSAR v President of the Legislative Council* [2017] 1 HKLRD 460, (CA). *See also Secretary for Justice v Leung Kwok Hung* [2019] HKEC 417, (CA), [50], where the Court of Appeal reaffirmed the legality of the interpretation of Standing Committee of the National People's Congress.
853. In Federal systems, it is common to have a federal list and state list of competencies, with residual powers left either with the federal authorities (as in India) or with state authorities (as in the USA), as well as a concurrent jurisdiction list which provides that in case of a conflict between federal law and state law on a subject in the concurrent list, federal law prevails.

autonomy and enjoy executive, legislative and independent judicial power, including that of final adjudication, in accordance with the provisions of this Law'. Article 12 of the Basic Law provides that 'the Hong Kong Special Administrative Region shall be a local administrative region of the People's Republic of China, which shall enjoy a high degree of autonomy and come directly under the Central People's Government'. The Hong Kong Special Administrative Region is responsible for the administration of all the affairs within the limits of its autonomy. The Central Government is only responsible for the defence and foreign affairs of the Hong Kong Special Administrative Region and affairs concerning either the relationship between the Hong Kong Special Administrative Region and the Central Government or matters falling exclusively within the jurisdiction of the Central Government.[854]

§2. Legislative Relationship Between Central Government and the Hong Kong Special Administrative Region

470. As we saw above, Hong Kong's Basic Law is a law passed by the NPC. Its interpretation and implementation is primarily left to the Hong Kong. The responsibility for the implementation of the Basic Law is vested in the Hong Kong legislature and the executive, who are to a significant extent free from any control from the Chinese Government. As far as the interpretation is concerned, the primary responsibility is vested in the Hong Kong judiciary, subject to an important limitation in respect of authoritative interpretations of certain Basic Law provisions.

471. The legislative relationship between the Chinese Central Government and the Hong Kong Special Administrative Region, in the light of 'One Country, Two Systems' may be summarized as follows: Hong Kong is governed by the Basic Law and Hong Kong laws that are not inconsistent with the Basic Law: the Chinese Constitution is not part of the internal constitutional framework of Hong Kong, although it might be useful in interpreting the Basic Law; national laws of China do not apply in Hong Kong unless they have been extended to Hong Kong under the Basic Law; Hong Kong legislation do not need to be approved by the Chinese Government to be effective in Hong Kong, although there is a mechanism by which the Chinese Government can invalidate Hong Kong legislation. The Chinese constitutional practice of the government being the ultimate authority to interpret law does not apply in Hong Kong except as provided by Article 158 of the Basic Law.[855]

472. The Chinese Constitution is the fundamental law of the State and has supreme legal authority. Hong Kong being an inalienable part of China, and in the

854. *See* the Preamble to the Basic Law.

855. As Yash Ghai wrote: 'When necessary [NPCSC] may provide an interpretation of laws and decrees, and in doing so it may either clarify the meaning of the law or extend it, thus negating the distinction between interpretation and law-making. In practice the [NPCSC] have preferred to provide guidance in the form of new provisions rather than straightforward interpretation.' Yash Ghai, *Hong Kong's New Constitutional Order: The Resumption of Chinese Sovereignty and the Basic Law* (Hong Kong University Press, 1997), 203.

absence of abdication by China of its sovereignty over Hong Kong, the Chinese Constitution must have binding force in Hong Kong. To use terminology that is used in relation to the UK Parliament in its relationship to the European Union it might be right to talk about 'self-imposed limitations' on the Chinese sovereignty over Hong Kong. In other words, the unique concessions that China has made in respect of Hong Kong through the enactment of the Basic Law, in pursuant of the Sino-British Joint Declaration, have to be respected by the Chinese Government. It can be argued that the Chinese Constitution has no application to Hong Kong to the extent its provisions are inconsistent with the letter and spirit of the Basic Law. Provisions in Chapters VII (External Affairs) and VIII (Interpretation and Amendment of the Basic Law) of the Basic Law highlight the fact that the system of government that Hong Kong has been given has no existence completely separate from Chinese constitutional principles.

473. Article 18 of the Basic Law clearly provides that Hong Kong will be governed by the Basic Law, laws previously in force in Hong Kong and legislation made by the Hong Kong legislature. Article 18 further provides that national laws will not apply in Hong Kong, except those that are incorporated in Annex III of the Basic Law, or those that are extended to Hong Kong by the Chinese Government in times of emergency. National laws that are extended to Hong Kong through incorporation in Annex III 'National Laws to be Applicable in the Hong Kong Special Administrative Region' do not take effect by themselves. They have to be made applicable in Hong Kong 'by way of proclamation or legislation in the Region'. The only situation where the Chinese Central Government may extend national laws to Hong Kong by making an order in that behalf is where at a time of emergency or war national unity or security is beyond the control of the Hong Kong Government: that too only where the situation in Hong Kong is beyond the control of the Hong Kong Government.

§3. Executive Relationship Between Central Government and the Hong Kong Special Administrative Region

474. The executive branch of the Hong Kong Special Administrative Region is headed by the Chief Executive and consists of the Department of Administration, the Department of Finance, the Department of Justice, and various bureaux, divisions and commissions (Article 60 of the Basic Law). Together they are referred to as the executive authorities and constitute the Hong Kong Government.[856] The Hong Kong Special Administrative Region shall, on its own, conduct its administrative affairs according to the relevant provisions of the Basic Law.[857] Most of its administrative affairs such as finance, banking, trade, industry, commerce, land-leasing and shipping are within the autonomy of the Hong Kong Special Administrative Region. National defence and foreign affairs are excluded from Hong Kong's

856. Basic Law, Art. 59.
857. *Ibid.*, Art. 16.

competence,[858] while some matters, such as aviation and external affairs, need to be handled together by both the Central Government and the Hong Kong Special Administrative Region Government.[859]

475. The Chinese Central Government is responsible for the foreign affairs and national defence of the Hong Kong Special Administrative Region.[860] Article 13(1) of the Basic Law provides: 'The Central People's Government shall be responsible for the foreign affairs relating to the Hong Kong Special Administrative Region.' In pursuance of its power under the Basic Law to establish an office in the Hong Kong Special Administrative Region to deal with foreign affairs,[861] the Ministry of Foreign Affairs has established the Office of the Commissioner of the Ministry of Foreign Affairs of the People's Republic of China in Hong Kong. Since reunification, the Hong Kong Special Administrative Region Government has maintained effective communication with the Office of the Commissioner of the Ministry of Foreign Affairs.[862]

476. Article 13(3) of the Basic Law provides that, 'The Central People's Government authorizes the Hong Kong Special Administrative Region to conduct relevant external affairs on its own in accordance with this Law.' The Basic Law is not clear on the difference, if any, between 'external affairs' and 'foreign affairs'. 'Relevant external affairs' appear to be those foreign affairs prescribed in Chapter VII of the Basic Law and some matters prescribed by relevant provisions in Chapters V and VI. They include the following:

(1) The Hong Kong Special Administrative Region may on its own, using the name 'Hong Kong, China', maintain and develop relations and conclude and implement agreements with foreign States and regions and relevant international organizations in the appropriate fields, including the economic, trade, financial and monetary, shipping, communications, tourism, cultural and sports fields.[863] The Hong Kong Special Administrative Region may, using the name 'Hong Kong, China', participate in international organizations and conferences not limited to States (Article 2(2)).
(2) With the authorization of the Central People's Government, the Government of the Hong Kong Special Administrative Region may conclude visa abolition agreements with foreign States or regions (Article 155).
(3) The Hong Kong Special Administrative Region may, if necessary, establish official or semi-official economic and trade missions in foreign countries (Article 156).

858. *Ibid.*, Arts 13 and 14.
859. *Ibid.*, s. 4 'Civil Aviation' of Ch. V 'Economy', and Ch. VII 'External Affairs'.
860. *Ibid.*, Arts 13(1) and 14(1).
861. *Ibid.*, Art. 13(2).
862. For details, *see* Hong Kong Yearbook, Chapter 1 'Constitution and Administration'. https://www.yearbook.gov.hk/2019/en/pdf/E01.pdf.
863. *See* Art. 151 of the Basic Law.

(4) The establishment of foreign consular and other official or semi-official missions in the Hong Kong Special Administrative Region shall require the approval of the Central People's Government (Article 157(1)).
(5) For international organizations and conferences limited to States, the Hong Kong Special Administrative Region may send representatives, as members of delegations of the People's Republic of China, to participate in international organizations or conferences or to attend in such other capacity as may be permitted by the Central People's Government and the international organization or conference concerned, and to express their views, using the name 'Hong Kong, China' (Article 152(1)).
(6) For negotiations at the diplomatic level, if they directly affect the Hong Kong Special Administrative Region, it may send representatives, as members of delegations of the Government of the People's Republic of China, to participate in them (Article 150).

477. Article 14(1) of the Basic Law stipulates that 'The Central People's Government shall be responsible for the defence of the Hong Kong Special Administrative Region' and that the Hong Kong Government shall be responsible for the maintenance of public order in the Region.[864] While the Central Government may station military forces in the Hong Kong Special Administrative Region, the military forces are prohibited from interfering in the local affairs of the Hong Kong Special Administrative Region. The garrison stationed in the Hong Kong may provide assistance in the maintenance of public order or in disaster relief, if Hong Kong makes a request to the Chinese Central Government for assistance.[865]

478. The garrison stationed in the Hong Kong Special Administrative Region is part of the Chinese national army. Accordingly, they should abide by Chinese national law. In addition, they should also abide by the laws of the Hong Kong Special Administrative Region because they are stationed in the Hong Kong Special Administrative Region.[866] To deal with any problems arising from the garrison being required to follow a national law and a Hong Kong law which may be in conflict with each other, the Standing Committee of the Eighth NPC adopted the Law of the People's Republic of China on Garrisoning the Hong Kong Special Administrative Region ('the Garrison Law') in December 1996, which came into effect on 1 July 1997 and was added to Annex III of the Basic Law.

479. Article 10 of the Garrison Law provides: 'The Hong Kong Special Administrative Region shall consult the Hong Kong Garrison when formulating any policy or drafting any legislation which concerns the Hong Kong Garrison.' Article 20 provides: 'Criminal offences committed by members of the Hong Kong Garrison shall be under the jurisdiction of the military judicial organs; but offences which are committed by members of the Hong Kong Garrison when not performing their official duties and in such violation of the personal right or property right of Hong Kong

864. *Ibid. See also* Art. 14(2).
865. *See* Art. 14(3) of the Basic Law.
866. *See* Art. 14(4) of the Basic Law.

residents or other persons who are not of the Hong Kong Garrison or otherwise in such contravention of the laws of the Hong Kong Special Administrative Region as to constitute crimes, shall be subject to the jurisdiction of the courts and the relevant law-enforcing organs of the Hong Kong Special Administrative Region.'

480. According to the Garrison Law, the garrison shall be subject to the direction of the Central Military Commission.[867] The expenditure for the garrison shall be borne by the Central People's Government.[868] The garrison shall perform the following defence functions and responsibilities: (1) preparing against any resisting aggression, and safeguarding the security of the Hong Kong Special Administrative Region; (2) carrying out the defence duties; (3) administering military facilities; and (4) handling foreign-related military affairs.[869]

481. The garrison may be involved in the security of Hong Kong. The Government of the Hong Kong Special Administrative Region may, when necessary, ask the Central People's Government for assistance from the garrison in the maintenance of public order and in disaster relief.[870] When the NPCSC decides to declare a state of war or, by reason of turmoil within the Hong Kong Special Administrative Region that endangers national unity or security and is beyond the control of the Hong Kong Special Administrative Region Government, decides that the Hong Kong Special Administrative Region is in a state of emergency, the garrison shall then perform its duties in accordance with the provisions of the national laws to be applied in Hong Kong Special Administrative Region by the Central People's Government.[871]

§4. Financial Relationship Between Central Government and the Hong Kong Special Administrative Region

482. Article 106 of the Basic Law provides that the Hong Kong Special Administrative Region shall have independent finances. The Hong Kong Special Administrative Region shall use its financial revenues exclusively for its own purposes, and they shall not be handed over to the Central Government. It also provides that the Central Government shall not levy taxes in the Hong Kong Special Administrative Region. Article 108 provides that the Hong Kong Special Administrative Region shall practise an independent taxation system and that the Hong Kong Special Administrative Region shall, taking the low-tax policy previously pursued in Hong Kong as reference, enact laws on its own concerning types of taxes, tax rates, tax reductions, allowances and exemptions, and other matters of taxation. Article 110 provides that the Government of the Hong Kong Special Administrative Region shall, on its own, formulate monetary and financial policies, safeguard the free

867. *See* Art. 3 of the Garrison Law.
868. *See* Art. 14(5) of the Basic Law.
869. *See* Art. 5 of the Garrison Law.
870. Basic Law, Art. 14.
871. *See* Art. 6 of the Garrison Law.

operation of financial business and financial markets, and regulate and supervise them in accordance with law. Article 111 recognizes that the authority to issue Hong Kong currency is vested in the Government of the Hong Kong Special Administrative Region. Article 116 provides that the Hong Kong Special Administrative Region shall be a separate customs territory. An important provision is Article 107 which provides as follows: 'The Hong Kong Special Administrative Region shall follow the principle of keeping expenditure within the limits of revenues in drawing up its budget, and strive to achieve a fiscal balance, avoid deficits and keep the budget commensurate with the growth rate of its gross domestic product.'[872]

§5. Cooperation Between the Central Government and the Hong Kong Special Administrative Region

483. The Central Government and the Hong Kong Special Administrative Region have reached three formal agreements on judicial cooperation: the 'Arrangement for Mutual Service of Judicial Documents in Civil and Commercial Proceedings between the Mainland and Hong Kong Courts'[873] the 'Arrangement concerning Mutual Enforcement of Arbitral Awards between the Mainland and Hong Kong Special Administrative Region,'[874] and the 'Arrangement on Reciprocal Recognition and Enforcement of Judgments in Civil and Commercial Matter by the Courts of the Mainland and of the Hong Kong Special Administrative Region Pursuant to Choice of Court Agreements between Parties concerned'.[875] Other important agreements include: 'Cooperative Arrangements between the Central Institute for Correctional Police of the Ministry of Justice and the Staff Training Institute of the Correctional Service Department of the Government of the Hong special Administrative Region' (2003), 'Customs Cooperative Arrangement between the Customs General Administration and the Hong Kong Customs and Excise Department' (2000), 'Mainland and Hong Kong Closer Economic Partnership Arrangement' (2003), Co-operation Arrangement on Legal Services for Commercial Matters and Arbitration was signed between the China Council for the Promotion of International Trade and the Hong Kong Department of Justice (2010), 'Agreement between the Mainland and Hong Kong on Achieving Basic Liberalization of Trade in Services in Guangdong' (2014), and the framework arrangement on exchange and mutual learning in legal aspects in the Greater Bay Area agreed between the Hong Kong Department of Justice and the Higher People's Court of Guangdong Province (2019).[876]

---

872. Yash Ghai has raised the concern that these seeming restrictions on fiscal competence of the Hong Kong Government may open the gateway for the Central Chinese Government to interfere in the very fiscal autonomy that has been bestowed on Hong Kong. *See* Yash Ghai, *Hong Kong's New Constitutional Order: The Resumption of Chinese Sovereignty and the Basic Law* (Hong Kong: Hong Kong University Press, 1997), at 150, and other relevant places.
873. Signed in Shenzhen on 14 January 1999.
874. Signed in Shenzhen on 21 June 1999.
875. Signed in Hong Kong on 14 July 2006.
876. *See*, for further information, https://www.doj.govhk/eng/topical/mainlandlaw.html.

Chapter 2. Interpretation of the Basic Law

§1. The Interpretation Authority of the Standing Committee of the National People's Congress

484. The NPCSC has the power to interpret the Constitution and statutes (national laws).[877] Basic Law being a national law the Standing Committee must have the authority to interpret it. This is recognized by Article 158 of the Basic Law which provides:

> The power of interpretation shall be vested in the Standing Committee of the National People's Congress.
>
> The Standing Committee of the National People's Congress shall authorize the courts of the Hong Kong Special Administrative Region to interpret on their own, in adjudicating cases, the provision of [the Basic Law] which are within the limit of the autonomy of the Region.
>
> The courts of the Hong Kong Special Administrative Region may also interpret other provisions of this Law in adjudicating cases. However, if the courts of the Region, in adjudicating cases, need to interpret the provisions of [the Basic Law] concerning affairs that are the responsibility of the Central People's Government, or concerning the relationship between the Central Authorities and the Region, and if such interpretation shall affect the judgments on the cases, the courts of the Region shall, before making their final judgments (which are not appealable), seek an interpretation of the relevant provisions from the Standing Committee of the National People's Congress through the Court of Final Appeal of the Region. When the Standing Committee makes an interpretation of the provisions concerned, the courts of the Region, in applying those provisions, shall follow the interpretation of the Standing Committee. However, judgments previously rendered shall not be affected.
>
> The Standing Committee of the National People's congress shall consult its Committee for the Basic Law of the Hong Kong Special Administrative Region before giving an interpretation of [the Basic Law].

485. Article 158 of the Basic Law apportions the function of interpreting the Basic Law between the NPCSC and the courts of the Hong Kong Special Administrative Region.[878] The allocation of the power of constitutional interpretation may be described in the following manner:

877. Article 67(1) and (4) of the Chinese Constitution.

878. On the part played by the Committee for Basic Law in interpretation, *see* Yash Ghai, 'The Intersection of Chinese Law and the Common Law in the Hong Kong Special Administrative Region' (2007) 37 *Hong Kong Law Journal* 363–405.

(1) The power of interpretation of the Basic Law is vested in the Standing Committee of the National People's Congress. The Standing Committee may exercise this power from time to time otherwise than in adjudication of cases.[879]
(2) Hong Kong does not have such a 'free-standing' power of interpretation. The courts of Hong Kong exercise their delegated power of interpretation in the course of adjudication, in the absence of any special jurisdiction to hand down advisory opinion, such as the jurisdiction that the Indian Supreme Court has been given when the President refers any question of law or fact of public importance for its advice (*see* Article 143 of the Indian Constitution).[880]
(3) Hong Kong courts may interpret Basic Law provisions 'which are within the limits of the autonomy of the Region' because the Standing Committee of the National People's Congress 'shall authorise' Hong Kong courts to exercise such jurisdiction.
(4) The power of Hong Kong Courts to interpret provisions which are not 'within the limits of the autonomy of the Region', namely Basic Law provisions 'concerning affairs which are the responsibility of the Central People's Government or concerning the relationship between the Central Authorities and the Region' is limited. While Hong Kong courts may interpret them, if an interpretation placed by a Hong Kong court will affect the decision of the case, the court having the final power of adjudication, namely the Court of Final Appeal, must seek a binding interpretation of such provision from the National People's Congress.[881] An interpretation given by the National People's Congress pursuant to such a request will have only prospective effect, in that the interpretation will be binding on the court as regards the case which gave rise to the request for interpretation and future cases, but will not affect any cases which have already been decided.[882]

---

879. As Sir Anthony Mason NPJ explained in *Lau Kong Yung v Director of Immigration* (1999) 2 HKCFAR 300, (CFA), 345: 'The Standing Committee's power to interpret laws is necessarily exercised from time to time otherwise than in the adjudication of cases. So the expression "in adjudicating cases" [in relation to interpretation by HK courts] makes it clear that the power of interpretation enjoyed by the courts of the Region is limited in that way and differs from the general and free-standing power of interpretation enjoyed by the Standing Committee under Art. 67(4) of the People's Republic of China Constitution and Art. 158(1) of the Basic Law.'

880. 'The well-established principle in our system [is] that the courts' role is adjudicative and not advisory': Ng *Ka Ling v Director of Immigration* (1999) 2 HKCFAR 4, (CFA), 30. For India, *see* Justice Vineet Kothari, 'Presidential Reference under Article 143 of the Constitution: Current Issues and Perspectives'. http://hcraj.nic.in/Paper-Speech/presidentialreference.pdf.

881. As the Court of final Appeal did in the course of hearing an appeal concerning the scope of state immunity. The interpretation was issued on 26 August 2011 (which appears as Instrument 24, appended to the Basic Law) and followed by the CFA. *See Democratic Republic of the Congo v FG Hemisphere Associates LLC (No 2)* (2011) 14 HKCFAR 395, (CFA).

882. As Art. 158 goes on to state: 'When the Standing Committee makes an interpretation of the provisions concerned, the courts of the Region, in applying those provisions, shall follow the interpretation of the Standing Committee. However, judgments previously rendered shall not be affected.'

(5) Where Hong Kong courts interpret a Basic Law provision in a way that is not acceptable for the Chinese Central Government, it is possible for the Standing Committee of the National People's Congress to offer a different interpretation, with prospective effect.[883]

(6) The Standing Committee of the National People's Congress exercises its power to interpretation not only consequent upon litigation in Hong Kong. For instance, it has issued three interpretations relating to the method for selection of the Chief Executive (in 2004), tenure of the Chief Executive (in 2005) and the adoption of universal franchise for Legislative Council elections (in 2007), all at the request of the Hong Kong Government.[884]

I. The Plenary Authority of the Standing Committee of the National People's Congress to Interpret the Basic Law

486. The Standing Committee of the National People's Congress (NPCSC) has 'free-standing' power of interpretation. It is free-standing or plenary because it can interpret any provision of the Basic Law and whether or not there is a request by the Hong Kong judiciary for an interpretation.[885] The Hong Kong Court of Final Appeal has confirmed that the NPCSC has plenary, free-standing and unqualified authority to interpret the Basic Law, including those provisions within the autonomy of the Hong Kong Special Administrative Region.[886] The exercise of this authority may be for the purpose of clearing doubts that may have arisen about the scope of a provision in order to provide guidance to relevant authorities or to correct what it deems a wrong interpretation by the Hong Kong Special Administrative Region courts.[887]

---

883. This happened, for instance, after the Court of Final Appeal decision in *Ng Ka Ling & Ors v Director of Immigration* (1999) 2 HKCFAR 4, (CFA). The Chief Executive submitted a report to the State Council referring to the serious problems the Government had encountered in implementing the decision, and the State Council requested the National People's Congress to interpret the relevant provisions of the Basic Law. The Decision of the National People's Congress, 'The Interpretation by the Standing Committee of the National People's Congress of Arts. 22(4) and 24(2)(3) of the Basic Law' was published in the Gazette in Hong Kong on 26 June 1999 and appears as Instrument 19 appended to the Basic Law.

884. The first of these three interpretations given in 2004 was seemingly given without any formal request by the Hong Kong Government. *See* Albert H.Y. Chen, 'The Constitutional Controversy of Spring 2004' (2004) 34 *Hong Kong Law Journal* 215.

885. As the first Chief Justice of Hong Kong explained in *Ng Ka Ling v Director of Immigration (No 2)* (1999) 2 HKCFAR 141, (CFA), clarifying its decision in *Ng Ka Ling v Director of Immigration* (1999) 2 HKCFAR 4, (CFA): 'The courts' judicial power is derived from the Basic Law. Article 158(1) vests the power of interpretation of the Basic Law in the Standing Committee. The courts' jurisdiction to interpret the Basic Law in adjudicating cases is derived by authorisation from the Standing Committee under Arts. 158(2) and 158(3). In our judgment on 29 January 1999, we said that the Courts' jurisdiction to enforce and interpret the Basic Law is derived from and is subject to the provisions of the Basic Law which provisions include the foregoing.'

886. *See Lau Kong Yung and others v The Director of Immigration* (1999) 2 HKCFAR 300, (CFA).

887. *See* Yash Ghai, *Hong Kong's New Constitutional Order*, (2nd edn, Hong Kong: Hong Kong University Press, 1999), 202. The power of the National People's Congress to issue authoritative constitutional interpretations was reaffirmed by the Court of Final Appeal in *Yau Wai Ching v Chief Executive of HKSAR* (2017) 20 HKCFAR 390, (CFA). The Court observed at [35] as follows: 'The

487. The first free-standing interpretation of the Basic Law by the Standing Committee was occasioned by an interpretation of Articles 22 and 24 by the Court of Final Appeal in *Ng Ka Ling v Director of immigration* which was contrary to the Hong Kong Government's understanding of those two provisions.[888] After the decision of the Court of Final Appeal was delivered, the Hong Kong Government referred the matter for interpretation by the Standing Committee and the legality of this power of interpretation was recognized by Hong Kong Court of Final Appeal.[889] The most recent free-standing interpretation was the interpretation of Article 104 on the meaning of the oath of allegiance, while a case was pending before the Court of First Instance.[890]

488. The Court of Final Appeal has stated that Hong Kong courts should adopt a common law approach to interpreting Basic Law. However, where the Standing Committee of the National Peoples' Congress has made an interpretation of the Basic Law pursuant to its power under Article 67(4) of the Chinese Constitution and Article 158 of the Basic Law, the courts were bound to follow it, although the common law canons of interpretation might not lead to the conclusion that the Standing Committee had reached.[891] The Court observed that in interpreting the Basic Law, the courts' role was to construe the language in order to ascertain the legislative intent as expressed in the language and that their task was not to ascertain the intent of the lawmaker on its own.[892]

NPCSC's power to interpret the Basic Law derives from Art. 67(4) of the Constitution of the PRC and is provided for expressly in the Basic Law itself in Art. 158(1) and is in general and unqualified terms. The exercise of interpretation of the Basic Law under PRC law is one conducted under a different system of law to the common law system in force in the Hong Kong Special Administrative Region and includes legislative interpretation which can clarify or supplement laws. An interpretation of the Basic Law issued by the NPCSC is binding on the courts of the Hong Kong Special Administrative Region. It declares what the law is and has always been since the coming into effect of the Basic Law on 1 July 1997' (footnotes omitted).

888. *Ng Ka Ling v Director of immigration* (1999) 2 HKCFAR 4, (CFA). The interpretation may be found in Instrument 19 appended to the Basic Law.

889. *Director of immigration v Chong Fung Yuen* (2001) 4 HKCFAR 211, (CFA).

890. Interpretation of Art. 104 of the Basic Law of the Hong Kong Special Administrative Region of the People's Republic of China by the Standing Committee of the National People's Congress (adopted by the Standing Committee of the Twelfth National People's Congress at its Twenty-Fourth Session on 7 November. 2016), (Instrument 26 appended to the Basic Law). *See* paras 465-466 above.

891. *Ibid.*, at 222. *See* '6.3 The Common law approach to interpretation', where Chief Justice Li observed: 'It is unnecessary for the purposes of this case to explore what assistance (if any) can be derived from extrinsic materials other than pre-enactment materials relating to context and purpose; in particular, whether post-enactment materials can be called in aid. For the purposes of this case, it is sufficient to state that on the common law approach which the courts are bound to apply in the absence of a binding interpretation by the Standing Committee, extrinsic materials, whatever their nature and whether pre or post-enactment, cannot affect interpretation where the courts conclude that the meaning of the language, when construed in the light of its context and purpose ascertained with the benefit of internal aids and appropriate extrinsic materials, is clear.'

892. *Ibid.*, at 224.

489. A truly free-standing interpretation is one given by the NPCSC without receiving a request from the Court of Final Appeal or the Hong Kong Government, as in 2004 and 2020. Those two interpretations were given at the request of the State Council of China.[893]

II. The Standing Committee of the National People's Congress' Interpretation upon Referral

490. The NPCSC may also exercise its power of interpretation at the request of the Court of Final Appeal. A request may be made only at the final stage of litigation 'before making their final judgment'. A party to litigation may request the courts to apply for an interpretation, and it is up to the court to decide whether it is appropriate to seek the guidance of the Standing Committee.[894] The Court of Final Appeal will seek such assistance only if it is satisfied that a provision of the Basic Law concerns the responsibility of the Central Government or the relationship between the Central Government and the Hong Kong Special Administrative Region. Moreover, an interpretation will only be sought if the interpretation would affect the judgment.[895] In *Ng Ka Ling*, the Court of Final Appeal held that it is up to the Court of Final Appeal to decide whether two conditions are satisfied: (1) the classification condition, that is, that the provision is an excluded provision (i.e., a provision that does not deal with a matter within Hong Kong's autonomous powers); (2) the necessity condition, that is, that the Court of Final Appeal in adjudicating the case needs to interpret the excluded provision, and such interpretation will affect the judgment on the case.[896] In *Vallejos v Commissioner of Registration*[897] the Court of Final Appeal refused to make an application under Article 158,

893. Discussed in paras 465-466 above. For a detailed account of how the Standing Committee came to offer this interpretation and constitutional issues arising from that interpretation, *see* Albert Chen, 'The Constitutional Controversy of Spring 2004' (2004) 34 *Hong Kong Law Journal* 215. So far there have been four interpretations without a referral by the Court of Final Appeal: (1) Arts 22 and 24, Right of abode; (2) Art. 7 of Annex 1, method of Selection of the Chief Executive; (3) Art. 53, the term of office of a succeeding Chief Executive for the remaining term of the vacating Chief Executive; (4) Art. 104, oath of allegiance.

894. The only interpretation given at the request of the Court of Final Appeal was on sovereign immunity. *Democratic Republic of the Congo v FG Hemisphere Associates LLC (No 1)* [2011] 14 HKCFAR 95, (CFA): 'Interpretation of Paragraph 1, Article 13 and Article 19 of the Basic Law of the Hong Kong Special Administrative Region of the People's Republic of China by the Standing Committee of the National People's Congress (Adopted at the Twenty Second Session of the Standing Committee of the Eleventh National People's Congress on 26 August 2011)', Instrument 24, appended to the Basic Law.

895. *See* Art. 158(2) of the Basic Law.

896. The dual test of classification and necessity was affirmed by the Court of Final Appeal in *Vallejos v Commissioner of Registration* (2013) 16 HKCFAR 45, (CFA), [110]–[112], and in *Democratic Republic of the Congo v FG Hemisphere Associates LLC (No 1)* (2011) 14 HKCFAR 95, (CFA), [83]. In the latter case, the Court of Final Appeal requested the Standing Committee of the National People's Congress to interpret the relevant Articles of the Basic Law and advise whether the courts of Hong Kong were free to continue to apply the pre-1997 common law practice relating to sovereign immunity. The Court of Final Appeal has said that it might have to revisit the dual test. *See Lau Kong Yung v Director of Immigration* (1999] 2 HKCFAR 300, (CFA), at 324.

897. (2013) 16 HKCFAR 45, (CFA).

for the reason that there was no question of interpretation that needed to be resolved. As the Court was able to ascertain the true meaning of Article 24(2)(4) of the Basic Law, a reference to NPCSC was unnecessary.[898]

§2. The Delegated Authority of the Courts in the Hong Kong Special Administrative Region

491. Article 158 of the Basic Law provides that the NPCSC shall authorize the courts of the Hong Kong Special Administrative Region to interpret on their own, in adjudicating cases, the provisions of the Basic Law falling within the limits of Hong Kong's autonomy. The courts of the Hong Kong Special Administrative Region may also interpret other provisions of the Basic Law (i.e., provisions which do not relate to matters within Hong Kong's autonomy). The jurisdiction to interpret 'other provisions' is subject to an important limitation. Article 158 proceeds to provide as follows: 'However, if the courts of the Region, in adjudicating cases, need to interpret the provisions of this Law concerning affairs which are the responsibility of the Central People's Government, or concerning the relationship between the Central Authorities and the Region, and if such interpretation will affect the judgments on the cases, the courts of the Region shall, before making their final judgments which are not appealable, seek an interpretation of the relevant provisions from the Standing Committee of the National People's Congress through the Court of Final Appeal of the Region. When the Standing Committee makes an interpretation of the provisions concerned, the courts of the Region, in applying those provisions, shall follow the interpretation of the Standing Committee. However, judgments previously rendered shall not be affected.'

I. The Constitutional Review Authority of the Courts of Hong Kong

492. Hong Kong Courts have the authority to question the legality of administrative action, deriving the authority to do so from common law. They also have the implied power to question constitutionality of legislation as Article 11 of the Basic Law provides that no law enacted by Hong Kong's legislature shall contravene the Basic Law. Article 8 of the Basic Law provides for the continuation of laws previously in force in Hong Kong, to the extent that they do not contravene any provision of the Basic Law or any law passed by Hong Kong's post-1997 legislature. Thus, the Basic Law enjoys the status of a paramount law that prevails over all other laws.[899]

493. While the authority of courts of Hong Kong to question constitutionality of legislation is straightforward, opinion is divided on whether they have the authority

898. *Ibid.*, [109]–[112].

899. The pre-1997 position is Hong Kong was no different. Hong Kong's legislature was bound by any laws and regulations made by the Imperial Government and by Hong Kong's own constitution, the Letters Patent.

to review acts of the NPC and the Standing Committee of the National People's Congress. The Court of Final Appeal stated in *Ng Ka Ling v Director of Immigration*[900] that Hong Kong courts have such authority. The Court of Final Appeal held that it has the power to examine whether there was a conflict between any acts of the NPC or the NPCSC on the one hand and the Basic Law on the other.[901] Soon after the judgment was delivered, the Director of Immigration sought a clarification of that part of the judgment because various interpretations had been put on that part of the judgment giving rise to much controversy. While it is not the usual practice for courts to issue clarifications of its decisions, unless the need for it arises in a subsequent case, the Court of Appeal agreed to take the exceptional course of issuing a clarification, in the exercise of its inherent power. The Court of Final Appeal issued the following clarification:

> The courts' judicial power is derived from the Basic Law. Article 158(1) vests the power of interpretation of the Basic Law in the Standing Committee. The courts' jurisdiction to interpret the Basic Law in adjudicating cases is derived by authorization from the Standing Committee under Articles 158(2) and 158(3). In our judgment on 29 January 1999, we said that the Court's jurisdiction to enforce and interpret the Basic Law is derived from and is subject to the provisions of the Basic Law which provisions include the foregoing. The Court's judgment on 29 January 1999 did not question the authority of the Standing Committee to make an interpretation under Article 158 which would have to be followed by the courts of the Region. The Court accepts that it cannot question that authority. Nor did the Court's judgment question, and the Court accepts that it cannot question, the authority of the National People's Congress or the Standing Committee to do any act which is in accordance with the provisions of the Basic Law and the procedure therein.[902]

494. When enacting the Basic Law, the NPC may be said to have imposed certain substantive and procedural restrictions upon itself with regard to the interpretation and amendment of the Basic Law. However, these are not limitations that are entrenched so as to be beyond retraction by the Chinese Government. The NPC may remove those limitations by amending the Basic Law. It may also restrictively interpret such self-imposed limitations so as to uphold its otherwise plenary power.

---

900. (1999) 2 HKCFAR 4, (CFA).
901. *Ibid.*, at 26: 'What has been controversial is the jurisdiction of the courts of the Region to examine whether any legislative acts of the National People's Congress or its Standing Committee (which we shall refer to simply as "acts") are consistent with the Basic Law and to declare them to be invalid if found to be inconsistent. In our view, the courts of the Region do have this jurisdiction and indeed the duty to declare invalidity if inconsistency is found. It is right that we should take this opportunity of stating so unequivocally.'
902. *See Ng Ka ling v Director of Immigration*, No 2 (1999] 2 HKCFAR 141, (CFA). The Court of Final Appeal did not change its view that it has jurisdiction to inquire whether any legislative act of the Central Government is inconsistent with the Basic Law (the relevant extract from the decision of the Court of Final Appeal is quoted in the immediately preceding footnote, note 902).

However, it might be argued that any such amendment of the Basic Law or interpretation of the Basic Law will have to be processed in accordance with the Basic Law's procedures.[903]

495. An important step in the interpretation process is that the duty of the Standing Committee to consult its Committee for the Basic Law, which was established by a decision of the NPC taken at the same time as the Basic Law was adopted.[904] The function of the Committee of the Basic Law is to study questions arising from the implementation of Articles 17, 18, 158 and 159 of the Basic Law and submit its views thereon to the NPCSC.[905] The Committee for the Basic Law consists of twelve members, six each from the mainland and the Hong Kong Special Administrative Region, including persons from the legal profession. The appointment is for a term of five years. The Hong Kong members are nominated jointly by the Chief Executive, the President of the Legislative Council and the Chief Justice of the Court of Final Appeal for appointment by the Standing Committee of the National People's Congress.[906]

496. The NPC must consult the Committee for the Basic Law before it decides: (a) to return an ordinance to Hong Kong with the effect that it is invalidated (Article 17); (b) to add to or delete from the list of Chinese national Laws in Annex III of the Basic Law (Article 18); (c) to issue an interpretation of the Basic Law; and (d) to amend the Basic Law. With its professionally qualified Hong Kong members the Committee for the Basic Law is in a position to draw the attention of the Standing Committee to the common law perspectives on the question referred to it for consultation, and in this way, there is a linking of the civil and common law traditions.[907] It is not clear whether the NPCSC must follow the opinions of the Committee for the Basic Law.[908]

903. *See* Art. 62 (the power of the National People's Congress power to amend the Constitution) and Art. 67 of the Chinese Constitution (the Standing Committee's power to interpret the Constitution and supervise its enforcement; and to enact and amend laws, with the exception of those which should be enacted by the National People's Congress); *see also* Art. 159 of the Basic Law (amendment of the Basic Law).

904. The National People's Congress approved on 4 April 1990 the recommendations made by the drafting committee of the Basic Law for the establishment of the Committee of Basic Law. *See* Instrument 15 appended to the Basic Law.

905. *Ibid.*, Cl. 3 of the Appendix, the proposal by the Drafting Committee for the Basic Law to establish a Committee for the Basic Law.

906. The Hong Kong members must be Chinese citizens, who are permanent residents of Hong Kong with no right of abode in any foreign country.

907. *See* Yash Ghai, *Hong Kong's New Constitutional Order*, (2nd edn, Hong Kong: Hong Kong University Press, 1999), 197–198.

908. Ji Pengfei said in his report to the National People's Congress on the draft of the Basic Law that the Committee for the Basic Law would enable the National People's Congress to 'heed fully the opinions of the people from all walks of life in Hong Kong' on whether the mater in question 'conforms' to the provisions of the Basic Law. The argument for 'advisory only' view is supported by the fact that only some of its members have legal qualifications. *See* Instrument 9 appended to the Basic Law 'Explanation on "Basic Law of the Hong Kong Special Administrative Region of the People's Republic of China" and its related Documents', dated 28 March 1990.

§3. AMENDMENT OF THE BASIC LAW

497. Article 159 sets out the procedure for amending the Basic Law.

'The power of amendment of [the Basic Law] shall be vested in the National People's Congress.

The power to propose bills for amendments to [the Basic Law] shall be vested in the Standing Committee of the National People's Congress, the State Council and the Hong Kong Special Administrative Region. Amendment bills from the Hong Kong Special Administrative Region shall be submitted to the National People's Congress by the delegation of the Region to the National People's Congress after obtaining the consent of two-thirds of the deputies of the Region to the National People's Congress, two-thirds of all the members of the Legislative Council of the Region, and the Chief Executive of the Region.

Before a bill for amendment to this Law is put on the agenda of the National People's Congress, the Committee for the Basic Law of the Hong Kong Special Administrative Region shall study it and submit its views.

No amendment to this Law shall contravene the established basic policies of the People's Republic of China regarding Hong Kong.'

498. Article 159(1) of the Basic Law recognizes that 'the power of amendment of [the Basic Law] shall be vested in the National People's Congress'. However, the remaining parts of Article 159 lay down a complex procedure for the amendment of the Basic Law involving various institutions of the Hong Kong Special Administrative Region.

499. The Standing Committee of the National People's Congress, the State Council, and the Hong Kong Special Administrative Region have the power to propose a bill for the amendment of the Basic Law. An amendment bill from the Hong Kong Special Administrative Region may be submitted to the NPC by the delegation of the Hong Kong Special Administrative Region only after obtaining the consent of two-thirds of the deputies of the Hong Kong Special Administrative Region to the National People's Congress, two-thirds of the Legislative Council and the Chief Executive.[909] The views of the Committee for the Basic Law have to be sought before an amendment bill is put on the agenda of the National People's Congress.[910]

500. The only substantive restriction upon the amendment of the Basic Law is that no amendment may contravene the established basic policies of China towards the Hong Kong Special Administrative Region.[911] Before the Legislation Law of the People's Republic of China (Order of the President No. 31 of 15 March 2000) which came into force on 1 September 2000, it could be argued that no clear distinction existed between amendment and interpretation, because an interpretation of a national law could be sought from the NPCSC to expand or restrict the meaning of

909. *See* Art. 159(1) of the Basic Law.
910. *See* Art. 159(2), *ibid.*
911. *See* Art. 159(3), *ibid.*

a provision in a national legislation, which would be hardly different in substance from amendment. After the coming into effect of the Legislation Law, there is a change of the situation. The new Law clearly provides that interpretation of a national law can only be sought from the NPCSC on one of the following two grounds: (1) the specific meaning of a provision needs to be further defined; or (2) after its enactment, new developments make it necessary to define the basis on which to apply the law.[912]

912. *See* Lin Feng, 'The Duty of Hong Kong Courts to Follow the NPCSC's Interpretation of the Basic Law: Are There Any Limits?' (2018) 48 *Hong Kong Law Journal* 167.

Chapter 3. District Administration

501. Hong Kong inherited from Britain a unitary system of government, with a central government and local authorities. The Basic Law has to all intents given up on the local government administration system. The British introduced a system of local government consisting of the Urban Council, the Regional Council and the District Boards in 1883, 1986 and 1982.[913] These three local authorities were replaced with provisional Urban Councils, Regional Councils and District Boards, which were in turn abolished.[914] Eighteen District Councils were established with effect from 1 January 2000 to replace the Provisional District Boards.[915]

502. The only local authority that operates today is the District Council. The District Administration Scheme, which was launched in 1982, with the establishment of the District Board system continues to be in operation. Under this scheme, there is a District Council and a district management committee in each of the Districts of Hong Kong. The aim of the district administration scheme is to achieve a more effective coordination of government activities in the provision of services and facilities at the district level, to ensure that the Government is responsive to district needs and problems and to promote public participation in district affairs.[916] The Home Affairs Department is responsible for the District Administration Scheme, community building and community involvement activities, rural public works and district minor works programmes, and the licensing of hotels and guesthouses, bedspace apartments and clubs. It promotes the concept of effective building management and works closely with other government departments to consistently improve the standard of building management in Hong Kong. In each of the districts, there is a District Officer, who heads the district office, and represents the government at district level. He is responsible for overseeing the operation of the scheme. He coordinates district programmes and ensures public participation in district affairs. He must see that the views of the District Council are taken into account and implemented, as far as possible. He mediates disputes between corporate bodies, such as building management bodies, and residents.[917] Since 1997, there have been significant changes to this regional administration framework.

---

913. P. Wesley-Smith, *Constitutional and Administrative Law in Hong Kong* (2nd edn, Hong Kong: Longman Asia Ltd, 1994), 131–133.
914. The Urban Council (Amendment) Ordinance (No 112 of 1997)) abolished the Urban Councils and replaced them with Provisional Urban Councils. The Regional Council (Amendment) Ordinance 1997 (No 113 of 1997) replaced the Regional councils with Provisional Regional Councils. These provisional councils were abolished by the Provision of Municipal Services (Reorganization) Ordinance (Cap. 552), s. 3. For unsuccessful challenges of the abolition of the local authorities, *see Wong Chung Ki v Chief Executive of HKSAR* [2000] HKEC 701, (CA), and *Chan Shu Ying v Chief Executive of the HKSAR* [2001] 1 HKLRD 405, (CFI).
915. District Councils Ordinance (Cap. 547).
916. *See* Home Affairs Department's website on District Administration: https://www.had.govhk/en/public_services/district_administration/admin_main.htm.
917. *Ibid.* For a brief account, *see* 'District Administration', in *Hong Kong: The Facts*, published by the Hong Kong Government, July 2018: https://www.govhk/en/about/abouthk/factsheets/docs/district_admin.pdf.

503. Before their abolition in 1997, the Urban Council and the Regional Council were empowered to deal with matters such as concerning the environment, food, hygiene, recreation and culture. The now-defunct Urban Council was responsible for administration in the urban areas, and the now-defunct Regional Council was responsible for administration in the rural areas. The duties of the Urban Council were discharged by the Urban Services Department. It also had a number of ward offices. The Regional Council carried out its work through the Regional Services Department, four functional select committees and a Liquor Licensing Board as well as nine geographically based committees.[918]

504. The District Boards had no such important administrative functions. They carried out coordinating functions and were sometimes treated no differently from other government advisory bodies. District Boards were not a form of local government, in the strict meaning of the term.[919] There were close ties between the Municipal Councils and the District Boards.[920] There were eighteen District Boards (nine urban District Boards and nine New Territories District Boards) during the colonial era, and currently there are eighteen District Councils for the eighteen districts.

505. There is an important local body called the Heung Yee Kuk, which represents the indigenous inhabitants of the New Territories.[921] The preamble to the Heung Yee Kuk Ordinance of 1997 (Cap. 1097) states the objective of the Ordinance as follows:

> (a) the Heung Yee Kuk has in the past served as a valuable advisory body to the Government on New Territories affairs and has been a forum where leaders of opinion in the Territories have been able to exchange views; and (b) it is now considered desirable that the Heung Yee Kuk should become a statutory advisory body with a constitution so framed as to ensure that it will as far as possible be truly representative of informed and responsible opinion in the New Territories. Heung Yee Kuk's major functions are (a) to promote and develop mutual cooperation and understanding among the people of the New Territories; (b) to promote and develop cooperation and understanding between the Government and the people of the New Territories; (c) to advise the Government on social and economic developments in the interests of the welfare and prosperity of the people of the New Territories; (d) to encourage the observance of all such customs and traditional usages of the people of the New Territories as are conducive to their welfare and to the preservation of public morality; and (e) to exercise such functions as they may be invited to from time to time by the Chief Executive.[922]

918. *Hong Kong 1996* (Hong Kong: Hong Kong Government, 1996), 12–13.
919. Norman Miners, *The Government and Politics of Hong Kong* (5th edn, Hong Kong: Oxford University Press, 1995), 175–176.
920. *Hong Kong 1996* (Hong Kong: Hong Kong Government, 1996), 13–14.
921. Norman Miners, *The Government and Politics of Hong Kong* (5th edn, Hong Kong: Oxford University Press, 1995), 177–178.
922. Section 9 of the Heung Kuk Ordinance (Cap. 1097) of the Laws of Hong Kong.

§1. The District Administration in Hong Kong Before 1997

506. In 1997, the Urban Council had 41 members, 32 of whom were returned by geographical constituency elections and 9 were returned by the 9 urban District Boards. The Regional Council had 32 members, 27 returned by geographical constituency elections and 9 by the 9 New Territories District Boards. There were 3 ex officio members from the Heung Yee Kuk. There was a total of 373 District Board members, of whom 346 were returned by geographical constituency elections and 27 were ex officio members from the Rural Committee.[923]

507. The Basic Law provides that 'district organizations which are not organs of political power may be established in the Hong Kong Special Administrative Region' and that 'the powers and functions of the district organizations and the method of their formation shall be prescribed by law'.[924] The meaning of the phrase, 'district organizations', is, however, not entirely clear. The Basic Law does not expressly say whether the existing local administrative bodies are the district organizations that 'may be established' in Hong Kong today.[925]

§2. The District Administration in Hong Kong Since 1997

508. The Urban Council, the Regional Council and the District Boards were dissolved on the handover. They were replaced by interim bodies, which were then called the Provisional Urban Council, the Provisional Regional Council and the Provisional District Boards, respectively. In addition to the members who served in these bodies immediately before the handover, there were nine new members appointed to the Provisional Urban Council, eleven appointed to the Provisional Regional Council and many more appointed to the Provisional District Boards. These interim bodies conducted business as described above.[926]

509. After an administrative review undertaken by the Government in 1998, it was decided that the Provisional Urban Council and the Provisional Regional Council would be dissolved at the end of 1999. Their powers were to be distributed among government departments and certain other public bodies. The Provisional District Boards had their first election in the Hong Kong Special Administrative Region in late 1999. In 2000, the Provisional District Boards were renamed the District Councils.[927] Today there are eighteen District Councils and together they have 458 members. District Council members belong to two categories: (1) members

923. *Hong Kong 1997 – A review of 1996* (Hong Kong: Hong Kong Government Printer, 1997), 10–14.
924. Articles 97–98.
925. Yash Ghai, *Hong Kong's New Constitutional Order: The Resumption of Chinese Sovereignty and the Basic Law*, (Hong Kong: Hong Kong University Press, 1997), 236–7.
926. *Hong Kong 1998* (Hong Kong: Hong Kong Special Administrative Region Government, 1999), 13–15 and 417–419.
927. *Hong Kong 1999* (Hong Kong: Hong Kong Special Administrative Region Government, 2000), 14–17, *see* the Provision of Municipal Services (Reorganization) Ordinance (Cap. 552) of the Laws of Hong Kong.

who are directly elected through geographical constituencies; and (2) the Chairmen of Rural Committees who are ex officio members of the District Council.[928] The term of office of the District Councils is four years. The first District Councils elections were held in December 1999, and the first term of District Councils commenced in January 2000. In their third term, which commenced in January 2008, District Councils consisted of 534 members, made up of as follows: (i) 405 directly elected members, through single constituency elections on the first-past-the-post system; (ii) twenty-seven Chairmen of Rural Committees who are ex officio members of the District Council; and (iii) 102 members appointed by the Chief Executive. The District Councils constituted after elections in January 2016, consist of 458 members, with 431 directly elected and 27 Rural Committee Chairmen.

510. The functions of the District Council are as follows:

(1) to advise the Government:
   (a) on matters affecting the well-being of the people in the District;
   (b) on the provision and use of public facilities and services within the District;
   (c) on the adequacy and priorities of Government programmes for the District; and
   (d) on the use of public funds allocated to the District for local public works and community activities; and
(2) where funds are made available for the purpose, to undertake:
   (a) environmental improvements within the District;
   (b) the promotion of recreational and cultural activities within the District; and
   (c) community activities within the District.[929]

511. The abolition of provisional Councils caused much disquiet in Hong Kong. In 2001, a former Provisional Regional Councillor unsuccessfully challenged these reforms in *Chan Shu Ying v Chief Executive of the Hong Kong SAR.*[930] Construing Article 97 of the Basic Law which recognized the role of district organizations not as 'organs of political power' but organizations to be consulted by the government on district administration and other affairs or to be responsible for providing services in such fields as culture recreation and environmental sanitation, the court held

928. District Council Ordinance (Cap. 547), s. 9. Rural Committees were set up by the British administration after the Second World War. They built upon a system of village representatives that the Japanese introduced in rural Hong Kong during their occupation of Hong Kong during the Second World War. A Rural Committee consists of village representatives of the geographical area of the Committee. Rural Committees are non-statutory and informal organizations but have representation in the District Councils and have voting rights in the Legislative Council functional constituency of Hung Yee Kuk. For Village Representatives and their role in Rural Committees, *see Secretary for Justice v Chan Wah* [2000] 3 HKCFAR 459, (CFA).

929. District Council Ordinance (Cap. 547), s. 61.

930. *Chan Shu Ying v Chief Executive of the HKSAR* [2001] 1 HKLR 405, (CFI).

that Article 97 was 'no more than an empowering provision. It does not create a constitutional obligation to establish [district organizations]'.[931] On the question whether the abolition of the elected councils denied the people's constitutional right to participate in the public life, Hartmann J held, recognizing the imperative of government policy, that there still remained an opportunity for the citizens to participate in civic affairs 'by way of open debate, consultation and advice [through the District Councils] to have a real influence on public affairs'.[932]

931. *Ibid.*, 424.
932. *Ibid.*, 422.

Part IV. Citizenship and the Administration of Justice

Chapter 1. Rules Concerning Nationality and the Relevance of Nationality

512. Article 15 of the Universal Declaration of Human rights declares that 'everyone has the right to a nationality' and that 'no one shall be arbitrarily deprived of his nationality or denied the right to change his nationality'.[933]

§1. NATIONALITY UNDER THE BRITISH ADMINISTRATION[934]

513. Under the British law, all those owing allegiance to the British Crown were 'British subjects' and accordingly all persons who were born in Hong Kong became British subjects. Any British subject had the right to enter and reside in the UK. In 1948, with the enactment of the British Nationality Act, there came into being a new status, that of Citizens of the United Kingdom and Colonies (CUKC) who retained their status as British subjects and their right to enter and reside in the UK. In 1962, the Commonwealth Immigrants Act took away the right of CUKCs not born in the UK or having a British passport to enter and reside in the UK. The Immigration Act of 1971 provided that only a *partial* had such a right. A CUKC was regarded as a partial, for example, if he or she was born or naturalized in the UK or could fulfil other strict requirements. The British Nationality Act of 1981 divided CUKCs into the following three categories: British Citizens, Citizens of British Dependant Territories and British Overseas Citizens.

514. The British Dependant Territories Citizenship (BDTC) was the one immediately relevant to Hong Kong. The British Nationality Act of 1981 provided transitional provisions to confer the status of BDTC on CUKCs and their dependants who had acquired that status by virtue of birth, registration or naturalization in a

933. *See*, for instance, 'Right to Nationality and Statelessness' at http://www.ohchr.org/EN/Issues/Pages/Nationality.aspx.

934. *See*, for a fuller account which this section draws upon, P. Wesley-Smith, *Constitutional and Administrative Law in Hong Kong* (2nd edn, Hong Kong: Longman Asia Ltd, 1994), 327–339; Johannes Chan, 'Nationality' in R. Wacks (ed.) *Human Rights in Hong Kong* (Hong Kong: Oxford University Press, 1992); Johannes Chan, 'Nationality and Permanent Residence' in Johannes Chan and C. L. Lim (eds) *Law of the Hong Kong Constitution* (Hong Kong: Sweet & Maxwell, 2015).

dependant territory, like Hong Kong. It also provided how a person could acquire BDTC status after the commencement of the Act. Only British Citizens were entitled to a British passport. Citizens of British Dependant Territories and British Overseas Citizens were entitled to an appropriate passport and to British consular protection while overseas. The effect of these changes was that people born in Hong Kong were denied an automatic right to enter and reside in the UK.

515. In 1986, an Order in Council was promulgated declaring that all BDTCs would lose that status upon the reversion of sovereignty to China in 1997. However, upon application, they were offered a new status, British National Overseas (BNO) status, when the Hong Kong Act 1985 was enacted. Section 2(1) of the Act enabled Her Majesty to pass an Order in Council to make provision whereby 'persons who are British Dependent Territories citizens by virtue of [a connection with Hong Kong] may before that date (or before the end of 1997 if born in that year before the relevant date) acquire a new form of British nationality the holders of which shall be known as British Nationals (Overseas)'. Holders of BNO passports had no right of abode in the UK. BNO passports were intended to be travel documents that probably confer their holders no consular protection anywhere in the world, despite their use of language to the contrary.[935]

516. In the wake of the 4 June Tiananmen Square protests in Beijing in 1989, the British Parliament enacted the British Nationality (Hong Kong) Act 1990, which imposed an obligation on the Secretary of State to grant British Citizenship to up to 50,000 people, together with their dependants, recommended by the Governor of Hong Kong. Under this scheme, holders of BDTC and BN(O) were entitled to apply for selection on point-based system. Those obtaining a British passport under that scheme enjoyed full British citizenship (including the right of abode in Britain) without having to fulfil the need for residence in Britain for the required number of years. The eligibility criteria were, however, very strict.[936]

§2. Nationality under the Basic Law

517. The Joint Declaration referred to the right of abode in the text of the agreement and referred to nationality only in a memorandum, which stated that 'all Hong Kong Chinese compatriots, whether they are holders of the BDTC or not, are Chinese nationals'. The memorandum also stated that Hong Kong BDTCs would cease to be such from 1 July 1997, and that no one could acquire that status in Hong Kong after that date. Those who had acquired that status previously would be eligible to receive travel documents issued by the British Government, which also gave them

935. Johannes Chan, 'Nationality' in R Wacks (ed.) *Human Rights in Hong Kong* (Hong Kong: Oxford University Press, 1992), at 483–485.

936. Roda Mushkat, *One Country Two International Legal Personalities: The Case of Hong Kong* (Hong Kong: Hong Kong University Press, 1997).

British consular protection abroad. It is in the light of this development that the Hong Kong (British Nationality) Order was made in 1986 to create the new status of BNO.[937]

518. The Basic Law provided for the application of several national laws in Hong Kong, including the Nationality Law of China.[938] However, it did not restate the above statement, 'all Hong Kong Chinese compatriots, whether they are holders of the BDTC or not, are Chinese nationals'. Therefore, Chinese Nationality Law governs the nationality status of Hong Kong residents upon 1997. The Nationality Law does not recognize dual nationality and creates difficulties for Chinese people who have acquired a foreign nationality.[939]

§3. Right of Abode

519. The right of abode or permanent residence may be obtained not only by Chinese nationals but also by others living in Hong Kong. The Basic Law has a list of six categories of people who enjoy the right of abode in Hong Kong as Hong Kong permanent residents:

(1) Chinese citizens born in Hong Kong before or after 1 July 1997;
(2) Chinese citizens who have ordinarily resided in Hong Kong for a continuous period of not less than seven years before or after 1 July 1997;
(3) persons of Chinese nationality born outside Hong Kong of those residents listed in categories (1) and (2);
(4) persons not of Chinese nationality who have entered Hong Kong with valid travel documents, have ordinarily resided in Hong Kong for a continuous period of not less than seven years and have taken Hong Kong as their place of permanent residence before or after 1 July 1997;
(5) persons under 21 years of age born in Hong Kong of those residents listed in category (4), before or after 1 July 1997; and
(6) persons other than those residents listed in categories (1)–(5), who, before 1 July 1997 had the right of abode in Hong Kong only.[940]

520. There has been much litigation on the meaning of 'ordinary residence' necessary for the purpose of acquiring permanent residence in Hong Kong. In *Fateh Muhammad v Commissioner of Registration*, it was held that the expression 'ordinarily resident' must be given its natural and ordinary meaning depending on the

937. Peter Wesley-Smith, *Constitutional and Administrative Law in Hong Kong* (Hong Kong: Longman Asia Ltd, 1994), 332–333 and Johannes Chan, 'Nationality' in Raymond Wacks (ed.) *Human Rights in Hong Kong* (Hong Kong: Oxford University Press, 1992), 479.

938. Annex II and Art. 18.

939. *See* generally Tung-Pi Chen, 'The Nationality Law of the People's Republic of China and the Overseas Chinese in Hong Kong, Macao and Southeast Asia' (1984) 5 *New York Law School Journal of International and Comparative Law* 281.

940. Article 24 of the Basic Law.

context in which the expression appears.[941] In *Fateh*, residence while serving a substantial term of imprisonment or detention in a training or detention centre was not regarded as part of the required period of ordinary residence.[942] In *Fayomi v Secretary for Security*, it was held that several interrupted periods of time that an applicant had spent in Hong Kong on visitor visas could not be counted towards the period of ordinary residence.[943] In *Vallejos v Commissioner of Registration*[944] it was held that foreign domestic helpers' visa prevented them from satisfying the requirement of 'ordinary residence'. They are permitted to live in Hong Kong only for the purpose of being employed as a domestic helper on contract with a specific employer for two years. Their visas expressly state that their stay in Hong will not be counted as being for the purpose of settlement in Hong Kong. At the end of their two-year contract they have to return home for two weeks before they could enter on a new similarly restricted two-year contract. It was held that these distinguishing features result in the residence of foreign domestic helpers in Hong Kong being qualitatively so far-removed from what would traditionally be recognized as 'ordinary residence' as to justify concluding that they do not, as a class, come within the meaning of 'ordinarily resident' for the purpose acquiring permanent residence in Hong Kong.[945]

I. The Right of Abode of the 'Returning Residents'

521. In the years immediately before the handover, quite a number of Hong Kong residents left Hong Kong, in fear of perceived uncertainties and problems under Chinese administration, but many of them returned home having acquired foreign passports. The Chinese Government was willing to let them retain their right of abode, notwithstanding their foreign nationality, as long as they had returned to

941. *Fateh Muhammad v Commissioner of Registration* (2001) 4 HKCFAR 278, (CFA), 283–284. In *Vallejos v Commissioner of Registration* (2013) 16 KCFAR 45, (CFA), the Court of Final Appeal observed that the expression 'ordinarily resident' in Art. 24(2)(4) of the Basic Law was open-textured as a matter of language and inherently capable of assuming different meanings in different contexts. It was always necessary to examine the factual position of the person claiming to be ordinarily resident to see whether there were any special features affecting the nature and quality of his or her residence. If such features existed, one asked whether they resulted in that person's residence being qualitatively so far-removed from what would traditionally be recognized as 'ordinary residence' as to justify concluding that he or she was not 'ordinarily resident'. This was necessarily a question of fact and degree. *See* [80]–[82].

942. *Fateh Muhammad v Commissioner of Registration* (2001) 4 HKCFAR 278, (CFA), 284. Section 2(4)(b) of the Immigration Ordinance (Cap. 115) provides that 'a person shall not be treated as ordinarily resident in Hong Kong … during any period … of imprisonment or detention pursuant to the sentence or order of any court'. Resorting to the *de minimis* principle, Bokhary PJ was willing to concede that a period of imprisonment of 'trivial duration' may not break the continuity of residence (*Fateh Muhammed* at p. 283). In *Asif Ali v Director of Immigration* [2011] HKEC 868, (CA), the Court of Appeal held that an order of a court that a person be detained in custody pending trial is not to be regarded as an order of detention capable of interrupting the period of residence.

943. *Fayomi v Secretary for Security* [2009] HKEC 2039, (CFI).

944. (2013) 16 KCFAR 45, (CFA).

945. *Ibid.*, [89].

Hong Kong prior to 1997. This concession was further expanded with the enactment of the Immigration (Amendment) Ordinance 1997. The relevant provision (section 6 of Schedule 1 of the Ordinance) stated that such a returning resident could retain the right of abode in Hong Kong in the following circumstances:

(a) he had 'settled in Hong Kong immediately before 1 July 1997';
(b) he had returned 'to settle in Hong Kong within the period of eighteen months commencing on 1 July 1997'; or
(c) he had returned after the above said eighteen months, 'but only if he has not been absent from Hong Kong for a continuous period of not less than thirty-six months'.[946]

522. According to section 2(d) of Schedule 1 of the Immigration Ordinance, a person who can satisfy one of those conditions is treated as a permanent resident under the fourth category of permanent residents, namely, persons not of Chinese nationality who have entered Hong Kong with valid travel documents, have ordinarily resided in Hong Kong for a continuous period of not less than seven years, and have taken Hong Kong as their place of permanent residence before or after 1 July 1997.

II. The Right of Abode of Non-Chinese Nationals

523. In order to acquire the right of abode, a non-Chinese must have entered Hong Kong with a valid travel document, resided in Hong Kong for a continuous period of seven years immediately before applying for permanent residence and taken Hong Kong as his permanent place of residence.[947] 'Chinese citizens' are defined in the current Immigration Ordinance as Chinese nationals in accordance with the Chinese Nationality Law.[948] A person who is not of Chinese descent may obtain Chinese nationality by naturalization. While a person not of Chinese descent may acquire Chinese nationality by naturalization, children of such a naturalized Chinese national do not automatically acquire Chinese nationality. They themselves have to successfully apply for naturalization.[949] A Chinese national by naturalization is considered to be a Chinese citizen and may obtain a Hong Kong Special Administrative Region passport under the Hong Kong Special Administrative Region Passports Ordinance (Cap. 539).

524. Whereas a Chinese citizen has only to prove that he has resided in Hong Kong for a period of seven years before or after the establishment of the Hong Kong

946. Section 6 of Sch. 1.
947. Basic Law, Art. 24(4). These requirements have been examined in several cases. On the principles applicable, the most instructive decisions are in *Prem Singh v Director of Immigration* (2003) 6 HKCFAR 26, (CFA), and *Commissioner of Registration v Registration of Persons Tribunal* [2000] 2 HKLRD 523, (CA), affirmed by the Court of Final Appeal in *Fateh Muhammad v Commissioner of Registration, Registration of Persons Tribunal* (2001) 4 HKCFAR 278, (CFA).
948. Section 1 of Sch. 1 of the Immigration Ordinance (Cap. 115).
949. *Azan Aziz Marwah v Director of Immigration* [2008] HKEC 2087, (CFI).

Special Administrative Region, a non-Chinese citizen must additionally prove that he completed a period of seven years of ordinary residence 'immediately before' making the application for right of aboard. It has been held that the drawing of such a distinction was not discriminatory. As Bokhary PJ observed in the Court of Final Appeal case of *Fateh Muhammad v Commissioner of Registration* 'different treatment of citizens and non-citizens in regard to the right of abode is a common, if not invariable, feature of the laws of countries throughout the world, including those with constitutions which prohibit discrimination'.[950]

525. The Immigration Ordinance provides as follows:

A person shall not be treated as ordinarily resident in Hong Kong

a. during any period in which he remains in Hong Kong:
   - with or without the authority of the Director, after landing unlawfully, or
   - in contravention of any condition of stay, or
   - as a refugee, or
   - while detained in Hong Kong, or
   - while employed as a contract worker, who is from outside Hong Kong, under a Government importation of labour scheme, or
   - while employed as a domestic helper who is from outside Hong Kong,[951] or
   - as a member of a consular post within the meaning of Consular Relations Ordinance (Cap. 557), or
   - as a member of the Hong Kong Garrison, or
   - as a holder of a prescribed Central People's Government travel document or
b. during any period of imprisonment or detention pursuant to the sentence or order of any court.[952]

III. The Right of Abode of Children Born in China of Hong Kong Residents

526. Article 24(3) provides that persons of Chinese nationality born outside Hong Kong of Chinese citizens, who are Hong Kong permanent residents, are permanent residents of Hong Kong. Where such a person is born in China, the question is whether such a person is governed by Article 22 of the Basic Law, which provides that 'for entry into the Hong Kong Special Administrative Region, people from other parts of China must apply for approval. Among them, the number of persons who enter the Region for the purpose of settlement shall be determined by the competent authorities of the Central People's Government after consulting the government of the Region.' The Immigration (Amendment) (No. 3) Ordinance 1997

950. *Fateh Muhammad v Commissioner of Registration* (2001) 4 HKCFAR 278, (CFA), 285.
951. On this, *see Vallejos v Commissioner of Registration* (2013) 16 HKCFAR 45, (CFA).
952. Section 2(4).

provided that a person of Chinese nationality born in China of permanent residents of Hong Kong must possess a one-way exit permit issued by mainland Chinese authorities in order to lawfully enter Hong Kong. In *Ng Ka Ling and Others v Director of Immigration*,[953] the Court of Final Appeal held that Article 22 of the Basic Law refers to residents of China, other than those who have the right of abode in Hong Kong. Where a person who is born in China is a permanent resident of Hong Kong by virtue of his parents' right of abode in Hong Kong, Article 22 has no application: He is a permanent resident of Hong Kong and has the right to enter Hong Kong.[954] In *Chan Kam Nga v Director of Immigration*[955] the question was whether a Chinese national born outside Hong Kong would be entitled to permanent residence in Hong Kong, where his parents of Chinese citizenship obtained permanent residence in Hong Kong only after the birth of such person. The Court of Final Appeal saw no reason to limit the benefit of Article 24 to Chinese nationals born outside Hong Kong only if his parents were permanent residents of Hong Kong at the time of his birth.

527. In all these cases, the children in question were born in China and claimed to be permanent residents of Hong Kong because of the permanent residence status of their parents who held Chinese citizenship. Some of these children had unlawfully landed in Hong Kong while others had overstayed in Hong Kong. None of them had a certificate of entitlement issued by the relevant mainland Chinese administrative authority to enter Hong Kong. One child was born out of wedlock to a woman who had no permanent residence in Hong Kong, whereas the father had acquired Hong Kong permanent residence.

528. The validity of three sets of provisions in the Immigration Ordinance was challenged in Hong Kong courts. The first two provisions were in issue in *Ng Ka Ling* and *Cheung Lai Wah* and the third provision was in issue in *Chan Kam Nga*. They are:

(1) A person of Chinese nationality born in China of Hong Kong permanent residents holding Chinese citizenship could apply for permanent resident status only if he had entered Hong Kong for that purpose after obtaining a certificate of entitlement.

---

953. *Ng Ka ling v Director of Immigration* (1999) 2 HKCFAR 4, (CFA).

954. In *Ng Ka ling v Director of Immigration* (1999) 2 HKCFAR 4, (CFA), Chief Justice Andrew Li, delivering the judgment of the Court of Final Appeal, found that the legislative provision which required a permanent resident of Hong Kong born in China to produce a one-way exit permit was contrary to the Basic Law: 'Considering the language of Article 24 and Article 22(4), in our view, "people from other parts of China", including among them persons entering for settlement referred to in Article 22(4), do not include permanent residents of the Region upon whom the Basic Law confers the right of abode in the Region. Persons with permanent resident status under the Basic Law are not, as a matter of ordinary language, people from other parts of China. They are permanent residents of this part of China. Nor is it correct to describe them as persons entering for the purpose of settlement. Their status is that of permanent residents of the Region. They do not enter the Region for the purpose of settlement. They are permanent residents with the right to enter the Region and to remain as long as they wish': (1999) 2 HKCFAR 4, (CFA), 35.

955. (1999) 2 HKCFAR 82.

(2) The Immigration Ordinance recognized that an illegitimate child of a woman who is a Hong Kong permanent resident is entitled to Hong Kong permanent residence. However, where the child is born out of wedlock to a woman who is not a Hong Kong permanent resident, the child could not rely on the permanent residence status of his father unless the mother legitimated her relationship by marrying the man.
(3) A person of Chinese nationality who is born outside Hong Kong of parents who are not Hong Kong permanent residents at the time of his birth, but who acquired permanent residence thereafter, was not entitled to permanent residence.

529. In *Ng Ka ling v Director of Immigration*, the Court of Final Appeal found all the above statutory provisions to be unconstitutional:[956]

(1) a Chinese national born in China of Hong Kong permanent residents was by that fact alone a Hong Kong permanent resident and did not need any special permission to enter Hong Kong;
(2) it would be discriminatory to deny an illegitimate child the benefit of his father's permanent resident status unless the parents legitimated their marriage subsequently (the mother having died soon after the childbirth);
(3) whether the parents were permanent residents at the time of birth or became so only after the child was born was not a relevant factor, in the light of the importance of the concept of unity of the family.

530. The Hong Kong Government, which was dissatisfied with the decision of the Court of Final Appeal, requested the NPCSC to reinterpret the relevant provisions of the Basic Law. The Standing Committee disagreed with the views expressed by the Court of Final Appeal and held that:

(a) a person of Chinese nationality born in China of Hong Kong permanent residents could apply for permanent resident status only if he had entered Hong Kong for that purpose after obtaining a certificate of entitlement; and
(b) a person of Chinese nationality born outside Hong Kong of persons who were not Hong Kong permanent residents at the time of the birth was not entitled to permanent residence.[957]

531. The interpretation did not disturb the Court of Final Appeal's decision regarding the provision of the Immigration Ordinance, which denied an illegitimate child the benefit of its father's permanent resident status unless the parents married thereafter.

956. *Ng Ka ling v Director of Immigration* (1999) 2 HKCFAR 4, (CFA).
957. *Lau Kong Yung v Director of Immigration*; (1999) 2 HKCFAR 300, (CFA).

532. New categories of cases have come before Hong Kong courts. In *Chong Fung*, the Court of Final Appeal held that the Standing Committee's reinterpretation of the Basic Law did not consider the case of a person of Chinese nationality born in Hong Kong. The Court held that such a person does not have to satisfy the criterion that his parents were Hong Kong permanent residents at the time of his birth, it being sufficient that his parents acquired permanent residence subsequent to his birth.[958]

533. In *Tam Nga Yin*, the Court of Final Appeal considered whether a person of Chinese nationality adopted as child by persons with Hong Kong permanent residence qualified for Hong Kong permanent residence. The Court held that the Standing Committee's interpretation did not cover the case of adopted children and went on to interpret the relevant provisions of the Basic Law and concluded that an adopted child did not qualify for the right of abode in Hong Kong.[959] There have been several cases concerning those affected by the interpretation exercise.

534. In *Ng Siu Tung and Others v Director of Immigration*,[960] the Court of Final Appeal observed that Article 22(4) referred to entry into the Hong Kong Special Administrative Region, and not into Hong Kong, which clearly indicated that what Article 22(4) intended to regulate was the entry after 1 July 1997 when Hong Kong became a Special Administrative Region. Those who had arrived before 1 July 1997 were entitled to have their status verified and to exercise their right of abode in the Hong Kong Special Administrative Region without the need to having a one-way exit permit. The Court of Final Appeal held that: 'Persons who had entered Hong Kong prior to 1 July 1997, whether illegally or otherwise and continued to stay beyond 1 July 1997 cannot be said to be entering the Hong Kong Special Administrative Region when they entered before that date. There was then no Hong Kong Special Administrative Region and Art. 22(4) of the Basic Law had not then taken effect.'[961]

535. The Court of First Instance in *Commissioner of Registration v Registration of Persons Tribunal*[962] held that a person who had been granted permanent residence in Hong Kong before the Basic Law came into effect would not automatically be entitled to permanent residence under the Basic Law: 'There is no dispute that the statutory criteria governing whether a person is a permanent resident of Hong Kong are different before and after July 1997 upon the establishment of the Hong Kong Special Administrative Region. Thus, someone who was a permanent resident of Hong Kong before July 1997 would only … be regarded as a permanent resident after July 1997 if he also meets the post-July 1997 statutory criteria.'[963]

958. *Director of Immigration v Chong Fung Yuen* (2001) 4 HKCFAR 211, (CFA).
959. *Tam Nga Yin and Others v Director of Immigration* (2001) 4 HKCFAR 644, (CFA).
960. (2002) 5 HKCFAR 1, (CFA).
961. *Ibid.*, [167].
962. [2015] HKEC 369, (CFI).
963. *Ibid.*, [20].

536. The third requirement (that the applicant has taken Hong Kong as his place of permanent residence) was examined by the Court of Final Appeal in *Prem Singh v Director of Immigration*[964] and *Gutierrez v Commissioner of Registration.*[965] As the Court of Final Appeal observed in *Gutierrez*, *Prem Singh* had held that:

> the wording, and especially the tense used by Art. 24(2)(4) in requiring persons concerned to 'have taken Hong Kong as their place of permanent residence', meant that an applicant, when putting forward his claim for verification by the Director, had to be able to point to facts which had already occurred permitting him to say that he had, starting at some prior point in time, already taken Hong Kong as his place of permanent residence. This was so while recognising that the permanence requirement imports 'the quality of a past, present and future commitment to establishing and maintaining a permanent residence in Hong Kong.' It was held that the permanence requirement 'makes it necessary for the applicant to satisfy the Director both that he intends to establish his permanent home in Hong Kong and that he has taken concrete steps to do so'. He must, in other words, show that his residence here is 'intended to be more than ordinary residence and that he intends and has taken action to make Hong Kong, and Hong Kong alone, his place of permanent residence', meaning that he intends to reside in Hong Kong 'permanently or indefinitely, rather than for a limited period'.[966]

964. (2003) 6 HKCFAR 26, (CFA).
965. (2014) 17 HKCFAR 518, (CFA).
966. *Gutierrez v Commissioner of Registration* (2014) 17 HKCFAR 518, (CFA), [20]. The Court of Final Appeal in *Gutierrez* had to consider whether a child, whose mother, a foreign domestic helper who was not qualified to claim permanent residence in Hong Kong, had to satisfy the requirement of having taken as the place of his permanent residence, which it answered in the affirmative. At [54], it held that 'the permanence requirement laid down by Art. 24(2)(4) of Basic Law requires a child or young adult applicant who is a non-Chinese national born in Hong Kong and whose application is made before he reaches the age of 21 to meet the criteria established by this Court in *Prem Singh v Director of Immigration*, taking into account his individual circumstances, including any action taken or arrangements made by himself or by a parent or legal guardian on his behalf or for his benefit which tend to show that such child or young adult has taken Hong Kong as his place of permanent residence'.

Chapter 2. Fundamental Rights and Liberties

§1. General

537. Hong Kong's transition from a British Crown Colony to a special administrative region of the People's Republic of China paved the way for constitutional protection of fundamental rights and freedoms. The first step was taken in 1991 when the British administration promulgated the Hong Kong Bill of Rights Ordinance (Cap. 383) 'to provide for the incorporation into the law of Hong Kong of provisions of the ICCPR as applied to Hong Kong; and for ancillary and connected matters'.[967] Article 39 of the Basic Law provides that 'the provisions of the International Covenant on Civil and Political Rights, the International Covenant on Economic, Social and Cultural Rights, and international labour conventions as applied to Hong Kong shall remain in force and shall be implemented through the laws of the Hong Kong Special Administrative Region'. While through the instrumentality of the Basic Law and the Bill of Rights, the ICCPR enjoys virtually direct application in Hong Kong, no local statute has been passed to incorporate the ICESCR into Hong Kong law. However, the ICESCR has inspirational value.

538. In *Chan Mei Yee v Director of Immigration*, Cheung J said that 'the way in which the ICCPR and ICESCR are formulated clearly supports the argument that the latter covenant is promotional in nature. However, even though it is promotional in nature, it does not mean that the ICESCR cannot be used as a framework in which government decisions or discretions are to be considered'.[968] Bokhary NPJ was prepared to give more persuasive authority to ICESCR when he said in *Ho Choi Wan v Hong Kong Housing Authority* that 'If it were necessary to do so in order to establish that the Authority is duty-bound to provide affordable housing, it might well be possible to pray the ICESCR powerfully in aid of construing the Housing Ordinance to impose that duty [namely a duty to provide affordable housing].'[969] In 2003 in the second report submitted to the United Nation's Committee on Economic Social and Cultural Rights, the Hong Kong Government stated that 'It is true that there is no single law – corresponding to the Hong Kong Bill of Rights Ordinance in relation to the ICCPR that incorporates the ICESCR into Hong Kong's domestic legal order. However, ICESCR provisions are incorporated into our domestic law through several Articles of the Basic Law (for example Articles 27, 36, 37 137, 144 and 149), and through provisions in over 50 Ordinances.'[970]

---

967. Long Title of the Hong Kong Bill of Rights Ordinance (Cap. 383). We will *see* below in the discussion on the Bill of Rights as a source of human rights that the Bill of Rights Ordinance is an ordinary statute with no special constitutional status, but that courts continue to make frequent references to the Hong Kong Bill of Rights, as if it has such special constitutional status.

968. *Chan Mei Yee v Director of Immigration* [2000] HKEC 788, (CFI), [67].

969. *Ho Choi Wan v Hong Kong Housing Authority* (2005) 8 HKCFAR 628, (CFA), [67].

970. This extract of the report is cited in *Kong Yunming v Director of Social Welfare* (2013) 16 HKCFAR 950, (CFA), [174]. *See* the Fourth Report submitted in February 2020, where the Hong Kong Government reasserts that 'it is neither necessary nor appropriate to incorporate all the provisions of the Covenant directly into the laws of Hong Kong' (para. 2.2). Noting the absence of comprehensive legislation to incorporate the ICESCR into Hong Kong law (unlike the Hong Kong Bill of

539. Hong Kong's Basic Law, which came into operation on 1 July 1999, contains a separate chapter, namely Chapter III, dedicated to 'Fundamental rights and Duties of Residents' and solemnly declares, as one of the general principles of the Basic Law, that 'the Hong Kong Special Administrative Region shall safeguard the rights and freedoms of the residents of the Hong Kong Special region and of other persons in accordance with [the Basic Law]'.[971]

540. The idea of the rule of law is the essential foundation of common law and many ideas that are now universally recognized as enforceable human rights have evolved in common law. In the following subsections, we will examine the importance of the common law, the Basic Law and the Bill of Rights as sources of human rights in Hong Kong and how they complement each other.[972]

I. Common Law as a Source of Human Rights

541. The common law is based on ideas of fairness and justice and upholds the rule of law.[973] The judiciary, while it defers to the legislature and the administration in compliance with the doctrine of separation of powers, considers as paramount the protection of individual rights against unlawful, arbitrary or discriminatory government action.[974] Common law proceeds on the basis that what is not unlawful is lawful. The words of Sir Robert Megarry V-C in *Malone v Commissioner of Police of the Metropolis (No. 2)* may be adapted for Hong Kong: '[Hong Kong] is not a country where everything is forbidden except what is expressly permitted.'[975] Thus, it is lawful for a person to smoke in a public place, unless there is a statutory prohibition against it, while most people would view it with 'disfavour'.[976] As a procedural aspect of that assumption, courts in criminal cases will require the prosecution to

Rights to incorporate the ICCPR) the report says: 'We consider that a sectoral approach with specific measures to deal with different fields covered by the Covenant could more effectively protect Covenant rights than the mere reiteration in domestic law of the Covenant provisions' (para. 2.4). https://www.cmab.govhk/en/issues/prc_10.htm.

971. Basic Law, Art. 4.

972. *See* generally Anton Cooray, 'International and Domestic Sources of Human Rights in Harmony: The Hong Kong Experience', (1990) 4 *Yearbook Law & Legal Practice in East Asia* 71–94. Robert Ribeiro, 'The Influence of the Strasbourg Court's Influence in Hong Kong'. https://www.hkcfa.hk/filemanager/speech/en/upload/1196/The%20Influence%20of%20the%20Strasbourg%20Court's%20jurisprudence%20in%20Hong%20Kong%20.pdf.

973. *See*, for instance, *KMM v Torture Claims Appeal Board* [2016] 1 HKLRD 568, (CA), [4] where Lam V-P referred to the 'fairness at common law' in considering whether a costs order should be made against the Torture Claims Appeal Board. For a stimulating account of the embodiment of rule of law in Common Law, *see* T.R.S. Allan, 'The Rule of Law as the Law of Reason: Consent and Constitutionalism', (1999) 115 *Law Quarterly Review* 221–244.

974. In *Ghulam Rbani v Secretary for Justice* [2014] HKEC 420, (2014) 17 HKCFAR 138, (CFA), [18] Ribeiro PJ said: 'The right to personal freedom and the concomitant right to be protected from arbitrary arrest or detention form part of the bedrock of the common law.'

975. [1979] Ch. 344, 357, (ChD). Lord Goff expressed a similar sentiment in *Attorney General v Observer and Times Newspapers* [1990] 1 AC 109, at 283, (HL).

976. As Sir Robert Megarry V-C said in *Malone v Commissioner of Police of the Metropolis (No 2)* [1979] Ch 344, (ChD), at 366: 'The notion that some express authorisation of law is required for acts which meet with "general disfavour", and "offend against proper standards of behaviour", and

establish the illegality of the defendant's actions. Every person is presumed to be innocent until the contrary is proved. Courts will assume that no person may be found guilty of an offence who had no accompanying guilty mind, and will import the requirement of *mens rea* into penal statutes, unless the legislation has by clear words made a particular statutory offence one of strict or absolute liability.[977]

542. It is a well-established rule of statutory interpretation that legislation must be interpreted in the context of the common law background to the enactment of the statutory provision in question.[978] While common law prevails over common law when they are in conflict, courts must guard against any erosion of fundamental principles of common law in the absence of a clear legislative intention to make such inroads into the common law.[979] It must be kept in mind that it is for the salutary purpose of improving and modernizing law that a well-intentioned legislature abolishes or modifies common law.[980]

543. In the absence of a constitution which makes it possible for the courts to declare legislation unconstitutional, it is possible for legislation to take away fundamental rights and to contravene the rule of law. In order to guard against such possibility courts construe legislation as restrictively as possible to protect fundamental rights, on the presumption that the legislature does not intend to take away citizens'

---

so on, would make the state of the law dependent on subjective views on indefinite concepts, and would be likely to produce some remarkable and contentious results.'

977. *Gammon (HK) Ltd v Attorney General of Hong Kong* [1985] AC 1, (PC), 14. *See also Hin Lin Yee v HKSAR* (2010) 13 HKCFAR 142, (CFA), and *Kulemesin v HKSAR* (2013) 16 HKCFAR 195, (CFA).

978. Any valid exercise in interpretation must be contextual which means that the passage in issue is to be read not only in the context of the enactment as a whole but also in the context of existing common law, where relevant, of legislative history and of other statutes *in pari materia*: *Bennion on Statutory Interpretation* (6th edn, LexisNexis, 2013) p. 540. Having referred to this rule of interpretation, Stock NPJ observed in *HKSAR v Leung Chun Kit Brandon* (2018) 21 HKCFAR 298, (CFA), [20], that it is beneficial to examine how a statutory rule that obtains in Hong Kong evolved in England in the backdrop of the common law prevailing there.

979. 'It is a well-established principle of construction that a statute is not to be taken as effecting a fundamental alteration in the general law unless it uses words that point unmistakably to that conclusion': *National Assistance Board v Wilkinson* [1952] 2 QB 648, (QB), 661, per Devlin J. That principle has been referred to as 'a principle of legal policy that law should be altered deliberately rather than casually, and that Parliament should not change either common law or statute law by a sidewind, but only by measured and considered provisions'. (Bennion on Statutory Interpretation (6th ed.), 741) *See HKSAR v Leung Chun Kit Brandon* (2018) 21 HKCFAR 298, (CFA), [57], per Stock NPJ.

980. *See HKSAR v Liang Yaoquiang* (2017) 20 HKCFAR 1, (CFA), where the Court of Final Appeal examined the defence of provocation which operates as a partial defence to a charge of murder, reducing the offence of murder for which the penalty of life imprisonment is fixed by statute to the lesser offence of manslaughter for which the penalty is in the discretion of the sentencing judge. Defence of provocation was originally a common law defence which now operates subject to legislative modification, mainly the abolition of the common law rule on what would constitute provocation. *See HKSAR v Liang Yaoquiang* (2017) 20 HKCFAR 1, (CFA), [6] and [7].

rights.[981] Where, as in Hong Kong, the legislature is controlled by a paramount constitution, any legislation that contravenes the constitution would be unconstitutional.

544. An important presumption in favour of individual freedom is that Parliament does not intend to deprive the individual of his fundamental right of access to courts.[982] The right of access to courts is now recognized in Hong Kong both by the Bill of Rights (Article 10) and the Basic Law (Article 35).

545. Access to courts is not an absolute right.[983] Legislation may impose a minimum monetary limit that must be passed for it to be litigated.[984] It has also been held that the imposition of modest court fees is not a denial of access to the courts.[985] In the area of criminal law, private prosecutions may be taken over by the Secretary of Justice and even discontinued.[986] Legislation may provide only for one avenue of litigation and not another. For instance, an election petition and not a judicial review application may be made available to challenge the legality of the Chief Executive elections.[987] Legislation may limit the scope of the remedy available. For instance it may provide that an administrative decision may be challenged by way

---

981. As Lord Russell of Killowen CJ famously said in relation to an unreasonable by-law: 'the Court might well say, "Parliament never intended to give authority to make [rules that are oppressive, manifestly unjust or unequal in application], they are unreasonable and ultra vires".' *Kruse v Johnson* [1898] 2 QB 91, (QB), 100. The oft-quoted words of Lord Hoffmann, uttered in the context of freedom of expression, deserve repetition here: 'Fundamental rights cannot be overridden by general or ambiguous words. This is because there is too great a risk that the full implications of their unqualified meaning may have passed unnoticed in the democratic process. In the absence of express language or necessary implication to the contrary, the courts therefore presume that even the most general words were intended to be subject to the basic rights of the individual': *R v Secretary of State for the Home Department, Ex p Simms* [2000] 2 AC 115, (HL), 131. Interestingly, Lord Hoffmann invoked the idea of principle of legality to achieve what could be achieved by constitutionally entrenched human rights: 'In this way the courts of the United Kingdom, though acknowledging the sovereignty of Parliament, apply principles of constitutionality little different from those which exist in countries where the power of the legislature is expressly limited by a constitutional document.' (*ibid.*)
982. '[T]he right of a citizen to access a court or tribunal and thereby to access justice is a right of the highest constitutional importance and legislation removing that right is prima facie contrary to the rule of law, as recognised in decisions such as *Anisminic Ltd v Foreign Compensation Commission* [1969] 2 AC 147, (HL). Clear and explicit words are required to justify a restriction to the constitutional right of unimpeded access to courts and tribunals': *Jhuti v Royal Mail Group Ltd* [2018] ICR 1077, (Employment Appeal Tribunal), 1086.
983. '[I]t has been established in the jurisprudence of the European Court of Human Rights in relation to the closely analogous right of access under art. 6(1) of the European Convention on Human Rights, that such right is by its nature not absolute, but may be subject to limitations. Such limitations are valid if they pursue a legitimate aim, are proportionate to that aim and are not such as to impair the very essence of the right.' *Ng Yat Chi v Max Share Ltd* (2005) 8 HKCFAR 1, (CFA), [73].
984. *See* above Part II, Ch. 5, §5, I. Original Civil Jurisdiction of the District Court.
985. *Re Grotch* [2012] 2 HKLRD 309, (CFI).
986. *See Ng Chi Kueng v Secretary for Justice* [2016] 2 HKLRD 1330, (CFI), where it was held that the Secretary for Justice's right, under s. 14(1) of the Magistrates Ordinance (Cap. 227), to assume the conduct of a private prosecution, even with a view to discontinuing it, was a permissible restriction on the right of access to courts.
987. *Leung Chun Ying v Ho Chun Yan Albert* (2013) 16 HKCFAR 735, (CFA).

of statutory review for legality and not a review of merits, as in the case of an appeal on questions both law and facts.[988] It is common for legislation to prescribe time limits within which an action has to be instituted in court. Even a short period of time within which action has to be instituted would be valid, if justified. For instance, a seven-day limit to lodge an election petition challenging the election of the Chief Executive has been considered to be a proportionate restriction on the right of access to courts.[989]

546. An interesting issue that courts had to deal with in Hong Kong is whether denial of a second appeal constitutes a denial of access to courts. In *Solicitor and Law Society of Hong Kong v Secretary of Justice*[990] it was held to be an impermissible denial of access to courts to deny an appeal to the Court of Final Appeal from the decision of the Court of Appeal, in the absence of a valid justification. In *Incorporated Owners of Po Hang Building v Sam Woo Marine Works Ltd,*[991] the Court of Final Appeal upheld the restriction on an appeal to the Court of Final Appeal from a decision of the Court of Appeal to be justifiable. The provision in question was section 63B of the District Court Ordinance (Cap. 336), which provides that 'no appeal lies from a decision of the Court of Appeal as to whether or not leave to appeal to it should be granted'. The Court of Final Appeal said that having the Court of Appeal screen out cases which had no reasonable prospect of success on appeal, promoted proper and efficient use of judicial resources and the avoidance of oppressive and unproductive appeals. In the context of the District Court, a court of limited jurisdiction, the statutory scheme also aimed to maintain reasonable proportionality between litigation costs and the amounts at stake by restricting the available tiers of appeal. In *China International Fund Ltd v Dennis Lau & Ng Chun Man Architects & Engineers (HK) Ltd,*[992] the Court of Appeal upheld the validity of section 84(4) of the Arbitration Ordinance (Cap. 609) which provided that the Court of First Instance may in its discretion not allow an appeal to the Court of Appeal from its decision from an arbitration award. In arriving at this decision, the Court of Appeal took into account the nature of the arbitration process, as well as the limited residuary jurisdiction that the Court of Appeal has to grant leave to appeal. The Court of Appeal observed that the limitation in section 84(4) must be 'read down' so as to preserve the 'residual jurisdiction' of the Court of Appeal to intervene in an

988. *See Lee Yee Shing Jacky v Inland Revenue Board of Review* [2012] 2 HKLRD 981, (CA), where it was held that the absence of an appeal against the decision of the Board of Review (on appeal from the tax assessment made by the Commissioner of Inland Revenue) was not a denial of access to courts, because there was access to courts by way of case stated, which was hardly different from judicial review proceedings. In a judicial review proceeding, though the court does not conduct a 'merits review' it could declare the decision in question unreasonable or irrational or an abuse of discretion, a determination which cannot be reached without some evaluation of the merits of the decision.

989. *Leung Chun Ying v Ho Chun Yan Albert* (2013) 16 HKCFAR 735, (CFA).

990. *Solicitor and Law Society of Hong Kong v Secretary of Justice* (2003) 6 HKCFAR 570, (CFA). The provision in question, s. 13 of the Legal Practitioners Ordinance (Cap. 159) was amended in 2005, removing the words 'the decision of the Court of Appeal on any such appeal shall be final'. *See* further para. 356 above.

991. (2017) 20 HKCFAR 240, (CFA).

992. [2015] 4 HKLRD 609, (CA).

extreme situation where not granting leave to appeal would compromise fairness of judicial process.[993] In determining the legality of such exclusionary provisions courts ask whether exclusion or restriction is proportionate, applying the four-step test identified in *Hysan Development co Ltd v Town Planning Board*:[994] The restriction on the right of appeal must: (i) pursue a legitimate aim; (ii) be rationally connected to advancing that aim; (iii) be no more than is necessary to accomplish that aim; and (iv) strike a fair balance between the general interest and any individual rights intruded upon.[995]

547. Access to courts does not necessarily mean that every dispute, be it criminal or civil, should be litigated only in ordinary courts of law. It is a feature of contemporary legal systems that special tribunals are more suitable than ordinary courts of law to deal with disputes arising in specific contexts, such as tax or labour disputes.[996] In order to ensure fair administration of justice, it is necessary that where a special tribunal exercises a jurisdiction otherwise exercised by a court of law safeguards must be in place for judicial supervision by way of an appeal or judicial review.[997] It is generally recognized that the conferment of special adjudicative powers on tribunals is constitutional unless the conferment of such powers on a special tribunal conflicts with the constitutional provision that judicial power must be exercised by the judiciary alone. Article 10 of the Bill of Rights protects equality before courts and tribunals, and although Article 35 of the Basic Law guarantees access to courts, and omits tribunals, it has been said that the requirement of access to courts would be satisfied if there is access to a properly constituted tribunal.[998]

993. *Ibid.*, [24]. In *American International Group Inc v Huaxia Life Insurance Co Ltd* (2017) 20 HKCFAR 503, (CFA), the Court of Final Appeal affirmed the correction of the approach adopted by the Court of Appeal in *China International Fund Ltd v Dennis Lau & Ng Chun Man Architects & Engineers (HK) Ltd* [2015] 4 HKLRD 609, (CA). For 'reading down' as a technique of remedial interpretation, *see* below paras 615-617.

994. (2016) 19 HKCFAR 372, (CFA), [134]–[135].

995. *Incorporated Owners of Po Hang Building v Sam Woo Marine Works Ltd* (2017) 20 HKCFAR 240, (CFA), [34].

996. 'Many countries have found that the complexity of their social organisation and legislation calls for the establishment of specialised tribunals to serve as the first port of call for citizens who wish to contest official decisions on such matters as taxation, social security, and planning permission. Such specialised tribunals (which are not courts) perform the function of ascertaining and evaluating the facts relevant to a matter within their special expertise. There is almost invariably a right of appeal from a specialised tribunal to a court, but often the appeal is restricted to questions of law': *Jauffur v Commissioner of Income Tax* [2007] 1 LRC 561, (PC), [1], per Lord Walker.

997. *See Lee Yee Shing Jacky v Inland Revenue Board of Review* [2012] 2 HKLRD 981, (CA). Citing *Begum v Tower Hamlets London Borough Council* [2003] 2 AC 430, (HL). *See also Interush Ltd v Commissioner of Police* [2019] HKEC 110, (CA).

998. The Basic Law is an instrument which sets out fundamental principles rather than detailed provisions like an ordinary statute. One would not expect the Basic Law to give a detailed definition of courts and tribunals. The use of tribunals is so prevalent in Hong Kong that it will need a strong case to justify the exclusion of tribunals from coming under the general word "courts".' *A Solicitor v Law Society of Hong Kong* [2004] HKEC 219, (CA), [65], per Woo VP. It is clear, however, that many administrative tribunals are not in a strict sense courts of law, which alone are authorized to exercise judicial power. *See Stock Exchange of Hong Kong Ltd v New World Development Co Ltd* (2006) 9 HKCFAR 234, (CFA), [46], [62] and [63]. Obviously, certain rights protected by Article 35 of the Basic Law would apply only to courts of law, and not to administrative tribunals which

548. Courts presume that Parliament does not intend to take away property except with justification and fair compensation.[999] However, courts have struck a balance between rights of the subject and the need for regulatory legislation by holding that, where legislation imposes limitations on the use and development of land, short of expropriation of land, the property owner has no common law right to be compensated.[1000]

549. The rule of law dictates that laws must be predictable,[1001] and that they must not be unequal and arbitrary.[1002] Courts will construe legislation so as to be consistent with the rule of law and invalidate any administrative action that is arbitrary and thus ultra vires. In determining the scope of administrative discretion, courts have imposed a procedural limitation on administrative authorities, so that no decision affecting rights of the subject may be taken without giving him a fair

---

may have some trappings of a court of law. When Art. 35 refers an individual's right of 'access to the courts', right of 'choice of lawyers for representation in the courts', right 'to judicial remedies' and 'right to institute legal proceedings in the courts against the acts of the executive authorities and their personnel', what are envisaged are ordinary court of law alone. As was observed in *Stock Exchange case* (above) the right to legal representation (as in a court of law) does not apply with the same rigour to proceedings before an administrative tribunal. On tribunals which are in essence courts of law, *see Bribery Commissioner v Ranasinghe* [1965] AC 172, (PC). *See* for an analysis of Privy Council cases from Sri Lanka, which are instructive of the meaning of judicial power, M J A (Anton) Cooray, *Judicial Role under the Constitutions of Ceylon/Sri Lanka: An Historical and Comparative Study* (Lake House Publishers, 1983).

999. *See Colonial Sugar Refining Co. Ltd v Melbourne Harbour Trust Commissioner* [1927] AC 343, (PC), where Lord Warrington of Clyffe said (at 359) that 'a statute should not be held to take away private rights of property without compensation unless the intention to do so is expressed in clear and unambiguous terms'. This has been cited for instance in *Wah Yick Enterprises v Building Authority* (1999) 2 HKCFAR 170, (CFA), 180, and *Kaisilk Ltd v Urban Renewal Authority* [2004] 1 HKLRD 907, (CA), [32]. The oft-quoted words of Lord Hoffmann, uttered in the context of freedom of expression, deserve repetition here: 'Fundamental rights cannot be overridden by general or ambiguous words. This is because there is too great a risk that the full implications of their unqualified meaning may have passed unnoticed in the democratic process. In the absence of express language or necessary implication to the contrary, the courts therefore presume that even the most general words were intended to be subject to the basic rights of the individual': *R v Secretary of State for the Home Department, Ex p Simms* [2000] 2 AC 115, (HL), 131. The Lands Resumption Ordinance (Cap. 124) provides for payment of compensation upon land resumption.

1000. *See Fine Tower Associates Ltd v Town Planning Board* [2008] 1 HKLRD 553, (CA), where Stock JA said at [17]: 'It can safely be postulated as a general proposition that regulatory restriction on use, imposed in the public interest, that does not amount to a taking or deprivation of the property, gives no right to compensation: *see Grape Bay Ltd v A-G of Bermuda* [2000] 1 WLR 574, (PC). But it is well established that action adversely affecting use of property, despite falling short of formal expropriation, may in certain circumstances nonetheless properly be described as deprivation, in which case there is a right to compensation. To ascertain whether there has been a deprivation, the court looks to the substance of the matter rather than to the form.' *See* further VI, The Right to Private Property below.

1001. 'Considerations of certainty and fairness entitle the court, in ascertaining and giving effect to the true intention of the legislature, to presume that the legislature intends that law should be certain, and therefore predictable, and that a person should not be penalised except under clear law': Cheung CJHC in *T v Commissioner of Police* [2013] 4 HKLRD 384, (CA), [21] citing Bennion on Statutory Interpretation (5th edn, 2008), pp. 799–807 and 825–831.

1002. For a stimulating account of the embodiment of rule of law in Common Law, *see* T.R.S. Allan, 'The Rule of Law as the Law of Reason: Consent and Constitutionalism', (1999) 115 *Law Quarterly Review* 221–244.

opportunity to be heard.[1003] A significant development in administrative law has been the recognition that judicial review of administrative action is founded not on the technical legal ground of ultra vires (without or beyond the power given by statute) but the substantive principle of rule of law which promotes good governance.[1004]

550. Hong Kong courts have frequently asserted that certain fundamental rights, which are enshrined in the Hong Kong Bill of Rights, are in fact firmly established in the common law. As Litton J said in *Chim Shing Chum v Commission of Correctional Services*,[1005] 'it rarely happens that the Bill of Rights operates in an area of human activity not already covered by the laws of Hong Kong'.[1006] In *R v Kevin Egan*,[1007] a Deputy Judge of the High Court observed that Article 10 of the Hong Kong Bill of Rights merely declared the relevant common law principles and did not enlarge the common law. In *R v Cheung Ka Fai*, the Court of Appeal held that admissibility of evidence was governed by common law and refused to accept a human-rights-based exception to admissibility of evidence where evidence had been obtained in pursuance of a breach of human rights.[1008] In *Stock Exchange of Hong Kong v New World Development Ltd* Ribeiro PJ said that the applicability of the common law principles of fairness made it unnecessary to embark on a parallel inquiry into the applicability of Article 10 of the Bill of Rights.[1009] Observing the overlap between common law and fundamental rights Ribeiro PJ has said: 'The right to personal freedom and the concomitant right to be protected from arbitrary arrest or detention form part of the bedrock of the common law.'[1010] There are numerous cases where English courts have emphasized that common law principles are capable of protecting personal freedoms without resort to human rights conventions. For instance in a case in respect of freedom of speech Laws LJ said: 'I do not therefore think it necessary, on this part of the case, to place any reliance on the jurisprudence of the European Court of Human Rights; the common law is a sufficient arena for the debate.'[1011]

1003. *See*, for instance, *X v Securities and Futures Commission* [2012] 4 HKLRD 296, (CFI).
1004. *See* Dawn Oliver, 'Is the Ultra Vires Rule the Basis of Judicial Review?' (1987) *Public Law* 543–569, Paul P. Craig, 'Ultra Vires and the Foundations of Judicial Review', (1998) 57:1 *Cambridge Law Review* 63–90. *See* para. 722 below.
1005. *Chim Shing Chum v Commission of Correctional Services* (1996) 6 HKPLR 313, (CA), 322.
1006. In *R v Cheung Ka Fai* [1995] 2 HKCLR 184, (CA), 196, Litton PJ said: 'The Bill of Rights is part of the fabric of the law of Hong Kong. It is not a self-contained code. It would be an extraordinary thing if, by applying the normal rules of evidence and procedure, a piece of evidence is admissible and yet, by the operation of s. 6(1) of the Bill of Rights Ordinance, it should be inadmissible. This would, in effect, be to operate a dual system of justice. In our judgment, s. 6(1) has no such effect.' It must however be said that a common law rule which falls foul of the constitution will be invalid to the extent of such inconsistency.
1007. *R v Kevin Egan* (1993) 3 HKPLR 277, (HC), 285.
1008. *R v Cheung Ka Fai* [1995] 2 HKCLR 184, (CA).
1009. *Stock Exchange of Hong Kong v New World Development Ltd* (2006) 9 HKCFAR 234, (CFA), [94].
1010. *Ghulam Rbani v Secretary for Justice* [2014] 17 HKCFAR 138, [18], CFA.
1011. *David Miranda v The Secretary of State for the Home Department et al* [2014] 1 WLR 3140, (DC), [41].

II. Legislation as a Source of Human Rights

551. It is common for the domestic legislature to pass laws to protect citizen's rights. Criminal procedure law is an important area where rights of persons suspected of or charged with an offence are entitled to a variety of rights. Among them are the right against self-incrimination and procedural safeguards to protect suspects from unlawful interference with their rights. Since the enactment of the Bill of Rights in 1991, a number of laws have been passed for the purpose of furthering the protection of fundamental rights and freedoms. These include the Sex Discrimination Ordinance,[1012] the Disability Discrimination Ordinance,[1013] the Martial Status Discrimination Ordinance[1014] and the Personal Data (Privacy) Ordinance.[1015] For the effective implementation of these laws, the Government has set up the Equal Opportunities Commission and the Office of the Privacy Commissioner for Personal Data.

III. Hong Kong Bill of Rights as a Source of Human Rights

552. The Bill of Rights Ordinance was passed in 1991 'to provide for the incorporation into the law of Hong Kong of provisions of the International Covenant on Civil and Political Rights as applied to Hong Kong; and for ancillary and connected matters' (the Long title). Section 2(3) of the Ordinance provided that:

> in interpreting and applying this Ordinance, regard shall be had to the fact that the purpose of this Ordinance is to provide for the incorporation into the law of Hong Kong of provisions of the International Covenant on Civil and Political Rights as applied to Hong Kong.

553. The Hong Kong Bill of Rights was not enacted as a constitutional document. It was incorporated in an ordinary statute, namely the Hong Kong Bill of Rights Ordinance. Building on the common law principle of statutory interpretation that whenever there is an inconsistency between two statutes passed by the same legislature, the previous statute stands repealed to the extent of such inconsistency, the now-defunct section 3 of the Bill of Rights Ordinance provided as follows:

(1) All pre-existing legislation that admits of a construction consistent with this Ordinance shall be given such a construction.
(2) All pre-existing legislation that does not admit of a construction consistent with this Ordinance is, to the extent of the inconsistency, repealed.[1016]

1012. Cap. 480 of the Laws of Hong Kong.
1013. Cap. 487 of the Laws of Hong Kong.
1014. Cap. 527 of the Laws of Hong Kong.
1015. Cap. 486 of the Laws of Hong Kong.
1016. Section 3 Bill of Rights Ordinance (Cap. 383) was repealed by Ordinance 2 of 1998, as it was considered to be incompatible with the Basic Law (Bill of Rights Ordinance (Cap. 383), s. 3). *See*

554. As the Hong Kong legislature could not bind its successors, it could not declare that any future legislation inconsistent with the Bill of Rights Ordinance should be ineffective. The powers of the Legislative Council could be restricted only by Hong Kong's constitution, the Letters Patent. Therefore, the Letters Patent were amended to provide for the effective protection of the rights enshrined in the Hong Kong Bill of Rights against legislative intrusion. The Letters Patent did not, however, provide for any entrenchment of the Bill of Rights, but of the ICCPR.

555. Article VII of the Letters Patent, which dealt with 'Governor, with advice and consent of Council to make laws', was amended by adding a new paragraph, namely paragraph (5):

> The provisions of the ICCPR, adopted by the General Assembly of the United Nations on 16 December 1966, as applied to Hong Kong, shall be implemented through the laws of Hong Kong. No law of Hong Kong shall be made after coming into operation of the Hong Kong Letters Patent 1991 (No. 2)[1017] that restricts the rights and freedoms enjoyed in Hong Kong in a manner which is inconsistent with that Covenant as applied to Hong Kong.[1018]

556. The now-defunct section 4 of the Bill of Rights Ordinance provided that courts must use the Covenant as a standard for guidance in interpreting future legislation: 'All legislation enacted on or after the commencement date shall, to the extent that it admits of such a construction, be construed so as to be consistent with the International Covenant on Civil and Political Rights.'

557. The combined effect of Article VII(5) of the Hong Kong Letters Patent and sections 3 and 4 of the Hong Kong Bill of Rights Ordinance, prior to 1 July 1997 when all the above provisions ceased to exist, may be summarized as follows:

Attorney General of Hong Kong v Lee Kwong-Kut [1993] A. C. 951, (PC), where the Privy Council held that, being in conflict with the Art. 11(1) of the Bill of Rights, s. 30 of the Summary Offences Ordinance had been repealed by s. 3(2) of the Bill of Rights Ordinance. Section 3 was repealed by Ordinance 2 of 1998, as it was considered to be incompatible with the Basic Law.

1017. The Hong Kong Letters Patent 1991 (No 2), which introduced para. (5) of Art. VII came into force on 8 June 1991, the same day on which the Hong Kong Bill of Rights Ordinance became operative.

1018. The Covenant was incorporated into the laws of Hong Kong only as applied to Hong Kong. The words 'as applied to Hong Kong' qualify the full operation of the Covenant in Hong Kong. The reason is that the UK when it ratified the Covenant in 1976 undertook to fulfil its obligation under the Covenant in respect of Hong Kong subject to certain reservations. The most important reservation was that the UK Government would not apply the Covenant guarantee of universal and equal franchise and free elections requiring the establishment of an elected Executive Council or Legislative Council in Hong Kong. The Hong Kong Bill of Rights Ordinance states in s. 13 in Part III, 'Exceptions and Savings', that Art. 21 of the Hong Kong Bill of Rights, 'Right to participate in public life', does not require the establishment of an elected Executive or Legislative Council in Hong Kong.

(1) all pre-existing Hong Kong ordinances had to be construed as far as possible in a manner consistent with the Hong Kong Bill of Rights Ordinance;[1019]
(2) any pre-existing Hong Kong ordinance which did not admit of such a construction was invalid to the extent of such inconsistency;[1020]
(3) all subsequent ordinances had to be construed as far as possible in a manner consistent with the Covenant as applied to Hong Kong;[1021] and
(4) any subsequent ordinance, which did not admit of such a construction, had no legal effect.[1022]

558. The Hong Kong Letters Patent ceased to be operative in Hong Kong with effect from 1 July 1997 when Hong Kong became part of China. As a result, the now-defunct Letters Patent cannot be relied on to give any constitutional status to the ICCPR as a standard for determining the validity of Hong Kong legislation. As we shall see, courts may rely on the ICCPR to test the validity of Hong Kong ordinances because the Basic Law incorporates the covenant into Hong Kong law and gives it constitutional status.

559. The Hong Kong Bill of Rights Ordinance, unlike the Hong Kong Letters Patent, continues to be operative in the Hong Kong Special Administrative Region under Article 8 of the Basic Law, which provides for the continued operation of ordinances passed by the Legislative Council prior to 1997. Article 160 of the Basic Law provides that upon the establishment of the Hong Kong Special Administrative Region, the laws previously in force in Hong Kong shall be adopted as laws of the Region except for those that the NPCSC declares to be in contravention of the Basic Law. The NPCSC declared sections 2(3), 3 and 4 of the Bill of Rights Ordinance to be inconsistent with the Basic Law and expressly declared them to be in contravention of the Basic Law.[1023] As a result, currently there is no provision in the Hong Kong Bill of Rights Ordinance enabling the courts:

1019. *See* Hong Kong Bill of Rights Ordinance, s. 3(1), repealed by Ordinance No 2 of 1998.
1020. *Ibid.*, s. 3(2) repealed by Ordinance No 2 of 1998.
1021. *Ibid.*, s. 4 repealed by Ordinance No 2 of 1998.
1022. *See* Hong Kong Letters Patent, Art. VII(5), not in operation in Hong Kong since 1 July 1997.
1023. Article 160 of the Basic Law further provides that if any laws are later discovered to be in contravention of the Basic Law, they shall be amended or cease to have force in accordance with the procedure prescribed by the Basic Law. It was held in *HKSAR v Hung Chan Wa* (2006) HKCFAR 614, (CFA), that 'laws' in Art. 160 is a reference to legislation and not judicial decisions. Li CJ explained at [11]: 'The crucial question is whether on its proper interpretation, the phrase "the procedure as prescribed by this Law" at the end of Art. 160(l) covers judicial procedure. If it does, judgments of the courts determining pre-1 July 1997 laws to be in contravention of the Basic Law would only have prospective effect, since the article provides that the law in question "shall cease to have effect" in accordance with the procedure prescribed. Such a result would be extraordinary. Article 160 would be according to such judgments a treatment which represents a radical departure from the established common law position. Further, a sharp distinction would have to be drawn between pre-1 July 1997 laws and post-1 July 1997 laws. Whereas a court judgment determining a post-1 July 1997 law to be in contravention of the Basic Law would operate retrospectively as well as prospectively in accordance with the common law position, a wholly different rule would prevail in relation to a judicial declaration of contravention in relation to a pre-1 July 1997 law. Article 160 should not be interpreted to lead to such an extraordinary result in the absence of clear words.'

(1) to use the Bill of Rights Ordinance as an aid to interpreting pre-existing ordinances, or to invalidate inconsistent pre-existing ordinances (as previously provided by section 3);
(2) to use the ICCPR as applied to Hong Kong as an aid to interpreting subsequent legislation (as previously provided by section 4); or
(3) to have regard to the ICCPR in interpreting the Bill of Rights Ordinance (as previously provided by section 2(3)).

560. The Chinese authorities decided to repeal sections 2(3), 3 and 4 of the Hong Kong Bill of Rights Ordinance because they did not want the Hong Kong Bill of Rights Ordinance to have a constitutional or quasi-constitutional status. Without those sections, the Hong Kong Bill of Rights Ordinance is an ordinary statute, embodying in Part II 'The Hong Kong Bill of Rights' a list of rights, which in no legal sense prevents the Hong Kong legislature from enacting a law inconsistent with it. It is, however, abundantly clear that the Hong Kong Bill of Rights Ordinance can be invoked to question the validity of subsidiary legislation or administrative action, since any subsidiary legislation or administrative action inconsistent with any ordinary legislation is ultra vires and of no effect. Where a subsidiary legislation provides for a disciplinary procedure that completely bars legal representation at a police disciplinary proceedings it would contravene Article 10 of the Bill of Rights, right to a fair and public hearing, and would be invalid.[1024] In *LK v Director of Immigration* it was argued unsuccessfully in the Court of First Instance that the Director of Immigration had failed to consider whether the removal of the applicant, an overstayer, from Hong Kong amounted to cruel and inhuman treatment under Article 3 of the Bill of Rights.[1025]

561. Where a person wishes to question the constitutionality of legislation on human rights grounds, he will have to show an inconsistency between the impugned statute and a provision of the Basic Law. Constitutionality of legislation cannot be questioned simply on the ground that it is inconsistent with the Bill of Rights because the Bill of Rights Ordinance is not of a higher authority than other Hong Kong ordinances. So, in the Court of Final Appeal of *B v Commissioner of the Independent Commission Against Corruption*,[1026] the applicant relied on Article 5(1) and Article 11(1) of the Bill of Rights as well as Article 28 of the Basic Law in support of the constitutional principle of legal certainty which it was argued was breached by the legislation in question.[1027]

1024. *Lam Siu Po v Commissioner of Police* (2009) 12 HKCFAR 237, (CFA).
1025. [2016] HKEC 1730, (CFI).
1026. [2010] 13 HKCFAR 1, (CFA).
1027. *See also A v Commissioner of Independent Commission Against Corruption* (2012) 15 HKCFAR 362, (CFA), where the court observed as follows:

> The expression 'privilege against self-incrimination' is a convenient one. It stands for a fundamental right, being the right not to self-incriminate. That persons have this right is a fundamental principle of the common law. And this right is guaranteed by our constitution the Basic Law. In *Koon Wing Yee v Insider Dealing Tribunal* (2008) 11 HKCFAR 170, [81], the Court referred to 'the privilege against self-incrimination as an integral part of the right to a fair trial

562. There is, however, increasing recognition of the Hong Kong Bill of Rights as a constitutional instrument. For instance, in *W v Registrar of Marriages* Chief Justice Ma said: 'The constitutional provisions relied on by the appellant are primarily Art. 37 of the Basic Law and art 19(2) of the Hong Kong Bill of Rights.'[1028]

563. The prevailing judicial view in Hong Kong is that the Hong Kong Bill of Rights Ordinance incorporates the ICCPR into Hong Kong law. As Cheung J said in the judicial review case of *Mok Chi Hung v Director of Immigration*:[1029] 'The International Covenant on Civil and Political Rights, as applied in Hong Kong, is by way of the Bill of Rights Ordinance.' As we shall see, the Basic Law incorporates the ICCPR into Hong Kong's law, and the ICCPR also has a direct effect in Hong Kong because of the Basic Law. Courts, however, continue to refer to the provisions of the Hong Kong Bill of Rights Ordinance when examining the effect of the ICCPR provisions. This judicial attitude is also justified because of Article 38 of the Basic Law which provides as follows: 'Hong Kong residents shall enjoy the other rights and freedoms safeguarded by the laws of the Hong Kong Special Administrative Region.' Thus because of the differences between the rights enshrined, and the manner in which they are worded, in the Hong Kong Bill of Rights and the Basic Law, as is set out below, it is legitimate for the courts to have resort to the Hong Kong Bill of Rights. It has now come to be accepted that the Hong Kong Bill Rights has 'constitutional status': 'As is well established, the Hong Kong Bill of Rights Ordinance, which enacts the Hong Kong Bill of Rights, implements the International Covenant on Civil and Political Rights so that the Hong Kong Bill of Rights is given constitutional status by [Article 39 of the Basic Law].'[1030]

---

which is closely linked to the presumption of innocence'. The right to a fair trial is guaranteed by Art. 87 of the Basic Law as well as by Art. 10 of the Hong Kong Bill of Rights which instrument is entrenched by Art. 39 of the Basic Law. Article 87 of the Basic Law guarantees the presumption of innocence, and so does Art. 11(1) of the Hong Kong Bill of Rights.

1028. *W v Registrar of Marriages* (2013) 16 HKCFAR 112, (CFA), [58].

1029. *Mok Chi Hung v Director of Immigration* [2001] 2 HKLRD 125, (CFI), 291, echoing the sentiment expressed by the Court of Final Appeal in *HKSAR v Ng Kung Siu* (1999) 2 HKCFAR 442, (CFA), 455) – the *Flag desecration* case. Quoted with approval by the Court of Final Appeal in *Lau Cheong et al v HKSAR* (2002) 5 HKCFAR 415, [32]: 'The Hong Kong Bill of Rights Ordinance (Cap 383), in fact provides for the incorporation of the provisions of the ICCPR into the laws of Hong Kong.'

1030. Ribeiro PJ in *HKSAR v Fong Kwok Shan Christine* (2017) 20 HKCFAR 425, (CFA), [14]. *See also* to the same effect, Ribeiro PJ in *Ghulam Rbani v Secretary for Justice* [2014] 17 HKCFAR 138, (CFA), [95]. The clearest statement of the significance of the Bill of Rights in Hong Kong's constitutional framework is perhaps the one given by Ribeiro PJ in *Comilang Milagros Tecson v Director of Immigration* (2019) 22 HKCFAR 59, (CFA), [24]: 'our courts have consistently held that by enacting [the Bill of Rights] the fundamental rights guaranteed by [it] … have not merely been incorporated domestically but, by virtue of [Art. 39 of the Basic Law], incorporated as part of the Basic Law and given constitutional effect. This is the consequence of [Art. 39(2) of the Basic Law] which protects the rights and freedoms of Hong Kong residents against restrictions which contravene [provisions of … the ICCPR as applied to Hong Kong and incorporated via [the Bill of Rights].' Fok PJ said less emphatically in *HKSAR v Md Emran Hossain* (2016) 19 HKCFAR 679, (CFA), [21]: 'In a system governed by the rule of law, it is axiomatic that adjudicative processes must be fair and impartial and observably so: justice must not only be done, it

564. Section 7 of the Hong Kong Bill of Rights Ordinance expressly provides that the Ordinance only binds '(a) the Government and all public authorities; and (b) any person acting on behalf of the Government or a public authority'.

565. Part III of the Bill of Rights Ordinance sets out some exceptions and savings, of which section 11 is quite significant: 'As regards persons not having the right to enter and remain in Hong Kong, this Ordinance does not affect any immigration legislation governing entry into, stay in and departure from Hong Kong, or the application of any such legislation.' Section 11 of the Bill of Rights excluded from the scope of the provisions of the Bill of Rights immigration legislation governing entry into, stay in and departure from Hong Kong and the application of such legislation.[1031] The words 'stay in' were given a broad meaning in *GA v Director of Immigration* to include the right to work. Ma CJ said that:

> the provision is intended to [exclude] immigration legislation that deals with each stage of a person's stay in Hong Kong … from entry through his or her stay in Hong Kong, to departure. This includes of course whether permission should be given to be in Hong Kong in the first place, the purpose for which that permission is to be granted to enter Hong Kong and the duration of the stay. It must also, from an immigration control point of view, generally cover the activities which a person in Hong Kong may be permitted to carry out and in my view must cover the aspect of whether a person should be permitted to work. Whether a person who, not having the right to enter and remain in Hong Kong, is permitted to work during his or her stay is, one would clearly have thought, eminently a matter of immigration control. Particularly in a place like Hong Kong, which has considerable economic attractions to many people, the need to control immigration and to control the number or type of people who may wish to work here, can easily be seen.[1032]

566. The rights and freedoms set out in the Hong Kong Bill of Rights and the corresponding rights and freedoms in the ICCPR are as follows: Entitlement to rights without distinction (HKBOR Article 1; ICCPR Articles 2 and 3), equality before the law and equal protection of the law (HKBOR Article 22; ICCPR Article 26), rights of minorities (HKBOR Article 23; ICCPR Article 27), right to life (HKBOR Article 2; ICCR Article 6), freedom from torture and inhuman treatment

---

must be seen to be done. This is particularly important in respect of those charged with, or convicted of, criminal offences since personal liberty will often be at stake. These principles are firmly embedded in the laws of Hong Kong at a constitutional level and also in its domestic law: rights under the International Covenant on Civil and Political Rights are given constitutional protection under Art. 39 of the Basic Law and are applied in Hong Kong through the Hong Kong Bill of Rights Ordinance (Cap. 383).'

1031. *Comilang Milagros Tecson v Director of Immigration* (2019) 22 HKCFAR 59, (CFA), following *Ng Ka Ling v Director of Immigration* (1999) 2 HKCFAR 4, (CFA), *Secretary for Justice v Lau Kwok Fai* (2005) 8 HKCFAR 304, (CFA), *Vallejos v Commissioner of Registration* (2013) 16 HKCFAR 45, (CFA), and *A v Director of Immigration* (2014) 17 HKCFAR 60 applied).

1032. (2014) 17 HKCFAR 60, (CFA), [30].

(HKBOR Article 3; ICCPR Article 7), freedom from slavery (HKBOR Article 4; ICCPR Article 8), liberty and security of person (HKBOR Article 5; ICCPR Article 9), rights of persons deprived of liberty (HKBOR Article 6; ICCPR Article 10), no imprisonment for breach of contract (HKBOR Article 7; ICCPR Article 11), liberty of movement (HKBOR Article 8; ICCPR Article 12), non-permanent residents may be expelled only in stated circumstances (HKBOR Article 9; ICCPR Article 12), equality before courts and right to a fair hearing (HKBOR Article 10; ICCPR Article 14.1), rights of persons accused or convicted of a criminal offence (HKBOR Article 11; ICCPR Article 14.2–14.7), prohibition against creation of retrospective offences (HKBOR Article 12; ICCPR Article 15), right to recognition as a person (HKBOR Article 13; ICCPR Article 16), right to privacy, family, home, correspondence, honour and reputation (HKBOR Article 14; ICCPR Article 17), freedom of thought conscience and religion(HKBOR Article 15; ICCPR Article 18), freedom of opinion and expression (HKBOR Article 16; ICCPR Article 19), right of peaceful assembly (HKBOR Article 17; ICCPR Article 21), freedom of association (HKBOR Article 18; ICCPR Article 22), rights in respect of marriage and family (HKBOR Article 19; ICCPR Article 23), rights of children HKBOR Article 20; ICCPR 24), right to participate in public life (HKBOR Article 21; ICCPR Article 25).

567. A comparison of the rights and freedoms set out in the Basic Law and the Bill of Rights shows that some rights that are guaranteed by the Bill of Rights are not expressly referred to in the Basic Law. In such a situation, the theoretical question remains whether such right gains constitutional status because the Bill of Rights enjoys constitutional status or because the source of that right can be traced to the ICCPR which is given constitutional recognition by the Basic Law.

IV. The Basic Law as a Source of Human Rights

568. The Basic Law has attempted through many of its provisions to assure the people of Hong Kong that Hong Kong's system of governance, its way of life and its values would be left unchanged when People's Republic of China resumed sovereignty over Hong Kong. The General Principles of the Basic Law in Chapter 1 which guarantee that Hong Kong will enjoy a high degree of autonomy with its own legislature, the executive and the judiciary; that socialist policies will not be practised in Hong Kong; that the law and legal system of Hong Kong will continue to be maintained, contain two specific provisions in relation to the protection of fundamental rights and freedoms. Article 4 states that 'the Hong Kong Special Administrative Region shall safeguard the rights and freedoms of the residents of the Hong Kong Special Administrative Region and of other persons in the Region in accordance with law'. Article 6 provides that 'the Hong Kong Special Administrative Region shall protect the right of private ownership of property in accordance with law'.

569. The General Principles relating to protection of fundamental rights and freedoms are further elaborated in the substantive chapters of the Basic Law. The most relevant chapter is Chapter II of the Basic Law, which is entitled 'Fundamental Rights and Duties of Residents', and which runs from Article 24 to Article 42. Having defined in Article 24 who Hong Kong residents are, the Basic Law refers to a number of specific fundamental rights in Articles 25–37, namely equality, franchise, expression and assembly, freedom of the person, inviolability of home, privacy, movement, conscience, choice of occupation, access to legal advice and justice,[1033] social welfare and freedom of marriage. Article 38 provides that 'Hong Kong residents shall enjoy the other rights and freedoms safeguarded by the laws of the Hong Kong Special Administrative Region'.

570. Article 39 of the Basic Law is a pivotal provision. It states as follows: 'The provisions of the International Covenant on Civil and Political Rights, the International Covenant on Economic, Social and Cultural Rights, and international labour conventions as applied to Hong Kong shall remain in force and shall be implemented through the laws of the Hong Kong Special Administrative Region. The rights and freedoms enjoyed by Hong Kong residents shall not be restricted unless as prescribed by law. Such restrictions shall not contravene the provisions of the preceding paragraph of this Article.'

571. The application of the international conventions which are referred to in Article 39 of the Basic Law is examined in this chapter as well as in Part I, Chapter 1 'Treaties'. These conventions may be incorporated in Hong Kong by way of a statute, such as the Bill of Rights Ordinance, incorporating the whole of an international convention. There may also be piecemeal incorporation of selected provisions of international conventions. International conventions apply in Hong Kong only if they have been specifically incorporated but may have some persuasive influence on the courts when deciding cases and on the legislature when passing legislation.

572. Article 39 of the Basic Law has a special significance when it mandates that any restriction of fundamental rights must be in accordance with the conventions which are referred to in that provision. Importantly it prohibits any restrictions which are inconsistent with the ICCPR, as applied to Hong Kong. Thus, while the Hong Kong legislature has some discretion in determining whether non-residents should enjoy same rights and privileges as residents, it would be unconstitutional for the government to impose restrictions which are incompatible with the ICCPR which finds expression in the Bill of Rights. For this reason, the Hong Kong Bill of Rights, notwithstanding that it is an ordinary statute, has assumed constitutional importance. For instance, the right to equality of all persons as recognized by the Bill of Rights has been preferred to equality of residents of Hong Kong as recognized by the Basic Law.[1034]

1033. The right to access to courts is fortified by Art. 87 which states that 'in criminal or civil proceedings in the Hong Kong Special Administrative Region, the principles previously applied in Hong Kong and the rights previously enjoyed by parties to proceedings shall be maintained. Anyone who is lawfully arrested shall have the right to a fair trial by the judicial organs without delay and shall be presumed innocent until convicted by the judicial organs.'

1034. *See* Art. 22 of the Bill of Rights and Art. 25 of the Basic Law. Chief Justice Ma explained in *Fok Chun Wa v Hospital Authority* (2012) 15 HKCFAR 409, (CFA), [52]: 'A small point arises at once

573. Article 40 of the Basic Law is intended to protect 'the lawful traditional rights and interests of the indigenous inhabitants of the New Territories'.[1035] Traditional Rights protected by Article 40 are the rights and interests of indigenous inhabitants of the New Territories which they enjoyed at the time of the commencement of the New Territories Lease in 1898. They do not include any practice which only came into being after Britain took that lease unless such practice is traceable to previous rights and interests.[1036] Where there is a conflict between a fundamental human right recognized by the Basic Law, such as the right to equality, and 'the lawful traditional rights and interests of indigenous inhabitants', such rights and interests will prevail even if they are discriminatory and thereby infringe the right to equality.[1037] An indigenous villager who asserts a right or privilege under Article 40 must establish that the privilege in question was in existence in 1898. In *Chan Wah v Hang Hau Rural Committee and Anor*,[1038] it was held that there was no ancient right of indigenous people to exclude non-indigenous people from voting at the election of village representatives, and such exclusion was a violation of the right of franchise given by Article 26 of the Basic Law.[1039]

---

in relation to Art. 25 of the Basic Law in that the reference therein is to "Hong Kong residents". The first applicant [was] not at the commencement of the present proceedings [a Hong Kong resident]. … This is not a point of any great significance, however, given the reliance on Art 22 of the Hong Kong Bill of Rights. The constitutional right to equality of treatment is accordingly engaged for determination.'

1035. It is evident that to be an indigenous villager, the person, who can establish patrilineal descent from an ancestor who was a resident of a village in 1898, need not be resident in the village. Indeed, there is no requirement for the person to have ever resided in the village at all. With economic and social forces resulting in mobility, a number of indigenous villagers have left the villages and a number of non-indigenous villagers are now part of the villages': *Secretary for Justice v Chan Wah* (2000) 3 HKCFAR 459, 465, (CFA), *Secretary for Justice v Liu Wing Kwong* [2014] 2 HKLRD 155, (CFI); *Koon Ping Leung v Director,* [2012] HKEC 103, (CFI). For a comprehensive account, *see* Johannes Chan, 'Rights of New Territories Indigenous Inhabitants' in Chan & Lim, *Law of the Hong Kong Constitution* (2nd edn, Sweet & Maxwell, 2015).

1036. *Tse Kwan Sang v Pat Heung Rural Committee* [1999] 3 HKLRD 267, (CFI).

1037. The purpose of Art. 40 of the Basic Law was to protect after 1 July 1997 those rights and interests of indigenous inhabitants of the New Territories which could properly be regarded as their traditional rights and interests. It was clear to everyone concerned at the time of the drafting of the Basic Law that some such rights or interests might be open to objection on the ground that they were discriminatory in nature. It would thus not be consistent with the purpose of Art. 40 of the BL to allow such rights or interests to be challenged on the ground of discrimination or on other grounds of unlawfulness. *Kwok Cheuk Kin v Director of Lands* [2020] 1 HKLRD 988, (CFI), [128]. The Court of First Instance held to be constitutional the small house policy which granted every indigenous villager, who is a male person of 18 years and above and descended through the male line from a resident in 1898 of a recognised village, although this entitlement discriminated against women.

1038. *Chan Wah v Hang Hau Rural Committee and Anor* [1999] 2 HKLRD 286, (CFI), 291, where Findlay J said: 'It cannot possibly be so that there is a custom that indigenous villagers enjoy, to the exclusion of non-indigenous villagers, the right to choose village representatives under the Ordinance that only became law in 1959. That is nonsense.' The decision of the Court of First Instance was affirmed by the Court of Appeal: *Chan Wah v Hang Hau Rural Committee and Anor* [2000] 1 HKLRD 411, (CA), and the Court of Final Appeal: *Secretary for Justice v Chan Wah* (2000) 3 HKCFAR 459, (CFA), referred to in the following footnote.

1039. In *Secretary for Justice v Chan Wah* (2000) 3 HKCFAR 459, (CFA), 477, the Court of Final Appeal held that indigenous Chinese people could derive political rights under Art. 40 of the Basic Law only if they are 'implicit within the rights and interests expressly protected by Art. 40. This

574. The Basic Law appears to contain provisions that draw a distinction between Chinese and non-Chinese residents. For instance, a Chinese citizen who has, at any time, resided in Hong Kong for a continuous period of seven years is entitled to become a permanent resident. On the other hand, a non-Chinese citizen must have resided in Hong Kong for a continuous period of seven years immediately before he makes an application for permanent residence, and he must make a statutory declaration that he has taken Hong Kong to be his permanent place of residence.[1040]

575. Article 41 of the Basic Law provides that 'persons in the Hong Kong Special Administrative Region other than Hong Kong residents shall, in accordance with law, enjoy the rights and freedoms of Hong Kong residents prescribed in this Chapter'. The right to social welfare in Article 36 of the Basic Law, for instance, does not extend to non-residents.[1041]

576. As Stock VP explained in *Fok Chun Wa v Hospital Authority*, Article 41 which provides that all persons in Hong Kong shall enjoy the rights and freedoms prescribed in Chapter III of the Basic Law does not mean that non-residents should be accorded all the same privileges and benefits as residents, unqualified by considerations of residence status, or other connection with Hong Kong, and the impact of according such privileges and benefits, such as the freedom of occupation or the right to social welfare. He said:

---

would require the Court to conclude that the traditional right and interests cannot be adequately protected without the political rights contended for.' It was held that the electoral arrangements for village representative elections discriminated against non-indigenous villagers, by depriving them of the right to participate in election of village representatives inconsistently with Art. 21 of the Bill of Rights ('Every permanent resident shall have the right and opportunity ... without unreasonable restrictions: (a) to take part in the conduct of public affairs, directly or through freely chosen representatives'). This inconsistency with Art. 21, constitutionally safeguarded through Art. 39 of the Basic Law was saved by Art. 40 of the Basic Law. The Court of Final Appeal held that Art. 40 of the Basic Law preserved the traditional rights and interests of indigenous villagers. Any such right would be valid notwithstanding a conflict with Art. 39 of the Basic Law, which incorporated ICCPR provisions into the laws of Hong Kong. These traditional rights and interests include various property rights and interests such as exemption from Government rent and rates in respect of certain properties held by indigenous villagers and benefits relating to land granted to male indigenous inhabitants under what is known as the small house policy. The traditional rights do not include any political right or privilege and the rights do not include a right to elect a village representative to the exclusion of non-indigenous villagers. *See* 476–478.

1040. Keith JA in *Commissioner for Registration v Registration of Persons Tribunal & Anor* [1999] 3 HKLRD 199, (CFI), 209, refrained from commenting on whether the imposition of different criteria was discriminatory, but pointed out that if there was any discrimination, it was created by the Basic Law. Keith JA also did not find it necessary to determine whether the courts could question the validity of a Basic Law provision if it contravened the Bill of Rights. *See also Association of expatriate Civil Servants of Hong Kong v Secretary for the Civil Service & Anor* (1996) 6 HKPLR 333, (CA), 344–349.

1041. *Kong Yunming v Director of Social Welfare* (2013) 16 HKCFAR 950, (CFA), [23] and *MS v Director of Social Welfare* [2016] HKEC 344, (CFI).

The range of rights within Chapter III is broad and the degree to which rights of non-residents in Hong Kong at any given time may lawfully be circumscribed so as to differ from those enjoyed by residents must depend upon the context. So, for example, it is not possible to envisage circumstances in which it would be lawful to deprive a non-resident of the freedom from arbitrary detention or imprisonment. On the other hand, it would be a non-purposive construction that supposed that art 41 intended that non-residents be accorded all the same privileges and benefits as residents, unqualified by considerations of residence status, or other connection with Hong Kong, and regardless of the impact of according such privileges and benefits on Hong Kong residents, benefits such as the freedom of occupation (art 33) or the right to social welfare (art 36).[1042]

577. Franchise is not a right that is extended to all residents, let alone non-residents: It is a right that only permanent residents enjoy. Article 26 of the Basic Law states that 'permanent residents of the Hong Kong Special Administrative Region shall have the right to vote and the right to stand for election in accordance with law'. As will be explained in relation to the public service, 'the principal officials of the Hong Kong Special Administrative Region shall be Chinese citizens who are permanent residents of the Region with no right of abode in any foreign country and have ordinarily resided in Hong Kong for a continuous period of not less than 15 years'.[1043]

578. The Basic Law seems to perpetuate inequality in relation to the acquisition of the status of a permanent resident of Hong Kong. A basic requirement for acquisition of permanent residence is a seven-year continuous period of residence in Hong Kong immediately preceding the application for permanent residence. While this requirement applies equally to Chinese citizens and non-Chinese citizens, there is a further condition that a non-Chinese resident has to satisfy, namely, that he has taken Hong Kong to be his permanent place of residence: Article 24(4) of the Basic Law. The Immigration Ordinance requires applicants to show that they are 'settled' in Hong Kong at the time of application, in order to satisfy that he has taken Hong Kong to be his permanent place of residence. The statute provides that a person could be said to be settled if he is ordinarily resident in Hong Kong and 'he is not subject to any limit of stay in Hong Kong' or he has what is commonly known as 'unconditional leave to stay'. In *Prem Singh v Director of Immigration*, the Court of Final Appeal held Article 24(4) envisaged a situation where a person may be said to have taken Hong Kong as his permanent place of residence, even at a time his stay was subject to a limit on stay and that therefore the Immigration Ordinance

1042. *Fok Chun Wa v Hospital Authority* [2011] 1 HKLRD A1, (CA), [70]. *See also* Chief Justice Ma, delivering the judgment of the Court of Final Appeal affirming the decision of the Court of Appeal (2012) 15 HKCFAR 409, (CFA), [52].

1043. Basic Law, Art. 61.

conflicted with the Basic Law when it additionally required an applicant to be a person who had the right to unconditional stay at the time of the application.[1044]

579. Article 42 states the obvious: 'Hong Kong residents and other persons in Hong Kong shall have the obligation to abide by the laws in force in the Hong Kong Special Administrative Region.' Thus, although Chapter IV is titled 'Fundamental Rights and Duties of Residents' there is no list of fundamental duties as one could see in the Indian Constitution.[1045] The obligation in Article 42 to abide by the law does not impose any duty which would not have existed had that article been omitted. If Article 42 serves any purpose, it is in fact to reassure people of Hong Kong that they need obey only laws of Hong Kong (and any Chinese law that are in operation in Hong Kong under the Basic Law) and not laws of the People's Republic of China.[1046] A similar qualification applies to membership of the Legislative Council. Article 67 provides that 'the Legislative Council of the Hong Kong Special Administrative Region shall be composed of Chinese citizens who are permanent residents of the Region with no right of abode in any foreign country. However, permanent residents of the Region who are not of Chinese nationality or who have the right of abode in foreign countries may also be elected members of the Legislative Council of the Region, provided that the proportion of such members does not exceed 20 percent of the total membership of the Council.'

580. Article 105 is a significant recognition of right to property. It says that 'the Hong Kong Special Administrative Region shall, in accordance with law, protect the right of individuals and legal persons to the acquisition, use, disposal and inheritance of property and their right to compensation for lawful deprivation of their property. Such compensation shall correspond to the real value of the property concerned at the time and shall be freely convertible and paid without undue delay. The ownership of enterprises and the investments from outside the Region shall be protected by law.'

581. Article 120 provides that 'all leases of land granted, decided upon or renewed before the establishment of the Hong Kong Special Administrative Region which extend beyond 30 June 1997, and all rights in relation to such leases, shall continue to be recognized and protected under the law of the Region'. Articles 121, 122 and 123 provide specific protections relating to leased land.

582. Chapter III of the Basic Law lists not only civil and political rights but also social and economic rights. For instance, Article 33 provides that Hong Kong residents shall have the freedom of choice of occupation, and Article 34 provides that

1044. *Prem Singh v Director of Immigration* (2003) 6 HKCFAR 26, (CFA), especially [63].

1045. Article 51A of the Indian Constitution requires every Indian citizen to, for instance, 'uphold and protect the sovereignty, unity and integrity of India and to defend the country and render national service when called upon to do so'.

1046. *See* P.Y. Lo, *The Hong Kong Basic Law* (Hong Kong: LexisNexis, 2011), 271–272 citing Wang Shuwen's *Introduction to the Basic Law*.

Hong Kong residents shall have the freedom to engage in academic research, literary and artistic creation, and other cultural activities.[1047]

583. Apart from the differences between the Hong Kong Bill of Rights and the Basic Law regarding the scope and content of the human rights enshrined in the two documents, there is also a difference as to who are entitled to enjoy those rights and freedoms. The rights set out in the Hong Kong Bill of Rights may be enjoyed by everyone, whereas the Basic Law draws a distinction between permanent residents and non-permanent residents for the purpose of enjoyment of fundamental human rights enshrined in Chapter III of the Basic Law. Only permanent residents of Hong Kong have the right to vote and the right to stand for election.[1048] All residents, including non-permanent residents, may enjoy all other fundamental rights listed in Chapter III. Article 41 provides that 'persons in the Hong Kong Special Administrative Region other than Hong Kong residents shall, in accordance with law, enjoy the rights and freedoms of Hong Kong residents prescribed in this chapter'.

584. Constitutional entrenchment of what are called human rights or fundamental rights is the preferred means of guaranteeing that state agencies act consistently with the protection of such rights and that state agencies take sufficient measures to ensure that citizens fashion their behaviour in such a way that those fundamental rights are observed in private dealings. In this scheme of things, legislative and administrative action, and to some extent judicial action, may be challenged if it leads to an infringement of those fundamental rights, with the result that constitutionally protected rights operate in the public sphere, i.e., in dealings between state agencies[1049] and between citizens and state agencies,[1050] and not in the private sphere. In other words, constitutional guarantees seek to protect citizens against governmental action[1051] – or actions which are of a public nature.[1052] As far as the

---

1047. Since Art. 6 of the ICESCR has not been incorporated by legislation, Hong Kong recognises no constitutional right to work: *see GA v Director of Immigration* (2014) 17 HKCFAR 60, (CFA). It has also been held that there is no right to employment in a particular field of occupation: *Cheng Chun Ngai v Hospital Authority* [2004] HKEC 1375, (CFI). Hartmann J said at [35]: 'even when [Art. 33 of the Basic Law. Which guarantees "freedom of choice of employment"] is interpreted generously and purposively, it is not to be interpreted in an active sense, by which I mean that it does not guarantee the right of employment in any particular field of occupation. Whether employment can in fact be obtained will depend on the laws of supply and demand as they apply in the marketplace. The article, in my view, is to be interpreted rather in the light of what it seeks to prevent; namely, outside of issues of national service, should they ever arise, any form of conscription to particular fields of occupation.' In *Leung Sze Ho Albert v Bar Council of Hong Kong Bar Association* [2016] 5 HKLRD 542, (CA), it was held that the decision of the Bar Council refusing to permit a practising barrister to engage in neuro-beautology as a supplementary occupation, which was incompatible with his practice as a barrister, was not an unconstitutional infringement of freedom of choice of occupation under Art. 33 of the Basic Law.

1048. Basic Law, Art. 26.

1049. *See*, for instance, *Town Planning Board v Town Planning Appeal Board* [2014] 1 HKLRD 1056, (CFI).

1050. *See*, for instance, *Hysan Development Co Ltd v Town Planning Board* [2012] HKEC 1266, (CFI).

1051. *See*, for instance, *Leung Hon Wai v Director of Environmental Protection* [2014] HKEC 1459, (CA).

citizens are concerned, constitutional guarantees have vertical effect, meaning a citizen can sue a state agency for an infringement of his fundamental rights, but cannot sue another citizen for such infringement: In other words, the constitutional guarantees do not have a horizontal effect.

585. Section 7 of the Bill of Rights Ordinance expressly states that the Ordinance binds only: (a) the Government and all public authorities and (b) any person acting on behalf of the Government or a public authority. The scope of section 7(1) was considered in *Hong Kong Polytechnic University v Next Magazine Publishing Ltd*[1053] where the university sued the magazine in libel. The magazine sought interlocutory relief arguing that the university should desist from litigation because it would infringe the magazine's freedom of expression guaranteed by Article 16 of the Bill of Rights. The success of their argument rested on a technicality, namely whether the university could be regarded as a public authority within the meaning of section 7(1) of the Bill of Rights, which is bound by the Bill of Rights.

586. In *Hong Kong Polytechnic case*, Keith J held that the phrase 'government' refers to the legislative, executive and judicial organs of the state, and the phrase 'public authority' refers to bodies which are not a part of the legislative, executive and judicial branches of the Government of Hong Kong, but yet are considered to operate within the 'public sphere'. Keith J clarified that 'for a body to be considered a public authority for the purposes of s 7(1) of the [Hong Kong Bill of Rights] it is not sufficient for it to be entrusted with functions to perform for the benefit of the public and not for private profit: there must be something in its nature or constitution, or in the way in which it is run, apart from its functions, which brings it into the public domain. … it may take the form of public funding, of a measure of governmental control or monitoring of its performance, or some form of public accountability. But something which brings it into the public domain there must be.' It was held that although the university was not subject to government control, it was a public authority given the nature of its functions, the purpose for which those functions were performed and the fact that it was funded to a great extent from public funds.[1054]

587. As Chief Justice Andrew Li observed in *Secretary for Justice v Chan Wah:*

1052. This would be the case where a non-governmental body such as a government-funded university would be regarded as a public authority. *See Hong Kong Polytechnic University et al v Next Magazine Publishing Ltd* [1996] 2 HKLR 260, (CFI), [1997] HKLRD 514, (CA). Fundamental rights protection is inapplicable if the state agency or the public authority only exercises a power of a private nature, such as entering into a private land lease: *Chi Hong Ching Yuen Ltd v Director of Lands* [2014] HKEC 584, (CFI), *Chau Tam Yuet Ching v Director of Lands* [2013] 3 HKLRD 169, (CA), and *Hang Wah Chong Investment Co Ltd v Attorney General* [1981] 1 WLR 1141; [1981] HKLR 336, (PC), or deals with a purely domestic matter *Kwan Wan Chee Alisa v City University of Hong Kong* [2013] HKEC 232, (CFI).

1053. [1996] 2 HKLR 260, (HC).

1054. *Ibid.*, 264–265.

> In order to engage the Bill of Rights Ordinance at all, the Government or a public authority or a person acting on behalf of either of them must be involved since the Ordinance only binds them. This could be said to be the key into the Bill of Rights. If the body involved is not the Government or a public authority or a body acting on behalf of either of them, the Ordinance does not bind that body and there is no question of the Bill of Rights being engaged at all.[1055]

V. International Human Rights Conventions as a Source of Human Rights

588. We have already seen above how the ICCPR was incorporated in the Hong Kong Bill of Rights Ordinance in 1991. When ratifying the ICCPR the UK Government entered some reservations in relation to its application to Hong Kong. As a result, some provisions of the convention have not been reproduced in the Hong Kong Bill of Rights. For instance, ICCPR Article 1 on self-determination and Article 20 on war propaganda and hate speech are absent from the Bill of Rights. Sections 9–13 in 'Part III Exceptions and Savings' of the Bill of Rights Ordinance set out the modifications to the ICCPR provisions which have been incorporated in the Bill of Rights.

589. The Basic Law provides for the continued application of the ICCPR in Hong Kong.

Article 39 provides as follows:

> The provisions of the International Covenant on Civil and Political Rights, the ICESCR and international labour conventions as applied to Hong Kong shall remain in force and shall be implemented through the laws of the Hong Kong Special Administrative Region. The rights and freedoms enjoyed by Hong Kong residents shall not be restricted unless as prescribed by law. Such restrictions shall not contravene the provisions of the preceding paragraph of this Article.

590. The Basic Law thus not only provides for the continued application in Hong Kong of the ICCPR (and other conventions) together with a duty to implement them through local legislation, but it also entrenches the ICCPR in the sense that no right or freedom enjoyed by Hong Kong residents may be restricted in a manner inconsistent with the ICCPR (and other conventions).

1055. *Secretary for Justice v Chan Wah* (2000) 3 HKCFAR 459, (CFA), at 471. The Court of Final Appeal reaffirmed this principle in *Leung Lai Fong v Ho Sin Ying* [2009] HKEC 1188, (CFA).

§2. Interpretation of Human Rights

591. Dispute resolution is the court's central function. The adversarial nature of judicial proceedings means that the court's duty is to settle a dispute between two or more parties. In the absence of a dispute, a court cannot conduct an inquiry or a hearing and arrive at a decision. In other words, courts will not generally deal with hypothetical questions. There must be a question ripe for litigation.[1056] The Court of Appeal in *Chit Fai Motors Co Ltd v Commissioner for Transport* identified four general principles relating to how courts would deal with academic or hypothetical questions. They are:[1057]

(1) Where a question is purely hypothetical or academic in the sense that there are simply no events that have occurred that form the basis for the question to be answered, a court will not entertain it. However relevant or even important the question may be, the court will not give an advisory opinion on hypothetical facts. There are principally two reasons for this: first, the court's function is to adjudicate on real disputes, not imaginary ones and secondly, to decide on points of law or principle when there are no facts before the court is not only undesirable, it can have unfortunate or even dangerous consequences. …

(2) Sometimes, however, … the question before the court is said to be hypothetical or academic only because the real dispute that drove the parties to litigation (sometimes called the *lis*) happens no longer to be in existence at the time of the hearing, even though the relevant facts giving rise to the dispute were real and had actually taken place. For example, in a civil dispute, where the defendant has openly made an offer to a claimant giving him all he is entitled to and this has been accepted, the dispute no longer exists even though it once did. … .[1058]

(3) In the type of situation referred to in the previous paragraph, the court does have jurisdiction to hear and determine the question in issue. However, in deciding whether or not to do so (and this can be said to be a matter of discretion), the court will closely examine the relevance or utility of any decision. In the public law sphere, this may be easier to demonstrate than in relation to private rights. This is because very often in public or administrative law cases, the duties of public bodies fall to be exercised on a continuing basis not only in relation to the parties before the court but also perhaps to others in the future. In *R v Secretary of State for the Home Department, ex p Salem* [1999] 1 AC 450, the House of Lords reviewed the relevant authorities and stated that the court had a discretion whether

1056. 'In keeping with the Court's general practice, where a constitutional issue is raised but it is not necessary to determine that issue for the purpose of determining the appeal before it, the Court usually will not address that constitutional issue': *HKSAR v Wan Thomas* (2018) 21 HKCFAR 214, (CFA), [51]. *See also Fateh Muhammad v Commissioner of Registration* (2001) 4 HKCFAR 278, (CFA), 287 and *GA v Director of Immigration* (2014) 17 HKCFAR 60, (CFA), [42]. For a recent affirmation of the principle, *see H v Director of Immigration* [2020] HKEC 1867, (CFA), [49].

1057. [2004] HKEC 218, (CA), [20].

1058. This is discussed in detail in paras 596-598, below.

or not to determine the question before it even though there was no longer a lis: *see* 456G-H. However, the discretion was to be exercised with caution and the court should only do so where there was good reason in the public interest. At 457A-B, Lord Slynn of Hadley said this: 'The discretion to hear disputes, even in the area of public law, must, however, be exercised with caution and appeals which are academic between the parties should not be heard unless there is good reason in the public interest for doing so, as for example (but only by way of example) when a discrete point of statutory construction arises which does not involve detailed consideration of facts and where a large number of similar cases exist or are anticipated so that the issue will most likely need to be resolved in the near future.'

(4) In other public law contexts, the court may consider determining issues where, for example, there are conflicting decisions: see *R v Birmingham City Juvenile Court, ex p Birmingham City Council* [1988] 1 WLR 337, (CA).[1059]

592. Courts' reluctance to give advisory opinions, that is a ruling on a question of law not arising on the facts before the court, is well illustrated by the recent case of *Balaoro Marietta S v Secretary for Justice.*[1060] There, the pastor of a Christian Church sought a declaration that the performance of a same-sex marriage ceremony in Hong Kong would not contravene any provision of the Marriage Ordinance, section 30 of which stipulates that 'marriage' means 'the voluntary union for life of one man and one woman to the exclusion of all others'.[1061] It was held that while the performance of services in question would not bring about the legal consequences of a marriage that did not mean that such performance was unlawful or prohibited by law. The court referred to *MK v Government of HKSAR*,[1062] where it was held that the Government had no legal or constitutional obligation to provide, as an alternative to marriage, a legal framework for the recognition of same-sex relationships giving them the same rights and benefits enjoyed by opposite-sex married couples. Thus, the court pointed out that, as the Secretary of Justice admitted, any person who performs a same-sex marriage ceremony would not be celebrating a marriage properly so-called and cannot be said to be celebrating a marriage contrary to any provision of the Marriage Ordinance.[1063] Having observed that performing such a ceremony is not an offence, the court observed that in considering a judicial review application, it is not the judicial practice to give any advisory opinion, or prior assurance to the applicant that his proposed conduct would not give rise to any criminal liability.

1059. These four factors are reproduced, (with some text omitted) from *Chit Fai Motors Co Ltd v Commissioner for Transport* [2004] HKEC 218, (CA), [20], per Ma CJHC.
1060. [2020] 1 HKLRD 1138, (CFI).
1061. Marriage Ordinance (Cap. 181), s. 30.
1062. [2019] 5 HKLRD 259, (CFI).
1063. *Balaoro Marietta S v Secretary for Justice* [2020] 1 HKLRD 1138, (CFI), [27].

593. In exceptional circumstances courts may deal with a constitutional issue without there being before it a live controversy arising from an infringement of law.[1064] *Leung v Secretary for Justice*[1065] provides a good illustration of such an exceptional situation. This was a case where a person successfully mounted a direct challenge[1066] on the constitutionally of a statute, where he had not been adversely affected by any governmental decision. There the applicant a homosexual brought a judicial review proceeding challenging the legality of section 118C of the Crimes Ordinance which made it an offence for a man to engage in homosexual buggery with a man below the age of 21, whereas in relation to sexual intercourse between men and women the age limit for it to be an offence was 16 years.

594. The Court of Appeal held that while in normal circumstances a constitutional challenge will be made in the context of a decision that affects the applicant, 'there is considerable flexibility and that as a matter of form, it is permissible simply to target legislation rather than any particular judgment, order, decision or other proceeding that has directly affected the would be applicant. Nevertheless, in such a situation, the court will more closely look at an applicant's standing and whether or not he does have a sufficient interest to bring judicial review proceedings.'[1067]

595. As Hartmann J crisply put it when considering the judicial review application in the Court of First Instance: 'If his cause of action must be founded on the exercise of executive power by a public authority, he must bring about a relevant exercise of power by such an authority. In the present case that authority would have to be the police and the only way he could get the police to act would be to commit a [relevant] criminal offence or series of offences. In short, the applicant would have to break the law – risking imprisonment – in order to challenge it.' In such a situation the court may in its discretion grant declaratory relief, declaring what the law is and what the rights of the applicant are under the law. This may be described as a remedy of clarification.[1068] Hartmann J said: 'It seems to me that the Basic Law,

1064. *See R (Pretty) v DPP & Secretary of State for the Home Department (Intervener)* [2002] 1 AC 800, (HL), [116] per Lord Hobhouse of Woodborough; *R (Rusbridger) v A-G* [2004] 1 AC 357, (HL), [16]–[19] per Lord Steyn, and [32] per Lord Hutton. Chief Justice Ma said in *Leung v Secretary for Justice* (2006) 4 HKLRD 211, (CA), [28]: 'It is of course up to the court on a case-by-case basis to determine whether sufficiently exceptional circumstances exist to enable it to exercise the discretion to hear cases notwithstanding that future conduct or a hypothetical situation is involved. It serves no purpose to try to enumerate exhaustively these situations.'

1065. *Leung v Secretary for Justice* [2005] 3 HKLRD 657, (CFI), affirmed on appeal in *Leung v Secretary for Justice* [2006] 4 HKLRD 211, (CA). This case was distinguished in *Balaoro Marietta S v Secretary for Justice*, [2020] 1 HKLRD 1138, (CFI), which was discussed in the immediately preceding paragraph, where there were no exceptional circumstances justifying a departure from the general rule against advisory opinions.

1066. Hartmann J said in *Leung v Secretary for Justice* [2005] 3 HKLRD 657, (CFI), [56]: 'It seems to me that the Basic Law, in terms of its inherent structure and purpose, must allow for a remedy in appropriate circumstances to those who say that their fundamental rights have been undermined by primary legislation, and not an indirect remedy but a direct one, one that permits the courts to go direct to the legislation.'

1067. *Leung v Secretary for Justice* [2006] 4 HKLRD 211, (CA), [27].

1068. *Leung v Secretary for Justice* [2005] 3 HKLRD 657, (CFI), [57] and [64]. Section 21K of the High Court Ordinance (Cap. 4) provides that the court may grant declaratory relief where it considers

in terms of its inherent structure and purpose, must allow for a remedy in appropriate circumstances to those who say that their fundamental rights have been undermined by primary legislation, and not an indirect remedy but a direct one, one that permits the courts to go direct to the legislation. If it was otherwise there would be cases in which the Basic Law would hold out to Hong Kong residents the protection of fundamental rights while denying them the means of securing those rights.'[1069]

596. Similarly, where the dispute between the litigants is no longer live, courts would refuse to express its opinion on the law except in exceptional circumstances.[1070] *Chit Fai Motors Ltd v Commissioner of Transport* is a good example of the exception.[1071] There the applicant, a commercial operator of public light buses, contested the validity of a licence that the Commissioner had granted to a bus operator operating a free shuttle bus service between a residential development and a

---

it 'just and convenient'. Section 21K(2) provides that 'An application for a declaration ... may be made in accordance with rules of court by way of an application for judicial review, and on such an application the Court of First Instance may grant the application having regard to (a) the nature of the matters in respect of which relief may be granted by orders of mandamus, prohibition or certiorari; (b) the nature of the persons and bodies against whom relief may be granted by such orders; and (c) all the circumstances of the case, it would be just and convenient for the declaration to be made.' Ma CJHC said in *Leung v Secretary for Justice* [2006] 4 HKLRD 211, (CA), [28]: 'It is up to the court on a case-by-case basis to determine whether sufficiently exceptional circumstances exist to enable it to exercise the discretion to hear cases notwithstanding that future conduct or a hypothetical situation is involved.'

1069. *Ibid.*, [56].

1070. *HKSAR v Lam Kwong Wai* (2006) 9 HKCFAR 574, (CFA), [75], where Sir Anthony Mason NPJ gave some examples from England, including *R v Secretary of State for the Home Department, ex p Salem* [1999] 1 AC 450, (HL). *See also Fan Kin Nang v Commissioner of Inland Revenue* [2009] HKEC 1914, (CFI).

1071. *Chit Fai Motors Ltd v Commissioner of Transport* [2004] HKEC 218, (CA). *See Cheung Tak Wing v Communications Authority* [2018] 5 HKLRD 515, (CFI), where the Court of First Instance considered it appropriate to consider the legality of a decision made under the Broadcasting Ordinance (Cap. 562) which required television and radio licence holders to broadcast certain 'announcement in public interest', conveying the Government's proposals for reforming the method of selecting the Chief Executive, as they were of political in nature. While television and radio broadcasters were prohibited from broadcasting advertisements of a political nature without prior permission, that restriction did not apply to announcements in public interest. This was alleged to be discriminatory. By the time the substantive judicial review application was taken up, the reform proposals had been rejected by the Legislative Council, and the grant of relief including injunctions had become purely academic. The Court considered it appropriate to proceed with the hearing, although the controversy had ceased to be live, for the following reasons: (1) The challenges related to the question of the legality and constitutionality of the prevailing legislative scheme and policies of the Authority and the Director. The present case would assist the Authority and the Director going forward insofar as how they approach their duties. (2) The controversy in relation to the broadcast of government materials that could be argued to be political in nature might well arise again given the present circumstances in Hong Kong. (3) While the constitutional reform proposal did not gain the requisite amount of support by the Legislative Council in 2015, there might well be another round of constitutional reform and the same or similar types of advertisements would recur. (4) Any such advertisements under challenge could only be broadcast for a limited (likely to be short) period of time. Unless expedited, the time frame from application for leave up to full substantive hearing is likely to exceed the period of broadcast of any relevant advertisement. If the Court were to accede to any challenge on the 'academic' ground, it would be more difficult for the misuse of APIs for political advertising to be challenged and put

transport terminal, which adversely affected their business. The ground of challenge was that the Commissioner had not consulted any operators, like the applicant, who would be affected by granting a licence for a free shuttle bus service to a residential development. While the case was pending, the licence for the free shuttle bus service expired and was not renewed, and the Commissioner argued that the subject matter of litigation had become moot. The Court of Appeal held that while the dispute that gave rise to the litigation was no longer alive, there was the possibility of the grant of a new licence for a free shuttle bus service and therefore the applicant's contention that the Commissioner was under a duty to consult him was a live legal issue and not a mere academic question. The Court was also influenced by the fact that there was every likelihood of such future conflicts arising between free residential bus service providers and regular commercial bus operators, other than the two bus operators in the present case, and therefore a definitive ruling on the issue would make the law certain for those others.

597. A good illustration of courts determining a question of law if it is of public importance, even where the matter in question has become academic is *Secretary for Security v Sakthevel Prabakar.*[1072] There, the Secretary for Security sought leave to appeal against the Court of Appeal's decision quashing his decision to deport an asylum seeker, who had since then resettled in a third country. The Court of Final Appeal granted leave on the ground that it was in the public interest to determine the nature of the duty of the Government towards torture claimants. Following upon the grant of leave to appeal, the Court of Final appeal determined the appeal against the Secretary for Security and laid down detailed guidance on how the Secretary's duty must be performed in order to be constitutional.[1073]

598. *R v Director of Immigration*[1074] is a recent case where the court did not find any exceptional circumstances to rule on a point of law that was no longer a live issue, for the reason that there was no indication that the type of dispute in question was likely to arise in the future involving other asylum-seekers. The applicant who had entered Hong Kong illegally applied for non-refoulement, which the Director had refused. The rejection of his application was held to be unlawful. Having made the order by consent of the parties, the court considered the remaining issue, namely the validity of the government policy to screen non-refoulement applications to determine whether there is sufficient merit to further consider the claim. The court ruled against the applicant because when the judicial review application was decided in his favour the validity of the screening policy had become purely academic. It did not consider that this was an appropriate situation to make a declaration on the validity of the policy: 'the court has jurisdiction to determine an issue which has become academic, but such jurisdiction should be exercised with caution. The important consideration is whether it is in the public interest for the issue

---

right. (5) The challenge arose from real and not hypothetical facts. The Court considered the judicial review application and concluded that all the grounds of challenge had no merit. The judicial review application was dismissed.

1072. *Secretary for Security v Sakthevel Prabakar* (2003) 6 HKCFAR 397, (CFA).

1073. *Secretary for Security v Sakthevel Prabakar* (2004) 7 HKCFAR 187, (CFA).

1074. [2020] HKEC 1522, (CFI).

to be determined. A relevant, but by no means conclusive, consideration is whether the issue is likely or may well arise in future. Having regard to ... the lack of evidence that the Director has adopted, on a systemic level, an incorrect threshold for recognizing non-refoulement claims, this is clearly not an appropriate case for the court to entertain the intended challenge to the alleged Pre-Screening Policy. A serious consideration of the issue should take place only where there is some sufficient or proper evidence to the effect that the Director has adopted, on a systemic level, an incorrect threshold as alleged.'[1075]

599. We may momentarily digress and note that declaration is a private law remedy, and as a general rule, declaratory relief will be granted only on established facts: Where 'there is no dispute in existence or the dispute is based on purely hypothetical facts or if the dispute has ceased to be of any practical significance, the court's established practice is to refuse declaratory relief. The court will in particular refuse to give an advisory opinion sought by a plaintiff in the guise of declaratory relief in respect of a situation that has not arisen and may never arise.'[1076] The discretionary remedy of declaration plays an important role in public law. While a declaration is generally made in the context of facts before them, courts have not hesitated to grant declarations in the absence of a concrete dispute to settle.

600. The court might consider clarifying the law as a matter of public importance even where the matter before the court does not require such clarification. *Pang Yiu Hung v Commissioner of Police*[1077] provides a good illustration. There, a barrister made a judicial review application challenging the lawfulness of his arrest by the Organised Crime and Triad Bureau on the suspicion that he had committed the offence under section 25A of the Organised and Serious Crimes Ordinance (Cap. 455) of not disclosing to an authorized officer that knew or reasonably suspected that any property belonging to another person represented proceeds of crime. The suspicion that the barrister was alleged to have entertained was that his client would deposit proceeds of crime in the solicitor's client account. The applicant submitted that this statutory duty of disclosure conflicted with the client's common law right of legal professional privilege, 'which reflects a fundamental right of confidentiality between a client and his legal advisor, a right protected by the Basic Law'.[1078] Hartmann J concluded that section 25A did not abrogate or limit legal professional privilege and indeed operated within the broad framework of such privilege. However, at the request of the applicant the court issued a declaration that section 25A of the Organized and Serious Crimes Ordinance (Cap. 455) had not abrogated legal professional privilege. The respondents argued, citing the words of Godfrey V-P in *Cheung Man Wai v Director of Social Welfare* that 'the Court, even in public law proceedings, is loath to make any declaration in the nature of an advisory opinion

1075. *Ibid.*, [31]. *See also Poa Kwok Ho v Director of Social Welfare* [2019] HKEC 1521, (CFI).
1076. *Charter View Development Ltd v Golden Rich Enterprises Ltd* [2000] HKEC 340, (CA), Ribeiro JA, citing Zamir & Woolf, *The Declaratory Judgment* (2nd edn, London: Sweet & Maxwell) at p. 127.
1077. [2003] 2 HKLRD 125, (CFI).
1078. *Ibid.*, [22].

as to the true construction or effect of legislation. It is equally loath to make a declaration in a situation which can be described as academic or hypothetical, because such a declaration would not be grounded on any factual basis. And the Court will certainly not make a declaration unless it is satisfied that the making of that declaration will serve some useful purpose.'[1079] Hartmann J issued a declaration that section 25A does not cover information and communications communicated to counsel which are covered by legal professional privilege when taking instructions and rendering legal advice, but refused to issue a further declaration that section 25A, insofar as it relates to information or communications communicated to counsel which are covered by legal professional privilege contravenes the relevant provisions of the Basic Law and the Bill of Rights. Fundamental rights are entrenched in the Basic Law and elaborated in the Bill of Rights. Being in the nature of constitutional provisions these fundamental rights must be given a large and purposive interpretation.[1080] As the Court of Final Appeal recognized in *Ng Ka Ling v Director of Immigration*, a constitution is a living instrument meant to last for generations and flexible enough to suit ever changing circumstances.[1081] It is for this reason that the Court of Final Appeal in *Leung Kwok Hung v HKSAR* reiterated that 'it is well established in our jurisprudence that the courts must give such a fundamental right a generous interpretation so as to give individuals its full measure'.[1082] A parallel development has been that courts interpret ordinary legislation in the light of its context and purpose.[1083] It has also been repeatedly said that the context of a

1079. *Cheung Man Wai v Director of Social Welfare* [2000] 3 HKLRD 255, (CA), 259.

1080. In *Ng Ka Ling v Director of Immigration* (1999) 2 HKCFAR 4, (CFA), 28, speaking generally of the interpretation of the Basic Law, Li CJ observed as follows: 'The adoption of a purposive approach is necessary because a constitution states general principles and expresses purposes without condescending to particularity and definition of terms. Gaps and ambiguities are bound to arise and, in resolving them, the courts are bound to give effect to the principles and purposes declared in, and to be ascertained from, the constitution and relevant extrinsic materials. So, in ascertaining the true meaning of the instrument, the courts must consider the purpose of the instrument and its relevant provisions as well as the language of its text in the light of the context, context being of particular importance in the interpretation of a constitutional instrument.'

1081. *Ng Ka Ling v Director of Immigration* (1999) 2 HKCFAR 4, (CFA), 28.

1082. *Leung Kwok Hung v HKSAR* (2005) 8 HKCFAR 229, (CFA), [16], endorsing the view expressed in *Ng Ka Ling v Director of Immigration* (1999) 2 HKCFAR 4, (CFA), 28–29. For an affirmation of this approach, *see Ubamaka v Secretary for Security* (2012) 15 HKCFAR 743, (CFA), [5].

1083. While the courts must ascertain the intention of the legislature as manifested in a statute, statutory interpretation is not limited to 'seeking the meaning of words which [the legislature] used': *Black-Clawson International Ltd v Papierwerke Waldhof-Aschaffenburg AG* [1975] AC 591, (HL), 613. 'The modern approach is to adopt a purposive interpretation. The statutory language is construed, having regard to its context and purpose. Words are given their natural and ordinary meaning unless the context or purpose points to a different meaning. Context and purpose are considered when interpreting the words used and not only when an ambiguity may be thought to arise': *HKSAR v Cheung Kwun Yin* (2009) 12 HKCFAR 568, (CFA), [12], per Li CJ. *See also Secretary of Justice v Leung Kwok Hung* [2019] HKEC 417, (CA), where a purposive approach was adopted in interpreting the Oaths and Declarations Ordinance (Cap. 11) in the light of Art. 104 of the Basic Law. *See* [39]–[43].

statutory provision must be taken in its widest sense.[1084] Purposive interpretation does not justify giving a statutory provision a meaning that it is incapable of bearing.[1085]

601. While fundamental rights must be given a purposive interpretation to ensure widest possible scope for their operation, restrictions on a fundamental right must be narrowly interpreted, in order to ensure any erosion of fundamental rights are confined to the smallest lawfully possible space,[1086] the burden being on the Government to justify any restriction.[1087] Interpreting the scope of Article 36 of the Basic Law which protected social welfare rights, Chief Justice Ma explained in *Kong Yunming v Director of Social Welfare* the need for a valid reason for the restriction and for the restriction to be no more than necessary for such legitimate reason: 'Restrictions on rights protected by Art. 36 must pursue a legitimate societal aim and must be rationally connected with the achievement of that end, employing measures that do not make excessive inroads into the protected right. If the restriction is not rationally connected to the avowed legitimate purpose or if the inroads it makes into the protected right are manifestly without reasonable foundation, the Court may declare the measure unconstitutional.'[1088]

602. The rules of interpretation appropriate for a Bill of Rights in a common law jurisdiction have their origin in the common law rules of statutory interpretation. They take their special flavour from rules of constitutional interpretation first developed in the US. Bills of Rights are invariably modelled on international and regional human rights declarations and conventions, and, for that reason, interpretation of such international instruments naturally influences domestic courts. The result of

1084. *See HKSAR v Li Kwok Cheung George* (2014) 17 HKCFAR 319, (CFA), [37]; *HKSAR v Cheung Kwun Yin* (2009) 12 HKCFAR 568, (CFA), [13]; and *HKSAR v Lam Kwong Wai* (2006) 9 HKCFAR 574.

1085. *See* Millett LJ's often-cited warning in *China Field Ltd v Appeal Tribunal (Buildings) (No 2)* (2009) 12 HKCFAR 342, (CFA), [36]: 'There can be no quarrel with the principle that statutory provisions should be given a purposive interpretation, but there has been a distressing development by the courts which allows them to distort or even ignore the plain meaning of the text and construe the statute in whatever manner achieves a result which they consider desirable. It cannot be said too often that this is not permissible. Purposive construction means only that statutory provisions are to be interpreted to give effect to the intention of the legislature, and that intention must be ascertained by a proper application of the interpretative process. This does not permit the Court to attribute to a statutory provision a meaning which the language of the statute, understood in the light of its context and the statutory purpose, is incapable of bearing: *see HKSAR v Lam Kwong Wai* (2006) 9 HKCFAR 574, (CFA), [63].'

1086. 'It is common ground that the statutory provisions criminalising desecration of the national and regional flags restrict the freedom of expression. Before considering whether the restriction is justified, it is important to examine first the extent of the restriction. This is because when one comes to consider the issue of justification, one must have in mind what it is that has to be justified, in particular, whether it is a wide or limited restriction that has to be justified. The wider the restriction, the more difficult it would be to justify': *HKSAR v Ng Kung Siu* (1999) 2 HKCFAR 442, (CFA), 455–456.

1087. This flows from the common law rule that a person who pleads justification of its action must establish it. A restriction of a fundamental right would be justified if it is prescribed by law, reasonable, proportionate and necessary.

1088. *Kong Yunming v Director of Social Welfare* (2013) 16 HKCFAR 950, (CFA), [139].

this rich diversity of sources is that courts have a spectrum of choices ranging from solemn deference to legislative intention to adventurous judicial activism reaffirming that the judiciary is after all not the least dangerous branch of the government.[1089] These comments are apt to describe the judicial attitude to the interpretation of the Hong Kong Bill of Rights and the Basic Law in Hong Kong.

603. It is clear that the Hong Kong Bill of Rights Ordinance and the Basic Law must be interpreted according to common law canons of interpretation. 'In the Courts of Hong Kong it is the canons of construction under Hong Kong law which have to be applied, even to the interpretation of the Basic Law.'[1090] The Court of Final Appeal has reiterated this view.[1091]

604. The starting point of statutory interpretation is ascertaining 'the intention of the legislature as expressed in the language of the statute'.[1092] 'The exercise of interpretation requires the courts to identify the meaning borne by the language when considered in the light of its context and purpose. This is an objective exercise.'[1093] Rules of statutory interpretation must be used carefully in relation to constitutional documents, because a constitution is drafted in broad and ample style and lays down principles of width and generality.[1094] Courts must avoid 'the austerity of tabulated legalism' and go for a 'generous and purposive interpretation suitable to give the individual the full measure of the fundamental rights and freedoms enshrined [in the Constitution]'.[1095] These sentiments are reflected in the words of Chief Justice Li in the Hong Kong case of *Ng Ka Ling v Director of Immigration*:

1089. Anton Cooray, 'Bills of Rights and Constitutional Interpretation' in John Hatchard and Peter Slinn (eds) *Parliamentary Supremacy and Judicial Independence: A Commonwealth Approach* (London and Sydney: Cavendish Publishing Ltd, 1999).

1090. *Commissioner for Registration v Registration of Persons Tribunal* [1999] 3 HKLRD 199, (CFI), 212, per Keith JA.

1091. *Director of Immigration v Chong Fung Yuen* (2001) 4 HKCFAR 211, (CFA), 221. *See also* at 223, where it was said: 'The courts' role under the common law in interpreting the Basic Law is to construe the language used in the text of the instrument in order to ascertain *the legislative intent as expressed in the language.* Their task is not to ascertain the intent of the lawmaker on its own. Their duty is to ascertain *what was meant by the language used* and to give effect to *the legislative intent as expressed in the language.* It is the text of the enactment which is the law and it is regarded as important both that the law should be certain and that it should be ascertainable by the citizen.'

1092. *HKSAR v Cheung Kwan Yin* (2009) 12 HKCFAR 568, (CFA), [11], per Li CJ. As Lord Reid said in *Black-Clawson International Ltd v Papierwerke Waldhof-Aschaffenburg AG* [1975] AC 591, at 613, (HL): 'We often say that we are looking for the intention of Parliament, but that is not quite accurate. We are seeking the meaning of the words which Parliament used.' In other words, the intention of the legislature must be objectively ascertained.

1093. *Director of Immigration v Chong Fung Yuen* (2001) 4 HKCFAR 211, (CFA), 223–224.

1094. *Ministry of Home Affairs v Fisher* [1980] AC 319, (PC), 328, per Lord Wilberforce. As Li CJ put it in *Ng Ka ling v Director of Immigration* (1999) 2 HKCFAR 4, (CFA), 28: 'The adoption of a purposive approach is necessary because a constitution states general principles and expresses purposes without condescending to particularly and definition of terms. Gaps and ambiguities are bound to arise and, in resolving them, the courts are bound to give effect to the principles and purposes declared in, and to be ascertained from, the constitution and relevant extrinsic materials.'

1095. *Ministry of Home Affairs v Fisher* [1980] AC 319, (PC), 328.

> The courts should give a generous interpretation to the provisions of Chapter III [of the Basic Law] that contain ... constitutional guarantees in order to give to Hong Kong residents the full measure of fundamental rights and freedoms so constitutionally guaranteed.[1096]

605. In interpreting the Basic Law and the Hong Kong Bill of Rights, extrinsic materials are of particular relevance.[1097] The Privy Council in *Attorney General v Lee Kwong-kut,*[1098] however, expressed some reservations about the relevance of international human rights jurisprudence. These doubts have now been laid to rest. As the Court of Appeal observed in *Hung Chan Wa & another v HKSAR*: 'The exhortation in *A-G of Hong Kong v Lee Kwong-Kut* to common sense, to realism, to acknowledgment of difficult policy problems was just that and was, we suggest, not intended to set for Hong Kong a principled course different from the approach elsewhere that places due weight, as against policy considerations, upon the importance of fundamental rights, of which the presumption of innocence is one.'[1099]

606. While courts recognize the importance of their role as guardians of the rights of the subject, they also realize the equal importance of striking a right balance between the rights of the individual and the need to protect society as a whole. There will also be circumstances where the court might defer to the view of the legislature even if the legislative decision appears to be incompatible with a fundamental human right.[1100] In *HKSAR v Pun Ganga,*[1101] in upholding the validity of the imposition of mandatory sentence for murder, the Court of Appeal relied on the fact that the Legislative Council had extensively debated the suitability of such punishment before enacting the relevant legislative provision.

607. Hong Kong courts have been warned to not be too adventurous: 'While the Hong Kong judiciary should be zealous in upholding an individual's rights under the Hong Kong Bill, it is also necessary to ensure that disputes as to the effect of

---

1096. *Ng Ka Ling v Director of Immigration* (1999) 2 HKCFAR 4, (CFA), 29.

1097. 'Extrinsic materials which throw light on the context or purpose of the Basic Law or its particular provisions may generally be used as an aid to the interpretation of the Basic Law': *Director of Immigration v Chong Fung Yuen* (2001) 4 HKCFAR 211, (CFA), 224.

1098. [1993] AC 951, 967–968; [1993] 2 HKCLR 186, 200.

1099. *Hung Chan Wa & another v HKSAR* [2005] 3 HKLRD 291, (CA), [81]. Judicial decisions where international jurisprudence was found to be helpful and persuasive include: *Numeric City Ltd v Lau Chi Wing* [2016] 4 HKLRD 812, (CA); *Wong Chi Fung v Secretary for Justice* [2016] 3 HKLRD 835, (CFI); *Bewang International (Group) Holdings Ltd v Next Magazine Ltd* [2016] HKEC 1145, (CFI) and *Kwok Chuk Kin v Secretary for Constitutional and Mainland Affairs* [2015] 5 HKLRD 881, (CA).

1100. *R v DPP, ex p Kebilene* [2000] 2 AC 326, (HL), 380–381, followed in *HKSAR v Pun Ganga* [2001] 2 HKLRD 151, (CA), 169–170.

1101. [2001] 2 HKLRD 151, (CA), 169–170: 'In this area [mandatory sentence of life imprisonment] difficult choices may have to be made by the executive or the legislature between the rights of the individual and the needs of society. In some circumstances it will be appropriate for the courts to recognise that there is an area of judgment within which the judiciary will defer, on democratic grounds, to the considered opinion of the elected body or person whose act or decision is said to be incompatible with the Convention.'

the Bill are not allowed to get out of hand. The issues involving the Hong Kong Bill [of Rights] should be approached with realism and good sense and kept in proportion. If this is not done the Bill will become a source of injustice rather than justice and it will be debased in the eyes of the public. In order to maintain the balance between the individual and the society as a whole, rigid and inflexible standards should not be imposed on the legislature's attempts to resolve the difficult and intransigent problems with which society is faced when seeking to deal with serious crime. It must be remembered that questions of policy remain primarily the responsibility of the legislature.'[1102]

608. Section 6(1) of the Bill of Rights provides that a court or tribunal:

(a) in proceedings within its jurisdiction in an action for breach of this Ordinance; and
(b) in other proceedings within its jurisdiction in which a violation or threatened violation of the Bill of Rights is relevant;
(c) may grant such remedy or relief, or make such order in respect of such a breach, violation or threatened violation as it has power to grant or make in those proceedings, and, as it considers appropriate and just in the circumstances.

609. Courts have the power to rule unconstitutional any provision which is inconsistent with the Basic Law or the Bill of Rights, assuming that the Bill of Rights has constitutional status in Hong Kong.[1103] The view has been expressed that the court's power to strike down legislation is not limited to unconstitutional provisions but also extends to any provisions, which by themselves are innocuous but tend to infringe a fundamental right. In *Koon Wing Yee v Insider Dealing Tribunal*, Sir Anthony Mason NPJ said in relation to section 6 of the Bill of Rights:

> Section 6(1) should be interpreted in accordance with its wide language as conferring power to strike down a non-infringing provision where to do so best conforms with the legislative intention. To exercise the power in that way is not to thwart the will of the legislature but rather to respect its will and give effect to its intention by giving the legislation as effective an operation as it can be given consistently with the Bill of Rights. Section 6(1) should be construed, in accordance with its terms, as conferring a power which will enable the courts to resolve the tension which exists between the legislative will and the protection given by the Bill of Rights by striking down only that part of the

1102. Lord Woolf in *Attorney General of Hong Kong v Lee Kwong-kut* [1993] AC 951, (PC), 975. *See* Yash Ghai 'Sentinels or Liberty of Sheep in Woolf's Clothing? Judicial Politics and the Hong Kong Bill of Rights', (1997) 60 *Modern Law Review* 459–480.

1103. It is a well-established principle in the common law world that any legislation or administrative action that is inconsistent with any provision of the paramount constitution is invalid and of no effect to the extent of such inconsistency.

statute that causes the violation or breach, even if it does not itself infringe the Bill of Rights, when to do so best gives effect to the legislative intention.[1104]

610. Courts interpret a legislative provision not in isolation, but in the context of the entirety of the statute, adopting a purposive approach. As Bokhary PJ said in *Medical Council of Hong Kong v Chow Siu Shek*: 'When the true position under a statute is to be ascertained by interpretation, it is necessary to read all of the relevant provisions together and in the context of the whole statute as a purposive unity in its appropriate legal and social setting.'[1105] The court may look not only at the other provisions in the relevant statute but also similar provisions in other statutes. Bokhary PJ said: 'It is well-established that the context in which a statute is to be interpreted includes other statutes in pari materia i.e., other statutes dealing with comparable matters.'[1106] Where the scope of a statutory provision does not appear to be restricted or expanded by other provisions in the same statute, such section must be regarded as self-standing. In such a situation the principle set out in *Medical Council of Hong Kong v Chow Siu Shek* does not apply.[1107] Where the wide scope of a statutory provision would contravene a constitutional provision, whether its apparently wide scope is cut down by other provisions is a relevant question to ask.[1108] When the answer is in the negative, then the statutory provision will be unconstitutional.[1109]

611. Where courts find a legislative provision inconsistent with a constitutional provision it will try and give a remedial interpretation to the impugned legislative provision, instead of declaring it invalid. As Bokhary PJ explained in *HKSAR v Lam Kwong Wai*: 'The justification for engaging in remedial interpretation is that it enables the courts, in appropriate cases, to uphold the validity of legislation, albeit in an altered form, rather than strike it down. To this extent, the courts interfere less with the exercise of legislative power than they would if they could not engage in remedial interpretation.'[1110] However, courts will hesitate to place a remedial interpretation if the suggested change of language leads to a result wholly different from what the legislature intended, or where the proposed change requires careful consideration by the legislature.[1111] As Sir Anthony Mason NPJ observed in *HKSAR v*

1104. *Koon Wing Yee v Insider Dealing Tribunal* [2008] 3 HKLRD 372, (2008) 11 HKCFAR 170, (CFA), [113]. For a critical account of this case *see* Kevin Zervos, 'Constitutional Remedies under the Basic Law' (2010) 40 *Hong Kong Law Journal* 687, pp. 703–707.
1105. (2000) 3 HKCFAR 144, (CFA), 151.
1106. *Ibid.*, 516.
1107. *See Leung Kwok Hung v Secretary for Justice* [2020] HKEC 533, (CA).
1108. *Ibid.*, [277].
1109. *Ibid.*, [279].
1110. *HKSAR v Lam Kwong Wai* (2006) 9 HKCFAR 574, (CFA), [77].
1111. In *Wong Chi Fung v Secretary for Justice* [2016] 3 HKLRD 835, (CFI), it was unsuccessfully argued that the requirement that a person standing for election must have reached the age of 21 while an elector only needs to have reached the age of 18 was a disproportionate restriction. Thomas Au J said that assuming that the requirement was unconstitutional, the court would not be prepared to substitute 18 for 21 so that the same age requirement applies to both situation because 'What should be the proper choice of the minimum age of candidature is obviously a matter of

Lam Kwong Wai[1112] 'the implied powers of this Court include the obligation to adopt a remedial interpretation of a legislative provision which will, so far as it is possible, make it Basic Law-consistent. Only in the event that such an interpretation is not possible, will the Court proceed to make a declaration of contravention, entailing unconstitutionality and invalidity.'[1113]

612. Remedial interpretation is guided by the following principles:

(a) Subject to the limitations in (c) and (d) below, the court can exercise the power of remedial interpretation to depart from the unambiguous meaning of the legislative provision in order to give a Basic Law compliant effect to the same.
(b) In adopting a remedial interpretation, the court can interpret language in a statutory provision restrictively or expansively. It can also read in words which change the meaning of the provision.
(c) However, the court cannot adopt a meaning inconsistent with a fundamental feature of the legislative scheme or its essential principles. Whether an element in the statutory provision constitutes a fundamental feature or essential principle must be determined with regard to its place in the overall scheme of the legislation.
(d) Remedial interpretation does not empower the courts to make decisions for which they are not equipped such as choosing between various options which requires legislative deliberation or adopting a meaning which has important practical repercussions which the court is in no position to evaluate.[1114]

613. There are several instances where courts have adopted a remedial interpretation.[1115] The first technique is to read words in. A prominent example of this technique is the decision of the Court of Final Appeal in *W v Registrar of Marriages.* There, it was held that consistently with Article 37 of the Basic Law and Article 19(2) of the Hong Kong Bill of Rights ((Freedom of marriage), section 20(1)(d) of the Matrimonial Clauses Ordinance and section 40 of the Marriage Ordinance must be read and given effect so as to include within the meaning of the words 'woman'

political judgment for the legislature, but not one for the court to make in the name of remedial interpretation' [74], relying on *Kwok Cheuk Kin v Secretary for Constitutional and Mainland Affairs* [2015] 5 HKLRD 881, (CA), [6].

1112. *HKSAR v Lam Kwong Wai* (2006) 9 HKCFAR 574, (CFA).

1113. *Ibid.*, [78]. In *HKSAR v Hung Chan Wa* (2006) 9 HKCFAR 614, (CFA), [86], Sir Anthony Mason NPJ reconfirmed that the power to apply a remedial interpretation is an inherent or implied power of the courts.

1114. *Keen Lloyd Holdings Ltd v Commissioner of Customs and Excise* [2016] 2 HKLRD 1372, (CA), [97]. There the court held that there was no difference between domestic premises and non-domestic premises in considering whether the power of inspection without a judicial warrant was constitutional. The court interpreted the words 'domestic premises', in relation to which a warrant was required by statute, to read as simply 'premises' so that the requirement of prior authorization applied to both domestic and non-domestic premises.

1115. *HKSAR v Mohammed Khan Shamim* [2013] HKEC 469, (CA); *Keen Lloyd Holdings Ltd v Commissioner of Customs and Excise* [2016] 2 HKLRD 1372, (CA).

and 'female' a post-operative male-to-female transsexual person whose gender has been certified by an appropriate medical authority to have changed as a result of sex reassignment surgery.[1116]

614. Leung Chun Kwong v Secretary for Civil Service[1117] read with *Leung Chun Kwong v Secretary for Civil Service (No 2)*[1118] is another good example, where the Court of Final Appeal held that the civil service had discriminated against the applicant-civil servant who was in a same-sex marriage (recognized in New Zealand but not in Hong Kong) by denying to extend to him tax and spousal benefits available to married civil servants. There, in order to save the statute from being unconstitutional on the ground of discrimination based on sexual orientation, the words marriage, husband, and wife appearing in the Inland Revenue Ordinance were interpreted as if they referred to marriage including a marriage between persons of the same sex, and, husband and wife as 'a married person and his or her spouse'. *Yeung Chu Wing v Secretary for Justice* is another recent example. Section 1181(1) of the Crimes Ordinance provides that 'a man who commits an act of gross indecency with another man who is a mentally incapacitated person shall be guilty of an offence … '. There was no corresponding provision which create a similar offence in relation to women. In order to remedy this unconstitutional discrimination the court remedially interpreted the word 'man' as a reference to 'person', so it would include both a man and a woman: 'a person who commits an act of gross indecency with another person who is a mentally incapacitated person shall be guilty of an offence … '.[1119]

615. Another technique is reading down. Where a statutory provision could be given two meanings, a narrow meaning consistent with the constitution and the other a broader meaning inconsistent with the constitution, it could be saved by giving the narrow meaning. The opting for a restricted meaning is known as 'reading down'. As was said in relation to whether the burden of proving a fact can be placed on the defendant, which would breach the presumption of innocence: 'where there

1116. *W v Registrar of Marriages* (2013) 16 HKCFAR 112, (CFA), [225], where Ma CJ said: 'I hold that the right to marry guaranteed by our constitution extends to the right of a post-operative transsexual to marry in the reassigned capacity. This means, without any need to rely on freedom from arbitrary or unlawful interference with privacy, that the legislation concerned would be unconstitutional unless the words of gender therein are read to include gender acquired by sex reassignment surgery. If those words can be so read, they should be so read. In my view, they can be so read. And, by way of remedial interpretation, I so read them.'

1117. (2019) 22 HKCFAR 127, (CFA).

1118. (2019) 22 HKCFAR 282, (CFA).

1119. *Yeung Chu Wing v Secretary for Justice* [2019] 3 HKLRD 238, (CFI).

existed two reasonably possible interpretations of a statutory provision, one consistent with an international obligation or a constitutional requirement, the other inconsistent, then it should be presumed that the Legislature intended the meaning that was consistent: this was simply applying a canon of interpretation to a word or phrase as it appeared in context'.[1120]

616. *China International Fund Ltd v Dennis Lau & Ng Chun Man Architects & Engineers (HK) Ltd*[1121] provides another method of applying the technique of reading down. There, the Court of Appeal upheld the legality of section 84(4) of the Arbitration Ordinance (Cap. 609) which provided that the Court of First Instance may in its discretion not allow an appeal to the Court of Appeal from its decision from an arbitration award. In arriving at this decision, the Court of Appeal took into account the nature of the arbitration process, as well as the limited residuary jurisdiction that the Court of Appeal has in granting leave to appeal. The Court of Appeal observed that the limitation in section 84(4) must be 'read down' so as to preserve the 'residual jurisdiction' of the Court of Appeal to intervene in an extreme situation where not to grant leave to appeal would compromise fairness of judicial process.

617. In *HKSAR v Ng Po On*[1122] the court read down section 24 of the Prevention of Bribery Ordinance (Cap. 201), which places on the accused the burden of proving a defence of lawful authority or reasonable excuse. 'So read down, the accused would be required to raise the issue of reasonable excuse, supported by sufficient credible evidence to engender a reasonable doubt as to the prosecution's case [by placing only an evidential burden on the accused], but the prosecution would retain throughout the persuasive burden of proving non-compliance, encompassing a burden of negativing any purported reasonable excuse. Read this way, s 24 would be compatible with the constitutionally entrenched presumption of innocence.'[1123] In the recent case of *HKSAR v Yeung Ho Nam (No. 1)*,[1124] the Court of Appeal having determined that imposing a harsher sentence on a man engaging in a prohibited homosexual act (life imprisonment) than a much more lenient sentence on a person engaging in a prohibited heterosexual act maximum period of five years in prison) infringed equality before the law, read down the harsher sentence to bring it in line with the lesser sentence.

1120. *Hung Chan Wa v HKSAR* [2005] 3 HKLRD, (CA), [135]. Section 47 of the Dangerous Drugs Ordinance (Cap. 134) provided that a person who has dangerous drugs in his possession is presumed to know the nature of such drug, unless the contrary be proved. If this meant that the defendant had to prove the fact (persuasive burden) that would be inconsistent with the presumption of innocence protected by the Hong Kong Bill of Rights and the Basic Law. The court read down the words 'contrary be proved' to 'unless sufficient evidence is given to the contrary', thus only imposing an 'evidential burden of proof'. *Ibid.*, [138].
1121. [2015] 4 HKLRD 609, (CA).
1122. (2008) 11 HKCFAR 91, (CFA).
1123. *Ibid.*, [77].
1124. [2020] 1 HKLRD 91, (CA).

618. Another technique of remedial interpretation is to sever words from legislation in order to remove ambiguities and give a clearly ascertainable meaning to words of a statute. Where the remedy is one of severance, the test is whether the constitutional parts are distinct from the unconstitutional parts so that what is unconstitutional may be severed leaving what is constitutional intact.[1125] For instance in *Leung Kwok Hung v HKSAR*[1126] the relevant statutory provision (section 14(1) of the Public Order Ordinance (Cap. 245)) granted discretion to the Commissioner to object to a procession if he reasonably considered this was 'necessary in the interests of national security or public safety, public order (ordre public) or the protection of the rights and freedom of others'. It was held that the words '*order public'* did not have an easily verifiable scope and expunged the phrase *order public*. After removing the words 'order public', the commissioner's discretion in relation to public order, in the sense of law and order, satisfied the 'prescribed by law' requirement and the 'necessary in a democratic society' requirement.[1127]

619. Courts will hesitate to give a remedial interpretation if such an interpretation is fundamentally at odds with the legislative intention. Courts would not adopt a remedial interpretation if do so would be incompatible with the underlying thrust of the legislation, or would not go with the grain of it, or would call for legislative deliberation, or would change the substance of a provision completely, or would remove its pith and substance, or would violate a cardinal principle of the legislation. In such a situation it is a matter for the Legislative Council to take necessary curative measures.[1128]

620. Where courts declare a statutory provision unconstitutional, courts have inherent power in exceptional circumstances to issue a temporary validity order or suspend for a short period of time the operation of the declaration of invalidity. As Bokhary PJ explained in *Koo Sze Yiu v Chief Executive*: 'The rule of law involves meeting the needs of law and order. It involves providing a legal system able to function effectively. In order to meet those needs and preserve that ability, it must be recognised that exceptional circumstances may call for exceptional judicial measures. Temporary validity or suspension are example of what courts have seen as such measures.'[1129] In *Leung Kwok Hung v Chief Executive of HKSAR*[1130] the Court

1125. *Ng Ka Ling v Director of Immigration* (1999) 2 HKCFAR 4 at 37, (CFA), per Li CJ. When this case was heard in the Court of First Instance Keith J borrowed the language of 'blue pencil test' from the law of contract. *See Cheung Lai Wah v The Director of Immigration* [1997] HKLRD 1081, (CFI), 1095.

1126. (2005) 8 HKCFAR 229, (CFA).

1127. *Ibid.*, [82]–[85]. Section 14(1) of the Public Order Ordinance was amended in 2008 removing the words 'ordre public'. The section now reads: 'the Commissioner of Police may object to a public procession being held if he reasonably considers that the objection is necessary in the interests of national security or public safety, public order or the protection of the rights and freedoms of others' (amended by Ordinance No 10 of 2008, s. 12). At the same time, s. 14(5) was amended to a similar effect.

1128. *HKSAR v Lam Kwong Wai* (2006) 9 HKCFAR 574, (CFA), [66], citing *Bellinger v Bellinger* (Lord Chancellor intervening) [2003] 2 AC 467, (HL).

1129. *Koo Sze Yiu v Chief Executive* (2006) 9 HKCFAR 441, (CFA), [28]. Following the principles set out in *Koo Sze Yiu* case, the Court of Appeal in *Leung Kwok Hung v Secretary for Justice* [2020]

of First Instance declared section 33 of the Telecommunications Ordinance (Cap. 106) unconstitutional but gave that section temporary validity for six months and this was affirmed by the Court of Appeal.[1131] On appeal, the Court of Final Appeal replaced the order of temporary validity with suspension of the ruling for six months.[1132] Only a superior court of law has inherent jurisdiction. However, an inferior court or tribunal may suspend its ruling of unconstitutionality where it has implied statutory power to do so and where such exercise is necessary for the effective exercise of jurisdiction expressly conferred upon it.[1133]

621. Prospective overruling offers another means of tempering the harshness of a judicial declaration. The generally accepted view in the common law world is that a judge declares the law (declaratory theory) and does not make it (constitutive theory). Where a court finds that a previous judicial decision is wrong, it will declare it invalid. The same common law practice applies where a court finds that a legislative provision is invalid. In other words, if the judge finds a statute invalid, he simply declares such invalidity with the result that the impugned legislation or legislative provision is invalid from its inception – void *ab initio*. In effect, the judge has made a declaration that has retrospective effect: any act done or any omission made relying on the validity of the statute, before or after the judicial decision, has no legal effect. This seriously affects certainty of law: What government agencies purported to do in exercising power under the invalidated legislation and what people did on the assumption that such legislative provision and government action were valid becomes unauthorized or even illegal.[1134] A possible solution that courts may resort to is prospective overruling, whereby a court may declare that a legislative provision or a judicial precedent is invalid, but without retrospective effect.[1135]

622. There are two main forms of prospective overruling: (1) the judge declares that the declaration of invalidity will not have any retrospective effect: 'The ruling applies only to transactions or happenings occurring after the date of the court decision. All transactions entered into, or events occurring, before that date continue to be governed by the law as it was conceived to be before the court gave its ruling.'

---

1 HKLRD 80, (CA), refused an application by the Government for a suspension or a temporary validity order of the invalidity that the Court of Appeal declared, pending the determination of substantive issues by the Court of Appeal.

1130. [2006] HKEC 239, (CFI).

1131. [2006] HKEC 816, (CA).

1132. *Koo Sze Yiu v Chief Executive* (2006) 9 HKCFAR 441, (CFA).

1133. *Ocean Technology Ltd v Secretary for Justice* [2009] HKEC 124, (CFI) especially [16] and [28] following what Bokhary PJ had said in *PCCW-HKT Telephone Ltd v Telecommunications Authority* (2005) 8 HKCFAR 337, [36].

1134. As was said in *In re Spectrum Plus Ltd (in liquidation)* [2005] 2 AC 680, (HL), [7]: 'People generally conduct their affairs on the basis of what they understand the law to be. This "retrospective" effect of a change in the law of this nature can therefore have disruptive and seemingly unfair consequences.'

1135. *See* generally, on prospective overruling, Mary Arden [Lady Arden], *Human Rights and European Law: Building New Legal Orders* (Oxford University Press: 2015), Ch. 17 'Prospective Overruling'. This chapter was first published in (2004) 120 *Law Quarterly Review* 7–11.

(2) The ruling may affect the parties to the litigation, and in that limited sense retrospective:[1136] 'The ruling in its operation may be prospective and, additionally, retrospective in its effect as between the parties to the case in which the ruling is given. Or the ruling may be prospective and, additionally, retrospective as between the parties in the case in which the ruling was given and also as between the parties in any other cases already pending before the courts.'[1137] Prospective overruling may be appropriate where a retrospective invalidation of legislation has the effect of invalidating a large number of similar past acts.[1138] Hong Kong courts have in several cases considered whether prospective overruling is appropriate. Even assuming that courts of Hong Kong have the power to employ prospective overruling, there has so far been no appropriate case where the courts could resort to this device.[1139]

§3. A Select Survey of Human Rights in Hong Kong

I. The Right to Equality

623. The Basic Law, the Hong Kong Bill of Rights and the ICCPR recognize the importance of equality before the law.[1140] Article 25 of the Basic Law provides that all Hong Kong residents shall be equal before the law. Article 22 of the Bill of Rights, reproducing Article 26 of the ICCPR, provides: 'All persons are equal before the law and are entitled without any discrimination to the equal protection of the law. In this respect, the law shall prohibit any discrimination and guarantee to

---

1136. *See*, for instance, *Murphy v Attorney General* [1982] IR 241 (SC of Ireland).

1137. *In re Spectrum Plus Ltd (in liquidation)* [2005] 2 AC 680, (HL), [9]–[10].

1138. Sri Lanka provides a good illustration. In *Jailabdeen v Danina Umma* (1962) 64 Ceylon New Law Reports 419, the Supreme Court held that Quazi Courts exercised judicial power and its members had to be appointed by the Judicial Service Commission, just as other inferior judicial officers. Muslim Marriage and Divorce Act was held to be unconstitutional to the extent it enabled the Minister of Justice to appoint members of Quazi Courts. Since judicial decisions have retrospective effect, this meant that all decisions previously given by Quazi Courts concerning Muslim marriages and divorces were without any legal effect. Parliament had to step in and pass legislation declaring that any exercise of power or grant of any order by a Quazi was deemed not to be invalid by reason only of the fact that such Quazi had been appointed by the Minister. The Act, Quazis (Validation of Appointments) Act No 11 of 1965, was passed with a two-thirds majority, the majority required to pass constitutional amendments, since conferment of judicial power on an executive authority (namely the power of appointing judicial officers given to the minister) was contrary to the exclusive vesting of judicial power in the judiciary. Thereafter the Muslim Marriage and Divorce Act was amended so as to grant the power of appointing Quazis to the Judicial Service commission, so for the future (prospectively) the legislation would be constitution-compliant. *See* M J A (Anton) Cooray, 'Three Models of Constitutional Litigation: Lessons from Sri Lanka' (1992) 21 *Anglo-American Law Review* 430–448, at 436–438.

1139. *See HKSAR v Hung Chan Wa* (2006) 9 HKCFAR 614, (CFA), *HKSAR v Lam Kwong Wai* (2006) 9 HKCFAR 574, (CFA), where Sir Anthony Mason NPJ discusses prospective overruling in some fair detail, while Bokhary PJ opted to leave the question open.

1140. Article 25 of the Basic Law provides that all Hong Kong residents shall be equal before the law. Article 22 of the Bill of Rights, reproducing Art. 26 of the ICCPR, provides: 'All persons are equal before the law and are entitled without any discrimination to the equal protection of the law. In this respect, the law shall prohibit any discrimination and guarantee to all persons equal and effective protection against discrimination on any ground such as race, colour, sex, language, religion, political or other opinion, national or social origin, property, birth or other status.'

all persons equal and effective protection against discrimination on any ground such as race, colour, sex, language, religion, political or other opinion, national or social origin, property, birth or other status.'

624. Article 1 of the Hong Kong Bill of Rights provides that the rights recognized in the Bill of Rights shall be enjoyed without distinction of any kind, such as race, colour, sex, language, religion, political or other opinion, national or social origin, property, birth or other status; and that men and women shall have an equal right to the enjoyment of all civil and political rights set forth in the Bill of Rights. Article 1 might be described as a procedural guarantee that underpins all substantive fundamental rights, ensuring that rights such as access to free and independent courts are enjoyed by all persons without any discrimination. It may also be described as a substantive right in the sense that it requires all government agencies to take positive measures to ensure that this right is effectively implemented.

625. 'The constitutional right to equality is in essence the right not to be discriminated against. It guarantees protection from discrimination.'[1141] 'Discrimination is an insidious practice. Discriminatory law undermines the rule of law because it is the antithesis of fairness. It brings the law into disrepute. It breeds resentment. It fosters an inequality of outlook which is demeaning alike to those unfairly benefited and those unfairly prejudiced.'[1142] Equality thus demands that similarly situated persons be similarly treated and that differently situated persons be differently treated. Discrimination may take the following forms: (i) direct discrimination where the complainant is receiving treatment which is unfavourable when compared with treatment given to persons in 'relevantly similar situations' [where like cases are not treated alike]; (ii) direct discrimination where the complainant disadvantageously receives the same treatment as persons in significantly different situations receive [where unlike cases are treated in the same way]; and (iii) indirect discrimination where an ostensibly neutral criterion is applied which operates to the significant prejudice of a particular group.[1143] Where discriminatory treatment is alleged the first question to ask is whether there is a differential treatment on a prohibited ground, such as sex or race. The applicant will have to show that he has been treated, or will be treated, less favourably than individuals belonging to a comparator group. If this is established, the next question is whether such differential treatment by the administration is justified, or the differential treatment by legislation is proportionate.[1144]

1141. *Secretary for Justice v Yau Yuk Lung* (2007) 10 HKCFAR 335, (CFA), [1], per Li CJ.
1142. *Ghaidan v Godin-Mendoza* [2004] 2 AC 557, (HL), [9] per Lord Nicholls of Birkenhead, cited in *QT v Director of Immigration* (2018) 21 HKCFAR 324, (CFA), [28].
1143. *Rodriguez v Minister of Housing Gibraltar* [2009] UKPC 52, (PC), [13]–[15], referred to in *QT v Director of Immigration* (2018) 21 HKCFAR 324, (CFA), [33].
1144. As the Court of Final Appeal explained in *Leung Chun Kwong v Secretary for Civil Service* [2019] 22 HKCFAR 127, (CFA), [21]: 'In order to determine whether differential treatment is unlawful, the courts apply the same test used to determine if incursions into constitutionally protected rights are lawful (following *QT v Director of Immigration* (2018) 21 HKCFAR 324, (CFA), [84]–[86]). When applied in the context of an analysis of constitutionality, that test is usually referred to as

626. Where a law does apply differently to persons, such application is valid if there is a rational basis for the differential treatment.[1145] In the absence of a compelling justification for differential treatment, law must be applied in a non-discriminatory manner. In *M v Secretary for Justice* the Court of Appeal in rejecting a claim of disability discrimination observed that sections 6(a) and 8 of the Disability Discrimination Ordinance (Cap. 487) required a comparison of the complainant's treatment with the treatment of a suitable comparator (the comparator question). If less favourable treatment was established, the court should then decide whether the less favourable treatment was 'on the ground' of the complainant's disability (the causation question).[1146]

627. In determining whether there has been discriminatory treatment an objective 'but for' test must applied, so that intention or motive to discriminate is not a necessary condition of liability, although this may be relevant when determining the appropriate remedies:[1147] Requiring male prisoners to have their hair cut short has

---

the "proportionality" test. When applied in the context of determining whether differential treatment is unlawful, that test is usually referred to as the "justification" test.'

1145. A discriminatory measure is justifiable if it is taken in pursuance of a legitimate aim, rationally connected to that aim, and no more than reasonably necessary to accomplish it; *Secretary for Justice v Yau Yuk Lung* (2007) 10 HKCFAR 335, CFA. *See* the recent case of *Kwok Cheuk Kin v Director of Lands* [2020] 1 HKLRD 988, (CFI), [22] where it was observed that the small house policy was discriminatory, but that Art. 40 of the Basic Law recognises the validity of traditional rights of native villagers even if they are discriminatory. It was held that Art. 40 of the Basic Law protects one aspect of the small house policy, the grant to male persons and not female persons a 'free building licence', but not the other two aspects of the small house policy, 'private treaty grant' of land and 'exchange' of land. *Ibid.*, [2]. For a brief account of the small house policy, *see* 'Small House Policy' a research publication of the Legislative Council (2016). https://www.legco.gov.hk/research-publications/english/essentials-1516ise10-small-house-policy.htm.
Chan Yeuk Ming v Housing Authority [2012] HKEC 1239, (CFI), is a case where differential treatment in allocation of public housing (the divorced wife with custody of children favoured against the divorced husband) was considered to be justified.

1146. *M v Secretary for Justice* [2009] 2 HKLRD 298, (CA). Citing the Court of Appeal decision, Thomas Au J said in *Law Chi Yuen v Secretary for Education* [2016] 5 HKLRD 302, (CFI), at [64]: 'It is now established (and indeed is common ground) that to establish direct disability discrimination under s. 6(a) of the Disability discrimination Ordinance (read together with s. 8), the complainant has to show that:

(1) on a relevant comparison between the complainant with a disability and the comparator (that is, a person "without a disability"), he receives less favourable treatment (the comparator question); and
(2) such less favourable treatment is wholly or partially due to the complainant's disability (the causation question).' As was said in *L v Equal Opportunities Commission* [2002] HKEC 1390, (DC), quoting from *Chung v University of Sydney* [2001] FMCA 94: 'To substantiate a complaint of discrimination it is not sufficient for you to show that you have a disability and that you have suffered unfair treatment. It is necessary to show that at least one reason for being treated less favourably than other students is based on your disability.'

1147. *M v Secretary for Justice* [2009] 2 HKLRD 298, (CA), citing *Secretary for Justice v Chan Wah* (2000) 3 HKCFAR 459, (CFA), where the Chief Justice had adopted the 'but for' test enunciated by Lord Goff in *Birmingham City Council v Equal Opportunities Commission* [1989] AC 1155, 1194, (HL). The test is whether the victim of discrimination would have been afforded the same preferential treatment that others enjoyed, if not for the wrongful discrimination. Lord Goff's view

been held not to amount to sex discrimination simply because such a strict restriction was not imposed on female prisoners.[1148] Similarly, it has been held that putting a pre-operative male-to-female transgender person in the male section of a prison, where prisoners are either placed in the men's section or women's section, did not amount to sex or disability discrimination.[1149]

628. Li CJ in *Secretary for Justice v Yau Yuk Lung* reiterated the established criteria to determine when a differentiation can be said to be justified and legitimate:

(a) The difference in treatment must pursue a legitimate aim. For any aim to be legitimate, a genuine need for such difference must be established.
(b) The difference in treatment must be rationally connected to the legitimate aim.
(c) The difference in treatment must be no more than is necessary to accomplish the legitimate aim.[1150]

629. In *So Wai Lun v Hong Kong Special Administrative Region,*[1151] the Court of Final Appeal adopted the test that Justice Bokhary had suggested in *R v Man Wai-Keung (No 2)*: 'Clearly, there is no requirement of literal equality in the sense of unrelentingly identical treatment always. For such rigidity would subvert rather than promote true even-handedness. So that, in certain circumstances, a departure from literal equality would be a legitimate course and, indeed, the only legitimate course. But the starting point is identical treatment. And any departure therefrom must be justified. To justify such a departure it must be shown: one, that sensible and fair-minded people would recognize a genuine need for some difference of treatment; two, that the difference embodied in the particular departure selected to meet that

---

was cited with approval by the Court of Appeal in *Leung Kwok Hung (Long Hair) v Commissioner of Correctional Services* [2018] 2 HKLRD 933, (CA), at [86]. *See Law Chi Yuen v Secretary for Education* [2016] 5 HKLRD 302, (CFI), where a complaint of disability discrimination in education was upheld and *L v Equal Opportunities Commission* [2002] HKEC 1390, (DC), where a complaint of disability discrimination against the Equal Opportunities Commission by one of its employees failed.

1148. *Leung Kwok Hung (Long Hair) v Commissioner of Correctional Services* [2018] 2 HKLRD 933, (CA).

1149. *Navarro Luigi Recasa v Commissioner of Correctional Services* [2018] 4 HKLRD 38, (CFI).

1150. *Secretary for Justice v Yau Yuk Lung* (2007) 10 HKCFAR 335, (CFA), [20]. Also *see* Ma CJ in *Fok Chun Wa v Hospital Authority* (2012) 15 HKCFAR 409, (CFA), at [58]–[59] and *QT v Director of Immigration* (2018) 21 HKCFAR 324, (CFA), [21]–[23]. *See*, for successful litigation against discrimination, *Chan Choi Yin Janice v Toppan Forms (HK) Ltd* [2006] HKEC 2114 (DC) and *Waliyah v Yip Hoi Sun Terence* [2017] 1 HKLRD 1082 (DC), both of which concerned pregnancy discrimination. *See also Equal Opportunities Commission v Director of Education* [2001] 2 HKLRD 690, (CFI), where a point system adopted for transfer of students from primary schools to secondary schools was found to be discriminatory on the basis of sex.

1151. *So Wai Lun v Hong Kong Special Administrative Region* (2006) 9 HKCFAR 530, (CFA) The Court of Final Appeal rejected the argument that s. 124 of the Crimes Ordinance (Cap. 200) was unconstitutional when it made it an offence for a man to have unlawful sexual intercourse with a girl under the age of 16 when it was not an offence for a woman to have unlawful sexual intercourse with a boy under the age of 16, and observed at [28] that while s. 124 departs from identical treatment, such departure 'is justified by reference to genuine need, rationality and proportionality. It does not violate the equality guarantees of the constitution. In so holding we are not deferring to the legislature. Rather are we acknowledging the legislature's proper role.'

need is itself rational; and, three, that such departure is proportionate to such need.'[1152] It has been said that there is no material difference between the above *So Wai Lun* test and the *Man Wai-Keung* test.[1153]

630. In considering whether an alleged discrimination was justified, the courts are prepared to allow a 'margin of appreciation' to the decision-maker, in consideration of his expertise as well as the familiarity with the circumstances of the case relevant to his exercise of discretion. However, the court must determine as a matter of law and applying the proportionality test whether the alleged infringement was lawful. The burden is on the decision-maker to establish that any interference with the right is justifiable and proportionate.[1154]

1152. *R v Man Wai-Keung (No 2)* [1992] 2 HKCLR 207, at 217, appearing sub nominee *R v Man Wai-Keung* [1992] HKEC 304, (CA), [52]. It was held discriminatory and unlawful for s. 83XX(3)(a) of the Criminal Procedure Ordinance (Cap. 221) to a disqualify person who, on appeal, has been ordered to be retried, from benefitting from court's discretionary power to order his costs to be paid out of public funds, while such disqualification did not apply to an appellant who had not been so ordered. Bokhary J said at [1992] 2 HKCLR 207, 217–218; [1992] HKEC 304, [58]–[61]: 'There is no need to take away the power to make such awards whenever a retrial has been ordered. Such powers are discretionary in nature. And where the particular circumstances of the case are such that the absence of finality gives rise to an adequate basis for withholding such an award, the Court would always have a discretion to withhold it for that reason', and ordered that 'all appellants whose appeals against conviction have been allowed, including those who have been ordered to be retried, are entitled to ask this Court to exercise its discretion to order that their costs be paid out of public funds. And the Court will say "yes" if it is just to so order and "no" if it is not.' Section 83XX was subsequently repealed by Ordinance No 39 of 1996. In *Leung Kwok Hung (Long Hair) v Commissioner of Correctional Services* [2018] 2 HKLRD 933, (CA), at [54], the Court of Appeal recognised the importance of respecting social values prevalent in Hong Kong: 'Though the hair length restriction for male inmates appears to be stricter than that for female inmates, one must bear in mind that the standard conventions in our society for hair length for men and women are also different. Thus, in terms of these restrictions being a restraint imposed on inmates by reference to conventional standards in the society, there is no less favourable treatment between male and female inmates.' More relevantly, Lam VP observed as follows at [112]: 'The policy was set by the Commissioner who was entrusted by the legislature to issue such orders as may be necessary for the government of all institutions, *see* r 77(4) of the Prison Rules. The management of prison and maintenance of custodial discipline are matters within the expertise and professional judgment of the Commissioner. The courts are not equipped with the same professional expertise in the assessment of the significance of conformity in reformation and discipline.'
1153. *Secretary for Justice v Yau Yuk Lung* (2007) 10 HKCFAR 335, [2007] 3 HKLRD 903, (CFA), [20].
1154. *Kwok Hay Kwong v Medical Council of Hong Kong* [2008] HKEC 137, (CA), where the court struck down a restriction on medical practitioners' right to publicise basic information through public media about them and their services. *See also Fok Chun Wa v Hospital Authority* [2012] HKEC 471; (2012) 15 HKCFAR 409, (CFA), where it was held the different treatment of local and non-local women (Mainland women married to Hong Kong permanent resident and living in Hong Kong as visitors) in relation to hospital charges was justifiable. *See also Q v Commissioner of Registration* [2019] 1 HKLRD 1244, (CFI), where two female-to-male transgender persons unsuccessfully challenged the decision of the Commissioner not to change their gender from female to male on their Hong Kong identity card, it was held that the Commissioner had a narrow margin of appreciation in determining whether the applicants satisfied the requirements for changing the sex on the ID cards. The Commissioner's refusal on the ground that the applicants had not fully undergone sex reassignment surgery was held to be valid, because the requirements for a

631. Where the ground for differential treatment is suspect, intense scrutiny of the reasons for departing from non-discrimination is in order.[1155] Discrimination on the grounds of sex, race, nationality etc., which relate to an individual's personal characteristics are inherently suspect.[1156] On the other hand, where the legislature accords differential treatment to people in dealing with social problems, such as housing, courts would be reluctant to engage in such intense scrutiny because of traditional judicial deference to the judgment of the legislature.[1157] As was observed by four members of the Human Rights Committee in *Oulajin and Kaiss v Netherlands* (UN Doc CPR/C/46/D/406/1990): 'With regard to the application of Art. 26 of the Covenant in the field of economic and social rights, it is evident that social security legislation, which is intended to achieve aims of social justice, necessarily must make distinctions. It is for the legislature of each country, which best knows the socio-economic needs of the society concerned, to try to achieve social justice in the concrete context. Unless the distinctions made are manifestly discriminatory or arbitrary, it is not for the Committee to re-evaluate the complex socio-economic date and substitute its judgment for that of the legislatures of States parties.'[1158]

---

change in the ID card were for the legitimate aim of adopting a standard which was objective (to maintain consistency and certainty) and was fair to the general public (in addressing their concerns).

1155. For the US origins of the doctrine, *see* Richard H Fallon, 'Strict Scrutiny' (2007) 54 UCLA L Rev 1267.

1156. Where differential treatment based on grounds, such as race, sex or sexual orientation, is in issue, the court will scrutinize with intensity whether the difference in treatment is justified: The reasons must be cogent if such differential treatment is to be justified. *See Ghaidan v Godin-Mendoza* [2004] 2 AC 557, (HL), [19] per Lord Nicholls.

1157. *Ghaidan v Godin-Mendoza* [2004] 2 AC 557, (HL), [18]–[19] per Lord Nicholls of Birkenhead. *See also Raza v Chief Executive in Council* [2005] 3 HKLRD 561, (CFI). In *Yong Yunming v Director of Social Welfare* (2013) 16 HKCFAR 950, (CFA), Ribeiro PJ explained the applicable principles as follows, at [43]: 'As the Chief Justice noted in *Fok Chun Wah v Hospital Authority* (2012) 15 HKCFAR 409, (CFA), [66] " ... it would not usually be within the province of the courts to adjudicate on the merits or demerits of government socio-economic policies". Where the disputed measure involves implementation of the Government's socio-economic policy choices regarding the allocation of limited public funds without impinging upon fundamental rights or involving possible discrimination on inherently suspect grounds, the Court has held that it has a duty to intervene only where the impugned measure is "manifestly without reasonable justification:" *Fok Chun Wah v Hospital Authority* (2012) 15 HKCFAR 409, (CFA), [71] and [76]. That is a test initially applied by the European Court of Human Rights while according a broad margin of appreciation to member States in setting and implementing their socio-economic policies. As the Chief Justice points out, the margin of appreciation principle has previously been adapted to apply in the context of our domestic law. It is appropriate similarly to apply the "manifestly without reasonable foundation" test in our domestic context.'

1158. Cited in *Raza v Chief Executive in Council* [2005] 3 HKLRD 561, (CFI), where Hartmann J upheld a levy imposed on employers of domestic helpers on the ground that sensible and fair-minded people would recognize the genuine need for a difference in treatment between employers of higher-skilled workers (for whom there was a pressing economic need) and those who wished to take advantage of a labour importation scheme to bring in lower-skilled workers, including foreign domestic helpers, when Hong Kong had a surfeit of lower-skilled workers who themselves, unless given new skills, faced an uncertain future. He held that the difference in treatment by not imposing the levy on the former group of employers but imposing it on the latter group was both rational and proportionate.

632. *Secretary for Justice v Yau Yuk Lung* is a case where sexual orientation was regarded as an obvious example of discrimination. The question was whether it was constitutional to criminalize buggery between men when buggery between heterosexuals was not equally criminalized. Chief Justice Li said: 'Homosexuals constitute a minority in the community. The provision has the effect of targeting them and is constitutionally invalid. The courts have the duty of enforcing the constitutional guarantee of equality before the law and of ensuring protection against discriminatory law.'[1159]

633. Similarly, it would be discrimination on the ground of sexual orientation for the Director of Immigration to apply a policy of limiting eligibility for dependant visa to a spouse who is a party to a monogamous marriage between a man and a woman, thus excluding partners of a same-sex marriage. Such policy could not be said to be objectively justifiable as furthering the policy of restricting the number of persons permitted to work in Hong Kong while attracting talented persons to join the Hong Kong workforce 'by giving them the choice of bringing their dependants to live with them'. The restrictive policy was not rationally connected with the legitimate objective of strict immigration control.[1160] However, it would not be unlawful for the Commissioner of Registration to refuse an application by a female-to-male transgender person to change the gender entry stated in the Hong Kong identity card from female to male, provided that the criteria that he applies in considering such an application are legitimate. Balancing private rights and public interest is an important aspect in decision-making which may appear at first sight to be discriminatory.[1161]

634. In *So Wai Lun v Hong Kong Special Administrative Region,* a man had been prosecuted for having unlawful sexual intercourse with a girl below the age of 16. It was argued on his behalf that section 124 of the Crimes Ordinance was discriminatory because it criminalized the conduct of the male to the exclusion of the

---

1159. *Secretary for Justice v Yau Yuk Lung* (2007) 10 HKCFAR 335, (CFA), [29].

1160. *QT v Director of Immigration* [2018] 21 HKCFAR 324, (CFA). The unanimous judgment of the court explained at [101]: 'The usual standard of review in proportionality analyses (applicable to the justification exercise in equality cases) is that of reasonable necessity: the challenged policy or measure (assuming it to be rationally linked to the promotion of a legitimate aim) may be permitted to encroach upon the protected right only to an extent that is no more than reasonably necessary. It is the usual standard since, as pointed out in *Hysan Development Co Ltd v Town Planning Board* (2016) 19 HKCFAR 372, (CFA), at [131] … it reflects the essential purpose of the exercise: the Court's endeavour to accommodate acceptable limitations of constitutional rights in the pursuit of a legitimate societal interest while preserving to the maximum extent the guarantees laid down in the constitution.'

1161. *Q v Commissioner of Registration* [2019] HKEC 338, (CFI), where Thomas Au J said at [25]: 'The approval for the change of gender entry of an ID card therefore does not only concern with the card holder's private right, but also public interests. As a result, in deciding whether to approve a transgender person's application for a change of the gender entry on the ID card, the Commissioner has to engage in a balancing exercise against the said private and public interest. There was held to be no sex discrimination. *See also* footnote 1155, above. As Hartmann J said in *Democratic Party v Secretary for Justice* [2007] 2 HKLRD 804, (CFI), at [59], "respect for an individual's privacy will be narrower when it is brought in context with public life or is in conflict with other protected interests".'

female. The Court of Final Appeal observed that in enacting section 124, the legislature was entitled to take into account and weigh considerations such as the problem of teenage pregnancies; not criminalizing the female's conduct because that might deter her from reporting the matter; the legislature's role in resolving issues engaging society's code of sexual morality; and the extent to which it was for the legislature to form a view on issues such as whether the initiative in these matters was generally taken by the male, who was often older than the female.[1162] There has been some successful litigation challenging acts of harassment or discrimination (with award of damages assessed in a way akin to that under the traditional personal injuries litigation).[1163] For instance, in *Yuen Sha Sha v Tse Chi Pan*[1164] video-recording of a girl changing clothes was held to be sexual harassment. In *Ma Bik Yung v Ko Chuen*[1165] a taxi driver's refusal to help a passenger to put her wheelchair inside the taxi was considered to amount to disability discrimination and harassment. In *Ma Bik Yung v Ko Cheun* Li CJ examined the various remedies that are available to a victim of discrimination and said: 'the purpose of the legislation is to seek to eliminate discrimination and the prejudicial attitudes that may exist in society. It is important for the court to bear in mind that the remedies granted should ensure respect for the legislation and its purpose. In fashioning remedies, the court should be prepared, where necessary, to be innovative. At the same time, the court should be flexible and pragmatic in its approach to remedies.'[1166]

635. Hong Kong has passed four statutes to prohibit discrimination. While the human rights provisions in the Basic Law and the Bill of Rights seek to prevent discrimination by the government and public bodies, these ordinances are directed at private individuals, groups and organizations. These ordinances bind the government too. They are: Sex Discrimination Ordinance (Cap. 480), Race Discrimination Ordinance (Cap. 602), Disability Discrimination Ordinance (Cap. 487) and Family

---

1162. *So Wai Lun v Hong Kong Special Administrative Region* (2006) 9 HKCFAR 530, (CFA), [27]–[29]. The court cited *R v Man Wai-Keung (No 2)* [1992] 2 HKCLR 207, (CA), 217, where Bokhary J said: 'Clearly, there is no requirement of literal equality in the sense of unrelentingly identical treatment always. For such rigidity would subvert rather than promote true even-handedness. So that, in certain circumstances, a departure from literal equality would be a legitimate course and, indeed, the only legitimate course. But the starting point is identical treatment. And any departure therefrom must be justified. To justify such a departure it must be shown: one, that sensible and fair-minded people would recognise a genuine need for some difference of treatment; two, that the difference embodied in the particular departure selected to meet that need is itself rational; and, three, that such departure is proportionate to such need.'

1163. *See* generally Carole J. Petersen, 'Implementing Equality: An Analysis of Two Recent Decisions under Hong Kong's Anti-discrimination Laws' (1999) 29 *Hong Kong Law Journal* 178. *See Li Pui Ha v Wong So Kee Transportation Ltd* [2014] 4 HKLRD 254, (DC), a case of termination of employment for a physical disability and pregnancy, and *Yuen Wai Han v South Elderly Affairs Ltd* [2005] 2 HKLRD 277, (CA), a case of termination of employment on grounds of employee's pregnancy are illustrative of how damages are calculated for discriminatory treatment.

1164. *Yuen Sha Sha v Tse Chi Pan* [1999] 2 HKLRD 28, (DC).

1165. *Ma Bik Yung v Ko Chuen* (2006) 9 HKCFAR 888, (CFA). The decision of the District Judge upholding the complaint of disability discrimination and harassment is reported in [1999] 2 HKLRD 263 (DC).

1166. *Ma Bik Yung v Ko Chuen* (2006) 9 HKCFAR 888, (CFA), [32].

Status Ordinance (Cap. 527). Sex Discrimination Ordinance prohibits sex discrimination against women, men, married persons and pregnant women, and discrimination by way of victimization. The Ordinance addresses sexual harassment in employment, education and other fields, and identifies some likely discriminators, such as employers, trade unions and clubs. The Ordinance identifies other unlawful acts such as discriminatory practices, discriminatory advertisements, instructing or pressuring someone to act in a discriminatory way, and aiding unlawful acts.

636. Protection from discrimination is achieved not only by prohibiting discriminatory acts and practices. Sometimes the law must positively assist disadvantaged persons to reverse effects of discriminatory that they have been subjected to. Affirmative action as developed in US constitutional jurisdiction is the most effective means of positively eliminating effects of discrimination,[1167] which does not appear to have been put into practice in Hong Kong in any meaningful way. There are, however, some provisions in Hong Kong legislation on discrimination which promote the welfare of persons who face discrimination. Section 48 the Sex Discrimination Ordinance, 'Special Measures', provides that it is not unlawful to take measures to ensure that persons of a particular sex or marital status or who are pregnant have equal opportunities with other persons in circumstances in relation to which a provision is made by this Ordinance, or afford to such persons grants, benefits or programmes, whether direct or indirect, to meet their special needs in relation to employment, education, clubs or sport, or, the provision of premises, goods, services or facilities. Similar provision may be found in Disability Discrimination Ordinance (section 50), Race Discrimination Ordinance (section 49), and Family Status Ordinance (section 36).

II. The Right to Not Be Subjected to Torture, Cruel, Inhuman, or Degrading Treatment or Punishment

637. Article 3 of the Bill of Rights provides that 'no one shall be subjected to torture or to cruel, inhuman or degrading treatment or punishment. In particular, no one shall be subjected without his free consent to medical or scientific experimentation'. This right is not subject to any restrictions.[1168] This protection finds expression in Article 28 of the Basic Law too: 'No Hong Kong resident shall be subjected

1167. *See*, for instance, Terry H. Anderson, *The Pursuit of Fairness: History of Affirmative Action* (OUP: 2004) and John David Skrentny, *The Ironies of Affirmative Action: Politics, Culture, and Justice in America* (Chicago: University of Chicago Press, 1996).

1168. The Court of Final Appeal in *Ubamaka v Secretary for Security* (2012) 15 HKCFAR 743, (CFA), [9]–[11] observed that it was also clear from the highly persuasive jurisprudence of the European Court of Human Rights in Strasbourg and the House of Lords in relation to the closely analogous provisions of the European Convention on Human Rights that Art. 3 rights [torture and cruel, inhuman or degrading treatment or punishment] were absolute and non-derogable. The Court held that while the rights enumerated in the Bill of Rights are subject to the immigration reservation in s. 11 of the Bill rights, that section does not make any inroads into the non-derogable rights of persons who have no right to enter and remain in Hong Kong. Section 11 of the Hong Kong Bill of Rights provides as follows: 'As regards persons not having the right to enter and remain in

to arbitrary or unlawful arrest, detention or imprisonment. Arbitrary or unlawful search of the body of any resident or deprivation or restriction of the freedom of the person shall be prohibited. Torture of any resident or arbitrary or unlawful deprivation of the life of any resident shall be prohibited.' To enforce this right, the Legislative Council enacted the Crimes (Torture) Ordinance[1169] and the Fugitive Offenders (Torture) Order[1170] shortly before the handover.[1171]

638. The prohibition of torture, inhuman or degrading treatment, enshrined in Article 3 of the Bill of Rights and Article 28 of the Basic Law, was unsuccessfully pleaded in *Lai Hung Wai v Superintendent of Stanley Prison.*[1172] There a detainee for murder, aged 18, argued that indefinite detention at executive discretion contravened the protection against inhuman or degrading treatment. This argument was rejected for the reason that the term of detention was under regular review by an independent Review Board. Hartmann J said at paragraph 30:

> The indeterminate sentences of detention at Executive discretion imposed in Hong Kong on young offenders is monitored ... by a statutory system that looks to three fundamentals: first, service of a period of time to expiate the punitive elements of the offence; second, the rehabilitation of the offender and, third, the question of on-going risk to society. Those three fundamentals, it seems to me, are recognized internationally not only as being lawful but also in full compliance with evolving norms of what lies within the boundaries of just, rational and humane punishment.

639. The Court of Final Appeal in *Secretary for Security v Saktheval Prabakar* established an exacting standard of compliance with this constitutional right. In relation to a decision to deport an asylum seeker who complained of the danger of torture if returned, the Court observed that: 'The high standards of fairness should be approached as follows: (a) the potential deportee, who had the burden of establishing his torture claim, should be given every reasonable opportunity to establish that claim; (b) the claim must be properly assessed by the Secretary; and (c) where the claim was rejected, reasons should be given by the Secretary, which must be sufficient to enable the potential deportee to consider the possibilities of administrative and judicial review.'[1173]

Hong Kong, this Ordinance does not affect any immigration legislation governing entry into, stay in and departure from Hong Kong, or the application of any such legislation.'

1169. Cap. 427, Laws of Hong Kong.

1170. Cap. 5031, *ibid.*

1171. Hong Kong Special Administrative Region Government, *Report on the Hong Kong Special Administrative Region under the Convention Against Torture and Other Cruel, Inhuman or Degrading Treatment or Punishment* (Hong Kong: Printing Department, the Hong Kong Special Administrative Region Government, 1998), 2 and 15–22.

1172. *Lai Hung Wai v Superintendent of Stanley Prison* [2003] HKEC 1024, (CFI).

1173. *Secretary for Security v Saktheval Prabakar* (2004) 7 HKCFAR 187, (CFA), [44]. In *Re Hidayah* [2018] HKEC 2705, (CA), the Court of Appeal allowed an appeal against refusal to apply for review of the decision of the torture Claims Appeal Board, for the reason that the Board had failed

640. The Court of Final Appeal's high standard of compliance in *Secretary for Security v Saktheval Prabakar* was followed by the Court of Appeal in *ST v Betty Kwan*, where the Director of Immigration had denied a claim for asylum. The applicant's petition to the Chief Executive against that decision was rejected by an adjudicator without hearing the applicant. Directing the petition to be dealt with afresh, the Court of Appeal said: 'First and foremost, the ultimate question is one of fairness. Secondly, … the requirements of procedural fairness are flexible and closely conditioned by the legal and administrative context. … where life and limb are in jeopardy and [the torture] claimants' fundamental human right not to be subject to torture is involved, high standards of fairness must be observed by the decision-maker when making the relevant administrative decision. … Thirdly, an opportunity to make "worthwhile representations" or "effective representations" is an important requirement of fairness in most if not all situations. … Fourthly, it does not follow from the requirement of an opportunity to make worthwhile or effective representations that there must be an oral hearing held before a decision is made.'[1174] In *C v Director of Immigration and UNHCR*, the Court of Final Appeal applied the *Saktheval Prabakar principle* and emphasized that the Director of Immigration's decision to order the removal of a failed asylum seeker must be subjected 'to rigorous examination and anxious scrutiny to ensure that the required high standards of fairness had been met'.[1175]

641. The 'inhuman or degrading treatment or punishment' limb of Article 3 came up for interpretation before the Court of Final Appeal in *Lau Cheong v HKSAR*,[1176] where the appellants questioned the constitutionality of the imposition of mandatory sentence of life imprisonment for murder. The appellants had been convicted of murder causing the death of a person with the intention of causing grievous bodily harm. They unsuccessfully argued that:

(a) The rule that a person may be found guilty of murder where he had not the intention of causing death of the victim but the intention to causing grievous bodily harm to the victim is arbitrary. Courts must adopt a stricter standard and require that nothing less than an intention to kill or endanger life would be the requisite mens rea for murder. Rejecting this argument, the Court pointed out that 'as the law stands, [the defendant] may be convicted of murder without ever intending or foreseeing death as the consequence of his acts or omissions. It is sufficient if he intends to cause grievous bodily harm and death in fact

---

to give, or had given, insufficient reasons for its decision. For a similar decision, *see Nnaji Charles Anayo v Torture Claims Appeal Board* [2018] HKEC 3963, (CFI).

1174. *ST v Betty Kwan* [2014] 4 HKLRD 277, (CA), [22]–[26].

1175. *C v Director of Immigration and UNHCR* (2013) 16 HKCFAR 280, (CFA), [86]. Rejecting a constitutional challenge, the Court of Final Appeal held in *GA v Director of Immigration* (2014) 17 HKCFAR 60, (CFA), that it was a question of fact in each case whether the refusal of the Director to permit a mandated refugee or a screened-in torture claimant to work amounted to inhuman or degrading treatment. The imposition of a sentence that fits the offence is not inhuman or degrading treatment: *HKSAR v Hussain Shakil* [2012] HKEC 940, (CA).

1176. *Lau Cheong v HKSAR* (2002) 5 HKCFAR 415, (CFA), followed in *Tong Yu Lam v Long-Term Prison Sentences Review Board* [2008] HKEC 24, (CA), and in *HKSAR v Godson Ugochukwu Okuro* [2019] 2 HKLRD 451, (CA).

results'.[1177] This rule is founded on valid legal policy: 'A person may not subjectively intend or even foresee that he will cause death. He may desire to limit the consequences of his actions to the infliction of grievous bodily injury. However, as a matter of commonsense it is impossible to predict that the consequences of an intentional infliction of really serious bodily harm will necessarily be successfully limited and will not prove to be life-threatening.'[1178]

(b) Mandatory death sentence was arbitrary, in violation of the protection given in Article 28 of the Basic Law: 'No Hong Kong resident shall be subjected to arbitrary or unlawful arrest, detention or imprisonment.' Rejecting this argument, the Court observed as follows: 'Taking into account the inherent and unique gravity of the offence and the sentencing objectives of a mandatory life sentence as a whole, we are unable to accept that mandatory life imprisonment represents a manifestly disproportionate sentence so as to contravene Art. 28 on the grounds of arbitrariness. The legislative judgment that the offence of murder, having regard to its gravity, calls for a sentence of mandatory life imprisonment, even allowing for the different circumstances in which it may be committed, is tenable and rational. As such it is a legislative judgment which this Court should respect.'[1179] Although mandatory death sentence involves an indeterminate term of imprisonment, there is an administrative mechanism whereby individual circumstances of a convicted person are taken into account in releasing him after serving a period of time in prison. 'In accepting the legislative judgment, we give particular weight to the legislature's insistence on a statute-based regime for review by an independent board of all life sentences, with power to recommend conversion of such sentences to fixed terms and to direct conditional releases in appropriate cases.'[1180]

(c) Mandatory death sentence violated the guarantee in Article 3 of the Bill of Rights. This argument too was rejected. The Court observed that only punishments which were grossly disproportionate fell within Article 3 of the Bill of Rights. The threshold for establishing such disproportionality was either the same or higher than the threshold for arbitrariness (manifestly disproportionate).[1181] 'In assessing whether a sentence is grossly disproportionate one looks first at the circumstances of the offence and of the particular offender but that this: … does not mean that the judge or the legislator can no longer consider general deterrence or other penological purposes that go beyond the particular offender in determining a sentence, but only that the resulting sentence must not be grossly disproportionate to what the offender deserves.'[1182]

1177. *Lau Cheong v HKSAR* (2002) 5 HKCFAR 415, (CFA), [14].

1178. *Ibid.*, [49].

1179. *Ibid.*, [123].

1180. *Ibid.*, [125]. The Review Board was set up under the Long-Term Prison Sentence Review Ordinance (Cap. 524). On the functions of the Review Board, *see Tong Yu Lam v The Long-Term Prison Sentences Review Board* [2008] HKEC 2420, (CA) and *Nancy Ann Kissel v Long Term Prison Sentences Review Board* [2020] HKEC 1454, (CA).

1181. *Ibid.*, [130].

1182. *Ibid.*, [131], citing *R v Smith (Edward Dewey)* (1987) 34 SCC (3d) (Supreme Court of Canada) 97, 137, per Lamer J.

III. The Right to Liberty and Security of the Person

642. The well-established common law right to liberty and security of the person is now enshrined in the Bill of Rights and the Basic Law, which protect people against unlawful or arbitrary deprivation of liberty.[1183] Article 5(1) of the Bill of Rights provides as follows: 'Everyone has the right to liberty and security of person. No one shall be subjected to arbitrary arrest or detention. No one shall be deprived of his liberty except on such grounds and in accordance with such procedure as are established by law.' To a similar effect is Article 28 of the Basic Law: 'No Hong Kong resident shall be subjected to arbitrary or unlawful arrest, detention or imprisonment. Arbitrary or unlawful search of the body of any resident or deprivation or restriction of the freedom of the person shall be prohibited.' The effect of these two provisions is not to impose an absolute prohibition on arrest, detention or otherwise deprive a person of his liberty: What they make unlawful is any deprivation of liberty which is not authorised by substantive and procedural law.[1184] A deprivation is lawful provided that: (i) the grounds for deprivation of liberty and the procedure of effecting such deprivation is 'established by law'; and (ii) such legal procedures must meet the minimal requirements of fairness implied in the ICCPR.[1185] As regards the procedure, Article 5(2) protects the right of a person who is arrested to be informed of the reasons for arrest and to be informed of any charges against him; Article 5(3) protects the right of a person arrested or detained on a criminal charge to be brought before a judge and be tried within a reasonable time or be released; Article 5(4) enables a person who has been arrested or detained to challenge the lawfulness of his detention and be released if the deprivation of liberty is not lawful. Where a person has been arrested without giving him reasons, such arrest may become lawful if reasons are given later.[1186]

1183. Article 5(1) of the Bill of Rights and Art. 28 of the Basic Law.

1184. 'Whether an arrest or detention is arbitrary turns on the nature and extent of any departure from the substantive and procedural standards involved. An arrest or detention is arbitrary if it is capricious, unreasoned, without reasonable cause: if it is made without reference to an adequate determining principle or without following proper procedures': *Neilsen v A-G* [2001] 3 NZLR 143, (CA), [34]. In *Lau Cheong v HKSAR* (2002) 5 HKCFAR 415, (CFA), [47]–[48] this was considered by the Court of Final Appeal to be 'a useful formulation'.

1185. In *HKSAR v Coady* [2000] 2 HKLRD 195, (CA), 205, Keith JA said: 'the expression "in accordance with such procedure as are established by law" in Art. 5(1) [of the Bill of Rights] means such legal procedures as meet the minimal requirements of fairness impliedly agreed to by the signatories to the International Covenant on Civil and Political Rights.' *See Wong Tze Yam v Commissioner of Police (No 2)* [2011] 3 HKLRD 369, (CA), where the court having observed that a night time anti-crime operation by the police restricted the plaintiff's freedom of person, proceeded to consider whether the restriction imposed on him was a violation of the Basic Law. *See also A (Torture Claimant) v Director of Immigration* [2008] 4 HKLRD 752, (CA), where the Court of Appeal held that the power of detention under s. 32 of the Immigration Ordinance did not comply with Art. 5(1) of the Bill of Rights and therefore unconstitutional because s. 32 was silent on the circumstances under which the power to detain pending removal could be exercised.

1186. *See,* e.g., *Leung Kwok Hung v Secretary for Justice* [2010] 5 HKLRD 170, (CA), where the detainee had been given reasons six hours later. Lam J said at [6]: 'Arrest is a continuing act. It starts from the moment when the person concerned is taken into custody and continues up to the moment when he is released. In this process, even if at the moment when the plaintiff was taken into custody he was not aware of the charge against him, but if at a later time he was informed of

643. Under the common law, a person may be arrested or detained where he has committed a breach of the peace[1187] or where the arrestor reasonably believes that a breach of peace is imminent.[1188] The Court of Final Appeal has interpreted the words of section 50 of the Police Force Ordinance (Cap. 232) that a police officer may arrest a person 'who he reasonably believes will be charged' to mean 'who he reasonably believes will be charged on the basis of a reasonable suspicion that the arrested person is guilty of an offence to be charged'.[1189]

644. A person may be deprived of his liberty by the police, for instances: (a) when proof of his identity is checked; (b) when stopped, searched and detained; and (c) when arrested by the police. The Immigration Ordinance[1190] provides that a person must produce his identity card for inspection when requested by a police officer or other authorized person. Failure to do so, without reasonable excuse, is an offence.[1191]

645. Under the Police Force Ordinance, a person can only be stopped, searched and detained where he acts suspiciously or where he is reasonably suspected to have committed an offence, or being about to commit an offence, or intending to commit an offence.[1192]

---

the reasons for his arrest and had the opportunity to make an explanation, then from that moment onwards the arrest was lawful, *see*: *Lewis v Chief Constable of the South Wales Constabulary* [1991] 1 All ER 206, (CA).'

1187. *Albert v Lavin* [1982] AC 546, (HL).

1188. *R v Howell* [1982] QB 416, (CA), 426.

1189. *Yeung May Wan v HKSAR* (2005) 8 HKCFAR 137, (CFA), [66].

1190. Cap. 115 of the Laws of Hong Kong s. 17(c). The argument that the power of the police under this section breached the Bill of Rights was rejected in *Lo Hon-hin v R* [1993] HKEC 467, (CFI). For recent convictions for the offence, *see HKSAR v Yung Wai Leong* [2018] HKEC 1359, (DC) and *HKSAR v Chow Hei Choy* [2018] HKEC 1281, (DC).

1191. In *R v Fung Chi-Wood* [1991] 1 HKLR 654, (HC), where a Hong Kong resident was convicted of this offence, the High Court rejected the argument that s. 17(c) of the Immigration Ordinance was enacted to stem the influx of illegal immigrants and therefore should not be used except for the purposes of immigration control.

1192. Police Force Ordinance s. 54. *See HKSAR v Lam Chiu Yin* [2018] HKEC 847, (DC), where the District Court held to be valid an arrest by a police officer of a person under s. 54(2) which provides that if a police officer finds any person in any street whom he reasonably suspects of having committed or of being about to commit or of intending to commit any offence, it shall be lawful for the police officer:

(a) to stop the person for the purpose of demanding that he produces proof of his identity for inspection by the police officer;
(b) to detain the person for a reasonable period while the police officer enquires whether or not the person is suspected of having committed any offence at any time;
(c) to search the person for anything that is likely to be of value to the investigation of any offence that the person has committed, or is reasonably suspected of having committed or of being about to commit or of intending to commit; and

(d)to detain the person during such period as is reasonably required for the purpose of such a search.

646. Under the Police Force Ordinance, a person can only be arrested with a warrant,[1193] (there are procedural requirements for arresting a person with a warrant),[1194] or without a warrant (where the person to be arrested is reasonably believed to be charged with or reasonably suspected to be guilty of an offence for which the sentence is fixed by law or for which a person may be imprisoned on a first conviction or where service of summons is impracticable).[1195] An arrest does not become unlawful merely because it subsequently transpires that the offence was not in fact committed or not committed by the suspect arrested. If a police officer reasonably believed that an offence had been committed and, in pursuit of that reasonable belief, effected an arrest, the arrest is lawful no matter that it subsequently turns out that the offence was not committed, or was not committed by the arrested person.[1196] In practice, it is a question of fact whether a person is lawfully deprived of his liberty in accordance with the above statutory provisions.[1197] Under the current law, the police are allowed to use 'all means necessary to effect the arrest',[1198] meaning that they may only use reasonable force in making an arrest.[1199]

647. Under the Bill of Rights Ordinance, 'anyone arrested or detained on a criminal charge shall be brought promptly before a judge … and shall be entitled to trial within a reasonable time or to release. It shall not be the general rule that

1193. The Magistrates Ordinance (Cap. 227) provides that whenever an information or complaint in writing is laid before a magistrate alleging the commission of an indictable offence and the accused is not in custody, a magistrate may issue a warrant for the apprehension of the accused. The warrant must, among other things, order the accused to be brought before a magistrate to answer to the complaint or information, and to be further dealt with according to law.

1194. *See,* e.g., ss 73–74 of the Magistrates Ordinance (Cap. 227) of the Laws of the Hong Kong.

1195. Section 50 of the Police Force Ordinance. *See Yeung May Wan v HKSAR* (2005) 8 HKCFAR 137, (CFA). Powers of arrest may be granted by other legislations too. *See Attorney General v Ho Shek-Kwan* [1980] HKLR 64, (CA), where the court upheld the validity of an arrest without warrant under s. 10(1) of the Independent Commission Against Corruption Ordinance (Cap. 204) if the arresting officer reasonably suspects that the person to be arrested is guilty of an offence under that Ordinance, the Prevention of Bribery Ordinance (Cap. 201) or the Elections (Corrupt and Illegal Conduct) Ordinance (Cap. 554).

1196. *See HKSAR v Yeung May Wan* [2004] 3 HKLRD 797, (CA), [130]–[131]. On appeal the Court of Final Appeal did not agree with the Court of Appeal that the requirement of reasonable suspicion was satisfied: (2005) 8 HKCFAR 137, (CFA).

1197. In *Yeung May Wan v HKSAR* (2005) 8 HKCFAR 137, (CFA), it was said that the standard set by s. 50 of the Police Force Ordinance is one requiring the arresting officer to have formed, at the time of arrest, a genuine suspicion of guilt held on grounds which are objectively reasonable. What is needed to meet that standard in any particular case is a question of fact and degree. *See,* e.g., *Attorney General v Kong Chung-shing* [1980] HKLR 533, (CA), where the Court of Appeal expressed the view that the police could have been executing their duties lawfully in arresting a person if he was reasonably suspected of having committed an offence – even though the criteria for searching him were not satisfied. A similar view was expressed in *Lee Yim-ping v R* [1979] HKLR 454, (HC), despite the colourable entry of her home by the police.

1198. Section 50(2) of the Police Force Ordinance.

1199. Section 101A of the Criminal Procedure Ordinance (Cap. 221) of the Laws of Hong Kong. In *HKSAR v Osunwoke Ifeanyi John* [2018] HKEC 786, (CFI), [39] the court referred to the commentary of *R v Kelbie* [1996] Crim LR 802 at 804 entitled 'Use of Force': 'Whatever the purpose of the use of force, it cannot be lawful if the force used is greater than is reasonable in the circumstances to achieve the purpose. It can never be lawful to use unreasonable force.'

persons awaiting trial shall be detained in custody.'[1200] Furthermore, a defendant in a criminal trial can apply for bail in accordance with the existing statutory criteria.[1201]

IV. The Right to Be Presumed Innocent

648. The Bill of Rights contains a number of important safeguards for defendants facing criminal trial,[1202] the most prominent among them being the right to be presumed innocent until the contrary is proved,[1203] which is also recognized by the Basic Law.[1204] The common law principle of presumption of innocence is based on the premise that a person may not be held liable for the commission of an offence unless the prosecution proves beyond doubt that the defendant committed the prohibited act (*actus reus*) accompanied by a guilty mind, such as intention, recklessness or knowledge (*mens rea*).[1205]

649. It is not uncommon for the legislature to create statutory offences where the prosecution is required to establish only the *actus reus*.[1206] The statute may permit the defendant to set up a statutory defence such as that he has a licence to do the act which is otherwise unlawful or the common law defence of honest and reasonable

1200. Article 5(3). The strictness of the requirement that the detained person must be brought before a judge was explained by the Human Rights Committee in *Rostislav Borinsenko v Hungary* (Comm No 852/1999, 14 October 2002). *See R v William Hung* [1992] 2 HKCLR 90, (HC).

1201. *See* further A. Byrnes, 'The Bill of Rights and Remand in Custody Pending Trial: A Warning Shot?' (1991) 21 *Hong Kong Law Journal* 362 and J. Chan, 'Undue Delay in Criminal Trials and the Bill of Rights' (1992) 22 *Hong Kong Law Journal* 2. For Bill of Rights cases in this regard, *see,* e.g., *R v Lau Kwok Hung* [1992] 2 HKCLR 241, (HC). It is only in exceptional cases that bail pending the leave application hearing (as opposed to the hearing of the appeal) would be granted. Bail would not be granted unless there is at least some reasonable prospect of the applicant obtaining leave to appeal to the Court of Final Appeal and there is no real risk of the applicant absconding. Where those conditions are satisfied, an important consideration is whether a refusal of bail is likely to render the application nugatory by the passage of time: *Secretary for Justice v Wong Ho Ming* (2017) 20 HKCFAR 518, (CFA).

1202. Article 11.

1203. Article 11(1).

1204. Generally on the presumption of innocence, *see* 'Presumption of Innocence' in Simon Young, 'Human Rights', Chapter 19 of *Archbold: Hong Kong* (Sweet & Maxwell 2018).

1205. A distinction must be drawn between finding a person guilty of an offence, without establishing a guilty mind, and increasing the sentence for a proved offence taking the gravity of the factual situation. For instance, in *HKSAR v Minney* (2013) 16 HKCFAR 26, (CFA), it was held that where the trial judge is satisfied that the guilt of the defendant has been established, the judge could take into account various factors in passing sentence. In the present case which involved the offence of possession of dangerous drugs, the judge was correct to have considered the risk that the dangerous drugs could fall into the hands of others (so-called latent risk) in increasing the starting point of imprisonment. This did not mean that the court attributed to the defendant an intention to traffic in the drugs (a more serious offence of which he was not charged), but simply reflected the fact that the quantity and circumstances of their possession was such as to pose a risk to society.

1206. In *Kulemesin v HKSAR* (2013) 16 HKCFAR 195, (CFA), Ribeiro PJ explained the five ways statutory offences may deal with the *mens rea,* reformulating the five possible alternative mental elements he had previously identified in *Hin Lin Yee v HKSAR* (2010) 13 HKCFAR 142, (CFA), [96]. Ribeiro PJ said in *Kulemesin* case, at [82]:

belief that he was doing something permitted by law. If such a defence is available, the offence is referred to as a strict liability offence.

650. If the statue does not permit the defendant to set up any defence at all, such offence is referred to as an absolute offence.[1207] '(1) there is a presumption of law that *mens rea* is required before a person can be held guilty of a criminal offence; (2) the presumption is particularly strong where the offence is "truly criminal" in character; (3) the presumption applies to statutory offences, and can be displaced only if this is clearly or by necessary implication the effect of the statute; (4) the only situation in which the presumption can be displaced is where the statute is concerned with an issue of social concern, and public safety is such an issue; (5) even where a statute is concerned with such an issue, the presumption of *mens rea* stands unless it can also be shown that the creation of strict liability will be effective to promote the objects of the statute by encouraging greater vigilance to prevent the commission of the prohibited act.'[1208]

651. The presumption of innocence under Article 87 of the Basic Law and Article 11(1) of the Hong Kong Bill of Rights is expressed in absolute terms, but the right to be presumed innocent is not absolute. It is capable of derogation, but no

---

the five *Hin Lin Yee* alternatives need reformulation to address the possible alternative mental requirements relating to the consequences, and not just the circumstances, of the defendant's conduct. So modified, the five possible alternatives may be stated as follows (with references to the element of consequences here italicised):

(a) First, that the mens rea presumption persists and the prosecution must prove knowledge, intention or recklessness as to every element of the offence (the First Alternative);
(b) Second, that the prosecution need not set out to prove mens rea, but if there is evidence capable of raising a reasonable doubt that the defendant may have acted or omitted to act in the honest and reasonable belief that the circumstances *or likely consequences* of his conduct were such that, if true, liability would not attach, he must be acquitted unless the prosecution proves beyond reasonable doubt the absence of such exculpatory belief or that there were no reasonable grounds for such belief (the Second Alternative);
(c) Third, that the presumption has been displaced so that the prosecution need not prove mens rea but that the accused has a good defence if he can prove on the balance of probabilities that he acted or omitted to act in the honest and reasonable belief that the circumstances *or likely consequences* of his conduct were such that, if true, he would not be guilty of the offence (the Third Alternative);
(d) Fourth, that the presumption has been displaced and that the accused is confined to relying on the statutory defences expressly provided for, the existence of such defences being inconsistent with the second and third alternatives mentioned above (the Fourth Alternative); and
(e) Fifth, that the presumption is displaced and the offence is one of absolute liability so that the prosecution succeeds if the prohibited act or omission is proved against the accused, regardless of his state of mind regarding the relevant elements of the offence in question (the Fifth Alternative).'

1207. For the difference between strict liability and absolute liability, *see also HKSAR v Choi Wai Lun* (2018) 21 HKCFAR 167, (CFA), [39]–[42] and *Archbold Hong Kong*, (Sweet and Maxwell, Hong Kong: 2018), [18–28]–[18–29].

1208. *Gammon (Hong Kong) Ltd v Attorney General of Hong Kong* [1985] AC 1, (PC), 14.

derogation is valid unless it is justified. An encroachment on these rights by way of a presumption against the defendant or reverse onus of proof may be justified only if it has a rational connection with the pursuit of a legitimate aim and it is no more than necessary for the achievement of that legitimate aim. In the case of a reverse onus, the justification must be compelling.[1209] As Ribeiro PJ explained recently: 'A reverse onus derogates from the constitutional right to be presumed innocent. For such a derogation to be justified, it must pass the rationality and proportionality tests: the Court must be satisfied that the reverse onus has a rational connection with the pursuit of a legitimate aim and that it is no more than necessary for the achievement of that aim. If those tests are met, the Court must be satisfied overall that adoption of a reverse onus strikes a reasonable balance between the societal benefits promoted and the inroads made into the constitutionally protected presumption of innocence and that it does not place an unacceptably harsh burden on the individual.'[1210]

652. It being the duty of the prosecution to prove all the elements of an offence against the defendant, legislation may not require the defendant to prove any element of the offence. A statute may require the defendant to prove a defence, but if it is an indirect attempt to impose a burden on the defendant to prove an element of the offence, there is a reversal of the burden of proof. The issue then will be whether such arrangements are rational in light of the compelling social demand for their existence.[1211] This is indeed the approach of the Privy Council in determining two appeals together, the first from the Court of Appeal *Attorney General v Lee Kwong-kut*[1212] and the second from the High Court *Attorney General v Lo Chak-man.*[1213]

1209. *HKSAR v Lam Kwong Wai* (2006) 9 HKCFAR 574, (CFA), [21], per Anthony Mason NPJ and *HKSAR v Hung Chan Wa* (2006) 9 HKCFAR 614, (CFA). In *Secretary for Justice v Richard Ethan Latker* [2009] HKEC 132, (CA), the Court of Appeal held that the legislative requirement for an owner of a motor vehicle to disclose the identity of the driver of the vehicle, in certain circumstances such as when the driver of the vehicle is suspected of having committed an offence under the Road Traffic Ordinance (Cap. 374), was a valid derogation from the constitutional right to silence (an important aspect of presumption of innocence).

1210. *HKSAR v Choi Wai Lun* (2018) 21 HKCFAR 167, (CFA), [68] (footnotes in the quotation omitted).

1211. As the Court of Final Appeal succinctly stated in *HKSAR v Lam Kwong Wai* (2006) 9 HKCFAR 574, (CFA), [29]: 'Our first task is to ascertain the meaning of [the relevant section creating a reverse onus] according to accepted common law principles of interpretation as supplemented by any relevant statutory provisions. Our second task is to consider whether that interpretation derogates from the presumption of innocence and the right to a fair trial as protected by the Basic Law and the Bill of Rights Ordinance. If that question is answered "Yes", we have to consider whether the derogation can be justified and, if not, whether it could result in contravention of the Basic Law or the Bill of Rights Ordinance and consequential invalidity. If invalidity could result, then it will be necessary to decide whether the validity of the section or part of it can be saved by the application of any rule of construction, severance of the offending part, reading down, reading in or any other remedial technique available to the Court.'

1212. [1992] 2 HKCLR 76, (CA).

1213. [1980] HKLR 687, (HC). In *A-G of Hong Kong v Lee Kwong-Kut* [1993] AC 951, (PC); [1993] 2 HKCLR 186, (PC), the Privy Council held that exceptions from strict application of the fundamental rule that throughout a trial the burden was on the prosecution to prove the guilt of the defendant beyond reasonable doubt where permissible provided that the responsibility for showing the guilt of the defendant remained primarily that of the prosecution; and that a provision

653. In *A-G of Hong Kong v Lee Kwong-kut,*[1214] the disputed provision was (the now repealed) section 30 of the Summary Offences Ordinance,[1215] which provided that 'any person who is brought before a magistrate charged with having in his possession or conveying in any manner anything which may be reasonably suspected of having been stolen or unlawfully obtained and who does not give an account, to the satisfaction of the magistrate, how he came by the same, shall be liable to a fine of HKD 1,000 or to imprisonment for 3 months'. In *Lo Chak-man*, the provision in question was section 25 of the Drug Trafficking (Recovery of Proceeds) Ordinance.[1216] which provided as follows: 'person who enters into or otherwise concerned in an arrangement whereby ... the retention or control by or on behalf of another ... of the relevant person's proceeds of drug trafficking is facilitated ... knowing or having reasonable grounds to believe that the relevant person is a person who carries on or has carried on drug trafficking or has benefited from drug trafficking, commits an offence'. It was a defence to prove for instance 'that he did not know or suspect that the arrangement related to any person's proceeds of drug trafficking'.

654. The Privy Council struck down section 30 of the Summary Offences Ordinance holding that the accused was, in effect, asked to disprove the *mens rea* of the crime and this was irrational.[1217] It upheld section 25 of the Drug Trafficking (Recovery of Proceeds) Ordinance for the reason that there was no real shifting of the burden of proof to the accused. The Privy Council held that the essential ingredients of the offence under section 25(1)(a) of the Drug Trafficking (Recovery of Proceeds) Ordinance were those contained in that subsection, whereby the burden was on the prosecution to prove that the defendant had been involved in an arrangement relating to another person's proceeds of drug trafficking knowing or having reasonable grounds to believe that person was connected with drug trafficking; that although subsection (4) prescribed special defences which the defendant had to prove on a balance of probabilities, such an onus on the defendant was justifiable in the context of the war against drug trafficking; and that, accordingly, neither section 25(1) nor 25(4) infringed Article 11(1).

655. To benefit from a statutory presumption of fact the prosecution has to satisfy the courts that the presumed facts 'rationally and realistically [follow] from that

under which the prosecution had to prove to the requisite standard the important elements of the offence as identified from the substance and reality of the statutory language, but an onus was reasonably imposed on the defendant to establish a proviso or exemption or similar matter, would not infringe the right conferred by Art. 11(1) to be presumed innocent until proved guilty according to law. *See* [1993] AC 951, 969–972; [1993] 2 HKCLR 186, 197–199.

1214. *A-G of Hong Kong v Lee Kwong-Kut* [1993] AC 951; [1993] 2 HKCLR 186, (PC).

1215. Cap. 228 of the Laws of Hong Kong.

1216. Cap. 405, *ibid*. After this decision, s. 25 was amended.

1217. *A-G of Hong Kong v Lee Kwong-Kut* [1993] AC 951; [1993] 2 HKCLR 186, (PC), applying s. 3(2) of the Bill of Rights Ordinance which invalidated any existing law which was inconsistent with the Bill of Rights. *See also R v Chong Ah-choi* (1994) 4 HKPLR 375, (CA).

proved and also … the presumption is no more than proportionate to what is warranted by the nature of the evil against which society [required] protection'.[1218] This is, in reality, a question of degree. As Lord Bingham of Cornhill noted in *Sheldrake v DPP*: The justifiability of any infringement of the presumption of innocence cannot be resolved by any rule of thumb, but on examination of all the facts and circumstances of the particular provision as applied in the particular case.[1219] In *Hong Kong Special Administrative Region v Lam Kwong Wai*, the Court of Final Appeal suggested that wherever possible a reverse legal burden of proof must be read down as an evidential burden.[1220]

V. The Rights of Defendants in a Criminal Trial

656. The common law has put in place many safeguards to protect the interests of defendants facing criminal trial. There is a presumption of innocence in the defendant's favour[1221] and the law requires the case against him to be proved beyond reasonable doubt.[1222] A defendant has a right to remain silent to protect himself from self-incrimination.[1223] He has the right to a fair trial,[1224] to be tried in the

1218. *R v Sin Yau-ming* [1992] 1 HKCLR 127, 163, (CA). For examples of statutory presumptions invalidated by the courts, *see R v Sin Yau-ming* [1992] 1 HKCLR 127, (CA), *R v Lum Wai-ming* [1992] 2 HKCLR 221, (HC) and *R v Chong Ah-choi* (1994) 4 HKPLR 375; [1994] 2 HKCLR 263, (CA). For examples of statutory presumptions not invalidated by the courts, *see R v Chan Wai-ming* [1993] 1 HKCLR 51, (HC), *R v Kwong Kui Wing* [1996] 1 HKDCLR 15, (DC), *R v Choi Kai-on* [1995] 1 HKCLR 79, (CA).

1219. *Sheldrake v DPP* [2005] 1 AC 264, (HL), [21].

1220. *HKSAR v Lam Kwong Wai* (2006) 9 HKCFAR 574, (CFA). *See HKSAR v Ng Po On* [2008] 11 HKCFAR 91, (CFA), where *Lam Kwong Wai* principle was applied. *See also Fu Kor Kuen Patrick v HKSAR* (2012) 15 HKCFAR 524, (CFA), *Secretary for Justice v Chan Chi Wan Stephen* (2017) 20 HKCFAR 98, (CFA) and *HKSAR v Choi Wai Lun* (2018) 21 HKCFAR 167, (CFA). *See also* para. 617 above.

1221. *See* above, IV. Right to be Presumed Innocent, paras 648-655.

1222. The right to be presumed innocent is the basis of the cardinal rule that the prosecution has the burden of proving beyond reasonable doubt that the defendant is guilty of the offence charged: *HKSAR v Lam Kwong Wai* (2006) 9 HKCFAR 574, (CFA), at [23].

1223. Privilege against self-incrimination is a well-established common law rule, which is implied in Art. 11 of the Hong Kong Bill of rights, the right to be presumed innocent. This is not an absolute right and may be restricted by legislation, so long as they are not disproportionate or otherwise unconstitutional: *A v Commissioner of Independent Commission Against Corruption* (2012) 15 HKCFAR 362, (CFA). *See also HKSAR v Lee Ming Tee* (2001) 4 HKCFAR 133, (CFA), 156. Hong Kong Bill of Rights, Art. 11(2)(g), provides that 'In the determination of any criminal charge against him, everyone shall be entitled to the following minimum guarantees, in full equality … not to be compelled to testify against himself or to confess guilt.' Article 11(2)(g) 'only applies to persons who face a criminal charge and the immunity then conferred is only a testimonial immunity, namely, the right 'not to be compelled to testify against himself or to confess guilt'. It is therefore of a much narrower scope than the common law privilege against self-incrimination': *HKSAR v Lee Ming Tee* (2001) 4 HKCFAR 133, (CFA), 171.

1224. *See*, for reference to the common law right to a fair trial, *Ramachandran Subramanian v The General Medical Council* [2002] UKPC 3, (PC), referred to in *Securities and Futures Commission v Wong Yuen Yee* [2017] 1 HKLRD 788, (CFI). 'In Hong Kong the right to a fair trial is an essential principle of the judicial system. It is guaranteed by two provisions of our constitution the Basic law. They are: (i) Art. 39 which entrenches Art. 10 of the Hong Kong Bill of Rights (where there

presence of a jury in relation to serious offences.[1225] He has a right to 'discover' the evidence of the prosecution before the trial and to cross-examine witnesses.[1226] Exceptionally, he has a right to stay criminal proceedings, to prevent abuse of the court process. The abuse alleged may arise in many different forms. It may involve complaints about the methods used to investigate the offence; it may be based on the allegation that the defendant is being prosecuted more than once for what is in effect the same offence. It may be a misuse of the process of the court to escape statutory time limits, or prejudicial pretrial publicity.[1227]

657. Under the common law, a confession made by a defendant is admissible evidence against him only if it has been made voluntarily 'in the sense that it has not been obtained from the accused either by fear of prejudice or hope of advantage excited or held out by a person in authority or by oppression'.[1228] The Bill of Rights has given statutory recognition to this well-established rule of common law.[1229]

658. Entrapment is not a defence to a criminal offence: The court, however, may stay a criminal proceeding if the police officers had brought about an 'artificial state-created crime'. The burden is on the applicant to show that this had taken place and

---

is an express reference to the right to a fair hearing); and (ii) Art. 87 which preserves the principles previously applied in proceedings and the rights previously enjoyed by parties to proceedings': *Chan Tak Ming v HKSAR* (2010) 13 HKCFAR 745, (CFA), [12].

1225. Article 86 of the Basic Law provides: 'The principle of trial by jury previously practised in Hong Kong shall be maintained.' It has been judicially observed that Art. 86 'is clear and unambiguous. All that it is saying is that whatever principle applied in relation to jury trials prior to the Basic Law coming into effect would continue to apply thereafter. … The principle of trial by jury that applied prior to the Basic Law coming into effect was clear: an indictable offence was triable either by judge and jury, in the High Court, or by judge alone, in the District Court, at the discretion of the Attorney General': *Chiang Lily v Secretary for Justice* [2009] HKEC 254, (CFI), [16] and [19]. Affirmed by the Court of Appeal in *Chiang Lily v Secretary for Justice* [2009] HKEC 1562, (CA), where Ma CJHC said that there is no right to trial by jury and the Basic Law did not create such a right. Trial by jury evolved from the common law and became part of Hong Kong law when s. 5 of the Supreme Court Ordinance (Cap. 5) extended the application of English law to Hong Kong: *R v Wong King Chau* [1964] HKDCLR 94, (DC).
1226. For the common law duty of disclosure and lawful limitation of it by legislation, *see HKSAR v Yu Lik Wai William* [2019] 1 HKLRD 1149, (CA). For the common law right to cross-examine witnesses, *see Oei Hengky Wiryo v HKSAR (No 2)* (2007) 10 HKCFAR 49, (CFA).
1227. *HKSAR v Lee Ming Tee* (2001) 4 HKCFAR 133, (CFA), 148. Ribeiro PJ went on to say at 150: 'If it be said that judicial measures cannot always secure perfect justice to an accused, we should ask whether the ideal of perfect justice has not sounded in rhetoric rather than in law and whether the legal right of an accused, truly stated, is a right to a trial as fair as the courts can make it. Were it otherwise, trials would be prevented and convictions would be set aside when circumstances outside judicial control impair absolute fairness.' *See also HKSAR v Ng Chuen To Raymond* [2013] HKEC 1190, (CA), where the Court of Appeal followed *Lee Ming Tee* case.
1228. *Secretary for Justice v Lam Tat Ming* (2000) 3 HKCFAR 168, 177, (CFA). In *HKSAR v Chow Ho Yin* (2020) 23 HKCFAR 1, (CFA), the defendant argued unsuccessfully that his absence at a *voir dire* to determine the voluntariness of a confession he had made (because he was not granted an adjournment to seek medical attention) resulted in the denial of a fair trial. It was held that taking the whole of the proceedings into account, especially that his counsel were well instructed and present throughout the proceedings, there was no denial of a fair trial.
1229. *R v Yu Yem-kin* [1994] HKEC 52, (SC), and *R v Cheung Ka Fai* [1995] 2 HKCLR 184, (CA).

the standard of proof is an extremely high one.[1230] However, if a defendant is encouraged to commit an offence which he would not otherwise have committed, the court would likely treat that as a mitigating factor and entrapment may be considered as an abuse of court process resulting in exclusion of evidence by court.[1231] It has been held that a trial judge has jurisdiction to stay proceedings in a criminal trial on the basis that a defendant was subjected to entrapment. This was so even if the trial of the defendant could be conducted fairly. Before exercising his discretion to stay on the basis of entrapment, a trial judge would have to be satisfied that if the trial were to continue it would be an abuse of process, amounting to an affront to the public conscience with severe consequences for public confidence in the administration of justice. A stay on the basis of entrapment should only be granted in exceptional circumstances.[1232]

659. A defendant has a right to be tried in his presence, and to defend himself in person or through legal assistance of his own choosing.[1233] This is not an absolute right and courts have the power to proceed with a trial where, for instance, the defendant has deliberately absconded prior to the proceedings.[1234] In appropriate circumstances, the court may decide to continue with the criminal trial in the absence of the defendant.[1235]

1230. *HKSAR v Yu Cheuk San* [2004] HKEC 651, (CA), citing *R v Looseley* [2001] 4 All ER 897, (HL). Among several failed attempts to establish this requirement is *HKSAR v Fung Hin Wah Edward* [2012] 1 HKLRD 374, (CA).

1231. *HKSAR v Yu Lik Wai William* [2015] HKEC 1286, [172], (DC). The judge rejected the argument that there was entrapment in the instant case, a finding upheld by the Court of Appeal in *HKSAR v Yu Lik Wai William* [2019] 1 HKLRD 1149, (CA).

1232. *HKSAR v Wong Kwok Hung* [2007] 2 HKLRD 621, (CA). As Lord Steyn said in *R Latif* [1996] 1 WLR 104, 112, (HL): 'If the court always refuses to stay such proceedings, the perception will be that the court condones criminal conduct and malpractice by law enforcement agencies. That would undermine public confidence in the criminal justice system and bring it into disrepute. On the other hand, if the court were always to stay proceedings in such cases, it would incur the reproach that it is failing to protect the public from serious crime.' Cited in *HKSAR v Fung Hin Wah Edward* [2012] 1 HKLRD 374, [54], (CA).

1233. Hong Kong Bill of Rights Ordinance (Cap. 383) Art. 11(2)(d). 'The right to be present at court is vital. It is not only a right so that the defendant can participate by giving instructions and following the trial, but also so that he can see and hear the witnesses who are giving evidence against him. This is not only part of the process by which a defendant participates at trial, but is also a sanction by which the public can be confident that there are pressures on those witnesses who give adverse evidence against a defendant to tell the truth. To give an account of events in a witness statement or within the seclusion of a police station is one thing. It is quite another to have to stand up in public, face-to-face with a defendant, and repeat those assertions': *R v Taylor (David Jeremy)* [2008] EWCA Crim 680, (CA), [16], cited in *HKSAR v Chow Ho Yin* (2020) 23 HKCFAR 1, (CFA), [15].

1234. *R v Jones* [2002] UKHL 5, (HL), cited in *HKSAR v Chow Ho Yin* (2020) 23 HKCFAR 1, (CFA).

1235. While the trial judge has a discretion in this matter, it is a discretion that should be sparingly exercised and never if the defendant's defence would be prejudiced by his absence. In exercising the discretion, the judge must consider whether the absence of the defendant is voluntary or involuntary, whether the defendant has waived his right to be present, is the defendant legally represented, would the accused be prejudiced by his absence. *See HKSAR v Chow Ho Yin* (2020) 23 HKCFAR 1, (CFA).

660. A defendant cannot take part meaningfully in a criminal trial unless he understands what is being said and is able to present his case: he has a right to have the free assistance of an interpreter if he cannot understand or speak the language used in court.[1236] It is well recognized that a defendant would be denied the right to fair hearing if he does not have access to the services of an interpreter so he could understand the proceedings and effectively put forward his case. It is responsibility of the defendant to raise his concerns about the inadequacy of the interpretation facilities made available to him. On appeal against conviction or sentence, the onus is on the defendant-appellant to demonstrate what the defective interpretation was, how it impeded his understanding of the proceedings and how it may have affected the conduct of his defence. The burden is on the defendant to establish on the balance of probabilities that any deficiencies on the interpreter's part fell short of the standard expected of the interpreter so as to imperil a fair trial.[1237]

661. Under the common law, the trial judge may abort a criminal trial where a prosecution witness whose evidence is important is missing so as to ensure justice to the accused.[1238]

662. Article 11(2)(d) of the Hong Kong Bill of Rights Ordinance, which protects the right to legal representation, entitles the defendant 'to be informed, if he does not have legal assistance, of this right; and to have legal assistance assigned to him, in any case where the interests of justice so require, and without payment by him in any such case if he does not have sufficient means to pay for it'. In order to make free legal aid meaningful it is necessary that a defendant, who does not have sufficient means to pay for legal assistance, is made aware of the availability of legal aid. In view of the real risk that an unrepresented defendant may not have a fair hearing, compelling reasons would generally be required to satisfy an appellate court that such a defendant had not been prejudiced to some degree by the wrongful denial of free legal representation.[1239] It must be noted that there is no absolute right to legal representation, and that even in the case of impecunious defendants, or defendants who claim to be such, reasonable limits may be set upon the provision of financially assisted legal representation in that reasonable constraints can be placed by the relevant authority upon the provision of legal services in terms of financial means.[1240]

663. It appears that this right operates even where he is not entitled to legal aid under the legal aid scheme. For instance, an accused may not qualify for legal assistance because he has property worth above the qualifying threshold value but may not in fact be able to afford legal fees. In such a situation, while the court cannot

---

1236. Hong Kong Bill of Rights Ordinance (Cap. 383), Art. 11(2)(f).
1237. *HKSAR v Gutierrez* [2020] 2 HKLRD 720, (CA), [29]–[34].
1238. In *R v Yeung Chi chiu* (1994) 4 HKLY 195, (DC), a stay of proceeding was granted, because it would be unfair and contrary to Art. 11 of the Bill of Rights (right to a fair trial) to proceed in the absence of some material witnesses.
1239. *HKSAR v Wong Chi Kwong* [2011] 1 HKLRD 843, (CFI), [50].
1240. *See R v Fu Yan* [1992] 2 HKCLR 59, (CA) and *R v Chandra Thanwardas Mirchandani* [1992] 2 HKCLR 174, (CA).

order him to be supported by legal aid scheme, it may stay proceedings to prevent an abuse of process – as the accused would not be guaranteed a fair hearing.[1241] Article 11(2)(d) of the Bill of Rights does not confer an absolute right to legal aid.[1242] Eligibility of legal aid is dependent on two conditions: (1) the interests of justice involved in a particular case must require that legal aid be granted and (2) the person concerned must not have sufficient means to pay for it. In *R v Chandra Thanwardas Mirchandani* the Court of Appeal observed that there was nothing objectionable in principle with a person applying for legal aid under the Legal Aid in Criminal Cases Rules (Cap. 221) being subject to a means test to determine whether they had sufficient means to pay for legal advice. The Rules regulated the grant of legal aid in a manner wholly consistent with Article 11(2)(d).[1243]

664. Where a defendant is unrepresented, the trial judge must take appropriate measures to ensure that the defendant is not prejudiced by the lack of legal representation. Generally, the trial magistrate's duty in assisting an unrepresented accused does not go beyond advising him of his legal rights in matters of procedure and in law. In appropriate circumstances, it may be desirable for the magistrate or the trial judge to ask witnesses questions not so much to assist the accused but as to ascertain the truth and to ensure that justice is done. Further, his duty may include rendering some assistance to the accused by asking a few relevant questions. There is no duty on the part of the magistrate to conduct the defence as such or take over the cross-examination from the accused.[1244]

A defendant may argue that he did not receive a fair hearing because of negligence or incompetence of his legal representative.[1245]

665. The common law rights of a defendant are supplemented by rights guaranteed by the Bill of Rights.[1246] Under the Bill of Rights, a defendant is entitled, for

1241. *R v Wong Cheung-bun* [1992] 1 HKCLR 240 (HC). Where a defendant has not been advised of his right to legal assistance, proceedings may be liable to invalidation: *Hall v Commissioner of Correctional Services* [2015] 2 HKLRD 917, (CFI).
1242. *R v Chandra Thanwardas Mirchandani* [1992] 2 HKCLR 174, (CA).
1243. *Ibid.* It appears from the decision that the court has decided that there will no longer be provision of legal aid apart from that provided under the current legal aid scheme. M. Wilkinson & J. Chan, 'Abuse of the Criminal Process', in G. Heilbronn (ed.) *Modern Trends in Litigation* (Hong Kong: Hong Kong Law Journal Ltd, 1995) 58–59.
1244. Li J in *Chan Leung v R* [1979] HKLR 98, (HC), 105, where the High Court said: 'generally the trial magistrate's duty in assisting an unrepresented accused does not go beyond advising him of his legal rights in matters of procedure and in law. In appropriate circumstances it may be desirable for the magistrate or the trial judge to ask witnesses questions not so much to assist the accused but as to ascertain the truth and to ensure that justice is done. Further his duty may include some assistance to the accused by asking a few pertinent questions if such questions were apparently necessary. There is no duty on the part of the magistrate to conduct the defence as such or take over the cross-examination from the accused.' Followed in *R v Tam Kin Wing* [1997] HKLRD 333, (HC).
1245. *HKSAR v Cheng Kan* [1998] HKEC 1143, (CFI).
1246. Bill of Rights Ordinance, *see* Art. 11(2)(d) (on the right to defend oneself, etc.) and Art. 11(2)(e) (on the right to examine witnesses).

example, to 'be informed promptly and in detail in a language which he understands of the nature and cause of the charge against him'.[1247] Thus, where an important prosecution document, for example, a summons, is in a language that the defendant does not understand, the trial judge ought to explain it to him and adjourn the trial.[1248]

666. The defendant must have 'adequate time and facilities for the preparation of his defence'.[1249] It follows that the failure of the prosecution to provide important materials to the accused may constitute unfairness. This may enable the defendant to stay the criminal proceedings.[1250]

667. Of particular importance is the constitutional right 'to be tried without undue delay'.[1251] Undue delay in itself is insufficient: The accused must have, as a result of the undue delay, suffered prejudice (a point that is not easy to prove). Where the delay is substantial, prejudice will be presumed and it is up to the prosecution to rebut that presumption. The prejudice that he has suffered must be balanced with the public interest in having justice done.[1252]

668. The Bill of Rights reinforces the common law rule against double jeopardy when it provides that 'no one shall be liable to be tried or punished again for an offence for which he has already been finally convicted or acquitted in accordance with the law and penal procedure of Hong Kong'.[1253]

669. The Criminal Procedure Ordinance provides that a person convicted of an offence may appeal on the ground that there has been a 'miscarriage of justice', in

---

1247. *Ibid.*, Art. 11(2)(a).

1248. *Attorney General of Hong Kong v Tang Yuen-Lin* (1995) 5 HKPLR 631; [1995] 2 HKCLR 157, (CA).

1249. Article 11(2)(b).

1250. *See R v Flickinger* (1993) 3 HKPLR 677, (DC), and *R v Chu Kam-to* (1994) 4 HKPLR 472; 1994] HKEC 53, (SC). *See HKSAR v Lee Ming Tee and SFC (Intervener)* [2004] 1 HKLRD 513; (2003) 6 HKCFAR 336, (CFA).

1251. Article 11(2)(c). *See* Michael Wilkinson & Johannes Chan 'Abuse of the Criminal Process', in *Modern Trends in Litigation*, ed. Gary Heilbronn (Hong Kong: Hong Kong Law Journal Ltd, 1995), 59–78.

1252. *In re George Tan* [1991] 2 HKLR 400, (HC), *R v William Hung* [1994] 1 HKCLR 47, (CA), and *R v Deacon Chiu* (1993) HKEC 163, (SC). The Court of Final Appeal observed in *Ong Siu Sin Kevin v HKSAR* [2011] HKEC 986, (CFA), [14]–[15], that 'to establish undue delay within the article to merit a remedy, the applicant must demonstrate something more, such as a serious unjust effect upon his trial or upon him personally. Examples are that his defence has been prejudiced, or the fairness of his trial has been compromised, or that the delay has been oppressive. Such a list, of course, cannot be exhaustive. Everything depends upon the individual circumstances in which the court is called upon to exercise its discretion.'

1253. Article 11(6). This right is narrower than the common law right, under which a previous conviction for a similar offence by a non-local court too could be taken into account. *See Yeung Chun Pong v Secretary for Justice* [2006] HKEC 1517, (CA).

the sense that there has been an 'unsafe or unsatisfactory' conviction, a legally erroneous judgment or a 'material irregularity' in the trial.[1254] The Bill of Rights provides that everyone convicted of a crime has the right to have his conviction and sentence reviewed by a higher tribunal.[1255]

670. Another essential procedural safeguard is the rule against retrospective laws.[1256] Although this is a right in a criminal trial, the Court of Final Appeal has relied on it to invalidate a provision of the Immigration Ordinance that purported to deprive the right of abode of the children of the Hong Kong residents who had entered Hong Kong unlawfully or had overstayed their lawful stay in Hong Kong before the commencement of the relevant provisions of the Ordinance. The reason is that had this provision been allowed to stand, they would be potentially liable for immigration offences which were not offences at the time of their Commission.[1257] The Bill of Rights provides that:

> a heavier penalty [shall not] be imposed than the one that was applicable at the time when the criminal offence was committed. If, subsequent to the commission of the offence, provision is made by law for the imposition of a lighter penalty, the offender shall benefit thereby.[1258]

In practice, whether the accused is entitled to this specific right depends on the circumstances of his case.[1259]

1254. Section 83(1) of the Criminal Procedure Ordinance (Cap. 221) of the Laws of Hong Kong. As Lord Dunedin put it succinctly in *Robins v National Trust Co Ltd* [1927] AC 515, (PC) 518–519:

> 'miscarriage of justice means such a departure from the rules which permeate all judicial procedure as to make that which happened not in the proper sense of the word judicial procedure at all. There is, however, also another way of preventing the application of the rule. If it can be shown that the finding of one of the Courts is so based on an erroneous proposition of law that if that proposition be corrected the finding disappears, then in that case there is no finding at all.' As Bokhary PJ observed in *Tang Siu Man v HKSAR (No 2)* (1997-98) 1 HKCFAR 107, (CFA), 147: 'To allow an appeal just because something has gone wrong at the trial even though it has not resulted in a miscarriage of justice would not be doing justice.'

1255. Article 11(4), referred to in *Chong Ching Yuen v HKSAR* [2004] 2 HKLRD 681; (2004) 7 HKCFAR 126, (CFA).

1256. Article 12(1). 'Retrospective criminal laws are odious to most developed legal systems': Lord Mustill in *Chan Chi-hung v R* [1996] AC 442, (PC), 446 on appeal from Hong Kong. There, the Privy Council held that where the definition of a statutory offence is reformulated after the commission of an offence by a person but before he was sentenced, the sentence that can be imposed on him should not exceed the punishment that was lawful under the previously existing law.

1257. *Ng Ka ling Others v Director of Immigration* (1999) 2 HKCFAR 4, (CFA).

1258. Article 12(1).

1259. *R v Chan Chi-Hung* [1993] 2 HKCLR 212, (CA), affirmed by the Privy Council: [1995] 2 HKCLR 50, (PC).

VI. The Right to Private Property

671. Article 7 of the Basic Law provides as follows: 'The land and natural resources within the Hong Kong Special Administrative Region shall be State property. The Government of the Hong Kong Special Administrative Region shall be responsible for their management, use and development and for their lease or grant to individuals, legal persons or organizations for use or development. The revenues derived therefrom shall be exclusively at the disposal of the government of the Region.' Since all land in Hong Kong is government-owned, right of private property refers to any land use rights that a lessee enjoys under a government lease. In Hong Kong a person who has a government lease is conveniently called 'landowner'. When Article 6 of the Basic Law provides that 'The Hong Kong Special Administrative Region shall protect the right of private ownership of property in accordance with law', that would be a reference to limited rights of ownership that a lessee of government land enjoys. Article 105 provides that:

> The Hong Kong Special Administrative Region shall, in accordance with the law, protect the right of individuals and legal persons … to compensation for lawful deprivation of their property. Such compensation shall correspond to the real value of the property concerned at the time and shall be freely convertible and paid without undue delay.

672. 'Deprivation' in this context means not only physical taking but also 'regulatory taking'. Regulatory deprivation (or regulatory taking) refers to situations where a lawful government action affects the use and enjoyment of land to such an extent that it could be said that the landowner has been deprived of the beneficial or productive use of the land, although his legal title remains intact.[1260] Physical taking includes not only compulsory acquisition, or to use the Hong Kong terminology, resumption by the Government of leased land, but it also includes lesser degrees of physical deprivation by way of imposing planning restrictions on the use of the land. Restrictive planning controls are not mere incidents of land ownership: They engage property rights protected by Articles 6 and 105 of the Basic Law.[1261]

673. There has been much litigation on whether town planning restrictions on land use, such as building height, layout and set back restrictions may amount to

1260. *Fine Tower Associates Ltd v Town Planning Board* [2008] 1 HKLRD 553, (CA) [17]–[25]. It has been held that deprivation of a person's property by adverse possession is not within the scope of Art. 105. In *Harvest Good Development Ltd v Secretary for Justice* [2007] HKEC 1272, (CFI), [151], [145] Harman J said 'on a true construction, Art. 105 of the Basic Law, even as buttressed by Art. 6, seeks only to guarantee the right to compensation for lawful deprivation of property when that deprivation constitutes expropriation of property by the state or a state agency. … the statutory scheme governing adverse possession, while it provides for a transfer of rights between individuals, is not confiscatory in nature. There is no confiscation of land by the state for public purposes.' Appeal against this decision was dismissed by the Court of Appeal: *Harvest Good Development Ltd v Secretary for Justice* [2007] HKEC 2355, (CA).

1261. *Hysan Development Co Ltd v Town Planning Board* (2016) 19 HKCFAR 372, (CFA), [37]. *See also* [40] and [41].

deprivation of property rights prohibited by Article 105 and whether any restrictions on land-use has to satisfy the proportionality test. Courts have recognized that all land in Hong Kong belong to the Hong Kong Government, and that there are no freeholder rights (subject to some insignificant exceptions) and that where the administrative authorities have acted within the powers conferred by legislation, there is little room to succeed in Article 105 challenges.[1262] A significant change in the approach to the nature of the property rights protected by Articles 6 and 105 was signalled by the Court of Final Appeal, when it heard the appeal from the Court of Appeal. Justice Ribeiro, with the other four judges agreeing held as follows: (1) imposition of planning or building restrictions (regulatory takings) are within the scope of Articles 6 and 105 of the Basic Law just as deprivation/expropriation of property (physical takings) are; (2) property rights which are protected by Articles 6 and 105 are not absolute rights and may be subjected to restrictions; (3) such restrictions have to be justified; (4) in considering whether such restrictions are justified the applicable test is that of proportionality; (5) a legitimate planning restriction is proportionate unless the restriction is 'manifestly without reasonable foundation' and not where the restriction is 'no more than necessary' to advance the legitimate aim of the legislation or administrative measure in question (which is a stricter test).[1263]

674. It has been argued that certain statutory or administrative arrangements relating to town planning, building control, government leases and resumption of government land may be subject to judicial review either because of their questionable status or inadequate provision of compensation.[1264] Where compensation is payable, the award must correspond to the 'real value' of the land or property right affected. The concept of 'real value' is said to correspond to market value supplemented by other relevant valuation principles that were in place when the Basic Law came into effect.[1265]

1262. For a comprehensive review of the legal issues involved, *see Hysan Development Co Ltd v Town Planning Board* [2014] HKEC 1869, (CA).
1263. *Hysan Development Co Ltd v Town Planning Board* (2016) 19 HKCFAR 372, (CFA).
1264. Albert Chen, 'The Basic Law and the Protection of Property Rights' (1993) 23 *Hong Kong Law Journal* 31 and Anthony Law, 'Judicial Review of Government Leases in the Hong Kong Special Administrative Region' (1999) 29 *Hong Kong Law Journal* 240.
1265. *See* Lord Millett in *Director of Lands v Yin Shuen Enterprises Ltd* (2000) 6 HKCFAR 1, (CFA), [56]. *See* generally, Gordon N. Crudden, *Land Compensation and Valuation Law in Hong Kong* (3rd edn, 2009: LexisNexis) 641–644.

675. Article 29 of the Basic Law provides that 'the homes and other premises of Hong Kong residents shall be inviolable. Arbitrary or unlawful search of, or intrusion into, a resident's home or other premises shall be prohibited.'[1266] Common law and legislation impose a number of procedural and substantive limitations on the police in the exercise of powers of entry into homes and arresting people in their homes.[1267] An important safeguard is that a search warrant must be clear and precise.[1268] In cases where the citizen asserts that the property involved in the search is privileged, special rules will apply.[1269]

VII. The Right to Privacy

676. The Bill of Rights provides that 'no one shall be subjected to arbitrary or unlawful interference with his privacy, family, home or correspondence',[1270] and the Personal Data (Privacy) Ordinance[1271] implements the right to privacy.[1272] The scope of the Ordinance is limited to the protection of documented personal data and provision of guidelines for access to such information (subject to exceptions and exemptions).[1273] In *Jiang Enzhu v Lau Wai Hing*,[1274] it was held that the obligation to comply with requests for personal data falls only on a person who had received a request for disclosure. Where the request had been served on a person who held an official position in an unincorporated association and by the time of the prosecution that person has been succeeded by another, the successor could not be prosecuted for his predecessor's failure to comply with the request.

1266. For a thorough analysis of Art. 29, *see HKSAR v McCall Howard Kenneth* [2017] HKEC 2893, (CFI), [24]–[26]. This case concerned an alleged unlawful search of premises.
1267. *See*, e.g., *McLorie v Oxford* [1982] QB 1290, (DC) where it was held that once a police officer has completed the arrest of a person suspected of a violent crime, there was no right in common law to enter domestic premises without a warrant to search for or to cease the weapon. Lord Justice Donaldson said: 'Such is the importance attached by the common law to the relative inviolability of a dwelling house that we cannot believe that there is a common law right without warrant to enter one either in order to search for instruments of crime, even of serious crime, or in order to seize such an instrument which is known to be there. Certainly if there were, we would expect it to be reflected in the books and it is not.' It has been held that the requirement of lawfulness of the search applies whether the premises entered is domestic or non-domestic: Search without a warrant is lawful only where it is not practicable to obtain a warrant before a search is conducted. *See Keen Lloyd Holdings Ltd v Commissioner of Customs and Excise* [2016] 2 HKLRD 1372, (CA), [91]. The court applying a remedial construction read the words 'domestic premises' in s. 22 of the Import and Export Ordinance (Cap. 60) to mean 'premises or places'.
1268. *Re an Application by Messrs. Ip and Willis for Leave to Apply for Judicial Review* [1990] 1 HKLR 154, (HC), (on the use of language) and *Apple Daily Ltd v Commissioner of the ICAC (No 2)* [2000] 1 HKLRD 647, (CA) (on the compatibility of the scope of the search warrant with the law).
1269. *Shun Tak Holdings Ltd v Commissioner of Police* [1995] 1 HKCLR 48, (HC).
1270. Article 14.
1271. Cap. 486 of the Laws of Hong Kong.
1272. *See*, e.g., *Kwan Chi On v Hong Kong Baptist University* [1997] HKEC 114, (CFI).
1273. *See* generally Mark Berthold & Raymond Wacks, *Professional Guide: Data Privacy Law in Hong Kong* (Hong Kong: FT Law & Tax Asia Pacific, 1997).
1274. *Jiang Enzhu v Lau Wai Hing* [2000] 1 HKLRD 121, (CFI).

677. Article 14 of the Hong Kong Bill of Rights provides that:

(1) No one shall be subjected to arbitrary or unlawful interference with his privacy, family, home or correspondence, nor to unlawful attacks on his honour and reputation.
(2) Everyone has the right to the protection of the law against such interference or attacks.

Article 30 of the Basic Law provides as follows: 'The freedom and privacy of communication of Hong Kong residents shall be protected by law. No department or individual may, on any grounds, infringe upon the freedom and privacy of communication of residents except that the relevant authorities may inspect communication in accordance with legal procedures to meet the needs of public security or of investigation into criminal offences.'

This protection is in the nature of a procedural safeguard.[1275] It does not operate to exclude evidence that is admissible under normal rules of evidence and procedure. In *HKSAR v Muhammad Riaz Khan,*[1276] the defendant, who was convicted of conspiracy to traffic in drugs, had his private conversation with an undercover agent secretly taped. While admitting that there was a prima facie breach of the right to privacy, the Court of Appeal held that there was no absolute bar to the reception of evidence obtained in breach of the defendant's constitutional right. Such evidence could be admitted in the discretion of the court.[1277]

678. Right to privacy is not an absolute right. It may be subjected to restrictions which are proportionate. The recent case of *Junior Police Officers' Association of Hong Kong Police Force v Electoral Affairs Commission*[1278] is an example of a proportionate restriction. There, the applicants argued that since the names and addresses of all those who are on the electoral list are public information, police officers who are on the electoral list run the risk of their personal information being readily available to the protestors who would use it to attack them. The court rejected the judicial review application and upheld the validity of the electoral arrangements set out in legislation aimed at ensuring transparency in the electoral process. It was held in *Sham Wing Kan v Commissioner of Police*[1279] that while a person has privacy rights in the digital contents of his mobile phone, a police officer

---

1275. *Fok Lai Ying v Governor in Council* [1997] 7 HKLRD 111, (CA).
1276. (2012) 15 HKCFAR 232, (CFA).
1277. *Ibid.*, at [20] it was said: 'The test can be stated thus. Evidence obtained in breach of a defendant's constitutional rights can nevertheless be received if, upon a careful examination of the circumstances, its reception (i) is conducive to a fair trial, (ii) is reconcilable with the respect due to the right or rights concerned (iii) appears unlikely to encourage any future breaches of that, those or other rights.' *See also Ho Man Kong v Superintendent of Lai Chi Kok Reception Centre* (2014) 17 HKCFAR 179, (CFA).
1278. [2020] 2 HKLRD 631, (CFI).
1279. [2020] 2 HKLRD 529, (CA).

could search such contents of a mobile phone found on an arrested person, subject to measures to prevent undue interference with the right to privacy.[1280]

VIII. Freedom of Thought, Conscience, and Religion

679. Article 15 of the Bill of Rights guarantees the freedom of thought, conscience and religion. They are not absolute rights: they 'may be subject only to such limitations as are prescribed by law and are necessary to protect public safety, order, health, or morals or the fundamental rights and freedoms of others'.[1281] In *Lau Wong Fat v Attorney General*,[1282] the Court of Appeal did not consider the abolition of the Chinese customary rule that gives males the sole right of succession to land to be an infringement of the freedom of thought, conscience and religion.

680. The Basic Law protects religious organizations in respect of their property rights, their freedom to run religious and educational activities and schools, as well as their liberty to maintain normal relationships with religious organizations outside Hong Kong. However, governmental measures justly intended to ensure proper management of schools managed by religious bodies is not a breach of religious freedom.[1283]

IX. Freedom of Expression

681. The Bill of Rights provides as follows:

> Everyone shall have the right to freedom of expression; this right shall include freedom to seek, receive and impart information and ideas of all kinds, regardless of frontiers, either orally, in writing or in print, in the form of Article, or through any other media of his choice. The exercise of [this right] … carries with it special duties and responsibilities. It may therefore be subject to certain

1280. *See also HKSAR v Yu Lik Wai William* [2019] 1 HKLRD 1149, (CA), [283]–[284], where telecommunications interceptions and covert surveillance by law enforcement authorities, subject to protective measures, were upheld as a legitimate limitation on the right to privacy. As regards the proportionality analysis, there was justification for the use of executive authorisations and unsworn statements in writing, given the opportunistic and fluid nature of covert surveillance. The appropriate standard to apply was 'manifestly without reasonable foundation' given the wide margin of discretion appropriate for this operational efficiency justification. Given that executive authorisation permitted only covert surveillance with low levels of intrusion into privacy rights, it could not be said that the regime was without reasonable foundation.

1281. Article 15(3). Judicially recognized for instance in *Ubamaka v Secretary for Security* (2012) 15 HKCFAR 743, (CFA).

1282. *Lau Wong Fat v Attorney General* [1997] HKLRD 533, (CA).

1283. Article 141. *See Catholic Diocese of Hong Kong v Secretary for Justice* [2010] HKEC 163, (CA), affirmed by the Court of Final Appeal (2011) 14 HKCFAR 754, (CFA).

restrictions, but these shall only be such as are provided by law and are necessary ... for respect of the rights or reputations of others; or ... for the protection of national security or of public order (ordre public), or of public health or morals.[1284]

The Basic Law has a similar provision.[1285]

682. The freedom to seek, receive and impart information must be jealously guarded against governmental intervention.[1286] As Chief Justice Li explained in *HKSAR v Ng Kung Siu*:

> Freedom of expression is a fundamental freedom in a democratic society. It lies at the heart of civil society and of Hong Kong's system and way of life. The courts must give a generous interpretation to its constitutional guarantee. This freedom includes the freedom to express ideas which the majority may find disagreeable or offensive and the freedom to criticize governmental institutions and the conduct of public officials.[1287]

683. Freedom of expression is not an absolute right, and courts are prepared to accept reasonable restrictions on the right. Flag desecration cases provide a good illustration. *HKSAR v Ng Kung Siu*[1288] concerned desecrating the national flag and the regional flag by publicly and wilfully defiling them, in contravention of the National Flag Ordinance and the Regional Flag and Regional Emblem Ordinance.[1289] It was held that freedom of expression could in these circumstances be restricted in the interest of public order. In the context of the 'One Country, Two Systems' arrangement, the legitimate societal interests in protecting the national flag, and the legitimate community interests in the protection of the regional flag, were interests which were within the concept of public order.[1290] In *Cheung Tak*

1284. Article 16.
1285. Article 27.
1286. *See*, e.g., *Chim Shing Chung v Commissioner of Correctional Services* (1995) 5 HKPLR 570, (HC). This decision was set aside by the Court of Appeal: (1996) 6 HKPLR 313, (CA).
1287. *HKSAR v Ng kung Siu* (1999) 2 HKCFAR 442, (CFA), 455. *See also Leung Kwok Hung v HKSAR* (2005) 8 HKCFAR 229, (CFA), [2]. In *Kwok Hay Kwong v Medical Council of Hong Kong* [2008] HKEC 137, (CA), it was held that a complete ban on advertising by medical practitioners was unconstitutional. The Court of Appeal held that any restriction on freedom of speech must be justifiable and proportionate.
1288. (1999) 2 HKCFAR 442, (CFA).
1289. The National Flag and National Emblem Ordinance (Instrument A401) Ordinance and the Regional Flag and Regional Emblem Ordinance (Instrument A602).
1290. *HKSAR v Ng Kung Siu* (1999) 2 HKCFAR 442, (CFA), 457. Justifying the limitation on freedom of expression the Court of Final appeal observed, at 456, as follows: 'The prohibition of desecration of the national and regional flags by the statutory provisions in question is not a wide restriction of the freedom of expression. It is a limited one. It bans one mode of expressing whatever the message the person concerned may wish to express, that is the mode of desecrating the flags. It does not interfere with the person's freedom to express the same message by other modes.' It was held to be a justifiable and a necessary restriction on freedom of speech. In *HKSAR v Koo Sze Yiu* (2014) 17 HKCFAR 811, (CFA), reaffirming its decision in the previous case of *HKSAR v Ng*

Wing v Director of Administration[1291] it was held that the requirement of obtaining Director of Administration's prior approval to hold any public meeting in the forecourt of the Central Government Offices was a valid limitation of the right to freedom of expression and assembly. In *MTR Corp Ltd v Kwok Wing Kan*[1292] it was held that the MTR Corporation was within its rights to prohibit persons from having loud demonstrations inside a train station in breach of the relevant by-laws. Having regard to the size of their activities, the nature and primary purpose of the concourse concerned and of the station as a whole, and in all the relevant circumstances, the restriction on the freedom of expression was held to be a reasonable restriction.

684. Freedom of expression may be restricted in order to protect the judiciary from any unjustified interference.[1293] In determining whether such restriction is justified it must be borne in mind that 'no wrong is committed by any member of the public who exercises the ordinary right of criticising, in good faith, in private or public, the public act done in the seat of justice. The path of criticism is a public way: the wrongheaded are permitted to err therein: provided that members of the public abstain from imputing improper motives to those taking part in the administration of justice, and are genuinely exercising a right of criticism, and not acting in malice or attempting to impair the administration of justice, they are immune. Justice is not a cloistered virtue: she must be allowed to suffer the scrutiny and respectful, even though outspoken, comments of ordinary men.'[1294] A similar consideration apply in relation to media reporting of criminal proceedings. As Robert CJ said *in R v Shamsudin*, where the court refused an application by the Attorney General to impose restrictions on media reporting of a judicial proceeding:

> The burden – and it is a substantial one – must lie on those who seek a court order which offends what I perceive to be the fundamental rule: that criminal trials must be conducted publicly, and should be reported fully and fairly ... I think that these same principles apply to a partial restriction on reporting as they do to a sitting in camera or to a ban on all reporting.[1295]

Kung Siu (1999) 2 HKCFAR 442, (CFA), the Court of Final Appeal refused leave to appeal against the decision of the Court of Appeal that the prohibition of flag desecration was not an unconstitutional restriction of the right to hold opinions. The Court of Final Appeal observed that there was no need to revisit *Ng Kung Siu* case. The reference to 'time, place and circumstances' in *Ng Kung Siu* was not a general invitation to revisit the validity of decisions of the Court from time to time.

1291. [2020] 1 HKLRD 906, (CA).

1292. [2019] 5 HKLRD 385, (CFI).

1293. *Wong Yeung Ng v Secretary for Justice* [1999] 2 HKLRD 293, (CA). The decision of the Court of Appeal was confirmed by the Court of Final Appeal in *Wong Yeung Ng v Secretary for Justice* [1999] HKEC 1330, (CFA).

1294. *Ambard v A-G for Trinidad and Tobago* [1936] AC 322, (PC), 335 Lord Atkin. Quoted in *Wong Yeung Ng v Secretary for Justice* [1999] 2 HKLRD 293, (CA), 309.

1295. *R v Shamsudin* [1987] HKLR 254 (HC). (This is a case decided before the Bill of Rights came into effect, but the principle that restrictions may be placed on open justice still holds true.) *See HKSAR v Wu Wing Kit (No 1)* [2016] 3 HKLRD 386, (CA), where *Shamsudin* was referred to, the Court of Appeal held that it was permissible under the common law and the Bill of Rights to impose restrictions on open justice. The Court also referred to *TCWF v LKKS* [2013] HKEC 1197,

685. An important area where curtailment of the freedom of expression occurs is public media. It is common for the government to regulate television and telecommunication agencies.[1296] In relation to the power of the Telecommunications Authority to take criminal proceedings against an unlicensed broadcaster, the Court of First Instance in *Secretary for Justice v Ocean Technology Ltd* held licensing of radio broadcasting to be a permissible fetter on the freedom of expression in view of the fact that unrestricted access to the radio frequency spectrum in Hong Kong would run the risk of interfering with vital emergency services, operations of the Civil Aviation Department and listeners' right to receive transmission by existing radio stations. Stock JA said that a societal justification for a licensing regime should be obvious from a moment's contemplation of the chaos and interference with the rights of others that would result absent such a regime.[1297] The Court of Final Appeal in *HKSAR v Wong Yuk Man* refrained from examining the constitutionality of offences relating to unauthorized broadcasts since the convictions could be quashed on the grounds that what the suspects had done did not constitute the *actus reus* of the offence in question.[1298]

686. Apart from the above statutory regulatory framework, the law of defamation is also a major source of law controlling the Hong Kong media. In light of the constitutional right to free speech, the defence of fair comment in the tort of defamation has been given a liberal interpretation in order to favour the defendant.[1299] Public authorities, as opposed to government bodies,[1300] may sue for defamation.[1301]

687. In 1999–2000, the Law Reform Commission of the Hong Kong Special Administrative Region Government recommended the following proposals: setting up of a statutory Press Council to handle complaints concerning media infringement of privacy, establishment of a new cause of action for media infringement of

---

(CA), where a request to hold a hearing in private was rejected. *Asia Television Ltd v Communications Authority* [2013] 2 HKLRD 354, (CA), is a case where the court refused to hold a judicial review hearing in private. The principle that emerges from these cases is that any restriction on open justice must be justified as tending to ensure a fair trial and that the right to privacy in itself is not a sufficient justification. An important aspect of open justice is the reporting in public media of judicial proceedings, and it is only in exceptional circumstances that the court prohibits public reporting of ongoing proceedings. *See HKSAR v Wu Wing Kit* (No 1) [2016] 3 HKLRD 386, (CA).

1296. *See* the Broadcasting Ordinance (Cap. 562) and the Telecommunications Ordinance (Cap. 106).

1297. *Secretary for Justice v Ocean Technology Ltd* [2009] 3 HKEC 2114, (CFI), [66], [68] and [92]. The Court of Final Appeal refused leave to appeal: *Secretary for Justice v Ocean Technology Ltd* [2009] HKEC 806, (CFA).

1298. *HKSAR v Wong Yuk Man* (2012) 15 HKCFAR 712, (CFA).

1299. *Eastern Express Publishers Ltd v Man Ching* (1999) 2 HKCFAR 264, (CFA) and *Cheng v & another v Tse Wai Chun* (2000) 3 HKCFAR 339, (CFA).

1300. *Derbyshire County Council v Times Newspapers Ltd* [1993] AC 534, (HL).

1301. *Hong Kong Polytechnic University v Next Magazine Publishing Ltd* [1997] HKLRD 514, (CA). *See* Jill Cottrell, 'Courts, Freedom of Speech and Defamation', (1999) 7 *Asia Pacific Law Review* 205.

privacy and criminalization of stalking.[1302] It has been argued that implementation of these reforms will stifle freedom of the press. As an industry response to the Law Commission report, perhaps to avoid the setting up of a statutory Press Council, after months of consultation and discussion, eleven newspapers and two journalists' associations, namely the Hong Kong News Executives' Association and the Hong Kong Federation of Journalists formed a Hong Kong Press Council in 2000, which receives and handles public complaints in accordance with its constitution and rules of procedures.

688. Concerns have been expressed that the offence of sedition,[1303] would stifle criticism of the state is inconsistent with freedom of expression.[1304] There is, at present, a law forbidding unauthorized prejudicial disclosure of certain classes of State secrets (e.g., those relating to defence and foreign affairs) by civil servants in particular.[1305] There is no defence of public interest. Like sedition, this law has also been criticized by Hong Kong academics.[1306] Section 30 of the Prevention of Bribery Ordinance (Cap. 201) makes it an offence for anyone knowing or suspecting that an investigation into a bribery offence is taking place to disclose that fact to the person subject to the investigation or to anyone else or to the public. Section 30(1A) provided that the prohibition on disclosure ended when the suspect has been arrested. In *Ming Pao Newspaper Ltd v Attorney General*,[1307] Ming Pao newspaper published articles reporting that the Independent Commission Against Corruption into alleged irregularities at a government public auction of land and that the targets of the investigations have not yet been ascertained. While upholding the decision of the Magistrate that no offence had been committed since section 30 becomes applicable only where there is a suspect or an allegation of bribery offence against a specified person, the Privy Council upheld the validity of the offence of unauthorized disclosure of identity of subjects. The Privy Council affirmed the following three principles relevant to determining whether the restriction prescribed in section 30 was a valid restriction: (1) A constitution, and in particular that part of it which protects and entrenches fundamental rights and freedoms to which all persons in the

1302. *See* Sub-Committee on Privacy, the Law Reform Commission of Hong Kong, *Consultation Paper on the Regulation of Media Intrusion* (Hong Kong: The Law Reform Commission of Hong Kong, 1999), Sub-Committee on Privacy, the Law Reform Commission of Hong Kong, *Consultation Paper on Civil Liability for Invasion of Privacy* (Hong Kong: The Law Reform Commission of Hong Kong, 1999) and the Law Reform Commission of Hong Kong, *Stalking* (Hong Kong: The Law Reform Commission of Hong Kong, 2000).

1303. *See* ss 9–10 of the Crimes Ordinance (Cap. 200) of the Laws of Hong Kong.

1304. D. Clark, 'Sedition and Article 23', in P Wesley-Smith (ed.), *Hong Kong's Basic Law: Problems & Prospects* (Hong Kong: Faculty of Law, University of Hong Kong, 1990). In *Fei Yi Ming v R* (1952) 36 HKLR 133, (Appellate Jurisdiction) a case decided in the colonial era, a proprietor of a pro-China newspaper was punished for this offence for referring to anti-British propaganda from a mainland Chinese source.

1305. The Official Secrets Ordinance (Cap. 521) of the Laws of Hong Kong.

1306. Yash Ghai, 'Official Information: Government Secrets or Public Assets?' (1991) 21 *Hong Kong Law Journal* 78.

1307. *Ming Pao Newspaper Ltd v Attorney General* (1996) 2 HKLR 239, (PC). Section 30(1A) was repealed subsequent to the Privy Council decision and a new s. 30(1) added expanding the situations when the prohibition of disclosure ends, such as when a warrant has been issued for the arrest of the suspect.

state are to be entitled, is to be given a generous and purposive construction; (2) Any restrictions on the guaranteed right of freedom of expression which constitutes one of the essential foundations of a democratic society must be narrowly interpreted; (3) Any restrictions on the guaranteed right of freedom of expression must be proportionate to the aims sought to be achieved thereby. The question in issue was whether the prohibition of disclosure of information to the public was a proportionate response to the necessity to preserve the integrity of investigations into corruption, which the Privy Council answered by saying that it was a policy decision of the government 'which was eminently sensible and by no means disproportionate to the important objectives sought to be achieved'. The Privy Council went on to assert the relevance of the doctrine of margin of appreciation in the European Convention of Human Rights: 'Under the system of protection established by the Convention, it is for the national authorities to make the initial assessment both of the existence of a problem of public concern warranting measures of deprivation of property and of the remedial action to be taken.' The Privy Council was of the view that the policy decision to prohibit the publication of information of an ongoing investigation could not be described as 'so unreasonable as to be outside the State's margin of appreciation. Indeed, it appears to their Lordships to be a decision which was eminently sensible and by no means disproportionate to the important objectives sought to be achieved.'[1308]

689. The government has relied on breach of confidence to prevent leakage of confidential government information by a former member of the security service.[1309] The government may rely on public interest privilege to refuse disclosure in court of certain classes of information (e.g., those relating to effective necessary functioning of the Executive). So far, no comprehensive legislation has been enacted in Hong Kong on the provision of government information.[1310]

X. Freedom of Assembly and Association

690. Article 27 of the Basic Law provides as follows: 'Hong Kong residents shall have freedom of speech, of the press and of publication; freedom of association, of assembly, of procession and of demonstration; and the right and freedom to form and join trade unions, and to strike.' The Bill of Rights deals with these rights in two separate provisions: Article 17 'Freedom of Peaceful Assembly' and Article 18 'Freedom of Association'. Article 17 of the Bill of Rights is as follows: 'The

1308. *Ibid.*, 245–246. As the Privy Council explained: 'The aim is to prevent the suspect coming to hear of the investigation so that he will not take avoiding action by rearranging his affairs, destroying documents or even leaving the colony. This can only be achieved if disclosure is restricted in such manner as to see that the information does not reach him.'

1309. *Attorney General in and for the United Kingdom v South China Morning Post Ltd* [1988] 1 HKLR 143, (CA).

1310. In 1995, Hong Kong Government introduced a non-statutory Code of Access to Information to enable access to public information. The Code recognises the need for the community to be well informed about government services and the basis for government policies and decisions that affect individuals and the community as a whole, https://www.access.govhk/en/home/index.html.

right of peaceful assembly shall be recognized. No restrictions may be placed on the exercise of this right other than those imposed in conformity with the law and which are necessary in a democratic society in the interests of national security or public safety, public order (*ordre public*), the protection of public health or morals or the protection of the rights and freedoms of others.' Article 18 provides as follows:

(1) Everyone shall have the right to freedom of association with others, including the right to form and join trade unions for the protection of his interests.
(2) No restrictions may be placed on the exercise of this right other than those which are prescribed by law and which are necessary in a democratic society in the interests of national security or public safety, public order (ordre public), the protection of public health or morals or the protection of the rights and freedoms of others. This article shall not prevent the imposition of lawful restrictions on members of the armed forces and of the police in their exercise of this right.
(3) Nothing in this article authorizes legislative measures to be taken which would prejudice, or the law to be applied in such a manner as to prejudice, the guarantees provided for in the International Labour Organization Convention of 1948 concerning Freedom of Association and Protection of the Right to Organize as it applies to Hong Kong.

691. The Court of Final Appeal has emphasized the importance of the freedom of assembly,[1311] freedom association[1312] and the right to demonstrate.[1313] At the same time, courts have also recognized that these rights have to be reconciled with the larger public interest.[1314] For instance, in *Chee Fei Ming v Director of Food and Environmental Hygiene*, the Court of Appeal upheld the constitutionality of section 104A of the Public Health and Municipal Services Ordinance (Cap. 132) which provided that 'no bill or poster shall be displayed or affixed ... (b) on any Government land, except with the written permission of the Authority'. It was argued that a banner displayed in connection with a demonstration was not covered by this provision, and therefore it was unlawful to order the removal of a banner displayed by

1311. *Leung Kwok Hung v HKSAR* (2005) 8 HKCFAR 229, (CFA) [1].

1312. *See Blakeney-Williams v Cathay Pacific Airways Ltd* (2012) 15 HKCFAR 261, (CFA), [4], where Ma CJ said: 'The right to form and join trade unions is to be given a purposive and generous interpretation, in common with the approach of the courts in respect of all fundamental rights and liberties.'

1313. *Yeung May Wan v HKSAR* (2005) 8 HKCFAR 137, (CFA), [1].

1314. *See HKSAR v Chow Nok Hang* (2013) 16 HKCFAR 837, (CFA), [33], where Ribeiro PJ observed as follows: 'Demonstrators are therefore free to assemble and to convey views which may be found to be disagreeable, unpopular, distasteful or even offensive to others and which may be critical of persons in authority. Tolerance of such views and their expression is a hallmark of a pluralistic society. At the same time, it must be recognized that those freedoms are not absolute and demonstrators must ensure that their conduct does not go beyond the constitutional limits of those rights.' *See also T v Commissioner of Police* (2014) 17 HKCFAR 593, (CFA), where Ribeiro PJ said at [137]: '[the freedoms of expression and assembly] are of course of great importance, but they are not absolute and laws which impinge on them are valid if they pass the proportionality test which has often been applied in this jurisdiction'.

Falun Gong in a site where its members used to conduct 'static demonstration', such as a sit in. Rejecting the argument, the Court of Appeal held that 'Section 104A does not catch the use of banners or placards in a demonstration (whether mobile or static) which does not occupy the same spot with a degree of permanence and habitual regularity.' Lam V-P said: 'We agree with the Judge … that one of the legitimate objectives is the orderly, fair and prioritised allocation of public space for dissemination of ideas. Without some proper control in place, there would be chaotic scramble for the display of bill or poster. And there could also be chaotic scramble even in the context of the competing exercise of the right of demonstration by different political or social factions in our society.'[1315]

692. The Public Order Ordinance[1316] governs gatherings of people.[1317] The Commissioner of Police has to be notified of any such gathering in advance, unless they are exempted such as a meeting involving less than fifty persons.[1318] The number of people permitted to take part in gatherings where the Commissioner of Police is not notified may differ, depending on whether the gathering in question is a meeting or procession, and whether it takes place in public or private.[1319] He is given the power to prohibit gatherings or permit a gathering subject to conditions.[1320] If the affected person or organization is not satisfied with his decision, they may appeal to an Appeal Board.[1321] Failure to notify the Commissioner of Police when they have to is an offence of unauthorized assembly.[1322]

693. The above regulatory framework has not been generally welcomed in Hong Kong, and it has been argued that it is not compatible with the freedom of assembly.[1323] There have been quite a number of prosecutions in respect of demonstrations[1324] for various summary offences such as unauthorized assembly,[1325] unlawful

1315. *Chee Fei Ming v Director of Food and Environmental Hygiene* [2016] HKEC 1266, (CA), [45]. On the proper construction of s. 104A, *see* [32]–[47].
1316. The Public Order Ordinance (Cap. 245) of the Laws of Hong Kong.
1317. Section 7(2).
1318. Sections 7–8 and 13–13A.
1319. Sections 2, 7 and 13.
1320. Sections 9, 11, and 14–15.
1321. Sections 16 and 43–44.
1322. Section 17A.
1323. Roda Mushkat, 'Peaceful Assembly' in R. Wacks (ed.) *Human Rights in Hong Kong*, (Hong Kong: OUP, 1992).
1324. *Tse Chung v R* [1967] HKLR 452, (Appellate Jurisdiction), where the evidence only showed that the defendant was present at an unlawful assembly which was a protest against the police, the defendant opting not to give evidence. It was held on appeal that evidence to show that an assemblage of persons, whether it has a common object or any object at all, was engaged in offering violence to the police or indeed to members of the public is sufficient evidence to show that the assembly is an unlawful one. The Colony being in a disturbed state at the time of the offence the magistrate was entitled to take judicial notice of circumstances which were notorious. In *Chow Shui v R* [1979] HKLR 275, (HC), the appellants had been convicted of unlawful assembly arising out of an attempt to present a petition to the Governor. The genuine desire of the appellants to present a petition did not provide them with a reasonable excuse for taking part in the unlawful assembly. The conviction was upheld in the appeal court observing that the petition could have been equally well presented by one or two representatives, and a licence could have been sought in advance. In *R v To Kwan-hang and Tsoi Yiu-cheong* [1995] 1 HKCLR 251, (CA), it was held

assembly,[1326] disorderly behaviour,[1327] unauthorized collection of charitable funds,[1328] refusal to produce identity documents,[1329] and nuisance.[1330]

694. The right of assembly under the Bill of Rights does not cover assemblies that are not conducted peacefully.[1331] In *Yeung May Wan v HKSAR* the Court of Final Appeal dealt with charges brought in relation to a protest, one charge being creating an obstruction in a public place and held that the offence would be complete only if there was no lawful excuse for their behaviour. The Court observed that in determining the guilt or innocence of the defendants it has to give due weight to the right of expression and assembly recognized by Article 27 of the Basic Law. Bokhary PJ said:

> I think that the participants in a large or even massive assembly, procession or demonstration will often be able to say with justification that their point could not be nearly as effectively made by anything on a smaller scale. Subject to this, the most obviously relevant considerations are, I think, how substantial the interference is and how long it lasts. But other considerations can be relevant, too. These include, I think, whether the interference concerned had been recently preceded by another act or other acts of interference on another occasion or other occasions. What the public can reasonably be expected to tolerate

---

that Art. 17 of the Bill of Rights did not confer a right of assembly on those who conducted themselves in a disorderly, intimidating, insulting or provocative manner or a manner likely to lead to a breach of the peace. The right was to peaceful assembly. Section 18 of the Public Order Ordinance was held not to be inconsistent with the Bill of Rights. In *R v Fung Chi-wood* [1991] 1 HKLR 654, (HC), the defendants who had organized a protest against the proposed Basic Law were successfully prosecuted for unauthorized collection of funds and failure to produce their national identity cards. It was considered immaterial that the power to require production of a valid identity card might have been introduced to control illegal migration. *R v Li Wing-tat* [1991] 1 HKLR 731, (HC), concerned unauthorized use of loudhailers. The prosecution was held to be an abuse of process because the defendants had a legitimate expectation that the kind of breaches of law in question would not lead to prosecution, since the well-established practice had been simply to warn the offenders and not to prosecute. In *HKSAR v Sin Ka Ho* [2020] HKEC 854, (DC) the defendant was found guilty of participating in a massive riot outside the Legislative Council, while participating in a demonstration against the introduction of Fugitive Offenders and Mutual Legal Assistance in Criminal Matter Legislation (Amendment) Bill. The judge observed at [40]: 'The freedom of peaceful assembly enables members of the public to voice their criticisms, air grievances and seek redress on views they hold. However, the freedom of assembly is not absolute. Once a protester becomes involved in violence or the threat of violence, a breach of peace, then that protester crosses the line between constitutionally protected peaceful assembly and demonstration to an unlawful activity which is subject to legal sanctions. There is such a line to protect public order because society is prone to descend into anarchy if public order is not preserved.'

1325. Public Order Ordinance (Cap. 245) of the Laws of Hong Kong, s. 17A.
1326. Section 18.
1327. Section 17B.
1328. Section 4(17) of the Summary Offences Ordinance (Cap. 228) of the Laws of Hong Kong.
1329. Section 17C of the Immigration Ordinance (Cap. 115) of the Laws of Hong Kong.
1330. Section 4(29) of the Summary Offences Ordinance (now repealed).
1331. *See HKSAR v Wong Yuk Man* (2012) 15 HKCFAR 712, CFA where reference was made to *R v To Kwan-Hang* [1995] 1 HKCLR 251, (CA), and *Leung Kwok Hung v HKSAR* (2005) 8 HKCFAR 229, (CFA).

is a question of fact and degree. But when answering this question, a court must always remember that preservation of the freedom in full measure defines reasonableness and is not merely a factor in deciding what is reasonable.[1332]

695. In *Leung Kwok Hung v HKSAR*,[1333] the Court of Final Appeal pointed out that the freedom of peaceful assembly is a fundamental constitutional right, closely associated with the fundamental right of freedom of speech. The resolution of conflicts through open dialogue and debate is the essence of a democratic society, and a procession is a potent method of expression. Such fundamental right must be given a generous interpretation so as to give individuals its full measure, and restrictions on it must be narrowly interpreted. The burden is on the government to justify any restriction on freedom of assembly.[1334] *HKSAR v Fong Kwok Shan Christine*, where the defendants had been convicted of contravening the Administrative Instructions for Regulating Admittance and Conduct of Persons by displaying banners and shouting slogans in the public gallery while the Legislative Council was in session, it was held that the Administrative Instructions was not a disproportionate restriction on the freedom of expression: It was part of a statutory framework aimed at creating a secured and dignified environment in the Legislative Council complex conducive to the legislature carrying out its constitutional functions at its sittings without disruption or disturbance, while permitting members of the public to observe proceedings within the Chamber as an open legislative process.[1335] Properly construed in light of its context and purpose, the prohibitions were aimed at displays which entailed the risk of disorder in public galleries and which might disturb Legislative Council sittings and the rights of others observing the proceedings. While access to a government premises (the forecourt of the Central Government Offices which also served as an access to the Legislative Council premises) may be restricted to the public for meetings and demonstrations, it would be unjustifiable to restrict such access only to Sundays and public holidays, without reserving discretion to permit public access for such purposes when the intended use would not be expected to affect the normal working of the adjacent government departments.[1336]

1332. *Yeung May Wan v Hong Kong Special Administrative Region* (2005) 8 HKCFAR 137, (CFA), [144].

1333. *Leung Kwok Hung v HKSAR* (2005) 8 HKCFAR 229, (CFA).

1334. *Ibid.*, [1]–[2], [16]. *See also HKSAR v Chow Nok Hang* (2013) 16 HKCFAR 837, (CFA), [2], where Chan ACJ said: 'In construing the relevant statutory provisions which have the effect of restricting such right, the court must have regard to competing public interests, including the maintenance of public order and the rights and freedoms of others. The right balance has to be struck between the preservation of public order and the exercise of the individual's rights and freedoms and between the competing rights and freedoms of individuals or groups of individuals.' *See also HKSAR v Fong Kwok Shan Christine* (2017) 20 HKCFAR 425, (CFA).

1335. *HKSAR v Fong Kwok Shan Christine* (2017) 20 HKCFAR 425, (CFA).

1336. *Cheung Tak Wing v Director of Administration* [2018] 5 HKLRD 740, (CFI). Thomas Au J reminded at [71] that Ribeiro PJ in *Fong Kwok Shan Christine* (2017) 20 HKCFAR 425, (CFA), [42] and [44], emphasised that it is necessary to weigh up the manner, form and impact of each of the demonstrations at the sites concerned to decide whether a challenged restriction satisfies the proportionality test. This is so since the rights to freedom of expression and assembly extend to the manner in which the protestors wish to express their views and to the location where they wish to express and exchange their views.

696. The Societies Ordinance requires all societies that are established in Hong Kong to be registered by the Societies Officer, who may exempt a society or a branch from registration if he is satisfied that the society or the branch is established solely for religious, charitable, social or recreational purposes, or as a rural committee or a federation or other association of rural committees.[1337] Office-bearers may be criminally liable for failure to register their societies[1338] that are not exempted from the requirement of registration.[1339] The Societies Officer may disapprove the registration application, cancel the registration or prohibit the operation of a society.[1340] The Societies Officer may, after consultation with the Secretary for Security, cancel the registration or exemption from registration of a society or a branch: (a) if he reasonably believes that the cancellation is necessary in the interests of national security or public safety, public order, or the protection of the rights and freedoms of others; or (b) if the society or the branch is a political body that has a connection with a foreign political organization or a political organization of Taiwan.[1341] The Basic Law provides that:

> The Hong Kong Special Administrative Region shall enact laws … to prohibit political organizations or bodies of the Region from establishing ties with foreign political organizations or bodies.[1342]

697. The Societies Ordinance has been criticized on the ground that the term 'society' is ill defined in the Ordinance.[1343] The Societies Ordinance, which was designed to deal with triads or organized criminal groups, may stifle activities of societies that are set up for legitimate purposes.[1344]

XI. The Right to Participate in Public Life

698. According to the Bill of Rights:

> every permanent resident shall have the right and the opportunity, … without unreasonable restrictions to take part in the conduct of public affairs, directly or through freely chosen representatives; to vote and to be elected at genuine periodic elections which shall be by universal and equal suffrage and shall be held by secret ballot, guaranteeing the free expression of the will of the electors.[1345]

1337. The Societies Ordinance (Cap. 151) of the Laws of Hong Kong, ss 5 and 5A.
1338. Sections 5C and 5F.
1339. Section 5A(2).
1340. Sections 5A(3), 5D and 8.
1341. Sections 8 and 2.
1342. Hong Kong Basic Law, Art. 23.
1343. Roda Mushkat, 'Freedom of Association and Assembly', in Raymond Wacks (ed.) *Civil Liberties in Hong Kong* (Hong Kong: OUP, 1988), 172.
1344. *Ibid.*, 156.
1345. Hong Kong Bill of Rights, Art. 21.

The Basic Law has a similar clause.[1346]

699. There have been several successful judicial challenges of legislation which imposed unjustifiable restrictions on the right to participate in public life.[1347] In *Lau San Ching v Liu, Apollonia*,[1348] the returning officer had rejected the nomination paper of a candidate for the District Board election on the ground that he had not been ordinarily resident in Hong Kong in the preceding ten-year period, as required by the Electoral Provisions Ordinance (which was not adopted when Hong Kong became a Special Administrative Region in 1997). It was held that the ten-year requirement was inconsistent with Article 21 of the Bill of Rights. The High Court held that while there was a legitimate purpose in imposing a residential requirement, there was no rational basis for imposing a ten-year residential requirement, and that the requirement was disproportionate to the legitimate aim of the statute). In *Secretary for Justice v Chan Wah*,[1349] the Court of Final Appeal held that the requirement that only indigenous inhabitants could be candidates at the election of a rural village representative elections was unconstitutional. Li CJ observed at p. 474 that 'bearing in mind that the village representative by statute is to and in fact does represent the village as a whole (comprising both the indigenous and the non-indigenous villagers) and further has a role to play beyond the village level, the restriction on the ground of not being indigenous cannot be considered a reasonable restriction' on the right to participate in public life. The requirement that the returning officer must be satisfied that the Legislative Council election candidate has genuinely and truthfully pledged allegiance to the HKSAR at the time of submitting nomination papers has come up for discussion. It has been held that before the returning officer can decide whether the oath was genuine he had to afford an opportunity to the candidate address his concerns, and that his failure to do so resulted in invalidity of his decision.[1350] *Senior Non-expatriate Officers' Association v Secretary for the Civil Service*[1351] (on denial of the senior civil servants' right to participate in the elections of the selection committee for the formation of the first

---

1346. Hong Kong Basic Law, Art. 26.

1347. *Lau San Ching v Liu, Apollonia* (1995) 5 HKPLR 23, (HC) and *Secretary for Justice v Chan Wah* (2000) 3 HKCFAR 459, (CFA). *See also Lai Tak Shing v Secretary for Home Affairs* (2007) 10 HKCFAR 655, (CFA). *See also* the cases relating to the failure of Legislative Council members or persons nominated as contestants at Legislative Council elections to subscribe fully and correctly the oath of allegiance, discussed elsewhere in this work.

1348. (1995) 5 HKPLR 23, (HC).

1349. [2007] HKEC 1950, (CFA).

1350. *Chow Ting v Teng Yu Yan Anne (Returning Officer)* [2019] 4 HKLRD 459, (CA), affirmed by the Court of Final Appeal in *Au Nok Hin v Teng Yu Yan Anne* (2019) 22 HKCFAR 524, (CFA). *See also Lau Wing Hong v Chan Yuen Man Amy (Returning Officer) (No 2)* [2019] 5 HKLRD 1, (CFI); and *Lau Siu Lai v Kwok Wai Fun Franco (Returning Officer)* [2020] HKEC 931, (CFI). The requirement to give the candidate an adequate opportunity to present their case was held to have been satisfied in *Chan Ho Tin v Lo Ying Ki Alan* [2018] 2 HKLRD 7, (CFI). *See also Wong Tai Hoi v Au Nok Hin* [2018] 2 HKLRD 789, (CFI), where an elector brought an application for judicial review praying that the candidate who won a seat at the Legislative Council election was disqualified because he had not genuinely taken his oath of allegiance. The application was rejected on the technical ground that the proper procedure was to bring an election petition.

1351. *Senior Non-expatriate Officers' Association v Secretary for the Civil Service* (1997) 7 HKPLR 91, (HC).

government of Hong Kong) and *Chau Tsun Kiu v Secretary for Justice* (the right of candidates at Legislative Council elections to send letters to electors free of postage) are examples of unsuccessful challenges.[1352]

700. There has been much controversy surrounding the electoral arrangements in Hong Kong.[1353] In *Lee Miu Ling v Attorney General*, the use of functional constituencies in Legislative Council elections was unsuccessfully challenged.[1354] The argument that corporate voting in functional constituencies is unconstitutional has been rejected.[1355]

701. The Bill of Rights guarantees the right 'to have access, on general terms of equality, to public service in Hong Kong'.[1356] Expatriate civil servants unsuccessfully challenged the civil service localization programme of the Hong Kong Government on the ground that localization granted more rights to local officers and thereby discriminated against non-locals, although certain aspects of the scheme such as the prohibition of non-local officers on contract terms transferring to permanent positions were held to be in breach of the Bill of Rights: *Association of Expatriate Civil Servants of Hong Kong v Secretary for the Civil Service.*[1357] Since the handover, the new civil service reform package proposing a reduction of remuneration and fringe benefits has, again, provoked a constitutional crisis.[1358]

XII. The Right to Social Welfare

702. The Basic Law provides that 'Hong Kong residents shall have the right to social welfare in accordance with the law. The welfare benefits and retirement security of the labour force shall be protected by law.'[1359] However, the reality in Hong

1352. *Chau Tsun Kiu v Secretary for Justice* [2014] 5 HKLRD 414, (CFI).
1353. On the right to vote in Hong Kong, *see* generally Simon Young, 'The Meaning of the Right to Vote in Hong Kong', (1997) 42 *McGill Law Journal* 649. The arrangements for Legislative Council and Chief Executive elections are noted elsewhere in this monograph.
1354. *Lee Miu Ling v Attorney General* [1995] 5 HKLY 196, (CA). *See* Albert Chen, 'The Legal Foundation of the Legislative Council Election 1995' in H. Kuan, S. Lau. K Louie & T. Wong (eds) *The 1995 Legislative Council Elections in Hong Kong*, (Hong Kong: Hong Kong Institute of Asia-Pacific Studies, The Chinese University of Hong Kong, 1996); and Gladys Li, 'The Right to Vote and to Be Elected: "Through the Looking-Glass"' in George Edwards & Johannes Chan (eds) *Hong Kong's Bill of Rights: Two Years Before 1997* (Hong Kong: Faculty of Law, University of Hong Kong, 1995).
1355. The Court of Appeal upheld corporate voting particularly in the light of the development of the electoral system in Hong Kong: *Chan Yu Nam v Secretary for Justice* [2010] HKEC 1893, (CA).Stock V-P gave an excellent account of the development of the electoral system. Leave to appeal was refused by the Court of Final Appeal [2012] HKEC 94.
1356. Bill of Rights, Art. 21.
1357. *Association of Expatriate Civil Servants of Hong Kong v Secretary for the Civil Service* (1996) 6 HKPLR 333, (CA).
1358. Anton Cooray, 'Public Sector Reform in Hong Kong: Some Legal Aspects' (1999) 8 *Public Administration and Policy* 23.
1359. Hong Kong Basic Law, Art. 36.

Kong is that 'the [social security] system [is] a patchwork of laws and administrative practices; the benefits that it conferred were more in the nature of [grace] than right ... The right or benefit to housing is not ... provided for in legislation.'[1360] Article 145 of the Basic Law provides that on the basis of the previous welfare system, the Government of Hong Kong Special Administrative Region shall, on its own, formulate policies on the development and improvement of the welfare system in the light of economic conditions and social needs. In *Kong Yunming v Director of Social Welfare* a Mainland woman who arrived in Hong Kong to join her husband, who died the next day, was denied comprehensive social security assistance on the ground that she did not meet the residence requirement of seven years. At the time the Basic Law was promulgated, the residence requirement was only one year, which was increased to seven years in 2004. The Court of Final Appeal held that the one-year requirement was part of the previously existing law, protected by Article 36, continued to be operative under the Basic Law. Social welfare rights protected by Article 36 were subject to modification in accordance with Article 145, which did not preclude the elimination or reduction of particular welfare benefits if that proved necessary to develop, improve or maintain the sustainability of the welfare system as a whole. However, any restriction had to be rationally connected with the accomplishment of a legitimate social aim and the means employed proportionate. As the right to social welfare was not a fundamental right but a right which intrinsically involved the government setting rules determining eligibility and benefit levels, the residence requirement would only be held to be disproportionate if it was manifestly without reasonable foundation. The Court held that the seven-year rule did not satisfy the requirements of the proportionality analysis, rejecting the government's argument that the restriction was adopted to ensure the sustainability of the social security system. It refrained from determining whether the one-year residence requirement too was unconstitutional, in the absence of any argument in that behalf.[1361]

§4. LIMITATIONS ON HUMAN RIGHTS

703. Many rights that are enumerated in the Bill of Rights may be restricted so long as the restrictions are 'provided by law'[1362] or 'imposed in conformity with the law'[1363] 'and are necessary in a democratic society in the interests of national security or public safety, public order (*ordre public*), the protection of public health or morals or the protection of the rights and freedoms of others'.[1364] The Bill of Rights specifically states:

1360. Yash Ghai, *Hong Kong's New Constitutional Order: The Resumption of Chinese Sovereignty and the Basic Law*, (2nd edn, Hong Kong: Hong Kong University Press, 1999), 437–438 (footnotes omitted).
1361. *Kong Yunming v Director of Social Welfare* (2013) 16 HKCFAR 950, (CFA).
1362. Bill of Rights, Art. 16.
1363. *Ibid.*, Art. 17.
1364. *Ibid.*

> nothing in [the Ordinance] is to be interpreted as implying for the Government or any authority, group or person any right to engage in any activity or perform any act aimed at the destruction of any of the rights and freedoms recognized in the Bill of Rights or at their limitation to a greater extent that is provided for in the Bill.[1365]

Some rights enshrined in the Bill of Rights are not expressly subject to restrictions. Notwithstanding this, it has been said that they may still be limited. But such seemingly absolute rights may be 'subject only to such reasonable limits prescribed by law as can be demonstrably justified in a free and democratic society'.[1366]

1365. Bill of Rights, s. 2(4). *See* Yash Ghai, 'Derogations and Limitations in the Hong Kong Bill of Rights' in Johannes Chan & Yash Ghai (eds) *The Hong Kong Bill of Rights: A Comparative Approach*, ed. Johannes Chan & Yash Ghai (Hong Kong, Singapore and Malaysia: Butterworths Asia, 1993), 161–201, especially at 180–194.

1366. *R v Sin Yau-ming* [1992] 1 HKCLR 127, (CA).

Chapter 3. Constitutional Problems of Minorities (Protection of Minorities and Group Rights)

704. Hong Kong's population is predominantly Chinese. As of 2016, about 92% of the Hong Kong's population is ethnic Chinese. The Filipinos are the largest minority community (about 2.5%) and the Japanese are the smallest among the known ethnic groups (about 0.1%).[1367] A large section of the ethnic minority communities are female domestic helpers.[1368] In Hong Kong, there are close to 40,000 non-Chinese Muslims and 15,000 Hindus.[1369] In *Lau Wong Fat v Attorney General*,[1370] where a law that abolished the discriminatory customary law of succession to rural land was challenged, it was unsuccessfully argued that the Chinese indigenous inhabitants of the New Territories constituted an ethnic minority for the purposes of the Bill of Rights.

705. Minority communities are entitled to constitutional protection of their rights under the Hong Kong Bill of Rights Ordinance and the Basic Law. The Hong Kong Bill of Rights Ordinance provides that 'persons belonging to ethnic, religious or linguistic minorities shall not be denied the right, in community with the other members of their group, to enjoy their own culture, to profess and practise their own religion, or to use their own language'.[1371] The Basic Law provides that 'lawful traditional rights and interests of the indigenous inhabitants of the New Territories shall be protected by the Hong Kong Special Administrative Region'.[1372]

§1. Religious Freedom

706. Article 32 of the Basic Law provides that Hong Kong residents have freedom of conscience, freedom of religious belief, and freedom to preach and to conduct and participate in religious activities in public. In *Chu Woan Chyi v Director of Immigration*,[1373] the Court of First Instance decided that Falun gong movement was a religious movement, although the movement itself did not recognize it as a religion. Importantly, Hartmann J laid down criteria that were relevant to deciding

1367. From the website of the Census and Statistics Department, the Hong Kong Special Administrative Region Government: https://www.bycensus2016.govhk/en/bc-mt.html.
1368. Survey on Ethnic Minorities in Hong Kong Released', press release of the Hong Kong Special Administrative Region Government, 2 January 2001. Available at the following website of the Hong Kong Special Administrative Region Government: https://www.censtatd.govhk/press_release/pressReleaseDetail.jsp?pressRID=-2429.
1369. *Hong Kong 2000* (Hong Kong: Hong Kong Special Administrative Region Government, 2001), 382.
1370. *Lau Wong Fat v Attorney General* [1997] HKLRD 533, (CA).
1371. Bill of Rights, Art. 23.
1372. Hong Kong Basic Law, Art. 40.
1373. *Chu Woan Chyi v Director of Immigration* [2007] HKEC 553, (CFI).

what is a religion. In relation to the law of trusts, it has been held that ancestral worship prevalent among the Chinese cannot be funded under a charitable trust because the beneficiaries of ancestral worship are the members of the family rather than the general public.[1374]

707. Article 141 of the Basic Law provides that religious organizations have the right, in accordance with law, to acquire, use, dispose of, and inherit property, and the right to receive financial assistance. Religious organizations may, according to their previous practice, continue to run seminaries and other schools, hospitals, and welfare institutions and to provide social services. It also provides that religious organizations and believers in the Region may also maintain and develop their relations with religious organizations and believers elsewhere. It was held in *Catholic Diocese of Hong Kong v Secretary for Justice*[1375] that the fact that religious organizations are permitted to operate according to the 'previous practice' – namely the practice before 1997 – did not mean that the government was barred from making gradual changes to the existing educational, social and welfare policies as long as those policies were formulated in accordance with the Basic Law.

§2. Family Law

708. Matrimonial law is an area where there might arguably be some infringement of minority rights. According to section 40 of the Marriage Ordinance, a marriage means 'a voluntary union for life of one man and one woman to the exclusion of others'. Adopting a remedial interpretation, the Court of Final Appeal held in *W v Registrar of Marriages,* that a post-operative male-to-female transsexual whose gender has been certified by an appropriate medical authority to have changed as a result of sex reassignment surgery falls within the meaning of woman for the purpose of this provision, thereby avoiding the need to declare section 40 invalid.[1376] Marriages can be celebrated in any of the licensed places of worship.[1377] Accordingly, as long as the administrative procedures are complied with, persons belonging to any religious community may celebrate their marriage in their place of religious worship.

1374. Anton Cooray, 'Customary Rights of the New Territories Inhabitants, Equality of Sexes and the Basic Law', paper presented at the University of Hong Kong, Hong Kong Bill of Rights: The Final Year Seminar, 8 June 1996, referring to the then Legislator Christine Loh's argument for the abolition of the custom. *See also* Anton Cooray, 'The Non-recognition of Chinese Ancestral Worship Trusts as Charitable Trusts in Hong Kong: With Some South Asian Comparisons', (2002) 8:1 *Third Sector Review* 153–172.

1375. *Catholic Diocese of Hong Kong v Secretary for Justice* [2007] 4 HKLRD 483, (CFI). Affirmed by the Court of Appeal [2010] HKEC 163, (CA), and Court of Final Appeal (2011) 14 HKCFAR 754, (CFA).

1376. *W v Registrar of Marriages* (2013) 16 HKCFAR 112, (CFA).

1377. Marriage Ordinance (Cap. 181), s. 19. Marriages may be celebrated by civil celebrants or in places of worship.

709. Hong Kong law recognizes monogamous marriages only.[1378] Any person who, being married, marries any other person during the life of the former husband or wife commits bigamy.[1379] The second marriage will be void. Hence, a Muslim cannot marry more than one wife in Hong Kong, although polygamous Muslim law marriages are recognized in some other jurisdictions. Under the common law, a domestic court will determine the validity of a marriage in accordance with the law of the country where the parties have their domicile at the time of their marriage.[1380]

710. Minorities may face other personal status problems. For instance, Hong Kong courts cannot entertain a petition for divorce, in respect of a polygamous marriage.[1381] However, Hong Kong courts do recognize a divorce obtained in the country where the parties are domiciled, as long as the divorce is lawful in that country.[1382]

711. An important aspect of protecting the rights of the family is the protection that the law accords to children. There are three directly relevant Hong Kong statutes: Protection of Children and Juveniles Ordinance (Cap. 213); Prevention of Child Pornography (Ord. 579) and Child Abduction and Custody (Cap. 512). The Protection of Children and Juveniles Ordinance (Cap. 213) makes provision for guardianship, custody and control of children and juveniles in need of care and protection (section 34). It also provides that any person who unlawfully takes or causes to be taken any child or juvenile out of the possession and against the will of the father or mother or of any other person having the lawful care or charge of such child or juvenile shall be guilty of an offence punishable on conviction on indictment by imprisonment for two years (section 26). The Prevention of Child Pornography Ordinance (Cap. 579) is intended to prohibit the production, possession and publication of child pornography; to prohibit the use, procurement or offer of persons under the age of 18 for making pornography or for live pornographic performances; and to extend the application of certain sexual offence provisions of that Ordinance to acts committed against children outside Hong Kong. The Child Abduction and Custody Ordinance (No. 512) incorporates into the law of Hong Kong provisions of the Convention on Civil Aspects of International Child Abduction which was signed at the Hague on 25 October 1980. The Court of First Instance has the jurisdiction to hear and determine an application under the Convention and importantly 'make a declaration that the removal of a child from Hong Kong, or the retention of the child outside Hong Kong, was wrongful within the meaning of Article 3 of the Convention'.

1378. Marriage Reform Ordinance (Cap. 178), s. 4.
1379. Offences Against the Person Ordinance (Cap. 212), s. 45.
1380. *Ali v Ali* [1966] 1 All ER 664, (DC) and *Hussain v Hussain* [1982] 3 All ER 369, (CA).
1381. Matrimonial Causes Ordinance (Cap. 179), s. 9.
1382. *Ibid.*, s. 59.

§3. Racial Discrimination

712. Hong Kong is a party to the International Covenant on the Elimination of All Forms of Racial Discrimination. In 1997, the Hong Kong Government conducted a study to see whether there was evidence of racial discrimination in Hong Kong, by examining the position of the non-Chinese people in areas such as education, employment, health and social welfare, and law and order. The study concluded that in the situations where there was differential treatment of Chinese and non-Chinese, the problem was basically caused by reasons other than racial discrimination. Moreover, it was found that there was no serious tension between racial groups in Hong Kong.[1383] In 2004, the Hong Kong Government issued another consultation paper 'Legislating against Racial Discrimination: A Consultation Paper'. In pursuance of this Hong Kong passed a Race Discrimination Ordinance (Cap. 602) in July 2008, which came into effect on 10 July 2009, to protect people against discrimination, harassment and vilification on the ground of their race, particularly in the areas of employment, education and social interaction.[1384] The Ordinance applies not only to the government but also to private individuals and groups or organizations. The Race Discrimination Ordinance states that where a person (discriminator) discriminates against another person (relevant person) if: (a) on the ground of the race of the targeted person, the discriminator treats the relevant person less favourably than the discriminator treats or would treat other persons; or (b) the discriminator applies a requirement or condition to the relevant person which the discriminator applies or would apply equally to persons not of the relevant person's racial group, but the number of persons who can comply with such condition is considerably smaller in that racial group, and the imposition of the condition or requirement is to the detriment of the person who cannot comply with it. Such a generally applicable condition or requirement is justifiable if it serves a legitimate objective and bears a rational and proportionate connection to the objective.[1385] The Ordinance contains detailed provisions in relation to discrimination such as discrimination and harassment in employment field (Part 3), discrimination in other fields (Part 4) and other unlawful acts (Part 5) such as discriminatory practices and advertisements, and vilification. *Re German Swiss International School Association Ltd*[1386] is a recent example where certain articles of association of a company were held to contravene the Ordinance.

1383. Home Affairs Branch of the Government Secretariat, *Equal Opportunities: A Study of Discrimination on the Ground of Race: A Consultation Paper* (Hong Kong: Hong Kong Government, 1997).

1384. Race Discrimination Ordinance (Cap. 602) of the Laws of Hong Kong. *See* Hong Kong's Third Report in the 'Fourteenth to Seventeenth Reports of the People's Republic of China under the International Convention on the Elimination of All Forms of Racial Discrimination, Part Two: Hong Kong Special Administrative Region' (2018). https://www.legco.govhk/yr17-18/english/panels/ca/papers/ca20180716-rpt20170406-e.pdf#:~:text=This%20report%20%28the%20Report%29%20is%20the%20third%20report,Racial%20Discrimination%20%28the%20Convention%29%2C%20as%20part%20of%20the.

1385. Section 4 of the Ordinance, slightly paraphrased. *See also* s. 5 (discriminating against a person on the ground of race of an associate of such person), s. 6 (discriminating against a person in order to victimise him), and s. 7 (racial harassment).

1386. [2020] HKEC 1616, (CFI).

§4. NATIONALITY LAW

713. Under the British administration, any person who had the right of permanent residence (equivalent to the current 'right of abode') in Hong Kong was entitled to a BNO Passport. Under the Nationality Law of China, which has been extended to Hong Kong, ethnic Chinese are entitled to Chinese nationality, meaning Chinese citizenship. In addition, it is possible for a person who is not of Chinese descent to obtain Chinese nationality by naturalization and obtain a Hong Kong passport.[1387] This area of law has already been discussed above in Part IV Citizenship and Administration of Justice, Chapter 1. 'Rules Concerning Nationality and the Relevance of Nationality'.

1387. *See Azan Aziz Marwah v Director of Immigration* [2008] HKEC 2087, (CFI).

Chapter 4. Judicial Control of Administrative Action

§1. Introduction

714. The doctrine of separation of powers recognizes a tripartite constitutional arrangement whereby the legislature makes law, the executive implements the law and the judiciary interprets the law and administers justice. In this scheme of things, the executive branch of the government must exercise its powers and functions within the parameters set out in the law – be it the Basic Law, legislation or the common law. Where an administrative agency acts beyond its power (by acting without authority, by exceeding its powers or by failing to confirm to the lawful procedure for the exercise of its powers) or in some other manner acts unlawfully (such as by exercising its discretionary powers arbitrarily), it is answerable to the ordinary courts of law. Through the exercise of their supervisory jurisdiction, courts act as an overseer of the administration and a defender of citizen's rights.[1388]

715. Judicial review of administrative action has its roots in the supervisory jurisdiction that the highest court of original jurisdiction in England – namely the High Court – exercised over inferior courts to ensure that they acted according to law,[1389] a jurisdiction which was later extended to cover administrative agencies. The supervisory jurisdiction of the High Court of England is not of legislative but of common law origin. The common law of judicial review has been supplemented by legislation or rules of courts.[1390] In Hong Kong, the Court of First Instance – the equivalent of the High Court of England – exercises supervisory jurisdiction over the administration. The Court of Appeal and the Court of Final Appeal participate in administrative law litigation in their capacity as appellate courts.

716. Administrative law and constitutional law constitute public law. Administrative law is the law relating to the control of government action and 'the primary purpose of administrative law, therefore, is to keep the powers of government within their legal bounds, so as to protect the citizen against their abuse'.[1391] 'Judicial review … provides the means by which judicial control of administrative action is

1388. *See* O. Hood Phillips & P. Jackson, *O. Hood Phillip's Constitutional and Administrative Law* (8th edn, London: Sweet & Maxwell Ltd, 2001), 23–29.
1389. This did not mean that inferior courts had no jurisdiction to determine questions of law: What the supervisory jurisdiction meant was that the High Court was able to review decisions made by inferior courts which were incorrect in law. *See In re Racal Communications Ltd* [1981] AC 374, (HL), explaining *Anisminic Ltd v Foreign Compensation Commission* [1969] 2 AC 147, (HL).
1390. Generally on administrative law, *see* H.W.R. Wade & C.F. Forsyth, *Administrative Law* (11th edn, Oxford University Press, 2014).
1391. *Ibid.*, p. 4.

exercised. The subject matter of every judicial review is a decision made by some person (or body of persons) whom I call the "decision-maker" or else a refusal by him to make a decision.'[1392]

717. Principles of judicial review of administrative action as developed in England are closely adhered to by Hong Kong Courts. While greater emphasis is placed on English case law, Hong Kong courts have not been slow to refer to jurisprudence developing in other common law jurisdictions. The exercise of judicial review is regulated by legislation and subsidiary legislation, namely the High Court Ordinance[1393] and the Rules of High Court.[1394]

718. Judicial review of administrative action is traditionally based on the idea of ultra vires, namely that an administrative body must act *intra vires* (within its authority) and that if it acts ultra vires (outside or in excess of its authority) such acts are unlawful. Ultra vires may be substantive or procedural. Substantive ultra vires occurs when an administrative decision is made 'outside the range of power conferred on' the administration. Procedural ultra vires occurs where an administrative decision is made in breach of 'a prescribed procedure'.[1395]

719. Administrative decisions illustrative of substantive ultra vires may be grouped under two headings: (1) decisions that are made outside the powers conferred on the administration and (2) decisions that are an abuse of power. The latter heading encompasses those administrative decisions: (a) made for an improper purpose; (b) made after taking irrelevant considerations into account or not taking relevant considerations into account; (c) made in bad faith; and (d) made after fettering discretionary power. Procedural ultra vires refers mainly to administrative decisions taken in breach of what are known as principles of natural justice.[1396]

720. In *Council of Civil Service Unions v Minister for the Civil Service*,[1397] Lord Diplock reformulated the traditional grounds of judicial review. He said:

> one can conveniently classify under three heads the grounds on which administrative action is subject to control by judicial review. The first ground I would

1392. *Council of Civil Service Unions v Minister for the Civil Service*, [1985] 1 AC 374, (HL) 408, per Lord Diplock. We saw above in Part IV, Ch. 2, §2 Interpretation of Human Rights, that judicial review may be appropriate in certain circumstances even when no administrative decision affecting the applicant has yet been made.

1393. High Court Ordinance (Cap. 4) of the Laws of Hong Kong, ss 12(2)(a), 21I, 21J, 21K, 22A and 25.

1394. Order 53 'Rules of High Court: Applications for Judicial Review'. On judicial review procedure, *see* Richard Gordon & Johnny Mok, *Judicial Review in Hong Kong* (2nd edn, Hong Kong: LexisNexis, 2014).

1395. O. Hood Phillips & P. Jackson, *O. Hood Phillip's Constitutional and Administrative Law*, (8th edn, London: Sweet & Maxwell Ltd, 2001), 699. H.W.R. Wade & C.F. Forsyth, *Administrative Law* (11th edn, Oxford University Press, 2014), 27–28.

1396. O. Hood Phillips & P. Jackson, *O. Hood Phillip's Constitutional and Administrative Law* (8th edn, London: Sweet & Maxwell Ltd, 2001), 699–713.

1397. *Council of Civil Service Unions v Minister for the Civil Service* [1985] AC 374, (HL).

> call 'illegality', the second 'irrationality' and the third 'procedural impropriety'. That is not to say that further development on a case by case basis may not in course of time add further grounds.

Lord Diplock explained the three grounds as follows:

> (i) By 'illegality' as a ground for judicial review I mean that the decision-maker must understand correctly the law that regulates his decision-making power and must give effect to it.
> (ii) By 'irrationality' I mean what can by now be succinctly referred to as 'Wednesbury unreasonableness'. It applies to a decision which is so outrageous in its defiance of logic or of accepted moral standards that no sensible person who had applied his mind to the question to be decided could have arrived at it.
> (iii) I have described the third head as 'procedural impropriety' rather than failure to observe basic rules of natural justice or failure to act with procedural fairness towards the person who will be affected by the decision. This is because susceptibility to judicial review under this head covers also failure by an administrative tribunal to observe procedural rules that are expressly laid down in the legislative instrument by which its jurisdiction is conferred, even where such failure does not involve any denial of natural justice.[1398]

721. This threefold classification has been referred to and followed in Hong Kong, just as in common law jurisdictions generally.[1399] It must be noted, as Lord Diplock himself admitted in *Civil Service Union*, that the three grounds are not exclusive and there may be cases where courts may have to take a broader view of grounds of attack.[1400]

722. There is a more recent view that the true basis of judicial review is the need to ensure good governance and administration.[1401] Perhaps built on this is the judicial view that, particularly in relation to situations where fundamental rights are involved, rule of law provides guidance to developing judicial review. In *Alconbury case* Lord Hoffmann, while recognizing the centrality of the doctrine of ultra vires, said: 'When ministers or officials make decisions affecting the rights of individuals, they must do so in accordance with the law. The legality of what they do must be

1398. *Ibid.*, 410–411.
1399. Most recently by the Court of Final Appeal in *HLB Hodgson Impey Cheng v Hong Kong Institute of Certified Public Accountants* (2013) 16 HKCFAR 460, (CFA), [3].
1400. *See*, e.g., Lord Donaldson MR in *R v Panel on Takeovers and Mergers, ex p Guinness* [1990] 1 QB 146, (CA) at 160 where he observed: 'In the context of the present appeal he might have considered an innominate ground formed of an amalgam of his own grounds with perhaps added elements, reflecting the unique nature of the panel, its powers and duties and the environment in which it operates … .'
1401. *See* Dawn Oliver, 'Is the Ultra Vires Rule of the Basis of Judicial Review?' (1987) *Public Law* 543.

subject to review by independent and impartial tribunals. … The principles of judicial review give effect to the rule of law. They ensure that administrative decisions will be taken rationally, in accordance with a fair procedure and *within the powers conferred by Parliament.*'[1402] In *C v Director of Immigration & United Nations High Commissioner for Refugees (Intervener)* Mason NPJ explained how the rule of law as the basis of judicial review could extend the boundaries of judicial review: said that '[while ultra vires doctrine retains its utility] it is now accepted that the foundation of judicial review is the rule of law. The rule of law as a foundation has the advantage that it extends judicial review to the exercise of non-statutory powers, including prerogative and common law powers, and it is capable of extending to administrative powers of non-government agencies, these being powers the exercise of which would not necessarily have attracted judicial review on the statutory ultra vires theory.'[1403] Courts invoke the rule of law not as a replacement for the doctrine of ultra vires, but as a means of enhancing what the courts of law could do to ensure that administration respects the rule of law. The invocation of the rule of law is indeed not novel. It is a well-established rule of statutory interpretation that 'Unless there is the clearest provision to the contrary, Parliament must be presumed not to legislate contrary to the rule of law. And the rule of law enforces minimum standards of fairness, both substantive and procedural.'[1404] In Hong Kong, where the legislature is bound by the Basic Law, any legislative provision that is expressly or impliedly inconsistent with the paramount Constitution is unconstitutional and of no legal effect.[1405]

723. The introduction of the Bill of Rights in 1991 as well as the incorporation of fundamental rights in the Basic Law has provided an important impetus to judicial review of administrative action. Where an administrative body has complied with the strict requirements of a law, but the law is inconsistent with the constitutional fundamentals, such action is invalid as being unconstitutional.[1406] The number of applications for leave for judicial review is on the ascent but not many applications have been successful. The number of applications heard and the number of successful applications in the recent years are as follows: 103 and 51 in 2011, 161 and 72 in 2012, 182 and 67 in 2013, 168 and 84 in 2014, 259 and 67 in 2015, 228 and 26 in 2016 and 1,146 and 16 in 2017.[1407]

1402. *R (Alconbury Developments Ltd) v Secretary of State for the Environment, Transport and the Regions* [2003] 2 AC 295, (HL), 73 (emphasis added).
1403. *C v Director of Immigration & United Nations High Commissioner for Refugees (Intervener)* (2013) 16 HKCFAR 280, (CFA), [77].
1404. *R v Secretary of State for the Home Department ex p Pierson* [1998] AC 539, (HL), 591, Lord Steyn.
1405. 'The difficulty about [the UK doctrine of sovereignty of Parliament], as experience in many countries has shown, is that certain fundamental rights need to be protected against being overridden by the majority. No one has yet thought of a better form of protection than by entrenching them in a written constitution enforced by independent judges.' *Matadeen v Pointu* [1998] 1 AC 98, (PC), 109–110, Lord Hoffman.
1406. *See QT v Director of Immigration* (2018) 21 HKCFAR 324, (CFA), *Leung Chun Kwong v Secretary for Justice* (2019) 22 HKCFAR 127, (CFA).
1407. Information provided by the Hong Kong Government. http://gia.info.govhk/general/201802/28/P2018022800345_278993_1_1519793382371.pdf.

724. The jurisdiction of the ordinary courts of law over the administration must be viewed in the context of administrative tribunals that have been set up to settle disputes between administrative agencies and citizens, or disputes arising in a profession, such as the Town Planning Appeal Board (Town Planning Ordinance (Cap. 131)), Building Appeal Tribunal (Buildings Ordinance (Cap. 123), Part 6), Immigration Appeal Tribunal (the Immigration Ordinance (Cap. 115), section 2AD), Telecommunications Appeal Board (Telecommunications Ordinance (Cap. 106)) and the Market Misconduct Tribunal (Securities and Futures Ordinance (Cap. 571), Part XIII). A particularly important tribunal is the Administrative Appeals Board, which deals with appeals against decisions taken by certain specified administrative agencies, such as licensing decisions made under the Employment Ordinance (Cap. 57), the Dangerous Goods Ordinance (Cap. 295), the Wild Animals Protection Ordinance (Cap. 170) or the Marine Fish Culture Ordinance (Cap. 353). The members of the Administrative Appeals Board must be persons who are qualified for appointment as District judges.[1408] Decisions of administrative tribunals are subject to judicial review.[1409]

725. Administrative tribunals perform an important function in settling disputes in an efficient and cost-effective way, thereby reducing the workload of the courts. They are, however, not courts of law which exercise the judicial power of the Region, as envisaged in Article 80 of the Basic Law. As Justice Lam explained in *Lee Yee Shing Jacky v Inland Revenue Board of Review:* 'the mere resemblance of a process to the judicial process to ensure fairness cannot be the acid test for deciding whether the decision-maker was exercising the judicial power of the state. Ultimately, one has to examine the nature, function and character of the decision in question in order to determine whether it involves the exercise of the judicial power of the state which by law reserves exclusively for the judiciary.'[1410]

1408. The Administrative Appeals Board Ordinance (Cap. 442), s. 6.

1409. *See*, for instance, *Town Planning Board v Town Planning Appeal Board* [2015] HKEC 1151, (CA), *Sky Ace Enterprises Ltd v Appeal Tribunal (Buildings)* [2016] HKEC 1318, (CA), *Li Wai Hung Cesario v Administrative Appeals Board* [2015] HKEC 2080, (CFI), and *Hong Kong Telecommunications (HKT) Ltd v Communications Authority* [2015] HKEC 1590, (CA).

1410. *Lee Yee Shing Jacky v Inland Revenue Board of Review* [2011] HKEC 261, (CFI), [68]. The Board of Inland Revenue Board was held to be an administrative and a judicial, body, and Lam J said at [79]: 'if the primary decision is an administrative one, the constitutional right of access to the courts manifests itself in the form of the exercise by the court of its supervisory jurisdiction through judicial review. It is then for the court to decide on the facts and circumstances in each case the extent to which the court could intervene (including intervention on the basis of errors of material facts).' The decision of the Court of First Instance was affirmed by the Court of Appeal: [2012] 2 HKLRD 981, (CA). *See Stock Exchange of Hong Kong Ltd v New World Development Co Ltd* (2006) 9 HKCFAR 234, (CFA), [46], [62] and [63], Where it was held that when Art. 35 of the Basic Law referred to 'the courts' it meant the judiciary and nothing else. Art. 35 applied to courts of law, that is, the courts entrusted with the exercise of independent judicial power in the HKSAR. The Disciplinary Committee of the Stock Exchange was not a court of law. *See also Luk Ka Cheung v Market Misconduct Tribunal* [2009] 1 HKLRD 114, (CFI) where it was held that the Market Misconduct Tribunal did not exercise judicial power: 'It does not oust the jurisdiction of the criminal courts in Hong Kong, nor does it usurp their function. It is established to perform a regulatory and protective role in Hong Kong's financial markets. It is there to ensure that those

726. An important development in ensuring administrative justice is the introduction of the Ombudsman. The Ombudsman has the power to investigate into complaints of maladministration. The Ombudsman Ordinance also enables the Ombudsman to conduct an investigation of his own motion, called direct investigations, for instance, when he receives anonymous complaints or when a matter of unfairness in government administration becomes common knowledge.[1411] The Ombudsman has no powers of enforcement but may order *ex gratia* payments against public authorities and make non-binding recommendations to improve public administration. His recommendations are generally heeded to by public authorities.[1412]

§2. Administrative Agencies Are Subject to Judicial Review

727. Judicial review of administrative action is concerned with the actions of the administration. In a strict sense, administration refers to the constitutive parts of the government such as ministers of government and government departments. However, in view of the developments which have led to the creation of many non-governmental bodies to perform functions which were previously performed by the government, judicial review has been extended to cover such bodies too. It is common to class any agencies that are amenable to judicial review as public authorities or public bodies. However, in this section we categorize the agencies which are amenable to judicial review as (1) public bodies; and (2) bodies analogous to public bodies, in view of the restrictive interpretation of 'public body' in Interpretation and General Clauses Ordinance (Cap. 1), as meaning the government and its constitutive parts. This will also overcome any difficulty in categorizing self-regulatory bodies created by contract rather than by legislation which have been held to be amenable to judicial review.

I. Public Bodies

728. The main focus of judicial review is on the government, be they the Central Government or local government authorities. According to the Interpretation

engaged in market misconduct do not profit from their wrongs. In a fairly general sense, it performs a function that protects and benefits the interests of society as a whole. But it does not determine criminal guilt nor impose penal sanction. Certainly, it wields extensive powers and indeed it must act judicially. But one thing it does not do is to exercise the judicial power of the HKSAR' (at p. 142).

1411. *See* generally, Anton Cooray, 'Ombudsman in Asia: A Case-Study of Hong Kong and Sri Lanka' in Roy Gregory & Philip Giddings (eds) *Righting Wrongs: The Ombudsman in Six Continents* (Netherlands: IOS Press, 2000) 75–91 and 'Hong Kong's Ombudsman: The First Decade', (1999) 3 *The International Ombudsman Year Book* 71.

1412. Anton Cooray, 'Some Reflections on the Legislative Context of the Hong Kong Ombudsman', (2009) 17:1 *Asia Pacific Law Review* 53–72.

and General Clauses Ordinance (Cap. 1) 'public body' includes the Executive Council, the Legislative Council, any District Council, any department of the government and any undertaking by or of the government. Any of these public bodies are amenable to judicial review. Even acts of the Chief Executive in Council may be reviewed by the courts: All decisions of the Chief Executive (whether in the Executive Council or not) other than 'acts of state such as defence and foreign affairs',[1413] are subject to judicial review: *see*, for example, *Hong Kong Television Network Ltd v Chief Executive in Council*[1414] (refusal to grant a television programme service licence), *Yau Ka Po v Chief Executive in Council*[1415] (decision to approve a draft outline zoning plan) and *Lister Assets Ltd v Chief Executive in Council*[1416] (decision to approve a railway scheme). Similarly, the Secretary for Justice is not above the law. However, except where abuse of process occurs, his prosecutorial decisions are not amenable to judicial review.[1417]

729. As seen in the chapter on 'District Administration', there is only one local government authority: the District Council, which was formerly known as the District Board. Until 2000, there were two other local government authorities: the Urban Council and the Regional Council. The Urban Council and the Regional Council exercised administrative powers[1418] and were subject to judicial review.[1419]

730. Hong Kong being an integral part of China, the Central People's Government may exercise administrative powers over Hong Kong. It is highly controversial whether the decisions of the Central Chinese Government are subject to the

1413. Hong Kong Basic Law, Art. 19 of the Basic Law.

1414. *Hong Kong Television Network Ltd v Chief Executive in Council* [2016] 2 HKLRD 1005, (CA).

1415. *Yau Ka Po v Chief Executive in Council* [2016] HKEC 239, (CFI).

1416. *Lister Assets Ltd v Chief Executive in Council* [2012] HKEC 1043, (CFI), affirmed by the Court of Appeal [2013] HKEC 605.

1417. *See RV v Director of Immigration* [2008] 4 HKLRD 529, (CFI), where it was held that Art. 63 of the Basic Law, which provides '[t]he Department of Justice ... shall control criminal prosecutions, free from any interference', enshrined the Secretary for Justice's independence to control criminal proceedings as he thought best and in the exercise of that power, the Secretary for Justice was free of both political interference and 'judicial encroachment' (following *Re C (Bankrupt)* [2006] 4 HKC 582, (CA)) but that this was a power that had to be exercised within constitutional limits. On a true construction of the Basic Law, the courts had jurisdiction to judicially review the Secretary for Justice's power to control criminal prosecutions and to determine whether he had or had not acted within the limits of his constitutional power. Hartmann J went on to observe that the Secretary for Justice's prosecutorial independence was a linchpin of the rule of law. Only in truly exceptional circumstances could the court hold that the Secretary for Justice had acted outside of his very broad constitutional powers. Such very limited cases might include where the Secretary for Justice acted on political instruction, in bad faith or fettered his discretion by a rigid policy. In *D v Director of Public Prosecutions* [2015] 4 HKLRD 62, (CFI), the Court of First Instance held that the Director of Prosecutions' decision not to prosecute a person for indecently assaulting his domestic helper was amenable to judicial review. Granting leave to pursue a judicial review application, the Court held that it was reasonably arguable whether the decisions came within exceptional circumstances, such as dishonesty and bad faith, or had exceeded the constitutional limits. *See also Wong Yuk Kwan v Secretary for Justice* [2016] HKEC 1392, (CFI).

1418. P. Wesley-Smith, *Constitutional and Administrative Law*, (2nd edn, Hong Kong: Longman Asia Ltd, 1994), 131–134.

1419. *See*, e.g., *Ng Enterprises Ltd v Urban Council* [1997] AC 168, (PC).

supervisory jurisdiction of the Hong Kong courts.[1420] In *Ng Ka Ling & Ng Tan v Director of Immigration,*[1421] Andrew Li CJ ruled that the Hong Kong Special Administrative Region courts were competent to challenge any administrative acts of the Sovereign, other than acts of state, in accordance with the provisions of the Basic Law.[1422]

II. Bodies Analogous to Public Bodies

731. An important feature of the British system of government is the creation of administrative agencies to support the work of government departments. This practice has been followed in Hong Kong too. Unlike government departments, such agencies may not be directly accountable to the Legislative Council, but the investiture of pubic duties in them makes them subject to judicial review.[1423] While it is easy to state such a broad principle, in practice, it is not easy to determine whether a given body of persons is or is not a public body for the purpose of judicial review jurisdiction.

732. Where a government department or public body is privatized or partially privatized (e.g., by listing their shares in the stock market), it is not clear whether it will be still amenable to judicial control.[1424] Such is the case of the Mass Transit Railway Corporation originally established in 1975 as a statutory corporation by the Mass Transit Railway Corporation Ordinance (Cap. 270).[1425] Since 2000, it has been a public limited company incorporated under the Companies Ordinance, and not a public body.[1426]

733. Statutory authorities, meaning bodies created by statute, are generally regarded as being amenable to judicial review.[1427] Examples are the Hong Kong Stock Exchange, the Town Planning Board and the Hong Kong Housing Authority. In *Re Applications by Chow Chin-wo and Others for Judicial Review*, the court

1420. *See* generally Lin Feng, 'The Constitutional Crisis in Hong Kong: Is it Over?' (2000) 9:2 *Pacific Rim Law & Policy Journal* 281, for the different views of the Chinese Government and the Hong Kong Special Administrative Region courts.

1421. *Ng Ka Ling v Director of Immigration* (1999) 2 HKCFAR 4, (CFA).

1422. *Ibid.*, 26. For an analysis of the approach of the Court of Final Appeal in this case, *see* Johannes Chan et al. (eds), *Hong Kong's Constitutional Debate: Conflict over Interpretation* (Hong Kong: Hong Kong University Press, 2000) and Bing Ling, 'Can Hong Kong Courts Review and Nullify Acts of the National People's Congress?' (1999) 29 *Hong Kong Law Journal* 8.

1423. H.W.R. Wade & C.F. Forsyth, *Administrative Law*, (11th edn, Oxford: Oxford University Press, 2014), Ch. 5.

1424. Lord Woolf, 'The Importance of the Principles of Judicial Review', in *Law Lectures for Practitioners* 1996 (Hong Kong: Hong Kong Law Journal Ltd, 1996), 69–71.

1425. Cap. 270, repealed by Mass Transit Railway Corporation Ordinance No 13 of 2000 (Cap. 556).

1426. Mass Transit Railway Corporation Ordinance (Cap. 556), s. 60.

1427. *See Secretary for Justice v Commission of Inquiry Re Hong Kong Institute of Education* [2009] HKEC 411, (CFI), where a commission of inquiry appointed under statutory authority was held to be amenable to judicial review.

assumed that the Insider Dealing Tribunal was amenable to judicial review.[1428] The Hong Kong Arts Development Council has been held to be amenable to judicial review.[1429] Universities, which are not part of the government but perform an important public function, are amenable to judicial review (*see Leung Chak Sang v Lingnan University*).[1430] While a statutory body is generally amenable to judicial review, not all of its decisions are subject to judicial review. Only decisions which have a strong public element are amenable to judicial review, thus excluding decisions of a private commercial nature.[1431]

734. Where a government department contracts out the performance of its public functions to a private entity, it is contrary to the principle for the citizen's protection to be reduced through such organizational choice. The solution would be to hold the private entity responsible in public law for the way it carries out the function that has been shifted from the public agency.[1432]

735. In the eighth edition of his book *Administrative Law*, Professor Craig, having reviewed the more recent developments, made the following observation. 'While the department or agency may still be subject to public law, it may in reality be difficult to show that it has broken such principles where the activity has been contracted out. It is therefore especially important to decide whether the private party to whom the activity has been contracted out is also subject to public law. The

1428. *Re Applications by Chow Chin-wo and Others for Judicial Review*, [1987] HKLR 73, 76, (HC), where Kempster JA said: 'In the absence of argument to the contrary I have no hesitation in making the necessary preliminary finding that, constituting as they do an inquisitorial body with statutory duties to perform, the members of the Insider Dealing Tribunal of Hong Kong are amenable to the process of judicial review at the instance, at least, of persons affected by their determinations in circumstances where no alternative remedy exists.'

1429. *Wong Hui Yin v Hong Kong Arts Development Council* [2004] HKEC 1102, (CFI). The Hong Kong Arts Development Council is a body corporate, created by the Hong Kong Arts and Development Council Ordinance (Cap. 472), which is a public body for the purposes of the Prevention of Bribery Ordinance (Cap. 201). The interpretation section of the Prevention of Bribery Ordinance adopts the definition of public bodies in the Interpretation and General Clauses Ordinance and the following: 'any board, commission, committee or other body, whether paid or unpaid, appointed by or on behalf of the Chief Executive or the Chief Executive in Council; and any board, commission, committee or other body specified in Schedule'.

1430. *Leung Chak Sang v Lingnan University* [2001] HKEC 297, (CFI). In *Hong Kong Polytechnic University v Next Magazine Publishing Ltd* [1996] 2 HKLR 260, (HC), 264, a case concerning a human rights claim, Keith J offered the following useful guidance: 'In my view, for a body to be a public authority ..., it is not sufficient for it to be entrusted with functions to perform for the benefit of the public and not for private benefit: there must be something in its nature or constitution, or in the way in which it is run, apart from its functions, which brings it into the public domain. It is unnecessary for me to identify what that might be: it may take the form of public funding, of a measure of government control or monitoring of its performance, or some form of public accountability.' *See also Tan Shih Ying v City University of Hong Kong* [2013] 1 HKLRD 675, (CFI) and *Yu Hung Hsua Julie v Chinese University of Hong Kong* [2016] 5 HKLRD 393, (CA).

1431. *See Metteograssi SpA v The Airport Authority* [1998] 2 HKLRD 213, (CA) and *Ngo Kee Construction Co Ltd v Hong Kong Housing Authority* [2001] HKEC 16, (CFI).

1432. P.P. Craig, *Administrative Law*, (8th edn, London: Sweet & Maxwell, 2016), 5-018. But *see R v Servite Houses ex parte Goldsmith* (2000) 2 LGR 55, (QB), and its criticism in Craig's 8th edn, 27-025.

courts have however been reluctant to hold that such private parties are subject to the procedure of judicial review. This is regrettable.'[1433]

736. A body incorporated under the Companies Ordinance[1434] is a private body, although it has a comprehensive constitution governing the relationship between it and its members. In *Ho Man-fat (No. 2) v The Royal Hong Kong Jockey Club*,[1435] the court admitted that the exercise of monopolistic powers by a private body over matters of public importance could, in an appropriate case, make it subject to judicial review. The Court of Appeal has held that the Hong Kong Rifle Association, an incorporated company, despite being the sole governing body for the sport of shooting in Hong Kong and being funded mainly by the government, did not exercise any powers of a public nature, sufficient to be subject to judicial review.[1436]

737. Agencies which are not created by statute, but formed as self-regulatory agencies, may also be subject to judicial review because of the importance of the functions of a public law nature they exercise. The importance of the nature of the functions rather than the source of power is illustrated amply by the fact that the Panel on Takeovers and Mergers is a non-statutory body in Britain while its Hong Kong counterpart is a creature of statute.[1437] In *Pacific Century Insurance Co. Ltd v Insurance Claims Complaints Bureau*,[1438] Hartmann J laid down the following useful guidelines in determining whether a non-statutory body that is closely allied to the exercise of governmental powers is subject to judicial review:

> The mere fact that a body lacking statutory, prerogative or common law powers, has been incorporated into a scheme of public regulation does not, of itself, mean that it is amenable to judicial review. No single factor is determinative. ... Is there then a public element in the present matter; in short, by its incorporation into a regulatory scheme underpinned by the Ordinance, has the [body] at all material times been carrying out a public function?[1439]

738. Hartmann J held that the non-statutory insurance complaints bureau in question (that was formed by the insurance profession as a limited liability company) was a public body:

1433. P.P. Craig, *Administrative Law*, (8th edn, London: Sweet & Maxwell, 2008), 5-018.

1434. Companies Ordinance (Cap. 32) of the Laws of Hong Kong.

1435. *Ho Man-fat (No 2) v The Royal Hong Kong Jockey Club* [1976] HKLR 452, (HC). *Cf. R v Disciplinary Committee of the Jockey Club, ex parte Aga Khan* [1993] 1 WLR 909, (CA).

1436. *Hong Kong Rifle Association v Hong Kong Shooting Association* (No 2) [2013] HKEC 980, (CA).

1437. The non-statutory panel in Britain (*R v Panel on Takeovers and Mergers, ex parte Datafin Plc* [1987] 1 QB 815, (CA)) and the non-statutory panel in Hong Kong (*Panel on Takeovers and Merger v William Cheng Kai Man* [1995] 2 HKLR 302, (PC)) have both been held to be amenable to judicial review in respect of their decisions which are of a public law nature.

1438. *Pacific Century Insurance Co. Ltd v Insurance Claims Complaints Bureau* [1999] 3 HKLRD 720, (CFI).

1439. *Ibid.*, 731.

> It was intended and has become a scheme which binds all of Hong Kong's personal insurance businesses and which thereby gives to a broad section of the general public a fast, efficient avenue for redress of complaints. As such, the Bureau has at all material times carried out a public function of conciliation and arbitration, if not as a surrogate of government, at least as an extension of government policy. ... The jurisdiction of the Bureau in terms of the scheme was not founded solely on contract as all members joining after the commencement of the scheme were obliged to do so.[1440]

§3. THE SCOPE OF ADMINISTRATIVE ACTION

739. 'The distinction often made between legislative and administrative acts is that between the general and the particular. A legislative act is the creation and promulgation of a general rule of conduct without reference to particular cases; an administrative act cannot be exactly defined, but it includes the adoption of a policy, the making and issue of a specific direction, and the application of a general rule to a particular case in accordance with the requirements of policy of expediency or administrative practice. Legal consequences flow from this distinction. Since the general shades off into the particular, to discriminate between the legislative and the administrative by reference to these criteria may be a peculiarly difficult task, and it is not surprising that the opinions of judges as to be proper characterisation of the statutory function is at variance.'[1441]

740. This distinction is important because generally there is little judicial control over the legislative process. In *Rediffusion (Hong Kong) Ltd v Attorney General of Hong Kong*, the plaintiffs sought a declaration that it would not be lawful for the Legislative Council of Hong Kong to pass a particular Bill, together with an injunction to restrain the members of the council from passing it. It was held that the Privy Council had jurisdiction to entertain the claim, but, by a majority, the action should be dismissed summarily as disclosing no cause of action. The Privy Council held that: (a) the conduct of the Legislative Council in passing a Bill which, if enacted, would be repugnant to an Act of Parliament cannot affect the legal rights of anyone; (b) if the Governor does not assent, the Bill will never become law; if he does, the Ordinance will be void and inoperative; (c) an infringement of a person's legal rights can only occur when steps are taken to enforce the void Ordinance.[1442] The

1440. *Ibid.*, 731–735, where the judge also made reference to 'bodies whose origins owed nothing to exercise of governmental power but which had been woven into the fabric of public regulation'. The Bar Council of the Hong Kong Bar Association has been held to be amenable to judicial review: *Leung Sze Ho Albert v Bar Council of Hong Kong Bar Association* [2015] HKEC 2009, (CFI).

1441. De Smith, Woolf & Jowell, *Judicial Review of Administrative Action* (5th edn, Sweet & Maxwell, 1995), 1006, para. A-011-A-012, as cited by the Court of Appeal in *Julita F Raza v Chief Executive in Council* [2006] HKEC 1339, (CA).

1442. *Rediffusion (Hong Kong) Ltd v Attorney General of Hong Kong* [1970] AC 1136, [1970] HKLR 231, (PC).

Privy Council also observed that there can be no reason in public policy why members of the Legislative Council should not debate, pass and present to the Governor a Bill that cannot have any effect as law in the Colony.[1443]

741. Hong Kong courts have continued to defer to the legislature in respect of its internal working. They recognize that the Legislative Council is the master of its own procedure, so long as it acts consistently with the Basic Law. In *Leung Kwok Hung v President of the Legislative Council (Filibuster)*, having held that Legislative Council members have no unrestricted right to speak in the Chamber, the Court of First Instance did not consider it necessary to intervene in the proceedings of the Council. The Court rejected the claim that the President had acted ultra vires in imposing limits on the length of Council debates.[1444]

742. Judicial review of administrative action may occasion the review of constitutionality of legislation. It is now generally accepted in Hong Kong that a 'facial challenge', or a direct challenge of constitutionality of legislation, may be made through a judicial review application. In other words, a judicial review application may direct itself at declaring that an ordinance is inconsistent with the Basic Law. *Koo Sze Yiu v Chief Executive of the HKSAR*[1445] provides an excellent example. There, two political activists challenged the constitutionality of section 33 of the Telecommunications Ordinance (Cap. 106) under which the Chief Executive could order interception of messages. As to their standing to bring such an attack by way of judicial review, Mr Leung and Mr Koo relied on two matters. For their standing (*locus standi*) of the conventional kind, they relied on their avowed belief that, as political activists who have had their brushes with the law, they were themselves targets of covert surveillance. They also asserted the right to maintain a facial challenge. For their standing to maintain such a challenge, they relied on their interest, as members of the public, in seeing that covert surveillance is not practised save constitutionally.[1446] As Hartmann J observed when hearing the judicial review application in the Court of First Instance,[1447] neither applicant could say for certain that he had been the subject of covert surveillance or that his private communications with others had been monitored by state agencies. However, having regard to their

1443. *Ibid.* Lord Morris of Borth-y-Gest dissented and held that if a proposed Bill appears to be clearly unconstitutional, courts should have the power to declare that the legislature is incompetent to debate and pass it.

1444. *Leung Kwok Hung v President of the Legislative Council (Filibuster)* [2012] HKEC 745, (CFI), applying *Leung Kwok Hung v President of the Legislative Council [2007] 1 HKLRD* 387, (CFI) (prohibition of amending of bills which had a charging effect); and *Cheng Kar Shun v Li Fung Yin* [2011] 2 HKLRD 555, (CFI) (power to summon witnesses).

1445. (2006) 9 HKCFAR 441, (CFA).

1446. When the matter came to be decided by the Court of First Instance, from where the appeal came up in final appeal in *Koo Sze Yu* case, Hartmann J explained why s. 33 was unconstitutional: 'In respect of telecommunications – the most common subject of the covert monitoring of private communications – s 33 of the Telecommunications Ordinance, Cap 106, gives a general power to the Chief Executive to order the interception of telecommunications. As the applicants said, it is an open-ended power and has not, in terms of the statute itself or any regulations made under it, been made subject to any restrictions or means of independent oversight.' *Leung Kwok Hung v Chief Executive of HKSAR* [2006] HKEC 239, (CFI), [23].

1447. *Leung Kwok Hung v Chief Executive of HKSAR* [2006] HKEC 239, (CFI).

shared history of activism, both believed that it is more likely than not. Hartmann J referred to *Klass v Germany* (1978) 2 EHRR 214, where the European Court observed that, when a state institutes secret surveillance of individuals, if those individuals could not, by reason of their lack of knowledge of the surveillance, challenge the lawfulness of the manner in which the state carries out secret surveillance then the protections afforded under the Convention would largely be rendered a nullity. The court therefore accepted that individuals may, under certain conditions, claim to be victims of alleged violations of their right to privacy by the mere existence of legislation permitting covert measures. In such a situation courts could grant a declaration of unconstitutionality of legislation.[1448] The most recent instance where such a challenge succeeded is *Yeung Chu Wing v Secretary for Justice*, where it was conceded by both parties that certain provisions of the Crimes Ordinance (Cap. 200) discriminated against homosexuals. Those provisions were declared unconstitutional.[1449]

743. Often, constitutionality of legislation arises where, for instance, an administrative authority exercises a discretionary power which satisfies the requirements set out in the enabling statute, but such statutory provision contravenes a constitutional requirement. While an exercise of administrative discretion under such provision is *intra vires* the enabling statute, it is ultra vires the constitution. In *QT v Director of Immigration*,[1450] it was argued that the Immigration Ordinance enables the Director of Immigration to act in a discriminatory manner, inconsistent with the constitutional right to equality. SS had entered into a same-sex civil partnership with QT under the UK Civil Partnership Act 2004. They both entered Hong Kong and had lived for some time, SS on an employment visa and QT on a visitor visa. Subsequently, QT unsuccessfully applied for a dependent visa which would allow her to take up employment. Her application was rejected by the Director of Immigration, applying the immigration policy that while encouraging talented people to join the Hong Kong work force 'by giving them the choice of bringing in their dependants to live with them in Hong Kong', admission must be strictly controlled in view of Hong Kong's dense local population and competitive job market. The Director argued that its policy or practice of granting dependent visas only to spouses who are party to a marriage within the meaning of the Marriage Ordinance (Cap. 181) – namely a marriage between a man and a woman – was one way of keeping employment visas at a manageable level. QT's judicial review application failed in the Court of First Instance where it was held that, in the context of immigration control, the Director was entitled to draw a line between married and unmarried persons (including persons in a same-sex relationship) since these two categories of persons were sufficiently different to justify the differential treatment under the policy and, accordingly, neither the policy nor the refusal of a dependent

1448. In *Leung Kwok Hung v Chief Executive of HKSAR* [2006] HKEC 239, (CFI), Hartmann J held that s. 33 was inconsistent with the constitutional guarantees contained in Arts 30 and 39 of the Basic Law and Art. 14 of the Bill of Rights and issued a declaration to the effect that s. 33 of the Telecommunications Ordinance, insofar as it permits the interception and inspection of telecommunication messages, was unconstitutional.

1449. [2019] 3 HKLRD 238, (CFI).

1450. [2016] HKEC 587, (CFI); [2017] 5 HKLRD 166, (CA); and (2018) 21 HKCFAR 324, (CFA).

visa discriminated on the basis of sexual orientation. Having concluded that the Director did not act in a discriminatory manner the court did not consider it necessary to deal with the argument that the Marriage Ordinance was unconstitutional on the ground that it enabled the Director to act in a discriminatory manner.[1451]

744. Disagreeing with the judge's conclusion, both the Court of Appeal and the Court of Final Appeal held that the Director had discriminated against the applicant.[1452] The Court of Appeal held that although denying the right to marry to same-sex couples did not constitute discrimination on account of sexual orientation, it did not necessarily follow that using marital status as a condition to enjoy other rights or benefits could never be discriminatory. Since persons who are in a same-sex relationship cannot enter into a valid marriage in Hong Kong, there was indirect discrimination against persons who had entered into a same-sex marriage. There was no inherent or obvious link between the immigration policy of keeping employment visas under tight control and refusing a dependant visa to a person who was in a recognized civil partnership which in the UK was as legal as a conventional marriage.[1453]

745. The Court of Final Appeal affirmed the decision of the Court of Appeal and observed that in the context of immigration, there was no obvious difference between homosexual civil partners and heterosexual married couples: each status was recognized under UK law, and homosexual couples and heterosexual couples were capable of having equivalent interdependent and interpersonal relationships. It was objectionable to use the difference in status alone as a reason for any difference in treatment. In the absence of a necessary connection between the aim to be achieved and the means employed to meet that objective, the distinction drawn between these two categories of persons as a means of controlling immigration was discriminatory and invalid. Since the dispute could be resolved by considering whether the Director had applied immigration policy in a discriminatory manner, there was no occasion to consider whether the Marriage Ordinance was discriminatory and consequently unconstitutional.[1454]

746. Not all administrative decisions would be amenable to judicial review. Only those decisions that are made in the public law domain or which involve a public law element are amenable to judicial review. A decision, even when taken by

1451. *QT v Director of Immigration*, [2016] HKEC 587, (CFI).

1452. *QT v Director of Immigration* [2017] 5 HKLRD 166, (CA), and (2018) 21 HKCFAR 324, (CFA).

1453. *QT v Director of Immigration* [2017] 5 HKLRD 166, (CA).

1454. *QT v Director of Immigration* (2018) 21 HKCFAR 324, (CFA), [25]. The court observed as follows: 'Article 37 of the Basic Law provides that the freedom of marriage of Hong Kong residents and their right to raise a family freely shall be protected by law. However, it has not been argued that this makes marriage available to same-sex couples. … [T]he European Court of Human Rights (ECtHR) has held in relation to the comparable right to marry under Art. 12 of the European Convention on Human Rights (ECHR), that that provision "does not impose an obligation on contracting states to grant same-sex couples access to marriage". As the point has not been argued, it is unnecessary to say anything more.' [26]. *See also Leung Chun Kwong v Secretary for Civil Service* (2019) 22 HKCFAR 127, (CFA), where reasoning in *QT v Director of Immigration* (2018) 21 HKCFAR 324, (CFA), was followed.

a body which is amenable to judicial review, is not reviewable if it lacks this important element. For instance, where a public body enters into a transaction, which may equally be entered into by private persons and entities, such as leasing land, the mere presence of a public law element does not transform such transaction into one that is amenable to judicial review. As said in *Chau Tam Yuet Ching v Director of Lands:* 'The mere presence of some public element in the Government's decisions is not sufficient to transform such decisions into public law decisions. After all, the Government administers land in Hong Kong, whether qua landowner or landlord or covenantee, for the benefit of the general public and it is difficult to imagine a case where a public official can make such decision without affecting the public interest either directly or indirectly. Even if one confines oneself to the consideration of the quantum of the premium for a modification of a term of the lease (a classic case of commercial decision), the money received will go to the general revenue and as such have an impact on public finance.'[1455] Situations where a public law element is said to be absent may be illustrated with reference to three categories of cases: (1) cases concerning contracts of employment; (2) commercial decisions; and (3) functions of public authorities which are governed by private law.

747. (1) *Cases concerning contracts of employment*: The first category of cases relates to contracts of employment. Judicial review will be appropriate even where a civil servant or public officer is dismissed under the provision of an employment contract, when the authority acts in compliance with an existing statutory regime of dismissal under which there are comprehensive procedural requirements for sacking of staff.[1456] With the implementation of the civil service reforms, as a part of which new entrants to civil service are appointed on contract terms, judicial review may not be appropriate as the contracts are governed by private law principles.[1457]

1455. *Chau Tam Yuet Ching v Director of Lands* [2013] 3 HKLRD 169, (CA), [23]. This case concerned the Director of Land's decision to cancel two land licences for breach of their terms. It was argued that the Director was acting under a statutory regime and, therefore, was carrying out a public function. Rejecting this argument the court observed that at [22]: 'it is beyond argument that decisions to grant and to cancel (on the ground of the breach of the terms of the licence) a licence for the occupation of unleased land are not susceptible to public law challenges. Such decisions are, like decisions to grant, modify or terminate a Government lease, the grant or modification or termination of a short-term waiver, "commercial decisions" which are guided by the interest of the Government as landowner or landlord and governed by private law such as the law of contract, the law of landlord and tenant and land law.' The judge referred to a series of cases where this principle has been applied: *Hang Wah Chong Investment Co Ltd v Attorney General* [1981] HKLR 336, (PC); *Canadian Overseas Development Co Ltd v Attorney-General* [1991] 1 HKLY 20; *Polorace Investments Ltd v Director of Lands* [1997] HKLY 491; *Rank Profit Industries Ltd v Director of Lands* [2009] 1 HKLRD 177, (CA) and *Rank Profit Industries Ltd v Director of Lands* [2009] HKEC 1021, (CFA); *Anderson Asphalt Ltd v Secretary for Justice* [2009] 3 HKLRD 215, (CFI).

1456. *Sit Ka Yin Priscilla v Equal Opportunities Commission* [1998] HKEC 911, (CFI).

1457. Anton Cooray, 'Public Sector Reform in Hong Kong: Some Legal Aspects' (1999) 8 *Public Administration and Policy* 23.

Of course, much will still depend on whether there is 'a public law element sufficient to justify judicial review' of the decision relating to the particular contract in question.[1458] As Sir John Donaldson MR explained in *R v East Berkshire Health Authority, ex p Walsh*:

> Parliament can underpin the position of public authority employees by directly restricting the freedom of the public authority to dismiss, thus giving the employee 'public law' rights and at least making him a potential candidate for administrative law remedies. Alternatively, it can require the authority to contract with its employees on specified terms with a view to the employee acquiring 'private law' rights under the terms of the contract of employment. If the authority fails or refuses to thus create 'private law' rights for the employee, the employee will have 'public law' rights to compel compliance, the remedy being mandamus requiring the authority so to contract or a declaration that the employee has those rights. If, however, the authority gives the employee the required contractual protection, a breach of that contract is not a matter of 'public law' and gives rise to no administrative law remedies.[1459]

748. (2) *Commercial decisions*: The second category of cases concerns commercial contracts, which are generally not amenable to judicial review. *Ngo Kee Construction Co. Ltd v Hong Kong Housing Authority* provides a good example.[1460]

1458. *See*, for instances, where judicial review was not available in the absence of the requisite public law element: (i) *Sit Ka Yin Priscilla v Equal Opportunities Commission* [1998] HKEC 911, (CFI), where an employee was dismissed by the Equal Opportunities Commission, a public body, which had statutory power to employ persons. The decision was held not amenable to judicial review quoting the words of Sir John Donaldson MR in *R. v East Berkshire Health Authority ex p. Walsh* [1984] 3 WLR 818, (HL), 826: 'Employment by a public authority does not per se inject any element of public law. Nor does the fact that the employee is in a "higher grade" or is an "officer". This only makes it more likely that there will be special statutory restrictions upon dismissal or other underpinning of his employment;' (ii) *Cheng Chun Ngai v Hospital Authority* [2004] HKEC 1375, (CFI), where too the aggrieved employee was not eligible to apply for judicial review because the public authority had statutory power to employ him but the terms of employment were not regulated by legislation; (iii) *Tan Shih Ying v City University of Hong Kong* [2012] HKEC 1678, (CFI), where it was held that a public element would be present only if there were special statutory provisions either restricting the freedom of a public authority to dismiss its employees or requiring the public body to contract with them on specified terms; and (iv) *Chan Tak Cheung v Commissioner of Police* [2002] HKEC 880, (CFI), where a police officer was unsuccessful in his judicial review application challenging the Commissioner's decision not to promote him. Chung J said at [29]: 'The applicant has not been able to point to any [public element]. I agree … that the decisions … relate exclusively to whether a police officer should be appointed (or promoted) to a higher rank. The respondent was exercising a power or function like any ordinary employer in the private sector.'

1459. *R v East Berkshire Health Authority, Ex p Walsh* [1984] QB 152, (CA), 165.

1460. *Ngo Kee Construction Co. Ltd v Hong Kong Housing Authority* [2001] HKEC 16, (CFI). The judge referred to *R v Panel on Takeovers and Mergers, ex p Datafin Plc* [1987] QB 815, (CA), where it was said that a decision of a pubic body is not amenable to judicial review where: (1) the decision is commercial in nature, such as the purchase of goods or services or a tendering process, so the public body is acting like a private body; (2) there is no statutory underpinning of the decision and the public body is left to decide on the substance and procedure of the decision-making process; (3) there is no allegation of fraud, corruption or bad faith.

There the court held that the Housing Authority's decision to suspend the applicant company from tendering for any project for twenty-four months was not amenable to judicial review, as the decision was of a commercial nature. It was held that judicial review did not apply to decisions of a public body where the decision was commercial in nature, such as the purchase of goods or services or a tendering process, so that the public body was acting like a private body. However, judicial review will be appropriate if the contractual decision was tainted with any 'fraud, corruption or bad faith'.[1461] Evidence of bad administration or failure to consider relevant factors in reaching a commercial decision would not justify judicial control, unless such evidence established fraud, corruption or bad faith.[1462] In *Re an Application by Yau Fook Hong Co. Ltd and another for Judicial Review*, it was held that the power of the Director of Lands to consider and select from among tenders for land exchange was derived from a private agreement and governed by private law, and accordingly judicial review was not the appropriate remedy for the aggrieved party.[1463]

749. (3) *Functions of public authorities which are governed by private law*: The third category of cases relates to government decisions concerning government-owned leased land. In Hong Kong, all land is government owned, and there are no landowners in Hong Kong in the sense of having a freehold interest. Government *qua* landlord frequently makes decisions affecting rights of the lessees. Courts have consistently held that the government's exercise of powers under lease agreements fall within the private law domain and are not subject to judicial review.[1464]

750. In Hang Wah Chong Investment Co. Ltd v Attorney General of Hong Kong, Lord Edmund-Davies said:

> The various Conditions of Sale well illustrate the wide range of roles played by the Director in exercising his discretion. As regards some of the conditions, the Director's role may, almost certainly, be that of protector of the public interest. The vital question is whether for the purposes of special conditions 6 and 7 he can properly be regarded as being entitled to act in his capacity of land agent for the Crown. It is not open to serious doubt that those conditions

---

1461. *Matteograssi SpA v Airport Authority* [1998] 2 HKLRD 213, (CA), especially at 221 where Mortimer VP observed that 'there is no universal test to determine whether a decision by a pubic body is amenable to judicial review. In borderline cases, this is a question of impression and degree'.

1462. *Lee Shing Yue Construction Co. Ltd v Director of Architectural Services* [2001] 1 HKLRD 715, (CFI).

1463. *Re an Application by Yau Fook Hong Co. Ltd and another for Judicial Review* [1985] HKLR 42, (HC).

1464. *See* Anthony Law, 'Judicial Review of Government Leases in the Hong Kong Special Administrative Region' (1999) 29 *Hong Kong Law Journal* 240 and Anton Cooray, 'Government as Ground Landlord and Land Use Regulator: The Hong Kong Experience' in Tsuyoshi Kotaka & David L. Callies (eds), *Taking Land: Compulsory Purchase and Regulation in Asian-Pacific Countries* (USA: University of Hawaii Press, 2002), 96–142. For useful statements of the principle and its application, *see Rank Profit Industries Ltd v Director of Lands* [2008] HKEC 773, (CA), *Cheung Shing Scrap Metals Recycling Ltd v Director of Lands* [2009] HKEC 813, (CFI), *Anderson Asphalt Ltd v Secretary for Justice* [2010] HKEC 1645, (CA), and *Re Wong Kwai Leung* [2016] HKEC 800, (CFI).

relate directly to the landlord's interests, economic and otherwise, and their Lordships conclude that the Director was entitled to act, and did act, in that role when granting his qualified approval to the applicants' plans in 1976. On that view, can it properly be said that it is for the Crown to establish the reasonableness of the demand for a premium? In the light of Viscount *Tredegar v Harwood* [1929] AC 72, (HL), their Lordships are of the opinion that the question requires a negative answer. ... It is sufficient, for present purposes, simply to say that, the applicants seeking a concession from their landlords in relation to the development of land leased, the landlords were entitled to make the granting of that concession conditional upon the payment of a premium.[1465]

751. The fact that the Hong Kong Government is the sole landlord does not mean that every decision that the government takes as the landlord is governed by private law. Such decisions may be questioned through judicial review proceedings if there is a public law element. In *Wong Pei Chun v Hong Kong Housing Authority*,[1466] the government had gone back on its promise that residents of a certain village would be permitted to live there indefinitely and not be resettled. It was held that, it being an abuse of power to resile from that promise, the decision was amenable to judicial review.[1467] In relation to decisions that the Hong Kong Government may make in relation to land leases, Keith J explained in *Hong Kong and China Gas Co. Ltd v Director of Lands*: 'The mere fact that the decision challenged relates to a Crown lease which is governed by the law of contract is not decisive. The true question is whether the making of the particular decision in question relating to a Crown lease amounts to the performance of a function within the public domain.'[1468]

1465. *Hang Wah Chong Investment Co. Ltd v Attorney General of Hong Kong* [1981] HKLR 336, (PC), 342.

1466. *Wong Pei Chun v Hong Kong Housing Authority* [1996] 2 HKLR 293, (HC), 299.

1467. The court recognized that serving notice to quit on tenants was a matter of public law, and judicial review was appropriate as theirs was a breach of promise that those tenants would be allowed to occupy the village indefinitely.

1468. *Hong Kong and China Gas Co. Ltd v Director of Lands* [1997] HKLRD 1291, (CFI), 1295. Keith J explained at 1296 why the decision was amendable to judicial review: 'A private developer need only have regard to its own economic interests. However, in deciding whether to extend the Company's lease, the Director of Lands had to have regard to a host of competing interests. Essentially, he had to balance the interests of the community at large in having an emergency and maintenance gas depot in Tsuen Wan, against the disadvantage of the current site being unavailable to other potential lessees at a significant premium in the event of the lease being extended. Ultimately, what the Director of Lands had to decide, therefore, was whether these considerations justified a departure from the "general" policy in the policy statement which would "normally" be applied to public utility companies (upon the assumption that the site was still being used for the purpose for which the lease was originally granted). In view of the competing interests which the Director of Lands had to balance in the context of the application of an important policy statement relating to the extension of large numbers of Crown leases in the New Territories, I have concluded that his decision whether or not to extend the Company's lease was made by him in the exercise of his public functions, and is therefore amenable to judicial review.' Affirmed by the Court of Appeal (decided on 22 May 1998) [2006] HKEC 444, (CA).

752. A brief mention is warranted of legislative attempts to confer finality on administrative decisions, where it becomes necessary to consider to what extent they succeed in excluding judicial review. The underlying principle is that, being the highest court of original jurisdiction in Hong Kong, the Court of First Instance has supervisory jurisdiction over administrative agencies, except where the enabling legislation clearly intends that the jurisdiction of the administrative decision-maker is exclusive. The old distinction between errors of law that went to jurisdiction and errors of law that did not is no longer a determining factor. Any error of law that could be shown to have been made by an administrative agency in the course of reaching their decision on matters of fact or of administrative policy would result in their having asked themselves the wrong question with the result that the decision they reached would be a nullity.[1469]

753. *Kwan Shung King v Housing Appeal Tribunal*[1470] concerned a provision in the Housing Ordinance (Cap. 283) that a decision of the Housing Appeal Tribunal on appeal from a Housing Authority's decision, such as to terminate a tenancy on the ground of breach of the tenancy agreement, 'shall be final'. The court held that a finality clause does not oust the jurisdiction of the Court of First Instance to enquire into and determine the legality of such final decision. In *Gurung Bhakata Bahadur v Director of Immigration*,[1471] the Director of Immigration had refused permission for the applicant to stay in Hong Kong and, on appeal, the Chief Executive had affirmed the Director's decision. The application for judicial review challenging the decisions of the Director of Immigration and the Chief Executive was met with the argument that section 64(3) of the Interpretation and General Clauses Ordinance barred the judicial review application. Section 64(3) of the Interpretation and General Clauses Ordinance provided as follows: 'The conferring by any Ordinance of a right of appeal or objection to the Chief Executive-in-Council shall not prevent any person from applying to the High Court for an order of mandamus, certiorari, prohibition, injunction or any other order, *instead of* appealing or making an objection to the Chief Executive-in-Council, where an application for such an order would lie, but no proceedings by way of mandamus, certiorari, prohibition, injunction or other order shall be taken against the Chief Executive-in-Council in respect of any such appeal or objection to the Chief Executive-in-Council or any proceedings connected therewith.' Mainly relying on the italicized words 'instead of' the Director argued that a person aggrieved by a decision of the Director had to choose between two remedies: (1) a petition or an appeal to the Chief Executive or (2) recourse to judicial review, one excluding the other. Rejecting this argument the court held that on an ordinary construction of section 64(3), and applying the common law presumption that access to the courts was not to be denied save by the clearest language, an aggrieved person seeking to challenge the decision of the Director could both appeal to the Chief Executive and challenge the Director's decision by way of judicial review. The court observed that an appeal to the Chief

1469. *Anisminic Ltd v Foreign Compensation Commission (No. 2)* [1969] 2 AC 147, (HL).
1470. [2000] 2 HKLRD 764, (CFI).
1471. [2001] 3 HKLRD 225, (CFI).

Executive was only an administrative remedy and not a judicial remedy.[1472] On appeal the Chief Executive would be concerned with merits of the case whereas judicial review is concerned with legality of the Director's decision: In the absence of plain language to the contrary, it would be unsafe to infer that the legislature intended that a person who had a justifiable grievance on both the merits and the lawfulness of a decision must be forced to elect to proceed on only one. Hartmann J explained what the section intended to exclude: 'while s. 64(3) concedes that rights of appeal to the Chief Executive do not prevent an aggrieved person from also (or only) seeking judicial review of an administrative authority's decision, it purports to protect from similar challenge the valid decisions of the Chief Executive made when he is called upon to decide such appeals.' In other words, section 63(4) prevents judicial review of the decision of the Chief Executive unless he has acted without or in excess of jurisdiction. In the instant case the Chief Executive had affirmed the decision of the Director and had not made a separate decision. Thus, for instance if the Director's decision was ultra vires and thus a nullity, there would be no decision for the Chief Executive to adopt.[1473] Hartmann J was satisfied that 's. 64(3) of the Interpretation Ordinance does not prevent the applicant from seeking to judicially review the decision of the Chief Executive-in-Council if it can be shown that the Chief Executive-in-Council "has done or failed to do something in the course of the [appeal] inquiry which is of such a nature that its decision is a nullity".' There appears to be three ways of challenging a decision of Director of Immigration: (1) a judicial review application on the ground that the decision of the director is unlawful; (2) an appeal to the Chief Executive on the merits of the Director's decision; (3) judicial review of the Chief Executive's decision on appeal on the ground that it is unlawful.

§4. The Grounds of Judicial Review

I. Acting Without or in Excess of Jurisdiction

754. Being creatures of statute, legal persons may do only what they are authorized by the parent statute to do. An administrative agency acts *intra vires* when it exercises a power that it has been expressly granted. However, even where there is no express grant of power, courts may be willing, by applying 'a purposive approach', to decide that an administrative agency has implied power to do what it

1472. 'The Chief Executive in Council, when considering any appeal or objection to him (whether by way of petition or otherwise, and whether such appeal or objection is made by virtue of any Ordinance or otherwise) shall act in an administrative or executive capacity and not in a judicial or quasi-judicial capacity and shall be entitled to consider and take into account any evidence, material, information or advice in his absolute discretion': Interpretation and General Clauses Ordinance, s. 64(4).

1473. As Chung J said in *Akram v Secretary for Security* [2000] 1 HKLRD 164, (CFI), 177: 'The Governor-in-Council merely decided that the applicant's appeal was rejected. The Governor-in-Council did not make a separate order from the one made by the Secretary for Security earlier. Hence, once the deportation order is found to be a nullity, there is nothing to which the decision to reject the appeal can "attach".'

has done. The courts imply powers in order to make the exercise of express powers of the administrative agency meaningful and effective, so long as the recognition of such implied power is not inconsistent with the purpose of the legislation in question. For instance, where a law confers a general power on a government authority to regulate land development, it is permissible to imply that it has the power to specify the kinds of buildings that can be erected therein.[1474]

755. In *PCCW-HKT Telephone Ltd v Secretary for Commerce and Economic Development,* the Court of Final Appeal held that the Secretary had exceeded his licensing powers when he decided to impose fees which would generate more income that would exceed the reasonable amount required for the provision of services. In the absence of plain and unmistakable words, a power to license which was an element in a regulatory scheme did not extend to authorize the imposition of a 'fee' which in substance was a tax on the activity to be conducted under the licence. The budgeting for notional tax and dividends was to create a surplus to be transferred to the general revenue. The surplus was not fortuitous. A declaration was granted declaring that the Secretary had acted ultra vires in deciding to impose a licence fee at a level than was necessary so that its effect was to impose a tax on licensees.[1475] To delegate one's power when not empowered by the statute to do so is a clear example of acting ultra vires.[1476]

1474. *Auburntown Ltd v Town Planning Board* [1994] 2 HKLR 272, (HC). In *Lo Siu Lan v Hong Kong Housing Authority* (2005) 8 HKCFAR 363, (CFA), [32], Li CJ explained the relevant rules in relation to demarcating the power of the Housing Authority as follows: 'The capacity of a statutory corporation must be ascertained from a proper interpretation of the statute.' As was stated by Lord Watson in *Elizabeth Dowager Baroness Wenlock v River Dee Co* (1884–1885) LR 10 App Cas 354, (HL), at 362–363 'whenever a corporation is created by Act of Parliament, with reference to the purposes of the Act, and solely with a view to carrying these purposes into execution, I am of opinion not only that the objects which the corporation may legitimately pursue must be ascertained from the Act itself, but that the powers which the corporation may lawfully use in furtherance of these objects must either be expressly conferred or derived by reasonable implication from its provisions'. Li CJ also referred to what was said in *Bonanza Creek Gold Mining Co Ltd v The King* [1916] 1 AC 566, (PC), at 577–578: 'It is a mistake to start by assuming that the Legislature meant to create a corporation with a capacity resembling that of a natural person, and then to ask whether there are words in the statute which cut down such capacity. The question is simply one of the proper interpretation of the statute creating the corporation with a view to ascertaining the scope of the legitimate objects of the corporation.'

1475. *PCCW-HKT Telephone Ltd v Secretary for Commerce and Economic Development* (2017) 20 HKCFAR 592, (CFA). *See also Man Hing Medical Suppliers (International) Ltd v Director of Health* [2015] 3 HKLRD 224, (CFI) where it was held that the Director had acted ultra vires when he ordered the recall of a Chinese medicinal product, on the suspicion that it was an unregistered Chinese medicine. The Director did not have express authority to recall a product, nor could it be said that such power was incidental to his power to 'seize, remove and detain any [Chinese medicine] which he has reasonable cause to suspect is in the possession of any person in contravention of [the relevant sections]'. It was held that the power to recall was not reasonably necessary for the effective exercise of the express power to seize, remove and detain. The court observed that it would be contrary to principle to imply such power merely because a recall would be more convenient and desirable than having inspectors go to every premises and outlet which sold the Chinese medicinal products to confiscate them, particularly when there was no evidence that the power to seize and remove would not be effective without a power to recall. The court followed

756. Ng King Tat Philip v Post Release Supervision concerned the scope of the power of the Post Release Supervision Board. The applicant, a transferred prisoner, (meaning a person sentenced in a place outside Hong Kong and transferred to Hong Kong to serve the term of imprisonment or a part of it), argued that the word 'prisoner' in the relevant statute did not include a transferred prisoner, and therefore the Board had no power to make a supervision order on him. Adopting a purposive interpretation, the court held that although there was no express provision relating to transferred prisoners, the word 'prisoner' included a transferred prisoner and rejected the argument that the resultant supervision order was ultra vires.[1477]

757. In *Ng Enterprises Ltd v Urban Council,*[1478] a licensing case, the Privy Council specifically pointed out that 'a power to regulate an activity *prima facie* does not give the [administration] the power to prohibit the activity totally'. The Privy Council also observed that whether 'partial prohibition' is permissible is a matter of statutory construction. In *Medical Council of Hong Kong v Chow Siu Shek,*[1479] the question was whether a medical practitioner whose name had been removed from the register of medical practitioners for a specified period of time was entitled to be restored to the register automatically at the end of the period, unlike in the case where a medical practitioner's name had been struck out indefinitely, in which case the Medical Council had discretion in allowing or not allowing restoration his name to the register of medical practitioners. The Court of Final Appeal held that the Medical Council had discretionary power in relation to both situations. In order to determine the scope of the Council's power, the Court of Final Appeal referred to relevant canons of statutory interpretation and, in particular, made reference to regulatory schemes in other legislations. In the case of the applicant in this case, the reason for the refusal to restore his name was that since removal from the register he had been convicted of an offence. All registered medical practitioners whose names had been removed from the Register, including those whose names had only been removed for a specified period, were covered by section 25(3) which

---

Hazell v Hammersmith and Fulham London Borough Council [1992] 2 AC 1, (HL), and *PCCW-HKT Telephone Ltd v Telecommunications Authority* (2005) 8 HKCFAR 337, (CFA), [39], [44]–[45] and [52].

1476. *See Rowse v Secretary for Civil Service* [2008] 5 HKLRD 217, (CFI), [232]. *Tam Chi Ming v Medical Council of Hong Kong* [2008] 1 HKLRD 24, (CFI), is an illustrative case. In considering an application by a medical practitioner to have his overseas medical qualification recognised in Hong Kong, the Education and Accreditation Committee of the Medical Council sought the advice of the College of Cardiology which gave an unfavourable opinion, without giving adequate reasons for it. Having received the advice, and without satisfying itself that the College of Cardiology's advice could be relied upon, the committee recommended to the Medical Council that the application be rejected. In these circumstances, there was found to be an unlawful delegation of the Medical Council's decision-making power to the College of Cardiology.

1477. *Ng King Tat Philip v Post Release Supervision* [2010] HKEC 1306, (CFI). Contrast *T v Commissioner of Police* (2014) 17 HKCFAR 593, (CFA), where the power of the police to enforce a licence requirement was held to have been exercised unlawfully, because the event in question could not have been within the contemplation of the relevant Ordinance defining the place where the event was taking place – a place 'to which the general public is admitted'.

1478. *Ng Enterprises Ltd v Urban Council* [1997] AC 168, (PC), 177.

1479. *Medical Council of Hong Kong v Chow Siu Shek* (2000) 3 HKCFAR 144, (CFA).

made it relevant to restoration whether that person had 'been convicted ... of any offence punishable with imprisonment' or had otherwise 'been guilty of misconduct in a professional respect ... '.

758. If an administrative agency wrongly decides that it has jurisdiction to deal with a matter, it would be acting without jurisdiction. The error need not necessarily relate to their jurisdiction. The House of Lords, in *Anisminic Ltd v Foreign Compensation Commission*,[1480] set out the principle as follows:

> any error of law that could be shown to have been made by [the decision-making body] in the course of reaching their decision on matters of fact or of administrative policy would result in their having asked themselves the wrong question with the result that the decision they reached would be a nullity.[1481]

759. Whether an administrative agency has a certain power, and if so, the manner in which it has to be exercised, are questions of law to be decided by a court of law, on a true interpretation of legislation or administrative regulation. The interpretation of non-statutory guidance or instructions too, if they relate to the scope or the manner of exercising a power, fall to be interpreted by courts of law.[1482] In *Mobil Petroleum Co. Inc. v Registrar of Trade Marks*, the Registrar of Trademarks had followed a restrictive view of what matters she had to have regard to, which had since been departed from, in determining how she ought to exercise her powers. Following the restrictive judicial view, which no longer represented correct view, she felt obliged, before exercising any discretion, to consider only the adequacy of the explanation for the delay, and she reached her decision on that basis. The prevalent and correct view was that all relevant matters (including the adequacy of any reason for the delay) must be considered so that the 'overall justice' of the case would be met. The law had been settled by the time of the Registrar's decision, and she made an error of law which materially affected her decision-making process. The decision was ultra vires.[1483]

1480. *Anisminic Ltd v Foreign Compensation Commission* [1969] 2 AC 147, (HL).

1481. 'The breakthrough made by *Anisminic* was that, as respects administrative tribunals and authorities, the old distinction between errors of law that went to jurisdiction and errors of law that did not, was for practical purposes abolished.' *In re Racal Communications Ltd* [1981] AC 374, (HL), 383.

1482. *See Shiu Wing Steel Ltd v Director of Environmental Protection and Airport Authority (Interested Party) (No 2)* (2006) 9 HKCFAR 478, (CFA). There the court held that the interpretation of the Technical Memorandum and the Study Brief, which were not subsidiary legislations, was the responsibility of the court. *See* [23]. As Sir Gerard Brennan NPJ explained at [24]: 'In the present case, the Court must find the meaning of the relevant provisions of the Technical Memorandum and the Study Brief and the procedure they prescribe in order to determine the scope of the Director's power to approve the environmental impact assessment report. Only in that way can the Court determine whether the power was validly exercised or whether the purported approval fell outside the scope of the power.'

1483. *Mobil Petroleum Co. Inc. v Registrar of Trade Marks* [2001] 1 HKLRD 225, 242, (CFI). On materiality of the error in law, the court explained that the mere existence of a mistake in law did not per se vitiate a decision. What must be shown was an error in the actual making of the decision

II. Review of Facts and Evidence

760. While questions of law are for the supervisory court, questions of fact are for the decision-maker. So long as the decision-maker has acted within the law, he may go right or he may go wrong. A court of supervisory jurisdiction does not engage in a merits review. In planning law, it is well established that whether a thing is a material consideration is a question of law whereas the weight that may be given to a material consideration is a matter for planning judgment.[1484] As we shall *see* below, if the finding of the decision-maker is unreasonable or irrational, the decision-maker acts outside his power. Similarly, where the evidence available to the tribunal is not reasonably capable of supporting its finding, it would be acting beyond its jurisdiction by arriving at a finding that is untenable in law.[1485]

761. Where a planning authority relies on what is considered a material consideration, such as the financial viability of a proposed development, there must be sufficient evidence to show that the consideration is material for its decision. In *Capital Rich Development Ltd v Town Planning Board*, the Court of Appeal held that the Town Planning Board did not have sufficient evidence to come to its finding that the proposed urban renewal scheme would not be financially viable if the applicant's land were to be excluded from the development site.[1486] The decision-maker must have sufficient evidence to support its determination. In *Smart Gain Investment Ltd v Town Planning Board* it was held that, in rejecting the objection to a proposed statutory land-use plan, the Town Planning Board did not have sufficient evidence to support its determination that the applicant's land was suitable for inclusion in a proposed conservation area, blighting its development prospects.[1487] Similarly, in *Oriental Generation Ltd v Town Planning Board* the Court of First Instance held that the Town Planning Board had 'manifestly insufficient' evidence to support

---

which affected the decision itself. Here, the Registrar believed that she was obliged, before exercising any discretion, to consider only the adequacy of the explanation for the delay, and reached her decision on that basis. But there were other factors which, if considered, might have influenced her decision. The decision would be set aside and the matter referred back to the Registrar.

1484. *See Tesco Stores Ltd v Secretary of State for the Environment* [1995] 1 WLR 759, (HL), 780, per Lord Hoffman: The law distinguishes between 'the question of whether something is a material consideration and the weight which it should be given. The former is a question of law and the latter is a question of planning judgment, which is entirely a matter for the planning authority.' *See also* Anton Cooray, 'Planning Law' in *Halsbury's Laws of Hong Kong* Vol. 48 (2018), [385.270]. In the context of the town Planning Board considering representations made to it regarding a proposed land-use zoning Au J said in *Chan Ka Lam v Chief Executive in Council* [2017] HKEC 2527, (CFI), [67], that it is trite that the court in judicial review is not to engage in a merits review of the Town Planning Board's decision and to substitute its own view with that of the Town Planning Board.

1485. *Allison v General Medial Council* [1894] 1 QB 750, (CA), 760: 'if there was no evidence upon which the council might fairly and reasonably say that the plaintiff had been guilty of "infamous conduct in a professional respect," they went beyond the jurisdiction given to them by the Act in entertaining the case and proceeding to adjudicate upon it. If there was no such evidence, they ought to have declined to interfere'; *R v Roberts* [1908] 1 KB 407, (CA), 423: 'if there was no evidence on which any tribunal could reasonably come to the conclusion to which the auditor has come the superior Courts have a jurisdiction to quash the surcharge'.

1486. *Capital Rich Development Ltd v Town Planning Board* [2007] 2 HKLRD 155, (CA).

1487. *Smart Gain Investment Ltd v Town Planning Board* [2007] HKEC 1964, (CFI).

its decision in imposing site restrictions in a land-use zone whereby developers were required to keep a 20 m wide gap between buildings to be constructed.[1488] Unless the finding of the administrative body is wholly unsupported by the evidence, it is not the function of the Court to interfere merely because it would have formed a different view as to credibility of the witnesses or would have drawn a different inference on the evidence.[1489]

III. Failure to Exercise Discretion

762. Failure to exercise discretionary powers may take place where an administrative agency misconstrues the law in reaching the conclusion, for instance, that it has no discretionary power.[1490] Where the administrative regulations are clear and leaves no room for deviation from them, an administrative authority cannot be faulted for refusing to so deviate and exercise discretion.[1491] An administrative agency would be acting ultra vires if it departs from a government policy through a misinterpretation of the policy.[1492] Slavish adherence to government policy, however, would amount fettering of discretion.[1493] There is a principle of public law that

1488. *Oriental Generation Ltd v Town Planning Board* [2014] HKEC 1868, (CFI), [112].

1489. *See Yeung Cheong Fat v Investigation Committee Appointed Pursuant to S6 of the Public Service (Disciplinary) Regulations and S10 of the Public Service (Administration) Order* 1997 [2005] HKEC 65, (CFI), [21] where A To (Deputy Judge) very correctly observed as follows: 'in an application for judicial review, the court is not so much concerned with the wisdom of a decision but with the propriety of the decision-making process. As Lord Brightman said in *Chief Constable of North Wales Police v Evans* [1982] 1 WLR 1155, (HL), judicial review is not an appeal from a decision, but a review of the manner in which the decision was made. It is not the function of this Court to conduct a detailed analysis of the minutiae of the evidence presented and the findings made by the Investigation Committee. Thus, unless the finding of the Investigation Committee is wholly unsupported by the evidence, it is not the function of this Court to interfere merely because it would have formed a different view as to credibility of the witnesses or would have drawn a different inference on the evidence.'

1490. *Wing On Co. Ltd v Building Authority* (1996) 6 HKPLR 432, (CA).

1491. *Li Kim Ming v Housing Authority* [2016] HKEC 1201, (CFI). The court observed at [81] that 'the evidence shows that the allocation of public housing by the Housing Department under the Scheme has always been strictly made in accordance with the rules set out in the relevant Circular Memorandum through the priority regime expressly set out therein. There is in fact nothing provided in the Scheme to give the Housing Department or Housing Authority discretion to consider personal or individual circumstances of the Scheme applicants.'

1492. *Hong Kong Television Network Ltd v Chief Executive in Council* [2015] HKEC 646; [2015] 2 HKLRD 1035, (CFI). The Communications Authority recommended approving all three licensing applications it received for provision of domestic free television broadcasts, there being no prescribed limit on the number of licences that could be granted. The Chief Executive in Council decided to grant only two licences, on the ground that a gradual and orderly approach should be adopted in granting licences. The Chief Executive's decision was quashed, the court holding that on a proper construction, the meaning of the policy of no pre-set limit was that no licence applications should be rejected unless there are physical or technological constraints. Thomas Au J of the view that the absence of a limit prescribed by legislation (and as explained by the administration in the Legislative Council) was consistent with the underlying objectives of the policy, including that of positively opening up the television market and having a market-driven approach in the licensing regime. The court held that as a consequence of not adhering to the established policy the refusal of the licence application amounted to a frustration of the applicant's legitimate

a minister who is granted a discretionary power must not improperly fetter the exercise of his discretion. In a case such as this, however, a minister has to lay down a firm policy in order to ensure consistency of decision-making.

763. Should administrative decision-makers publish a policy to explain how their discretionary powers will be exercised? In relation to Article 5 of the European Convention on Human Rights on right to liberty and security, corresponding to Article 5 of the Hong Kong Bill of Rights, the UK Supreme Court in *R (Lumba) v Secretary of State for the Home Department* identified three propositions in relation to policy: First, it must not be a blanket policy admitting of no possibility of exceptions. Second, if unpublished, it must not be inconsistent with any published policy. Third, it should be published if it will inform discretionary decisions in respect of which the potential object of those decisions has a right to make representations.[1494] On the third point, Lord Dyson disagreed with the Court of Appeal's view that there was no general rule and that the detention of persons pursuant to unpublished policies was not in itself a reason for holding that the decisions to detain them were unlawful. Lord Dyson said that the Court of Appeal were wrong on this issue 'both as a matter of common law and human rights law'.[1495] This statement has not been accepted in Hong Kong as a general statement of unrestricted application.[1496]

764. In *Ghulam Rbani v Secretary for Justice,*[1497] Ribeiro PJ offered a measured opinion of the importance of having a published policy. He said that 'there is no public law duty generally requiring decision-makers to publish policies setting out their criteria for exercising statutory discretionary powers. The absence of such published policies does not of itself constitute a breach of a public law duty. However,

expectation. On appeal, the Court of Appeal disagreed: *Hong Kong Television Network Ltd v Chief Executive in Council* [2016] 2 HKLRD 1005, (CA). The Court of Appeal held that the policy of no pre-determined limit on licences that could be issued did not prevent the Chief Executive from taking all material considerations into account including the public interest in not approving all the three applications. *See*, for a discussion of the Court of Appeal decision, para. 781, below.

1493. If an authority blindly adheres to a policy laid down in advance without applying its mind to the special circumstances of an individual case, it is not exercising its discretion lawfully: *Bromley LPC v Greater London Council* [1983] 1 AC 768, (HL) referred to in *Lam Hei Ying v Hong Kong Housing Authority* [2001] HKEC 82, (CFI). Also *see Rowse v Secretary for Civil Service* [2008] 5 HKLRD 217, (CFI), [129]. In *Lai Tak Shing v Director of Home Affairs* [2006] HKEC 1873, (CA), the Court of Appeal held that the Secretary of Home Affairs had acted ultra vires when he failed to exercise his statutory discretion on whether to add new villages to the schedule of the Ordinance which regulated village representative elections, by rigidly following a government policy not to add any new villages. However, the Court of Final Appeal disagreed: It was not a mere government policy but a binding legislative policy to restrict elections to the villages listed in the legislation and therefore the Secretary had no discretion in the matter. Justice Bokhary PJ said: 'It was the clear intention of the Legislature to confine future village representative elections to those villages already on the list where elections had been held in 1999. I would respectfully disagree with the Court of Appeal that this was merely a policy and not the legislative intent.' *Lai Tak Shing v Secretary for Home Affairs* (2007) 10 HKCFAR 655, [50], CFA.

1494. *R (Lumba) v Secretary of State for the Home Department* [2012] 1 AC 245, (UKSC), [20].

1495. *Ibid.*, [27].

1496. *See* paras 765, below where Ribeiro PJ explained the *Lumba* case.

1497. (2014) 17 HKCFAR 138, (CFA).

especially where executive detention is involved, if the powers concerned are so broad and so lacking in specificity that legitimate doubts may arise as to the basis on which they are exercised in a particular case, published policies setting out relevant criteria may introduce the transparency needed as a safeguard against arbitrariness. This is of particular importance as a safeguard against arbitrary detention, but whether such a concern arises depends on case-specific considerations.'[1498] Justice Ribeiro explained that administrative discretion is a means of achieving flexibility in decision-making; where the legislature grants broad powers, it authorizes the administration to make regulations or issue less formal guidance notes and practice notes to guide those who seek redress; where there is no provision for making such formal or less formal rules, the administration may publish policies in order to promote consistency, certainty and fairness; 'Where this is done, those affected may have a legitimate expectation that the policies will be adhered to, although the decision-maker may be able to justify departing from those policies for good reason. It is necessary as a matter of public law to strike a balance between on the one hand, preserving a beneficial discretion which is not excessively fettered; and providing transparency to promote non-arbitrary decision-making on the other. Whether a public law duty to publish policies arises therefore depends very much on the nature of the discretionary power concerned and how it is exercised.'[1499]

765. Ribeiro PJ considered Lord Dyson's above-quoted statement and said that the statement was made in the context of unlimited detention powers that the UK administration enjoyed and said the problem in *R (Lumba) v Secretary for the Home Department* was not that there was no published policy: There was a published policy but the Secretary had applied an unpublished policy while purporting to apply the written policy. Thus, interpreted in context, Lord Dyson's view did not suggest that a decision taken by an administrative decision-maker would be unlawful, unless he had published the policy guiding the exercise of discretion.[1500] Justice Ribeiro appreciated the difficulty a person would have preparing for representations to be made in support of his application to the decision-maker in the absence of sufficient guidelines. He concluded: 'where the power is conferred in terms capable of giving rise to genuine doubts as to the basis of its exercise and thus preventing or significantly hampering the making of such representations in particular cases, a public law duty may arise requiring the publication or disclosure of relevant criteria or reasons. Where the power involves interference with personal freedom, recognition of such a public law duty is necessary to avoid executive detentions lacking transparency and possibly involving arbitrariness.'[1501]

766. There is failure to exercise discretion if a decision-maker obeys superior orders rather than exercise his discretionary power. In *In re Hong Kong Hunters' Association Ltd*,[1502] the Director of Agriculture and Fisheries had taken a decision

1498. *Ibid.*, [66].
1499. *Ibid.*, [67].
1500. *Ibid.*, [72] and [74].
1501. *Ibid.*, [76]–[77].
1502. *In re Hong Kong Hunters' Association Ltd* [1980] HKLR 179, (HC).

not to issue hunting licences anymore, because of a directive from the Executive Council. Since the prevailing law (the Wild Animals Protection Ordinance) at the time clearly conferred a discretionary power to consider any application for hunting licences on a case-by-case basis, his decision was null and void. The High Court observed: 'he has not exercised his discretion because he felt his discretion was fettered by the directive of the Executive Council and he has indicated generally that he would not renew any hunting licences'.[1503]

767. Silver Mountain Investments Ltd v Attorney General[1504] is a case where the applicant failed to prove that the administrative agency had fettered its discretion. There the Land Development Corporation proposed a comprehensive land development and negotiated with the landowners to acquire their land for this purpose. Having failed in negotiations, the Corporation turned to the Governor to resume the land. The landowners argued that the Corporation was under duty to explore the possibility of developing the land in cooperation with the landowners, without making up its mind that having a single developer was the right way to proceed with the development. The Privy Council held that the landowners had not put forward any practicable scheme for development by them and that deciding to develop the land without their participation was not an instance of fettering discretion. It is well established that: 'The principle against fettering discretion does not prevent public authorities upon which a discretionary power has been conferred guiding the implementation of that discretion by means of a policy or a rule that is within the scope of its conferred powers. The principle directs attention to the attitude of the decision-maker, preventing him from rigidly excluding the possibility of any exception to that rule or policy in a deserving case.'[1505] 'When Parliament confers a discretionary power exercisable from time to time over a period, such power must be exercised on each occasion in the light of the circumstances at that time. In consequence, the person on whom the power is conferred cannot fetter the future exercise of his discretion by committing himself now as to the way in which he will exercise his power in the future. He cannot exercise the power *nunc pro tunc* (meaning "now for then"). By the same token, the person on whom the power has been conferred cannot fetter the way he will use that power by ruling out of consideration on the future exercise of that power factors which may then be relevant to such exercise.'[1506]

1503. Li and Garcia JJ.

1504. *Silver Mountain Investments Ltd v Attorney General* [1994] 2 HKLR 297, (PC).

1505. De Smith's Judicial Review (6th edn, 2007) para. 9-004, cited in Hong Kong cases including *Inglory Ltd v Director of Food and Environmental Hygiene* [2012] HKEC 710, (CFI) and *Fairland Overseas Development Co Ltd v Secretary for Justice* [2007] 4 HKLRD 947, (CFI).

1506. Lord Browne-Wilkinson in *R. v Secretary of State for the Home Department, Ex p. Venables* (1998) AC 407, (HL), 496–497. Cited with approval by the Court of Appeal in *Lai Tak Shing v Director of Home Affairs* [2006] HKEC 1873, (CA), [24].

IV. Use of Discretionary Powers for Improper Purpose

768. It is presumed that law gives powers to be used for the purposes for which they are given and not in bad faith for unauthorized or improper purposes. It is very rarely that an administrative officer will act in bad faith, for instance as a measure of political victimization. Courts use the description 'bad faith' not only in respect of intentionally dishonest behaviour, but whenever an administrative officer has acted unreasonably or on improper grounds. In *Lee Ma-loi v Commissioner of Inland Revenue*,[1507] the Court of Appeal observed that abuse of power did not connote behaviour to which opprobrium should necessarily attach.[1508]

769. Where a decision-making body has 'acted capriciously' and not 'fairly and properly', its decision is amenable to judicial review.[1509] As Wade and Forsyth have observed 'it is extremely rare for public authorities to be found guilty of intentional dishonesty: Normally they are found to have erred, if at all, by ignorance or misunderstanding'.[1510] *R v Fung Chi-wood*[1511] is a case where the court had to decide whether a police officer could, under the Immigration Ordinance,[1512] require a person, who is not suspected of being an illegal immigrant, to prove his identity. The court rejected the argument that the sole purpose for which the stop and ascertain residence status was to stem the influx of illegal immigrants. The police officers could not be said to have misunderstood the objective of the statute and used their powers for an exterior purpose (in this case in connection with a protest held by Hong Kong residents).

770. A successful challenge on the grounds of improper purposes was made in *Lee Ma-loi v Commissioner of Inland Revenue*.[1513] There, the police found a large sum of money in a fishing boat belonging to the applicant and suspected that it was proceeds from smuggling activities. The police did not have sufficient evidence to press charges and asked the Inland Revenue to confiscate the money. The Inland Revenue wrote to the applicant that they suspected that the money represented profits he made from fishing and any connected activities and demanded payment of the sum as tax due. The Inland Revenue directed the police to turn over the money to them. On a judicial review application, it was held that the powers under the Inland Revenue Ordinance had been used for a purpose unconnected with the purposes of

1507. *Lee Ma-loi v Commissioner of Inland Revenue* [1992] HKLY 30, (CA).
1508. *See* H.W.R. Wade & C.F. Forsyth, *Administrative Law* (11th edn, Oxford: Oxford University Press, 2014), 354–5.
1509. *In re 11–13 Sands Street, Hong Kong* [1994] HKDCLR 7, (DC), 7–8 (headnote).
1510. H.W.R. Wade & C.F. Forsyth, *Administrative Law* (11th edn, Oxford: Oxford University Press, 2014), 354.
1511. *R v Fung Chi-wood* [1991] 1 HKLR 654, (HC).
1512. Immigration Ordinance (Cap. 115) of the Laws of Hong Kong.
1513. *Lee Ma-loi v Commissioner of Inland Revenue* [1992] 1 HKLR 200, (HC).

that Ordinance. The Revenue powers were used to deprive the citizen of his property, which the police could not accomplish under criminal legislation. The Court of Appeal rejected the appeal by the Commissioner of Inland Revenue against this finding.[1514]

V. Taking Irrelevant Considerations into Account

771. Administrative decision-makers must not take irrelevant considerations into account. However, the difficulty is that very often a law does not state clearly what considerations may be taken into account in making administrative decisions. In *Wing On Co Ltd v Building Authority,*[1515] the Court of Appeal usefully listed two categories of considerations that must be taken into account in any decision-making process: (1) those that the legislation requires expressly or by necessary implication to be taken into account, and (2) those that the decision-maker may take into account. Thus, the Court held that factors such as traffic generation at or around the site in question could be taken into account alongside with the planning considerations in deciding whether to approve the proposed building work by a landowner.

772. In practice, 'relevant factors include: (a) statutory criteria, (b) any relevant policies, (c) the merits of the individual case'.[1516] Random examples of irrelevant considerations include whether a club's facilities are restricted to its members and not open to the public in determining whether to grant a gaming licence[1517] and the availability of parallel disciplinary proceedings abroad in deciding whether to grant a stay of the local proceedings.[1518] Where there is a complaint of taking irrelevant considerations into account, there is invariably an accompanying complaint of failure to take relevant considerations into account.[1519]

VI. Failure to Take Relevant Considerations into Account

773. Just as an administrative body must refrain from taking into account any irrelevant considerations, it must take into account any relevant considerations. *Oriental Generation Ltd v Town Planning Board* is a good example of a Hong Kong case where an administrative decision was held to be invalid for failure to take relevant considerations into account. There, the Town Planning Board had imposed a

1514. *Lee Ma-Loi v Commissioner of Inland Revenue* [1992] HKLY 30, (CA).

1515. *Wing On Co Ltd v Building Authority* (1996) 6 HKPLR 432, (CA), at 439 *per* Godfrey JA, citing with approval the judgment of Simon Brown LJ in *R v Somerset County Council, ex p Fewings* [1995] 1 WLR 1037, (CA), 1049.

1516. David Clark & Gary McCoy, *Hong Kong Administrative Law* (2nd edn, Hong Kong: Butterworths Asia, 1993), 316.

1517. *Chan Yat-san v Attorney General* [1975] HKLR 503 (HC). The court was unconcerned that the decision-maker repeatedly refused to give reasons for the refusal of a licence. This view is of doubtful value today in view of the increasing emphasis on fair and open government.

1518. *Nomura International (Hong Kong) Ltd v Securities and Futures Commission* (1997–1998) 1 HKCFAR 250, (CFA).

1519. *See Orrico Philippe v Municipal Services Appeals Board* [2014] HKEC 1388, (CFI).

no-building area restriction purportedly to minimize obstruction to views to and from some historical buildings, but no visual impact assessment had been prepared and presented to the Board for its consideration. The Court of Appeal held that the Board had 'manifestly failed to give due consideration to relevant considerations before it reached its decision'.[1520]

774. In considering whether an administrative agency has taken relevant considerations into account, the court must decide as a matter of law what considerations are relevant. Where an administrative agency has taken all relevant considerations into account, it is a matter for the discretion of the administrative agency, and not for the courts, to decide what weight should be attached to those considerations.[1521] Courts would intervene only if the administrative authority has acted unreasonably in the *Wednesbury* sense or irrationally. On the other hand, in *Silver Mountain Investments Ltd v Attorney General*,[1522] the Town Planning Board had designated an area within an Outline Zoning Plan as a 'Comprehensive Development Area' including land belonging to the appellant. The Board rejected the appellant's objection to the zoning that it was preferable for the appellant to develop their land independently of the proposed comprehensive development. When appellants refused to sell the land to the Corporation, the Land Development Corporation recommended to the Governor in Council that the appellant's land be resumed for a public purpose. In rejecting the appeal, the Privy Council held that, so long as the relevant considerations had been duly taken into account, it was left to the professional judgment of the Town Planning Board to decide whether or not the appellant's land should be included within the Comprehensive Development Area and for the Land Development Corporation to recommend resumption of the affected land.

1520. *Oriental Generation Ltd v Town Planning Board* [2014] HKEC 1868, (CFI). *See Waddington Ltd v Securities and Futures Commission* [2018] HKEC 3334, (CFI) where a decision taken by the Securities and Futures Commission was invalid for its failure to take a relevant consideration into account.

1521. *Tesco Stores Ltd v Secretary State for the Environment and Ors* [1995] 1 WLR 759, 764G, frequently cited in Hong Kong, for instance, by the Court of Appeal in *Chan Kam Choi v Commissioner of Correctional Services* [2016] HKEC 1787, [28]. As Hartmann J explained in *Building Authority v Appeal Tribunal (Buildings) & Estoree Ltd* [2003] HKEC 947, (CFI), and cited in *Sky Ace enterprise Ltd v Appel Tribunal (Buildings)* [2016] HKEC 1318: '[The Court of First Instance] is not an appellate court. It does not evaluate the strengths and weaknesses of the evidence. The assessment of relevant facts and the weighing of relevant considerations are a matter for the Appeal Tribunal, more especially [where] the Tribunal is a specialist professional body … . Only on the basis of *Wednesbury* unreasonableness may the Tribunal's determination be set aside if it is found otherwise to be correct in law.'

1522. *Silver Mountain Investments Ltd v Attorney General* [1994] 2 HKLR 297.

VII. Irrationality and Proportionality

775. Irrationality evolved from 'Wednesbury unreasonableness'.[1523] Where an administrative agency has acted within its powers and followed all the relevant procedural requirements, but yet arrives at a conclusion no sensible person would have arrived at, such a decision is irrational and therefore objectively indefensible. The authority is said to have acted beyond its jurisdiction. In such a case, the court intervenes 'not as an appellate authority to override the decision of the local authority but as a judicial authority which is concerned, and concerned only, to see whether the local authority have contravened the law by acting in excess of the powers which Parliament has confided in them' (*Wednesbury* case at 234). A good example of an administrative decision tainted by irrationality may be found in *Building Authority v Appeal Tribunal (Buildings) (re Methodist Church)* where the Appeal Tribunal had classified a land when there was insufficient evidence to support such classification.[1524] Where a land developer requests an extension of a short-term lease to deal with some unfinished business, the Director of Lands should at least consider his proposal before turning down the request for extension. A blunt refusal might, in an appropriate case, amount to an irrational decision.[1525]

776. As a matter of practice, it is difficult to find as irrational a decision made by a body consisting of a large number of persons. As Waung J explained in a planning case concerning a decision of the Town Planning Board: 'when there is a Board of that size and such a diversity of distinguished backgrounds, it seems to me that the task of establishing irrationality turns from the very difficult to the almost impossible. ... Whether the court is convinced that on the planning decision, the Board is wrong or that the Board ought to act differently is to my mind really irrelevant. Planning merits do not enter into judicial review. The court can and should only interfere if it can be clearly shown that there was an aberration by the Board. The Board was master of its own house. It could take into account many factors articulated or not.'[1526]

1523. *Associated Provincial Picture Houses Ltd v Wednesbury Corp.* [1948] 1 KB 223, at 230, where Lord Greene said: 'It is true to say that, if a decision on a competent matter is so unreasonable that no reasonable authority could ever have come to it, then the courts can interfere. That, I think, is quite right; but to prove a case of that kind would require something overwhelming. Lord Greene went on to emphasise that in considering whether a decision in question is unreasonable: 'It is not what the court considers unreasonable, a different thing altogether.'

1524. *Building Authority v Appeal Tribunal (Buildings) (re Methodist Church)* [2015] 5 HKLRD 108, (CFI).

1525. *Hong Kong and China Gas Co. Ltd v Director of Lands* (decided on 22 May 1998) [2006] HKEC 444, (CA).

1526. *R v Town Planning Board, ex parte Kwan Kong Co. Ltd* (1995) 5 HKPLR 261, 286, (HC). *Oriental Generation v Town Planning Board* [2014] HKEC 1868, (CFI), an instance where the Court of First Instance found that a decision of the Town Planning Board (in imposing a building height restriction to preserve a local view corridor) was arbitrary and irrational, since the need to preserve a local view corridor provided no sensible justification for imposing the proposed height restriction. While it is rare that a court disturbs a finding of a specialist government agency, courts would not hesitate to intervene if there is a compelling reason to do so. The Court observed at [83] and [85]: 'The planning authority is entitled to exercise its aesthetic judgment and conclude that a towering building, with a height which is incompatible with the surrounding building

777. It is often said that the rationality of regulatory measures is a matter of subjective judgment. Where an administrative agency has been entrusted with a discretionary power to decide (for instance, where prison administrator has been given the power to restrict prisoners' access to reading materials) the administrative officer, and not a court exercising supervisory jurisdiction, has the discretion to decide. So long as the administrative officer acts within the power given to him, does not act arbitrarily or maliciously or with bad motives or after taking irrelevant considerations into account or taking irrelevant considerations into account (which all will render his decision ultra vires, or takes his action outside his lawful authority) his decision has to be upheld in a court of law even if the judge himself might prefer to arrive at a different discretionary decision.[1527]

778. Proportionality is directly relevant where legislation or administrative action is challenged as being in conflict with a fundamental right.[1528] In determining whether a restriction is justified, the court has to be satisfied that it has been

---

heights and overall building height profile, would cause adverse visual impacts on the ridgelines as a whole. ... We live in a dynamic city with its citizens always moving around. Since the view of a particular object may vary dramatically at different viewpoints, the choice of a particular viewpoint for imposing building control to deal with possible visual impacts on the object needs to be made very carefully. Otherwise, given Hong Kong's crowded condition, drawing of view corridors from randomly or arbitrarily selected viewpoints for the purpose of imposing building height control on buildings would easily lead to confusion and unfairness.'

1527. *See Chim Shing Chung v Commissioner of Correctional Services* [1996] 6 HKPLR 313, (CA). There the prison authorities had removed the horse-racing supplement from a newspaper that a prisoner had received from outside. The prisoner's judicial review application against censorship was successful in the High Court where the judge held the relevant regulation to be irrational because (i) there was no causal connection between access to racing information and illegal gambling, admittedly a serious concern in prisons; (ii) the racing supplement was not the only part of the newspaper that contained racing information; and (iii) censorship was ineffective in controlling gambling in prisons. This decision was overturned by the Court of Appeal observing that the relevant regulation laid down a policy and it would be inappropriate for a court to second-guess government policy, citing the oft-quoted words of Lord Diplock in *Council of Civil Service Unions v Minister for the Civil Service* [1985] 1 AC 374, 411E, (HL): 'the reasons for the decision-maker taking one course rather than another do not normally involve questions to which, if disputed, the judicial process is adapted to provide the right answer'. And, as Lord Brightman had said in *Chief Constable of the North Wales Police v Evans* [1982]1 WLR 1155, 1173F, (HL): 'Judicial review is concerned, not with the decision, but with the decision-making process. Unless that restriction on the power of the court is observed, the court will ... under the guise of preventing the abuse of power, be itself guilty of usurping power.' In *Chim Shing Chung v Commissioner of Correctional Services* [1996] 6 HKPLR 313, (CA), Litton V-P observed at [23] that: 'Competing policy considerations are not matters which courts of law can properly weigh. These are matters of value judgment based on priorities which the decision-maker considers relevant.' Applying these principles to the High court's decision that the prohibition imposed on the prisoner was irrational, Litton V-P said at [30]: 'As can be seen from the reasons given by the judge, he had, in effect, stepped into the Commissioner's shoes to judge the merits of the policy. The "casual connection" between removing racing supplements and the diminution of gambling cannot be "proved"; it is a matter of value judgment. Effectiveness of policy is a matter of degree. These are matters for the Commissioner's judgment, not the court's.'

1528. For a recent example, *see Chee Fei Ming v Director of Food and Environmental Hygiene (No 2)* [2018] 4 HKLRD 517, (CFI), where the Court of First Instance held unconstitutional the requirement of prior permission to display banners on government land as an unjustifiable restriction of

clearly established that the restriction is necessary to achieve a legitimate aim.[1529] In *HKSAR v Lam Kwong Wai* Sir Anthony Mason NPJ explained this aspect of the proportionality test in these terms: 'The next question is whether the means employed, namely the creation of the persuasive onus, is necessary to achieve the legitimate aim. In this respect, the means employed must be no more than is necessary to achieve that aim. If the means employed go beyond what is necessary in that sense, the restriction or limitation on the right, in this case the persuasive onus, is disproportionate and there is an absence of the requisite proportionality between the means employed and the legitimate aim.'[1530] In the light of the decision of the Court of Final Appeal in *Hysan Development Co Ltd v Town Planning Board* the proportionality test involves a four-step analysis:

(1) the restriction or limitation must pursue a legitimate aim;
(2) the restriction or limitation must also be rationally connected to that legitimate aim;
(3) the restriction or limitation must also be no more than was necessary to accomplish that legitimate aim; and
(4) where an encroaching measure had passed the three-step test, the analysis should incorporate a fourth step, asking whether a reasonable balance had been struck between the societal benefits of the encroachment and the inroads

---

freedoms of expression, assembly and demonstration, but rejected the argument that the prior permission requirement was a disproportionate restriction on the fundamental rights in question.

1529. *See*, for instance, Sir Anthony Mason in *HKSAR v Lam Kwong Wai* (2006) 9 HKCFAR 574, [21], CFA and *Kwok Cheuk Kin v Secretary for Constitutional and Mainland Affairs* [2015] 5 HKLRD 881, [19]–[33]. *See R v Sin Yau-ming* [1992] 1 HKLR 127, where it was held that a limitation on the presumption of innocence may be implied, even though the right was not subject to any explicit limitation. Such implied limitation was subject to proportionality test, which is applied with strict scrutiny.

1530. *HKSAR v Lam Kwong Wai* (2006) 9 HKCFAR 574 at [43]. In *HKSAR v Choi Wai Lun* (2018) 21 HKCFAR 167, (CFA), the Court of Final Appeal considered whether the imposing of a reverse onus on a defendant was proportionate. Ribeiro PJ explained at [68] and [69]: 'A reverse onus derogates from the constitutional right to be presumed innocent. For such a derogation to be justified, it must pass the rationality and proportionality tests: The Court must be satisfied that the reverse onus has a rational connection with the pursuit of a legitimate aim and that it is no more than necessary for the achievement of that aim. If those tests are met, the Court must be satisfied overall that adoption of a reverse onus strikes a reasonable balance between the societal benefits promoted and the inroads made into the constitutionally protected presumption of innocence and that it does not place an unacceptably harsh burden on the individual. … In my view, construing s. 122(2) [of the Crimes Ordinance (Cap. 200), which was designed to protect persons under the age of 16 from sexual exploitation] as imposing a burden on the accused to prove on the balance of probabilities that he honestly and reasonably believed that the girl in question was aged 16 or more passes those tests. It is rationally connected with the legitimate aim of giving heightened protection to vulnerable underaged girls and is no more than necessary to achieve such a level of protection. The inroad it makes into the presumption of innocence as the price of promoting necessary protection of a vulnerable class strikes a reasonable balance in the context of a fair trial for the accused.'

made into the constitutionally protected rights of the individual, asking in particular whether pursuit of the societal interest resulted in an unacceptably harsh burden on the individual.[1531]

779. Where the court considers constitutionality of a legislative measure in an area where government policy is a major consideration, the courts, in applying the proportionality test, must allow a greater margin of appreciation to the legislature. As was observed in *Fok Chun Wa v Hospital Authority* (2012) 15 HKCFAR 409, the court would not interfere unless the solution in question was manifestly beyond the spectrum of reasonableness. There the Court of Final Appeal upheld the constitutionality of a discriminatory requirement that non-resident spouses of Hong Kong residents to pay higher hospital charges than would be payable by Hong Kong resident spouses. The Court of Final Appeal observed that using residential status as the dividing line was only a mere question of general social or economic policy, and the entitlement to subsidized health services was not a fundamental concept which goes to the heart of any society as the term was used. In *Kong Yunming v Director of Social Welfare*,[1532] the Court of Final Appeal considered the right to social welfare benefits protected by Article 36 of the Basic Law[1533] which was subject to modification under Article 145[1534] (Hong Kong Government may formulate policies on the basis of the previous system of social welfare) and applied the manifestly without reasonable foundation test.[1535]

1531. *Hysan Development Co Ltd v Town Planning Board* (2016) 19 HKCFAR 372, CFA, [134]–[135], per Ribeiro PJ, with all the other judges concurring. For a slightly different formulation of the four-step 'structured test' of proportionality, *see* Wade & Forsyth, *Administrative Law* (11th edn, OUP, 2014), 307.

1532. *Kong Yunming v Director of Social Welfare* (2013) 16 HKCFAR 950, CFA.

1533. Article 36: 'Hong Kong residents have the right to social welfare in accordance with law. The welfare benefits and retirement security of the labour force shall be protected by law.'

1534. Article 145: 'On the basis of the previous social welfare system, the Government of the Hong Kong Special Administrative Region shall, on its own, formulate policies on the development and improvement of this system in the light of the economic conditions and social needs.'

1535. *Kong Yunming v Director of Social Welfare* (2013) 16 HKCFAR 950, [43] 'insofar as the disputed restriction in the present case is rationally connected to a legitimate societal aim espoused by the Government, the restriction will only be held to be disproportionate if it is manifestly without reasonable foundation'. *See also Keen Lloyd Holdings Ltd v Commissioner of Customs and Excise* [2016] 2 HKLRD 1372 [59], (CA), in relation to the 'broad concept of arbitrariness'. With reference to the decision of the Court of Final Appeal in *Lau Cheong v HKSAR* (2002) 5 HKCFAR 415, (CFA), the Court of Appeal set forth the broad concept of arbitrariness: (a) Something lawful may nonetheless be arbitrary. (b) Arbitrariness is to be construed broadly to include elements of inappropriateness, injustice and lack of predictability. (c) The concept of arbitrariness has developed to embrace within it the concept of manifest or gross disproportion in addition to its traditional meaning of 'capricious, unreasoned or without reasonable cause'. A statutory provision can also be challenged as arbitrary if it is manifestly disproportionate. (d) A high threshold must be crossed before a statutory provision can be struck down as arbitrary by reason of it being manifestly disproportionate. Ribeiro PJ explained in *Hysan Development Co Ltd v Town Planning Board* (2016) 19 HKCFAR 372, (CFA), [138], how the idea of marginal appreciation has entered the domestic constitutional jurisprudence: 'At the supra-national level of the ECtHR, the margin of appreciation doctrine involves the recognition that on certain issues, the Court should allow Member States latitude to decide on the legitimacy of their societal aims and the means to achieve them since they are better placed to make the assessment. Similar considerations have led the Court at a domestic level to allow the legislative and executive authorities latitude or a "margin

780. Where the enabling legislation is constitutional, being a proportionate restriction of a fundamental right, the legality of any action taken under such legislation is measured by ordinary rules relating to legality of administrative action. In other words, the only question would be whether the administrative action is *intra vires* the enabling statute. In *Hong Kong Television Network Ltd v Chief Executive in Council*, the Court of Appeal held that the TV licensing regime as set out in the Broadcasting Ordinance (Cap. 562) constituted a justifiable and proportionate restriction of the fundamental right of freedom of expression. Chueng CJHC said that where the legislative scheme is a justifiable proportionate restriction prescribed by law, a discretionary decision taken under such scheme not to grant a licence may not be challenged as a disproportionate restriction on the freedom of expression. 'All [that an aggrieved applicant] has is a right to be considered in accordance with the licensing regime for a licence to do so. Following from that, in reviewing the decision to grant or refuse its application, all one has to do is to look at whether the decision of the CE in Council was unlawful, or was unreasonable in the public law sense, or was otherwise arbitrary or procedurally improper; in other words, the conventional public law grounds.'[1536] Cheung CJHC referred to a different view expressed by the House of Lords in *Belfast City Council v Miss Behavin Ltd* involving an application for a licence to use premises as a sex shop which was refused by the local city council, which appears to suggest that the refusal must be reviewed in accordance with the proportionality test as a Convention right was involved, despite that there was no challenge against the licensing system itself.[1537] Cheung CJHC said: 'It is unnecessary to resolve this difference in approach. In any event, it should be pointed out that even under a conventional public law review, given that freedom of expression is involved, the intensity of review has to be a heightened one so as to be commensurate with the fundamental right at stake.'[1538]

VIII. Procedural Impropriety

781. Following procedural requirements is as important as respecting substantive rights: 'it is imperative that the procedure laid down in the relevant statutes must be properly observed. The provisions of the statutes in this respect are supposed to provide safeguards for Her Majesty's subjects. Public bodies and Ministers

---

of discretion" to do the same, applying the "manifestly without reasonable foundation" standard in such cases.' As Ma CJ observed in *Fo Chun Wa v Hospital Authority* (2012) 15 HKCFAR 409, (CFA)[75], 'outside the area of socio-economic or other general policy matters, where fundamental concepts or core-values are involved, the court will be particularly stringent or intense in the application of the justification test. But in the area of socio-economic or other general policy matters, attempts to search for more and more alternatives to the solution that was adopted in any one case, should be discouraged. This, I reiterate, is not the role of the court.'

1536. [2016] 2 HKLRD 1005, (CA), [103].

1537. [2007] 1 WLR 1420, (HL). On the slow admission of proportionality to replace irrationality in administrative law, *see* Sir Philip Sales, 'Rationality, Proportionality and the Development of the Law' (2013) *Law Quarterly Review* 223.

1538. *Hong Kong Television Network Ltd v Chief Executive in Council* [2016] 2 HKLRD 1005, (CA), [106].

must be compelled to observe the law.'[1539] An administrative authority must observe any mandatory statutory procedures that are binding on it. For instance, an administrative decision would be invalid if the decision-maker failed to properly conduct a consultation as required by legislation,[1540] and give proper consideration to representations made in the consultation.[1541] It is generally agreed that administrative decision-making process must be open to the public in order to ensure public confidence in the fairness of the process. In the case of the now-defunct Insider Dealing Tribunal, which usually held its hearing in the public, it was held that the Tribunal breached the principle of 'open justice' when it excluded the public when it consulted its legal counsel.[1542]

A. Rules of Natural Justice

782. Failure to observe the rules of natural justice is the classic illustration of procedural impropriety. Article 10 of the Hong Kong Bill of Rights provides: 'In the determination of any criminal charge against him, or of his rights and obligations in a suit at law, everyone shall be entitled to a fair and public hearing by a competent, independent and impartial tribunal established by law.' This echoes the two limbs of the common law rule of natural justice: (1) the *audi alteram partem* rule or the right to a fair hearing and (2) the rule against bias or the right to be judged by an impartial tribunal.[1543] As Lord Browne-Wilkinson has observed 'where wide powers of decision-making are conferred by statute it is presumed that Parliament implicitly requires the decision to be made in accordance with the rules of natural justice'.[1544] We must briefly mention the use of 'duty to act fairly' and the duty to observe the rules of natural justice. The earlier view was that rules of natural justice are applicable when an administrative agency exercises a quasi-judicial function, and one reason for adopting the terminology of the duty to act fairly was to overcome that technical difficulty. Another reason is that duty to act fairly may be better suited to ensure fairness in situations where a full hearing is not called for. For all practical purposes, the duty to observe rules of natural justice (mainly the fair hearing) and the duty to act fairly may mean the same thing.[1545]

1539. *Bradbury v Enfield LBC* [1967] 1 WLR 1311, (CA), 1325, per Danckwerts LJ.
1540. *Tang Shuk Chun v Director of Food and Environmental Hygiene* [2015] HKEC 2422, (CFI).
1541. It is necessary for proper consideration to be given to representations made in the consultation and the government authority must 'have embarked on the consultation process prepared to change course, if persuaded by it to do so': Woolf, Jowell & Le Sueur (eds) *De Smith's Judicial Review* (7th edn, Sweet & Maxwell, 2013), 7-055 cited with approval in *Hysan Development co Ltd v Town Planning Board* [2014] HKEC 1869, (CA), [166].
1542. *Dato Tan Leong Min v Insider Dealing Tribunal* [1999] HKEC 1580, (CA).
1543. As Lord Denning said in *Kanda v Government of Malaya* [1962] AC 322, (PC), 337: 'The rule against bias is one thing. The right to be heard is another. Those two rules are the essential characteristics of what is often called natural justice. They are the twin pillars supporting it. The Romans put them in the two ways: *Nemo judex in causa sua* and *Audi alteram partem*. They have recently been put into two words, 'Impartiality' and 'Fairness'.
1544. *R v Secretary of State for the Home Department ex p Pierson* [1998] AC 539, (HL), 550.
1545. *See* Paul Craig, *Administrative Law* (8th edn, Sweet and Maxwell, 2016), 12-009 and 12-010 'Natural Justice and Fairness'.

1. The Right to a Fair Hearing

783. The purpose of giving a person, against whom a charge has been made a genuine, meaningful opportunity to present his case is to ensure that the decision-maker does not make up its mind influenced by only the charge and its own view of the veracity and gravity of the charge. *Kam Wai Hung v Secretary for Justice* is illustrative of how an opportunity to be heard given to the person charged may fall short of the right to a fair hearing.[1546] Hartmann J observed that a letter addressed to a junior police officer imposing a severe penalty and asking him to 'show cause' against it would lead any reasonable observer to conclude that at the very least there was a real likelihood that the matter had already been determined.[1547]

784. The right to a fair hearing requires that a defendant must be given notice of the charge against him and be allowed to present his case. A good illustration may be taken from the recent spate of litigation concerning the requirement that any candidate at any Legislative Council or District Council Election must be given an adequate opportunity to respond to any concerns that the returning officer may have about the genuineness of the oath of allegiance a candidate has taken. The returning officer must give the candidate a reasonable opportunity, before the decision is made, to respond to any materials intended to be relied upon by the returning officer for a decision that the candidate's nomination is invalid. Failure to do so would amount to a material irregularity in the election process.[1548]

785. Whether a person has been denied a fair hearing must be considered in the context of the entirety of the relevant process. In *X v Securities and Futures Commission*,[1549] X was being investigated by the Hong Kong Monetary Authority for

1546. *Kam Wai Hung v Secretary for Justice* [2002] HKEC 495, (CFI).

1547. *Ibid.*, [30].

1548. *See*: (i) *Chow Ting v Teng Yu Yan Anne (the Returning Officer)* [2019] 4 HKLRD 458, (CFI), where the returning officers considered whether an opportunity must be given to the candidate but decided against it; (ii) *Lau Wing Hong v Chan Yuen Man Amy (Returning Officer) (No 2)* [2019] 5 HKLRD 1, (CFI), where the returning officer had not considered whether the candidate must be given an opportunity to make representations, having concluded that even if such an opportunity had been given the decision would have been the same in view of the materials that she, the returning officer, had reviewed; and (iii) *Lau Siu Lai v Kwok Wai Fun Franco (Returning Officer)* [2020] HKEC 931, (CFI), where the returning officer had determined that in view of the material that he had before him, giving the candidate an opportunity to make representations would have made no difference to this determination. Chow J, at [23], explained why an opportunity ought to have been given: 'While the contents of the substantive constitutional requirement [namely taking the oath of allegiance] is a matter of law, whether she did satisfy such requirement is a question of fact. The determination of that question of fact is not a straight-forward one such as whether she has reached the age of 21, or whether she is a Chinese citizen and a permanent residence of the HKSAR, being some other eligibility requirements for nomination as a candidate under s 37(1) of the [Legislative Council Ordinance (Cap. 542)]. The determination of whether Ms Lau satisfied the substantive constitutional requirement raises some fine or intricate questions of whether she had sufficiently changed her previous stance [that Hong Kong is not an inalienable part of China, and therefore her publicly expressed view goes against what she affirms in the oath of allegiance] and genuinely and truly intended to uphold the Basic Law and pledge allegiance to the HKSAR, being matters which … should be determined objectively.'

1549. [2012] 4 HKLRD 296, (CFI).

alleged misconduct. Based on the Authority's findings and its own investigations, the Securities and Futures Commission issued notice of proposed disciplinary action, stating the nature of the charge, supporting evidence and reasons for the proposed disciplinary action, together with relevant documents. X's request for disclosure of further documents was declined on the ground of public interest immunity. X applied for judicial review of the refusal on the ground of denial of a reasonable opportunity to be heard. The court rejected the application on the grounds that: (i) the charge which X needed to address were clearly stated in the letter; (ii) the charge was based on the disclosed documents and not the other undisclosed documents; (iii) the undisclosed documents were irrelevant to the matter that the Authority and the Commission had to decide; and (iv) if the letter did not provide sufficient evidence, X would have an opportunity of further pursuing the matter at a review of the Commission's decision by an independent appeals tribunal chaired by a judge. The court rejected the judicial review application because looking at the entire scheme of the disciplinary proceedings it could not be said that the applicant was denied a fair hearing or a reasonable opportunity to be heard, citing the words of Ribeiro PJ: 'It is, however, clear that Article 10 ["In the determination of any criminal charge against him, or of his rights and obligations in a suit at law, everyone shall be entitled to a fair and public hearing by a competent, independent and impartial tribunal established by law"] ... does not require every element of the protections conferred to be present at every stage of the determination of a person's rights and obligations, but only that such protections should be effective when the determination is viewed as an entire process, including as part of that process such appeals or judicial review as may be available'.[1550]

786. Notice of the charge must provide sufficient information in order for him to be able to present an adequate reply. In *Caltex Oil Hong Kong Ltd v Governor in Council*,[1551] the applicants objected to a road works scheme that would adversely affect one of their petrol service stations. There occurred several rounds of communication between the relevant government department and the applicants. During this consultation the applicants were not given sufficient information in time for them to make a full submission. Moreover, when the proposed road works scheme was submitted to the Governor in Council for approval, not all the information provided by the applicants was forwarded to the Governor in Council. It was held that the Governor was under a duty to act fairly towards an objector when considering an objection to a proposed roadworks scheme and there was failure of this duty.[1552] In *Fine Tower Associates Ltd v Town Planning Board*, it was held that where the Board has received qualified advice from government departments on which it based its decision, it was under a duty to disclose it to the affected parties (persons

1550. *Lam Siu Po v Commissioner of Police* (2009) 12 HKCFAR 237, (CFA), [109], Ribeiro PJ.
1551. *Caltex Oil Hong Kong Ltd v Governor in Council* [1995] 1 HKLR 122, (HC).
1552. *Ibid.* Sears J said: 'Although the Ordinance only says that the Governor in Council shall consider the objection, this involves the Governor in Council, that is, the members of Executive Council, knowing first the precise details of the objection, secondly the administration's answer to the objection and, thirdly, the objector's comments, if any, on the administration's answer of which the objector would not have been aware at the time of lodging his objection. It is only in this way that the Governor in Council can act fairly' (at p. 125).

making representations against a proposed land-use plan) so they could present counterarguments.[1553] In *Oriental Generation Ltd v Town Planning Board*, the Court of First Instance held that non-disclosure of information to the applicant, who objected to a land-use plan, vitiated the decision of the Board.[1554]

787. In *Pearl Securities Ltd v Stock Exchange of Hong Kong Ltd*,[1555] a company was denied membership of the Hong Kong Stock Exchange by a blackballing balloting system, which was not an open and transparent system. It was held that the selection system was flawed because the applicant company was not given 'sufficient particularity to enable the company to address those concerns if it [wanted] to'. As Justice Keith explained, 'all that [was] necessary [was] for the company to be informed of the nature of the members' concerns and the gist of any information on which those concerns were based'.[1556]

788. Where the government decides to resume land, the affected landowner (the lessee) must be given an opportunity make representations. *Fok Lai Ying v Governor in Council* reiterated this principle but held on facts that there had been no breach of the principle. There, an approved land-use plan drastically interfered with the applicant's use of the land. In order to implement the land-use policy set out in the plan, the government decided to resume the applicant's land. The applicant, by her solicitors, sent in a written objection and asked for its consideration by the Executive Council, which was duly considered. The applicant was told that the answers of officials to her objection would also be put before the Executive Council. She was given an opportunity to raise any further questions. In the event she raised none. Accordingly, there was nothing unfair, arbitrary or unlawful in the consultation procedure.[1557] As regards the approach to the interpretation of the Governor's power to resume land for a public purpose, the Court of Appeal said that in the absence of any express provision granting an opportunity to affected landowners to make representations, 'the common law requires that it must be done with fairness … to all concerned'. The Court added, however that 'fairness cannot be strained to such an extent as to frustrate the object of the statute'. While recognizing that an affected person must have an opportunity to make representations which should be duly considered, the Court of Appeal rejected the idea that the Governor was obliged to conduct a comprehensive inquiry, involving not only the affected landowner. The Privy Council agreed that the affected landowner has been afforded a fair opportunity to be heard. However the Privy Council found it difficult to

---

1553. *Fine Tower Associates Ltd v Town Planning Board* [2005] HKCU 504, (CFI), where Hartmann J said that 'a principal limitation placed on the Board's freedom to create its own unfettered procedures is the statutory obligation to ensure that an objector is able to exercise his right to make representations, which must mean representations in respect of all relevant matters not merely some, and to have those representations considered before the Board comes to a decision. But the right to make representations is worth little if material factors which may weigh against an objector are not disclosed to the objector so that he may speak to them' [41].

1554. *Oriental Generation Ltd v Town Planning Board* [2014] HKEC 1868, (CFI), [94] and [97], following *Caltex Oil Hong Kong* case.

1555. *Pearl Securities Ltd v Stock Exchange of Hong Kong Ltd* [1999] 2 HKLRD 243, (CFI).

1556. *Ibid.*, 258.

1557. *Fok Lai Ying v Governor in Council* [1997] HKLRD 111, (CA).

endorse the Court of Appeal's view on the nature of the inquiry required: 'The judgment of the Court of Appeal in this case and the judgment of a Full Bench of the High Court in the earlier *K.O.Y. case*[1558] depend ultimately on the ideas that to superimpose on the statutory language requirements apt to lead to protracted exchanges or something akin to a public inquiry would be to frustrate the purposes of the Ordinance.'[1559,1560]

789. The duty to hear the affected party is meaningful if the decision-maker has heard the representations: 'He who decides must hear'. Where the decision-maker is a collective body, it is important that the members of such body who are present at the time of its determination had heard the affected party. If those who participate in the determination had been absent from the hearing, it cannot be said that the affected party has been given an adequate hearing by the decision-maker. In the context of the Town Planning Board it has been held that while it is not practicable for all members who participate in the decision-making to be present throughout the proceedings of the Board (because of the constraints of time on them who are not full time members of the Board), it is essential that all Board members involved in making the decision must be adequately informed of the contents of such representations by the time they come to deliberate and decide upon them.[1561]

790. While it is universally accepted that decisions affecting citizens must be taken in compliance with the rules of natural justice, there is no consistency in case law regarding what different aspects of natural justice must be present in an individual case. This problem relates mainly to the requirements of a fair hearing, which are diverse. They include: (a) the right to a public and oral hearing; (b) the right to cross-examine the opponents; (c) the right to legal representation; and (d) the right to have reasons for decisions. Under the common law rules on procedural fairness, there was no absolute right to have counsel address a tribunal or question witnesses.

1558. *In re Application by K.O.Y. Investment Co Ltd* [1983] HKLR 28 (HC).

1559. *Fok Lai Ying v Governor in Council* [1997] HKLRD 810, (PC).

1560. *Ibid.*, 820. At 811 Lord Cooke of Thornton quoted from *R v Secretary of State for the Home Department, ex p Doody* [1994] 1 AC 531, (HL), 560, where Lord Mustill said that fairness requires that: '(1) where an Act of Parliament confers an administrative power there is a presumption that it will be exercised in a manner which is fair in all the circumstances. (2) The standards of fairness are not immutable. They may change with the passage of time, both in the general and in their application to decisions of a particular type. (3) The principles of fairness are not to be applied by rote identically in every situation. What fairness demands is dependent on the context of the decision, and this is to be taken into account in all its aspects. (4) An essential feature of the context is the statute which creates the discretion, as regards both its language and the shape of the legal and administrative system within which the decision is taken. (5) Fairness will very often require that a person who may be adversely affected by the decision will have an opportunity to make representations on his own behalf either before the decision is taken with a view to producing a favourable result; or after it is taken, with a view to procuring its modification; or both. (6) Since the person affected usually cannot make worthwhile representations without knowing what factors may weigh against his interests fairness will very often require that he is informed of the gist of the case which he has to answer.'

1561. *Oriental Generation Ltd v Town Planning Board* [2014] HKEC 1868, (CFI), [127]. *See also Hysan Development co Ltd v Town Planning Board* [2014] HKEC 1869, [166], (CA), citing *R (Hill) v Institute of Chartered Accountants* [2014] 1 WLR 86, (CA).

Tribunals had a discretion whether to permit legal representation. The mode and extent of legal representation that should be permitted at a hearing depended on the needs of fairness in the circumstances and what was proportionate. There is no comprehensive list of factors that a tribunal should have regard to in deciding this, but such factors include the seriousness of the charge and potential penalty; whether any points of law are likely to arise; the capacity of the individual to present his own case; procedural difficulties; the need for reasonable speed in making the adjudication; and the need for fairness among the individuals concerned. It might well be that a blanket exclusion of legal representation is likely in most cases to offend the principles of fairness.[1562]

791. In situations where there is no significant impact on rights of the individual, there need not be an oral hearing, and a 'hearing conducted in writing' is considered sufficient.[1563] The Court of Appeal's decision in *De Kantzow (Peter) v Appeal Tribunal*[1564] provides another example where the Court was satisfied that there was no need for an oral hearing.

792. The right to cross-examine the opponent and his witnesses is not an indispensable requirement of a fair hearing. However, there are situations where denial of cross-examination constitutes a serious procedural impropriety. In a case concerning disciplinary proceedings where the essential issue was whether a prosecution witness, who had been called by an adjudicator to give expert evidence, was telling the truth or was seeking to cover up for himself or others by blaming the applicant, the credibility of that witness was of the greatest relevance to the matters before the adjudicator. Accordingly, to deny the applicant a fair opportunity of cross-examining as to credit was a form of procedural impropriety sufficiently serious to justify the court concluding that there had been a substantial denial of natural justice unless the actual material was clearly and manifestly inadequate to make any effective impression on the witness' credibility.[1565]

793. Another aspect of a fair hearing is the right to legal representation. In *Stock Exchange of Hong Kong Ltd v New World Development Co. Ltd*,[1566] the Court of Final Appeal held that there is no absolute right to be legally represented before an

1562. *Stock Exchange of Hong Kong Ltd v New World Development Co. Ltd* (2006) 9 HKCFAR 234, (CFA), [101].

1563. *See Re an Application by Wong Chik-wai for Judicial Review* [1986] HKLR 478, (HC).

1564. [1991] HKLY 743, (CA).

1565. *Re Ngai Kin Wah* [1986] HKLY 8, (HC), 244.

1566. (2006) 9 HKCFAR 234, (2006) 9 HKCFAR 234, (CFA). *See Rowse v Secretary for Civil Service* [2008] 5 HKLRD 217, (CFI), where the Court of First Instance held that the denial of legal representation was fatal to the proceedings of a committee of inquiry. There, the Secretary for the Civil Service who had discretion to allow legal representation refused to do so in the absence of compelling reasons, whereas in the opinion of the court the test was a less strict one of whether fairness required grant of legal representation. *See* [129]. Hartmann J held that denial of legal representation might have materially prejudiced the applicant in the presentation of his case. *See* [141].

administrative tribunal – even a tribunal with the power to impose heavy penalties – but there is a discretion vested in the tribunal to permit legal representation if fairness requires it. Ribeiro PJ said:

> The common law principles of fairness operate flexibly, requiring the tribunal to respond reasonably to the requirements of fairness arising in each case, balancing any competing interests and considering what, if any, limits may proportionately be imposed on legal representation in consequence (at [101]). The argument is sometimes made not that the defendant did not have legal representation, but that the incompetence of this legal representative resulted in the denial of a fair hearing. The Hong Kong Court of Final Appeal has adopted a view expressed in Australia that a legal representative has a wide discretion in the conduct of his client's case: 'As a general rule, a party is bound by the conduct of his or her counsel, and counsel have a wide discretion as to the manner in which proceedings are conducted. Decisions as to what witnesses to call, what witnesses to our score not to ask, what lines of argument to pursue and what points to abandon, are all matters within the discretion of counsel and frequently involve difficult problems of judgment, including judgment as to tactics. The authorities concerning the rights and duties of counsel are replete with emphatic statements which stress both the independent role of the barrister and the binding consequences for the client of decisions taken by a barrister in the course of running a case'.[1567] The courts have recognised that in some exceptional instances, an error of sufficient proportion and consequence, amounting to 'fragrant incompetence' will enable the court to intervene and avert a miscarriage of justice.[1568]

794. Some statutes prohibit legal representation in certain tribunals for administrative reasons.[1569] In *Lam Siu Po v Commissioner of Police* [2009] 4 HKLRD 575, Regulations 9(11) and 9(12) of the Police (Discipline) Regulations (Cap. 232A, Sub.Leg.) prohibited legal representation in a police disciplinary inquiry. The Court of Final Appeal held this to be unconstitutional and contrary to Article 10 of the Hong Kong Bill of Rights, which guarantees the right to a fair hearing.

2. The Rule Against Bias

795. The rule against bias[1570] requires that there should not be any real bias or likelihood of bias on the part of the decision-maker. Real bias is quite difficult to

1567. This view expressed by Gleeson CJ of the South Wales Court of Criminal Appeal in *R v Birks* (1990) 48 Aust Crim R 385, 390, was adopted by the Court of Final Appeal in *Chong Ching Yuen v HKSAR* (2004) 7 HKCFAR 126, (CFA), [47].

1568. *Chong Ching Yuen v HKSAR* (2004) 7 HKCFAR 126, (CFA), [49].

1569. *See,* e.g., the Small Claims Tribunal Ordinance and the Labour Relations Ordinance.

1570. 'It has been authoritatively held that there is no difference between the common law test for bias and the requirement under ECHR 6(1) of an independent and impartial tribunal: *see Lawal v Northern Spirit Ltd* [2003] ICR 856, (HL), (HL), [14] (Lord Steyn), *R v Abdroikov* [2007] 1 WLR

prove.[1571] Apparent bias can arise because of: (i) a pecuniary or other direct interests; or (ii) a reasonable apprehension arising from the facts of the case. As Lord Browne-Wilkinson observed in the *Pinochet (No. 2)* case, '[the rule against bias] has two very similar but not identical implications. First, it may be applied literally: if a judge is in fact a party to the litigation or has a financial or proprietary interest in its outcome then he is indeed sitting as a judge in his own cause. In that case, the mere fact that he is a party to the action or has a financial or proprietary interest in its outcome is sufficient to cause his automatic disqualification. The second application of the principle is where a judge is not a party to the suit and does not have a financial interest in its outcome, but in some other way his conduct or behaviour may give rise to a suspicion that he is not impartial, for example because of his friendship with a party. This second type of case is not strictly speaking an application of the principle that a man must not be judge in his own cause, since the judge will not normally be himself benefiting, but providing a benefit for another by failing to be impartial.'[1572]

796. *Dimes*[1573] is a classic example of a case of financial interest and *Pinochet* [2000] 1 AC 119 is an example of a non-pecuniary interest both falling within the first category that Lord Browne-Wilkinson called 'automatic disqualification'. The test applicable for the second category of cases, namely cases of apparent bias, is as follows:

2679, [14] (Lord Bingham) and *O'Neill v HM Advocate (No 2)* [2013] 1 WLR 1992, (SC), [47] (Lord Hope of Craighead DPSC). In my view, the same conclusion follows in Hong Kong in respect of the right to an independent and impartial tribunal under BOR 10': *HKSAR v Md Emran Hossain* (2016) 19 HKCFAR 679, (CFA), [31]. The fair-minded observer would be aware of the judicial oath and that judges would generally try to live up to the high standard which it imposed. That observer would expect that a single judge who had previously refused leave to appeal would hear the renewed application for leave with an open mind and with a readiness to grant leave to appeal if persuaded by the arguments advanced to the Full Court and the deliberations of his judicial colleagues. This was not to say that there might never be circumstances in which the fair-minded and informed observer would consider there to be a real possibility that a single judge who had refused leave to appeal might be biased on a subsequent hearing of the underlying merits of the case.

1571. *Incorporated Owners of Finance Building v Bright Hill Management Consultants Co Ltd* [2010] 3 HKLRD 1, (CA), illustrates how a claim of apparent bias is easier than a claim of actual bias to establish. There, D had failed to prove that the judge was actually biased against it because of some observation that the judge had made in the course of the proceedings. The judge had accepted that the criticisms he made of D's directors were mistaken. There might not have been actual bias, but there was an appearance of bias on his part.

1572. *R v Bow Street Metropolitan Stipendiary Magistrate ex p. Pinochet Ugarte (No 2)* [2000] 1 AC 119, (HL), 132–133.

1573. *Dimes v Proprietors of Grand Junction Canal* (1852) 3 HL Case 759.

> The court must first ascertain all the circumstances which have a bearing on the suggestion that the judge was biased. It must then ask whether those circumstances would lead a fair-minded and informed observer to conclude that there was a real possibility, or a real danger, the two being the same, that the tribunal was biased.[1574]

This formulation was adopted by the Court of Final Appeal in *Deacons v White & Case LLP*.[1575]

797. In *Panel on Takeovers & Mergers v Cheng Kai Man, William*,[1576] a member of the Panel on Takeovers and Mergers asked the Securities and Futures Commission whether an investigation should be conducted in relation to a takeover action that might possibly have been made in breach of the takeover code. The Panel was appointed by the Commission to inquire into disputes in takeover cases. The member happened to be a director of a company that was given a non-exclusive mandate to acquire the shares in question. When a listing company subsequently had to face inquiry by the Panel, it contended that the member was biased. However, the Privy Council dismissed its claim by holding that the financial interest of the member was far too remote to fall foul of the rule against bias.

798. It is a question of fact whether a person is disqualified from being a member of a decision-making body because of his close connection with a matter to be decided by it. In *Wong Pun Cheuk v Medical Council of Hong Kong and the Attorney General*,[1577] the Director of Medical and Health Services was disqualified to act as the Chairman of the Medical Council. The subsidiary legislation in question conferred a power on the Director to refer to the Medical Council for inquiry of any cases where he was of the opinion that a medical practitioner was using dangerous drugs for purposes other than medical treatment. After inquiry, the Council could recommend to the Director the withdrawal of the authorization of the medical practitioner in question to possess or supply dangerous drugs. Thus, the Director did act not only as the prosecutor by referring suspected cases to the Medical Council but

---

1574. *In re Medicaments and Related Classes of Goods (No 2)* [2001] 1 WLR 700, (CA), [85], per Lord Philips MR. *See Rowse v Secretary for Civil Service* [2008] 5 HKLRD 217, (CFI), [69]. In *HKSAR v Md Emran Hossain* (2016) 19 HKCFAR 679, (CFA), the Court of Final Appeal did not see a breach of the rule against bias when a single judge who refused leave to appeal participated in the hearing of the application to review the refusal. The Court was of the view that a fair-minded observer would be aware of the judicial oath and that judges would generally try to live up to the high standard which it imposed. That observer would expect that a single judge who had previously refused leave to appeal would hear the renewed application for leave with an open mind and with a readiness to grant leave to appeal if persuaded by the arguments advanced to the Full Court and the deliberations of his judicial colleagues. This was not to say that there might never be circumstances in which the fair-minded and informed observer would consider there to be a real possibility that a single judge who had refused leave to appeal might be biased on a subsequent hearing of the underlying merits of the case.

1575. (2003) 6 HKCFAR 322, (CFA).

1576. [1995] 2 HKLR 302, (PC).

1577. [1964] HKLR 47, (HC), 79.

also as judge in his capacity as the chairman of the Council. This conflicted with the maxim that 'a person must not be a judge in his own cause'.[1578]

799. On the other hand, it has been held proper for the Secretary for Planning, Environment, and Lands and the Director of Planning to be members of the Town Planning Board. The two senior public officers, when lawfully acting as members of the board, were not acting as members of the Planning Department of the government. Members of the Planning Department who were called upon to assist the Board in its deliberations were present as advisers, not as parties to adversarial proceedings. They were not acting in furtherance of some private interest of the Planning Department: they were serving the public interest in putting their knowledge and expertise at the service of all the members of the board. In the peculiar circumstances of Hong Kong, it was unrealistic to regard their presence on the board, which was authorized by statute, as necessarily importing systemic bias. Whatever might be the impression of an observer who was not in possession of the full facts, there was no real danger of bias on the part of the two public officers.[1579] It has been held that while members of the Town Planning Board were entitled to have some predispositions on policies,[1580] 'the court had to made an assessment, putting itself in the shoes of a fair-minded and informed observer, having due regard to the statutory scheme in question, as to whether there was a real risk that the members' minds were closed by predetermination'.[1581] The Court in *Oriental Generation* case, also held against the argument of apparent bias, pointing out that while official members of the Board may legitimately have some predispositions by reason of their earlier involvement in the preparation of land-use plans they should not allow such predispositions to overwhelm the determination of the Board or pre-empt any meaningful and fair consideration of the relevant planning issues.[1582]

800. It is standard practice of many deliberative bodies for a member of the body to declare any conflict of interest he may have in relation to any matter that is before it. Where the conflict of interest is likely to affect his ability to impartially contribute to its proceedings, the member could be required to abstain from participating in its deliberations. The body might decide that the member should not even receive any information or documents in relation to the matter in respect of which he has a conflict of interest.[1583]

1578. *Dr Z v Education and Accreditation Committee Medical Council of Hong Kong* [2011] HKEC 1209, (CFI), is an illustrative case where overlapping membership may give rise to an appearance of bias.
1579. *Real Estate Developers Association v Town Planning Board* (1996) 6 HKPLR 179.
1580. As is the case in England. *See R (Lewis) v Redcar & Cleveland BC* [2009] 1 WLR 83, (CA).
1581. *Town Planning Board v Oriental Generation Ltd* [2014] HKEC 1868, (CFI), [56] citing *Redcar case*.
1582. *Ibid.*, [64].
1583. The practice of the Town Planning Board provides a good illustration. *See Town Planning Board: Procedure and Practice*, Chapter II 'Declaration of Interests'. https://www.info.govhk/tpb/en/about_us/Procedure_Practice/PxP_revised_May2014_Part%20II.pdf.

801. Where a judge considers that he has, or appears to have, a conflict of interest which might result in his not being able to bring an impartial and independent mind to the resolution of the question that he is required to decide, the judge must recuse himself from hearing the case. He may decide to do so on his own, or after considering a recusal application made by a party to litigation. In *Komal Patel v Chris Au*[1584] the recusal application alleged apparent bias on the part of the judge and the court held that the test to be applied is reasonable apprehension of bias: 'The court must first ascertain all the circumstances which have a bearing on the suggestion that the judge was biased. It must then ask whether those circumstances would lead a fair-minded and informed observer to conclude that there was a real possibility that the tribunal was biased.'[1585] In the particular circumstance the judge was not convinced that he needed to recuse himself.

802. In *Falcon Private Bank Ltd v Borry Bernard Edouard Charles Ltd*[1586] the Court of Final Appeal held that the refusal by the judge to recuse himself was not justifiable. There, the trial judge, who had dismissed several applications by the defendant to resist enforcement of a series of orders for disclosure of information regarding large sums of money alleged to have been wrongfully received by him, had on several occasions criticized the defendant and his counsel. The defendant made a recusal application which the judge rejected. On the defendant's appeal, the Court of Appeal held that the judge's uncompromisingly expressed finding that the defendant's legal representatives had deliberately misled the Court, repeated in a series of decisions spanning more than six months, would inevitably lead a fair-minded and informed observer to conclude that there was a real possibility that the tribunal had lost its detachment and would approach the case with its mind closed to persuasion by those advisers, thus undermining judicial impartiality. The Court of Final Appeal refused to interfere with that conclusion and observed that a judge must not automatically recuse himself just because he had seriously criticized counsel or solicitors appearing in a case.[1587] '[I]f a judge made criticisms without any discernible rhyme or reason or which were obviously unfair and unreasonable, this might be factored into what the fair-minded and informed observer might apprehend in terms of apparent bias. Conversely, if the criticisms appeared capable of being justified, any appellate court would be slow to conclude from the mere fact of such criticisms, that the fair-minded and informed observer would apprehend a risk of bias. But even if the criticisms were or might be justified, if they were couched in terms or made in a context which raised doubts as to whether the judge could continue to adjudicate with the detachment and impartiality essential to the judicial process, his recusal might be properly required. … Where a judge finds it necessary to criticise the legal representatives of a party appearing in a case, the question

1584. [2016] 1 HKLRD 328, (CFI). *See Chau Siu Woon v Cheung Shek Kong* [2013] 3 HKLRD 49, (CA), for another unsuccessful recusal application.
1585. *Ibid.*, at [8], citing *Deacons v White & Case LLP* (2003) 6 HKCFAR 322, (CFA), [20]–[24] and *Falcon Private Bank Ltd v Borry Bernard Edouard Charles Ltd* (2014) 17 HKCFAR 281 at [11].
1586. (2014) 17 HKCFAR 281, (CFA).
1587. *Ibid.*, [29].

of whether recusal should follow requires all relevant circumstances to be taken into account and policy considerations to be balanced against each other.'[1588]

B. Duty to Give Reasons

803. The duty is a function of due process, and therefore of justice. Its rationale has two principal aspects. The first is that fairness requires that the parties, especially the losing party, should be left in no doubt why the tribunal decided the dispute the way it did. The second is that a requirement to give reasons concentrates the mind; if it is fulfilled, the resulting decision is much more likely to be soundly based on the evidence than if it is not.[1589] A duty to give reasons may be imposed by legislation expressly[1590] or by implication.[1591] The common law does not, as a matter of principle, require reasons to be given for decisions made,[1592] but 'just because Parliament had ruled that some tribunals should be required to give reasons for their reasons, it [does not follow] that common law is unable to impose a similar

1588. *Ibid.*, [36] and [37].

1589. *Flannery and Another v Halifax Estate Agencies Ltd. (trading as Colleys Professional Services)* [2000] 1 W.L.R. 377, (CA), 381.

1590. *See Leung Kwok Hung v HKSAR* (2005) 8 HKCFAR 229, (CFA), where the Public Order Ordinance (Cap. 245) was in issue. Section 13A requires at least one week's notice of a proposed procession consisting of more than thirty persons on a public highway or thoroughfare or in a public park to be given to the Commissioner of Police, who has a discretion to accept shorter notice where he is reasonably satisfied that a week's notice could not have been given. Where the Commissioner decides not to accept notice of less than one week, he must give reasons for this decision as soon as practicable. Similarly, the Commissioner may object to the holding of the public procession of which he has been duly notified, if such objection is necessary in the interest of national security or public safety, public order or protection of the rights and freedoms of others. His objection and the reasons must be notified in writing to the organizer: s. 14. He may instead impose conditions on his approval of the procession. If he decides to do so, he must inform the organizer of his decision with reasons why such conditions are necessary: s. 15.

1591. *See Oriental Daily Publisher Ltd v Commissioner for Television and Entertainment Licensing Authority* (1997–1998) 1 HKCFAR 279, (CFA), affirming the decision of the Court of Appeal. Li CJ went a step further: 'It is possible that the duty may be put on a wider ground than implication as a matter of statutory construction. It may be said to arise under the common law in the following way. Considering the character of the tribunal, the kind of decision it has to make and the statutory framework in which it operates, the requirements of fairness demand that the tribunal should give reasons; there being no contrary intention in the statute' (at 289).

1592. *Amoy Properties Ltd v The Committee for Takeovers and Mergers and the Commissioner for Securities* [1989] 1 HKLR 170, (HC). In *CP Ships USA LLC v Chief Executive of Hong Kong Special Administrative Region* [2007] HKEC 858, (CFI), the Chief Executive had given reasons why he refused a petition against the decision of the Customs Department to return a shipment of guns that had been imported by the applicant without a permit. The judge observed that while the Chief Executive must listen to any explanations given by the petitioner, he also had to take into account wider policy considerations, which are not legal considerations, into account. Compelling him to disclose those reasons 'may force him to "legalism". He may be compelled to express a subtle or difficult balancing of a wide range of non-legal considerations (some of which may only be intuitively grasped by virtue of his experience as an administrator) in a legal language which is wholly unsuited to the task. Indeed, even if he were able sufficiently to articulate his motivations, ultimately they could not be justiciable by a Court in a judicial review.' At [82]. The Court of Appeal agreed that the Chief Executive was not under a duty to give reasons: [2007] HKEC 1714, (CA).

requirement upon other tribunals, if justice so requires'.[1593] It has been said that it is incorrect to assume that 'there now exists any rule of common law or of procedural fairness to the effect that a public authority must always give reasons for its decisions. Nor … does there exist a duty generally to give reasons subject only to reasonable exceptions that have evolved by way of empirical experience.'[1594] There are two classes of situations where a duty to give reasons may arise: (1) where the subject matter is an interest so highly regarded by the law (e.g., personal liberty), fairness requires that reasons be given as of right; (2) where the decision appears aberrant, fairness may require reasons to be given. In *Pearl Securities Ltd v Stock Exchange of Hong Kong Ltd,* Keith J explained what an aberrant decision is: 'A decision will have the appearance of being aberrant if it is t markedly out of line with decisions which the decision-maker regularly makes on the topic. Such a decision will normally require reasons to be given for it.'[1595] When there is a duty to give reasons or where in the absence of a mandatory duty to do so the administrative officer proceeds to give reasons for the decision in question, the reasons so given must be clear and sufficient.[1596]

1593. *R v Civil Service Appeal Board ex p Cunningham* [1991] 4 All ER 310, 318, per Lord Donaldson, cited in *Wong Wai Tak v Secretary for the Civil Service* [2001] HKEC 167, (CFI). Keith J said in *Re Solicitor* [1999] 3 HKLRD 406, 414, (CA), that whether a tribunal should be required to give reasons depended upon whether in the particular circumstances of the case fairness required seasons to be given. In *Oriental Daily Publisher Ltd v Commissioner for Television and Entertainment Licensing Authority* (1997–1998) 1 HKCFAR 279, (CFA), where the duty to give reasons was held to be an implied statutory duty, Li CJ went a step further: 'It is possible that the duty may be put on a wider ground than implication as a matter of statutory construction. It may be said to arise under the common law in the following way. Considering the character of the tribunal, the kind of decision it has to make and the statutory framework in which it operates, the requirements of fairness demand that the tribunal should give reasons; there being no contrary intention in the statute' (at p. 865).

1594. Hartmann J in *So Chung v Commissioner of Correctional Services* [2001] HKEC 91, (CFI), and cited by him in *Wong Wai Tak v Secretary for the Civil Service* [2001] HKEC 167, (CFI).

1595. *Pearl Securities Ltd v Stock Exchange of Hong Kong Ltd* [1999] 2 HKLRD 243, (CFI), 261. Sound public administration demands that when reasons are required or are provided for an administrative decision they should be clear as well as sufficient to the circumstances: *Capital Rich Development Ltd v Town Planning Board* [2007] 2 HKLRD 155, 97, (CA), per Stock JA. *See B v Torture Claims Appeal Board* [2015] 1 HKLRD 681, (CFI), where it was held that the Board was under a duty to give reasons because its decision had a significant effect on the applicants' torture claims and there was no right to appeal against the decision.

1596. As Stock JA explained in *Capital Rich Development Ltd v Town Planning Board* [2007] 2 HKLRD 155, (CA), [97]: 'Sound public administration demands that when reasons are required or are provided for an administrative decision, they should be clear as well as sufficient to the circumstances. The provision of adequate and clear reasons, where reasons are required by law, is a function of sound administration because transparency is more likely to promote confidence in public administration than is opacity, and also because the very requirement to provide clear reasons against the background of the particular issues raised itself encourages a disciplined approach to the issues at hand. But, most obviously, the requirement is based on fairness, so that the person or body adversely affected by a decision should have an adequate indication of the reasoning process, enabling him to know whether the decision-maker has addressed his grievance and whether there may be a basis for challenging the decision': *see Leung Kwok Hung v HKSAR* (2005) 8 HKCFAR 229, (CFA), where it was held that the Commissioner of Police under the Public Order Ordinance (Cap. 245) was under a duty to give reasons for objecting to the holding of a public procession or for imposing conditions on his approval of such a public procession. Li CJ explained at [59]: 'The duty is to give adequate reasons. Plainly, the bald assertion of a conclusion would

804. It is now well recognized that there is a growing trend towards accepting duty to give reasons as part of common law. As Elias LJ observed in *R (Oakley) v South Cambridgeshire District Council*:[1597] 'It is firmly established that there is no general obligation to give reasons at common law … .' However, the tendency increasingly is to require them rather than not. Indeed, almost twenty years ago, when giving judgment in *Stefan v General Medical Council* [1999] 1 WLR 1293, (PC), 1301, Lord Clyde observed: 'There is certainly a strong argument for the view that what was once seen as exceptions to a rule may now be becoming examples of the norm, and the cases where reasons are not required may be taking on the appearance of exceptions.'[1598] Having cited the above words of Elias LJ in *R (Oakley) v South Cambridgeshire District Council*, Lisa Wong J added in *Trustees of Church of England in Diocese of Victoria, Hong Kong v Town Planning Board*: 'The time may have come for the courts in Hong Kong to recognise that there is a general duty for an administrative body to give reason, unless there is a proper justification for not doing so.'[1599]

805. If a decision-maker does not give reasons for its actions, the court might well conclude that there were no reasons for the decision. However, the law also allows evidence to be admitted to elucidate or, exceptionally, correct or add to the reasons given by an administrative body, although evidence could not be admitted to fundamentally alter or contradict the reasons given. The function of such evidence should generally be 'elucidation not fundamental alteration nor contradiction'.[1600]

IX. Legitimate Expectation

A. Procedural Legitimate Expectation

806. Procedural legitimate expectation demands that, where a promise has been given that a particular procedural process will be adopted, for instance that the person to be affected will be given an opportunity to be heard before an adverse decision is made, and the promisee had relied on the promise to their detriment, such promise must be honoured.

---

not be sufficient. Where the Commissioner decides to object or to impose conditions, the reasons given must be sufficient to show that he has properly applied the proportionality test in making his decision.'

1597. [2017] 1 WLR 3765, (CA), [29]–[30].

1598. Referred to by the Supreme Court in *R (CPRE Kent) v Dover District Council* [2018] 1 WLR 108, (SC), [52], [54].

1599. *Trustees of Church of England in Diocese of Victoria, Hong Kong v Town Planning Board* [2020] HKEC 412, (CFI), [78]. In *Chow Oi Tong Amy v Hong Kong Housing Authority* [2020] HKEC 1383, (CFI), [26], Alex J agreed.

1600. *Smart Gain Investment Ltd v Town Planning Board* [2007] HKEC 1964, (CFI), [72]; *Popular Signs Ltd v Radiation Board* [2010] HKEC 41, (CFI), [78].

807. The leading case on procedural legitimate expectation is the Privy Council decision in *Attorney General v Ng Yuen Shiu.*[1601] There the Hong Kong Government had announced that it would interview illegal immigrants from Macau in determining whether they would be allowed to stay in Hong Kong, while making it clear that it would not allow all interviewees to stay in Hong Kong. In response to this announcement, Mr Ng, an illegal immigrant from Macau, surrendered to the Immigration Department and a removal order was made against him immediately. It was held that because of the promise made by the government, Mr Ng was entitled to demand a hearing before being deported. Accordingly, the court prohibited the Immigration Department from issuing a removal order against him. In *Fok Ho Chiu v Chinese Temples Committee*,[1602] the court held that a legitimate expectation arose that there will be a particular way of assessing the tenders. Claims of procedural legitimate expectation were rejected in *Television Broadcasts Ltd v Communications Authority*[1603] and *Tong Wai Ting v Secretary for Education.*[1604]

B. Substantive Legitimate Expectation

808. Today, legitimate expectation can be relied on to assert substantive rights. In *R. v North and East Devon HA Ex p. Coughlan*, the Court of Appeal held that if a public body exercising a statutory function made a promise as to how it would behave in the future that induced a legitimate expectation of a benefit that was substantive, rather than merely procedural, to frustrate that expectation could be so unfair that it would amount to an abuse of power. The promise must be honoured unless there is a sufficient overriding interest to justify a departure from what had previously been promised.[1605] In *Council for Civil Service Unions v Minister for Civil Service*,[1606] the House of Lords held that a policy that had been implemented for some time should not normally be withdrawn without consulting those affected.

1601. *Attorney General v Ng Yuen Shiu* [1983] 2 AC 629, (PC).

1602. *Fok Ho Chiu v Chinese Temples Committee* [2003] HKEC 1183, (CFI), which concerned selection of temple keepers by the Chinese Temples Committee by calling tenders. The complainant was a former temple keeper whose tender was unsuccessful, who argued that the respondent, in disregard of its promised procedure, took account only of the tender price at the second stage of consideration. Upholding argument of frustration of the procedural legitimate expectation, Chung J said: 'there has been made a clear and unambiguous representation on behalf of the Respondent that the knowledge, experience and abilities of the tenderers would be taken into account by the selection committee of the Respondent not only at the pre-qualified test stage but also at the tender stage. In my judgment, that is sufficient to found an argument based on legitimate expectation. This was a statement of procedure represented by the Respondent to the Applicant and his fellow temple keepers' [32].

1603. *Television Broadcasts Ltd v Communications Authority* [2013] HKEC 729, (CFI).

1604. *Tong Wai Ting v Secretary for Education* [2009] HKEC 1867, (CFI).

1605. *R v North and East Devon HA Ex p. Coughlan* [2001] QB 213, (CA). The substantive legitimate expectation is part of Hong Kong Law. *See Ng Siu Tung v Director of Immigration* (2002) 5 HKCFAR 1, (CFA), which is discussed in the next paragraph.

1606. *Council for Civil Service Unions v Minister for Civil Service* [1985] AC 374.

809. In *Ng Siu Tang v The Director of Immigration*,[1607] the Court of Final Appeal held that substantive legitimate expectation was part of Hong Kong law and set out the principles relating to legitimate expectation. It observed that in the absence of any overriding reason of law or policy excluding its operation, failure to keep a promise may amount to an abuse of power. Where a legitimate expectation has arisen, the decision-maker must take that into consideration and if effect is not to be given to the expectation, there must be cogent reasons to support such decision. The analysis of the doctrine of legitimate expectation as given in *Ng Siu Tang v The Director of Immigration* has been helpfully summarized in *Hong Kong Television Network Ltd v Chief Executive in Council*[1608] as follows:

(1) Generally speaking, a legitimate expectation arises as a result of a promise, representation, practice or policy made, adopted or announced by or on behalf of the Government.
(2) While it is essential that the Government and the relevant government agency remain free to change its policy, the adoption of a new policy does not relieve a decision-maker from his duty to take account of a legitimate expectation.
(3) The law requires that a legitimate expectation arising from a promise or representation be properly taken into account in the decision-making process so long as to do so falls within the power, statutory or otherwise, of the decision-maker.
(4) Unless there are reasons recognized by law for not giving effect to legitimate expectations, then effect should be given to them; fairness also requires that, if effect is not given to the expectation, then the decision-maker should express its reasons so that they may be tested by the court when the decision is challenged.
(5) Even if the decision involves the making of a political choice by reference to policy considerations, the decision-maker must make the choice in the light of the legitimate expectation.
(6) If the decision-maker fails to do so, the decision will be vitiated by reason of a failure to take into account a relevant consideration; the failure to take account of the legitimate expectation constitutes an abuse of power and once the court has established such an abuse, it may ask the decision-maker to exercise his discretion by taking the legitimate expectation into account.

810. At a time when Hong Kong had not yet adopted substantive legitimate expectation, it was held that where a very clear statement is made by the government promising a right to occupy a certain land for good, it was a misuse of power for the government to breach its promise by serving quit notice on them.[1609]

1607. *Ng Siu Tang v The Director of Immigration* (2002) 5 HKCFAR 1, (CFA). For a successful judicial review founded on legitimate expectation, *see Hong Kong Television Network Ltd v Chief Executive in Council* [2015] HKEC 646; [2015] 2 HKLRD 1035, (CFI).

1608. [2015] 2 HKLRD 1035, (CFI), [69].

1609. *Wong Pei Chun v Hong Kong Housing Authority* [1996] 2 HKLR 293, (HC).

811. In *United Grand Ltd v Town Planning Board,*[1610] it was argued unsuccessfully that the Town Planning Board acted ultra vires when it down-zoned land owned by the applicant. One of the arguments was that since fourteen previous successive plans relating to the land had given it a higher development potential (plot ratio of 2.1), a legitimate expectation was raised that such development potential would not be reduced by way of a new replacement plan. It was also argued that the Town Planning Board ignored the non-statutory Outline Plan, which guided the making of statutory plans and which prescribed a lower development potential. The judge observed that by reading the successive plans and looking at the matter in context, there was no clear and unambiguous representation that there was a development right or guaranteed right to develop to a plot ratio of 2.1. Nor could it be said the Board had clearly and unambiguously represented that the Layout Plan and the planning intentions stated on it would not be considered nor that they would be ignored. There was, in short, no proper basis for the claimed expectation to arise.[1611]

812. An applicant will succeed on the ground of legitimate expectation only where the government has breached the specific promise it has made. In *Hong Kong and China Gas Co. Ltd v Director of Lands*, this requirement was not satisfied. There, the government had promised to renew a special purpose land lease as long as the land is used for that special purpose. Since the applicant was not using the land for that purpose, the government was not bound to renew the lease.[1612] The court observed that in order to invoke the doctrine of legitimate expectation, the statement relied on must be 'clear, unambiguous and devoid of relevant qualification'.

813. Determining whether a published public policy has made a specific promise is a matter of interpreting the policy, which is a question of law. Thus, what matters is not how the decision-maker understood the policy, but how the courts would objectively understand the meaning of the policy. Courts do not interpret policy as if they are legislative provisions.[1613] What Ouseley J said in *R v Financial Ombudsman Service Ltd, ex p Norwich & Peterborough Building Society* in relation to the

1610. *United Grand Ltd v Town Planning Board* [2006] HKCU 1781, [2006] HKEC 1971, (CFI).

1611. For a discussion of the scope of judicial review of decisions concerning premium payments, *see* Albert Chen, 'The Basic Law and the Protection of Property Rights' (1993) 23 *Hong Kong Law Journal* 31, 47.

1612. *Hong Kong and China Gas Co. Ltd v Director of Lands* (decided on 22 May 1998) [2006] HKEC 444, (CA). *See also Ho Choi Wan v Hong Kong Housing Authority* (2005) 8 HKCFAR 628, (CFA), where the Court of Final Appeal rejected the argument that an administrative practice of regular review and (upward) revision of public housing rents which prevailed before the adoption of the statutory regime of 1997 in question did not give rise to a legitimate expectation because: (1) that administrative practice operated under a statutory regime with less restrictions on decision-making by the Housing Authority than currently; and (2) during inflationary times, unlike at the current time when there were deflationary pressures. *See* [52]–[55]. *See also Building Authority v Appeal Tribunal* (Buildings [2013] 4 HKLRD 52, (CA).

1613. *Shiu Wing Steel Ltd v Director of Environmental Protection & Airport Authority (No 2) (Third Party),* (2006) 9 HKCFAR 478, (CFA), where it was held that a government policy which binds an administrative agency must be given its proper meaning; but since the policy is not a legislative provision, the court should interpret it in a 'practical down-to-earth way'.

banking code provides useful guidance: 'The code ... is a material consideration for the Ombudsman to take into account. If he misinterprets it, he will have failed to take it into account. It has one meaning. Although people may reasonably differ as to that meaning, it is for the courts to decide what that one meaning is because it is for the courts to decide whether a material consideration has been ignored. The code cannot have as many meanings as reasonable people might attribute to it, all of which have to be considered. The code is to be applied by banks and other deposit-taking institutions; their compliance officers and customers cannot all say that their differing interpretations are right because reasonable.'[1614] Further, in interpreting a policy, the court should adopt a purposive common-sense approach, having regard to its context and purpose, and will presume that the drafter did not intend to produce consequences which are objectionable or undesirable, or absurd, or unworkable or impracticable, or merely inconvenient, or anomalous or illogical, or futile or pointless.[1615]

814. Sometimes, the true scope of an assurance given by the government may be misunderstood. Where it is argued that a certain practice gives rise to a legitimate expectation, the test is whether, on a fair understanding of the conduct relied upon, it would reasonably have been understood by those to whom it was directed to amount to a clear and unambiguous representation as to future conduct.[1616] *Ho King-kwan v Attorney General of Hong Kong*[1617] provides a good illustration. There, in 1978, notice was served on the applicant requiring him to remove an unauthorized structure erected on the roof of a building. Following negotiations between the Building Authority and the applicant, it was agreed that instead of removing the illegal structure, he would carry out some modifications in order to make it comply with fire safety requirements. The reason for this under-enforcement was due to the lack of manpower to effectively enforce the Building Regulations. Alterations were done, and a notice of compliance was issued in 1979. While the modified structure satisfied some concerns of the Building Authority in relation to fire safety, it was still an unauthorized structure. Later in 1984, when the Building Authority had sufficient manpower to enforce Building Regulations, a fresh notice was issued requiring the demolition of the illegal structure, because the structure in some respects still remained a threat to the fire safety of the building. Rejecting the argument that the 1979 compliance notice created any substantive legitimate expectation, Kempster JA said (at page 1511):

1614. [2002] EWHC 2379, (QB), [71].

1615. *Ibid.*, [70] and *Law Mei Mei v Airport Authority* [2018] 4 HKLRD 312, (CFI), [40]. *See*, for a recent discussion of legitimate expectation, *Sunevision Holdings Ltd v Hong Kong Science and Technology Parks Corp* [2020] HKEC 465, (CFI), where the legitimate expectation ground did not succeed.

1616. *Li Kim Ming v Housing Authority* [2016] HKEC 1201, [55], (CFI), where it was held that the absence of precedent cases does not create a legitimate expectation that a decision as the one in question will never be taken: [60]. It must also be noted that there cannot be a legitimate expectation that a public authority would act contrary to the terms of a statute or any statutory requirements it is bound to follow. *See R v Secretary of State for Education and Employment ex p Begbie* [2000] 1 WLR 1115, (CA).

1617. *Ho King-kwan v Attorney General* [1986] HKLR 1148, (CA).

> I cannot, for my part, accept the submission that the applicant's legitimate expectation was that no further enforcement action would ever be taken against him on the basis of fire-hazard so long as there was no change in the nature or disposition of the roof structure; an expectation which would imply an intolerable fetter on the Authority's discharge of its statutory duties.

815. What if a public authority makes a promise in error? 'Where the court is satisfied that a mistake was made by the minister or other person making the statement, the court should be slow to fix the public authority permanently with the consequences of that mistake. That is not to say that a promise made by mistake will never have legal consequences. It may be that a mistaken statement will, even if subsequently sought to be corrected, give rise to a legitimate expectation, whether in the person to whom the statement is made or in others who learnt of it, for example where there has been detrimental reliance on the statement before it was corrected. The court must be alive to the possibility of such unfairness to the individual by the public authority in its conduct as to amount to an abuse of power.'[1618]

816. In *In re Heland Investment Ltd*,[1619] it was held where a building plan had been approved on the basis of a land-use plan, it would be wrong to reject a revised building plan under a new land-use plan which had since then been adopted:

> a citizen should not be deprived of his right, for which he has a legitimate expectation, by a public authority, when the public authority has through its own failure to apply lawful principles in its decision-making process prevented the citizen from obtaining those rights.[1620]

§5. The Bill of Rights and Fairness

817. Hong Kong's Bill of Rights has had a significant influence on ensuring fairness in administrative justice. Article 10 of the Bill of Rights provides that 'all persons shall be equal before the courts and tribunals. In the determination of … [one's] rights and obligation in a suit at law, everyone shall be entitled to a fair and public hearing by a competent, independent and impartial tribunal established by law.'[1621]

1618. *R v Secretary of State for Education and Employment ex parte Begbie* [2000] 1 WLR 1115, 1127, (CA), per Peter Gibson LJ.
1619. *In re Heland Investment Ltd* [1994] 2 HKLR 158, (HC).
1620. *Ibid.*, at 160.
1621. For a good analysis of Art. 10, *see Lam Siu Po v Commissioner of Police* (2009) 12 HKCFAR 237, (CFA), where a prohibition of legal representation in disciplinary proceedings was held to be incompatible with Art. 10 of the Bill of Rights.

818. Article 10 reinforces the common law protection of natural justice and confers the right to procedural fairness and equality in litigation.[1622] The protection offered by Article 10, however, applies only in the circumstances stated in it. For instance, an administrative decision does not attract the application of Article 10 of the Bill of Rights Ordinance where the administrative decision to a large extent is policy based.[1623]

819. Article 10 of the Bill of Rights applies where there is 'a determination', whereas common law requirements may apply even where a final decision has not been made.[1624] The Town Planning Board, for example, does not have the final say over the making of plans under the Town Planning Ordinance (its decision is subject to confirmation by the Chief Executive in Council). As it makes no 'determination', its procedure does not have to comply with this constitutional right.[1625]

820. The determination must be a determination of 'rights or obligation at a suit at law'. These may include legal ownership rights[1626] and 'rights' in land development and commercial ventures.[1627] The requirement of a 'suit at law' does not limit the application of Article 10 to judicial proceedings alone.[1628]

1622. *R v Town Planning Board, ex parte Kwan Kong Co. Ltd* (1995) 5 HKPLR 261, (HC). Fair hearing requirement demands, for instance, that sufficient information must be given to the defendant to enable him to understand the nature of the allegations and to respond: *Asia Television Ltd v Communications Authority (No 2)* [2013] 3 HKLRD 618, (CA); the decision-maker has to impartial: *See*, for instance, *Wong Tak Wai v Commissioner of Correctional Services* [2010] 4 HKLRD 409, (CA) and *Television Broadcasts Ltd v Communications Authority* [2016] 2 HKLRD 41, (CFI); hearings must be held in public unless there are compelling reasons to deviate from this requirement: *HKSAR v Wu Wing Kit (No 1)* [2016] HKLRD 386, (CA).

1623. *Ma Wan Farming Ltd v Chief Executive in Council* [1998] 1 HKLRD 514, (CA).

1624. *In Re Caltex Oil Hong Kong Ltd* [1995] 1 HKLR 122, (HC), is a case where the approval by the Governor in Council of a road works scheme was successfully challenged on the ground that an affected person had not been given an opportunity to make objections. The arguments were founded on common law and there was no reference to the Bill of Rights. *Ma Wan Farming Ltd v Chief Executive in Council* [1998] 2 1 HKLRD 514, (CA), is a case dealing with the approval of a roads scheme, this time challenged, but unsuccessfully, relying on Art. 10 of the Bill of Rights.

1625. *R v Town Planning Board, ex parte Auburntown Ltd* (1994) 4 HKPLR 194, (HC), *Kwong Kong Co. Ltd v Town Planning Board* (1996) 6 HKPLR 237, (CA), and *Real Estate Developers Association v Town Planning Board* (1996) 6 HKPLR 179, (HC). In *Town Planning Board v Oriental Generation Ltd* [2014] HKEC 1868, (CFI), the Court of First Instance felt bound by the decision in *Kwan Kong* case and was content to consider the arguments in the context of the common law right to a fair hearing. The Court held that the procedure adopted by the Board in hearing objections to a proposed plan was unfair and the resultant decision of the Board was invalid. The Court of Appeal too considered itself bound by *Kwan Kong* decision and relied on the concept of fairness in the common law which gives 'more flexibility in application' [55].

1626. *Business Rights Ltd v Building Authority* (1994) 4 HKPLR 43, (CA) and *Ma Wan Farming Ltd v Chief Executive in Council* [1998] [1998] 1 HKLRD 514, (CA).

1627. *R v Town Planning Board, ex parte Auburntown Ltd* (1994) 4 HKPLR 194, (HC) and *Real Estate Developers Association v Town Planning Board* (1996) 6 HKPLR 179, (HC).

1628. *See The Queen v The Town Planning Board ex parte The Real Estate Developers Association of Hong Kong* [1996] 2 HKLR 267, (HC).

821. Article 10 does not always require an oral hearing, and in appropriate circumstances the decision may be based on written material submitted by the affected party. *Business Rights Ltd v Building Authority* concerned an appeal to the Building Appeal Tribunal from a decision of the Building Authority to order a building closure. The relevant legislation empowered the Appeal Tribunal to determine whether the appellant has shown 'good cause' that an appeal is merited, on the basis of written submissions of the appellant without affording him an oral hearing. Litton JA, delivering the judgment of the Court of Appeal, said:

> There must be many circumstances where the 'substance of the matter' relating to an appeal is so lacking in merit that a tribunal can with confidence conclude that no 'good cause' has been shown. I cannot see how it could be suggested that such a provision infringes a fundamental human right: without such a provision, the tribunal would be deprived of the ability to dismiss an appeal in limine, where it is wholly lacking in merit, or is frivolous and vexatious. How can this be in the public interest: particularly where the public might be at risk, relating to the exercise of discretion by the Building Authority covering such things as dangerous buildings (section 26), defective buildings (section 26A), or dangerous hillsides (section 27A).[1629]

822. To the extent that Article 10 requires open justice, a hearing by members of the decision-making body in the absence of the parties may be unconstitutional.[1630] In addition, justice and fairness demands that a 'fair procedure including a reasonable opportunity of objection' must be followed in taking decisions that affect citizen's rights.[1631] Open justice also requires that judicial proceedings are held in public and that the public have access to information concerning litigation, unless there are special considerations. In *HKSAR v Wu Wing Kit (No. 1)* the Court of Appeal held that where open administration of justice would frustrate the ultimate aim of doing justice between the parties concerned, it was a most important, if not decisive, consideration when balancing the interests, rights and freedoms involved, to decide whether open justice should be restricted, and if so, by what means and to what extent. Where there was a risk that justice could not be done, the court must balance that risk against competing considerations.[1632]

1629. *Business Rights Ltd v Building Authority* [1994] 2 HKLR 341, 347, (CA).
1630. *R v Town Planning Board, ex parte Auburntown Ltd* (1994) 4 HKPLR 194, (HC), where Rhind J said at p. 294: 'My guess would be that the Board's hearings in the present case were not "public", but that would be a shortcoming easily rectified by the Board for the future since there, is nothing in the Town Planning Board which constrains the Board from its hearings being "public" when [hearing objections to a proposed plan].' The Ordinance was amended in 2004 to provide for the proceedings of the Board to be held in public.
1631. *Fok Lai Ying v Governor in Council* [1997] HKLRD 810, 820, (PC).
1632. *HKSAR v Wu Wing Kit (No 1)* [2016] 3 HKLRD 386, (CA).

§6. Practice and Procedure of Judicial Review

823. Jurisdiction to consider judicial review applications, in the first instance, is given to the Court of First Instance, from where an appeal may be taken to the Court of Appeal and to the Court of Final Appeal. Order 53 of the Rules of High Court, 'Application for Judicial Review', deals with procedural matters relating to judicial review applications. Rule 1A, the interpretation section, provides that a judicial review application may be made to question the lawfulness of (a) a legislative enactment or (b) a decision, action or failure to act in relation to the exercise of a public function. A judicial review application may not only be directed at a public authority but may also be sought in relation to a non-public authority if it exercises a public function.

824. Where a person seeks an order of mandamus, prohibition or certiorari or an injunction to restraint a person from holding any office which he is not entitled to hold, it must be by way of judicial review. Alternatively, a declaration may be sought. Where the sole purpose of litigation is to seek an award of damages or restitution or recovery of money judicial review is not appropriate. However, where a judicial review application is made seeking an order of certiorari, mandamus or prohibition, or an injunction to restraint a person from holding office, the application may also seek a monetary award.[1633]

825. An application for judicial review may be made only with the leave of the court (rule 3(1)). An application for leave is made ex parte (rule 3(2)). The judge may determine the application for leave without a hearing, unless a hearing is requested in the notice of application and need not sit in open court (rule 3(3)). The court must not grant leave unless it considers that the applicant has 'a sufficient interest in the matter to which the application relates' (rule 3(7)). An application for leave to apply for judicial review must be made promptly and in any event within three months from the date when grounds for the application first arose unless the court considers that there is good reason for extending the period within which the application has to be made.[1634] The fact that an application has been made within three months will be insufficient if the court considers that it should have been submitted much earlier in order to satisfy the requirement of 'promptness'.[1635] The reason for the requirement of promptness is that litigation must be concluded in a timely manner so as not to unduly hinder the administrative process.[1636] The applicant must serve the order granting leave on the respondent and any interested parties, as directed by the court (rule 4A).

1633. Order 53, rule 1: 'Cases appropriate for application for judicial review'.
1634. Order 53, rule 4. On justifications for extending the period, *see Re Right Centre Co Ltd* [1990] 1 HKLR 250, (HC).
1635. *See Re Right Centre Co Ltd* [1990] 1 HKLR 250, (HC), citing *R. v Stratford-on-Avon District Council, ex parte Jackson* [1985]1 WLR 1323, (CA); and *BI v Director of Immigration* [2016] 2 HKLRD 520, (CA).
1636. *Lo Siu Lan v Hong Kong Housing Authority* [2004] HKEC 1541, [34], (CA).

826. The court will grant leave to proceed with the application if there is an arguable case. The granting of leave to apply for judicial review is a matter for the court's discretion to be exercised judicially. Settling the uncertainty as to whether what is needed is an arguable case or a potentially arguable case (i.e., on further consideration at a subsequent hearing an arguable case might be demonstrated), Li CJ in *Po Fun Chan v Winnie CW Cheung* held as follows: 'The purpose of the leave requirement would be better served by the adoption of the arguability test instead of the potential arguability test. The granting of leave to apply for judicial review is a matter for the court's discretion to be exercised judicially. The test which should be applied is the arguability test. Under this test, arguability must mean reasonable arguability. A claim for relief which is not reasonably arguable could not be regarded as arguable. A reasonably arguable case is one which enjoys realistic prospects of success. Whilst the test adopted represents a higher threshold than the potential arguability test, claims which are reasonably arguable would be given leave to go forward under it. It is in the public interest that challenges which are not reasonably arguable should not be given leave to proceed.'[1637]

827. We may briefly set out the remedies that a successful applicant may obtain through a judicial review application. High Court Ordinance of 1986 (Cap. 4) provides for the grant of orders of mandamus, prohibition and certiorari closely following the previously operative prerogative writs of mandamus, prohibition and certiorari (section 21I) and injunction (section 21J). An order of certiorari may be issued to quash an unlawful administrative decision. For instance, in *Television Broadcasts Ltd v Communications Authority*,[1638] the Court of First Instance granted an order of certiorari quashing the decision of the Communications Authority for imposing unjustified sanctions on the applicant in breach of Article 10 of the Hong Kong Bill of Rights; mandamus, which would usually accompany an order of certiorari, lies to require a public authority to perform a function as required by law. In *Tung, Jeremy v Dental Council of Hong Kong*,[1639] the Court of First Instance quashed the Dental Council's decision to remove the applicant's name from the register of dentist and ordered it to reconsider the restoration of the applicant's name to the list, to be determined by a freshly appointed panel; prohibition is an order to prevent a public authority from taking a particular course of action, which is unlawful. In *Attorney General v Ng Yuen Shiu*,[1640] the Privy Council endorsed the decision of the Court of Appeal granting an order of prohibition preventing the Director of Immigration from executing the removal order until he had given the applicant an opportunity to be heard; an injunction, which has entered the public law area from the private law sphere, may be issued to restrain any public officer or holder of an office created by any enactment from doing something that they are not entitled to

---

1637. *Po Fun Chan v Winnie CW Cheung* (2007) 10 HKCFAR 676, (CFA), [15].
1638. *Television Broadcasts Ltd v Communications Authority* [2016] 2 HKLRD 41, (CFI).
1639. *Tung, Jeremy v Dental Council of Hong Kong* [2012] HKEC 1151, (CFI).
1640. *Attorney General v Ng Yuen Shiu* [1983] 2 AC 629, (PC).

do and, if the case so requires, declare the office to be vacant (section 21J). In addition, the court may, instead of granting an order, make a declaration of what the lawful thing would be to do in the circumstances of the case.[1641] Another remedy that has been borrowed from the sphere of private law and adapted to the needs of public law is damages, which may accompany any order that the court may grant.

§7. STANDING

828. A judicial review application may be brought only by a person who has an interest in the matter: He must have 'sufficient interest' to bring an action for judicial review.[1642] The requirement of sufficient interest can be easily satisfied if the applicant for judicial review is 'an aggrieved party', a phrase that is often used in legislation granting a right of appeal or statutory review, or a 'person affected' by an administrative wrongdoing.[1643] Courts are, however, sympathetic to applications made in the public interest, although the applicants themselves may not be affected any more than members of the general public.[1644] In *Business Rights Ltd v Building Authority*,[1645] the Court of Appeal was of the opinion that those who had no right to occupy a building that was subject to a closure order had, under the Bill of Rights Ordinance, no standing to object to it. Where a person belonging to a class of persons (e.g., a trade union) is prejudiced by an administrative action, the whole class

---

1641. High Court Ordinance (Cap. 4), s. 21K (2) recognizes the power of the Court of First Instance to grant a declaration. *See AA v Securities and Futures Commission* [2016] HKEC 998, (CFI).

1642. High Court Ordinance (Cap. 4) provides that no application for judicial review shall be made unless the leave of the Court of First Instance has been obtained in accordance with rules of court and the court shall not grant leave to make such an application unless it considers that the applicant has a sufficient interest in the matter to which the application relates (s. 21K(3) and 21K(7)).

1643. To require that the applicant is affected by an administrative wrongdoing has the effect of ensuring that leave is not granted to a meddlesome busybody. It is true that the words 'sufficient interest' have been liberally construed: Yet, an applicant must still have some interest in the matter to warrant leave being granted to him to challenge a public decision: *see R v Monopolies and Mergers Commission, ex p Argyll Group Plc* [1986] 1 WLR 763, (CA), at 773; *Li Jen Fei et al v Director of Immigration* [1994] 1 HKLR 253, (CA); *Wong Chi Kin, re* [2014] HKEC 1590, (CA). However, as Dyson LJ explained in *R (Feakins) v Secretary of State for Environment* [2004] 1 WLR 1761, (CA), [23]: 'if a claimant has no sufficient private interest to support a claim to standing, then he should not be accorded standing merely because he raises an issue in which there is, objectively speaking, a public interest. As Sedley J said in *R v Somerset County Council, Ex p Dixon* [1997] JPL 1030, (QB), when considering the issue of standing, the court had to ensure that the claimant was not prompted by an ill motive and was not a mere busybody or a troublemaker. Thus, if a claimant seeks to challenge a decision in which he has no private law interest, it is difficult to conceive of circumstances in which the court will accord him standing, even where there is a public interest in testing the lawfulness of the decision, if the claimant is acting out of ill-will or for some other improper purpose. It is an abuse of process to permit a claimant to bring a claim in such circumstances. If the real reason why a claimant wishes to challenge a decision in which, objectively, there is a public interest is not that he has a genuine concern about the decision, but some other reason, then that is material to the question whether he should be accorded standing.' Cited in *Re Wong Chi Kin* [2014] HKEC 1590, (CA).

1644. *See*, for instance, *BI v Director of Immigration* [2016] 2 HKLRD 520, (CA).

1645. *Business Rights Ltd v Building Authority* (1994) 4 HKPLR 43, (CA).

of persons has *locus standi* in a judicial review action.[1646] In a series of politically sensitive cases, the Hong Kong judiciary took a restricted view of standing; *see Lee Miu Ling v Attorney General*[1647] (persons who were neither candidates nor electors of a functional constituency could challenge the legality of functional constituencies) and *Ng King Luen v Rita Fan*[1648] (a citizen had no standing to impugn the constitutionality of the Provisional Legislative Council because he was motivated by purely political considerations). These decisions must now be viewed with caution in view of the more liberal approach that the courts adopt in determining whether a person has sufficient interest, whereby an applicant who is not directly affected by the contested administrative action may nevertheless be permitted to proceed in view of the general public importance of the question that he has raised.

829. Whether an applicant has 'sufficient interest' is considered both at the application for leave stage and at the substantive hearing. At the stage of considering an application for leave, the court has to be satisfied that the applicant has a prima facie or arguable case. At this stage, the court does not usually require the applicant to prove that he has sufficient interest in the matter that he wishes to bring before the court, although the court will not entertain mere busybodies. As Sedley J said in *R v Somerset County Council, ex. p Dixon* (1998) 75 P&CR 175, 183–184:

> Public law is ... about wrongs – that is to say misuses of public power; and the courts have always been alive to the fact that a person or organization with no particular stake in the issue or the outcome may, without in any sense being a mere meddler, wish and be well placed to call the attention of the court to any apparent misuse of public power. If an arguable case of such misuse can be made out on an application for leave, the court's only concern is to ensure that it is not being done for an ill motive. It is if, on a substantive hearing, the abuse of power is made out that everything relevant to the applicant's standing will be weighed up, whether with regard to the grant or simply to the form of relief.

830. At the substantive hearing, the question of sufficient interest may be considered again. However, it is only one of the many matters that the court will take into account. As the Court of Appeal observed in *Anderson Asphalt Ltd v Town Planning Board*,[1649] it is common ground that where leave has been granted to an applicant to move for judicial review, the Court is more concerned about merits at the substantive hearing and that the standing of an applicant is only one of the factors to be weighed in the balance.

1646. *Association of Expatriate Civil Servants v Chief Executive of the Hong Kong Special Administrative Region* [1998] 1 HKLRD 615, (CFI).
1647. *Lee Miu Ling v Attorney General* [1995] 5 HKLY 196, (CA).
1648. *Ng King Luen v Rita Fan* [1997] 7 HKPLR 281, (HC).
1649. *Anderson Asphalt Ltd v Town Planning Board* [2007] 3 HKLRD 18, (CA).

831. We may make a brief reference to an important recent development in judicial review which is closely allied to the liberalization of the rules on *locus standi*, namely the recognition that special concessions must be made in the award of costs in public interest litigation. Litigations concerning issues of general public importance which the public interest requires to be resolved are referred to as public interest litigation. The decision of the Court of Final Appeal in *Town Planning Board v Society for Protection of the Harbour Ltd*[1650] is one of the early examples where the courts took into consideration the fact that they should exercise their discretion in favour of the applicant where 'proceedings are commenced to vindicate the public interest … rather than to assert or enforce some private right or interest. … Also relevant is the fact that, but for the commencement of the proceedings by the [the applicant], the public interest in securing compliance with the law would not have prevailed and resulted in the resolution of fundamental legal issues. Likewise relevant are the manifest public importance of the case (the protection of the Harbour) and the Society's limited finances dependent as they are on public donation.' In *Scott v Government of the HKSAR*,[1651] Hartmann J said: 'If an action is brought in the public interest, often as a test case, so that the law may be clarified and if that clarification will benefit a large class of persons or the public generally, those circumstances may warrant a court in making a costs order that does not follow the event.'

832. A further development in concessions made to applicants in public interest litigation is the making of protective costs orders (PCO), whereby the court may make an order as to costs at the commencement of the proceedings or at any stage before the conclusion of the case. These orders enable an applicant to proceed, in appropriate circumstances, without the fear of being subjected to a costs order if their case were to fail. The Court of First Instance in *Designing Hong Kong Ltd v Town Planning Board*,[1652] affirmed by the Court of Appeal and the Court of Final Appeal,[1653] clearly set out the principles relating to such orders, in the light of the *Corner House Principles*, set out in *R (Corner House Research) v Secretary of State for Trade and Industry*.[1654] The *Corner House Principles* and factors are:

(1) A PCO may be made at any stage of the proceedings, on such conditions as the court thinks fit, provided that the court is satisfied that:
   (a) the issues raised are of general public importance;
   (b) the public interest requires that those issues should be resolved;

1650. *Town Planning Board v Society for Protection of the Harbour Ltd (No 2)* (2004) 7 HKCFAR 114, (CFA).

1651. *Scott v Government of the HKSAR* [2004] 2 HKLRD 989, (CFI), [15].

1652. *Designing Hong Kong Ltd v Town Planning Board* [2015] HKEC 688, (CFI).

1653. *Designing Hong Kong Ltd v Town Planning Board* [2017] HKEC 309, (CA); (2018) 21 HKCFAR 237, (CFA).

1654. *R (Corner House Research) v Secretary of State for Trade and Industry* [2005] 4 All ER 1, (CA). In *Designing Hong Kong Ltd v Town Planning Board*, (2018) 21 HKCFAR 237, (CFA), [20], the Court of Final Appeal agreed with the view expressed in previous relevant Hong Kong cases that *R (Corner House Research) v Secretary of State for Trade and Industry* [2005] 4 All ER 1, (CA), provides useful guidance in Hong Kong.

(c) the applicant has no private interest in the outcome of the case;
(d) having regard to the financial resources of the applicant and the respondent and to the amount of costs that are likely to be involved, it is fair and just to make the order; and
(e) if the order is not made, the applicant will probably discontinue the proceedings and will be acting reasonably in so doing.

(2) If those acting for the applicant are doing pro bono this will be likely to enhance the merits of the application for a PCO.
(3) It is for the court, in its discretion, to decide whether it is fair and just to make the order in light of the consideration set out above.

§8. Who May Be the Respondent?

833. As explained above, administrative litigation may be directed at government bodies, statutory bodies or even agencies created by contract. The governing criterion is not the source of power, but the nature of the power exercised by an agency. If the power is of a public law nature then judicial review is appropriate: where an agency which is amenable to judicial review engages in an activity of a private nature, such as entering into a contract, judicial review is generally not appropriate. However, even when engaged in an activity of a private nature, the agency is required to comply with public law requirements, such as not to abuse discretionary powers or not to act arbitrarily, and judicial review will be available to question the procedure leading to the conclusion of that activity.[1655]

1655. On the private and public law divide, *see Lee Shing Yue Construction Co Ltd v Director of Architectural Services* [2001] 1 HKLRD 715, 727–728, (CFI).

Chapter 5. Legal Position of Aliens

834. Anyone other than a person who has the right of abode[1656] or the right to land[1657] in Hong Kong requires an entry visa or permit to work, study, take up residence or stay in Hong Kong as a visitor longer than the visa free period.[1658] A reservation in the Hong Kong Bill of Rights Ordinance states as follows: 'Regarding persons not having the right to enter and remain in Hong Kong, this Ordinance does not affect any immigration legislation governing entry "into, stay in and departure from Hong Kong, or the application of any such legislation".'[1659]

835. An applicant for a visa for employment or investment must possess a special skill, knowledge or experience not readily available in Hong Kong and be able to make a substantial contribution to Hong Kong. There are different categories of employment visa: non-Mainland resident professionals, mainland talent and professionals, non-Mainland resident entrepreneurs, non-local graduates and quality immigrants. There are also special visa schemes for domestic helpers and imported workers. Other categories include training, students and dependants.[1660]

1656. Permanent residents of Hong Kong enjoy the right of abode. Right of abode means the right to land in Hong Kong, to be free from any conditions of stay (including a limit of stay) in Hong Kong, not to be deported or removed from Hong Kong. Immigration Ordinance (Cap. 115), s. 7.
1657. A person, who was a permanent resident immediately before 1 July 1997, but did not become a permanent resident of the Hong Kong Special Administrative Region, will have the right to land in Hong Kong Special Administrative Region. He will be free from any conditions of stay and will not be liable to be removed. Immigration Ordinance (Cap. 115), s. 2AAA.
1658. Visitors from most countries do not require a visa to travel to Hong Kong as a visitor. The visa free period of stay varies from country to country.
1659. Hong Kong Bill of Rights Ordinance (Cap. 383), s. 11, in Part III 'Exceptions and Savings'.
1660. *See* the website of the Hong Kong Immigration Department: http://www.immd.govhk/eng/services/index.html.

Part V. Special Problems

Chapter 1. War, Treaty and Foreign Affairs Powers

§1. General

836. As has been seen above, the Chinese Central Government is responsible for foreign affairs relating to Hong Kong and for the defence of Hong Kong, but there is a fair degree of delegation to Hong Kong of defence and foreign affairs matters. The Chinese Ministry of Foreign Affairs has established an office in Hong Kong to deal with foreign affairs, and the Chinese Central Government has stationed military forces in Hong Kong for the purposes of defence of Hong Kong.

I. Foreign Affairs

837. The Chinese Central Government authorizes Hong Kong to conduct relevant external affairs in accordance with the Basic Law.[1661] The external affairs powers within the competence of the Hong Kong Government are as follows:

(1) Representatives of the Hong Kong Government may participate in negotiations at the diplomatic level directly affecting Hong Kong conducted by the Central Government. They will so participate as members of the Chinese delegation.[1662]
(2) Hong Kong may maintain and develop relations and conclude and implement agreements with foreign States and relevant organizations in areas such as trade, finance, shipping, communication, and sports. Hong Kong must in these matters use the name 'Hong Kong, China'.[1663]
(3) Representatives of the Hong Kong Government may participate in international organizations and conferences, limited to States and directly affecting Hong Kong. They must so participate as part of the Chinese delegation. They may also attend in some other capacity as permitted by the Central Government and the organization or conference concerned. They must then use the name 'Hong Kong, China'.[1664]

1661. Basic Law, Art. 13.
1662. *Ibid.*, Art. 150.
1663. *Ibid.*, Art. 151.
1664. *Ibid.*, Art. 152.

(4) Hong Kong may, using 'Hong Kong, China', participate in organizations or conferences not limited to states.[1665]
(5) The Central Government must take steps to ensure that Hong Kong retains its status in any international organization, in one capacity or another, if China is a member of such organization. Where China is not a member of such an organization, the Central Government must necessitate Hong Kong's continued participation, 'where necessary'.[1666]
(6) Whether an international treaty to which China is a party should be applicable to Hong Kong is a matter for the Central Government to determine 'in accordance with the circumstances and needs of the Region, and after seeking the views of the government of the Region'. International agreements to which China is not a party but which are implemented in Hong Kong may continue to be implemented in Hong Kong.[1667]
(7) The Hong Kong Government has been authorized by the Central Government to issue passports and other travel documents. It has the power to apply immigration controls on entry into, stay in, and departure from Hong Kong by persons from foreign countries.[1668] The Central Government will assist or authorize the Hong Kong Government to conclude visa abolition agreements with foreign States.[1669]
(8) Hong Kong may establish official or semi-official economic and trade missions in foreign countries. Hong Kong must report the establishment of such missions to the Central Government for record.[1670]

838. The establishment of foreign consular and other official or semi-official missions in Hong Kong requires the approval of the Central Government. Consular and other official missions established in Hong Kong by states which have formal relations with China may be maintained. According to the circumstances of the case, consular and other official missions established in Hong Kong by states which have no formal relations with China may be permitted to remain or be changed to semi-official missions. States not recognized by China may only establish non-governmental institutions in Hong Kong.

II. Defence Powers

839. While the Chinese Central Government is responsible for the defence of Hong Kong, the Government of Hong Kong is responsible for the maintenance of public order in Hong Kong.[1671] Military forces stationed by the Central Government in Hong Kong for defence must not interfere in Hong Kong's local affairs.[1672]

1665. *Ibid.*
1666. *Ibid.*
1667. *Ibid.*, Art. 153.
1668. *Ibid.*, Art. 154.
1669. *Ibid.*, Art. 155.
1670. *Ibid.*, Art. 156.
1671. *Ibid.*, Art. 14.
1672. *Ibid.*

840. The Government of Hong Kong may ask the Chinese Central Government for assistance from the garrison in the maintenance of public order and in disaster relief.[1673] When there is a state of emergency, the Central Government may issue an order applying the relevant national laws to Hong Kong.[1674]

841. Foreign warships require special permission of the Central Government to enter the ports of Hong Kong.[1675] Similarly, foreign State aircrafts require special permission of the Central Government to enter Hong Kong.[1676]

1673. *Ibid.*
1674. *Ibid.*, Art. 18.
1675. *Ibid.*, Art. 126.
1676. *Ibid.*, Art. 129.

Chapter 2. The Taxing and Spending Powers

§1. General

842. It has not been suggested that the taxing statutes in force in Hong Kong prior to 1 July 1997, such as, notably, the Inland Revenue Ordinance 1947 (Cap. 112), contravene the Basic Law; consequently, these statutes remain in force under Article 8. So, too, do the cases, both from Hong Kong and from other Common Law jurisdictions, relevant to their interpretation. Since the handover, the territory's various taxing statutes have been repeatedly amended. These amendments have all been minor, but the cumulative effect has been substantial. In particular, the Inland Revenue Ordinance 1947 is considerably lengthier and more complex than it was in 1997; and administration and compliance have become correspondingly more burdensome. Equally, in tax cases as in cases of other kinds, Hong Kong's courts refer to post-handover decisions from other jurisdictions.[1677] The territory's tax system has thus survived the handover not only intact but also largely unchanged.[1678] In particular, there has been no change in the territory's basic policy of imposing only light and relatively simple taxes.

843. The provisions of the Basic Law dealing with taxation and expenditure are in some respects an unexceptional continuation of the Westminster tradition from which they were derived; in other respects, they are unique. Taking, first, the unexceptional measures, taxes and public spending fall to be proposed by the Special Administrative Region Government (i.e., the Executive), but must be sanctioned by the Legislature, in accordance with the Westminster tradition. Thus, Article 62(4) of the Basic Law authorizes and requires the Government to 'draw up and introduce [in the Legislative Council] budgets and financial accounts'; and Article 64 provides that the Government 'shall obtain approval from the [Legislative] Council for taxation and public expenditure'. In accordance with the Westminster Model, Article 48(3) authorizes and requires the Chief Executive '[t]o sign budgets passed by the Legislative Council'; but Article 48(3) also, in accordance with Hong Kong's position as part of China, requires him to 'report the budgets and final accounts to

1677. It is in this context worth noting *Commissioner of Inland Revenue v Cosmotron Manufacturing Ltd* [1997] 1 WLR 1288, (PC). The case is a unique constitutional oddity, in that the Privy Council gave its judgment before 1 July 1997 (as, of course, it had to, if it was to give judgment at all), but it did not give its reasons until after the handover.

1678. On the Hong Kong Government's taxing and spending powers generally, *see* Yash Ghai, *Hong Kong's New Constitutional Order: The Resumption of Chinese Sovereignty and the Basic Law*, (2nd edn, Hong Kong: Hong Kong University Press, 1999), Ch. 6; Richard Cullen, 'Revenue Law in Hong Kong: The Future', in Raymond Wacks (ed.) *The New Legal Order in Hong Kong,* (Hong Kong: Hong Kong University Press, 1999); and Norman Miners, *The Government and Politics of Hong Kong* (5th edn, Hong Kong: Oxford University Press, 1998). The author of this chapter is grateful to the authors of each of these works and also to Michael Dowdle and Rajesh Sharma for sharing their views on its subject matter. The best general work on Hong Kong tax law is Peter Willoughby & Andrew Halkyard, *Encyclopaedia of Hong Kong Taxation* (Butterworths, Hong Kong, 1993, loose-leaf). On the history of the territory's tax system, *see* M. Littlewood, *Taxation Without Representation: The History of Hong Kong's Troublingly Successful Tax System* (Hong Kong: Hong Kong University Press, 2010).

the Central People's Government for the record'. Also unexceptionally, Article 108 specifically authorizes and requires the Special Administrative Region to 'enact laws ... concerning types of taxes, tax rates, tax reductions, allowances and exemptions, and other matters of taxation'.[1679] Article 73(2) authorizes the Legislative Council to 'examine and approve budgets introduced by the Government' and Article 73(3) authorizes it to 'approve taxation and public expenditure'.[1680] In accordance with this provision, the Special Administrative Region Government has continued the pre-1997 practice of authorizing its expenditures by means of an annual Appropriation Ordinance.

844. Thus, as in the British and other British-derivative systems, the Hong Kong Special Administrative Region legislature has a veto over the Executive in matters of taxation and public spending. In Hong Kong, as in other jurisdictions, this veto is obviously of very great constitutional importance. In Hong Kong, however, it would appear to be of even greater importance than elsewhere. The reason is that, under Hong Kong's 'Executive-led' system of government,[1681] this power of veto seems to be by far the most important means by which the Legislature can actively exercise power. The reason for this, in turn, is as follows. The Legislative Council can decline to endorse proposals for legislation initiated by the Government; the Legislative Council's *passive* power is therefore considerable: it can stop the Government from doing what it wants to do. But the Legislative Council's authority to initiate legislation is very closely circumscribed. In particular, Article 74 of the Basic Law provides that: 'Members of the Legislative Council of the Hong Kong Special Administrative Region may introduce bills in accordance with the provisions of this Law and legal procedures. Bills which do not relate to public expenditure or political structure or the operation of the government may be introduced individually or jointly by members of the Council. The written consent of the Chief Executive shall be required before bills relating to government policies are introduced.'[1682] There is obviously room for debate as to the interpretation of Article 74, but plainly the competence of the Legislative Council to legislate against the wishes of the Chief Executive is so restricted as to be inconsequential.[1683]

845. The Legislative Council could, however, decline to pass the budget. That is, it could decline to pass the Government's annual Appropriation Bill. This has never happened, either before 1 July 1997 or since, though on several occasions the opposition has been substantial. What the consequences would be is, therefore,

1679. In other respects, however, as will be seen, Art. 108 is exceptional.

1680. It is worth noting that, although the intended meaning of these provisions seems plain enough, their drafting is less than entirely satisfactory.

1681. The Executive-led Government is a feature that the Basic Law retained from the pre-1997 colonial system of government.

1682. Presumably this means, most importantly, that the legislation must not entail any cost to the government.

1683. For an analysis of the scope and importance of Art. 74, *see* Yash Ghai, *Hong Kong's New Constitutional Order: The Resumption of Chinese Sovereignty and the Basic Law*, (2nd edn, Hong Kong: Hong Kong University Press, 1999). There are also other constraints on the legislative competence of the Legislative Council. *See* above, Part II, Ch. 3, Legislature.

unclear. It seems reasonable, though, to regard the Basic Law as effectively giving the Legislative Council power to provoke a constitutional crisis, should it wish to do so, by withholding its support for the Appropriation Bill. The Legislative Council could also, therefore, attempt to use the possibility of provoking such a crisis as a means – as the last resort, perhaps the *only* effective means – of persuading the Chief Executive to initiate or, at least, endorse legislation wanted by the Legislative Council. The Basic Law also provides, however, in Article 51, for the making of provisional appropriations if the legislature declines to endorse the budget. Article 51 is as follows:

> If the Legislative Council of the Hong Kong Special Administrative Region refuses to pass the budget introduced by the government, the Chief Executive may apply to the Legislative Council for provisional appropriations. If appropriation of public funds cannot be approved because the Legislative Council has already been dissolved, the Chief Executive may, prior to the election of the new Legislative Council, approve provisional short-term appropriations according to the level of expenditure of the previous fiscal year.[1684]

846. Also relevant is Article 52, which provides that the Chief Executive 'must resign' in a variety of circumstances, including the following: 'When, after the Legislative Council is dissolved because it refuses to pass a budget or any other important bill, the new Legislative Council still refuses to pass the original bill in dispute.'[1685]

847. The provisions of the Basic Law pertaining to the Special Administrative Region Government's taxing and spending powers are exceptionable in three main respects. First, they provide for what is sometimes described as a 'fiscal firewall', by which is meant the total separation of the public finances of the territory and the Mainland. Second, they require the Special Administrative Region Government to attempt, at least, to balance its budgets. And, third, they accord constitutional, or at least, quasi-constitutional, status to Hong Kong's 'low tax policy'.

§2. The 'Fiscal Firewall'

848. The 'fiscal firewall', that is, the separation of the Hong Kong Special Administrative Region Government's finances from those of the Central People's Government, is established by Articles 106 and 108 of the Basic Law. Article 106 provides as follows:

1684. The drafting of this provision leaves room for improvement, also. In particular, first, the term 'short-term' is imprecise. Second, the meaning of 'according to' is unclear. Art. 51 authorizes the Chief Executive to approve short-term appropriations 'according to the level of expenditure of the previous fiscal year'. This appears to limit the Chief Executive's authority, but 'according to' presumably means something other than 'of no more than'. The scope of the authority conferred on the Chief Executive by Art. 51 is, thus, unclear.

1685. Basic Law, Art. 52(3).

> The Hong Kong Special Administrative Region shall have independent finances. The Hong Kong Special Administrative Region shall use its financial revenues exclusively for its own purposes, and they shall not be handed over to the Central People's Government. The Central People's Government shall not levy taxes in the Hong Kong Special Administrative Region.

849. Article 108 provides in part[1686] as follows:

> The Hong Kong Special Administrative Region shall practise an independent taxation system.[1687]

850. The firewall is based also on Article 18, which provides that 'National laws shall not be applied in the Hong Kong Special Administrative Region except those listed in Annex III', for the national laws listed in Annex III to the Basic Law do not include any tax statutes. The nature of the firewall is demonstrated also by the existence of what is in substance a tax treaty between the Hong Kong Special Administration Region and the Central Government in Beijing.[1688] Of course, it is not a treaty, because a treaty is an agreement between sovereign States; it is for this reason that the instrument is called an 'arrangement'. But its substance and form are very similar to tax treaties generally. In this connection, it is relevant to note also that the other double tax treaties to which China is a party do not cover Hong Kong.[1689]

851. During the colonial period, the British Government extracted substantial revenues from Hong Kong in the form of the 'Defence Contribution', which the Colonial Government was obliged to pay to the British Government ostensibly for Britain's defence of the colony from outside aggression. In fact, however, it was only until about 1958 that the British Government maintained seriously that it could defend the colony militarily. British troops were stationed in Hong Kong right up until midnight of 30 June 1997; but it was not pretended that the reason for this was

1686. The whole of Art. 108 is reproduced in para. 859 below.

1687. For the Hong Kong Inland Revenue Department's position, *see* Commissioner of Inland Revenue, *Departmental Interpretation and Practice Notes No 29: Tax Relations between the Hong Kong Special Administrative Region and the People's Republic of China*, August 1997. The substance of the Commissioner's position seems uncontroversial.

1688. Arrangement between the Mainland of China and the Hong Kong Special Administrative Region for the Avoidance of Double Taxation and the Prevention of Fiscal Evasion with respect to Taxes on Income, 21 August 2006, as modified by protocols executed on 31 January 2008, 27 May 2010 and 1 April 2015. *See also* Commissioner of Inland Revenue, Departmental Interpretation and Practice Notes No 44 (Revised): Arrangement between the Mainland of China and the Hong Kong Special Administrative Region for the Avoidance of Double Taxation and the Prevention of Fiscal Evasion with respect to Taxes on Income, August 2008.

1689. *See* Commissioner of Inland Revenue, Departmental Interpretation and Practice Notes No 29: Tax Relations between the Hong Kong Special Administrative Region and the People's Republic of China, August 1997.

to defend the colony from aggressors. Rather, it would appear that it suited the British Government's own purposes to have troops present in Hong Kong. Perhaps also it was thought that these troops would prove useful in the event of serious domestic unrest. They were also used to patrol the border. In any event, the Chinese Government has deprived itself of the opportunity to follow the British practice in this regard by incorporating in the Basic Law Article 14, which provides, among other things, as follows: 'Expenditure for the garrison [of the People's Liberation Army troops stationed in Hong Kong] shall be borne by the Central People's Government.'

852. There would appear to be several methods by which the Central Government could, if it wished, circumvent the spirit of Article 106 without contravening it. For example, it could impose a tax on the exportation of water from the Mainland to Hong Kong, because the territory is heavily dependent on the Mainland for water. Electricity, gas, meat, vegetables and various other goods are also imported from the Mainland in large quantities, and all of these, too, would be reasonably expeditious subjects of taxation. It may be that taxes of this nature would be contrary to, in particular, China's World Trade Organization obligations. It is possible also, however, that such difficulties could be overcome by imposing charges rather than taxes. In the case of utilities provided by state-related entities, it seems likely that this would be feasible. To date, however, the Central Government's behaviour has been in this respect exemplary: it appears to have made no attempt whatever to extract revenues from Hong Kong other than of course through normal commercial endeavour.

853. It seems reasonable to suppose that, in the event of serious national need, the fiscal firewall would come down; and that the Central Government would cease to deprive itself of the revenues it might raise in Hong Kong. If this were to happen, presumably it would be done by requiring the Special Administrative Region's Government to transfer funds to the Central Government and by requiring the Special Administrative Region's Government to raise taxes to this end if necessary. While fiscal reserves have grown from HKD 860 billion in 2017 to HKD 11,000 billion in 2020, in the current uncertain times Hong Kong, having budget deficit in 2020 for the first time in fifteen years, is expected to run a deficit budget for the coming five years;[1690] it is doubtful whether Hong Kong would be able to transfer substantial revenues without increasing taxes. It would be possible for the Central Government to raise funds from Hong Kong by extending its own tax system to cover the territory, whether by extending existing taxes or establishing new ones especially for Hong Kong. The latter method would appear however to be, at best, extremely cumbersome administratively. While it would be possible for the Central Government to raise revenues from Hong Kong either directly (by imposing its own taxes in the territory) or indirectly (by requiring the Special Administrative Region's Government to transfer funds to the Central Government), either method would appear to

1690. The 2020–2021 Budget, the budget speech, paras 168 and 174. The Hong Kong Government holds various tangible and financial assets in addition to the fiscal reserves, such as, notably, the Exchange Fund.

require either the amendment of the Basic Law or the declaration of a 'state of emergency' under Article 18. It is possible, however, that the amendment of the Basic Law so as to permit radical tax reform would run counter to Article 159 which provides, among other matters, that 'No amendment to this Law shall contravene the established basic policies of the People's Republic of China regarding Hong Kong.'

§3. THE 'BALANCED BUDGET' REQUIREMENT

854. Hong Kong's constitutional 'balanced budget' requirement is contained in Article 107 of the Basic Law, which provides as follows:

> The Hong Kong Special Administrative Region shall follow the principle of keeping expenditure within the limits of revenues in drawing up its budget, and strive to achieve a fiscal balance, avoid deficits and keep the budget commensurate with the growth rate of its gross domestic product.

855. The desirability and feasibility of constitutional 'balanced budget' requirements has long been a matter of considerable interest in many parts of the world, notably in the US at both federal and state level. Article 107 thus demonstrates one method by which it has been done. It is important to notice, though, that Article 107 allows considerable flexibility. It does not require that the Special Administrative Region's Government actually balance its budgets, but only that it 'strive' to do so. Similarly, it does not require that the Government keep expenditure within the limits of revenue; but only that it 'follows the principle' of doing so. What this means is obviously debatable.

856. From 1945 until 1997, the Hong Kong Government almost always operated at a surplus, as a result of sustained and rapid economic growth and relatively low public spending. Since 1997, it has sometimes operated at a deficit. It has been maintained that a single annual deficit does not necessarily entail non-compliance with Article 107; rather, it is said, Article 107 requires only that the Government balance its budgets over some longer period of time. For example, in 1999, the Financial Secretary included in his Budget Speech the following statement:

> In these circumstances, a deficit budget in the short term is entirely consistent with the provisions of the Basic Law, provided that it is set in the context of a return to balanced budgets over the medium term. From a macro-economic point of view, returning to a fiscal balance over the medium term is prudent and rational. It would be inflexible and unreasonable to try to achieve a strict balance year after year.[1691]

1691. Sir D. Tsang, 1999 Budget Speech, para. 102.

But it is not clear whether Article 107 can properly be interpreted in this way; nor is it clear, if the interpretation is correct, what is meant by 'the short term' and 'the medium term'.

857. It is important to note also that Article 107 requires far more than that the Special Administrative Region's Government attempt merely to balance its budgets. It requires also that the Government 'strive to ... keep the budget commensurate with the growth rate of its gross domestic product'. Presumably, this is intended to mean that the Government must strive not to increase public spending as a proportion of GDP, even if it could do so without running a deficit. In other words, Article 107 is intended not only to ensure balanced budgets but also as an oblique protection against increased public spending and higher taxes. It is worth noting in this connection that the principle that public spending should expand no faster than the economy itself was a key element from the 1960s, if not earlier, in the Colonial Government's philosophy of public finance. The principle has not only obvious attractions but also a serious flaw: it was never explained by the Colonial Government, and has yet to be explained by the Special Administrative Region's Government, why it should be accepted that the current level of public spending, expressed as a percentage of GDP, is optimal.

858. The vagueness of Article 107 suggests that it was not intended to be justiciable. In other words, it suggests that it was not intended that any person or other applicant would be able to obtain a remedy through the courts for non-compliance by the Government. In other words, it seems likely that Article 107 is essentially symbolic – that it is 'directory' rather than 'mandatory'.[1692] Nonetheless, the symbolism is powerful, as is evidenced by the fact that debates on how the Special Administrative Region's Government might best respond to its occasional budgetary difficulties have made repeated reference to it.

§4. The Constitutional Status of the Low Tax Policy

859. Article 108 of the Basic Law provides as follows:

> The Hong Kong Special Administrative Region shall practise an independent taxation system. The Hong Kong Special Administrative Region shall, taking the low tax policy previously pursued in Hong Kong as reference, enact laws on its own concerning types of taxes, tax rates, tax reductions, allowances and exemptions, and other matters of taxation.

860. The first limb of Article 108 is a key component of the fiscal firewall; the second authorizes the Special Administrative Region's Government to legislate on 'matters of taxation' and also accords constitutional status to the 'low tax policy'

1692. *See* Yash Ghai, *Hong Kong's New Constitutional Order: The Resumption of Chinese Sovereignty and the Basic Law*, (2nd edn, Hong Kong: Hong Kong University Press, 1999), 243.

for which Hong Kong has long been famous. Again, however, it seems likely that the reference to the 'low tax policy' is essentially symbolic rather than justiciable. In any event, it is obviously imprecise in the extreme. First, the term 'low tax policy' is obviously vague. Second, 'taking' a policy 'as reference' does not necessarily mean adhering to it. Article 108 specifically empowers the Special Administrative Region to enact laws 'concerning ... tax reductions', but tax increases are not expressly authorized. Although the drafting is curious, it would presumably be wrong to base on it an *eijusdem generis* interpretation to the effect that the Special Administrative Region is not authorized to increase taxes at all.

861. It seems likely that the Basic Law's reference to Hong Kong's 'low tax policy', like its references to the balancing of the budget, is symbolic rather than justiciable. The Special Administrative Region's Government has sometimes experienced budgetary difficulties which were, at least by its own fortunate standards, quite serious. Should it experience further difficulties, it seems likely that it would seek to redress these by increasing taxes (i.e., raising existing taxes or introducing new ones or both), and also by cutting spending and operating deficits financed either by borrowing or from the Government's accumulated reserves. For example, the Government might seek to increase the taxes on income provided for by the Inland Revenue Ordinance, for example, by simply raising the rates of tax, or it might seek to establish a general indirect tax of the kind usually called Goods and Services Tax or GST (in New Zealand, Australia, Canada and Singapore) or Value Added Tax or VAT (in other countries). Presumably, any increases in taxation will encounter opposition from those affected. Moreover, it seems likely that increased taxes are likely to arouse greater opposition than unbalanced budgets, because people are more likely to oppose higher taxes than the running down of the Government's reserves. It seems likely, then, that the justiciability of Article 108 will at some point be put to the test. Opponents of new or increased taxes could presumably give themselves standing by simply declining to pay. The Government would then be obliged to commence proceedings to collect the tax unpaid; and the opponent of the tax would be afforded an opportunity to raise before a court the compatibility of the taxing legislation with the Basic Law.

862. There is very considerable interest, not only in the US but also elsewhere, in the possibility of imposing constitutional constraints on the Governments' powers of taxation,[1693] and yet such constraints are in fact rare. Indeed, the drafters of the Basic Law to some extent based Article 108 on an analysis of the theoretical

1693. *See*, in particular the works of J.M. Buchanan, such as J.M. Buchanan & Richard E. Wagner (eds), *Fiscal Responsibility in Constitutional Democracy* (Leiden: Martinus Nijhoff, 1978); Geoffrey Brennan & James M. Buchanan, *The Power to Tax: Analytical Foundations of a Fiscal Constitution* (Cambridge: Cambridge University Press, 1980); and JamesM. Buchanan & Richard A. Musgrave, *Public Finance and Public Choice: Two Contrasting Visions of the State* (Cambridge, MA: MIT Press, 1999).

literature on this subject.[1694] Article 108 is therefore of some significance in the field of comparative and theoretical fiscal constitutionalism.[1695]

863. In addition, there are a number of other provisions in the Basic Law which bear directly or indirectly on the Special Administrative Region's Government's taxing and spending powers. Article 7, which deals with land and natural resources, provides that 'the revenues therefrom [i.e., from land and natural resources] shall be exclusively at the disposal of the government of the [Special Administrative Region]'.[1696] Article 36 provides as follows: 'Hong Kong residents shall have the right to social welfare in accordance with law. The welfare benefits and retirement security of the labour force shall be protected by law.' Related to Article 36 is Article 145, which provides as follows:

> On the basis of the previous social welfare system, the Government of the Hong Kong Special Administrative Region shall, on its own, formulate policies on the development and improvement of this system in the light of the economic conditions and social needs.

These provisions are consistent with the socialist tradition of according constitutional status to social and economic rights, but their meaning and justiciability are unclear.

864. Chapter V of the Basic Law (particularly Articles 110–119) deals with various matters relating to the territory's economy. Some of these (in addition to Articles 106, 107 and 108, which are examined above) bear on matters relevant to the taxing and spending powers. For example, Article 114 provides as follows: 'The Hong Kong Special Administrative Region shall maintain the status of a free port and shall not impose any tariff unless otherwise prescribed by law.' And Article 116 provides, among other things, as follows: 'The Hong Kong Special Administrative Region shall be a separate customs territory.'

865. Chapter VII (Articles 150–157) of the Basic Law deals with the Hong Kong Special Administrative Region's Government's authority in connection with external affairs. Some of these powers bear on matters of taxation directly (e.g., the

1694. *See* Yash Ghai, *Hong Kong's New Constitutional Order: The Resumption of Chinese Sovereignty and the Basic Law*, (2nd edn, Hong Kong: Hong Kong University Press, 1999), Ch. 6.

1695. *See* P. Vitu, *Hong Kong:* 'Fiscal Constitutionalism and the Basic Law', December 1999 *Asia-Pacific Tax Bulletin* 404.

1696. Discussed above.

negotiation of tax treaties)[1697] or indirectly (e.g., the Special Administrative Region's membership of international organizations such as the World Trade Organization).[1698]

1697. The Colonial Hong Kong Government appears to have had little interest in entering into double tax treaties. Since 1997, however, the SAR Government has embarked on an ambitious programme of entering into such treaties. Currently, Hong Kong has a network of thirty-seven comprehensive double tax treaties, plus a number of more narrowly focused treaties.

1698. For a closer analysis of Ch. VII of the Basic Law, *see* Part V, Ch. 1 'War, Treaty, and Foreign Affairs Powers'.

Chapter 3. Emergency Laws (Legislation under Emergency Powers for War or under Other Extraordinary Circumstances)

§1. General

866. Hong Kong being a Special Administrative Region of China, both the Chinese Government and the Hong Kong Government have powers to declare an emergency and to bring in special legislative and administrative controls. The authority of the Central Government to act in emergencies derives from the Basic Law. The powers of the Hong Kong Government to exercise emergency powers flow from local legislation.

867. Article 14 of the Basic Law clearly provides that the Chinese Central Government is responsible for the defence of Hong Kong and permits the stationing of military forces in Hong Kong for that purpose. These forces may not intervene in local affairs of Hong Kong, but they may assist in the 'maintenance of public order and in disaster relief' at the request of the Hong Kong Government.

868. Article 18 of the Basic Law provides that the Central Government may declare an emergency in Hong Kong if by reason of turmoil within Hong Kong which endangers national unity or security and is beyond the control of the Hong Kong Government. In such an emergency situation, the Central Government may, by order, apply relevant national laws in Hong Kong. Whether there is such an emergency is to be decided by the NPCSC and, on the face of it, Article 18 seems to permit the Central Government to extend any law to Hong Kong, whether or not such laws are consistent with the Basic Law provisions concerning fundamental rights.[1699]

869. The Hong Kong Government is responsible for the maintenance of public order in Hong Kong[1700] and must accordingly have the power to legislate for that purpose. Hong Kong already has two important statutes, which were passed during the British administration, which relate to emergencies and maintenance of public order. They are the Emergency Regulations Ordinance (Cap. 241) of 1922 and the Public Order Ordinance (Cap. 245) of 1967. These two laws are part of Hong Kong law because of the guarantee given in Article 8 of the Basic Law that laws previously in force would continue to be effective in Hong Kong, as long as they do not contravene the Basic Law.

1699. *See* Yash Ghai, *Hong Kong's New Constitutional Order: The Resumption of Chinese Sovereignty and the Basic Law*, (2nd edn, Hong Kong: Hong Kong University Press, 1998), at 416–418.
1700. Basic Law, Art. 14.

§2. LEGISLATION ON SECURITY

I. The National Security Law

870. Article 23 of the Basic Law, which appears as the last article in 'Chapter II Relationship between the Central Authorities and the Hong Kong Special Administrative Region', imposes an obligation on Hong Kong Government to pass legislation for national security as well as security in the region: 'The Hong Kong Special Administrative Region shall enact laws on its own to prohibit any act of treason, secession, sedition, subversion against the Central People's Government, or theft of state secrets, to prohibit foreign political organizations or bodies from conducting political activities in the Region, and to prohibit political organizations or bodies of the Region from establishing ties with foreign political organizations or bodies.' As discussed elsewhere in this work,[1701] the Government made a failed attempt in 2003 to pass legislation to implement Article 23. The proposed Bill had to be abandoned in view of widespread public opposition to it. One of the reasons for the public anxiety of what was conceived to be draconian restrictions on fundamental freedoms that the Basic Law had guaranteed was that there had been in those years no notable movements against the Chinese Government or in favour of Hong Kong severing its ties to China.[1702]

871. If 2003 was a period of relative calm, the hard-hitting SARS pandemic notwithstanding, the last few years have been seriously troubled times for Hong Kong. Perhaps the first notable and well-orchestrated manifestation of public unease in recent years about the uncertain future direction of Hong Kong was the 'Occupy Central' movement which emerged in 2013 as a direct response to the decision taken by the Chinese Central Government to thwart local demands for democratic electoral reforms. While the resultant protest movement lasted only four months, September-December 2014, public demand for democratic reform continued unceasingly. By 2019 it had grown into a demand for true autonomy and, in some corners, an independent Hong Kong. Just as the 2003 protests were generated by proposed legislation to implement Article 23 of the Basic Law and the 2014 protest movement was prompted by the delaying of democratic electoral reforms, the 2019 protest movement was triggered by a proposed law that would allow Hong Kong to extradite suspects of crime to countries such as China and Taiwan with whom Hong Kong had not concluded an extradition treaty. This was widely perceived by the people to be an attempt by China to facilitate extradition of political activists to China, on the pretext of having committed criminal offences, for prosecution and punishment under a less than satisfactory system of criminal procedure.

872. The popular uprising which began as a show of resistance to the proposed bill soon became – developing on the Occupy Central movement – a movement calling for free and fair elections founded on universal franchise and, as widely

1701. *See* above [107]–[108].
1702. Albert Chen, 'Comment: How Hong Kong Law Will Change When Article 23 of the Basic Law Is Implemented' (2003) *Hong Kong Law Journal* 1.

believed, march towards independence. Just as in 2014, and in a much more pronounced manner, the Government had to face violent public protests which frequently led to indiscriminate damage to public and private property and assaults on police officers and civilians who would challenge them and, as before, attacks on protestors by those who opposed them. Hong Kong, which the late UK Premier Margaret Thatcher once famously described as a place where there was no democracy but where rule of law prevailed, was soon becoming a city in turmoil and out of control. The chaotic situation was not helped by the onset of the COVID-19 pandemic that severely affected the Hong Kong economy. If there were no reasons in 2003 for legislation of the type envisaged by Article 23 of the Basic Law, as Professor Albert Chen had assessed, there appeared to be every reason for strong measures to protect national security and to strengthen the hands of the Hong Kong Government. The passing of a regulation under the Emergency Regulations Ordinance (Cap. 241) banning face covering in public gatherings did not prove effective as people openly disobeyed it. Disagreeing with the Court of First Instance, the Court of Appeal ruled that the regulation was not constitution-compliant if the police resort to the power given by it in relation to authorized assemblies and gatherings. On appeal to the Court of Final Appeal the ruling of the Court of Appeal on that point was not contested.[1703]

873. It is in this context that the Chinese Government decided that effective legislation and law enforcement measures were urgently needed in Hong Kong, particularly to prevent the rising anti-Chinese movement. The result was the passing of a fairly detailed national law of China, consisting of sixty-six Articles: 'The Law of the People's Republic of China on Safeguarding National Security in the Hong Kong Special Administrative Region' (popularly known as the National Security Law) especially made for and extended to Hong Kong under the enabling provision in the Basic Law, Article 18. This law was enacted pursuant to a decision made by the National People's Congress on 'establishing and improving the legal system and enforcement mechanisms for safeguarding national security in the Hong Kong Special Administrative Region'.[1704]

874. As seen elsewhere in this work, the NPCSC has the authority to extend Chinese national law to Hong Kong. This can be done under Article 18 of the Basic Law in one of two ways: (1) by adding a national law to Annex III of the Basic Law. However, as Article 18 provides 'Laws listed in Annex III to [the Basic Law] shall be confined to those relating to defence and foreign affairs as well as other matters

1703. *Kwok Wing Hang v Chief Executive in Council* (2020) 3 HKCFAR 518, (CFA), [106].

1704. 'Decision of the Standing Committee of the National People's Congress on the Addition to the List of National Laws in Annex III to the Basic Law of the Hong Kong Special Administrative Region of the People's Republic of China', appended to the Basic Law of Hong Kong as Instrument 9. The Hong Kong Government promulgated the National Security Law on 30 June 2020 and on the same day gazetted 'Implementation Rules relating to measures that Hong Kong law enforcement authorities may take in handling cases endangering national security', including rules for search of premises, restricting persons under investigation from leaving Hong Kong, seizing and freezing properties used or intended to be used for the commission of an offence endangering national security, and interception of communications. *See* Instrument A406A.

outside the limits of the autonomy of the Region as specified by this Law'; (2) exceptionally, 'in the event that the NPCSC decides to declare a state of war or, by reason of turmoil within the Hong Kong Special Administrative Region which endangers national unity or security and is beyond the control of the Government of the Region, decides that the Region is in a state of emergency, the Central People's Government may issue an order applying the relevant national laws in the Region'. The NPCSC made the National Security Law specifically for Hong Kong and extended it to Hong Kong, using the first method.

875. It is too early to make any meaningful comments on the practical impact that the National Security Law will have on Hong Kong, its relationship with the Chinese Central Authorities, its common law system – particularly the judicial system – and the scope of the 'One Country, Two Systems' model of power sharing. What can be done is to highlight the main provisions of the law to show the National Security Law's wide scope.

876. The purposes of the National Security Law are: (a) ensuring full implementation of the 'One Country, Two Systems' policy; (b) preventing, suppressing and punishing acts of secession, subversion, terrorism and collusion with foreign countries or elements to endanger national security in relation to Hong Kong; (c) maintaining prosperity and stability of the Hong Kong Special Administrative Region; and (d) protecting lawful rights and interests of Hong Kong residents (Article 1). The law goes on to provide that in Hong Kong fundamental rights would be respected and rule of law upheld. It makes special reference to the presumption of innocence, the right of an accused person to defend himself and the rule against double jeopardy (Articles 4 and 5).

877. The National Security Law enjoys primacy over Hong Kong law – legislation or common law – which is inconsistent with it (Article 62), a status the Basic Law enjoys.[1705] The power of interpreting the National Security Law is vested in the NPCSC (Article 65). Hong Kong Courts are likely, as evident from the first case on National Security Law in the Court of First Instance, *Tong Ying Kit v HKSAR*, to approach the interpretation of the National Security Law, applying common law rules of interpretation, which they have consistently applied in interpreting the Basic Law, including generous and purposive approach towards provisions protecting fundamental rights and a restrictive approach towards any limitations on such rights, reading a statutory provisions in the context of the entirety of the statute, and giving an interpretation which makes it, as far as possible, consistent with the Basic Law.[1706]

1705. In the first case where the constitutionality of the National Security Law was challenged, *Tong Ying Kit v HKSAR* [2020] HKEC 2586, (CFI), decided on 21 August 2020, the court left undecided the question whether the Basic Law itself must yield to the National Security Law, as that question was not relevant to the determination of the dispute before the court. *Ibid.*, [26].

1706. *See* the explanation of the *Tong Ying Kit v HKSAR* in the follow up bail application case, *HKSAR v Tong Ying Kit* [2020] HKEC 2621, (CFI), [7]–[10], decided on 25 August 2020.

878. Article 7 reminds the Hong Kong Government of its yet unfulfilled duty to pass legislation as stipulated in the Basic Law [in Article 23] to safeguard national security, as soon as possible; Article 8 says that it is the Hong Kong Government's duty to fully enforce the National Security Law and laws in force to ensure national security; Article 9 requires Hong Kong Government to 'strengthen its work on safeguarding national security and prevention of terrorist activities' and states that the Hong Kong Government 'shall take necessary measures to strengthen public communication, guidance, supervision and regulation over matters concerning national security, including those relating to schools, universities, social organizations, the media, and the internet'. Article 10 states as follows: 'The Hong Kong Special Administrative Region shall promote national security education in schools and universities and through social organisations, the media, the internet and other means to raise the awareness of Hong Kong residents of national security and of the obligation to abide by the law.' Article 11 makes the Chief Executive accountable to the Chinese Central Government for affairs relating to safeguarding national security in Hong Kong.

879. For the implementation of this law, two special agencies have been established: the Office for Safeguarding National Security of the Central People's Government in the Hong Kong Special Administrative Region and the Committee for Safeguarding National Security. The Office for Safeguarding National Security is established and funded by the Chinese Central Government and made up of staff 'jointly dispatched by relevant national security authorities under the Central People's Government' (Articles 48 and 51). Chapter V deals with this Office. The Office has a mandate to analyse and assess developments in relation to safeguarding national security in Hong Kong provide opinions and make proposals on major strategies and important policies for safeguarding national security; oversee, guide, coordinate with, and provide support to the Region in the performance of its duties for safeguarding national security; collect and analyse intelligence and information concerning national security; and handle cases concerning offences of endangering national security (Article 49). The work of the Office and its staff in accordance with the National Security Law is not subject to the jurisdiction of the Hong Kong Government (Article 60). The Office is expected to work in collaboration with the Liaison Office of the Chinese Government in Hong Kong, the Office of the Commissioner of Foreign Affairs in Hong Kong and the Hong Kong Garrison of the Chinese People's Liberation Army (Article 52). Relevant departments of the Hong Kong Government must facilitate and support the work of the Office, and must 'stop any act obstructing the performance of such mandate and hold those who commit such act liable in accordance with the law' (Article 61). The Office is expected to establish a mechanism of coordination with the Committee for Safeguarding National Security (which is discussed in the next paragraph) to oversee and provide guidance on the work of the Committee (Article 53). Upon approval of the Chinese Central Government of a request of the Hong Kong Government or, by the Office itself, exercise jurisdiction over a case concerning an offence endangering national security if: (a) the case involves a foreign country or external elements making it difficult for Hong Kong to exercise jurisdiction over the case, or (b) a serious situation occurs where the Hong Kong Government is unable to effectively enforce the

National Security Law, or (c) there is a major and imminent threat to national security (Article 55). Such a case is outside the jurisdiction of Hong Kong authorities: investigation will be initiated by the Office, prosecution will be by a prosecuting body designated by the Supreme People's Procuratorate of China, adjudication will be by a court designated by the Supreme People's Court of China (Article 56), and the Criminal Procedure Law of China and other relevant Chinese laws will govern the whole process (Article 57). Relevant Hong Kong authorities must comply with measures taken by the Office (Article 57).

880. The second agency, the Committee for Safeguarding National Security, is set up by Hong Kong Government and consists of certain designated principal government officials. The Committee is responsible for affairs relating to national security. It will work 'under the supervision of and accountable to the Central People's Government' (Article 12). The Committee has a National Security Officer, designated by the Chinese Central Government, to advice on matters relating to the duties and functions of the Committee (Article 15). Article 13 provides for a Secretariat to work under the committee and its Secretary-General is to be nominated by the Chief Executive and appointed by the Chinese Government. The Committee has extensive powers of 'making work plans, and formulating policies for safeguarding national security in the Region; advancing the development of the legal system and enforcement mechanisms of the Region for safeguarding national security; and coordinating major work and significant operations for safeguarding national security in the Region' (Article 14). The committee is well insulated from outside scrutiny and control: 'No institution, organization or individual in the Region shall interfere with the work of the Committee. Information relating to the work of the Committee shall not be subject to disclosure. Decisions made by the Committee shall not be amenable to judicial review' (Article 14).

881. The National Security Law also requires the setting up of a special division for the purpose of implementing the National Security Law in the Police Department and the Department of Justice. Hong Kong's Police Force must establish a department for safeguarding national security with law enforcement capacity (Article 16). This department will be headed by a person appointed by the Chief Executive after seeking written opinion of the Office for Safeguarding National Security. The department may recruit 'qualified professionals and technical personnel from outside the Hong Kong Special Administrative Region to provide assistance in the performance of duties for safeguarding national security' (Article 16). The powers of the department include the power of: (i) planning, coordinating and enforcing measures and operations for safeguarding national security; (ii) investigating offences endangering national security; and (ii) investigating offences endangering national security (Article 17).

882. The Department of Justice of the Hong Kong Special Administrative Region is required to establish a specialized prosecution division responsible for the prosecution of offences endangering national security and other related legal work. The head of the department is appointed by the Chief Executive after seeking the written opinion of the Office for Safeguarding National Security. The appointment of prosecutors of this division may be done only with the consent of the Committee for Safeguarding National Security (Article 18).

883. Article 19 requires the Financial Secretary to set up a special fund to meet the expenses of safeguarding national security including for the establishment of relevant posts, 'which are not subject to any restrictions in the relevant provisions of the laws in force in the Region'.

884. Except in cases where Article 55 applies (namely those initiated by the Office for Safeguarding National Security) where jurisdiction is vested with Mainland Chinese authorities, Hong Kong shall have jurisdiction over offences under the national Security Law (Article 40). In hearing such cases the courts are aware of the clear statements made in the National Security Law that: Human rights shall be respected and protected in safeguarding national security in Hong Kong (Article 4), the principle of the rule of law shall be adhered to in preventing, suppressing and imposing punishment for offences endangering national security (Article 5), and a person is presumed to be innocent until convicted by a judicial body (Article 5).[1707] Article 41 of the National Security Law provides that '[the National Security Law] and the laws of the Hong Kong Special Administrative Region shall apply to procedural matters, including those related to criminal investigation, prosecution, trial, and execution of penalty, in respect of cases concerning offence endangering national security over which the Region exercises jurisdiction.' For instance, in determining whether to grant bail in a case involving security offences, the courts would follow the principles that have been well established in Hong Kong read together with Article 42 which provides that 'no bail shall be granted to a criminal suspect or defendant unless the judge has sufficient grounds for believing that the criminal suspect or defendant will not continue to commit acts endangering national security'. Rejecting the argument that Article 42 suggests that a person may be granted bail only if there is admission by the defendant that he has committed an act endangering national security, the Court of First Instance did not see a conflict between Article 42 and the common law.[1708]

885. Marking a notable departure from Hong Kong's judicial practice, the Chief Executive has been authorized to nominate judges from the Magistrates' Courts, District Courts, Court of First Instance, Court of Appeal and the Court of Final Appeal for the purpose of handling cases concerning offences endangering national

1707. *Tong Ying Kit v HKSAR* [2020] HKEC 2586, (CFI), [39].

1708. In *Tong Ying Kit v HKSAR* [2020] HKEC 2586, (CFI), [30], the Court of First Instance observed as follows: '[A]ll that Article 42(2) does is to direct the judge dealing with an application for bail to consider the question of whether an accused person may, if bail is granted and while on bail, commit acts endangering national security. There is no question of the accused person being required to acknowledge, or admit, guilt before he can make an application for bail. Neither is the judge required to first form a view that the accused person has already committed acts endangering national security before considering the question of whether that person may commit such acts in future.'

security. In designating such judges, the Chief Executive may consult the Chief Justice of the Court of Final Appeal and Committee for Safeguarding National Security (Article 44).[1709] What Article 44 says is that the Chief Executive must designate a panel of judges (this is not a term used in the National Security Law), which is valid for a period of twelve months, and not that the Chief Executive must nominate judges to hear a particular case.[1710] Any judge who has made any statement or behaved himself in any manner endangering national security is not eligible for such nomination. Any judge who has been included in the list of nominated judges makes any statement or behaves in any manner endangering national security, will be taken off the list (Article 44, paragraph 2).

886. The Secretary of Justice may direct a non-jury trial by a panel of three judges of the Court of First Instance of offences endangering national security, for instance on the grounds of the protection of State secrets, involvement of foreign factors in the case, and the protection of personal safety of jurors and their family members (Article 46). A certificate issued by the Chief Executive is conclusive that an act involves national security, or, the relevant evidence involves State secrets, when such questions arise in the adjudication of a case (Article 47).

887. Chapter III of the National Security Law deals with offences and penalties. The listed offences are secession, subversion, terrorist activities, collusion with a foreign country or with external elements to endanger national security. It is helpful to set out the offences in some detail.

888. Secession refers to organizing, planning, committing or participating in any of the following acts, whether or not by force or threat of force, with a view to committing secession or undermining national unification: (1) separating the Hong Kong Special Administrative Region or any other part of the People's Republic of China from the People's Republic of China; (2) altering by unlawful means the legal status of the Hong Kong Special Administrative Region or of any other part of the People's Republic of China; or (3) surrendering the Hong Kong Special Administrative Region or any other part of the People's Republic of China to a foreign country (Article 20). It is an offence to incite, assists in, abet or provide pecuniary or other financial assistance or property for the commission by other persons of an offence of secession (Article 21).

1709. 'Offences endangering national security' is a reference to offences under Hong Kong law or the National Security Law which endanger national security. As the Court First Instance said in *Tong Ying Kit v HKSAR* [2020] HKEC 2586, (CFI), [37], '"acts endangering national security" means offences under the National Security Law and not just any act which may in some way be said to endanger national security'.

1710. *Tong Ying Kit v HKSAR* [2020] HKEC 2586, (CFI), [54]. The judge quoted from a statement made by the Chief Justice of the Court of Final Appeal on 20 July 2020 relating to Art. 44 to the following effect: 'The listing and handling of cases, the assignment of which judge or judges are to handle cases or appeals will be determined by the court leader of the relevant level of court. These are matters within the sole responsibility of the Judiciary.' https://www.info.gov.hk/gia/general/202007/02/P2020070200414.htm.

889. Subversion refers to organizing, planning, committing or participating in any of the following acts by force or threat of force or other unlawful means with a view to subverting the State power shall be guilty of an offence: (1) overthrowing or undermining the Chinese system of government; (2) overthrowing the Chinese or Hong Kong Government; (3) seriously interfering in, disrupting, or undermining the performance of duties and functions by the Chinese or Hong Kong Government; or (4) attacking or damaging the premises and facilities used by the Hong Kong Government to perform its duties and functions, rendering it incapable of performing its normal duties and functions (Article 22). It is an offence to incite, assist in, abet or provide pecuniary or other financial assistance or property for the commission by other persons of the offence of subversion (Article 23).

890. The offence of terrorism is committed by any person who organizes, plans, commits, participates in or threatens to commit any of the following terrorist activities causing or intended to cause grave harm to the society with a view to coercing the Central People's Government, the Government of the Hong Kong Special Administrative Region or an international organization or intimidating the public in order to pursue political agenda: (1) serious violence against a person or persons; (2) explosion, arson, or dissemination of poisonous or radioactive substances, pathogens of infectious diseases or other substances; (3) sabotage of means of transport, transport facilities, electric power or gas facilities, or other combustible or explosible facilities; (4) serious interruption or sabotage of electronic control systems for providing and managing public services such as water, electric power, gas, transport, telecommunications and the internet; or (5) other dangerous activities which seriously jeopardize public health, safety or security (Article 24). Some of these reflect the acts of vandalism and destruction caused during the 2019–2020 democracy protests in Hong Kong. It is an offence to provide support, assistance or facility such as training, weapons, information, funds, supplies, labour, transport, technologies or venues to a terrorist organization or a terrorist, or for the commission of a terrorist activity; or to manufacture or illegally possess substances such as explosive, poisonous or radioactive substances and pathogens of infectious diseases or use other means to prepare for the commission of a terrorist activity (Article 26). It is an offence to advocate terrorism or incite the commission of a terrorist activity (Article 27).

891. It is an offence to steal, spy, obtain payment or unlawfully provide state secrets or intelligence concerning national security for a foreign country or an institution, organization or person outside China, Hong Kong and Macao; to request a foreign government or an institution, organization or person outside China, Hong Kong and Macao, or directly receives instructions, control, funding or other kinds of support from a foreign government or an institution, organization or person outside China, Hong Kong and Macao to commit any of the following acts: (1) waging a war against the People's Republic of China, or using or threatening to use force to seriously undermine the sovereignty, unification and territorial integrity of the People's Republic of China; (2) seriously disrupting the formulation and implementation of laws or policies by the Government of the Hong Kong Special Administrative Region or by the Central People's Government, which is likely to cause serious consequences; (3) rigging or undermining an election in the Hong Kong Special Administrative Region, which is likely to cause serious consequences; (4) imposing sanctions or blockade, or engaging in other hostile activities against the Hong Kong Special Administrative Region or the People's Republic of China; or (5) provoking by unlawful means hatred among Hong Kong residents towards the Central People's Government or the Government of the Region, which is likely to cause serious consequences (Article 29).

892. The above offences may be committed by a corporation or an unincorporated body, for which the punishment is a fine. Where such an entity if found guilty and sentenced their operations will be suspended or their licence or permit revoked (Article 31). Any proceeds obtained from the commission of an offence under the National Security Law, including grants and rewards, shall be seized and confiscated (Article 32). Where a person is found guilty of a terrorism offence, in addition to a sentence of imprisonment he may have his property confiscated (Articles 25, 26 and 27) may have his property confiscated in addition to life imprisonment. The sentences of imprisonment imposed on a person guilty of an offence may range from a maximum term of five years, with no minimum period specified, short-term detention or restriction (Article 23), through ten years with a minimum of three years, (as in Article 25) to life imprisonment, with a minimum of ten years (as in Article 20).[1711] A non-permanent Hong Kong resident who contravenes any provision of the National Security Law, but not prosecuted, may be deported (Article 34). Civic disabilities are imposed on any person who is convicted of an offence endangering national security (Article 35). An offence under the National Security Law may be committed: (a) in Hong Kong by any person; or (b) outside Hong Kong by a permanent resident or an incorporated or unincorporated body set up in Hong Kong; and (c) in the case of an offence under the National Security Law against Hong Kong committed by any person from outside the region (Articles 36, 37 and 38).

II. Emergency Regulations Ordinance

893. The plenary nature of the powers that the Emergency Regulations Ordinance (Cap. 241) confers on the Chief Executive has been noted in the chapters dealing with subordinate legislation[1712] and the Executive.[1713] The Emergency Regulations Ordinance provides as follows: 'On any occasion which the Chief

1711. Upholding the validity of these provisions the Court of First Instance observed that it is permissible to prescribe a fixed penalty such as life imprisonment, or a maximum period of imprisonment with a minimum term, giving discretion to the judge to determine the appropriate sentence in a given case: *Tong Ying Kit v HKSAR* [2020] HKEC 2586, (CFI), [66], citing *Yau Kwong Man v Secretary for Security* [2002] HKEC 1142, (CFI).

1712. *See* Part I, Ch. 6 'Subordinate Rules and Regulations'.

1713. *See* Part II, Ch. 4 'The Executive'.

Executive in Council may consider to be an occasion of emergency or public danger he may make any regulations whatsoever which he may consider desirable in the public interest.'[1714]

894. The purposes for which the Chief Executive may make regulations include, for example, arrest, detention, exclusion and deportation; appropriation, control, forfeiture and disposition of property; amending any enactment, suspending the operation of any enactment and applying any enactment with or without modification; requiring persons to do work or render services; and the apprehension, trial and punishment of persons offending against the regulations or against any law in force in Hong Kong.[1715] Regulations may provide for punishment of offenders, including mandatory life imprisonment and forfeiture of property.[1716]

895. The power to declare war by necessary implication arising from the Basic Law is with the Central Government. Article 18 of the Basic Law provides that 'in the event the Standing Committee of the National People's Congress decides to declare a state of war'; it can order the application of relevant national laws in Hong Kong. It may also be argued that if in an emergency situation the Chief Executive decides to exercise his powers under Hong Kong law and the Central Government decides to invoke Article 18 of the Basic Law, the powers of the Central Government should prevail.

III. Bill of Rights Ordinance

896. The Hong Kong Bill of Rights Ordinance permits derogations from the Bill of Rights. Section 5 of the Ordinance, which deals with 'Public Emergencies', provides as follows:

1. In time of public emergency which threatens the life of the nation and the existence of which is officially proclaimed, measures may be taken derogating from the Bill of Rights to the extent strictly required by the exigencies of the situation, but these measures shall be taken in accordance with law.
2. No measure shall be taken under Subsection (1) that:
   a. is inconsistent with any obligation under international law that applies to Hong Kong (other than any obligation under the International Covenant on Civil and Political Rights);
   b. involves discrimination solely on the ground of race, colour, sex, language, religion or social origin; or

1714. Emergency Regulations Ordinance (Cap. 241), s. 2(1).
1715. *Ibid.*, s. 2.
1716. *Ibid.*, s. 3.

c. derogates from Articles 2 [right to life], 3 [prohibition of torture], 4(1) and (2) [prohibition of slavery], 7 [no imprisonment for breach of contract], 12 [prohibition against retrospective penal legislation], 13 [right to recognition as a person] and 15 [freedom of thought, conscience and religion].

Chapter 4. The Constitutional Relationship Between Church and State

897. Hong Kong is a secular state. It has no state religion and is not committed to the promotion of a particular religion or religious institution.[1717] However, Hong Kong recognizes the importance of religious freedom. The Hong Kong Bill of Rights and the Basic Law contain provisions designed to promote freedom of religion. Reflecting Article 18 of the ICCPR, Article 15 of the Bill of Rights provides that everyone is entitled to freedoms of thought, conscience and religion. This freedom includes the freedom to have or to adopt a religion or belief of one's choice, and freedom, either individually or in community with others and in public or private, to manifest his religion or belief in worship, observance, practice and teaching. Of these the freedom of thought, conscience and religion are considered absolute, whereas the freedom to manifest one's religion or belief may be subjected to restrictions.[1718] Such restrictions must be necessary to protect public safety, order, health, or morals or the fundamental rights and freedoms of others.[1719] Article 32 of the Basic Law provides that Hong Kong residents have the freedom of conscience and freedom of religious belief. Religious freedom includes the freedom to preach and to conduct and participate in religious activities in public.

898. Article 141 of the Basic Law provides that the Government of Hong Kong must not restrict the freedom of religious belief, interfere in the internal affairs of religious organizations or restrict religious activities. Religious organizations have been guaranteed the right to acquire, use and dispose of land, to inherit property and to receive financial assistance. Religious organizations and believers in Hong Kong may maintain and develop their relations with religious organizations and believers elsewhere.[1720] Religious organizations may, according to previous practice, continue to run seminaries and other schools, hospitals and welfare institutions, and to provide other social services.[1721]

1717. The Constitution of Sri Lanka, on the other hand, imposes a duty on the State to give Buddhism the 'foremost place' and to 'protect and foster' Buddhism. *The Constitution of the Democratic Socialist Republic* of Sri Lanka of 1978, Art. 9.

1718. *See* generally on the freedom of religion in the Commonwealth, Anton Cooray, 'The Protection and Promotion of Religious Rights: A Commonwealth Survey', (2001) *Sri Lanka Journal of International Law* 12, 153–179.

1719. Hong Kong Bill of Rights, Art. 15.

1720. *See also* Basic Law, Arts 148 and 149.

1721. *Ibid.*, Art. 141.

Select Bibliography

Allan, T R S. 'The Rule of Law as the Law of Reason: Consent and Constitutionalism' (1999) 115 *Law Quarterly Review* 221–244.

Allan, T R S. 'Judicial Deference and Judicial Review: Legal Doctrine and Legal Theory' (2011) *Law Quarterly Review* 96-117.

A W Bradley, K D Ewing & C J S Knight. *Constitutional and Administrative Law* (17th edn, Pearson 2018).

Chan, Johannes. 'Hong Kong's Administrative Complaints System' (1996) 26 *Hong Kong Law Journal* 339–368.

Chan, Johannes. 'The Status of the Bill of Rights in the Hong Kong Special Administrative Region' (1998) 28 *Hong Kong Law Journal* 152–155.

Chan, Johannes. 'Hong Kong's Bill of Rights: Its Reception of and Contribution to International and Comparative Jurisprudence' (1998) 47 *International and Comparative Law Quarterly* 306–336.

Chan, Johannes. 'Some Reflections on Remedies in Administrative Law' (2009) 39 *Hong Kong Law Journal* 321–337.

Chan, Johannes. 'Basic Law and Constitutional Review: The First Decade' (2007) 37 *Hong Kong Law Journal* 407–448.

Chan, Johannes, Fu, HL & Ghai, Yash (eds). *Hong Kong's Constitutional Debate: Conflict Over Interpretation* (Hong Kong: Hong Kong University Press, 2000).

Chan, Johannes & Ghai, Yash (eds). *The Hong Kong Bill of Rights: A Comparative Approach* (Hong Kong: Butterworths Asia, 1993).

Chan, Johannes & Lim, CL (eds). *Law of the Hong Kong Constitution* (2nd edn, Hong Kong: Sweet and Maxwell, 2015).

Chan, Johannes. 'Reconciliation of the NPCSC's Power of Interpretation of the Basic Law with the Common Law in the HKSAR' (2000) Hong Kong Law Journal 657.

Cheek-Milby, Kathleen. *A Legislature Comes of Age: Hong Kong's Search for Influence and Identity* (Hong Kong: Oxford University Press, 1995).

Chen, Albert. 'The Basic Law and Protection of Property Rights' (1993) 23 *Hong Kong Law Journal* 31–78.

Chen, Albert. 'The Legal Foundation of the Legislative Council Election 1995' in H.C. Kuan et al. (eds) *The 1997 Legislative Council Elections in Hong Kong* (Hong Kong: Hong Kong Institute of Asia-Pacific Studies, Chinese University of Hong Kong, 1996).

Chen, Albert. 'Prosecutorial Discretion, Independence and Accountability' (1998) 28 *Hong Kong Law Journal* 406–411.

Chen, Albert H.Y. 'The Interpretation of the Basic Law: Common Law and Mainland Chinese Perspective' (2000) 30 *Hong Kong Law Journal* 380–431.
Chen, Albert Chen. 'Comment: How Hong Kong Law Will Change When Article 23 of the Basic Law is Implemented' (2003) 33 *Hong Kong Law Journal* 1.
Chen, Albert H.Y. 'The Constitutional Controversy of Spring 2004' (2004) 34 *Hong Kong Law Journal* 215–226.
Chen, Albert & Lo, PY. 'The Judicial Perspective of "Separation of Powers" in the Hong Kong Special Administrative Region of the People's Republic of China' (2018) 5:2 *Journal of International and Comparative Law* 337–362.
Clark, David & Gerard McCoy. *Hong Kong Administrative Law* (Singapore: Butterworths, 1993).
Cooray, Anton. 'Three Models of Constitutional Litigation: Lessons from Sri Lanka' (1992) 21 *Anglo-American Law Review* 430–448.
Cooray, Anton. 'Toward More Efficient Administration: Citizen's Charter in the United Kingdom and Hong Kong's Performance Pledge Programme' (1993) 2:2 *Hong Kong Public Administration* 159-176.
Cooray, Anton. 'Accountability and Choice: New Directions in the Delivery of Public Services', in Jane Lee & Anthony Cheung (eds) *Public Sector Reform in Hong Kong: Future Directions* (Hong Kong: Chinese University of Hong Kong Press, 1994) 209–230.
Cooray, Anton. 'Asian Customary Laws through Western Eyes: A Comparison of Sri Lankan and Hong Kong Colonial Experience', in Louis A. Knafla & Susan W.S. Binnie (eds) *Law, State, and the Society: Essays in Modern Legal History* (Canada: University of Toronto Press, 1995) 145–177.
Cooray, Anton. 'Hong Kong in China: The Promise of One Country, Two Systems' (1997) 42 *McGill Law Journal* 752–760.
Cooray, Anton. 'Bills of Rights and Constitutional Interpretation' in John Hatchard & Peter Slinn (eds), *Parliamentary Supremacy and Judicial Independence: A Commonwealth Approach* (London and Sydney: Cavendish Publishing Co., 1999) 59–64.
Cooray, Anton. 'Hong Kong's Ombudsman: The First Decade' (1999) 3 *The International Ombudsman Yearbook* 71–88.
Cooray, Anton. 'International and Domestic Sources of Human Rights in Harmony? The Hong Kong Experience' (1999) 4 *Yearbook Law & Legal Practice in East Asia* 71–94.
Cooray, Anton. 'Public Sector Reform in Hong Kong: Some Legal Aspects' (1999) 8 *Public Administration and Policy* 23–26.
Cooray, Anton. 'Ombudsman in Asia: A Case-Study of Hong Kong and Sri Lanka' in Roy Gregory & Philip Giddings (eds) *Righting Wrongs: The Ombudsman in Six Continents* (Netherlands: 10S Press Co., 2000) 75–91.
Cooray, Anton. 'The Protection and Promotion of Religious Rights: A Commonwealth Survey' (2001) 12 *Sri Lanka Journal of International Law* 153–179.
Cooray, Anton. 'Government as Ground Landlord and Land Use Regulator: The Hong Kong Experience' in Tsuyoshi Kotaka & David L. Callies (eds) *Taking Land: Compulsory Purchase and Regulation in Asian-Pacific Countries* (Honolulu: University of Hawaii Press, 2002) 96–142.

Cooray, Anton. 'The Non-recognition of Chinese Ancestral Worship Trusts as Charitable Trusts in Hong Kong: With Some South Asian Comparisons' (2002) 8:1 *Third Sector Review* 153–172.

Cooray, Anton. 'Constitutional Law and Human Rights' (fourth reissue, 2019) 16 *Halsbury's Laws of Hong Kong*.

Cooray, Anton. 'Some Reflections on the Legislative Context of the Hong Kong Ombudsman' (2009) 17:1 *Asia Pacific Law Review* 53–72.

Cooray, Anton. 'Hong Kong's Court of Final Appeal: The Development of the Law in China's Hong Kong' (2014) 22:1 *Asia Pacific Law Review* 157–159.

Cooray, Anton. Book review of Simon Young and Richard Cullen's *Electing Hong Kong's Chief Executive* in (2011) 41 *Hong Kong Law Journal* 879–881.

Cooray, Anton & Anthony Law. 'Legislative Guidelines on the Use of Extrinsic Materials in Statutory Interpretation: Is Hong Kong Ready?' (2001) 9:1 *Asia Pacific Law Review* 23–44.

Cooray, Anton. 'Standards of Judicial Behaviour and the Impact of Codes of Conduct' in Shimon Shetreet and Christopher Forsyth (eds.), *The Culture of Judicial Independence: Conceptual Foundations and Practical Challenges* (Leiden: Martinus Nijhoff, 2012), 349-361.

Cooray, Anton. 'The Environment' (2013 reissue), 25 *Halsbury's Laws of Hong Kong*.

Cooray, Anton. 'Entering the Political Thicket: The Role of the Judiciary as an Arbiter in Relation to Making and implementation of Public Policy', in Shimon Shetreet (ed.) *The Culture of Judicial Independence: Rule of Law and World Peace* (Leiden: Brill Nijhoff, 2014), 200-216.

Cooray, Anton. 'Town Planning' (5th reissue, 2018), 48 *Halsbury's Laws of Hong Kong*.

Cooray, Anton. *Environmental Law in Hong Kong* (2nd edn, The Netherlands: Wolters Kluwer, 2018).

Cooray, Anton. 'Developing an Indian Constitutional Jurisprudence Drawing on Judicial Thinking in the Rest of the Common Law World' in Giuseppe Franco Ferrari (ed.), *Judicial Cosmopolitanism: The Use of Foreign Law in Contemporary Constitutional Systems* (Leiden: Brill Nijhoff, 2020), 177–194.

de Smith, S A. 'Westminster's Export Models: The Legal Framework of Responsible Government' (1961) 1 *Journal of Commonwealth Political Studies* 2.

De Smith, Woolf & Jowell's. *Judicial Review of Administration* (London: Sweet & Maxwell, 1995).

Elliott, Mark & Christopher Forsyth. 'The Rule of Law in Hong Kong: Immigrant Children, the Court of Final Appeal and the Standing Committee of the National People's Congress' (2000) 8:1 *Asia Pacific Law Review* 53–75.

Fallon Richard H. 'Strict Scrutiny' (2007) 54 *UCLA Law Review* 1267.

Friedmann, Wolfgang. 'Limits of Lawmaking and Prospective Overruling' (1966) 29:6 *Modern Law Review* 593-607.

Ghai, Yash. 'Sentinels of Liberty or Sheep in Woolf's Clothing? Judicial Politics and the Hong Kong Bill of Rights' (1997) 60 *The Modern Law Review* 459–480.

Ghai, Yash. *Hong Kong's New Constitutional Order: The Resumption of Chinese Sovereignty and the Basic Law*. (2nd edn, Hong Kong: Hong Kong University Press, 1999).

Ghai, Yash. 'The Intersection of Chinese Law and the Common Law in the Hong Kong Special Administrative Region' (2007) 37 *Hong Kong Law Journal* 363–405.

Han Zhu and Albert H Y Chen, 'The Oath-taking Cases and the NPCSC Interpretation of 2016: Interface of Common Law and Chinese Law' (2019) 49 Hong Kong Law Journal 381.

Hood Phillips, O. & Jackson, P. *Constitutional and Administrative Law*, (8th edn, London: Sweet & Maxwell, 2000).

Jowell, Jeffrey. 'Judicial Deference: Servility, Civility or Institutional Capacity?' (2003) *Public Law* 592-601.

Leckey, Robert. 'Remedial Practice Beyond Constitutional Text' (2016) 64:1 *The American Journal of Comparative Law* 1-136.

Law, Anthony M.W. 'Judicial Review of Government Lease in the Hong Kong Special Administration Region' (1999) 29 *Hong Kong Law Journal* 240–266.

Leung, Priscilla Mei-Fun. *The Basic Law of the Hong Kong Special Administrative Region: From Theory to Practice* (Hong Kong: LexisNexis Butterworth & Co, 1998).

Leung, Priscilla Mei-Fun. *The Hong Kong Basic Law: Hybrid Common Law and Chinese Law* (Hong Kong: LexisNexis, 2007).

Lin, Feng. 'The Constitutional Crisis in Hong Kong: Is It Over?' (2000) 9 *Pacific Rim Law and Policy Journal* 281–315.

Lin, Feng. *Constitutional Law in China* (Hong Kong: Sweet & Maxwell Asia, 2000).

Lin, Feng. 'Constitutionality of the Co-location Arrangement at the West Kowloon High-Speed Rail Terminus' (2017) 47 *Hong Kong Law Journal* 699–732.

Li, Feng 'The Duty of Hong Kong Courts to Follow the NPCSC's Interpretation of the Basic Law: Are There Any Limits?' (2018) 48 *Hong Kong Law Journal* 167–190.

Lo, PY. *The Hong Kong Basic Law* (Hong Kong: LexisNexis, 2011).

Lo, PY. *The Judicial Construction of Hong Kong's Basic Law: Courts, Politics and Society after 1997* (Hong Kong: Hong Kong University Press, 2014).

Lo, Shiu-Hing. An Analysis of Sino-British Negotiations over Hong Kong's Political Reform (1994) 16:2 *Contemporary Southeast Asia* 178–209.

Lo, Shiu-Hing and Yu, Wing-yat. 'Election and Democracy in Hong Kong: The 1998 Legislative Council Election' (1999) 4 *Contemporary Asian Studies* 1–68.

Miners, Norman. 'The Governor, the Secretary of State and the Prerogative of Mercy' (1987) 17 *Hong Kong Law Journal* 77.

Miners, Norman. *The Government and Politics of Hong Kong*, (Updated 4th edn, Hong Kong: Hong Kong University Press, 1989).

Miners, Norman. *The Government and Politics of Hong Kong*, (Updated 5th edn, Hong Kong: Hong Kong University Press, 1998).

Mo, John Shijian. 'Transfer of Sovereignty and Application of an International Convention: CISG in China in the Context of "One Country, Two Systems"' (2015) 2:1 *Journal of International and Comparative Law* 61–86.

Mushkat, Roda. *One Country, Two International Personalities: The Case of Hong Kong* (Hong Kong: Hong Kong University Press, 1997).

Mushkat, Roda. 'Assessing a Key Facet of the Rule of Law in Post-1997 Hong Kong' (2014) 1:2 *Journal of International and Comparative Law* 313–325.

Nichol, Gene R. 'Ripeness and the Constitution' (1987) 54:1 *The University of Chicago Law Review* 153-183.

Norton-Kyshe & James William. *The History of the Laws and Courts of Hong Kong from the Earliest Period to 1898* (Hong Kong: Vetch and Lee Ltd, 1971).

Petersen, Carole. 'Implementing Equality: An Analysis of Two Recent Decisions under Hong Kong's Anti-Discrimination Laws' (1999) 29 *Hong Kong Law Journal* 178–194.

Ramsden, Michael. 'Reviewing the United Kingdom's ICCP Immigration Reservation in Hong Kong Courts' (1994) 63(3) *International and Comparative Law Quarterly* 635–663.

Ramsden, Michael. 'Judging Socio-Economic Rights in Hong Kong' (2018) 16:2 *International Journal of Constitutional Law* 447–469.

Rao, Geping. 'The Application of the International Covenant on Civil and Political Rights to Hong Kong' (1993) 2:1 *Pacific Rim Law & Policy Journal* 9-35.

Ribeiro, Robert. 'The Influence of the Strasbourg Court's Jurisprudence in Hong Kong' in Marek Zubik (ed.), *Human Rights in Contemporary World: Essays in Honour of Professor Leszek Garlliski* (Wydawnictwo Sejmowe, Warszawa, 2017) https://www.hkcfa.hk/filemanager/speech/en/upload/1196/The%20Influence%20of%20the%20Strasbourg%20Court%E2%80%99s%20jurisprudence%20in%20Hong%20Kong%20.pdf.

Roberts-Wray, Sir Kenneth. *Commonwealth and Colonial Law* (London: Stevens, 1966).

Wang, Guiguo & Priscilla M.F. Leung. 'One Country, Two Systems: Theory into Practice' (1998) 7 *Pacific Rim Law and Policy Journal* 279–321.

Wacks, Raymond (ed.). *Human Rights in Hong Kong* (Hong Kong: Oxford University Press, 1992).

Wesley-Smith, Peter. *Constitutional and Administrative Law in Hong Kong* (2nd edn. Hong Kong: Longman, 1994).

Wesley-Smith, Peter. *The Sources of Hong Kong Law* (Hong Kong: Hong Kong University Press, 1994).

Wesley-Smith, Peter & Albert Chen. *The Basic Law and Hong Kong's Future* (Hong Kong: Butterworths, 1998).

Yap, Po Jen. 'Constitutional Review under the Basic Law: The Rise, Retreat and Resurgence of Judicial Power in Hong Kong' (2007) 36:2 *Common Law World Review* 166–191.

Yap, Po Jen. 'Legislative Oaths and Judicial Intervention in Hong Kong' (2017) 47 *Hong Kong Law Journal* 1–15.

Yap, Po Jen. 'Interpreting the Basic Law and the Adjudication of Politically Sensitive Questions' (2007) 6:3 *Chinese Journal of International Law* 543–564.

Yap, Po Jen & Jiang, Zixin. 'Co-location is Constitutional' (2018) 48 *Hong Kong Law Journal* 37–50

Young, Simon. 'Restricting Basic Law Rights in Hong Kong' (2004) 34 *Hong Kong Law Journal* 109–132.

Young, Simon. 'Does it Matter if Restrictions on the Right to Social Welfare in Hong Kong Are Prescribed by Law or Policy?' (2014) 44 *Hong Kong Law Journal* 25.

Young, Simon. 'Human Rights', Chapter 19 of *Archbold: Hong Kong* (Sweet & Maxwell 2018).

Young, Simon & Cullen, Richard. *Electing Hong Kong's Chief Executive* (Hong Kong: Hong Kong University Press, 2010).

Young, Simon & Yash Ghai (eds). *Hong Kong's Court of Final Appeal: The Development of the Law in China's Hong Kong* (Cambridge: Cambridge University Press: 2014).

Table of Cases

A v Commissioner of Independent Commission Against Corruption (2012) 15 HKCFAR 362, CFA
A (Torture Claimant) v Director of Immigration [2008] 4 HKLRD 752, CA
A Solicitor v Law Society of Hong Kong [2004] HKEC 219, CA
AA v Securities and Futures Commission [2016] HKEC 998, CFI
Agrila Ltd and Others v Commissioner of Rating and Valuation [1999] HKEC 1486, LT
Agrila Ltd and Others v Commissioner of Rating and Valuation [1999] HKEC 793, CA
Akram v Secretary for Security [2000] 1 HKLRD 164, CFI
American International Group Inc v Huaxia Life Insurance Co Ltd (2017) 20 HKCFAR 503, CFA
Amoy Properties Ltd v The Committee for Takeovers and Mergers and the Commissioner for Securities [1989] 1 HKLR 170, HC
Anderson Asphalt Ltd v Secretary for Justice [2009] 3 HKLRD 215, CFI
Anderson Asphalt Ltd v Secretary for Justice [2010] HKEC 1645, CA
Anderson Asphalt Ltd v Town Planning Board [2007] 3 HKLRD 18, CA
Appeal Tribunal v Peter A. de Kantzow and Another [1992] 1 HKLR 55, CA
Apple Daily Ltd v Commissioner of the ICAC (No. 2) [2000] 1 HKLRD 647, CA
Asia Dyeing Co. Ltd and Others v The Authority [1990] 1 HKLR 263, CA
Asia Television Ltd v Communications Authority [2013] 2 HKLRD 354, CA
Azan Aziz Marwah v Director of Immigration [2008] HKEC 2087, CFI
Asif Ali v Director of Immigration [2011] HKEC 868, CA
Association of Expatriate Civil Servants of Hong Kong, The v The Chief Executive of HKSAR [1998] 1 HKLRD 615, CFI
Association of Expatriate Civil Servants of Hong Kong v Secretary for the Civil Service (1996) 6 HKPLR 333, CA
Association of Expatriate Civil Servants of Hong Kong v Secretary for the Civil Service [1998] 1 HKLRD 701, CFA
Attorney General, In and For the United Kingdom v South China Morning Post Ltd [1988] 1 HKLR 143, CA
Attorney General v Chan Foo [1990] 2 HKLR 428, CA
Attorney General v Chan kei-lung [1977] HKLR 312, CA
Attorney General v Chan Wah-chuen [1988] 2 HKLR 559, HC
Attorney General v Cheung King-chow [1990] 1 HKLR 659, HC
Attorney General v David Chiu Tat-Cheung [1992] 2 HKLR 84, CA

Table of Cases

Attorney General v Ho Shek-Kwan [1980] HKLR 64, CA
Attorney General v Kong Chung-shing [1980] HKLR 533, CA
Attorney General v Lee Kwong-kut [1992] 2 HKCLR 76, CA
Attorney General v Tang Yuen-Lin (1995) 5 HKPLR 631, CA
Attorney General v Tsang Kwok-kuen [1971] HKLR 266, FC
Auburntown Ltd v TPB [1994] 2 HKLR 272, HC
Azan Aziz Marwah v Director of Immigration [2008] HKEC 2087, CFI
B v Commissioner of the Independent Commission Against Corruption (2010) 13 HKCFAR 1, CFA
B v Torture Claims Appeal Board [2015] 1 HKLRD 681, CFI
Balaoro Marietta S v Secretary for Justice [2020] 1 HKLRD 1138, CFI
Bertschy v R [1967] HKLR 739, FC
Bewang International (Group) Holdings Ltd v Next Magazine Ltd [2016] HKEC 1145, CFI
Bird v English Schools Foundation and Another [1998] HKLRD (Yrbk) 513, CA
Building Authority v Appeal Tribunal (Buildings) [2013] 4 HKLRD 52, CA
Building Authority v Appeal Tribunal (Buildings) [2015] 5 HKLRD 108, CFI
Building Authority v Appeal Tribunal (Buildings) & Estoree Ltd [2003] HKEC 947, CFI
Building Authority v Appeal Tribunal (Buildings) (re Methodist Church) [2015] 5 HKLRD 108, CFI
Business Rights Ltd v Building Authority (1994) 4 HKPLR 43, CA
C v Director of Immigration and UNHCR (2013) 16 HKCFAR 280, CFA
Caltex Oil Hong Kong Ltd v Governor in Council [1995] 1 HKLR 122, HC
Canadian Overseas Development Co Ltd v Attorney-General [1991] 1 HKLY 20
Capital Rich Development Ltd v Town Planning Board [2007] 2 HKLRD 155, CA
Catholic Diocese of Hong Kong v Secretary for Justice [2007] 4 HKLRD 483, CFI
Catholic Diocese of Hong Kong v Secretary for Justice [2010] HKEC 163, CA
Catholic Diocese of Hong Kong v Secretary for Justice (2011) 14 HKCFAR 754, CFA
Chan Choi Yin Janice v Toppan Forms (HK) Ltd [2006] HKEC 2114, DC
Chan Ho Tin v Ying Ki Alan [2018] 2 HKLRD 7, CFI
Chan Ka Lam v Chief Executive in Council [2017] HKEC 2527, CFI
Chan Kam Nga v Director of Immigration (1999) 2 HKCFAR 82, CFA
Chan Leung v R [1979] HKLR 98, HC
Chan Mei Yee v Director of Immigration [2000] HKEC 788, CFI
Chan Noi Heung v The Chief Executive in Council [2009] 3 HKLRD 413, [2009] HKCU 377, CA
Chan Noi Heung v The Chief Executive in Council [2009] HKEC 459; [2009] HKCU 417, CFA
Chan Pui Sze v Wang Jue [2019] HKEC 3355, CFI
Chan Shu Ying v Chief Executive of the Hong Kong Special Administrative Region [2001] 1 HKLR 405, CFI
Chan Tak Cheung v Commissioner of Police [2002] HKEC 880, CFI
Chan Tak Ming v HKSAR (2010) 13 HKCFAR 745, CFA
Chan Tak Shing v Chief Executive of the Hong Kong Special Administrative Region [1999] 2 HKLRD 389, CA

Chan Wah v Hang Hau Rural Committee and Anor [1999] 2 HKLRD 286, CFI.
Chan Wah v Hang Hau Rural Committee and Anor [2000] 1 HKLRD 411, CA
Chan Wah v Hang Hau Rural Committee and Anor (sub nominee Secretary for Justice v Chan Wah) (2000) 3 HKCFAR 459, CFA
Chan Yat-san v Attorney General [1975] HKLR 503, HC
Chan Yeuk Ming v Housing Authority [2012] HKEC 1239, CFI
Chan Yu Nam v Secretary for Justice [2010] HKEC 1893, CA
Chang Lan-Sheung v The Attorney General [1968] HKLR 487, FC
Charter View Development Ltd v Golden Rich Enterprises Ltd [2000] HKEC 340, CA
Chau Tam Yuet Ching v Director of Lands [2013] 3 HKLRD 169, CA
Chau Hon-leung v Kong Kwok-choi and others [1975] HKLR 529, FC
Chau Tam Yuet Ching v Director of Lands [2013] 3 HKLRD 169, CA
Chau Tsun Kiu v Secretary for Justice [2014] 5 HKLRD 414, CFI
Chau Woan Chyi v Director of Immigration [2007] HKEC 553, CFI
Chong Yu On v Kwan SH Susan [2020] 2 HKLRD 407, CA
Chow Ting v Teng Yu Yan Anne (the Returning Officer) [2019] 4 HKLRD 459, CFI
Chee Fei Ming v Director of Food and Environmental Hygiene [2018] 4 HKLRD 517, CFI
Chee Fei Ming v Director of Food and Environmental Hygiene [2016] HKEC 1266, CA
Chen Chong Gui v The Chief Executive [1999] 1 HKLRD 693, CFI
Cheng v Tse Wai Chun (2000) 3 HKCFAR 339, CFA
Cheng Chun Ngai v Hospital Authority [2004] HKEC 1375, CFI
Cheng Kar Shun v Hon Li Fung Ying [2011] 2 HKLRD 555, CFI
Cheung Kong Holdings Ltd v Chan Wai Yip Albert [2001] HKEC 307, CFI
Cheung Lai Wah v The Director of Immigration [1997] HKLRD 1081, CFI
Cheung Man Wai v Director of Social Welfare [2000] 3 HKLRD 255, CA
Cheung Moon Hoi Jeff v Administrative Appeals Board [2016] HKEC 1241, CA.
Cheung Ng Sheong Steven v Eastweek Publisher Ltd [1995] HKLY 1453, (1995) 5 HKPLR 428, CA
Cheung Shing Scrap Metals Recycling Ltd v Director of Lands [2009] HKEC 813, CFI
Cheung Tak Wing v Communications Authority [2018] 5 HKLRD 515, CFI
Chi Hong Ching Yuen Ltd v Director of Lands [2014] HKEC 584, CFI
Chiang Lai Wan v Tang Siu Tong [1998] HKEC 225, CFI
Chiang Lily v Secretary for Justice [2009] HKEC 254, CFI
Chiang Lily v Secretary for Justice [2009] HKEC 1562, CA
Chief Executive of HKSAR v President of Legislative Council [2016] HKEC 2487, CFI
Chief Executive of HKSAR v President of Legislative Council [2017] 1 HKLRD 460, CA
Chief Executive of HKSAR v President of Legislative Council [2017] 4 HKLRD 115, CFI
Chief Executive of HKSAR v President of Legislative Council [2019] HKEC 417, CA
Chim Pui Chung v President of the Legislative Council [1998] 2 HKLRD 552, CFI

Chim Shing Chung v Commissioner of Correctional Services (1995) 5 HKPLR 570, HC
Chim Shing Chung v Commissioner of Correctional Services (1996) 6 HKPLR 313, CA
China Field Ltd v Appeal Tribunal (Buildings) (No 2) (2009) 12 HKCFAR 342, CFA
China International Fund Ltd v Dennis Lau & Ng Chun Man Architects & Engineers (HK) Ltd [2015] 4 HKLRD 609, CA
China International Fund Ltd v Dennis Lau & Ng Chun Man Architects & Engineers (HK) Ltd [2015] HKEC 2707, CFA
Chit Fai Motors Ltd v Commissioner of Transport [2004] HKEC 218, CA
Chiu Koon-kwong v R [1969] HKLR 254, FC
Chiu Tat-cheong, David and Chiu Te-ken, Deacon, In re [1992] 2 HKLR 57, HC
Chiu Tat-cheong, David and Chiu Te-ken, Deacon, (*sub nominee, In re Attorney General v David Chiu Tat-Cheung* [1992] 2 HKLR 84, CA
Chong Ching Yuen v HKSAR [2004] 2 HKLRD 681; (2004) 7 HKCFAR 126, CFA.
Chow Chin-wo and Others for Judicial Review, Re Applications by [1987] HKLR 73, HC
Chow Oi Tong Amy v Hong Kong Housing Authority [2020] HKEC 1383, CFI
Chow Shui v R [1979] HKLR 275, HC
Chu Woan Chyi v Director of Immigration [2007] HKEC 553, CFI
Circumwealth Co. Ltd v Attorney General [1993] 2 HKLR 193, HC
Comilang Milagros Tescon v Director of Immigration [2018] HKEC 753, CA
Comilang Milagros Tecson v Director of Immigration (2019) 22 HKCFAR 59, CFA
Commissioner for Registration v Registration of Persons Tribunal [1999] 3 HKLRD 199, CFI
Commissioner for Registration v Registration of Persons Tribunal [2000] 2 HKLRD 523, CA
Commissioner for Registration v Registration of Persons Tribunal [2015] 2 HKLRD 369, CFI.
Commissioner of Inland Revenue v Perfekta Enterprises Ltd [2018] HKEC 3302, CFA
Competition Commission v W Hing Construction Co Ltd (No 2) [2019] 3 HKLRD 46, Competition Tribunal
Cowie v Attorney General (1948) 32 HKLR 156, SC
CP Ships USA LLC v Chief Executive of HKSAR [2007] HKEC 858, CFI
CP Ships USA LLC v Chief Executive of HKSAR [2007] HKEC 1714, CA
D v Director of Public Prosecutions [2015] 4 HKLRD 62, CFI
Dato Tan Leong Min v Insider Dealing Tribunal [1999] HKEC 1580, CA
David Lam Shu-Tsang v Attorney General [1977] HKEC 140, CA.
De Kantzow (Peter) v The Appeal Tribunal [1991] HKLY 2, HC
De Kantzow (Peter) v Appeal Tribunal [1991] HKLY 743, CA
Deacons v White & Case LLP (2003) 6 HKCFAR 322, CFA
Democratic Party v Secretary for Justice [2007] 2 HKLRD 804, CFI
Democratic Republic of the Congo v FG Hemisphere Associates LLC (No 1), (2011) 14 HKCFAR 95, CFA
Designing Hong Kong Ltd v Town Planning Board [2015] HKEC 688, CFI

Designing Hong Kong Ltd v Town Planning Board [2017] HKEC 309, CA
Designing Hong Kong Ltd v Town Planning Board (2018) 21 HKCFAR 237, CFA
Director of Immigration v Chong Fung Yuen (2001) 4 HKCFAR 211, CFA
Director of Lands v Yin Shuen Enterprises Ltd (2003) 6 HKCFAR 1, CFA
Dr Z v Education and Accreditation Committee Medical Council of Hong Kong [2011] HKEC 1209, CFI
Eastern Express Publisher Ltd v Mo Man Ching (1999) 2 HKCFAR 264, CFA
Equal Opportunities Commission v Director of Education [2001] 2 HKLRD 690, CFI
Export-Import Bank of China v Taifeng Textile Group Co Ltd [2018] HKEC 2210, CFI
Fairland Overseas Development Co Ltd v Secretary for Justice [2007] 4 HKLRD 947, CFI
Falcon Private Bank Ltd v Borry Bernard Edouard Charles Ltd (2014) 17 HKCFAR 281, CFA
Fan Kin Nang v Commissioner of Inland Revenue [2009] HKEC 1914, CFI
Fateh Muhammad v Commissioner of Registration [2001] 2 HKLRD 659, CFA
Fayomi v Secretary for Security [2009] HKEC 2039, CFI.
Fei Yi Ming and Lee Tsung Ying v R (1952) HKLR 133, Appellate Jurisdiction
Financial Services and Systems Ltd, Re [2007] HKEC 1230, CFI
Fine Tower Associates Ltd v Town Planning Board [2008] 1 HKLRD 553, CA
Fok Chun Wa v Hospital Authority [2008] HKEC 2161, CFI
Fok Chun Wa v Hospital Authority [2011] 1 HKLRD 1A, CA
Fok Chun Wa v Hospital Authority (2012) 15 HKCFAR 409, CFA
Fok Ho Chiu v Chinese Temples Committee [2003] HKEC 1183, CFI
Fok Lai Ying v Governor in Council [1997] HKLRD 111, CA
Fok Lai Ying v Governor in Council [1997] HKLRD 810, PC
Fu Kor Kuen Patrick v HKSAR (2012) 15 HKCFAR 524, CFA
GA v Director of Immigration (2014) 17 HKCFAR 60, CFA
German Swiss International School Association Ltd, re [2020] HKEC 1616, CFI
Grotch, Re [2012] 2 HKLRD 309, CFI
Ghulam Rbani v Secretary for Justice [2014] 17 HKCFAR 138, CFA
Gurung Bhakta Bahadur v Director of Immigration and Another [2001] 3 HKLRD 225, CFI
Gurung Kesh Bahadur v Director of Immigration [2001] 3 HKLRD 32, CA
Gurung Kesh Bahadur v Director of Immigration (2002) 5 HKCFAR 480, CFA
Gutierrez v Commissioner of Registration (2014) 17 HKCFAR 518, CFA.
HKSAR v Chan Pak Hoe [2012] HKEC 941, CFA
HKSAR v Cheng Kan [1998] HKEC 1143, CFI
HKSAR v Cheung Kwai Choi [2018] HKEC 2910, CFI
HKSAR v Cheung Kwun Yin (2009) 12 HKCFAR 568, CFA
HKSAR v Choi Wai Lun (2018) 21 HKCFAR 167, CFA
HKSAR v Chow Hei Choy [2018] HKEC 1281, DC
HKSAR v Chow Ho Yin (2020) 23 HKCFAR 1, CFA
HKSAR v Chow Nok Hang (2013) 16 HKCFAR 837, CFA
HKSAR v Coady [2000] 2 HKLRD 195, CA
HKSAR v Godson Ugochukwu Okuro [2019] 2 HKLRD 451, CA

HKSAR v Fong Kwok Shan Christine (2017) 20 HKCFAR 425, CFA
HKSAR v Fung Hin Wah Edward [2012] 1 HKLRD 374, CA
HKSAR v Hung Chan Wa (2006) 9 HKCFAR 614, CFA
HKSAR v Hussain Shakil [2012] HKEC 940, CA
HKSAR v Koo Sze Yiu (2014) 17 HKCFAR 811, CFA
HKSAR v Lam Chiu Yin [2018] HKEC 847, DC
HKSAR v Lam Kwong Wai (2006) 9 HKCFAR 574, CFA
HKSAR v Lee Ming Tee (2001) 4 HKCFAR 133, CFA
HKSAR v Lee Ming Tee and SFC (Intervener) (2003) 6 HKCFAR 336, CFA
HKSAR v Leung Chun Kit Brandon (2018) 21 HKCFAR 298, CFA
HKSAR v Li Man Tak [2006] HKEC 1724, CA
HKSAR v Li Kwok Cheung George (2014) 17 HKCFAR 319, CFA
HKSAR v Liang Yaoquiang (2017) 20 HKCFAR 1, CFA
HKSAR v Ma Wai Kwan, David [1997] HKLRD 761, CA
HKSAR v McCall Howard Kenneth [2017] HKEC 2893, CFI
HKSAR v Md Emran Hossain (2016) 19 HKCFAR 679, CFA
HKSAR v Minney (2013) 16 HKCFAR 26, CFA
HKSAR v Ng Chuen To Raymond [2013] HKEC 1190, CA
HKSAR v Ng Kung Siu and Another (1999) 2 HKCFAR 442, CFA
HKSAR v Ng Po On [2008] 11 HKCFAR 91, CFA
HKSAR v Osunwoke Ifeanyi John [2018] HKEC 786, CFI
HKSAR v Pang Hiu San (2014) 17 HKCFAR 545, CFA
HKSAR v Pun Ganga Chandra [2001] 2 HKLRD 151, CA
HKSAR v Shum Wai Kee [2018] HKEC 2225, CFA
HKSAR v Shum Wai Kee [2019] HKEC 283, CFA
HKSAR v Sin Ka Ho [2020] HKEC 854, (DC
HKSAR v Tong Ying Kit [2020] HKEC 2621, CFI
HKSAR v Tsang Chun Ying [2016] HKEC 1044, CFI
HKSAR v Tse Hin Yeung [2016] HKEC 1524, CA
HKSAR v Wan Thomas (2018) 21 HKCFAR 214, CFA
HKSAR v Wong Kwok Hung [2007] 2 HKLRD 621, CA
HKSAR v Wong Yeung Tat [2015] HKEC 2796, CFI
HKSAR v Wong Yuk Man (2012) 15 HKCFAR 712, CFA
HKSAR v Wu Wing Kit (No. 1) [2016] 3 HKLRD 386, CA
HKSAR v Yeung May Wan [2004] 3 HKLRD 797, CA
HKSAR v Yu Cheuk San [2004] HKEC 651, CA
HKSAR v Yu Lik Wai William [2015] HKEC 1286, DC
HKSAR v Yu Lik Wai William [2019] 1 HKLRD 1149, CA
HKSAR v Yung Wai Leong [2018] HKEC 1359, DC
H v Director of Immigration [2020] HKEC 1867, CFA
Hall v Commissioner of Correctional Services [2015] 2 HKLRD 917, CFI
Harvest Good Development Ltd v Secretary for Justice [2007] HKEC 1272, CFI
Harvest Good Development Ltd v Secretary for Justice [2007] HKEC 2355, CA
Heland Investment Ltd, In re [1994] 2 HKLR 158, HC
Hero v The Director of Planning [2011] HKEC 1305, CFI
Hero v The Director of Planning [2012] HKEC 991, CA
Hidayah, re [2018] HKEC 2705, CA

Hin Lin Yee v HKSAR (2010) 13 HKCFAR 142, CFA.
HLB Hodgson Impey Cheng v Hong Kong Institute of Certified Public Accountants (2013) 16 HKCFAR 460, CFA
Ho Choi Wan v Hong Kong Housing Authority (2005) 8 HKCFAR 628, CFA
Ho Chun Yan Albert (2012) 15 HKCFAR 686, CFA
Ho King-kwan v Attorney General [1986] HKLR 1148, CA
Ho Man-fat (No. 2) v The Royal Hong Kong Jockey Club [1976] HKLR 452, HC
Ho Man Kong v Superintendent of Lai Chi Kok Reception Centre, (2014) 17 HKCFAR 179, CFA
Home Restaurant Ltd v The Attorney General [1987] HKLR 237, HC
Hong Kong and China Gas Co. Ltd v Director of Lands [1997] HKLRD 1291, CFI
Hong Kong and China Gas Co. Ltd v Director of Lands (decided on 22 May 1998) [2006] HKEC 444, CA
Hong Kong and Shanghai Banking Corp. v Chan Yiu-Wah and Another [1988] 1 HKLR 457, CA
Hong Kong Hunters' Association Ltd, In re [1980] HKLR 179, HC
Hong Kong Polytechnic University v Next Magazine Ltd [1996] 2 HKLR 260, HC
Hong Kong Polytechnic University v Next Magazine Publishing Ltd [1997] HKLRD 514, CA
Hong Kong Rifle Association v Hong Kong Shooting Association (No. 2) [2013] HKEC 980, CA
Hong Kong Telecommunications (HKT) Ltd v Communications Authority [2015] HKEC 1590, [2015] 2 HKLRD 1035, CFI.
Hong Kong Television Network Ltd v Chief Executive in Council [2016] 2 HKLRD 1005, CA
Horsfield Leslie Grant v Chief Executive of HKSAR [2020] HKEC 971, CFI
Hui Sin Hang v Chief Executive in Council [2016] HKEC 608, CFI
Hung Chan Wa & another v HKSAR [2005] 3 HKLRD 291, [2005] HKEC 967, CA
Hysan Development Co Ltd v Town Planning Board [2014] HKEC 1869, CA.
Hysan Development Co Ltd v Town Planning Board (2016) 19 HKCFAR 372, CFA
Incorporated Owners of Finance Building v Bright Hill Management Consultants Co Ltd [2010] 3 HKLRD 1, CA
Inglory Ltd v Director of Food and Environmental Hygiene [2012] HKEC 710, CFI
In re 11–13 Sands Street, Hong Kong [1994] HKCLR 7, DC
Interush Ltd v Commissioner of Police [2019] HKEC 110, CA
Ip and Willis for Leave to Apply for Judicial Review, Re an Application by [1990] 1 HKLR 154, HC
Jeremy Tung v Dental Council of Hong Kong [2012] HKEC 1151, CFI
Jiang Enzhu v Lau Wai Hing Emily [2000] 1 HKLRD 121, CFI
Jill Spruce v The University of Hong Kong [1991] 2 HKLR 444, CA
Julita F Raza v Chief Executive in Council [2006] HKEC 1339, CA
Junior Police Officers' Association of Hong Kong Police Force v Electoral Affairs Commission, [2020] 2 HKLRD 631, CFI
Kaisilk Ltd v Urban Renewal Authority [2004] 1 HKLRD 907, CA
Kam Lan Koon and Others v Secretary for Justice [1998] 2 HKLRD 875, CFI
Kam Wai Hung v Secretary for Justice [2002] HKEC 495, CFI

Kao, Lee and Yip v Donald Koo Hoi Yan (2009) 12 HKCFAR 830, (CFA) and *BT v CBY* [2020] HKEC 1300, CA
Keen Lloyd Holdings Ltd v Commissioner of Customs and Excise [2016] 2 HKLRD 1372, CA
Keung Siu Wah v A-G [1990] 2 HKLR 238, CA
Komal Patel v Chris Au [2016] 1 HKLRD 328, CFI
Kong Chi-ien Rediffusion (HK) Ltd v Attorney General (1919) 14 HKLR 48, FC
Kong Yunming v Director of Social Welfare [2009] HKCU 912, CFI
Kong Yunming v Director of Social Welfare [2012] HKEC 229, CA
Kong Yunming v Director of Social Welfare (2013) 16 HKCFAR 950, CFA
Koo Sze Yiu v Chief Executive (2006) 9 HKCFAR 441, CFA
Koon Ping Leung v Director, [2012] HKEC 103, CFI
Koon Wing Yee v Financial Secretary [2013] 1 HKLRD 76, CA
Koon Wing Yee v Insider Dealing Tribunal (2008) 11 HKCFAR 170, CFA
K.O.Y. Investment Co Ltd, In re an application by [1983] HKLR 28, HC
Kulemesin v HKSAR (2013) 16 HKCFAR 195, CFA
Kwan Chi On v Hong Kong Baptist University [1997] HKEC 114, CFI
Kwan Kong Co Ltd v Town Planning Board [1995] (1995) 5 HKPLR 261, HC
Kwan Kong Co. Ltd v Town Planning Board [1996] 2 HKLR 363, CA
Kwan Shung King v Housing Appeal Tribunal [2000] 2 HKLRD 764, CFI
Kwan Wan Chee Alisa v City University of Hong Kong [2013] HKEC 232, CFI
Kwan Yiu-wing v R [1996] HKLR 752, Appellate Jurisdiction
Kwok Cheuk Kin v Director of Lands [2020] 1 HKLRD 988, CFI
Kwok Cheuk Kin v Leung Chun Ying [2017] HKEC 926, CFI
Kwok Chuk Kin v Secretary for Constitutional and Mainland Affairs [2015] 5 HKLRD 881, CA.
Kwok Hay Kwong v Medical Council of Hong Kong [2008] HKEC 137, CA
Kwok Wing Hang v Chief Executive in Council (No 2) [2020] 1 HKLRD 1, CFI
Kwok Wing Hang v Chief Executive in Council (2020) 23 HKCFAR 518, CFA
Kwong Mile Services Ltd v Commissioner of Inland Revenue (2004) 7 HKCFAR 275, CFA
KMM v Torture Claims Appeal Board [2016] 1 HKLRD 568, CA
L v Equal Opportunities Commission [2002] HKEC 1390, DC
LK v Director of Immigration [2016] HKEC 1730, CFI
Lai Hung Wai v Superintendent of Stanley Prison [2003] HKEC 1024, CFI
Lai Tak Shing v Director of Home Affairs [2006] HKEC 1873, CA
Lai Tak Shing v Secretary for Home Affairs (2007) 10 HKCFAR 655, CFA
Lam Hei Ying v Hong Kong Housing Authority, Appeal Tribunal [2001] HKEC 82, CFI
Lam Siu Po v Commissioner of Police (2009) 12 HKCFAR 237, CFA
Lam Yuk-ming v Attorney General [1980] HKLR 815, CA
Lau Cheong v HKSAR (2002) 5 HKCFAR 415, CFA
Lau Hei Wing, re [2016] 3 HKLRD 652, CFI
Lau Kong Yung v Director of Immigration; (1999) 2 HKCFAR 300, CFA
Lau Kwok Fai v Secretary for Justice [2003] HKEC 711, CFI
Lau Ping v R [1970] HKLR 343, HC
Lau San Ching v Liu, Apollonia (1995) 5 HKPLR 23, HC

Lau Siu Lai v Kwok Wai Fun Franco (Returning Officer) [2020] HKEC 931, CFI
Lau Tong Ming v Director of Lands [2018] HKEC 3304, CFI
Lau Wing Hong v Chan Yuen Man Amy (Returning Officer) (No 2) [2019] 5 HKLRD 1, CFI
Lau Wong Fat v Attorney General (1997) HKLRD 533, CA
Law Chi Yuen v Secretary for Education [2016] 5 HKLRD 302, CFI
Law Mei Mei v Airport Authority [2018] 4 HKLRD 312, CFI
Law Society of Hong Kong v Solicitor [2004] HKEC 1423, CA.
Lee Ma-loi v Commissioner of Inland Revenue and Another [1992] 1 HKLR 200, HC
Lee Ma-loi v Commissioner of Inland Revenue and Another [1992] HKLY 30, CA
Lee Miu Ling v Attorney General [1995] 5 HKLY 196, CA
Lee Shing Yue Construction Co. Ltd v Director of Architectural Services [2001] 1 HKLRD 715, CFI
Lee Yee Shing Jacky v Inland Revenue Board of Review [2011] HKEC 261, CFI
Lee Yee Shing Jacky v Inland Revenue Board of Review [2012] 2 HKLRD 981, CA
Lee Yim-ping v R [1979] HKLR 454, HC
Leung v Secretary for Justice [2006] 4 HKLRD 211, CA
Leung Chak Sang v Lingnan University [2001] HKEC 297, CFI
Leung Chun Kwong v Secretary for Civil Service (2019) 22 HKCFAR 127, CFA
Leung Chun Kwong v Secretary for Civil Service (No 2), (2019) 22 HKCFAR 282, CFA
Leung Chun Ying v Ho Chun Yan Albert (2013) 16 HKCFAR 735, CFA
Leung Chung Hang Sixtus v President of Legislative Council [2019] 1 HKLRD 292, CFI
Leung Fuk Wah Oil v Secretary for Justice [2015] HKEC 1752, CFA
Leung Hiu Yeung (2018) 21 HKCFAR 20, CFA
Leung Hon Wai v Director of Environmental Protection [2014] HKEC 1459, CA
Leung Kwok Hung v Chief Executive of HKSAR [2006] HKEC 239, CFI
Leung Kwok Hung v Chief Executive of HKSAR [2006] HKEC 816, CA
Leung Kwok Hung (Long Hair) v Commissioner of Correctional Services [2018] 2 HKLRD 933, CA
Leung Kwok Hung v HKSAR (2005) 8 HKCFAR 229, CFA
Leung Kwok Hung v Legislative Council Secretariat [2004] HKEC 1203, CFI.
Leung Kwok Hung v President of Legislative Council [2007] 1 HKLRD 387, CFI
Leung Kwok Hung v President of the Legislative Council (Filibuster) [2012] HKEC 745, CFI
Leung Kwok Hung v President of Legislative Council (No. 1) (2014) 17 HKCFAR 689, CFA
Leung Kwok Hung v Secretary for Justice [2010] 5 HKLRD 170, CA
Leung Kwok Hung v Secretary for Justice [2020] 1 HKLRD 80, CA
Leung Kwok Hung v Secretary for Justice [2020] HKEC 533, CA
Leung Kwok Hung v Secretary for Justice [2020] HKEC 1817, CA
Leung Lai Fong v Ho Sin Ying [2009] HKEC 1188, CFA
Leung Lai Kwok Yvonne v Chief Secretary for Administration [2015] HKEC 1034, CFI.

Leung Sze Ho Albert v Bar Council of Hong Kong Bar Association [2015] HKEC 2009, CFI
Leung Sze Ho Albert v Bar Council of Hong Kong Bar Association [2016] 5 HKLRD 542, CA
Li Bun and Others v R [1957] HKLR 89, Appellate Jurisdiction
Li Hong Mi v Attorney General (1918) 13 HKLR 6, FC
Li Jen Fei et al v Director of Immigration [1994] 1 HKLR 253, CA
Li Kim Ming v Housing Authority [2016] HKEC 1201, CFI
Li Pui Ha v Wong So Kee Transportation Ltd [2014] 4 HKLRD 254, DC
Li Wai Hung Cesario v Administrative Appeals Board [2016] HKEC 1325, CA
Lister Assets Ltd v Chief Executive in Council [2012] HKEC 1043, (CFI)
Lister Assets Ltd v Chief Executive in Council [2013] HKEC 605, CA
Lo Hon-hin v R [1993] HKEC 467, CFI
Lo Siu Lan v Hong Kong Housing Authority [2004] HKEC 1541, [34], CA
Lo Siu Lan v Hong Kong Housing Authority (2005) 8 HKCFAR 363, CFA
Lum Yuk-ming & Ors v Attorney General [1980] HKLR 815, CA
Lui Chi Hang Hendrick v Independent Police Complaints Council (No 2) [2020] 2 HKLRD 911, CFI
Luk Ka Cheung v Market Misconduct Tribunal [2009] 1 HKLRD 114, CFI
M v Secretary for Justice [2009] 2 HKLRD 298, CA
Ma Bik Yung v Ko Chuen [1999] 2 HKLRD 263, DC
Ma Bik Yung v Ko Chuen (2006) 9 HKCFAR 888, CFA
Ma Kwai Chun v Leong Siu Chung [2001-2003] HKCLRT 286, CA
Ma Kwai Chun v Queeny KY Au-Yeung [2002] CHKEC 4914, CFI
Ma Wan Farming Ltd v Chief Executive in Council [1998] 1 HKLRD 514, CA
Man Hing Medical Suppliers (International) Ltd v Director of Health [2015] 3 HKLRD 224, CFI
Mathnasium Center Licensing LLC v Chang Chi Hung (no 2) [2019] 4 HKLRD 565, CFI
Matteograssi SpA v Airport Authority [1998] 2 HKLRD 213, CA
Max Share Ltd & Another v Ng Yat Chi [1997] HKLRD 1255, CFA
Medical Council of Hong Kong v Chow Siu Shek (2000) 3 HKCFAR 144, CFA
MK v Government of HKSAR [2019] 5 HKLRD 259, CFI
Mobil Petroleum Co. Inc. v Registrar of Trade Marks [2001] 1 HKLRD 225, CFI
Mohan v McElney [1983] HKLR 308, CA
Mok Chi Hung v Director of Immigration [2001] 2 HKLRD 125, CFI
Morning Post Ltd and Others [1988] 1 HKLR 143, CA
MS v Director of Social Welfare [2016] HKEC 344, CFI
MTR Corp Ltd v Kwok Wing Kan [2019] 5 HKLRD 385, CFI
Mutual Luck Investment Ltd v The Attorney General [1997] HKLRD 1097, HC
Nam Pei Hong (Holding) Ltd v The Stock Exchange of Hong Kong Ltd [1998] 2 HKLRD 910, CFI
Nancy Ann Kissel v Long Term Prison Sentences Review Board [2020] HKEC 1454, CA
Navarro Luigi Recasa v Commissioner of Correctional Services [2018] 4 HKLRD 38, CFI
Ng Che-foon and Another v R [1968] HKLR 439, Appellate Jurisdiction

Ng Chi Kueng v Secretary for Justice [2016] 2 HKLRD 1330, CFI
Ng Ka Ling v Director of Immigration (1999) 1 HKCFAR 4, CFA
Ng Ka Ling v Director of Immigration (No 2) (1999) 2 HKCFAR 141, CFA
Ng King Luen v Rita Fan (1997) 7 HKPLR 281, HC
Ng King Tat Philip v Post Release Supervision [2010] HKEC 1306, CFI.
Ng Shek Wai v Medical Council of Hong Kong [2015] 2 HKLRD 121, CFI *v*
Ng Siu Tung v Director of Immigration (2002) 5 HKCFAR 1, CFA
Ng Yat Chi v Max Share Ltd (2005) 8 HKCFAR 1, CFA
Ngai Kin Wah, Re [1986] HKLY 8, HC
Ngo Kee Construction Co. Ltd v Hong Kong Housing Authority [2001] HKEC 16, CFI
Nnaji Charles Anayo v Torture Claims Appeal Board [2018] HKEC 3963, CFI
Noise Control Authority v Step In Ltd [2005] 1 HKLRD 702, CFA
Nomura International (Hong Kong) Ltd v Securities and Futures Commission (1997-98) 1 HKCFAR 250, CFA
Numeric City Ltd v Lau Chi Wing [2016] 4 HKLRD 812, CA
Oei Hengky Wiryo v HKSAR (No 2) (2007) 10 HKCFAR 49, CFA
Official Receiver v Zhi Charles (2015) 18 HKCFAR 467, CFA
Ong Siu Sin Kevin v HKSAR [2011] HKEC 986, CFA
Oriental Daily Publisher Ltd v Comr for Television and Entertainment Licensing Authority (1997-1998) 1 HKCFAR 279, CFA
Oriental Generation Ltd v Town Planning Board [2014] HKEC 1868, CFI
Orrico Philippe v Municipal Services Appeals Board [2014] HKEC 1388, CFI.
Pacific Century Insurance Co. Ltd v Insurance Claims Complaints Bureau [1999] 3 HKLRD 720, CFI
Pagtama Victorina Alegre v Director of Immigration [2016] HKEC 85, CFI
Pan American Airways Inc v R [1959] HKLR 366, FC
Pan World Airways Incorporated Ltd v The Queen [1959] HKLR 366, FC.
Pang Tak Kwai v Commissioner of Correctional Services and the Chief Executive [2000] HKEC 1298, CFI
Pang Tak Kwai v Commissioner of Correctional Services and the Chief Executive [2001] HKEC 1139, CA
Pang Yiu Hung v Commissioner of Police [2003] 2 HKLRD 125, CFI
Pagtama Victorina Alegre v Director of Immigration [2016] HKEC 85, CFI
PCCW-HKT Telephone Ltd v The Secretary for Commerce and Economic Development [2016] HKEC 1089, CA
PCCW-HKT Telephone Ltd v Telecommunications Authority (2005) 8 HKCFAR 337, CFA
Pearl Securities Ltd v Stock Exchange of Hong Kong Ltd [1999] 2 HKLRD 243, CFI
Po Fun Chan v Winnie CW Cheung (2007) 10 HKCFAR 676, CFA
Poa Kwok Ho v Director of Social Welfare [2019] HKEC 1521, CFI
Polorace Investments Ltd v Director of Lands [1997] HKLY 491, CA
Pong Wai Ting v Attorney General (1925) 20 HKLR 22, SC
Popular Signs Ltd v Radiation Board [2010] HKEC 41, [78], CFI
Prem Singh v Director of Immigration (2003) 6 HKCFAR 26, CFA
Q v Commissioner of Registration [2019] 1 HKLRD 1244, CFI

Quebostock Ltd v The Building Authority and Another [1986] HKLR 467, CA
QT v Director of Immigration [2016] 2 HKLRD 583, CFI
QT v Director of Immigration [2017] 5 HKLRD 166, CA
QT v Director of Immigration [2018] 21 HKCFAR 324, CFA
R v Chan Chi-Hung [1993] 2 HKCLR, CA
R v Chan Wai-ming (No. 1) (1991) 1 HKPLR 292, CA
R v Chan Wai-ming [1993] 1 HKCLR 51, HC
R v Chandra Thanwardas Mirchandani [1992] 2 HKCLR 174, CA.
R v Chau Ping [1990] 2 HKLR 462, CA
R v Cheung Ka Fai [1995] 2 HKCLR 184, CA
R v Choi Kai-on [1995] 1 HKCLR 79, CA
R v Chong Ah-choi and others [1994] 2 HKCLR 263, CA
R v Chu Kam-to and Another (1994) 4 HKPLR 472, HC
R v Chu Kwok Fai [1973] HKLR 107, HC
R v Deacon Chiu Te-ken; R v David Chiu Tat-Cheung (1993) 3 HKPLR 483, HC
R v Deputy District Judge Lee, ex parte Chow Po-bor (1993) 3 HKPLR 101, HC
R v Director of Immigration [2020] HKEC 1522, CFI
R v Flickinger (1993) 3 HKPLR 677, DC
R v Fu Yan [1992] 2 HKCLR 59, CA
R v Fung Chi-wood [1991] 1 HKLR 654, HC
R v E.C. Harris [1991] 1 HKLR 389, CA
R v Hui Kwok Fai (1993) 3 HKPLR 752, DC
R v Kevin Egan (1993) 3 HKPLR 277, HC
R v Kwong Kui Wing [1996] 1 HKDCLR 15, DC
R v To Lam sin (1952) 36 HKLR 1, SC
R v Lam Tak-ming and Another (1991) 1 HKPLR 222, DC
R v Lau Kwok Hung (No. 1) (1991) 1 HKPLR 19, HC
R v Lau Kwok Hung (No. 2) (1992) 2 HKPLR 261, HC
R v Li Tat [1993] 2 HKCLR 203, CA
R v Li Wing-tat [1991] 1 HKLR 731, HC
R v Lum Wai-ming [1992] 2 HKCLR 221, HC
R v Man Wai-Keung (No 2) [1992] 2 HKCLR 207, CA
R v Mirchandani (1992) 2 HKPLR 196, CA
R v Ng Tung-Fong [1992] 1 HKCLR 114, CA
R v Ng Shing-man [1960] HKDCLR 211, DC
R v Secretary for Civil Service and the Attorney General of Hong Kong, ex parte the Association of Expatriate Civil Servants (1995) 5 HKPLR 490, HC
R v Shamsudin [1987] HKLR 254, HC
R v Mohamed Hashim Shamsudin [1987] HKLR 254, HC
R v Sin Yau-ming (1991) 1 HKPLR 88, [1992] 1 HKCLR 127, CA
R v Tam Kin Wing [1997] HKLRD 333, HC
R v To Kwan-hang and Tsoi Yiu-cheong (1994) 4 HKPLR 356, CA
R v Town Planning Board, ex parte Auburntown Ltd (1994) 4 HKPLR 194, HC
R v The Town Planning Board ex parte The Real Estate Developers Association of Hong Kong [1996] 2 HKLR 267, HC
R v William Hung (1992) 2 HKPLR 49, HC
R v Wong Cheung-bun (1992) 2 HKPLR 82, HC

R v Wong Hing-yuk [1989] 1 HKLR 251, CA
R v Wong King Chau [1964] HKDCLR 94, DC
R v Wright, ex parte Lau Wing-wo (1993) 3 HKPLR 126, HC
R v Yeung Chi chiu and Another (1994) 4 HKPLR 677, DC
R v Yu Yem-kin [1994] HKEC 52, SC
Raza v Chief Executive in Council [2006] HKEC 1339, CA
Rank Profit Industries Ltd v Director of Lands [2008] HKEC 773, CA
Rank Profit Industries Ltd v Director of Lands [2009] HKEC 1021, CFA
Registrar of Hong Kong Institute of Certified Public Accountants v Wong Tak Man Stephen [2016] HKEC 1859, CA
Real Estate Developers Association v Town Planning Board (1996) 6 HKPLR 179, HC
Rediffusion (Hong Kong) Limited v The Attorney General and Others [1968] HKLR 277, HC.
Review of Sentence, Re Applications for [1972] HKLR 370, HC
Right Centre Co Ltd, Re [1990] 1 HKLR 250, HC
Rowse v Secretary for the Civil Service [2008] 5 HKLRD 217, CFI
RV v Director of Immigration [2008] HKEC 412, CFI
Scott v Government of the HKSAR [2004] 2 HKLRD 989, CFI
Secretary for Justice v Buk Chui Ying [2008] 5 HKLRD 185, CA
Secretary for Justice v Chan Wah (2000) 3 HKCFAR 459, CFA
Secretary for Justice v Chan Chi Wan Stephen (2017) 20 HKCFAR 98, CFA
Secretary for Justice v Chan Wah (2000) 3 HKCFAR 459, CFA
Secretary for Justice v Commission of Inquiry Re Hong Kong Institute of Education [2009] HKEC 411, CFI.
Secretary for Justice v Lam Tat Ming (2000) 3 HKCFAR 168, CFA
Secretary for Justice v Lau Kwok Fai (2005) 8 HKCFAR 304, CFA
Secretary for Justice v Richard Ethan Latker [2009] HKEC 132, CA
Secretary for Justice v Leung Kwok Hung [2020] HKEC 1118, CA
Secretary for Justice v Leung Kwok Hung [2019] HKEC 417, CA
Secretary for Justice v Liu Wing Kwong [2014] 2 HKLRD 155, CFI
Secretary for Justice v Lo King Fat [2015] HKEC 2688, CA
Secretary for Justice v Ocean Technology Ltd [2009] HKEC 2114, CFI
Secretary for Justice v Ocean Technology Ltd [2009] HKEC 806, CFA
Secretary for Justice v Wong Chi Fung (2018) 21 HKCFAR 35, CFA
Secretary for Justice v Wong Ho Ming (2017) 20 HKCFAR 518, CFA
Secretary for Justice v Yau Yuk Lung (2007) 10 HKCFAR 335, CFA
Secretary for Security v Saktheval Prabakar (2004) 7 HKCFAR 187, CFA
Secretary for Transport v Delight World Ltd [2007] 1 HKLRD 647, CFA
Securities and Futures Commission v Wong Yuen Yee [2017] 1 HKLRD 788, CFI
Senior Non-expatriate Officers' Association v Secretary for the Civil Service (1997) 7 HKPLR 91, HC
Sham Wing Kan v Commissioner of Police [2020] 2 HKLRD 529, CA
Shiu Wing Steel Ltd v Director of Environmental Protection & Airport Authority (No 2) (Third Party), (2006) 9 HKCFAR 478, CFA
Shum Kwok Sher v HKSAR (2002) 5 HKCFAR 381, CFA

Shun Tak Holdings Ltd and Others v Commissioner of Police [1995] 1 HKCLR 48, HC
Singway Co. Ltd v The Attorney General [1974] HKLR 275, Original Jurisdiction
Sit Ka Yin Priscilla v Equal Opportunities Commission [1998] HKEC 911, CFI
Sky Ace Enterprises Ltd v Appeal Tribunal (Buildings) [2016] HKEC 1318, CA
Smart Gain Investment Ltd v Town Planning Board [2007] HKEC 1964, [72], CFI
So Chung v Commissioner of Correctional Services [2001] HKEC 91, CFI
So Wai Lun v HKSAR (2006) 9 HKCFAR 530, CFA
Solicitor, Re [1999] 3 HKLRD 406, 414, CA
Solicitor (24/07) v Law Society of Hong Kong (2008) 11 HKCFAR 117, CFA
Solicitor and Law Society of Hong Kong v Secretary for Justice [2003] 6 HKCFAR 570, CFA
ST v Betty Kwan [2014] 4 HKLRD 277, CA
Stock Exchange of Hong Kong Ltd v New World Development Co. Ltd (2006) 9 HKCFAR 234, CFA
Sunevision Holdings Ltd v Hong Kong Science and Technology Parks Corp [2020] HKEC 465, CFI
Sung Man Cho v The Superintendent of Prisons [1931] HKLR 62, FC
Syed Agha Raza Shah v Director of Health [2020] HKEC 802, CFI
T v Commissioner of Police [2013] 4 HKLRD 384, CA
T v Commissioner of Police (2014) 17 HKCFAR 593, CFA
T v The Judiciary [2018] CHKEC 709, DC
Tam Chi Ming v Medical Council of Hong Kong [2008] 1 HKLRD 24, CFI
Tam Hing-yee v Wu Tai-wai [1992] 1 HKLR 185, CA
Tam Kei Kam v HSBC International Trustee Ltd [2014] HKEC 1189, CA
Tam Nga Yin and Others v Director of Immigration (2001) 4 HKCFAR 644, (CFA)
Tan Shih Ying v City University of Hong Kong [2012] HKEC 1678, CFI
Tang Shuk Chun v Director of Food and Environmental Hygiene [2015] HKEC 2422, CFI.
Tang Siu Man v HKSAR (No 2) (1997-98) 1 HKCFAR 107, CFA
Tang Ping-hoi v Attorney General [1987] HKLR 324, HC
TCWF v LKKS [2013] HKEC 1197, CA
Television Broadcasts Ltd v Communications Authority [2016] 2 HKLRD 41, CFI
Thomas Lai, Re [2014] HKEC 334, CFI
TO Wong & Co. Ltd v Leung Pui [1957] HKLR 417, Appellate Jurisdiction
Tong Wai Ting v Secretary for Education [2009] HKEC 1867, CFI
Tong Yu Lam v Long-Term Prison Sentences Review Board [2008] HKEC 24, CA
Town Planning Board v Oriental Generation Ltd [2014] HKEC 1868, CFI
Town Planning Board v Society for Protection of the Harbour Ltd (No. 2) (2004) 7 HKCFAR 114, CFA
Town Planning Board v Town Planning Appeal Board [2014] 1 HKLRD 1056, CFI
Town Planning Board v Town Planning Appeal Board [2015] 3 HKLRD 490, CA
Town Planning Board v Town Planning Appeal Board (2017) 20 HKCFAR 196, CFA
Trustees of Church of England in Diocese of Victoria, Hong Kong v Town Planning Board [2020] HKEC 412, CFI
Tse Cho, Re [1979] HKLR 339, HC

Tse Chung v R [1967] HKLR 452, Appellate Jurisdiction
Tse Hung Hing v Medical Council of Hong Kong [2010] 1 HKLRD 111, CFI
Tse Kwan Sang v Pat Heung Rural Committee [1999] 3 HKLRD 267, CFI
Tsui Kin Kwok Johnnie v Commissioner of Police [2010] HKEC 134, CFI
Tung, Jeemy v Dental Council of Hong Kong, [2012] HKEC 1151
Ubamaka Edward Wilson v Secretary for Security (2012) 15 HKCFAR 743, CFA
United Grand Ltd v Town Planning Board [2006] HKCU 1781, CFI
United States of America and Johnny Eng Sui-hang, Re (1991) 1 HKPLR 298, MC
Vallejos v Commissioner of Registration (2013) 16 HKCFAR 45, CFA
W v Registrar of Marriages (2013) 16 HKCFAR 112, CFA
Waddington Ltd v Securities and Futures Commission [2018] HKEC 3334, CFI
Wah Yick Enterprises Co. Ltd v Building Authority [1999] 1 HKLRD 237, CA
Wah Yick Enterprises Co. Ltd v Building Authority [1999] 1 HKLRD 840, CFA
Waliyah v Yip Hoi Sun Terence [2017] 1 HKLRD 1082, DC
Winfat Enterprise (HK) Ltd v Attorney General [1983] HKLR 211, HC
Winfat Enterprise (HK) Ltd v Attorney General [1984] HKLR 32, CA
Wing On Co. Ltd v Building Authority (1996) 6 HKPLR 432, CA
Wong Chi Fung v Secretary for Justice [2016] 3 HKLRD 835, CFI
Wong Chi Kin, re [2014] HKEC 1590, CA
Wong Chik-wai for Judicial Review, Re an application by [1986] HKLR 478, HC
Wong Chung Ki v Chief Executive of HKSAR [2000] HKEC 701, CA
Wong Ho Ming v Secretary for Justice [2020] HKEC 1132, CFI
Wong Hoi Tang v Hospital Authority [2001] HKEC 1468, CFI
Wong Hon, Re [1959] HKLR 601, FC
Wong Hui Yin v Hong Kong Arts Development Council [2004] HKEC 1102, CFI
Wong Kei Kwong v Principal Assistant Secretary for Civil Service [2008] HKEC 261, CFI
Wong Kwai Leung, Re [2016] HKEC 800, CFI
Wong Kwong-shing Trading as Ka Wah Motors Co. v Attorney General [1975] HKLR 654, CFI
Wong Pei Chun and Others v Hong Kong Housing Authority [1996] 2 HKLR 293, HC
Wong Pun Cheuk v Medical Council of Hong Kong and the Attorney General [1964] HKLR 47, (HC)
Wong Tak Wai v Commissioner of Correctional Services [2010] 4 HKLRD 409, CA
Wong Ti Hoi v Au Nok Hin [2018] 2 HKLRD 789, CFI
Wong Tze Yam v Commissioner of Police (No 2) [2011] 3 HKLRD 369, CA
Wong Wai Tak v Secretary for the Civil Service [2001] HKEC 167, CFI.
Wong Yeung Ng v Secretary for Justice [1999] 2 HKLRD 293, CA
Wong Yeung Ng v Secretary for Justice [1999] HKEC 1330, CFA
Wong Yuk Kwan v Secretary for Justice [2016] HKEC 1392, CFI.
X v Securities and Futures Commission [2012] 4 HKLRD 296, CFI
Yao Man Fai George v Director of Social Welfare, [2011] 1 HKLRD A2, CFI
Yau Fook Hong Co. Ltd and Another for Judicial Review, Re an application by [1985] HKLR 42, HC
Yau Ka Po v Chief Executive in Council [2016] HKEC 239, CFI
Yau Kwong Man v Secretary for Security [2002] HKEC 1142, CFI

Yau Wai Ching v Chief Executive of HKSAR (2017) 20 HKCFAR 390, CFA
Yeung Cheong Fat v Investigation Committee Appointed Pursuant to S6 of the Public Service (Disciplinary) Regulations and S10 of the Public Service (Administration) Order 1997 [2005] HKEC 65, CFI
Yeung Chu Wing v Secretary for Justice [2019] 3 HKLRD 238, CFI
Yeung Chun Pong v Secretary for Justice [2006] HKEC 1517, CA
Yeung May Wan v HKSAR (2005) 8 HKCFAR 137, CFA
Yeung Tin Leung v The Chief Executive [2005] HKEC 373
Yu Hung Hsua Julie v Chinese University of Hong Kong [2016] 5 HKLRD 393, CA
Yuen Sha Sha v Tse Chi Pan [1999] 2 HKLRD 28, DC
Yuen Wai Han v South Elderly Affairs Ltd [2005] 2 HKLRD 277, CA
Yung Chi Keung v Protection of Wages on Insolvency Board (2016) 19 HKCFAR 469, CFA
X v Securities and Futures Commission [2012] 4 HKLRD 296, CFI, Privy Council decisions on appeal from Hong Kong
Attorney General v Ng Yuen Shiu [1983] 2 AC 629, PC
Attorney General of Hong Kong v Lee Kwong-Kut, [1993] AC 951; [1993] 2 HKCLR 186, PC
Attorney General v Lo Chak-man (1993) 3 HKPLR 72, PC
Chan Chi-hung v R [1996] AC 442, (1995) 5 HKCFAR 1, PC
Chien Sing Shou v The Building Authority [1967] HKLR 352, PC
Commissioner of Inland Revenue v Cosmotron Manufacturing Ltd [1997] 1 WLR 1288, PC
Elvira Vergara and Another v Attorney General [1989] 1 HKLR 233, PC
Fok Lai Ying v Governor in Council (1997) 7 HKPLR 327, PC
Gammon (HK) Ltd v Attorney General of Hong Kong [1985] AC 1, PC
Hang Wah Chong Investment Co. Ltd v Attorney General of Hong Kong [1981] 1 WLR 1141, [1981] HKLR 336, PC
Henderson Real Estate Agency Ltd v Lo Chai Wan (1996) 7 HKPLR 1, PC
Hinge Well Co Ltd v Attorney General [1988] 1 HKLR 32, PC
Ming Pao Newspapers Ltd v Attorney General [1996] AC 907, PC
Ng Enterprises Ltd v Urban Council [1997] AC 168, PC
Panel on Takeovers & Mergers v Cheng Kai Man William [1995] 2 HKLR 302, PC
R v Chan Chi-Hung [1995] 2 HKCLR 50, PC
Rediffusion (Hong Kong) Ltd v Attorney General of Hong Kong [1970] AC 1136; [1970] HKLR 231, PC
Silver Mountain Investments Ltd and Another v Attorney General and Another [1994] 2 HKLR 297, PC

United Kingdom

Agricultural, Horticultural and Forestry Industry Training Board v Aylesbury Mushrooms Ltd [1972] 1 WLR 190, QB
Albert v Lavin [1982] AC 546, HL
Ali v Ali [1966] 1 All ER 664, Probate Divorce & Admiralty Division
Allison v General Medial Council [1894] 1 QB 750,760, 63, CA
Ambard v A-G for Trinidad and Tobago [1936] AC 322, PC
Anisminic Ltd v Foreign Compensation Commission [1969] 2 AC 147, HL

Associated Provincial Picture Houses Ltd v Wednesday Corporation [1948] 1 KB 223, CA
Attorney-General v Great Eastern Railway Co (1880) 5 App Cas 473, HL
Attorney General v Observer and Times Newspapers [1990] 1 AC 109, at 283, HL
Attorney General v Ryan [1980] AC 718, PC
B (A Minor) v DPP [2000] 2 AC 428, HL
Begum v Tower Hamlets London Borough Council [2003] 2 AC 430, HL
Belfast City Council v Miss Behavin Ltd [2007] 1 WLR 1420, HL
Belfast Corporation v O.D. Cars Ltd [1960] AC 490, HL
Bellinger v Bellinger (Lord Chancellor intervening) [2003] 2 AC 467, HL
Black-Clawson International Ltd v Papierwerke Attorney General [1975] AC 591, HL
Bonanza Creek Gold Mining Co Ltd v The King [1916] 1 AC 566, PC
Boodram v Trinidad and Tobago [2002] 1 Cr App R 103, PC
Bradbury v Enfield LBC [1967] 1 WLR 1311, CA
Breen v Amalgamated Engineering Union [1971] 2 QB 175, CA
Bribery Commissioner v Ranasinghe [1965] AC 172, PC.
Chenard & Co v Arissol [1949] AC 127, PC
Chief Constable of North Wales Police v Evans [1982]1 WLR 1155, HL
Colonial Sugar Refining Co. Ltd v Melbourne Harbour Trust Commissioners [1927] AC 343, PC
Commissioner of Customs and Excise v Cure and Duley Ltd [1962] 1 QB 340, QB
Council of Civil Service Unions v Minister for the Civil Service [1985] AC 374, HL
David Miranda v The Secretary of State for the Home Department et al [2014] 1 WLR 3140, DC
Derbyshire County Council v Times Newspapers Ltd and Others [1993] AC 534, HL
Dimes v Grand Junction Canal (1852) 3 HLC 759, HL
Dunkley v Evans [1981] 3 All ER 285, QB
Edwards (Inspector of Taxes) v Bairstow and Another [1956] AC 14, HL
Elizabeth Dowager Baroness Wenlock v River Dee Co (1884-1885) LR 10 App Cas 354, HL
Fagernes, The [1927] P 311, CA
Felstead v R [1914] AC 534, HL
Flannery and Another v Halifax Estate Agencies Ltd. (trading as Colleys Professional Services) [2000] 1 W.L.R. 377, CA
Fraser v Mudge [1975] 1 WLR 1132, CA
Gentel v Rapps [1902] 1 KB 160, KB
Ghaidan v Godin-Mendoza [2004] 2 AC 557, HL
Grape Bay Ltd v A-G of Bermuda [2000] 1 WLR 574, PC
Hazell v Hammersmith and Fulham London Borough Council [1992] 2 AC 1, HL
Hinds v R [1977] AC 195, PC
Hodge v R (1883) 9 AC 117, PC
Hussain v Hussain [1982] 3 All ER 369, CA
Jauffur v Commissioner of Income Tax [2007] 1 LRC 561, PC
Jhuti v Royal Mail Group Ltd [2018] ICR 1077, (Employment Appeal Tribunal)
Kruse v Johnson [1898] 2 QB 91, QB
Lewis v Chief Constable of the South Wales Constabulary [1991] 1 All ER 206, CA

McLorie v Oxford [1982] 1 QB 1290, QB
Malone Commission of Police of the Metropolis (No. 2) [1979] Ch. 344, Ch D
Medicaments and Related Classes of Goods (No. 2), In re [2001] 1 WLR 700, CA
Minister for Aboriginal Affairs v Peko-Wallsend Ltd (1986) 66 ALR 299, HC
Ministry of Home Affairs v Fisher [1980] AC 319, PC
National Assistance Board v Wilkinson [1952] 2 QB 648, QB
O'Reilly v Mackman [1983] 2 AC 237, HL
Padfield v Minister of Agriculture, Fisheries and Food [1968] AC 997, HL
Powell v May [1946] 1 KB 330, KB
Racal Communications Ltd, In re [1981] AC 374, HL
R (Alconbury Developments Ltd) v Secretary of State for the Environment, Transport and the Regions, HL
R (CPRE Kent) v Dover District Council [2018] 1 WLR 108, SC
R (Corner House Research) v Secretary of State for Trade and Industry [2005] 4 All ER 1
R (Feakins) v Secretary of State for Environment [2004] 1 WLR 1761, CA
R (Hill) v Institute of Chartered Accountants [2014] 1 WLR 86, CA
R (Kambadzi) v Secretary of State for the Home Department (Bail for Immigration Detainees intervening) [2011] 1 WLR 1299, SC
R (Lewis) v Redcar & Cleveland BC [2009] 1 WLR 83, CA
R (Lumba) v Secretary of State for the Home Department [2012] 1 AC 245, UKSC
R (Oakley) v South Cambridgeshire District Council [2017] 1 WLR 3765, CA
R (Pretty) v DPP & Secretary of State for the Home Department (Intervener) [2002] 1 AC 800, HL
R (Rusbridger) v A-G [2004] 1 AC 357, HL
R v Birmingham City Juvenile Court, ex p Birmingham City Council [1988] 1 WLR 337, CA
R v Bow Street Metropolitan Stipendiary Magistrate ex p Pinochet Ugarte (No. 2) [2000] 1 AC 119, HL
R v Chief Immigration Officer, Heathrow Airport and Another, Ex parte Salamat Bibi [1976] 1 WLR 979, CA
R v Dairy Produce Quota Tribunal for England and Wales, ex. p Caswell [1990] 2 AC 738, HL
R v DPP, ex p Kebilene [2000] 2 AC 326, HL
R v Disciplinary Committee of the Jockey Club, ex parte Aga Khan [1993] 1 WLR 909, CA
R v East Berkshire Health Authority, ex p Walsh [1985] QB 152, CA
R v Endfield L.B.C., ex parte T.F. Unwin (Roydon) Ltd [1989] C.O.D. 466, DC
R v Financial Ombudsman Service Ltd, ex p Norwich & Peterborough Building Society [2002] EWHC 2379, QB
R v Gough [1993] AC 646, HL
R v Holmes, ex parte Sherman and Another [1981] 2 All ER 612, DC
R v Howell [1982] QB 416, QB
R v Immigration Appeal Tribunal ex p Begum Manshoora [1986] Imm AR 385, QB
R v Immigration Appeal Tribunal ex p Joyles [1972] 1 WLR 1390, DC
R v Latif [1996] 1 WLR 104, HL
R v Looseley [2001] 4 All ER 897, HL

R v Lord Chancellor, ex p Witham [1998] 2 WLR 849, QB
R v Monopolies and Mergers Commission, ex p Argyll Group Plc [1986] 1 WLR 763, CA
R v North and East Devon HA Ex p. Coughlan [2001] QB 213, CA
R v Northumberland Compensation Appeal Tribunal, ex parte Shaw [1952] 1 KB 338, CA
R v Panel on Takeovers and Mergers, ex p Datafin Plc [1987] 1 QB 815, CA
R v Panel on Takeovers and Mergers, ex p Guinness [1990] QB 146, CA
R v Roberts [1908] 1 KB 407, 423, CA
R v Secretary of State for Education and Employment ex p Begbie [2000] 1 WLR 1115, CA
R v Secretary of State for Home Affairs, ex parte Bhajan Singh [1976] Q.B. 198, QB
R v Secretary of State for the Home Department, ex parte Brind and Others [1991] 1 AC 696; [1991] 2 WLR 588, HL
R v Secretary of State for the Home Department, ex p Doody [1994] 1 AC 531, HL
R v Secretary of State for the Home Department, ex p Fayed [1998] 1 WLR 763, CA
R v Secretary of State for the Home Department ex p Mohammed Hussain Ahmed [1999] Imm AR 22, CA
R v Secretary of State for the Home Department ex p Pierson [1998] AC 539, HL
R v Secretary of State for the Home Department, ex p Salem [1999] 1 AC 450, HL
R v Secretary of State for the Home Department, Ex p Simms [2000] 2 AC 115, HL
R v Secretary of the State for the Home Department and Others, ex parte Tarrant and Another [1984] 1 All ER 799, QB
R v Secretary of State for Social Services exp Association of Metropolitan Authorities [1986] 1 WLR 1, QB
R v Servite Houses ex parte Goldsmith (2001) 33 HLR 35, QB
*R v Somerset County Council, ex. p Dixon (*1998) 75 P&CR 175; [1997] JPL 1030, QB
R v Somerset County Council, ex p Fewings [1995] 1 WLR 1037.
R. v Stratford-on-Avon District Council, ex parte Jackson [1985]1 WLR 1323, CA
R v Sussex Justices, ex parte McCarthy [1924] 1 KB 256, KB
R v Taylor (David Jeremy) [2008] EWCA Crim 680, CA
R v Thames Magistrates' Court, ex parte Polemis [1974] 1 WLR 1371, QB
Ramachandran Subramanian v The General Medical Council [2002] UKPC 3, PC
Robins v National Trust Co Ltd [1927] AC 515, PC
Rodriguez v Minister of Housing Gibraltar [2009] UKPC 52, PC
Sheldrake v DPP [2005] 1 AC 264, HL
Sirros v Moore [1975] 1 QB 118, CA
South East Asia Fire Bricks Sdn. Bhd. v Non-Metallic Mineral Products Manufacturing Employees Union and Others [1981] AC 363, PC
Spectrum Plus Ltd (in liquidation) [2005] 2 AC 680, HL
Stefan v General Medical Council [1999] 1 WLR 1293, PC
Tesco Stores Ltd v Secretary of State for the Environment [1995] 1 WLR 759, HL
Tredegar v Harwood [1929] AC 72, HL

Westminster Bank Ltd v Minister of Housing and Local Government [1971] AC 508, HL

Australia

Chung v University of Sydney [2001] FMCA 94, Federal Magistrates Court of Australia
Commonwealth v Grunseit (1943) 67 CLR 58, CA
Craig v South Australia (1995) 69 ALJR 873; 131 ALR 595, HC.
Minister of State for Immigration and Ethnic Affairs v Teoh (1994–1995) 183 CLR 273, HC
R v Birks (1990) 48 Aust Crim R 385, New South Wales Court of Criminal Appeal
Tien v Minister for Immigration and Multicultural Affairs (1998) 159 ALR 405, Fed Court of Australia

Canada

R v Smith (Edward Dewey) (1987) 34 SCC (3d), *SCRJR-MacDonald v Canada* [1995] 3 SCR 199, SC
Royer v Mignault (1988) 50 DLR (4th) 345

New Zealand

Neilsen v A-G [2001] 3 NZLR 143, CA
R v Shaheed [2002] 2 NZLR 377, CA
R v Uljee [1982] 1 NZLR 561, CA

Others

Murphy v Attorney General [1982] IR 241 (SC of Ireland).
Oulajin and Kaiss v Netherlands (UN Doc CPR/C/46/D/406/1990)
Rostislav Borinsenko v Hungary (Comm No. 852/1999, 14 October 2002)
Van Raalte v The Netherlands (1997) 24 EHRR 503

Table of Statutes

1994, Administrative Appeals Board Ordinance (Cap. 442)
1998, Adaptation of Laws (Nationality Related Matters) Ordinance (No 22 of 1998)
1983, Air Pollution Control Ordinance (Cap. 311)
1995, Airport Authority Ordinance (Cap. 483)
1993, Amusement Games Centres Ordinance (Cap. 435)
1976, Animals and Plants (Protection of Endangered Species) Ordinance (Cap. 187) (repealed by Protection of Endangered Species of Animals and Plants Ordinance Cap. 586)
1975, Antiquities and Monuments Ordinance (Cap. 53)
1963, Arbitration Ordinance (Cap. 341)
2000, Broadcasting Ordinance (Cap. 562)
1955, Buildings Ordinance (Cap. 123)
1978, Census and Statistics Ordinance (Cap. 316)
2001, Chief Executive Election Ordinance (Cap. 569)
1997, Chinese Nationality (Miscellaneous Provisions) Ordinance (Cap. 540)
1928, Chinese Temples Ordinance (Cap. 153)
1976, Chinese University of Hong Kong Ordinance (Cap. 1109)
2004, Clearing and Settlement Systems Ordinance (Cap. 584)
1991, Clubs (Safety of Premises) Ordinance (Cap. 376)
1968, Commissions of Inquiry Ordinance (Cap. 86)
1932, Companies Ordinance (Cap. 32)
2000, Consular Relations Ordinance (Cap. 557)
1994, Consumer Goods Safety Ordinance (Cap. 456)
1977, Consumer Council Ordinance (Cap. 216)
1997, Copyright Tribunal Ordinance (Cap. 528)
1997, Costs in Criminal Cases (Cap. 492)
1976, Country Parks Ordinance (Cap. 208)
1993, Crimes (Torture) Ordinance (Cap. 427)
1971, Crimes Ordinance (Cap. 200)
1994, Criminal Jurisdiction Ordinance (Cap. 461)
1899, Criminal Procedure Ordinance (Cap. 221)
1969, Dangerous Drugs Ordinance (Cap. 134)
1956, Dangerous Goods Ordinance (Cap. 295) (A previous version was promulgated in 1873, amending the law in respect to the carriage and deposit of dangerous goods.)
1995, Disability Discrimination Ordinance (Cap. 487)

Table of Statutes

1999, District Councils Ordinance (Cap. 547)
1953, District Court Ordinance (Cap. 336)
1986, Domestic Violence Ordinance (Cap. 189)
1989, Drug Trafficking (Recovery of Proceeds) Ordinance (Cap. 405)
1995, Dumping at Sea Ordinance (Cap. 466)
2000, Elections (Corrupt and Illegal Conduct) Ordinance (Cap. 554)
1997, Electoral Affairs Commission Ordinance (Cap. 541)
1981, Electoral Provisions Ordinance (Cap. 367) (not adopted as law of HKSAR)
1964, Employees Compensation Ordinance (Cap. 282)
1922, Emergency Regulations Ordinance (Cap. 241)
1992, Employees Retraining Ordinance (Cap. 423)
1968, Employment Ordinance (Cap. 57)
1967, English Schools Foundation Ordinance (Cap. 1117)
1997, Environmental Impact Assessment Ordinance (Cap. 499)
1935, Exchange Fund Ordinance (Cap. 66)
1997, Family Status Discrimination Ordinance (Cap. 527)
1988, Film Censorship Ordinance (Cap. 392)
1997, Fugitive Offenders Ordinance (Cap. 503)
1977, Guardianship of Minors Ordinance (Cap. 13)
1959, Heung Yee Kuk Ordinance (Cap. 1097)
1975, High Court Ordinance (Cap. 4)
1995, Hong Kong Arts and Development Council Ordinance (Cap. 472)
1991, Hong Kong Bill of Rights Ordinance (Cap. 383)
1995, Hong Kong Court of Final Appeal Ordinance (Cap. 484)
1993, Hong Kong Reunification Ordinance (Not given a Chapter number. Appears as Instrument A601)
1997, Hong Kong Special Administrative Region Passports Ordinance (Cap. 539)
1073, Housing Ordinance (Cap. 283)
1971, Immigration Ordinance (Cap. 115)
1972, Import and Export Ordinance (Cap. 50)
1974, Independent Commission Against Corruption (Cap. 204)
1947, Inland Revenue Ordinance (Cap. 112)
1983, Insurance Companies Ordinance (Cap. 41)
2006, Interception of Communications and Surveillance Ordinance (Cap. 589)
1966, Interpretation and General Clauses Ordinance (Cap. 1)
1996, Judicial Officers (Tenure of Office) Ordinance (Cap. 433)
1975, Judicial Officers Recommendation Commission Ordinance (Cap. 92)
1975, Judicial Service Commission Ordinance (Cap. 65) (repealed)
1887, Jury Ordinance (Cap. 3)
1972, Labour Tribunal Ordinance (Cap. 25)
1900, Lands Resumption Ordinance (Cap. 124), before 1998 known as Crown Lands Resumption Ordinance.
1974, Lands Tribunal Ordinance (Cap. 17)
1966, Legal Aid Ordinance (Cap. 91)
1964, Legal Practitioners Ordinance (Cap. 159)
1997, Legislative Council Ordinance (Cap. 542)
1985, Legislative Council (Powers and Privileges) Ordinance (Cap. 382)

1965, Limitation Ordinance (Cap. 347)
1932, Magistrates Ordinance (Cap. 227)
1876, Marriage Ordinance (Cap. 181)
1970, Marriage Reform Ordinance (Cap. 178)
1971, Married Persons Status Ordinance (Cap. 182)
1980, Marine Fish and Culture Ordinance (Cap. 353)
1995, Marine Parks Ordinance (Cap. 476)
1999, Mass Transit Railway Corporation Ordinance (Cap. 270) (repealed)
2000, Mass Transit Railway Corporation Ordinance (Cap. 556)
1967, Matrimonial Causes Ordinance (Cap. 179)
1972, Matrimonial Proceedings and Property Ordinance (Cap. 192)
1953, Merchant Shipping Ordinance (Cap. 281)
1990, Merchant Shipping (Prevention & Control of Pollution) Ordinance (Cap. 413)
1933, Miscellaneous Licences Ordinance (Cap. 114)
1997, National Flag and National Emblem Ordinance (Cap. 2401)
1988, New Territories Leases (Extension) Ordinance (Cap. 150)
1988, Noise Control Ordinance (Cap. 400)
1972, Oaths and Declarations Ordinance (Cap. 11)
1974, Official Languages Ordinance (Cap. 5)
1997, Official Secrets Ordinance (Cap. 521)
1989, Ombudsman Ordinance (Cap. 397), previously known as Commissioner of Administrative Complaints Ordinance of 1988
1994, Organised and Serious Crimes Ordinance (Cap. 455)
1993, Parent and Child Ordinance (Cap. 429)
1988, Pension Benefits (Judicial Officers) Ordinance (Cap. 401)
1949, Pensions Ordinance (Cap. 89)
1995, Personal Data (Privacy) Ordinance (Cap. 486)
1995, Pharmacy and Poisons Ordinance (Cap. 138)
1948, Police Force Ordinance (Cap. 232)
1971, Prevention of Bribery Ordinance (Cap. 201)
1991, Private Bills Ordinance (Cap. 69)
1999, Provision of Municipal Services (Reorganization) Ordinance (Cap. 552)
1983, Public Finance Ordinance (Cap. 2)
1960, Public Health and Municipal Services Ordinance (Cap. 132)
1967, Public Order Ordinance (Cap. 245)
1950, Public Service Commission Ordinance (Cap. 93)
2008, Race Discrimination Ordinance (Cap. 602)
1973, Rating Ordinance (Cap. 116)
1997, Railways Ordinance (Cap. 519)
1990, Recognition of Trusts Ordinance (Cap. 76)
1986, Regional Councils Ordinance (Cap. 385) (repealed in 1999)
2017, Regional Flag and Regional Emblem Ordinance (Instrument A602)
1984, Road Traffic Ordinance (Cap. 374)
1900, Securities (Insider Dealing) Ordinance (Cap. 395)
1989, Securities and Futures Commission Ordinance (Cap. 24)
2002, Securities and Futures Ordinance (Cap. 571)
1935, Separation and Maintenance Orders Ordinance (Cap. 16)

Table of Statutes

1995, Sex Discrimination Ordinance (Cap. 480)
1975, Small Claims Tribunal Ordinance (Cap. 338)
1949, Societies Ordinance (Cap. 151)
1933, Summary Offences Ordinance (Cap. 228)
1866, Suppression of Piracy Ordinance No 2 of 1866 (repealed)
1843, Supreme Court Ordinance No 15 of 1843 (repealed)
1962, Telecommunications Ordinance (Cap. 106)
1970, Theft Ordinance (Cap. 210)
1939, Town Planning Ordinance (Cap. 131)
1943, Trade Boards Ordinance (Cap. 63)
1954, Trade Marks Ordinance (Cap. 43)
1958, University of Hong Kong Ordinance (Cap. 1053)
1973, Urban Council Ordinance (Cap. 101) (Repealed)
1964, Variation of Trusts Ordinance (Cap. 253)
1982, Vocational Training Council Ordinance (Cap. 1130)
1980, Waste Disposal Ordinance (Cap. 354)
1980, Water Pollution Control Ordinance (Cap. 358)
1996, Whaling Industry (Regulation) Ordinance (Cap. 496)
1976, Wild Animals Protection Ordinance (Cap. 170)

Index

The numbers here refer to paragraph numbers.

Index

Index

Index

www.ingramcontent.com/pod-product-compliance
Lightning Source LLC
LaVergne TN
LVHW011103300926
849160LV00008B/268
* 9 7 8 9 4 0 3 5 3 4 3 2 9 *